D0843317

Caradoc Evans
The Devil in Eden

Caradoc Evans
The Devil in Eden

John Harris

SEREN

Seren is the book imprint of
Poetry Wales Press Ltd
Nolton Street, Bridgend, Wales

www.serenbooks.com
facebook.com/SerenBooks
Twitter: @SerenBooks

Hardback – 978-1-78172-435-4
Ebook – 978-1-78172-436-1
Kindle – 978-1-78172-437-8

A CIP record for this title is available from
the British Library

The publisher works with the financial assistance
of the Welsh Books Council

Printed in Perpetua by Akcent Media Ltd

Contents

Preface

I came to Caradoc Evans when I came to his native county. My drive to and from work at Aberystwyth took me through New Cross, the hamlet where Brynawelon, the Evanses' wartime home, rears up from the pavementless road; close by was Capel Horeb, the chapel he regularly attended (a private dwelling now) and behind it the small hillside cemetery with his neglected grave at the top. In Aberystwyth's public library I met his smiling face in the Evan Walters charcoal sketch given to the library by his widow Marguerite. In the Thirties they and Marguerite's son Nicholas had lived in the town, renting part of Queen's Square House, a stylish corner residence across the road from the Town Hall. The young Dylan Thomas had visited them there and from "the great Caradoc Evans" reference in *Portrait of the Artist as a Young Dog* I knew that Dylan was an admirer. I also knew the one big thing about Evans: that he was "the hammer of the Welsh" and, by some distance, "the best-hated man in Wales". Here was a local writer who stirred the strongest passions, alive enough in legend but very little read.

In the post-war years he survived through a few anthologised stories and briefly through the 1953 edition of *My People* published by Dennis Dobson. Welcoming its re-issue in 1967, the *Guardian* doubted if many better short stories had been published since *My People* first appeared. Some thirty years later the same paper carried a provocative piece placing Evans among the twentieth century's forgotten authors, their books mostly buried in the slagheap of fiction. My efforts at staying his slide into oblivion gave rise to fresh editions of the better work: his first three short-story collections, his Faber novel *Nothing to Pay*, and the wartime novella *Morgan Bible*, a late return to form.

Earliest of all was a Caradoc Evans miscellany published by Seren with a substantial biographical introduction. I was curious about the man, about what in his own dark acres had prompted such staggering fiction. What kind of life had he led, and what did he do besides writing? But the immediate requirement was a comprehensive bibliography, with as many as possible of his fugitive pieces in periodicals and newspapers. In a spat with Richard Hughes, Evans himself had said that if an author's personality is to be judged by his work, then the entire output should be taken into account. I looked closely at his Fleet Street years, charting the posts he occupied and the people he moved among: publishers, editors, journalists and writers. Most crucial was Andrew Melrose, the Scottish Presbyterian publisher brave enough to take on *My People*, a book not really to his taste and guaranteed to give offence. But "If you get sincerity and style you get literature at its best," he told the *Christian World*, "and though I justified the book by reasons of its sincerity, I had more than a suspicion that I was really publishing literature."

The Fleet Street research yielded some hoped-for uncollected fiction and more hidden newspaper pieces to swell the impassioned polemics that shook the Welsh daily press. His distinctive showing in Ideas was a complete surprise. In his "You and the Editor" column Evans warmly engaged with readers from every corner of Britain on topics raised by the penny weekly's postbag; and this at the time of his narrow, combative exchanges with critics in Wales – the contrast is remarkable, and wholly refreshing. In all, the material unearthed made possible a chronicle of Evans's public career. What was lacking were the resources that might allow a fuller, more personal history: the private letters, notebooks and diaries that form the backbone of most biographies. Evans with some truth apologized for being the world's worst correspondent. He was never a "natural writer"; almost everything he wrote was painfully crafted, and outside his column in *Ideas* he shows little sign of the relaxed conversational style more suited to correspondence – he clearly had no wish to put before others his innermost thoughts and feelings. Between 1939 and 1944 he sporadically kept a journal, an absorbing document as it stands but with little self-examination. For something of this one has to look to his brief "Self-Portrait"; to personal asides in articles, interviews and newspaper letters; to the talks he gave in the 1920s (some surviving in typescript, all partially reproduced in the press).

Others spoke about him. For the childhood years we have an articulate headmaster's view of his pupils and their community, a few words from playground pals, and the fuller recollections of one or two Rhydlewis residents. Fortunately, we also have the ground-breaking work of David Jenkins: his classic *Agricultural Community in South-West Wales* and his study of Evans's family background (in the *Anglo-Welsh Review*). For one member of that family, his nephew Howell Evans, the turning-point was Caradoc's failure to enter secondary school; bright enough at board school, he surely would have done so had money not been a problem. But it was, and in consequence the lad was doomed to drapery. Much can be gathered of his shop days from *Nothing to Pay*, an unusually autobiographical novel from an author whose previous fiction, the "realistic fantasies" that made his name, consciously concealed his personality. Yet the characters he created in part reflected himself; he and they had all been "cradled in Welsh Non-conformity"; what he disliked about them he recognised in himself. "The only evil we see in another man is the likeness of our own evil," he would have us believe.

Drapery brought Evans to London where a fellow shop assistant, Duncan Davies from Lampeter, introduced him to the thrills of the city. A prominent union activist, Davies became Caradoc's closest, most loyal friend, shaping his radical politics and encouraging his literary ambitions. He had trodden the night-school path his younger colleague would take, through the Working Men's College and – in Caradoc's case – out of drapery altogether. Davies's letters to Caradoc's widow Marguerite are quite indispensable for these years.

With the move into journalism other witnesses appear. An acknowledged Fleet Street "character", and following *My People* and the riot over *Taffy*, something of a minor celebrity, Evans drew comment from fellow writers and journalists. An arresting figure, they agreed, in looks, dress and manner: tall and lean, dark-haired, gaunt of face, with dark, penetrating eyes, high cheekbones, large mouth and prominent nose. He spoke quietly and quickly in a marked Welsh accent. His black, broad-brimmed hat was a fixture, as were his glasses, horn-rimmed or rimless, dangling on a thick cord. Sporting country-tweed suits early on, by the end he had taken to an outlandish mishmash of separates, as detailed descriptions attest – from Gwyn Jones, Glyn Jones, George Green and others (with similar fascination they dwelt on his face).

As to his behaviour, again there is some consensus: "A man of moods", "a volcano capped with ice", "a professional enemy". The theatre journalist Raymond Marriott echoed this last remark: Evans was a born provoker, a man who relished conflict and needed his opponents. But one had to look behind his words of anger, his colourful cursing of this and that, to gauge how genuine were the emotions they seemingly expressed; likewise with his lavish praise, of particular individuals and the whole profession of journalism. Barely into his twenties, Sewell Stokes worked for a while on *T.P.'s Weekly* and besides his deathless "best-hated man in Wales" tag, left some analysis of the boss. "Evans has more than a touch of genius, and his is a fine spirit struggling for self-expression through a mind which is brutal and often coarse.... In many of his moods, and he has many, he resembles Peter Pan. At heart he is a child. A disappointed one, perhaps, but at times, just an uncouth boy," disappointed that life didn't match his adolescent dreams.

Marguerite (as "Oliver Sandys") published an undervalued biography of her husband in 1946, the year after his death. "A maddening, though important, book", thought the Irish writer Frank O'Connor, the story of a stormy marriage where "we see the twisted sentimentalism of the Welshman protected by the abundant, good-humoured, extravagant sentimentality of the successful novelist, like a red-brick Nonconformist chapel in the shadow of an English parish church." O'Connor found Evans "a morose, hard-drinking violent man" – living proof of his own dictum that a Welshman was never happy for long. Gwyn Jones later confided that as he got to know Caradoc, the more he admired the writer, and the less he liked the man. It is quite impossible to like the Evans who tormented German-Jewish Pauline ("Paula") Block, a wartime live-in help at Brynawelon (Marguerite's biography makes no mention of this). Paula had reasons enough for hating Evans but her loathing had its bounds. "It is not in my character to condemn happenings and human failings outright. I have enough of them myself!"

Her words came to mind one summer's afternoon at New Cross where I'd been tidying up Evans's grave prior to a visit by an interested group. A curious neighbour, learning of my mission, directed me to a car parked beside the chapel. In the passenger seat sat an elderly gentleman who had known Caradoc Evans. Eagerly I approached him and, yes, he had known Caradoc, but it was a long time ago. I prompted his boyhood memories. "A strange man," was all he could say; "and his wife even stranger." "The artistic temperament," I suggested. Oh, but he didn't mean to be critical – "There's something wrong with us all."

In accounts of Evans's books I have freely plagiarised myself, treating them as events in his life and in the cultural life of his nation. *My People* and what was to follow met with astounding hostility in Wales. He defended himself ferociously, knowing he would never win because, "It does not matter what an author sees in his work, it is what the public sees in it." His truths were too unpalatable; if he had written goody-goody stories in Welsh, everybody would have said he was right. "I believe I am right. I know I am right! Because no one writing in sincerity can be wrong." The issues raised by *My People* swirled around him all his life. Establishment voices continued to deride him, new champions rallied to his side, but the debates I have not pursued much beyond his death.

I have also tried to temper psychological speculation based on accounts of behaviour. Contradictions abound in Evans: a bohemian peasant, a belligerent flatterer, a misogynistic feminist, one might say; a defamer of chapels he appreciatively attended; "the hammer of the Welsh" who claimed for ordinary Welsh folk a cultural level beyond that of their kind in England; and a worshipper of words who winced when called an artist. In admitting our contradictory natures we do not lose our sense of self, yet Howell Evans, closest to him within the family, failed to grasp his uncle's "self". He found him "baffling and unbalanced, not conventional in any sense". As for Caradoc's books, "He wrote about actual people and if they recognised themselves in that, too bad. They had no right to react as they did. They wanted him to sweep it all under the carpet." But Howell could not agree with the other controversial aspect of the writing: "the way he translated idiomatic Welsh into its literal English equivalent and put it into the mouths of his characters. That's easy and it's nasty because it makes the Welsh people look simple." And this perhaps has become the commonest Welsh position regarding Evans's fiction.

The apocrypha should be mentioned. Around Caradoc legends grew, dubious reports of what he said and did. The origins of them all are intriguing and one or two appear in this book. I was particularly pleased to tackle (albeit in an endnote) the ugly little story that mourners were paid to attend his funeral.

Endnotes make plain the many sources drawn upon for this study, prominent among them the Caradoc Evans archive in the Gwyn Jones Papers now deposited at National Library of Wales. I worked through this personal archive before it went to NLW and, thanks to Gwyn Jones's kindness, in the comfort of my own home. "We can't know too much about Caradoc," he urged me on; as he had encouraged Trevor L. Williams whose pioneering work on Evans gave me valuable bearings at the outset. There were unexpected boosts along the way, from Russell Davies's early articles showing (to me at least) that Evans's bold imaginative flights had some basis in fact, and from Ralph Maud, my summer neighbour. A leading Dylan Thomas scholar, he startled me by saying he thought Caradoc a greater writer than Dylan. "What a largely untapped source of drama and truth there is in the corpus of Caradoc Evans," ran his last letter from Vancouver. John Barnie stands beside him as another Evans enthusiast: while at *Planet* he published two handsome reprints of his work; and he led me back when, lost to London, I had put Caradoc aside. His generous offer to read draft chapters of my proposed biography was gratefully accepted and without his expert intervention the book might never have been finished.

Daughter of Marguerite's oldest friends, Monica Dunbar was herself close to Marguerite, preserving her letters and books, and in a delightful correspondence revealing more and more to me about her. She spoke of Caradoc with affection, as she did of Nicholas Sandys, with whom I became friendly during his spells at Aberystwyth. (Nick carried nothing relating to his mother – no book, letter or photograph – and was silent on their years together.) With like generosity Margaret Austin has shared her knowledge of Marguerite in Shropshire.

I am indebted also to others who over the years have offered their recollections of Caradoc, Marguerite and Nicholas, or else provided helpful information about them. It is a pleasure to record my thanks to Anita Arter, Robin Chapman, Sarah Clynch, Pierre Coustillas, Patricia Crowther, John Davies (New Cross & Aberystwyth), Maureen Davies (Llandysul), John Edmunds, Clifford Evans, Howell Evans, Miss Evans (Rhydlewis), Edmund Fryde, Ronald ("Ronnie") Hughes, David Russell Hulme, David Jenkins, Glyn Jones, Nest Lloyd (Llandysul), Violet Luckham, David Muspratt, Dilys Powell, Barbara Prys-Williams, Keidrych Rhys, Beti Richards, Martha S. Vogeler, Owain Wilkins and T. Ceiriog Williams. I must also thank the National Library for facilitating my research and Ceredigion Archives for answering specific queries. Both are friendly places to work in.

With its list of Evans reprints, Seren Books was the natural home for this biography; and where elements of its house style mystified me, compromise was admirably reached. At the back of my mind was Caradoc. The editors and publishers "have got us," he told a London writers' circle; "They hold the whip and the reins. Hence it is more profitable that we should go the way they bid us."

As their copyright holder, I have quoted without restriction from the published and unpublished writings of Caradoc and Marguerite. I believe that the bulk of other quotations are covered by fair usage. Where there is doubt, every effort has been made to contact relevant copyright holders but this has proved impossible in a small number of cases. We do, however, know Paula Block's wishes concerning her diary entries: "Let them shout out loud… to all who are interested and want to study and read them," she told Gwyn Jones. The publisher will be pleased to hear from anyone regarding copyright.

The Evan Walter portraits of Caradoc Evans and Countess Barcynska, in section 3, are reproduced by courtesy of the National Museum of Wales. The cover illustration of Evans is reproduced by courtesy of the National Library of Wales, as is the photograph of Dr Joshua Powell (section 1), and the "Tom Tit" sketch of Evans (section 2). The picture of the Evanses at Maidenhead (section 3) is reproduced with the permission of Topfoto. The "Cubist Caradoc" picture was skilfully reconstructed by Gwyn Martin.

For her fine analytical index I thank Marie-Pierre Evans; I trust the book lives up to it.

Finally, thanks to Rosalind for her patience and her sustaining tarka dal.

J.H., Aberystwyth, 2018

1

"I Remember Things":
Family and Boyhood in Rhydlewis
1878-93

In April 1916 Caradoc Evans, a thirty-seven-year-old Fleet Street journalist, looked back on the Cardiganshire landscape of his youth:

> Sometimes I think that man's natural labour is to dig and trim the soil, and sometimes I crave for the peace of the country. But soon I awake, and I remember things: badly-paid farm labourers; stunted, pale-faced children, whose bodies are starved and whose intellect is stifled at the hands of the village schoolmaster; sexless women, whose blood has been robbed by the soil; little villages hidden in valleys and reeking with malice.[1]

Such a response is startling, particularly in a son of rural Wales, but from Evans's boyhood in Rhydlewis, and the village presences he encountered there, came his view of life at large and most of what would fashion his own imaginative universe. It could be hardly have been otherwise, since "What we gather in our youth we commonly carry into our graves".

Though he called himself a peasant, his kinsfolk were people of substance. His father William Evans (1849-82) was the son of David and Sara Evans, tenants of Rhiwlug farm near Tregroes (north of Llandysul), in local terms a "large place" of some two hundred acres. There William remained until his marriage to Mary Powell (1848-1934). A vivacious young woman, privately educated at Cardigan and Lampeter, Mary was a Powell of Blaenbarre, another prosperous farm some five miles away at Rhydlewis, the village in the vale of the winding Ceri, a river that joins the Teifi below Newcastle Emlyn on its way to Cardigan and the sea. The Powells were influential land-owners, and besides Blaenbarre's one hundred and sixty acres, Mary's father William Powell (1820-75) owned two hundred more nearby – all this in a Troedyraur parish where most holdings barely made fifty acres. A cut above their neighbours, the Powells qualified as "gentlemen": members of a class which, as David Jenkins explains in his pioneering account of Caradoc Evans's family background, constituted a bridge between the local squirearchy and the rest of this rural society.[2]

William Powell (Caradoc's maternal grandfather) had married Mary Morgan, the daughter of John Morgan (1784-1871), described as "landed proprietor and registrar of births, deaths and marriages" in the 1851 census, and the owner of Broniwan, a thirty-two-acre smallholding on the easterly rise above the village (a little below the Methodist chapel Twrgwyn). At Broniwan William and Mary settled in with Mary's aging father

John. Their first child Mary (Caradoc's mother) was born there in 1848, followed in 1850 by Joshua, her brother who became a doctor-surgeon, much celebrated in the neighbourhood. Altogether, the Powell offspring numbered two girls and seven boys, two of the sons making good in America. Speaking of the Powells, David Jenkins emphasizes that "Caradoc's kinsmen were prominent and substantial people according to the standards of the day," and he notes an unusual mix of the serious and irreverent in their makeup: they were established community figures who somehow remained out- siders. He instances Mary's sister Ann, carelessly riding her horse through worshippers leaving a service at Hawen, the village's Congregational chapel. For the Powells were Calvinistic Methodists attending Twrgwyn, all except Caradoc's mother, who followed her own mother to Hawen where grandfather John had served as deacon for sixty years. As it happened, the obsessive teetotalism of John Green, the dictatorial minister of Twrgwyn, would drive one Powell son into the parish church, while sister Ann on marriage rebelled so far as to keep the Bronwydd Arms, a pub near Carmarthen.

Caradoc's parents, William Evans and Mary Powell, married on 4 January 1870. For family reasons they did so at Liverpool, where the Powells had business connections, and since the Evanses were Anglicans, the wedding took place at Liverpool's Welsh church, St David's, Brownlow Hill. Marriages between Nonconformists and Anglicans were rare in south-west Wales, if only because church people made up no more than a tenth of those attending places of worship; but such unions were not disapproved of provided that (as here) the respective families were socially matched. The new couple settled at Pantycroi, a thirty-five-acre holding hidden away on the Carmarthenshire side of the river Tyweli, two miles south of Llandysul. With the help of an agricultural servant, William Evans farmed a little as a sideline; described as "clerk" on his marriage certificate, he was employed in the Llandysul grocery business of David Lewis, another Tregroes man (the father of J.D. Lewis, founder of the Gomerian Press). There at Market Stores William Evans began his training as auctioneer and land surveyor, an apprenticeship marked by an act that would outrage local feeling and bring him lasting opprobrium.

It concerned the sale of Cwmgeist, a farm adjoining Rhiwlug, whose tenant Benjamin Jones, in company with other tenant farmers in Cardiganshire, had defied the wishes of his landlord by backing the Liberal candidate in the great transformative election of November 1868. This was before the 1872 Ballot Act introduced secret voting and at a time when, in the eyes of every squireen, land and vote went together. In a display of political vindictiveness Anglican-Tory landlords evicted a number (though not all) of those tenants who in open voting had not passively toed the line, thus promptly making them rebel-martyrs in the cause of Welsh Liberal-Nonconformity. So strong was public sympathy that no local auctioneers for the ensuing farm sales could be found – except in the case of Cwmgeist, which young William Evans, barely into his twenties, agreed to handle. He did so in two separate sales, on 30 August and 29 September 1870. The ignominy of the act long survived him; a great-grandson of the evicted tenant, the Unitarian minister D. Jacob Davies, remembered being reverently handed the Cwmgeist sale book ("Mr William Evans, Rhiwlug, Auctioneer" inscribed on its inside cover), testimony to the treachery at the heart of the Evans family – as William Evans had sold Cwmgeist so Caradoc his author-son was "now busy selling his country to the highest bidder".[3]

Some sense of the depth of this "treachery" can be gathered from J.N. Crowther's account of the November 1868 election at Rhydlewis.[4] Crowther, a committed Liberal, had been appointed headmaster of the village Board School there (Caradoc would become his pupil), and though ineligible to vote, he followed the campaign intensely. He attended the Cardigan hustings where the Tory candidate Edward Mallet Vaughan, scion of the house of Lisburne, cut an awkward, anxious figure. Behind the scenes the landlords and their agents were canvassing on his behalf, quietly turning the screws on tenants, playing on their fears of eviction – "A man's hearth and home are very dear to him." Even so, Crowther witnessed one resolute tenant farmer stride up to the polling booth and openly vote for the Liberal candidate, Evan Matthew Richards, with the estate agent glowering nearby.

The election result was carried by horseback, and "all the countryside seemed to be gathered at Rhydlewis that evening, so tense was the feeling everywhere". Walking the road between Capel Hawen and the village, Crowther heard "the thundering sound of a horse galloping down the hill from Penrhiwpal". Its shoes struck sparks in the moonlight, its rider shouting as he flashed by, "Evan Matthew Richards 232!" The horseman had ridden from Llandysul with the election result (Richards's majority was actually 156). At Rhydlewis a cheering, singing crowd paraded the valley for hours. "Blue is the Liberal colour in Cardiganshire, and on the following Sunday many of the men wore blue ties – some had blue bands around their hats! – and the women showed the colour in various ways." But euphoria turned to anxiety at the thought of what might happen come the spring. Fears were not misplaced; notices to quit were served on several of those who had voted according to their conscience and, crucially, had urged other tenants to do so. Eviction – "ruthless, vindictive" – duly followed for Crowther's "heroes of '68".

Despite all this, William Evans survived in the neighbourhood, operating out of Llandysul's High Street as auctioneer and surveyor for fully ten years. At Pantycroi he and Mary added to their family. A first child, David Hywel, lived a mere seven weeks (March-May 1871); his grave with its faded inscription is prominently positioned in front of Hawen, beside the grave of its founder-minister, Benjamin Evans. Over the next four years, two daughters and a son were born: Mary (in 1871), Sarah (1874) and William (1876). Then also at Pantycroi, on New Year's Eve 1878, came a second son, the writer David Caradoc Evans. Over "Caradoc" we need to pause; it was not his birth name. He was registered simply as "David", though the 1881 census return shows the two-year-old as "David Hywel", names once belonging to the Evanses' deceased first child. Nowhere else does "Hywel" appear in connection with Caradoc Evans. In school records he is "David C. Evans" and in the playground "Dafydd (or Dafi) Lanlas", the "Lanlas" acquired when his family settled at Lanlas Uchaf, Rhydlewis. "As 'Dafydd Lanlas' we all knew him. His name being David Caradoc Evans," wrote Annie Rees, a school companion.[5] What is clear is that "Caradoc" (or "Caradog"), by which the Welsh at large came to know him, was established prior to his joining the infants class and that his parents had when choosing it stepped outside family precedent and the common pool of Welsh given names.[6]

Towards the end of 1880, William Evans moved his family to Carmarthen town. He was now fully qualified, his auctioneer's licence granted on 11 September 1880; but whatever his professional achievements, his domestic life was in turmoil, largely on account of an explosive nature readily primed by drink. Marital strife drove an again pregnant Mary away from her husband and Carmarthen, probably sometime after April 1881 (when the census has them living at 3 Towy View Terrace). Her brother Joshua brought her back to Rhydlewis, together with three of her children; six-year-old Sarah remained with her father until grandmother Sara, recently widowed, took care of her at Rhiwlug. For William's time at Carmarthen proved short; barely into his thirties, he died of pneumonia on 17 January 1882.

In his brief troubled life, William Evans gained a full measure of notoriety. Dangerously handsome, he was known as a womaniser and talk of his drinking and immorality was widespread. More than one source attests to his suffering the ceffyl pren (the wooden horse), an act of public humiliation commonly inflicted upon individuals suspected of sexual misconduct. The ceffyl pren was no quiet settling of scores. Accounts speak of riotous torch-lit processions assembling late at night around the house of the accused; of victims being tied to the "horse" and paraded before neighbours awoken by gunshot so as not to miss the spectacle. This social punishment, flourishing in the early nineteenth century, had never wholly died out, sporadic instances occurring as late as the 1880s. Victims were mostly individuals unpopular on other grounds besides adultery, and local memory recalls William Evans as the last person in the Rhydlewis locality to suffer in this way: it seems he was carried on a wooden pole across the parish boundary to Aberbedw bridge, north of the village. Annie Rees, who (as Annie Owen) had attended school with Caradoc and knew his family's circumstances, gave the whole incident a dramatic setting:[7]

> ... here is the secret. His father [William Evans] was an <u>immoral</u> man – in those days if any man was found adulterous they made a "ceffyl pren" – an old custom, & carried it to the door. Mrs Evans at the time was expecting a child. She had such a shock that she collapsed. The child was born – an imbecile – Josi. Sir, isn't truth stranger than fiction?

This "truth" however is questionable. Joshua, the last Evans child (known as Josi), was indeed born physically and mentally handicapped, but at Carmarthen on 12 August 1881. It may have been that Mary, recently moved to Rhydlewis, had hurried back to Towy View Terrace for the birth of her son – during their months of separation her husband visited Rhydlewis – but Rees's interpretation of events more likely represents a wish of some in the village to believe that in poor blighted Josi the sins of the father had been visited upon the son. That Caradoc knew of his father's humiliation can be taken for granted, although he never directly mentioned it.

Time did not soften Rhydlewis's judgement of William Evans; in 1952 the Revd J.

Seymour Rees (Annie Rees's husband) spoke of him "falling into an early grave through his lusts".[8] The grave is at Tregroes, in St Ffraed's churchyard, where he is buried close by his parents, his brother and sister. William's headstone bears a suitably mournful epitaph, the Welsh version of Psalm 102:1: "My days are like a shadow that declineth; and I am withered like grass." We recall two preceding verses: "Mine enemies reproach me all the day; and they that are mad against me are sworn against me. For I have eaten ashes like bread, and mingled my drink with weeping." From the beginning Caradoc knew the fate of the outsider. His own mischievousness as a child was partly attributed to his father: "Caradoc, the son of a Church of England father, is an atheist. Quite a bad atheist", he has the local minister pronounce.[9]

Marriage to William Evans was widely considered the root of his wife's misfortunes and – most crucially – the reason why Caradoc's mother Mary received nothing of her father's estate after William Powell's death in April 1875. Within months of leaving Carmarthen, she found herself an impoverished widow with four small children to bring up. Her brother Joshua immediately helped, providing two homes for her, the first at Broniwan where he and Mary had been born and which he had now inherited. Medically qualified, with a practice at Newcastle Emlyn, the unmarried Joshua lived at Broniwan with Will and Howell, two younger brothers intent on following him into medicine. From Broniwan, Mary moved with her children to Lanlas Uchaf, a ten-acre smallholding further up the rise from Broniwan. It would be home for the rest of her life; there as "Mali Lanlas" she became something of a local character, and from her cottage the boy Caradoc would cross the fields to the Board School a mile or so below.

Discussing Mary Evans and her reputation within the locality, David Jenkins says that "sbortlyd" (sporty) was the adjective generally applied to her, a term not used in any pejorative sense but "meant to refer to the un-earnest inconsequential element, the attitude of unwillingness to take the world too seriously, which characterised Mary Evans as it did her brother Joshua Powell and other of her kin".[10] Mali opened her door to the banterers and leg-pullers, the more irreverent souls around. She was a teller of legendary tales; an obituary would note her "wealth of reminiscences concerning some of the older residents" and her knowledge of "the earlier days of Nonconformity in Cardiganshire".[11] One visitor, Marged Powell (not a relation), "a wrinkled little woman with a glass eye" who called in every day on her way for water from the well in Lanlas field, "knew everything that went on for miles around".[12] But the matter concerning Caradoc's mother that has dominated discussion of his childhood is her alleged expulsion from Hawen chapel for defaulting on her membership dues. The journalist Edward Wright first spoke of this occurrence (obviously at Caradoc's prompting) and assigned it a singular importance. In Wright's words, Mary Evans

> fell under the ban of the religious body to which she belonged. Like many other widow women, she was assessed to contribute to the treasury of the chapel. Lacking the money and having a heavy burden of young children, she would not pay and was, according to custom, treated as an outcast. All that Mr Evans has written is I think inspired by this event.[13]

Former Rhydlewis residents have refuted Wright's story, one dismissing it as "a complete fabrication, for there never was an assessment of contribution and plenty of members paid only a few shillings annually and if they paid nothing at all no one was excommunicated on those grounds".[14] Annie Rees also, though seeking to represent Mali honestly, found no hint of her having been expelled from the chapel. On the contrary, she recounts how her own father, then a senior deacon at Hawen, had with a friend given up a day's work to travel from farm to farm "begging for contributions to renovate the chapel":

> He called at Lanlas, Caradoc's home – He [Caradoc] was there. Mali his mother shouted in the yard [in Welsh] O damn you, the only time you come to see me is when you want need money. Half a minute now, father said, we're nearly starving. She turned on her heel. Good heavens! She said & in no time prepared a grand feast. She gave £1 & Caradoc did also.[15]

The poet Wil Ifan (Revd William Evans), a vocal opponent of Caradoc's, repeats this story. Dr Dan Evans, his father, was Hawen's minister at the time and Mary Evans a "respected worshipper" there.

Overall, Mali is remembered as an independent, high-spirited widow, with a ready sense of humour and a great deal of courage. If some found her prickly – "proud and unyielding", said one grandson – her bark was worse than her bite. Talk of her being an outcast seems as extravagant as the tale of her chapel expulsion. The exaggerations derived from Caradoc, who doubtless spoke feelingly to Edward Wright of his mother's straightened circumstances, her difficulties and disappointments, and the censure that might have come her way from the narrower spirits of Hawen. Cut off by her father, she had suffered an unfortunate marriage, and the widowhood that came in her thirty-fifth year left her yoked to a marginal ten-acre smallholding for the rest of her days.

There does seem to have been a break of sorts with the chapel. Mali attended Hawen through the ministries of David Adams and his successors, up to and during the long tenure of Dr Dan Evans (1901-27);[16] but she seems not to have been a regular chapelgoer in her later years. Caradoc went occasionally to Twrgwyn (as did Josi), either with his brother or his mother.[17] Hawen lay at the far end of the village below; Twrgwyn was just down the lane from Lanlas. That Mali chose to be buried at Twrgwyn, next to her brother Joshua, is unsurprising; that portion of burial ground, formerly part of Broniwan farm, had been gifted to Twrgwyn by the Powells, who were granted free pews in return.[18]

Mali Evans battled on at Lanlas almost alone. The children Mary and Will left for employment at Carmarthen. The younger daughter Sarah moved to Tresaith on marriage to a well-to-do farmer, Thomas Evans of Dyffryn Bern (close to the home of the novelist Allen Raine), while marriage to a Cardiff chemist eventually took Mary from the area. Will moved further away, to America no less, where his uncles William and Howell – Mali's brothers – had settled. Letters from him began to arrive, and a picture of himself in Chinese dress; he had settled in San Francisco from where in 1906 he seems to have written his last letter home. A heart-broken Mali, believing that he had perished in the

great April earthquake, would henceforth rarely speak of her eldest son.[19] At least
Caradoc kept in touch, all through his years in London returning home each summer
for a week or so. "During his stay, he hardly allowed his mother to move from her chair.
He made the beds, washed the floor, cleaned her boots and did a hundred and one little
jobs about the house for her."[20]

The severely disabled Josi remained at Lanlas. Meeting him first could be unsettling,
and his appearance disturbed Annie Rees: "very, very deformed in mind and body" she
records; "Honestly, the poor soul is hideous to behold: one eye larger than the other –
humped back – droop in one shoulder & swaying back and fore as he walks. He used to
tap our windows after dark if he saw a light. Nobody cared. We knew it was Josi."[21] The
chapel displayed similar tolerance: "A deacon would kneel in prayer. Josi used to go up
as well & kneel behind him & not move in utter reverence. You might think children
would laugh & people as well. Not a soul. They took it for granted." Such neighbourly
understanding was not infrequently called upon since Rhydlewis, as a past resident confirmed, had its share of the disabled, a consequence of rural inbreeding – "the coming
of the bicycle did much to curb congenital idiocy".[22] (The historian Kenneth O. Morgan
notes "the high prevalence of idiocy" in late nineteenth-century Cardiganshire.) Josi
remained a helpless son and the strain of looking after him must further have taxed his
mother. While on holiday, Caradoc did what he could to help. One summer he presented
Josi's measurements to an Aberaeron tailor, with the request that a suit be made from
them. The customer in question could not attend for a personal fitting. "And if you can't
make the suit to measure without a fitting," snapped Caradoc, "leave it at that."[23]

Caradoc first went to school from Broniwan, joining the local infants' class in January
1883, soon after his fifth birthday. Nine years later he left the village for employment
in Carmarthen. Thus his time at Rhydlewis was mostly his time at school there; he per-
ceived his community as a schoolboy and with a child's heightened awareness encountered
in successive headmasters two powerful presences. Their pedagogic skills he dismissed
more than once, as in his *Who's Who in Wales* (1921) entry with its reference to "Rhydlewis
(Cardiganshire) Board School, which he left untaught". Elsewhere he elaborates: "Next
to the preacher the schoolmaster was the worst tyrant in the place. He also was religious.
He taught me a little penmanship and a little English reading, but I never had a ghost of
an idea what I was reading."[24] School unfailingly aroused his anger and the "schoolin" in
Evans's fiction is always a creature of ridicule. Such attacks seemed the more provocative
in being aimed at the village's first headmaster, J.N. Crowther, an English incomer who
under his bardic name "Glanceri" won a place in Welsh literary circles. As it happens,
Crowther was not the object of Evans's scorn. On the contrary, he remembered him
with something approaching admiration.

John Newton Crowther (1847-1928) left home in the Pennines for Rhydlewis on
Friday morning, 4 January 1867. Battling through blizzards by road and rail, he managed
to reach Llandysul on Saturday evening. He was to take up the post of head teacher at
the Newgate British School, about to become in the wake of the 1870 Education Act

(establishing compulsory elementary education) the Rhydlewis Board School. Term began on Monday, 7 January, and the young man from Todmorden had to be there to take charge. He duly made it, as did the hardier of his pupils: twenty-eight struggled through deep snow, anxious to see the new headmaster.

At its site in the Ceri valley, a mile or so from the village, Rhydlewis Board School was typical of the larger rural creations in employing a principal teacher, a sewing mistress, and one or two pupil-teachers (likely recruits to the profession). Crowther himself was just nineteen, and had come to Wales as a trainee teacher at Bangor Normal College. Within three years of settling in Rhydlewis he had married a local girl Sarah Lloyd, who encouraged his love of things Welsh. He remained the village headmaster for more than twenty years, during which he kept a log, his weekly observations on progress at the school. All heads were charged with this task but Crowther proved unusually conscientious in this and readier than most to speak his mind.[25] Taken as a whole, his log-book entries provide a vivid record, not simply of happenings at school but of village life in general.

They picture an institution desperately trying to discipline a community whose habits were firmly fixed. The conflict is dramatized in Crowther's continuous analysis of attendance figures and his constant despair over absenteeism. He contended with two natural obstacles: child sickness and atrocious weather. Snow, gales and heavy rain regularly marked the winter – the playground streamed with water for days – while sickness was a year-round threat. Epidemics of whooping-cough, mumps and scarlet fever brought Caradoc's uncle, Dr Joshua Powell to the school; it emptied for a fortnight in February 1880, and again in October following an outbreak of scabs: one lad had to go home – "It was too sickening to go near him," Crowther records.

If winter meant foul weather and multiple sicknesses, other seasons saw farming pressures. Agriculture penetrated the school life, sometimes quite literally. "The Board should not allow pigs to be kept in the playgrounds of any of its schools," declared the H.M. Inspector's report of 1892. Disruption began in April with potato-planting; summer saw haymaking then the corn harvest, while October brought potato harvesting, a task whose impact on class attendance particularly angered Crowther, as did farm auctions ("so many of them!") which regularly closed the school. Once in a while demands of the land claimed pupils for longer periods. In 1883 a Standard III boy went absent for weeks working as a herd boy: his mother promised to bring him back provided the School Board refrained from prosecuting. Parents for their part, the cottagers and small farmers, desperately needed any little extra income that their children's casual labour might bring in.

Besides this farming activity, Rhydlewis's two chapels also might empty the school. Chapels dominated village life, with two attendances expected each Sunday (plus afternoon school for the young). Writing of the years before World War I, a Twrgwyn member recalls struggling to chapel on dark winter evenings, her mother carrying a candle-lit lantern to avoid the potholes. "Most of Saturday was a preparation for Sunday… and there were many extra jobs to be done": polishing boots and shoes (chapelgoers were smartly dressed), cleaning cutlery (hard work before stainless steel), lifting garden vegetables in preparation for Sunday dinner: "The Sabbath day cast its shadow on Saturday."[26] But chapel invaded the working week. During Caradoc's time, the school was closed, or attendance curtailed, because of chapel events requiring the presence of children, often as well-drilled performers. The list seems endless: monthly meetings at Twrgwyn, quarterly meetings of the Calvinistic Methodists, thanksgiving services, Sunday School festivals, singing festivals, Band of Hope tea parties, gatherings of the Good Templars and other temperance occasions, ordination services in neighbouring chapels. Nor was it simply a matter of losing the odd day here and there, for in a community where going to school was not an ingrained practice, a holiday granted early in the week marred attendance on subsequent days.

Throughout Cardiganshire head teachers battled to establish their schools and tried everything to bolster attendances. Survival depended upon it, since school grants – and teachers' pay – were linked to pupil numbers. John Crowther waved carrot and stick. After 1883, pupils regularly attending received tokens towards quarterly prizes, and he sacrificed time in the classroom to hunt down hardened absentees in their homes. His Board offered little support, a stance he construed as tacitly encouraging parents to withhold their children from school.[27] Such conflict marred his final years at Rhydlewis:

> I try tickets [tokens] and sweets and last Friday and today dismissed all those who had attended ten times at 4 instead of 4.30, but everything seems to fail in securing what might be called "good" attendance .... Even the promise of a "tea party" on May 11th seems to have no effect. (13 April 1888)
>
> The parents appear to have an idea that *their* children will pass, or ought to pass, and that we shall pass them somehow. The regular children do very well but we can do nothing with those we seldom or never see. (21 September 1888)

Chapels still disrupted work. Time could ill be spared for a music festival at Twrgwyn, and weekday services at Hawen spoiled attendances (which had fallen from an average 91 in 1887 to 70 in 1889). Stemming the decline took its toll of the headmaster ("gloomy, black-bearded, gooseberry-eyed" in Caradoc's sight). Forced to rest in November 1889, he now began to contemplate a move away.

Caradoc's deep-grained antipathy towards the spirit and practices of school was something that struck his later Aberystwyth friend George Green, a university lecturer in education. "He spoke – how truthfully I do not know, since reminiscences of this kind are not wholly to be trusted – of his punishment and bullying, of cramming; of utter indifference as to whether pupils were interested in what they were required to learn, or whether they understood it."[28] In fact, the Crowther headship was tolerable enough, though under him, and more certainly under his successor, the school appears as joyless and repressive, hampered by a stultifying curriculum and the strain of the annual inspection. The three R's ruled, buttressed by additional subjects entitling the school to extra revenue. Geography was popular at Rhydlewis; the boys took it on Tuesdays and Thursday while the girls were at their Sewing. Poetry and singing had their place.

Poetry meant memorizing set passages for recitation at the end-of-year examination; in 1883 Crowther proposed as set pieces Mark Antony on the death of Caesar, Wordsworth's "We are Seven" and Scott's "The Battle of Bannockburn". Favourites like Longfellow's "The Wreck of the Hesperus" were quickly learned, and to encourage faultless performance prizes of textbooks containing the poems might be awarded.

Rhydlewis especially cultivated singing. "Tell Me the Old, Old Story" and "Shall We Gather at the River" appear in the 1870s school repertoire, these hymns later joined by secular songs. The headmaster, a music fanatic, developed a pernicious sore throat as a result of his driven singing lessons. Young Caradoc ran less risk:

> When I was a boy in school, on the eve of an examination day my teacher said to me: "Don't you sing with the class tomorrow. Open your mouth and pretend." I opened my mouth and shaped words with my lips, and it was so that at the end of the singing the examiner turned to the teacher, saying: "The small bloke over there sings very well."[29]

At Rhydlewis some songs were in Welsh, though the primary school at this time was a conscious instrument for promoting the English language within a community that lived almost entirely through Welsh. Formal teaching in Welsh lay with the chapels (the Sunday class at Hawen offered instruction in grammar and composition). "Can't get them to speak English in the playground", Crowther admitted of the children, "because those who can play with those who can't." (Caradoc's extra-mural tuition from a land-surveyor briefly lodging at Lanlas had minimal impact, apart from teaching him a few English swear words.)

If his English and singing were shaky, his arithmetic was worse. Evans began his 1944 "Self-Portrait" with a reference to his discomfort in the subject:

> One of my schoolins used to stand sadly in front of me, cut a bit of Spanish [liquorice], pop it into his mouth, scratch his back head, and say: "There will be whiskers on eggs before the twelve times in your head. He was short and slim and had whiskers all over his face and in his nostrils and ears, and he produced a child a year without outside help."[30]

The veracity of this passage need not be questioned: Caradoc's difficulty with arithmetic is well attested, as is the headmaster's virility – eleven Crowther offspring enrolled at the school.

Evans's story "The Talent Thou Gavest" (*My People*) has this reflection on Eben, the lad who abandons school to tend sheep on the moor. "His life was lonely; books were closed against him, because he had not been taught to read; and the sense of the beautiful or the curious in Nature is slow to awake in the mind of the Welsh peasant." Outside his fiction, Evans said much the same of himself. He professed an inability to tell one tree from another or one bird, and he was ignorant of basic bovine mechanics despite having lived for years among cows. "I have fetched the cows home to be milked, and I have tried to milk them, and I have taken them back to their pasture, and I have herded them in the heat of a summer day to a place where there is water, and I have never noticed how a cow walks."[31] The neglect of "nature study" helped condition the grown man's response to the natural world. Never could he glorify nature, invest it with high significance – which sets him apart from the Welsh tradition of writing about the countryside. At least, as D. Jacob Davies observed, "He escaped the notable cruelty to animals that characterised the sons of farming communities… and still thrives and survives in all rural communities"; Davies had his "own excruciating boyhood memories of cruelty to man and beast in the same locality [as Evans's]", having once witnessed "the disembowelling of a badger on Christmas morning during a badger-baiting session with respectable men taking pleasure in… setting the dogs upon the hapless creature later."[32]

As for classroom discipline, in Cardiganshire board schools corporal punishment was the norm. Crowther hardly ever used it, recording in November 1877 that Stephen Morgan "is the only child who I have punished (corporeally) since Jan. 1874". That there were disciplinary problems is unsurprising, given that one teacher, assisted by a Sewing mistress and two juvenile pupil-teachers or monitors, had charge of an assortment of pupils aged from five to fourteen, about a third of whom attended school fitfully. The fussy grading of children into seven "standards" (excluding the Infants class) complicated matters, so that groups of children were inevitably left unattended at certain times of the day.

Overall, John Crowther's reputation was that of a successful teacher who consistently produced good results. Examiners congratulated him on his "persevering energy", a quality which began to strike some parents as unfeeling – wasn't he pushing his classes too hard? "Still some of us are accused (and myself in particular, I am informed) of unduly pressing or driving the children" (23 November 1888), but "all the classes have already commenced their poetry and a number of children know it all by heart. No pressure whatever has been used" (30 November 1888). The cramming approach is understandable, given a system of payment by results (to school and teachers) partly measured by exam success. This is Caradoc's charge against his school: facts stuffed in for mindless regurgitation, imagination and intellect unstirred. "Every subject is dull to the schoolboy, unless it is livened up and presented in an attractive form by the teacher. My experience is only of dull teachers; that is why I was a dull pupil."[33]

Crowther too was a victim of the system. A cultivated man, in December 1879 he took the unusual step of establishing a library within the school, its stock available to the community at large. Tuesday, 9 May 1882, saw delivery of a large parcel of books from London ("including some thirty volumes… a little commotion and excitement in consequence"). In May 1888 Hawen chapel arranged a competitive evening of music and literature in aid of new books. Yet the library caused dissension among borrowers (essentially over its siting) and eventually it ceased to function – Twrgwyn and Hawen picked over the remains. Crowther's humanising influence is evident elsewhere. He organised a successful summer outing for the school: "Started from Rhydlewis at 8.30am and arrived at Llangrannog about 10.30am. Tea provided for them at 3pm. Children roamed the sands and rocks. Sang a few tunes (Mr Sankey's) together on the sands and after a day of healthy enjoyment returned to Rhydlewis by 8.30pm." (One can't help thinking of "Greater Than Love", Evans's grim tale of a day trip to Llangrannog.) Back at school the headmaster, on impulse, took pupils out into the sunshine to read from *Robinson Crusoe*, from a life of General Gordon, and even from the local newspaper. "Enjoyed it greatly", he jotted down on 13 February 1884. Such expressions of pleasure are rare; more often he writes of ill-prepared pupils, hostile parents, indifferent Board members and endemic absenteeism – all threats to examination success. Now in his early forties, he had been looking for work elsewhere, and on 2 September 1890 he learned of his appointment as headmaster of the Cefnfaes British School. In November he left for Bethesda.

Time predictably mellowed his memories. His twenty-four years at Rhydlewis had been happy ones; there he had married, played a prominent part in community life, and had grounds for believing that his work as headmaster had not been fruitless or unappreciated. The School Board's chairman Dr Powell had been good enough to say that they were losing the chief brain of the neighbourhood – "That, no doubt, was an exaggeration." He would meet Caradoc Evans again and exchange with him views on literature. There could be no real affection between them, though a measure of mutual respect. Caradoc came to appreciate the exceptional energy that allowed Crowther a literary life outside his taxing job and the personal touches by which he humanised the classroom. "I left the Board School at the age of thirteen. My first teacher was Mr J.N. Crowther, a gentleman of remarkable literary instinct, and a keen student of the psychology of his pupils. But unfortunately for me he left the village when I was about ten; the remaining years in school I learnt nothing."[34]

"A whipper-snapper who claimed to be able to count with his eyes shut and sing louder than any other man in the district",[35] Thomas Elias took charge of the school on 9 January 1891. A native of nearby Glynarthen, Bangor-trained (like Crowther), he remained in post at Rhydlewis for the rest of his career, a span of forty-two years. In the month of Elias's appointment, Caradoc began his duties as temporary monitor. George Green explains how necessary was the post of monitor in devising a system of elementary education "so cheap that even those who did not believe in education hardly bothered to oppose it".[36] A twelve-year-old pupil was invited to become a temporary monitor and, following a period of probation, could expect to make the rank of full monitor. In this capacity the chosen pupil would arrive at school at 8 a.m., before the rest of the children assembled, for an hour or so of instruction (and pencil-sharpening duty) designed to enable him or her to teach the junior classes. At the age of fourteen a full monitor might graduate to pupil-teacher status, effectively becoming an apprentice to the principal teacher.

How far Caradoc proceeded with his apprenticeship is a matter of some debate. Local opinion has explained his bitterness towards school in terms of his lack of success there; more especially, his failure to be selected as a pupil-teacher.[37] J. Seymour Rees has him competing against a girl and dramatically missing out on the casting vote of a minister – there lies the root of Caradoc's antipathy towards the chapel.[38] Mrs Rees elaborates on the appointment as pupil-teacher, not of Caradoc, but of Elisabeth (Lizzie) Mary Owen (the novelist "Moelona").[39] It confirmed the extent of social stratification in a closed rural community: a cottage widow's son stood no chance against a farmer's daughter. Annie Rees's own brother, the son of a blacksmith, similarly suffered in competition with a farmer's daughter and, like Caradoc, had to seek his livelihood away from the area. *Plant y ffermwyr* were distinctly a peg or two higher than a cottager's or workman's children ("*O! dim ond plant gweithwyr*").[40]

The facts are that Caradoc, a Standard VI boy, became temporary monitor in the week beginning 19 January 1891, shortly after his twelfth birthday; the Board, with Uncle Joshua as chairman, confirmed his appointment at two shillings a week. 1891 saw staff changes. A pupil-teacher, another David Evans, left in June through ill health (he died six months later) and Lizzie Mary Owen, formerly a Standard VII girl, filled his post. Eighteen months older than Caradoc, she was appointed specifically as a probationary candidate for teacher-training on a monitor's salary, also two shillings a week. Caradoc may well have been rejected for the pupil-teacher vacancy in the light of Lizzie's candidacy but he did not leave school on account of her appointment. Indeed, in 1892 he in turn entered Standard VII and, as monitor, worked in harness with her. Nor does he seem to have failed any formal test of competency, although he did exit from school following a confrontation with the Board. This was over pay. In May 1892 Lizzie applied for, and was granted, an increase of a shilling a week (her three-year stint as pupil-teacher being then confirmed). Caradoc, though still a monitor, also asked for three shillings a week. At its meeting of 20 December 1892 (Dr Powell did not attend), the Board rejected his request on the grounds that he enjoyed the same salary as others in his position. On 3 February 1893 Elias noted that "D.C. Evans (monitor) has expressed his intention of giving up teaching this week", an intention promptly carried out – the minutes of the next Board meeting (21 February) duly noted his "retirement".

An alert, spirited schoolboy, Caradoc was reasonably at ease under Crowther and able enough to have been singled out as a potential teacher. Matters worsened under Elias. As monitor Caradoc fell short in two areas: his arithmetic remained below par and he found classroom discipline difficult. Besides absorbing the work of Standards VI and VII, he instructed the Infants and Standard II in his first year, and Standards II and III in his second. Controlling younger children taxed the best of monitors and reports of beatings are not infrequent. Caradoc's one taste of power (so he claimed) was his job as holiday scarecrow: "the crows challenged my authority and perched on my battered hat". As with crows, so with children: "the monitor (D.C. Evans) does not seem able to maintain anything like good discipline in the Infants Class. The children are by far too familiar with him" (13 April 1891). His arithmetic failing he never denied; "I hate figures," he confessed.[41] Crowther remembered him "sitting in a desk which happened to be in front of my own, struggling with the intricacies of simple arithmetic",[42] and Elias's log describes him as "exceedingly backward in Arith.". The inspector who examined Caradoc's classes of 1891 (and those of 1892) found matters more acceptable. "The Infants did, on the whole, well," he reported.

It was unfortunate that Evans's years at school should have coincided with Crowther's stressful exit and, more especially, Elias's uncomfortable initiation into headship. This is Evans's response to a man (a reader of a weekly he was editing), grieving that his son was unhappy at school:

> Such was the plight of one I knew: a higher salary enticed away his school-master, and a vain stripling with hanging lips, narrow forehead, and a rotten singing voice came into his place. His ways were harsh and his manner insolent and all who sat in his school did not learn anything. Your son… will have to remain in that school which is conducted by a fool for a set time, and when the set period is ended, may it please God to give him understanding.[43]

The passage demonstrates the depth of hostility towards Elias (who in turn loathed the author of *My People*). One senses too Caradoc's hurt at what he sees as Crowther's defection, a teacher who had glimpsed his potential. After Crowther came the reign of a cocksure novice.

"A whipper-snapper", "a vain stripling": the judgements seem confirmed in Elias's opening log-book entries. He denigrates Crowther for not having introduced drawing lessons and – of all things – for being soft on absenteeism. After one week of low attendance he writes (5 June 1891), "No special reason for this, save habitual irregularity having been tolerated in the past and the children still taking advantage of this leniency" (this of a predecessor who had driven himself to the point of nervous collapse in the effort to keep up numbers). By 1892 Elias was himself resorting to oranges as rewards for good attendance; later came sweets, bought out of his own pocket. Of his harsh ways and insolent manner there is likewise confirmation. The punishment of sending pupils back a Standard, sparingly used by Crowther, Elias adopted enthusiastically. He prided himself on academic rigour and a reputation for discipline. "Monday morning I had to punish 5 children for having played truant last Friday. It seems they had gone to the moor close by to gather bilberries. I do not think this offence will again be repeated" (20 July 1891). He is pictured as the stern disciplinarian by one of Caradoc's classmates who also became a journalist; David L. Evans (of the *Carmarthen Journal*) recalled how during the monitors' early morning hour with the teacher, the pomposities of Tom Elias reduced Caradoc to "a fit of uncontrollable laughter, to his consequent discomfort".[44] His reminiscences of "Dafi Lanlas" entertaining the other boys with playtime sermons suggest an amusing, mischievous lad, popular with his contemporaries. In fairness, once must say that the years following Caradoc's departure show Elias in a more favourable light; in those early days the young head teacher, conscious of his predecessor's high standing, strove fiercely to make his mark, his strident, overbearing manner masking a lack of natural authority.

As a child, Caradoc accompanied his mother to Hawen and in a 1944 "Self-Portrait" delivered a memorable blast against the chapel's most celebrated minister.

> There was a man who might have been Hitler's schoolin. He was Davydd Thomas,
> minister Capel Independents, the lanky red-bearded wisp who sneaked after sin like
> a tom-cat and slapped pulpit Bible and broke its back every half-year, and spat through
> his spiky teeth in denunciation. He denounced going to fairs, dablenning [drinking
> alcohol], going to church, voting for church parson, voting for a Tory, courting in or
> out of bed.[45]

"Davydd Thomas", actually David Adams (1845-1923), a boot maker's son from the
Cardiganshire hills above Talybont, had been a schoolmaster prior to his entering the
ministry; and Caradoc narrowly missed being one of his very first pupils. For following
teacher-training at Bangor, Adams was appointed headmaster at Rhydlewis, but at the
last minute he opted for Llanelli, thus allowing his college pal John Crowther, who
much preferred a rural posting, to remain in Wales.[46] Crowther remembered their first
meeting. The young Adams commanded attention, through his looks ("tall, slender... a
fairly thick crop of chestnut hair crowning the well-shaped forehead") and his quietly
determined opinions ("he would not, or could not, support or acquiesce in what he did
not believe"). The two became close companions at Bangor, walking around Garth point
each morning before classes began.

As Adams made possible Crowther's coming to Rhydlewis so, a decade later, the
headmaster brought his friend to the village. In autumn 1877 Adams, now a graduate
(having spent the intervening years in teaching and as a student at Swansea and Aberystwyth), wrote to express his willingness to preach in Hawen's untenanted pulpit with a
view to gaining a living there. Traditionally, Rhydlewis deacons favoured older, experienced
candidates over young college-trained men, but so urgently did Crowther press Adams's
case that in 1878 he was duly ordained Congregationalist minister of Hawen and Bryn-
gwenith. (When soon afterwards Adams married, the village school closed for Crowther
to attend the wedding.)

In the twists of his relations with David Adams, John Crowther liked to see God's
guiding hand: "Providence interfered in 1866 to send me and not Mr Adams to Rhydlewis,
and the same Divine Power made me, indirectly, the means of bringing him to Hawen
as minister of the Gospel. No, my friends, such things are not 'accidents'."[47] Perhaps
the same Divine Power sent Crowther to Bethesda in 1890, two years after Adams had
settled there. Evans saw it rather differently: "I knew one thing. Schoolins got their jobs
because they were religious Independents and the Independents were stronger than the
Methodists."

Caradoc's unremitting hostility towards Adams has puzzled most commentators.
They find it remarkable that he should have overlooked the gifts, not simply of David
Adams but of a long line of distinguished Hawen ministers. J.T. Jones ("John Eilian")
summed up conventional opinion when he insisted that "the people of Rhydlewis have
been ministered to, not by pusillanimous, oppressive and even cruel men, as Mr Caradoc
Evans makes out, but by a succession of men of noble character, of highest intellectual
attainment, and qualities in every way outstanding."[48] David Adams's academic and
literary achievements demonstrate his ability and he has his place in Welsh theology.

One further point about David Adams: he was, on the threshold of his ministry, a convinced ecumenicalist who additionally held that scientists should be met on their own grounds. He voiced his anger at Welsh Nonconformity's failings in these areas:

> If we were to ask what is the greatest obstruction to our understanding and realizing the benign catholic, tolerant, cosmopolitan spirit of New Testament Christianity, we should unhesitatingly reply that it is sectarian bigotry, sectarian animosities, arising from the infallibility which is always born of ignorance and want of culture... The pulpit in Wales is too often turned into a "Coward's Castle", whence the preacher fulminates against scientific men, and other proscribed heretics, with an air of self-complacent superiority which is quite sickening. These learned ignoramuses are already laughed at quietly by the wisest amongst their own congregation, and if the pulpit is to retain the power it has wielded and command the respect it has enjoyed in the past, it must certainly change its front in regard to many current questions that await solutions.[49]

The sentiments come close to Caradoc's – chapels, surrounded by every social ill, fixated on denominational rivalry and (he would add) the marginal issue of temperance – but what matters here is the differing outlets through which the two men censured Nonconformity's crippling sectarianism. Adams addressed a closed Welsh readership whereas Caradoc Evans sounded off in the pages of a Fleet Street newspaper, something Adams could never do; whatever Welsh Nonconformity's failings, its standing in the eyes of the English had to be maintained.

"It is rough marble that is given us for our substance, but it is Education that is to chisel it into a splendid form." This translated couplet,[50] from Adams's eisteddfod poem of 1877, epitomizes the high value that Welsh Nonconformity placed on education as a means of self-realisation and social advancement. (It was a means actively pursued by the local chapel hierarchy: of the sixty-six Rhydlewis children who received a secondary education between 1890 and 1912, thirty-two were the offspring of ministers and deacons.)[51] Adams's own career testified to the benefits of education – it raised him to a peak of social leadership – and his minister's skills as catechist charged many a denominational gathering where adults and children presented themselves for interrogation on scriptural passages. No one in this role was more eminent, or more feared, than David Adams. It was fear he evoked in young Caradoc. A newspaper interview of 1924 recounts his boyish terror of "David Adams, the slim, tyrannical, red-haired preacher, whose presence on the road caused children to clamber over the hedges to escape his wrath; and grown-up people who feigned delight in his talk found real joy in cursing him when he had passed on."[52]

"Mr David Adams made the people think as he thought and vote as he willed them to," Evans added, a point underscored by J.T. Jones: "Mr Adams and Mr Crowther were the two who did most to create public opinion at Rhydlewis."[53] Adams and Crowther were Congregationalists and – inevitably – political Liberals. Crowther actively "championed the Liberal cause with his pen, his election songs being very popular".[54] His emotions must have been mixed at the time of the 1868 election when, his school log-book entry records, he "had to reprove some of the boys for shouting after some Tories as they passed the schoolroom during playing-time." Hawen housed Liberal Party gatherings and children were not debarred – an enthused young Caradoc Evans lobbed a stone through the parson's window during a tithe riot of 1889.[55]

Working in tandem, Adams and Crowther propelled the teetotal cause. If less fanatical than Twrgwyn's John Green, Adams initiated a programme of temperance meet-ings (at which Caradoc sometimes recited), while Crowther distributed back numbers of the *Band of Hope Review* to children with exercise books "written carefully without blots". Crowther reflected on the prevalence of drink, sometimes in surprising quarters. In his very first month in the village he met one prominent minister over a pint in a pub and would witness another "so much under the influence of drink in the pulpit that he had difficulty standing up".[56] The temperance cause was winning, if slowly. Nor was drink the only taboo. At Blaenbarre, William Powell caught one of his sons in bed with a farm servant girl. "Jiw, jiw," he exclaimed, "what next? Smoking!" The Powells were more comfortable with drink (and perhaps with courting in bed) than they were with cigarettes. In Rhydlewis at large temperance remained the major concern with smoking a borderline issue, resisted by some as promotive of carnal indulgence. (It remained among Caradoc's local "temptashoons": "beer, cigarettes, cinemas").

As Crowther gave to the chapel, conducting the singing classes there,[57] so Adams kept an eye on the school. Crowther recorded the minister's visits as Board member (three in 1884), but even when not present in the flesh he might be brought to mind. As a composition exercise, one class was asked to reproduce all they could remember of "Mr. Adams' lecture on Ieuan Gwynedd [Revd Evan Jones, a Welsh Nonconformist exemplar] delivered at Hawen on Tuesday evening" (log-book entry, 9 March 1883). Ministers, of whatever stripe, served as bogeymen, their visits becoming occasions for displays of good behaviour. "Noisy girls," complained Crowther the day after one such visit, "asked them what the Rev. R. J. Lloyd would have thought had he called on Tuesday instead of Monday" (1 May 1885). The commotion at old Newgate schoolhouse on magic lantern evenings was more forgivable. Severe weather failed to dampen the turn-out of children in March 1886 – yet "their parents think it too cold for them to be in school", Crowther ruefully noted – and three years later another packed audience, Caradoc among them, warmed to slides of comic postcards and scenic views of north Wales. Tem-perance plates ("I've drunk my last glass") and a portrait of Gladstone, an idol of the Welsh, pointed up more serious concerns. The evening's entertainment had been funded by Uncle Joshua Powell, applause for whom rivalled that for the Gladstone slide.[58]

Both Crowther and Adams had literary ambitions and Crowther (as Glanceri) pub-lished much pastoral poetry. Welsh poetry, Caradoc would confess, was never to his taste. He did, however, point to one local influence, the underground verse satire associated with the Congregationalist minister Thomas Cynfelyn Benjamin (1850-1925). Edward Wright's early article on Evans paints Cynfelyn as "an old and broken man, who promised to be a master of eloquence but failed in his religious career, either from too

stubborn and independent a character or from too errant a way of life". He "spread his
verses by reciting them by the firesides of houses and in the hayfields, where he was
made welcome", and young Caradoc sat at his feet; for Cynfelyn "used to come to his
mother's house for milk, butter and other food, and to declaim the latest of his works".[59]
Evans must have spoken approvingly of the mendicant poet and Wright's account of the
man broadly accords with the facts.[60] Born at Capel Bangor, Cynfelyn Benjamin experienced mixed fortunes in south Wales before he moved to America where he trained
for the ministry. Back in Wales, in 1896 he took up the living of grim-faced Pisgah Independent Chapel, Talgarreg (some five miles north of Rhydlewis). There his preaching
began to be questioned, as did the brand of wit and playfulness he brought to the pulpit.
When a Pisgah faction began to work for his removal, Cynfelyn's response was to jot
down on postcards satiric verses on chapel leaders and mail them to their targets. But
the chapel always wins; in July 1905 his letter of resignation was accepted. From Talgarreg
he retired to Brynaraul, Rhydlewis, where his fortunes further declined. No chapel
would grant him a living; he preached the occasional sermon, driven to engagements
by pony and trap. (Eventually he returned to south Wales and died at Llwynypia workhouse
in 1925.)

    What of contact with Caradoc? The two might well have met at Lanlas, for Mali
Evans extended her hospitality to pedlar-preachers and various social misfits – "no tramp
or poor man ever left her door empty-handed", her *Welsh Gazette* obituary asserts – and
for years Cynfelyn was in easy reach of her. But the notion of Caradoc sitting at his feet
from childhood is fanciful. By the time Cynfelyn came to Talgarreg, Caradoc had found
employment in Cardiff and during Cynfelyn's Rhydlewis years he was making his way
in Fleet Street. These were also the years when Caradoc began to write stories. Cynfelyn
may have offered encouragement, for he took an interest in another local author – Evans's
friend, the satirist Sarnicol (Thomas Jacob Thomas) acknowledged his early influence –
and Evans on his holidays would surely have been drawn to the wayward wit and rebel,
a man doubtless more commanding in the flesh than on the page: *Odlau'r Awelon* (1906),
considered representative of his poetry, shows habitual sympathy for the underdog ("The
Persecuted Bird", "He Who Persecutes the Orphaned Girl", "Do Not Starve the Preacher")
but barely qualifies as satire.

On leaving school at fourteen, Caradoc would go to work as a draper's assistant in Carmarthen and angrily come to resent the circumstances that consigned him to "the densest
occupation in the world". He saw his talents as frustrated for want of a decent education,
something that might have been his had help been forthcoming from his mother's brother,
Dr Joshua Powell. It never was – and consequently he'd been driven into drapery. Evans
detested his uncle, placing him next to Adams and Elias in his pantheon of local demons
and weaving around him elaborate fantasies. Such loathing Rhydlewis folk have regarded
as wholly unwarranted. David Jenkins rightly speaks of the affection in which Dr Powell
was widely held; and as late as 1952, following Professor Gwyn Jones's extended radio
portrait of Caradoc Evans, Joshua's daughter, Mrs Evelyn Evans, could speak of the

many letters and messages received in protest at its unfair treatment of her father, "portrayed as a completely dishonourable person, guilty of the most shameful conduct". Trained at University College, London, Joshua Powell by 1875 had qualified as doctor and surgeon. For a time he worked as house surgeon at London's Royal Free Hospital before settling down to general practice, first at Rhydlewis and afterwards at Newcastle Emlyn, the market town where he remained for the rest of his life.[61] In 1883 he married Rachel Evans, Newcastle Emlyn born and bred. Two years his senior, she gave birth in her early forties to a daughter, Mary Evelyn, and a son Thomas (who followed his father into medicine). All the while Joshua flourished professionally, becoming the local Medical Officer of Health and a Justice of the Peace for Cardiganshire and Carmarthenshire.

The notices of his death – he died, after a short illness, from pleuropneumonia on 21 October 1917 – confirm the passing of a local hero. The *Carmarthen Journal* (2 November 1917) reported his funeral as the largest seen at Newcastle Emlyn. "Rich and poor came in crowds to pay the deceased their last tribute of respect." Relatives and friends sent mountains of flowers. Caradoc's mother attended, but not Caradoc. Within a lengthy encomium, the *Cardigan and Tivy-Side Advertiser* (26 October 1917) crystallized the reputation of the man (a political Unionist – Conservative in all but name[62] – but "no bigot" in spite of this):

> To his lasting credit it is said that power and influence were never used for self-aggrandisement. He sought nothing for himself. As he used to say – "My wants are few and easily supplied." What he did was for the benefit of others. This note of service for others was one of the dominating inspirations of his life, and explains the love and devotion with which he was regarded by all classes of the community.

Such sentiments are strikingly memorialised in a quotation incised on the rugged Gorsedd pillar of his grave at Twrgwyn. The verse, from Jeremiah, runs: "He judged the cause of the poor and needy; then it was well with him: was not this to know me? Saith the Lord." (His widow Rachel barely survived his passing, being buried alongside him at Twrgwyn one week later to the day.)

Caradoc's nephew, Howell Evans, glowingly confirmed Joshua's kindnesses.[63] When Howell's mother (Caradoc's sister Sarah) married Thomas Evans of Tresaith, Joshua "often sent a calf, a heifer, or a colt to their farm [Dyffryn Bern] with the excuse that he was overstocked (he had some land attached to his house), and that he was giving the animals to save having to destroy them". The poor were not charged for his medical services; on the contrary, he would raid his own pantry if patients were lacking in food. His very death stemmed from self-sacrifice. "One night he was summoned to a cottage 12 miles away where a child was dying of pneumonia. He knew there was poverty in that home and he cleaned out the pantry at his own home before going. When he arrived he had to make an immediate operation to relieve congestion of the lungs, caught the infection, and himself died a week or so later. The child lived and is alive today." Almost alone, Annie Rees hints at a darker side. While hailing Joshua Powell "the greatest doctor of the ages" and "an idol of the countryside", she mentions how his busy, scattered practice regularly took him away from his Newcastle Emlyn home. There were extended stays at Rhydlewis, for reasons rarely mentioned and at odds with his public image. In Rees's words, "Dr Powell [was] an enemy to himself through drink; coming to Rhydlewis to sober up, for a week at a time, though he was married." Another resident agreed that while Dr Powell was half-worshipped by the older people, and widely admired as the first ever doctor from the village, drink was a problem towards the end. She remembered his pony trotting home all the way to Newcastle Emlyn, this and the smell of cigars.[64]

Caradoc makes no mention of drink. His gripe against his uncle centred on his not coming forth with the means to secure his nephew an education. But Caradoc went further, at various times putting about the story – though not in print – of a loan which his mother had made to her brother, one that was never repaid. Lordly Joshua prospered mightily while Mali languished in poverty.[65] Evans held to this reading of events, telling George Green in the mid-1930s that,

> He could remember his mother, poor and unhappy, crying a great deal. He alleged that a close relative had taken advantage of her simplicity and trust to rob her of everything... [He] told me how he grew up, often meeting this man, well-to-do, respected, unctuous and patronising, and contrasting his prosperity with his mother's poverty and want. Whether the story is factually correct or not, I do not know, but that Caradoc believed it completely I am certain. He could not tell it without being carried away by bitterness and indignation.

The story of the loan is fanciful, however passionately Caradoc might have believed it. There *was* a loan from within the family, designed to set up Joshua in practice, and every penny he repaid. As for a refusal of help in the matter of Caradoc's education, his nephew Howell Evans had views on this, and on the likely role of Joshua's wife Rachel. "You ask about Dr Powell," wrote Howell to Caradoc's widow in 1945:

> Well, the position was that he was not sufficiently well established in Caradoc's early childhood to help, though if he were established, I doubt whether he would have helped with the education of Caradoc or his [Caradoc's] brother, William, and his sisters. Dr Powell was made a Dr. by his parents on condition that he trained his younger brothers (William & Howell) in the same profession. When the training of the brothers began (it was partly a matter of apprenticeship in those days), Dr Powell's wife told them over every meal that she was not going to house and feed them. The result was that the two brothers abandoned medicine and went to America...

It is generally accepted that Joshua was good to his sister Mary and that outwardly the two of them got on well. He brought her home from Carmarthen and she had assisted him as a nurse in the early days. Nonetheless, in Caradoc's eyes his uncle was a sinister, controlling presence, wielding power over the Powells at large and conspicuously failing to assist when a little of his wealth would have gone a long way. Mali seemingly requested no help to put her son through secondary school and none was volunteered, a circumstance which Evans sorely came to resent. George Bullock (Marie Corelli's biographer), who knew Evans in the Thirties, felt that one had only to hear him mention his early frustrations and the dismal years in drapery to understand why he wrote bitterly about Wales: "Impulses to avenge ourselves are not always directed towards the people who have deserved them. Usually those who are closest, and therefore the most vulnerable, become the target for aggressive manifestations."[66] Evans's most direct expression of Joshua loathing is, predictably, in the context of education: "After *My People* was published people began to talk about me. My uncle, whose memory I hate, noised it about that it was he who had me educated; but the village schoolmaster said: 'If Caradoc can write a book, the village idiot can write a new Bible.'" In Evans's eyes, not only had Joshua not helped his mother financially, he had taken from her; not only had he not given Caradoc an education, he had positively denied him one.

"Rich people have an insolent way of dealing with their poor relatives"; "Is it not written how that we must despise our poor relations?" Evans's words as journalist reflect his understanding of a hypocritical rich relation, one ready to dispense occasional favours the more to stress dependency upon him. Here was insidious captivity practised by an outwardly benevolent guardian. Yet Dr Powell gathered money and reputation: the two went hand in hand, material prosperity and public standing. "That is the way of the earth. If you struggle to put by a few pounds, you are called a miser. But put by thousands, and people will black your boots and whitewash your character."[67]

"What has been done in youth can never be undone in age," so wrote Mrs Gaskell. A west Wales childhood does not guarantee a Caradoc Evans. Many have written of their own happy days in south Cardiganshire and a few remember Caradoc, not as a doom-laden schoolboy, but as a well-liked, fun-loving lad preaching mock sermons in the playground, dispensing rough justice as monitor and mildly enjoying his privileges (one ex-pupil recalls how he promised to mark her sums right in return for an apple, "a special apple" he said). Village life had its many facets and why Evans chose the materials he did to furnish his fictional world is a matter of literary aptitude as well as of factual biography. Yet within a writer's personal biography it is commonly the earliest years that most intensely feed the imagination. And Caradoc's lot was a damaging one and went far to defining his nature: the loss at the age of four of a father against whom there was such obloquy;[68] the helplessness of a mother, dispossessed and widowed, before an uncle judged overbearing and hypocritical; the disappointments of school (abandoned, as he thought, by Crowther and humiliated by Elias), the tyranny of the chapel, which denied the life of the young. (Others have testified to the damage wrought on the sensitive child by the rigid codes of school and chapel.) The move to Carmarthen, at just fourteen, took him away from mother and home into a line of work that robbed him (so he came to feel) of his most precious years. Henceforth the world would seem a cruel, unforgiving place, ruled by those made untouchable by money. There was a message here, one he found articulated in George Gissing's *A Life's Morning* (1888). "Put money in thy purse; and again, put money in thy purse; for, as the world is ordered, to lack current coin is to lack the privileges of humanity, and indigence is the death of the soul." He committed the words to memory.

2

Draper's Assistant, Apprentice Journalist
1893-1913

In late February 1893 Caradoc joined Jones Brothers, the Market Hall drapery store in Carmarthen owned by cousins of his father, the brothers David and Llewelyn Rees Jones. His elder sister Mary looked after millinery there and brother Will had worked at the store prior to leaving for America. "Mother wanted to place her children in genteel trades," Evans explained, "The professions were out of the question." It was either drapery or working on the land, and "a draper – unlike a farmer – doesn't get wet".[1] His teaching ambitions frustrated, the boy had no choice but to move away from home. In this he was not alone. The 1890s saw a hastening outflow from around Rhydlewis as younger men sought opportunities in the coalfields and towns of the south. The depressed agricultural conditions of the 1880s severely struck Rhydlewis where holdings were uneconomically small (the 1881 census shows 57 per cent of farms in Troedyraur parish as of under fifty acres), a situation exacerbated by the lack of rail facilities for shifting produce to markets in the south; the rail network did not reach Newcastle Emlyn, the station serving Rhydlewis, until 1895.[2]

On the fringe of the western coalfield, Carmarthen shone as a prosperous beacon over the rural county. English, "the language of progress", was more in evidence there and it discomforted Caradoc. His stumbling command was a source of amusement for others but of agony to himself, especially so at Cardiff where customers insisted on using English and where for the first six months he felt "a load of difficulties tearing at my tongue".[3] *Nothing to Pay* (1930), the novel drawing most directly on his drapery years, talks of shop assistants using "the Carmarthen language, this language being a leavening of English and Welsh". In the novel, Boss at Carmarthen does what he can to prepare his apprentices for their chosen field. "He spoke to them not in Carmarthen English but in plain English, thus familiarizing them with the language of the draper in Swansea and Cardiff, in Bristol and Liverpool, and in Manchester and London."

Boss also helps them enjoy the high life of a thriving county town. "Every fair night he gave his apprentices half-a-crown each, screwed up in a piece of paper, in order that they might go and taste the glittering offers of the fair." Besides market and fair days, Carmarthen had its theatricals, the travelling "fit-up" companies performing mostly at the Assembly Rooms. The Johnstone players set up their stage in the market, their tent condemned by town preachers as "an evil thing of poles, ropes and canvas" and their actresses as "deep wells of sin". Those drawn to watch risked contamination. (When one of Caradoc's uncles suggested that the minstrel show he'd enjoyed at Swansea might be invited to Rhydlewis, a local minister preached against such abomination.) Yet these same pulpit-preachers struck Evans as having much in common with actors: always on show, they enjoyed a theatrical profession. Inevitably at Carmarthen, as he moved through his teens, Caradoc encountered drink and women. A London friend remembered being told "how on one occasion he ingratiated himself into the company of a buxom middle-aged actress whom he took into a public house where he 'stood' her several bottles of stout, and emerging he hoped that some of his shop-mates might see him – such a roaring and incredible 'Dog' he felt himself to be."[4] In *Nothing to Pay* this woman became the actress Florence Larney, to whom the young apprentice Amos Morgan succumbs in the fields one afternoon. Artistic, romantic, highly emotional, Florence acts as a counterweight to genteel, straight-laced Miss Owen, a picture of piety and rectitude, Amos's mothering colleague determined to save him from harm. Within Evans's own family Sarah Owen was seen as a cruel portrait of Mary, Caradoc's "prim and neat little sister", as Howell Evans described his aunt. Caradoc's behaviour would regularly embarrass her, especially his party piece of preaching from a stool in the shop the sermon he'd heard the previous Sunday. "He apparently had a very good memory, for he would go through the prayer first, almost verbatim. When he came to the sermon, he would use all the preacher's gesticulations... The 'hwyl', too, came in the right places at frequent intervals." The brothers Jones enjoyed the performance but "Mary, however, could not see the joke of it, and she was furious whenever Caradoc began to preach".[5] (Evans entertained serious thoughts of becoming a preacher, so it seems.)

Carmarthen gave Caradoc his first taste of "living-in", the much-abused system of employment whereby shop assistants were paid in part through the provision of board and lodgings. *Nothing to Pay* gives actual salaries. At Manchester House (its front "hung with bundles of towels and stockings, blouses and shirts, braces and ties, scarves and shawls, and rolls of oilcloth and calico and printed cotton and flannelette rest[ing] against the windows") Slim Jones, a senior assistant, gets £25 a year "and his eating and lodging". In contrast, a boy apprentice in his third year receives just £10 – thus the economic sense of employing apprentices straight from school. Caradoc began in haberdashery, where he learned about "spiffs", or the commission on goods judged difficult to shift, and about "squadding", the pre-breakfast preparation of the shop space for which an assistant was responsible. The widely detested living-in system was ameliorated at Carmarthen by an unusually humane employer who genuinely trained his assistants,[6] a boss who kept reasonable opening hours, provided spiffs on everything, and handed out bonuses on fair nights. "O iss, Boss was a bit of o-rait": Amos Morgan's rare tribute reflects Caradoc's high estimate of his distant relative, "not only the best Welshman I had met up to then, but... the best man I have ever met in my life".[7]

Caradoc remained apprenticed at Carmarthen for a little over three years, a conscientious assistant wishing to advance in his line of work. This meant moving to Cardiff, where he arrived in 1896 following a brief spell at Barry Dock, the freewheeling shipping town which graphically reinforced a cardinal tenet of commerce, that all money is clean ("The shilling of a harlot rings as true as that of the preacher's wife"). At Cardiff he was taken on by James Howell (1835-1909), founder and sole proprietor of the city emporium that bore his name (until 2008 when it became part of the House of Fraser chain). A Fishguard draper at first, Howell opened his Cardiff enterprise in 1865, a venture that grew prodigiously; in 1892 the premises moved to St Mary's Street, where Caradoc found a berth. All the while, James Howell gathered wealth; a farm son of Pembrokeshire, he bought a farm of his own, built the Park Hotel and cinema, and erected two baronial dwellings, each of which in time would serve as the city's Mansion House. A commanding figure in any assembly, Howell left a lasting impression on Caradoc, whose fictional portrayal rings true (he is Sam Samson in *Nothing to Pay*). Though Howell's success brought grudging admiration, he was judged despotic, harsh and unfeeling by his own commercial kind. In the novel his fear-ridden store resembles a military unit, its staff in rigid hierarchy simultaneously bullying juniors and grovelling before superiors.

> At nine o'clock the shop-walkers appeared, and they all wore frock coats and wavy moustaches, and not one was under six feet in height. They splayed their feet in comely order to their several departments, gravely murmuring: "Lavatory", whereupon the ladies, their scissors swinging from their waists, and the young men, their coats hanging from their arms, stepped to the basement to tidy themselves.

Wound up for the day, they fawn cash out of customers, curtseying and madaming, waddling around the showrooms like puppets.

"When I was a shop assistant", wrote Evans, "I never exercised my brain, nor was I asked to exercise my brain."The poverty of the draper's assistant is not simply material; it accompanies a barren personal life, a poverty of interests and a lack of social concern. At Sam's, only Burns is a critic ("worser than a socialistic", a colleague tut-tuts) and, looking at those around him, the sixty-three-year-old survivor concludes that "We Welsh are ideal shop assistants because we are meek and mild hypocrites and born liars." Nothing in Sam's store suggests otherwise, save for a reference to the fledgling Shop Assistants' Union whose leaders on their boxes in The Hayes revile their employers. For years gentility had defined the shop assistant and stifled the growth of trade unionism; shop assistants felt themselves a superior class of employee, a cut above the restless manual workers. But in 1889, stirred by local militancy in a national dock strike, the Cardiff Shop Assistants' Union came into being with the immediate aim of securing a 7 p.m. closing time. Recruitment quickened as other punishing aspects of living-in became targets, with Howell's employees to the fore.[8] There is no evidence that Evans joined the Union (his friendship with Union officers came later) but his socialism can be traced back to Cardiff.

There was life beyond the counter in an anglicised city of some 150,000 ("Get English teached you, mister. You're in Cardiff now," the young Amos is advised). Caradoc sneaked in twice for Marie Corelli's *The Sorrows of Satan* at the Theatre Royal and twice for Wilson Barrett's immensely popular religious melodrama, *The Sign of the Cross*. There were other nights out too:

Long ago in Cardiff, I worked in a draper's shop. In the daytime I was openly seen, selling things by the yard across a counter, but in the evening I might have been a different person. Dressed as I considered smartly, I went with another lad from the shop, to a music hall. Really a gentleman I felt in my best clothes and hoping no one in the auditorium would recognise me as the shop assistant, don't you know? Then, as I looked around me, admiring and, as I hoped, admired, my fool of a companion gave the whole show away. He took from his pocket a long pair of scissors, such as are only used in drapers' shops, and started to cut off his nails in full view of everyone! As his nails snipped off, I remember blushing terribly.[9]

In London, Evans would freely indulge his liking for music hall, that great popular working-class entertainment. Music hall and theatre excited him, as did new reading. According to a journalist friend, borrowing a library copy of Sir Walter Besant's *All Sorts and Conditions of Men* (1882) proved a life-changing experience.

The book fired his imagination. This wonderful London, this miraculous East End which Sir Walter described almost as thrillingly as another Sir Walter had once described the Highlands of Scotland – he must see it, at all costs. In a single day Wales had become too small a country to contain Caradoc Evans.

T. Michael (Tommy) Pope exaggerates,[10] though Evans did acknowledge the moral impact of Besant's novel. The book had stirred others, arousing real sympathy for the plight of the East End poor. Queen Victoria herself in 1887 opened the People's Palace in the Mile End Road, a local educational and recreational centre built by subscription as a tangible expression of this sympathy and a direct result of Besant's novel (in which the Palace is envisaged).

Reading also meant the *Western Mail*, a daily newspaper that came to stand for the disputatious, liberating city. At Rhydlewis news came courtesy of Sam Post, the postman whose joy in ill tidings was so great that Caradoc in a later light-hearted piece has him discarding letters that were cheery. "Sam's sayings gathered in the rolling, for a whispered secret is speedier than a shout in the highway: and though the stories were clothed differently at each telling, they were never false."[11] (Gossip defined the rural community, as communal opinion shaped the lives of those who lived there.) At Cardiff in the evenings, after twelve hours serving in the shop, Evans crossed St Mary's Street to the offices of the *Western Mail*, drawn by the clatter of printing machines. What sort of work went on inside? What sort of people wrote for newspapers? Sooner than he imagined, he would find out.

The south Wales years were important in his teenage awakening – he left for London in his twentieth year, having "put on the trousers of manhood". The 1890s were likewise critical in the history of south Wales. Accelerating expansion of the coalfields brought signs of a political and cultural reorientation. Caradoc shared in this: the Rhydlewis boy was now a reader, drawn to theatre and music hall, becoming more politically aware.

Fired or not by Besant, Caradoc took the draper's path to London, almost certainly in 1899, there to serve in shops for six more years. The self-discovery continued and with it a growing conviction that life had more to offer. A fellow shop assistant and close friend at this time, the Lampeter-born Duncan Davies, has left an invaluable record of Evans's early London days.[12] He recounts how he [Caradoc] first found employment in one appalling Kentish Town establishment. Housed on the premises, he shared a bedroom with nine other "slaves of the counter", working daily from 7 a.m. to 8 p.m. (on Saturdays up till midnight). There was no bathroom, which did not unduly depress him – he had never been accustomed to such a luxury (he would first see a bathroom many months later in a house in London's West End). Evans duly fled Kentish Town for Thomas Wallis's, a celebrated store on Holborn Circus where, if anything, conditions were worse. Of Wallis's regime Davies writes:

> The assistants were subjected to the harshest discipline. On starting their engagement they were furnished with a four-page brochure giving the "Rules" of the Establishment, breach of any of these Rules entailing fines varying from 3d. to half-a-crown. One fine was that of 3d. for being late at prayers in the morning – the day's work was ushered in… with prayers conducted by the curate of a local church, whose stipend was, at least partially, paid out of the "worshippers'" fines. Of these "Rules" Caradoc used to say wryly: "It is difficult enough to keep Moses' Ten Commandments but, when is came to Wallis' two hundred, I was whacked."[13]

Evans spoke of having been sacked from a succession of London draperies: in March 1901 he was certainly at Selby's on the Holloway Road, a large store owned and managed by James Selby, another Pembrokeshire man. The census return for that year shows a "David Evans" of Rhydlewis, one of fourteen assistants living in, together with a cook and two housemaids. The assistants – five men, three women – were mostly in their late teens and twenties (adding a couple of years, Evans gave his age as twenty-four).

Soon afterwards he arrived at the great Bayswater emporium of William Whiteley, the one place providing "everything from a pin to an elephant" – Harrods and Selfridges came afterwards. There Caradoc met Duncan Davies and worked beside Margaret Bondfield, another trade union activist (and later Labour MP) who had also been apprenticed to drapery at fourteen; she sold blouses, Caradoc umbrellas.[14] Conditions at Whiteleys were more tolerable; employees lived at Vine Court, Kensington, a nearby barrack-like building accommodating over four hundred staff in cubicles of between two and four men each. Sheer numbers made strict supervision impossible and the atmosphere stayed comparatively relaxed. The basement housed a large common room where men might gather for billiards, cards or conversation. All humanity could be savoured there: "Broken-down actors, barristers, journalists, seemed to be able to find a niche in that vast organisation".[15] But reading and writing were difficult. Duncan Davies recalls Caradoc grappling with Shakespeare and Dickens against an incessant buzz of talk. Again and again he would say, "If only I had a garret, and attic of my own somewhere, I should be as happy as a king." Things worsened when, encouraged by Davies, he registered for weekly evening classes, briefly at Whitechapel's Toynbee Hall, then at the Working Men's College.

The Working Men's College had been founded in 1854 by (among others) F.D. Maurice, Charles Kingsley and Thomas Hughes (author of *Tom Brown's Schooldays*), all inspired by Robert Owen's educational ideals; John Ruskin, Edward Burne-Jones, Lowes Dickinson and Leslie Stephen were among its early teachers. Evans joined classes on 27 October 1904.[16] For the first year he took composition, supported by additional grammar instruction and classes in history; during the second year he applied himself exclusively to composition. Between these years the College moved premises, from Great Ormond Street to the classic Edwardian educational building it still occupies on Crowndale Road, St Pancras.[17] Though a student for just two years, Evans benefited hugely from his time at Crowndale Road and always mentioned the College in his biographical summaries for reference books – it appears in every one of his otherwise constantly changing *Who's Who* entries. He sacrificed to attend, incurring fines for missing evening prayers at Whiteleys when classes ran late. He had sensed his means of liberation, as Howell Evans reflected:

> What caused Caradoc's frustration more than anything, I think, was the long struggle on a mere pittance from one drapery store to another. He hated the job intensely – long hours, poor food, no hope of saving any money, no hope of escape. And all the time he wanted to express himself, to preach at first, then to write; but without education he could do nothing. One can just imagine his sense of impotence when he thought of it all – the complete frustration of all he desired, all he lived for, by economic necessity. His fight for freedom, via the Working Men's College, must have been very grim, and only a man of the strongest will could have won through as he did.[18]

Tommy Pope mentions E. J. Turner as one tutor who took "considerable interest" in Caradoc's progress. Just two years older than his pupil, Ernest John Turner, son of a Kensington schoolmaster, had embarked on a successful career in the India Office after gaining a first-class Cambridge degree. His association with the Working Men's College was long and productive, and his examination papers suggest the grounding he offered in composition; a flexible prose was the aim, one that might tackle a job application and as well as a conventional essay. Another staff member looked over Caradoc, the octogenarian scholar-editor Dr F. J. Furnivall (reputedly the inspiration for Ratty in Kenneth Grahame's *The Wind in the Willows*); together with Turner, he encouraged Caradoc's short-story writing and possibly his wider ambition of abandoning shop work for journalism.[19]

It is tempting to speculate on what might have happened had Evans chosen to attend Morley College in Waterloo Road, for in 1904 the young Virginia Woolf began as tutor there. Her students resembled those at Crowndale Road. During Evans's years, manual workers made up more than 40 per cent of the students, the others being clerks, shop assistants and lower-paid professionals. Woolf described those in her own Wednesday composition class:

10 people: 4 men, 6 women... I have an old Socialist of 50 who thinks he must bring the Parasite (the Aristocrat)... into an Essay on Autumn; and a Dutchman who thinks – at the end of the class too – that I have been teaching him Arithmetic; and anaemic shop girls who say they would write more but they only get an hour for their dinner, and there doesn't seem much time for writing...

In a report she generalizes more sympathetically on those she taught in 1905:[20]

On the whole they were possessed of more intelligence than I had expected; though the intelligence was almost wholly uncultivated. But of this I am convinced; that it would not be hard to educate them sufficiently to give them a new interest in life; they have tentacles languidly stretching forth from their minds, feeling vaguely for substance, & easily applied by a guiding hand to something that [they] could really grasp.

These observations well fit Caradoc in his twenties; restless at work, responsive to guidance, and quietly convinced that he was fitted for something better than shop work.

His time at evening school, and at Whiteleys, nourished his political radicalism. The ethos of the Working Men's College was strongly Christian socialist – Furnivall praised it as "free from all stupid and narrow class humbug" – and its conception of education went beyond the narrowly functional. All the while, Whiteleys store saw much resolute union action organised by P.C. Hoffman and Duncan Davies, both officials of the fledging Shop Assistants' Union. In June 1901 Davies led thirteen banner-carrying Whiteleys staff in a West End march advertising a protest meeting against living-in, an event that effectively signalled the end of a hated employment regime.

Both a literary and political mentor, six years older than Caradoc, Davies introduced his Whiteleys' pal to the work of Robert Blatchford. Evans must have been drawn to Blatchford's personal odyssey, to his socialist ideals, to the outlook and tone of his celebrated *Clarion* newspaper. Of lower-class Congregationalist background, Blatchford left the army for a career in journalism, having taught himself to write largely by reading Bunyan and the Old Testament. "It was Blatchford's simple grandeur that led me to discover the English Bible," Evans explained. Another Evans friend-to-be, the writer Edwin Pugh, elaborates on this "simple grandeur", finding Blatchford's style "clear, strong, picturesque, easy and graceful, yet concise and full of pith". The weekly *Clarion*, founded in 1891 to champion those whose days were spent in "drudging toil, weary poverty and anxious care", gained a shop worker's ready support, but Blatchford's socialism had other dimensions. He directed his message against the panoply of organised religion and all its chill restrictions. To one minister objecting to the sale of Sunday newspapers he replied: "we expect the enmity of the Church... Parsons and ourselves are natural antagonists. We preach virtue, charity and humanity. They preach religion. The two are diametrically opposed to one another."[21] Here was a radicalism divorced from the chapel-riddled south Wales kind. The *Clarion* printed poetry and fiction, book and theatre reviews, and by marrying politics and literature opened up new cultural ·

vistas. Anti-puritan contributors were spreading a form of bohemianism among their lower-class Nonconformist readership,[22] and dabs of the bohemian colour Duncan Davies's picture of Evans at this time – his theatre and music-hall enthusiasms, his late-night suppers and drinking.

From village magic-lantern shows, through Carmarthen's fit-up companies and Cardiff's Theatre Royal, to London's theatreland was heady progression. Duncan Davies recalled the many stars they saw from the shilling gallery, Henry Irving, Ellen Terry, Beerbohm Tree among them. Surprisingly, he makes no mention of Marie Lloyd, though Evans pays striking tribute to the music-hall idol in his classic "Self-Portrait", where he credits her with having influenced his approach as story-teller. More celebrated writers have offered testimony to her gifts; "a born artist", thought the Woolfs; "a great woman", wrote T.S. Eliot, pointing to "the perfect expressiveness of her smallest gestures... all a matter of selection and concentration... her understanding of the people and sympathy for them".[23] This approach, her letting the audience fill in the blanks ("she tells a story not by what she says but by what she says not," wrote Evans),[24] might well have proved a helpful stylistic model, particularly as in Marie's case it was aimed at dishonest puritanism.

Arthur Machen, another Welshman in London, confirmed how the theatre might serve as a symbol of metropolitan gaiety, in contrast to the dull grey provincialism of home. He glossed atmospherically Thackeray's seemingly straightforward question, "Do you like the theatre?":

> – do you like the mingled gas and orange odours of the theatre, do you like the sound of the orchestra tuning, the sight of the footlights suddenly lightening, can you project yourself readily into the fantastic world disclosed by the rising curtain, and afterwards, do you like a midnight chop at Evans's, with Welsh rarebit to follow, and foaming tankards of brown stout, and then "something hot"; in fine, do you like to be out and about in the midst of gaiety at hours of the night when your uncles and aunts and all quiet country people are abed and fast asleep?[25]

Evans would have said "yes" to all these questions. The London stage, the vibrant music hall with its patterers and dancers, its melodrama and sentimentality, its audience participation and celebration of working-class values, all had captivated him. In time he would himself write for the theatre and, with fluctuating enthusiasm, much later support his second wife's theatrical ventures.

"Looking back on it all," Duncan Davies reflected, "I marvel at the wonderful times we had on our pitifully small incomes, but then 5/- would pay for a theatre seat, a very good supper at Gatti's and several pints of beer." Gatti's was a favourite; doubling as a music hall, it stayed open beyond midnight, so that Evans sometimes found himself locked out of Vine Court and forced to take lodgings for the night, or else wander the streets till daybreak. Other favourite restaurants included Rules in Maiden Lane, the Bedford Street Bodega and the Bun Shop on the Strand. Davies liked the Strand, "a delightful street full of quaint old taverns" where Caradoc enjoyed drawing out the ex-actors who gathered there. As for wonderful times on small incomes, Evans at Whiteleys earned some £35 per annum. With a further £25 or so in spiffs, and board and lodgings equivalent to some £50, he and other London drapery assistants were close to what was then the average income of £120 a year (one which might allow a young man to consider marriage). There were rooms enough for rent in central London, offering bed and board at 15/6d. a week (or even less); good suits could be bought for four guineas, a pair of boots for 15 shillings, and beer cost 4½d. a pint

Davies recognized in Evans a young man of exceptional gifts and "so far as love of study and literature was concerned a kindred spirit." Inseparable companions, in the evenings and on weekends they wandered Soho, explored the exotic East End, combed various second-hand bookstalls. Books piled on barrows might be had for between a halfpenny and a shilling; Charing Cross Road housed better, more expensive stuff. London's literary landmarks were eagerly sought out – "we could have taken full marks in an examination of Dickens' topography," judged Davies. Caradoc was steeped in Dickens, having spent one annual leave reading John Forster's massive biography in Kensington Gardens – a cardsharper at Whiteleys had swindled him out of money set aside for the annual trip to Rhydlewis.

In appearance, Caradoc struck him as "a tall, very dark young man wearing pince-nez with gold rims, with a length of thin, silk cord, always, I recollect, passed back behind the ear. He moved very rapidly in quick jerky movements – a sort of half-run, and always, when alone, seemed to be in a hurry. Of course, in our London explorations the pace was reduced to a leisurely amble."[26] As for Evans's personality, this was fixed in adolescence, acknowledged by himself and others over the years. "Very quick to take offence, but, very forgiving – the sun never went down on his wrath"; "he had a fury and a quick temper, but, he always had himself well in hand".[27] Occasionally Davies penetrated the fiery surface, and Caradoc's "curious impish whimsicality", to a "deep seriousness and sadness" beneath. "If this emerged at all, as it did sometimes, it was immediately suppressed by some humorous gibe. He had a great love for his mother and I have often seen him buy something from a shop window which he thought would please her, or his invalid brother, and he was very careful that no news went home but good news."[28]

Besides his reading and night-school studies, Evans while at Whiteleys had taken to short-story writing. "There are shop assistants in London today," wrote Thomas Burke (a short-story writer and Fleet Street companion), "who remember a thin, saturnine colleague of theirs who went from counter to counter begging for the paper overlaps of the boxes in which gloves are packed."[29] Evans could afford little for writing paper, so "Upon this glove box paper he made his first experiments in the short story."[30] In October 1904 came remarkable success: *Reynolds's Newspaper* accepted one of his efforts and paid him fifteen shillings. This story, untitled and printed anonymously, he always referred to as "A Sovereign Remedy" and it constitutes his very first publication. Caradoc caught the socialist Sunday – badge of emancipation for Mr Doran in Joyce's *Dubliners* – at an opportune moment: in summer 1904 the paper introduced a page-two weekly story and sought original contributions to intersperse with reprinted pieces. Buoyed by its appearance (23 October 1904), Evans had registered at the Working Men's College. With the need for a room of his own now more pressing, in early 1905 he quit Whiteleys for an Oxford Street store that permitted its staff to live out. He found accommodation on the second floor of a house in Northumberland (now Luxborough) Street, opposite Marylebone workhouse: a small back room in a dismal quarter but with space for a shelf of books and the peace enough for writing. "I doubt whether Caradoc ever enjoyed greater happiness than during those early days of deliverance from bondage."[31] (Years previously Anthony Trollope, then a post office clerk, had lodged in this same "very uninviting street... opposite the deadest part of the dead wall" of the workhouse.)

In summer 1905 Evans struck again when the *Free Lance* paid him a guinea for "The Star Turn", a story published in its 19 August issue; "he had shaken the tree of prayer and a little fruit had fallen to the ground".[32] The *Free Lance*, though short-lived, was a reputable paper founded by Clement Scott, the *Daily Telegraph*'s theatre critic. Acceptance of this second story settled Evans's mind. He would slip his drapery chains, continue writing stories, and hope for a break in journalism. With a working capital of two pounds ten, he threw up his Oxford Street job and found new lodgings at 41 Munster Square, off Regents Park. From this address he registered for his second year at the Working Men's College, his occupation now recorded as "clerk".[33]

The pull towards journalism was real, something more than romantic attachment to the externals of the trade, though this he had in plenty: Saturday evenings found him spellbound, pressed against the railings of the *News of the World* as the presses began to roll. As we have seen, the magic of printing had struck while at Cardiff, something he confessed to the *Western Mail*:

> In the evenings of those days I used to stand without your office and smell your ink and listen to the music of your machines, and wonder what sort of folk wrote for you, and printed you, and put you to bed, and what happened to you between bed-hour and the hour I had seen you waking up in the farmhouse kitchen, village shop, in smithy, in hayfield, and twice in the awful hands of the parish policeman, who rested against a hedge.[34]

His nephew Howell confirmed all this, of Caradoc glued to the grating at St Mary's Street, watching the rotary machines running off their editions. "He often spoke to me for hours when I was a small child about printing and he always described it as the most fascinating of arts."[35] Caradoc's article, "Children and News" (1923), probes the roots of this attachment:

> Youth cares little for the fooleries and vanities of the world; it hankers after the doings of the people of the world and its sights. It is hungry for news. It wants the lid lifted that the sunshine shall show up the things which it has been cheated of. To say all in a few words: it wants a newspaper.[36]

As with much else that motivated the man, the impulse to journalism lay in the restrictions of childhood. For him, newspapers stood for enlightenment and liberation. Such feelings come more readily to village youths yearning for a world outside. The writer-journalist Arthur Machen, who for a while would be close to Caradoc, vividly records the impact of London newspapers on another Welsh youth buried in the countryside:

> … for me the *Standard* and *Telegraph* became mystic documents of the highest interest and most vital consequence; these were the charts to the Terra Nova Incognita; every line in them came from the heart of the mystery and were written by men who were learned in all the wisdom of London. London papers I must have; so I set out to get them.[37]

He did so by walking four miles from his home (Llanddewi Rectory, Caerleon) to the W.H. Smith bookstall at Pontypool Road station for copies of the national dailies. "I would make my way out of the station and along the high road till I came to the stile, and alone under a tree or in the shelter of a friendly hedge I would open my papers, cut their pages, and plunge into the garden of delights."

However strong the motivation, Evans's journalistic ambitions might have seemed unrealistic, particularly as he still wrote English laboriously as an acquired second tongue and had reached his late twenties, past the point where most journalists began their career. Yet Fleet Street at this time had its encouraging aspects. Magazine publication enjoyed unprecedented growth as proprietors capitalized on technical advances in printing and papermaking and on improved transport networks for distributing their wares. Newly founded magazines strove to attract a readership whose tastes and interests were barely recognised by the more established journals. Fresh markets were opening up among people never before counted as readers. Evans was one of them, board-school educated, recently employed in a shop, imbibing *T.P.'s Weekly* at leisure moments. Founded by T.P. O'Connor in 1902, this penny literary paper published pieces by some reputable names (Bennett, Shaw and Wells) and serialised Conrad's *Nostromo* through much of 1904. The paper "exercised my brain and heated my imagination" – in Caradoc's case through fiction by Thomas Hardy, Arthur Morrison, and the French and Russian writers, Tolstoy especially ("the perfect story-teller").

In a sub-world beneath *T.P.'s Weekly* jostled more precarious magazines. Whatever their banner titles, their ingredients were much the same. There had to be "information", neatly packaged and easily assimilated, often as facts offered discretely or as answers to readers' queries. There were articles and sketches, some signed by celebrities though ghosted by old journalistic hands. Jokes and humour played their part (often pictorial), as did endless competitions with cash prizes. The presence of short stories, facile products of practised pens, gave most magazines a literary air. Readers wanted them, and editors sought them out. Best-selling novelists would occasionally contribute, along with fertile Edwardian belletrists and authors of serious standing. Fiction writers, whatever their hue, depended on journalism for a living.

These were the publications in Evans's sights as outlets for his fiction or, better still, as potential employers. There were reasons for optimism. At the turn of the century, journalists grew appreciably faster in number than did other categories of professional, and if the profession remained a humble one, poorly paid and with little job security (shop assistants were used to this, dismissal at a moment's notice), at least no formal qualifications were required. The gates of Fleet Street were wide and Evans felt ready to enter. He would begin by submitting his stories.

"But I found that though the gates of Fleet Street are wide, the ways of editors are exceedingly narrow. Down as the heart of a trusting maid whose lover has broken his pledge was my heart when all my work was rejected with printed compliments…"[38] For close on a year (late 1905 to October 1906) he remained unemployed, living precariously at Munster Square. He told Duncan Davies of the "happy discovery" of how to suppress one's appetite. "I bought a 2d packet of cigarettes in a shop in Wardour Street, and found that by smoking three of them, in rapid succession, they made me so sick that I could not look at food again that day. They saved me no end of money."[39] Then came a happy break, with the founding of yet another penny weekly designed to catch the popular market. The first issue of *Chat*, "the really new weekly for home and train", edited by one C.A. Farmer, a penniless adventurer, appeared on 13 October 1906 carrying a short story by Evans entitled "King's Evidence". It won him five guineas, a success he repeated two issues later with "An Inch from Death" (27 October). For the first story Caradoc kept the pseudonym "D. Evans Emmott" which had served for the *Free Lance* (the "Emmott" is something of a puzzle, having no obvious source). For "An Inch from Death" he wore a comic disguise as a precaution against *Chat's* reluctance to award a second five guineas to the same competitor. Accordingly, the paper announced its 27 October winner as "S. Wales, Lanlas, Rhydlewis, Cardigan". Soon afterwards came the prize most longed for, a job on *Chat* as apprentice sub-editor. Pieces by "Emmott" continue, but others are left to win the competitions.

The circumstances of appointment to this, the first of his Fleet Street posts, are amusingly recounted in a 1930 essay, "A Bundle of Memories":

> Presently I wrote to the editor-proprietor of a weekly paper and he answered that I could call upon him, and I called in my trade garments: black frock coat and trousers, a high stiff collar, a bulging black tie, a silk hat, yellow boots. He engaged me at three pounds a week, but he did not say any more about salary or pay me any; then at the end of the fourth week he asked me for ten pounds to save the paper from death. I borrowed the money and gave it to him. The paper must have had readers, for one afternoon a pawnbroker's assistant came to the office, saying that he wanted the editor to tell him how to get on, because his employer had told him to get out. The editor said: "God made you a journalist. Three pounds a week." From him he borrowed twenty pounds…

The facts here are essentially true, though Evans put abroad another version that had him winning not just the short-story prize but an editorial post that went with it. [40]

However obtained, and whether salaried or not (Evans mentions surviving on savings), the post with *Chat* offered far from humdrum experience:

> My editor was always waiting for a fluke. He used to say *Pearson's Weekly* was a failure until they saturated an issue with eucalyptus oil during a 'flu epidemic... We lived by the grace of a printer and a paper merchant, and for fuel we tore up the landlord's linoleum and broke up the landlord's shelves. Somehow a man who had a rich father was found and the father took over the liabilities and gave the editor a sum of money for himself and a sum with which to pay what was due to my colleague and me.

Fleet Street cherished notions of success by chance. *Titbits* and *Answers*, two giants among popular weeklies, had luck on their side, and *Pearson's Weekly* became their rival by means of a stunt, a prodigiously successful "missing word" competition where readers were asked to supply a blindingly obvious word omitted from a passage of verse. No such luck fell upon *Chat*, or *London Chat* as it quickly became:

> The rich man's son then sat in the editorial chair and he conducted the paper for the purposes of writing prose impressions of the London Salvage Corps and limerick impressions of some waitresses at a teashop, and obtaining books and theatre seats for nothing. The paper failed, as do all papers which are run by rich amateurs...

Failure came within a couple of years, the issue of 5 July 1908 being effectively the last (though unsold copies, masquerading as new weekly issues, were on sale until 10 October).

However perilous his initiation into Fleet Street, one positive for Evans was to have Edward Wright as a colleague, a gifted journalist brought in to bolster practices. J.A. Hammerton (later Sir John) considered Wright "a truly remarkable and quite unknown man of genius", one who could write with style and erudition on almost any topic under the sun (he produced some impressive pieces for the *Quarterly Review*, notably one on Anatole France). Evans learned the rudiments of editing from Wright, who gave his impressions of his pupil:

> We worked side by side on the sub-editor's table, and though he was a careful and improving hand at the routine business of make-up, as a writer he was at first deplorable. He was dogged and reticent... He thought and composed in Welsh, and then translated into English. Only when he could mechanically put in some slab of journalese was he saved the worry of wildly roundabout composition. I had the happiness of meeting him in his apprenticeship and seeing him suddenly become a master.[41]

We have little evidence of this mastery in the papers Evans worked on. As a writer he was rarely free-flowing, and if at *Ideas* he developed a highly engaging editorial voice, he was not a writing journalist (the few ad hoc pieces he produced reflect marked personal interests). He preferred the sub-editors' table, processing the efforts of others.

Although treated cavalierly in retrospect, the *Chat* years were not a waste. A ready outlet for his fiction, the paper (thanks to Wright) gave Evans some professional grounding and paid sufficiently well to allow another move of quarters: sometime in 1907 he vacated Munster Square for 65 Cavendish Buildings, Clerkenwell Road. On £3 a week he now felt able to take a yet more important step. Unbeknown to his mother, on Christmas Day 1907 at Holborn Register Office, he married Rosie Jessie Sewell, daughter of a deceased "jobmaster" – the title of one who hired out horses, carriages and drivers (London at the turn of the century was largely a horse-drawn society). Lambeth-born and living in Soho, Rose (as she came to be known) was at thirty-one a good year older than Caradoc and with her auburn hair the prettiest girl in London, so he told his anxious mother. The choice of an English wife startled folks at home. Some thought they understood: "And did you then, Caradoc bach, marry English money?" they approached him in the village.

The period from spring 1908 to summer 1913 forms a separate phase in Evans's journalistic career. It saw a succession of jobs with Amalgamated Press, part of the domain of Alfred Harmsworth (Viscount Northcliffe), founder of modern popular journalism. The jump from *Chat's* shoe-string enterprise to the giant Amalgamated Press was immense, though even within this empire Evans encountered one or two failures.

On leaving *Chat*, he joined the squad of assistants helping J.A. Hammerton, a master of the large-scale reference work, compile the *Harmsworth History of the World* – "the world's story told by famous men, with 10,000 pictures". The idea for this encyclopaedic publication was Arthur Mee's: he sensed the commercial possibilities of a serialised translation of Hans Helmolt's *World History*, suitably expanded by British experts and copiously illustrated. Northcliffe approved and, with translation rights secured, assigned Hammerton the editorial burden. Issued in fortnightly parts (priced 7d) and sold through newsagents, the *History* was an impressive achievement, making some £80,000 and cementing Harmsworth's reputation in the educational field. Hammerton's memoirs provide a glimpse of Evans at work. The tetchy Northcliffe was following behind the young assistant as he negotiated a door in the corridor. Casually, Evans let it swing back in the face of the advancing Chief:

> What a row this led to! Northcliffe came at once to me, reporting the fact that some member of the staff who had seen him coming lacked the courtesy to wait for a moment and hold the door open for him… "Who this fellow is I don't know. He must be some school-board person. (He had recently developed a strong prejudice against school-board manners.) Find him at once…" As well as I could I tried to smooth him down and to excuse the thoughtlessness of which he complained, feeling, I confess, entirely sympathetic to the unknown offender. It was some time before I discovered the guilty one. His name was Caradoc Evans, and out of the entire Harmsworth pay-roll at that time it would have been impossible to have named one less willing to behave in an offhand manner to the Chief.[42]

Evans's deference did not encompass all colleagues. "He confessed to me that he had seen a figure following him along the passage, but in the shadow he had assumed it to be that of Bart Kennedy!"[43]

With the completion of the *History of the World*, Evans switched in 1909 to another Harmsworth encyclopaedic venture, *The World's Great Books*. One more brainchild of Arthur Mee, and under his and Hammerton's joint editorship, potted versions of a thousand great books would be sold as "a literary self-education" in the Amalgamated's manner of fortnightly parts retailing at 7d. each. A large staff of "literary assistants" came together to hammer out the digests. As far as possible, the words of the originals were to be used (Hilaire Belloc and H. G. Wells potted their own books). Hammerton described the core of his team. "I can still see Tommy Pope, who so endeared himself to his fellow journalists that at his death in 1930 he had a better press than many who have achieved international fame; and Caradoc Evans... busy with stacks of guillotined pages from which everything had been deleted except biographies; J.A. Manson, then recently resigned from the chief editorship of Cassell's; W.A. Lewis Bettany, and Ladbroke Black, all working at top speed."[44] Shortly before his death, Tommy Pope filled in some detail:

> He [Caradoc Evans] and I had both been engaged at a salary of three guineas a week each – to help compile a new encyclopaedia which a well known London publishing house had embarked upon. The place was like a school. There was a large room in which the various assistants – some dozen or so in number – sat facing each other across a series of double desks. Smoking was allowed, but excessive talking discouraged – and, indeed, reprimanded. A certain number of words – I have forgotten how many – had to be provided by the end of the week. The hours were rigid – from half-past nine in the morning till six in the evening. No work, however, was done on Saturday. Evans and I inwardly chafed at the discipline but submitted with as much good grace as possible, occasionally relieving our overcharged feelings by cursing our immediate superiors when the day's work was done.[45]

Work of this nature surely left its mark. The necessity for elimination, for paring down text to a minimum, must have encouraged a disposition in Evans, both as journalist and creative writer.

Then, as now, the notion of a literary digest provoked amused condescension and mock testimonies appeared – "Freddy Welsh (the champion light-weight): 'Why was it never thought of before? I shall never read Chambers' *Vestiges of Creation* in the original again'". Serious endorsements were few, and by the towering standards of Amalgamated Press the project was deemed a failure. Sales of around 60,000, outstanding by most measures, fell far below the hundreds of thousands of Harmsworth's *History of the World*.

Caradoc's employment with Hammerton continued; recently married, he valued the security of Amalgamated Press. Wages were good, sufficient for him to buy a house in East Sheen, an Edwardian suburban extension south of Mortlake (with its convenient railway station) on the fringe of Surrey. In 1911 the Evanses settled at 26 Thornton Road, a red-brick terrace house with small-tile roof and wooden porch, three upstairs bedrooms and three rooms downstairs (including a sizeable living room and a kitchen).

Southwards, across Upper Richmond Road, lay East Sheen Avenue, where the novelist and critic Desmond Hawkins grew up. His autobiography evokes the East Sheen of his childhood in the twenties:

> There was a muffin-man, a tall striding figure carrying a tray of muffins on his head and swinging a large hand-bell. He strode along so briskly that I doubted if he could stop, but I suppose he intended to reach his recognised customers while his muffins were still warm. There was another man who sold cockles and winkles. My mother had a secret fondness for winkles, which were scorned socially as a low-class taste…
> A knife-grinder and a barrel-organ added their colour and sound to the Avenue but the two principal figures, who haunt me still, were of a different kind. One was a grim-faced woman, her features partly concealed by a black shawl, who sold lavender. She moved very slowly and she intoned her traditional cry very slowly… melancholy, deeply tragic. She appeared to bear witness to some ancient sorrow. The other figure was a seafarer of some kind… He carried nothing and offered no service … a weird sort of tuneless singing … a beggar, lacking a nose – sticking plaster there.
> Lamp-lighter at night. He carried a long pole in a rather ceremonial way, as a marching soldier carried a rifle, sloping against his shoulder. At the lamp he stopped, lifted his pole to turn the key in the base of the lantern and ignited the gas. That done, he cycled away around the corner to the next lamp. An orderly and satisfying life… creating these sudden balls of white light in the darkness and cycling onwards.[46]

From the literary encyclopaedia Evans moved to a new Northcliffe periodical, *Everybody's Weekly*. (Arthur Mee, meanwhile, had founded the *Children's Encyclopaedia*, which would become the *Children's Newspaper* and run for a remarkable forty-six years.) Conceived and initially edited by Hammerton, *Everybody's Weekly* aimed at the "very large body of readers ready for something more than the 'Bits' [*Titbits*] class of weekly, yet not quite so bookish in its tastes as the more limited public *T.P.'s Weekly* was then catering for so skilfully".[47] With a picture of Oswald Mosley ("founder of the Standard Bread Movement") on the cover, the new penny weekly first appeared on 11 March 1911. Early contributors included Arnold Bennett and H.G. Wells (quick to take advantage of yet another publishing outlet). Among the fiction are pieces by Edward Wright (late of *Chat*); Edwin Pugh, a friend and early model for Caradoc; and Joseph Keating ("John Beddoe's Garden of Gold: A Story of the Welsh Hills"). One more name catches the eye, that of "Oliver Sandys" who, twenty years later, would become the second Mrs Caradoc Evans. Here she contributes a story, while her husband Armiger Barclay offers advice on collecting antiques.

Everybody's Weekly never found its audience. With the issue of 8 September 1911 Hammerton relinquished his editorship and by the end of the year *Everybody's* had been absorbed into *Penny Pictorial Magazine*. Evans joined this more successful Northcliffe venture, on his way to the *Sunday Companion*. In her biography of her husband, Marguerite Evans (as Oliver Sandys) has Caradoc saying: "Then I was promoted to the *Sunday Companion* as editor. I was fairly well paid. There was no more poverty. I could swank a bit. I wore horn-rimmed glasses dangling on a thick cord for more swank."[48] The tone suggests Caradoc, and the facts derive from Duncan Davies, but nowhere does Evans directly record his editorship of the *Sunday Companion* – a significant Fleet Street post. That he worked for the paper is clear (he talks of "writing sermons and prayers for a religious weekly")[49] and almost certainly he sat at the subs desk. Northcliffe had founded the weekly in 1894 with the intention of quickening a moribund branch of journalism. Nonconformist in outlook, it avoided any single denominational viewpoint and in consequence its readership grew. Evans's joining the *Sunday Companion* suggests the regard in which his employers held him. He had served Amalgamated Press for a good four years, rising from the ranks of the encyclopaedists to the offices of what rapidly became the country's foremost religious weekly, with a circulation touching half a million.

Nor should one be too surprised that Evans worked on such a paper. His was always a love-hate relationship with the chapel. However violent his attack on Welsh religion, he declared himself proud to belong to a nation whose God was a preacher and whose heaven a chapel. Arriving in London, he was at first much taken with G.W. Foote, president of the National Secular Society and long-time editor of the *Freethinker*; besides his anti-religious pamphleteering, Foote dazzled as an orator and Evans enjoyed listening.[50] It proved a brief flirtation; his was a Welsh brand of radicalism, essentially Christian-spirited, grounded in the ethics of the Gospels. He harboured a "Puritanism in the soul", this combined with a strong emotionalism and an ingrained love of the word. "Between the ages of five and twelve I preached and prayed on the tops of hedges, in the fields, while scaring crows, and to the slumbering sheep on summer afternoons."[51] Pulpit language and dramatics excited him from the start, one sermon passage from childhood echoing in the mind:

> The Sun and Jonah rested over Nineveh. When the Sun and Jonah opened their eyes in the morning, a voice spoke saying: "Don't open your shop today, little man, because the parson's bumbailiffs are after you for the church tithe."
>
> Before the Sun and Jonah rested again, the church parson was brought so low in poverty that he had to strip his bed and eat the fleas. And when he found the first flea the Sun struck him with blindness.

"That sermon", commented Evans, "caused holy joy, a holy joy to ring through my head."[52]

Things were different in London, English pulpits pale by comparison. Still, Evans kept up sermon-tasting, even in English chapels. The evangelist "Gipsy" Smith impressed him at Bayswater and at Holborn's City Temple he felt the power of two great Congregationalists, Dr Joseph Parker and his successor R.J. Campbell. Such men were exceptions, and in the general decline of the sermon, of the power of the preacher to enthral, Evans saw the decline of Nonconformity. Chapel preachers could fall back on few indispensable clerical offices, a fact forcing Evans to consider that "maybe the world will be led to the Mount of Salvation by a man from Rome".[53] Meanwhile at the *Sunday Companion* he would fight the good Nonconformist fight. One would like to be able to trace the "sermons and prayers" he says he wrote for it. During 1912 and 1913 the *Companion* kept a settled format and core of regular contributors. Evans's name nowhere appears among them, nor can his hand be readily detected in any editorial column. The contrast of his next job, his four eventful years at *Ideas*, could hardly have been greater.

Earliest Stories: Cockney and Welsh

1904-08

B etween October 1904 and February 1908 Caradoc Evans published fourteen stories. Three are set in Wales, the rest being "cockney" tales, the first of which appeared in *Reynolds's Newspaper*, 23 October 1904. This most socialist of the Sundays enjoyed a solid working-class readership and Evans most likely knew it from his time in south Wales where in the 1890s sales were high.

"A Sovereign Remedy" centres on Elizabeth Hunt, "a physical wreck of fifty". By day she sweats in a tailor's shop, returning at night to her bedridden family. On a trip for food and medicine she loses a sovereign in the Soho mud; her terror at the loss is extreme, likened to a child's "before the lash of an unmerciful parent, or one that sees its mother in the grasp of the police". From the thieving crowd surrounding her a stranger approaches; he pretends to have found her sovereign but passes her a dud from his ample supply. In a butcher's shop minutes later the fake is detected and a policeman called. But Elizabeth escapes prosecution when, in a fit of remorse, the stranger enters the shop to confess his guilt.

Here are Evans's first published sentences:

> There is a curious, slimy mud in some parts of London that a few hours' rain works into a sinister paste that the feet flounder over as if it were the frozen slush of winter. Soho is one of these districts, and when the rain fell one afternoon in November, and the thermometer swelled up to sixty, there were horses down, three together, along Greek-street. Drivers were blasting the Vestry from their boxes, and those on foot planted each step in flat, cautious smacks over the mud.

The month of the year, the named location, the enveloping mud, the plight of horses and pedestrians, all echo the opening of *Bleak House*. The curse of poverty and cheating over money would become signature elements in Evans's fiction and "King's Evidence", the prize winner at *Chat* (13 October 1906), introduces one more staple ingredient – domestic violence. The ex-convict Joe Gray bullies his submissive wife and sickly son; only his spirited young daughter – a type Evans would be regularly drawn to – offers any resistance. She finds her father lying injured outside a pub after an encounter with the father of a lad against whom Joe has turned king's evidence. She leaves him unattended, though not before reclaiming the two shillings he had grabbed from the house earlier on. "King's Evidence" attempts more by way of cockney dialogue (with minimal authen-ticity, it must be said); the narrative voice, in contrast, essays a detached wit and irony, largely at the characters' expense (the model again is Dickens).

"The Prodigal Son" (*Chat*, 8 December 1906) reverses family exploitation. Another ex-convict, Ted Young, journeys from Devon to his parents in London. They welcome him unstintingly and readily bail him out when again he lands in trouble. His response is to flee in the night taking the family savings. "Our little Ted" is a little waster, yet his every shortcoming his parents blame on themselves. Evans frequently returned to the callous exploitation within family life, and to the figure of the Prodigal Son, but here it is palely schematised in a tale with little sense of place.

With "Her Royal Highness" (*London Chat*, 28 December 1907) Evans sets aside simple narrative for a story of atmosphere and feeling. A family death provides the central incident, this of Mrs Collins who dies in the presence of her daughter. Daisy is another lively, intelligent young woman resisting an abusive father where her mother has long since surrendered. At the house, the local priest prepares Mrs Collins for her end. Evans's first fictional clergyman is distanced from his flock by money and a bank of platitudes. There is dignity in the woman's reply to him, in her wish for rest and peace, not for life eternal:

> "No, I don't want no Gawd: and 'E don't want me. 'E never stopped Bill kickin' me"
>
> "But He was only trying you."
>
> "That ain't sport."

The understatement of the death scene, its shift into the present tense and run of short sentences, is a new departure:

> A long silence follows. Daisy hears the mice running over the floor. The ghostly sound frightens her.
>
> Hand clasping hand, they lay, mother and daughter, close together. Daisy sleeps, and when she wakes, her mother's eyes are wide open.
>
> She touches the white face and gazes into the staring eyes.
>
> "She's a goner," she says, gently disengaging her hand.

A like restraint characterizes "On the Morning" (*London Chat*, 24 August 1907). Here for once a family is united, though in ultimate adversity, the husband's execution. On the dreaded morning his wife and mother prepare for the journey to prison, their destination and reason for travelling only gradually dawning on the reader.

"On the Morning", "Her Royal Highness" and "A Sovereign Remedy" stand out among the London tales, most of which are pedestrian exercises in social realism. "I wrote Cockney stories after the manner of Edwin Pugh and Arthur Morrison," explained Evans in "Self-Portrait". Morrison's stories of East End life were brought together as *Tales of Mean Streets*, an 1894 collection whose popularity confirmed "mean streets" as a synonym for city slums (one Evans piece *Chat* headed "A Striking Mean Street Story" and *Reynolds's Newspaper* rejected Caradoc's neat title "A Sovereign Remedy" for the generic "A Plain Tale from the Streets"). Morrison's Bethnal Green world of petty

criminals and social outcasts, of drinking and domestic strife, provoked charges of fal-
sification and sensationalised "realism" of the kind *My People* would face. Morrison's
response accorded with Caradoc's. "If the community have left horrible places and
horrible lives before his [the author's] eyes, then the fault is the community's; and to
picture these places and these lives becomes not merely his privilege, but his duty."

Morrison had impact – close to death at the Hôtel d'Alsace, Oscar Wilde ordered
Morrison's novel *A Child of the Jago* (1896); *Tales of Mean Streets* stirred the social conscience
of young Guy Burgess at Eton – and he still has a reputation of sorts; whereas Edwin
Pugh has fallen into oblivion. Evans came to know him well and to publish him in *Ideas*.
Pugh's eye for the grotesque and his insistence on the meaner side of things again
prompted criticism of the kind Evans would meet: that his outlook lacked breadth and
charity. Yet Pugh's London working-class stories are softer, more sentimental, than Morrison's, and distinguished by a charged Cockney idiom – as in "The Master-Beggar":

> "I told one old geeser... as I was a father o' five. Builder's labourer – frozen out.
> I pitched the tale to her for nigh on ten minutes, an' she kep' on a-nodding her
> bloomin' napper an' sayin': 'Dear! dear!' all the time, sweet as squeeze. I tell you I
> thought I was on a fair cop. And what did it all amount to?"
> "Trac'?"
> "Wuss! Far wuss," the others replied.
> "'Yes,' she said, when I 'ad done. 'Very fly, my chal, but not fly enough. But if I'd
> a brighfull o' posh', she said, 'I wouldn't parker no wedge to you. Them children,'
> she said, 'Oh, five's too many, an' you so young. Make it three,' she said, 'an' two on
> 'em step 'uns. That'll suggest a designin' wider. Well cully,' she said, 'here's luck!' she
> said. 'I'm doin' the broken-down 'ouse keeper myself!' An' pratted off."

Though proud of his Welsh descent, Pugh was an out-and-out Londoner and it shows
in his often bemusing cockney slang. There is nothing comparable in Evans's earliest
pieces.

W. W. Jacobs was another writer whom Evans enjoyed. Nowadays almost forgotten,
Jacobs at one time rivalled Wodehouse as a popular humourist. Such was his reputation
at the beginning of the last century – he died in 1943 though wrote little after 1926 –
that Evans's placing of him with Tolstoy, Gorky, Turgenev, Maupassant, Flaubert and
Hardy in that group of great moderns whom he (Caradoc) had encountered in *T.P.'s
Weekly*, might not, in 1924, have seemed too extravagant. "The Monkey's Paw", Jacobs'
classic horror tale, sits outside his regular output. Like Pugh and Morrison, he wrote
of London low life, of the docklands in particular, in a flexible vernacular capable of
carrying a whole story. His was an original voice, and his talent for comic invention
made him a sensible model for a short-story writer wanting commercial success. Evans
would have relished the unstrained escape from naturalism, the liking for the bizarre
and grotesque, within a sturdy formal structure – "But oh! for the days of O. Henry
and W. W. Jacobs, when even the most banal story had a beginning, a middle and an end
and a surprise in the last paragraph was not considered too horribly vulgar," sighed

George Orwell in 1940 (strangely enough, when reviewing Penguin's *Welsh Short Stories*).

Behind every author treating of the London poor at the turn of the century loomed Charles Dickens. Evans, we have said, knew his novels, was steeped in their London topography, and well acquainted with the novelist's life. And what Evans knew of the life furthered his regard for the writing (as was so with his response to Blatchford and Thomas Burke, to Arthur Machen and W.H. Davies). The circumstances of Dickens's childhood – his family's sinking fortunes, the marks of disgrace, the indifference of those who had the shaping of his destiny, his suffering as a sensitive twelve-year-old in a relation's blacking factory – all have parallels in Caradoc's own boyhood. Other similarities strike us, not least the hatred of a Nonconformist minister and the dire experience of a schoolmaster. Although neither writer's youth lacked brighter moments, both Dickens and Evans bore the scars of childhood suffering; each resolved in early manhood to escape humiliation and, as artists, to point the abuse of the weak and defenceless and explore what in their society made such suffering possible. Dickens was Evans's pin-up. To the end he worked with a framed portrait of the novelist hung above his writing desk. Both men, Marguerite insisted, got "savage over injustice", but Caradoc got savage over human nature, "and one cannot do much about that".

Reading *T.P.'s Weekly* (22 July 1904), Evans might well might have digested Clement Scott's advice on the kind of story that his own paper, the *Free Lance*, would welcome (a year later it accepted Evans's "The Star Turn"). Scott's counsel is largely unexceptional: choose strong, dramatic stories with the fewest possible characters; get right to the point in the first three lines; avoid wordy dialogue; and end the story with a snap – "like a door that is suddenly closed". Two further comments catch the eye in the light of Evans's practices. Scott urges contributors to adopt a "plain, Bible English" and to "draft your story in rough, ruthlessly cut it down to one-half or one-third, and then lovingly and laboriously polish each sentence." If the Scott influence remains conjectural, Evans did take advice from another literary guru. Duncan Davies mentions that "he submitted one of his stories to Barry Pain for criticism, and Pain's opinion, though pointing out certain defects, was sufficiently favourable to encourage him to go on."[1] From the "Literary Correspondence College" this successful writer of working-class sketches offered guidance to novices, reiterated in his *First Lessons in Story Writing* (1908). Authors should speak with their own, not a borrowed, voice; information should be conveyed indirectly; detail is selected for its symbolic content. Pain's advice was sensible, as were his remarks on choice of subject matter. "Begin with some phase of life with which you are familiar… It is better, if possible, to take a phase of life which you have observed carefully some years before. That will have ripened in your mind. You will find it easier to avoid the bad mistake of reporting… and attain the artistic quality of transmuting." Dialogue was difficult at the best of times and "here especially you must transmute and not report".

This brings us to the Welsh stories of Evans's first phase. It is strange that he should nowhere mention them. The abandonment of fiction in 1908 he put down to the realisation that in his Cockney tales he was writing outside his own experience, about things he didn't know. He does refer to an early Welsh story, one apparently never published. "I filled a penny exercise book, both sides, with a Welsh love-story. 'This doesn't sound true.' I said to myself. 'Any Welsh preacher could have written it.' I let years go by."[2] The facts are rather different. Whatever else he might have suppressed, his last two published stories are Welsh ones, both of interest, and neither a love story. With the descriptive sketch "Taffy at Home: the humour and pathos of Welsh village life" (*London Chat*, 21 September 1907),[3] they form a triptych that might have been written in response to Barry Pain's injunction: "Begin with some phase of life with which you are familiar… which you have observed carefully some years before. That will have ripened in your mind."

What had ripened over the years was his boyhood village, the ironically named Manteg ("fair spot") of "Taffy at Home". He guides us through its past, naming himself as "Dai Lanlas" and "Mali Evans's boy". Manteg is isolated, ten miles from the nearest railway station, which gives it its personality. Habits of belief and behaviour are settled, the Revd Adams presides over "we the dissenters" – "Congregationalists are known as Dissenters in the rural parts of Wales", interpolates the author (after the manner of Arthur Morrison) – and the village actively protects itself from dangerously new-fangled English. Caradoc remembers David Adams's sad observations after "he caught him red-handed reading an English book". The child's salvation was imperilled; English might be the language of the church but "Welsh will be spoken in Heaven." A fluency in English seems not to have harmed Josiah Watkins, General Dealer, whose thatch cottage has given way to "a red-brick building, with large bow windows and grey Carnarvon tiles". The shopkeeper unites with the minister as hard-line shapers of opinion, though their relationship is not without friction. Josiah's taste for London theatre diminishes his chances of a deaconship, for Puritanism opposes play-acting in whatever shape or form. "Mr Adams denounced Howell Powell from the pulpit for blacking his face on New Year's Eve." The allusion is to a local custom of requesting calennig (a New Year gift) and, more generally, to the chapel's repression of pre-Nonconformist tradition and belief. In "Taffy at Home" the world beyond Nonconformity persists most tenaciously in superstitions connected with death. Only reprobates like Will Ty'r Avon and Robert the pig dealer reject the deadening Manteg ethos. If they too, in turn, succumb, the sketch ends on an upbeat, celebrating Shaki Rees and his cheating of the village of a keenly anticipated death. Subtitled "the humour and pathos of Welsh village life", "Taffy at Home" approaches Evans's local patch with no little wit and flair. His targets are precise and personal and rendered with the satirist's blend of comedy and affectionate contempt. Overall the tone is gentle, marks of the composition class remain, but materials are at hand for something altogether more weighty.

The theme of "The Pretender: a sketch of Welsh life" (*London Chat*, 11 January 1908) – attitudes to English in Welsh-speaking Wales – underlies the tale of a young drapery assistant returning home from London to her native village (again Rhydlewis, fixed by references to David Adams and "Dai Lanlas"). Maria affects showy airs, among them the stubborn pretence, after eighteen months abroad, of being better able to communicate in English. The villagers are shocked – and envious. Maria has London style, uses pink toothpaste and scented soap, wears high-heeled boots and "such garments that are too good even for a minister's daughter". To her parents Twmi and Sal, Maria's success is a source of pride and her hard-won command of English a social distinction which, together with her table manners, aligns her with the squire's niece. But rejection of Welsh carries perils. "Maria forgetting her language!" Sal exclaims, "She might as well forget her religion because to forget one is to forget the other…. Of what use are supplications uttered in any language but Welsh?" Evans was acquainted with this line of thinking, which held "that the Welshness of the revelation vouchsafed to the people of Wales [was] unique, and by definition different in important respects from that revealed in other languages to other people".[4] So intimately bound up with Welsh was chapel life that any challenge to the language was seen as threatening the religion.

A letter from Maria, translated by the scholar-postman, brings Twmi to Carmarthen, there to meet her at the railway station (itself a means of alien encroachment). On the journey home the girl's high-spirits suggest the moral danger of London life. "Occasionally she sang snatches of comic songs. Twmi asked if they were hymns. Maria laughed, said something in English, and then executed some movements with her feet." That their daughter's behaviour must damn them in the eyes of "the good Mr Adams" is sufficient for Twmi. If needs be, his bull will be sacrificed to exorcise the demon within her.

Manteg remains the setting of "The Man Who Wouldn't Die: a sketch of Welsh life" (*London Chat*, 8 February 1908); Rhydlewis buildings are named (Lanlas included) and "Josi Evans" figures as the most sympathetic of the squabbling Methodists. The action anticipates "The Glory That Was Sion's" (*My People*) in its preoccupation with a new burial ground, this to receive Anthony Penffos whose death looks imminent. If, for lack of space in the Methodist graveyard, the Congregational chapel were to receive him, then in time "the Dissenters" would claim him as their own. His fellow Methodists judge Anthony a worthless sinner, yet should he not be saved from their sectarian rivals? Unable to agree on an answer, the deacons approach Penffos to ascertain Anthony's own wishes in the matter. They learn that he's escaped to the south Wales collieries. He was sure the "new ground wouldn't agree with his health," explains his wife.

Set against the achievements of 1915, these Welsh stories may seem unremarkable, but they show a significant change of direction, a greater confidence in handling locale (incorporating satiric fantasy), and a more personal manner of expression. Evans is discovering his natural subject matter and a means of treating it; we sense a new ease in the writing. How seriously he thought himself an author at this stage is difficult to say. The *Chat* stories were means to an end and once established in journalism he seems to have put away fiction for work in the Northcliffe empire.[5]

"A Wild Welsh Editor Chained Up": Evans at *Ideas*

1913-17

S ometime in 1913 Caradoc severed his links with Amalgamated Press for a post on *Ideas*, a popular penny weekly owned by Edward Hulton, the Manchester newspaper proprietor who modelled himself on Northcliffe. The editor's chair did not immediately come his way; Hannen Swaffer recalls meeting Caradoc at the paper when Edgar Wallace was editor-in-chief and A.E. Wilson the senior assistant.[1] This fixes the period as late 1913, soon after *Ideas* moved from Manchester to Temple Chambers, off Fleet Street. Wallace lost his post in December 1913 following nine stressful months under Hulton, a man described by Wallace's biographer as "uncouth, dour, brutal and suspicious" and "a curious person to find running publications ostensibly devoted to popular lightheartedness and humour".[2] Wallace felt "something of the gloom of death lay upon him all the time I knew him" (ill-health forced Hulton's retirement in 1923, two years before his death at fifty-six), and the history of *Ideas* confirms his reputation as a boorish bully who hired and fired unpredictably. The paper had only been running since 1905 yet Wallace in 1913 had become its twentieth editor. The nineteenth, A.E. Wilson, was re-engaged on Wallace's dismissal and a year later, when Wilson relinquished the post for a second time (he would flourish as the *Star's* drama critic), the hemlock passed to Caradoc. "I was the twenty-first editor of a ten-year-old weekly," he accurately computed.[3]

His appointment dates from early 1915 – the "Davies, bach" in the 12 February issue shows a Welshman's touch – and he left some two-and-a-half years later, in June 1917, having set a record for occupancy of this trying editorial berth. Though Evans proved a dynamic editor, Thomas Burke was not alone in thinking that the post hardly matched a man of his ability. Indeed, only in 1923, when he moved into literary journalism, did there seem to be some consonance between Evans's standing as an author – *My People* shot him to prominence in November 1915 – and his daily work in Fleet Street. But this is the outsider's viewpoint. Evans seemed contented enough with his dual career and, like Machen at the *Evening News*, was grateful for a bread-and-butter job – as he believed would anyone who had suffered the brain death of drapery. He was a journalist rather than a writer, one of the many refugees from other occupations crowding into Fleet Street around the turn of the century; not a few were working-class men determined to get on in life. Such a one was Edgar Wallace, "prince of journalists" in Evans's eyes. Wallace had survived his Peckham board school, its "godlike teachers" and "evil blackboard", where "the fires were never lit" save for the reading of poetry. He had survived his Wesleyan chapel as well: "Church is a terrible experience for children – a cruel experience."[4] From similarly unpromising beginnings, Evans had gained the security of Amalgamated Press, there advancing in the field of the weeklies. The move to *Ideas* was natural for a man with this level of experience, and his elevation to editorship not so remarkable granted the history of the post; but coming in his thirty-sixth year, less than a decade after entering journalism, it must have been a source of pride and a vindication of his abandoning drapery.

    Ideas and other weeklies of its kind (*Titbits*, *Answers* and *Pearson's Weekly* were models) might be seen as degenerate successors to the "new journalism" born at the end of the nineteenth century. The phrase is Matthew Arnold's:

> We have had opportunities of observing a new journalism which a clever and energetic man [W.T. Stead] has lately invented. It has much to recommend it; it is full of ability, novelty, variety, sensation, sympathy, generous instincts; its one great fault is that it is *feather-brained*.[5]

Turning the pages of *Ideas*, one would not immediately disagree. "The great popular weekly" designed for family reading comprised twenty-four pages, mostly of gossip and chat, spiced with jokes, cartoons and regular circulation-boosting competitions – sales at this time topped two hundred thousand. Articles strive for the sensational, at least in presentation, often taking the form of "confessions" by minor players briefly near the centre of significant events. Fiction is served up in similar spirit: short stories and serials written to formula and excitedly puffed. But there were useful, practical features. The very title, *Ideas*, emphasized the paper's wish to provide an outlet for readers' queries, problems and suggestions. The cheaper magazines had long recognised the attractiveness of readers' contributions and *Ideas* encouraged this source of copy. Advice and information were set out in response to specific questions and much was made of the paper's crusading lawyers, ever ready to combat injustice. A dearth of reader submissions was never a problem, as a July 1915 article makes plain. Purporting to come from the editor's secretary ("a cross between a buffer state and a watch dog"), it talks of having tactfully to disappoint some predictable would-be contributors: minor actresses wanting major stories of their beauty and charity; old women with pet theories on preserving kittens; old men with pet theories on running the empire; inventors requiring a few hundred pounds capital; eager originators of sure-fire financial schemes; Cockney revolutionists (in touch with anarchists in Soho and Petrograd) with knowledge of an impending assassination; suburban drama companies seeking to redress the shocking neglect of their every production.

    The years of Caradoc's editorship were the years of the war. He himself did not serve, presumably because his Fleet Street job was deemed civilian work of national importance. (The Military Service Act of May 1916 called for the compulsory enlistment of all men between 18 and 41 regardless of their marital status – the Act of January 1916 had targeted single men – but exemption was still allowed on grounds of occupation, and here the editorial staff of newspapers qualified.) The war quickly affected the press.[6] All engrossing for journalists and readers alike, it provided far less copy than might be

imagined, and that of a monotonous nature. Stringent government censorship ensured
that practically every paper carried the same news about campaigns abroad and the war
effort at home. From the viewpoint of the press, this greatest of wars was being fought
in near silence.

By 1916 Fleet Street faced another problem: an acute shortage of paper and its consequently soaring price. The shortage stemmed from import restrictions (paper and
papermaking equipment were among the bulkiest goods crossing the seas), from the
destruction of shipping in a German submarine campaign, and from the general com-
mandeering of transport for military purposes. Feeling the pinch particularly, the dailies
responded by raising cover prices or reducing their number of pages. Pressure of space
meant the drastic compression of standard features and a serious cutback in coverage
of sport. The impact on the weeklies was mixed. Circulations suffered in that extra
copies could no longer be printed for casual sale and, within an issue, space was at a
premium. This Evans explains to Welsh readers who, having missed the opening instalment
of Edith Nepean's *Gwyneth of the Welsh Hills*, asked him to reprint it: "Boys bach – the
price of paper, the valuable inches of *Ideas* – I cannot" (4 May 1917). Yet the paper famine
actually worked to the weeklies' advantage in as much as advertisers, deprived of their
slots in the dailies, looked anew at the Sunday papers, the magazines and the regional
press. The weeklies generally did not need to increase prices – *Ideas* kept steady at one
penny – and held their own throughout the war.

Fixed in content and layout, *Ideas* showed little outward signs of its changing editors.
Evans's tenure began unobtrusively, with a stray word or two of Welsh, but his stamp
began to show in the regular "You and the Editor" column, a space allowing readers the
chance to sound off on whatever they wished. Evans took this feature in hand, weaving
a compelling weekly page from the gist of letters received and his reactions to them.
By 1916 it had become a rich source of opinion and reflection delivered in a quite unmis-
takeable style. Evans communicated freely with folk from all over Britain, and on a
range of topics – the contrast to the narrowly combative exchanges he was simultaneously
conducting through the press in Wales is refreshing. When stirred he could, even in *Ideas*,
be sharply forthright, but his prevailing tone is warm, playful and encouraging.

The editorial persona he carefully constructs, volunteering something about himself
but holding much back. One angry reader, sore at a rejection slip, challenged "What do
you know about short stories anyway? Have you ever written one?" Evans isn't tempted.
With his own literary troubles in mind, he responds:

> I am repentant. I should not have written the truth. Thus with most of us, indeed:
> we love the hypocrite and hate the prophet of evil. That I should have known. The
> Old Bible prophets spoke much truth, and their days were made very bitter. (21
> April 1916)

The wish to preserve anonymity is neatly conveyed in the line drawing heading Evans's
column. It shows the back of the editor bent over his desk, quill in hand. Readers
requesting a front view were denied on the grounds that his face wasn't attractive enough.

Once, somewhat obliquely, he elaborated on his objections:

> If you saw me, I wonder if you would buy *Ideas*. Years ago, at the time that I had just
> put on the trousers of manhood, a party of players performed in a wooden booth in
> the market place. I envied one – one who had black moustaches and who always
> smoked cigarettes; I envied him until on a snowy day I saw him in the street; he was
> without an overcoat, and on his feet were dancing pumps. I did not go to the booth
> any more. (11 May 1917)

The Carmarthen incident impressed the notion that the public and the personal were
not to be confused; if they were, then a professional's relationship with his audience
would suffer. As it was, Evans's relationship with his readers prospered. They regularly
complimented each other and the editor's easy charm ensured a stream of correspondence:
"the longer letters you write me, my lads and lasses, the better I like them" (25 August
1916), "but of all the letters I like, I like the 'Old Bloke' tone" (5 January 1917).

Old Bloke was Caradoc's nickname in Fleet Street. He enjoyed a relaxed familiarity
with his readers because he naturally identified with them. His village roots, his understanding of labouring-class aspirations, fixed his sympathies inalienably. The tyranny of
poverty, its psychological as well as physical dimension, he knew as personal truth. To a
reader who asked where one should go to experience poverty, Evans answers "Nowhere";

> You may live among the poor and as the poor, experiencing bad housing and want
> of food, administering black eyes and making sacrifices unto others, yet you will not
> know poverty any more as long as you have ten shillings in the post-office bank. (4
> May 1917)

"You and the Editor" served as pulpit and political platform. Like every popular newspaper,
Ideas could be counted pro-war; Britain was defending democracy against the Prussian
jackboot. Evans took pride in its appreciative following among the troops, whose letters
home could be drawn upon for occasional editorial copy. Servicemen are championed
at every turn, usually at the expense of those on whose behalf they fought. Until his
dismissal as editor, Evans thundered against the professional defenders of God, King
and Country. He urges pride in the common man, in "the very working classes that are
the backbone of our Army, Navy and industry". Soldiers might have to defer to rank
but on no account should civilians raise their hats to army officers – "strutting striplings
are given commissions" (29 November 1915). The war effort could be furthered on
many fronts. "Keep your pecker up, my lad," he cheers one family breadwinner targeted
by "silly women of the white-feather tribe"; "You are doing well. Those small brothers
of yours will grow up and the country may need them one day, and it won't be your
fault if they are not fit to respond to the call" (20 August 1915). Of those who taunt
others for not enlisting,

> The worst offenders are women and rich old men, both secure from active service
> by reason of sex and age. If they were half as patriotic as they would lead you to

believe, they would have sunk all their money long ago in Government funds. But
that was not to be: as is always usual, when the State is in real danger, it is the working
classes that come to the rescue. (30 July 1915)

Readers are left in no doubt that, besides war against the Germans, a civil war was
taking place at home. The notion that, in face of a national emergency, social divisions
were being swept aside he dismisses as fantasy; the truth was that they were intensifying.
It is striking how fiercely Caradoc saw the war in terms of class conflict and economic
injustice; and, as in his fiction, it's the enemy within who incur the greatest wrath –
"public servants drawing enormous salaries, ship-owners, munitions magnates and food
thieves wallowing in their profits" (13 October 1916). Week after week *Ideas* headlined
lower-class exploitation in the name of the war – munitions workers handling poisonous
chemicals on a "monstrously inadequate" six shillings a week; Belfast women weaving
aeroplane linen for "starvation wages" (3d. an hour). Standard wages were everywhere
depressed, in the countryside and town: farm labourers earn 15 shillings a week, London's
working mothers five shillings less.[7] It is the indifference of the better-off that angers.
"I wish the bright beauties in Parliament and elsewhere who talk about economy for
the working classes would try to live on thirty shillings a week... I have heard of women
who say that shopping, and riding in motor-cars, opening bazaars, attending public
dinners are awfully tiring" (24 March 1916).

As the war dragged on, wages in fact increased and in the Welsh coalfields especially
labour militancy sharpened. In July 1915 miners calling for a strike were straightway
branded "paytriots" – "Germany's Allies in Wales" howled the *Evening Standard*. Almost
alone, *Ideas* jumped to their defence. What about the owners?

> They advanced coal prices to ridiculous heights, and whenever the public became
> restive they pointed at the colliers as the culprits... Coal owners are making their
> fortunes. Many miners are practically working themselves to death... The owners,
> who are probably making more out of war coal profiteering than any other class,
> are concerned seriously about absenteeism. You see, absenteeism means less profit.
> But the owners are – oh! such patriots. (17 November 1916)

Throughout 1916 *Ideas* stayed fiercely radical, predominantly through one columnist,
Douglas Mount. The paper promoted him heavily, blazing him across its cover and
reprinting his pieces. He was new to journalism – Evans brought him to *Ideas* having
heard him speaking in public – but his impact was immediate. A New Tredegar man
reported that at mass meetings of the miners in his district Mount's articles were freely
quoted. Mount was quoted at Hyde Park as well, which is probably where Caradoc first
heard him, among the demagogues, revolutionists, anarchists and visionaries of Speakers'
Corner:

> The nation must be spring-cleaned. The slums where babies die and fever begins and
> consumption spreads must be swept away. The kennels of the poor that nestle under
> the comfortable houses of cathedral clergy, and on the rents of which deans and

> chapters batten, must be swept away. The jobbery and influence that control the
> Board of Education, Agriculture, War, Admiralty, and the whole Civil Service, must
> be swept away. (31 March 1916)
>
> 　　There are farm labourers today in the southern counties, men too old and racked
> with rheumatism to serve, but with families to feed, getting 11/- and 12/- a week!
> Deal with the farmers. Make them pay full rates. Today they pay half. Make them pay
> full income tax. They have swindled the Exchequer out of millions. (19 May 1916)

Only farmers could rival the coal owners in their profiteering from war. They greedily
pushed up prices, treated farm workers like slaves, exploited child labour and (so Mount
insisted) defaulted on income tax.

　　For conditions in Wales, Evans turned to his old school pal on the *Carmarthen Journal*.
D.L. Evans's damning reports spoke of wasted acres that could largely solve the food
problem were it not for the indolence of farmers and a shortage of suitable labour. Agricultural labour was scarce because Welsh farmers had never learned how to treat their
workers as human beings (they were now mistreating industrial English schoolboys).
Meanwhile, they basked in excessive prices (for butter especially) and heartlessly
expressed the wish that the war would continue until they had made enough to retire.
Military conscription barely touched them since they used "all manner of dodges and
backstairs influence to keep their burly sons at home to assist them in swelling their
bank balances with blood money" (27 October 1916).

　　In December 1916, Evans moved outside the pages of *Ideas* to write on what he
took to be a major cultural shift within the south Wales coalfield communities. He did
so in the *New Witness*, Cecil Chesterton's political weekly that earlier in the year had
published four of his *Capel Sion* stories. "The Welsh Miner" (7 December 1916) celebrates
the turning of the worm. Previously docile men who had suffered on the land, passively
taken their political opinions from the pulpit, were throwing off their shackles, coming
together in a remarkable show of strength. "No one can accuse the religious leaders of
the Rhondda Valley of aiding and abetting the miners to strike," wrote Evans:

> Most of the chapels are erected with the money of coal capitalists and upholstered
> with grocery, leather, and drapery money. The men in the pulpits are the paid servants
> of their employers, and often the paid agents of Liberal politicians. "Respect your
> rich betters" seems to be the motto of the coalfield preacher.

It is such distancing of the men, not simply from the coal owners but from their religious
and erstwhile political leaders, that impresses Evans. This shift is dramatic, with consequences beyond the reach of even the miners' representatives. "These strikes in Wales
have a deeper meaning than Mr [C.B.] Stanton can fathom. The people are awakening.
Nonconformity is bitten with its own teeth." For Evans, the politicised coalfield communities, increasingly emancipated from a backward-looking social leadership, carried
hope of a rebirth for the Welsh nation at large.

　　Faced with gross inequality, the miners deserved whatever they could get, as did working people at large. Nothing must depress their wages, not even well intentioned voluntary labour. In his own distinctive fashion he makes this point to a Bournemouth reader lamenting her boredom:

> Many of us are weary, and a few are weary of doing nothing. But weariness is our portion, for man lives by cash; and if there were many more like you, little woman, we would become more weary and get less cash. Work if you will, but take care that you receive full value for your labour. (11 May 1917)

"Man lives by cash"; "Love and poverty do not blend. Poverty does not blend with anything" (16 March 1917): these were lessons learned at Rhydlewis, from his years behind shop counters and his early struggles in Fleet Street. His socialism proclaimed human dignity and the equality of man. "I am unable to differentiate between the classes: a man is a man," he tells the correspondent who queries the worth of a working man's son poring over books and learning history dates; "if books and history dates are stupid, surely it is wrong that the son of a duke should pour [sic] over them" (14 July 1916). The word "man" he insists upon, for its natural dignity and rightness. He squirms when called "this gentleman". "Lady" likewise sickens; "woman" must be rehabilitated, rescued from the usage that confines it to servants. "A woman is a woman, and a nobler name for her, moves she in whatever circle, cannot be found" (28 April 1916); "ignorant persons imagine that it is vulgar to call anything by its proper name; it is vulgar to call anything except by its proper name" (7 July 1916). Evans's radicalism remained classically Welsh, its principles more moral than political, grounded in Christian notions of equality and entertaining no belief in man's unaided perfectibility.

Evans, with little prompting, pondered the human condition, and in a way that must have baffled many readers. He wished to believe that the universe was in the hands of a benevolent ruler and that life could be softened by love. To a young girl at odds with the world he writes: "I was like you at your age. Most of us were like you. But the years have brought much humility unto me. Today I look into the faces of passing people, and I discern not enmity against myself or against anyone, but much charity and understanding. So it shall be with you…" (29 September 1916). Yet these words, sensibly offered to a troubled adolescent, keep company with this:

> Sing you in beautiful words, my lad, you will never change the heart of man, and the best of men are hard and selfish. Even the sun pours spitefully into the poor man's home, and upon the poor woman's garment he seems to say: "I will intensify your poverty." (11 August 1916)

One reader, "James, Abertawe", provoked perhaps his bleakest reading of the way we are:

> We shall never have universal peace. At what time we shall not be fighting against a foreign enemy, we shall be fighting against our brothers and neighbours. Men will

not cease to covet that which is not theirs, howsoever loudly they will cry forth their honesty. The humble shall serve the boastful; the rich shall be as gods, and they shall do no wrong, for the laws will be in their keeping. (6 April 1917)

Professional problems seem to have intensified the bitterness on display. By spring 1917 it was becoming clear that his position at *Ideas* was in jeopardy. His personal campaign against the rich was ending in defeat; the laws did indeed seem to be in their keeping. "Strip us of this garment which we name 'Civilisation', and see what you find: a hard, cruel, and a selfish nature," Evans had written (20 October 1916); "We are incapable of sacrifice; none of us would lay down his life for another. We swear friendship to the man whom we think will do us good.... That is why I say we are not of today or yesterday; we began with the rocks and we will end in stone." Yet his despair somehow embraced a semi-mystical apprehension of the rightness of the world, of its sharp economy and purity of design:

> The fact that a thing is done or that man exists is proof enough that there is nothing in this planet that does not count. You may have your own theory as to who pulls the strings of this universe; but judging from that which is done, it is safe to say that the Power is never wasteful. He has some use, often terribly mysterious, for everything that has been created. (16 March 1917)

Crucial to this vision is a belief in the overriding worth of the individual, however beleaguered he or she may be. Readers should put less faith in others and more in themselves, inhabit "the certain today" and fight for their place within it. There might well be a cost, but "one is in the world to perform some definite work, and when that work is ended one is removed therefrom. The earth is fearsome: it exacts to the last drop of blood" (15 September 1916).

Such spiritual wrestlings sit strangely among the cartoons, competitions and football coupons of *Ideas*, though Evans wove them into his column with a style that pleased. His religion was plainly expressed. The kingdom of God is within us, and we alone know the claims it makes. On divisive issues like Sabbatarianism each person must be guided by conscience, for conscience and personal conviction are our surest guides. These, and continuous study of the Bible. "Lately you have referred frequently to the Bible", observed one reader (12 May 1916); "a lifetime's study of the Bible would not yield a tenth of its treasures,", Evans assured him. The ways of the chapel, on the other hand, must be regarded suspiciously. When another writes of having fallen foul of his minister and the chapel "headmen", Evans's sympathy stirs. "Fight your persecutors, and if you fight hard enough the minister's wife will come up to you and ask you to come to her house to tea. That is the moment when you must be strong. Do not go." (25 August 1916)

Comment on love and marriage forms another significant strand in the "You and the Editor" pages. These are topics that agitated readers constantly, and other weeklies soon channelled requests for guidance into a specialist "agony" column. From time to time

Caradoc gave himself to such matters. He considers what brings men and women together. Physical attributes may attract but they do not make for love. Addressing himself to men – women seem to know these truths – he speaks of "the intoxicating love hours" which must end in "the horrible awakening that her god's face is like the face of a man" (16 March 1917). A man should sense in his partner something that sets her apart from her sisters. The love so evoked is God's greatest gift and in its absence marriage cannot be contemplated. He puts this to a Carlisle reader who, during a holiday taken on his own, has been abandoned by his girlfriend:

> I can never understand why men want to marry women who have no love for them. If there is no love before marriage, there is none after marriage. So, my Carlisle lad, be you grateful, and set your affections to someone else; and when you have found another girl try and persuade her that her welfare is more in your eyes than your own. Try to do that, even if you do not believe it. (22 September 1916)

My Carlisle lad is presumed to be as egocentric as the next man. This the editor makes clear to female readers: that when a man frowns he expects the world of women to tremble and that a man undervalues whatever he can easily secure, "though that thing be to him as balm in Gilead" (13 August 1915). The last thing a woman should do is inflate male ego. Thus the advice to a woman who believes her man is drifting away from her:

> My dear Beatrice, you have forgotten the way to a man's heart. Let him not imagine that you are depressed, nor that you care for him, nor that you cannot get another fiancé. Laugh merrily, not spitefully, in his face, and give him to understand that you are jolly glad to be rid of him. Man's pride is easily hurt; and probably your fiancé will return to you. (21 April 1916)

Such guidance is offered in no great belief that it will ever be followed. The human mind is unfathomable and human emotions beyond the reach of counselling. People marry if they wish to, though all the world be against it. Evans sees the first year as particularly taxing and urges husbands not to neglect their wives for the sake of their pals (advice, it must be said, that he personally found hard to follow). Husband and wife should equally care for their child – "it is given to neither and to both" – and the extended family of in-laws be charitably embraced. Antipathies with time should fade away. "Probably in your patriarchal age all the bunch of you will sit at the same hearth and use the same tobacco from the same pouch and suck lozenges from the same box" (15 September 1916). The homely picture is balanced by others arising all-too-commonly from conflicts over money. As in his fiction, Evans's sympathies are here with wives, so often kept as hired servants but denied an adequate allowance.

> I detest the vain fool who gives his wife a sum of money for housekeeping and then demands a record of how she spends it. Unfortunately, men marry for other reasons than love. One man's mother or wife will die, and he will take into his house a woman

who will keep it clean and will not steal anything that is therein because she is the owner's wife, and she will not demand a settled salary as a hired woman would. (3 March 1916)

Infidelity presents the most painful challenge in marriage. Women, both wives and mistresses, write more willingly on this subject. Caradoc's advice is that straying husbands should be shunned: they never speak honestly about their wives, and a mistress is almost always discarded. To one wife who suspects her husband's infidelity the response is less categorical. Evans here writes with tenderness, urging honesty of feeling, forgiveness and reconciliation, and even offers to assist again, if he can:

> I am very sorry for you, "Troubled"; if the evil report which you heard was true, I am more sorry for Miss – who sows careless of the harvest she will be made to reap. But why do you believe the gossips and not your husband?… Remember from first to last the years that you have lived together: the joys that came to you and the difficulties that faced you. So let it come to pass that you go up to him saying: "I don't believe there was anything between you and Miss – Let us make it up, and we will never refer to it again." Do that, for I feel that the love which your husband has for you is as great as your love for him. And your love is neither dead nor crushed: it is a little bruised. Will you please write again? (31 March 1916)

Other times he refrained from counselling, as when a man in love with his brother's fiancée asks what he should do. "I do not know," comes the honest reply; "I do not know you, nor your brother, nor Millie. If that which you have done seems honest to you, continue; if it does not, discontinue" (12 January 1917). Conscience again was the surest guide. By 1917 Evans's own marriage had begun to founder. In December 1916 he talked of "blood-red matrimonial squabbles" and three months later declared that "matrimonial affairs have little concern for me".

Quotation from "You and the Editor" hardly suggests the full play of humour that brightened Caradoc's contributions. He could write straightforwardly enough, but where the issues were appropriate he readily adopts the preacher's mantle. Pulpit cadences are humorously deployed when broaching routine matters – "Little is my space, dear people, and fitting that I shall be brief. Did I hear one lifting his voice and say 'Briefer the better, old sport'?" – and bathos heightened when longer passages, self-consciously tuned, end with a blunt colloquialism. Towards the end of his editorship the self-mockery, the pulpit flights, become noticeably more audacious. "Not so much of your 'gather ye together in secret conclave' in the future," suggests a Stockport man (submitting a story in Geordie dialect). For the most part, readers seemed to have enjoyed their editor's way with words. They protest at the weeks of silence that preceded Evans's departure. One Gloucester fan picks up his tone. "I missed your editorial chat most dreadfully, and welcome its return with much gladness of heart. Fail not to say something each week" (18 May 1917).

Before glancing at the Welsh contributions to *Ideas*, it is worth mentioning just how much in passing Evans reveals about his early background. He refers to his Rhydlewis board school, to magic lantern shows there, to the theatrical troupe he saw at Carmarthen. He remembers farming routines and confesses he doesn't miss them. When a reader invites him to visit his farm in Wales, he replies:

> Many thanks. But I won't come. I have sowed potatoes and scattered seeds and pitched hay and tethered cows and hunted for someone's stray pigs on the tramping road on the Sabbath; and many other things: and I don't want to do them again. (15 September 1916)

Farm animals are basically commercial units, as any cowherd understands. "Now I have had a lot to do with cows," he once more tells his readers:

> I have milked them and cleaned their houses; I have herded them to the fair, and watched over them while strange men, who spoke with oaths and curses, bargained for them; and I have led many to the slaughter. But I did not know the manner by which a cow gets up on her feet. (24 December 1915)

His ignorance extends to trees – "I do not so much as know one tree from another" – and for much the same reason: "Who would give me twopence for saying 'This is a beech, and that an elm'?"[8] It typified Welsh rural indifference to much in the natural world, an unresponsiveness he largely shared, except when it came to animal suffering. Here his emotions are readily engaged, his column being peppered with tender references to cats and dogs and grief at their mistreatment.

Evans readily dispels romantic notions of country living, pointing to its poverty and squalor and the lot of wives and women forced into farmhouse drudgery. They are far removed from the creatures of musical comedy: "some of the petticoats I have seen hanging around the bodies of many of these women labourers are straightened stiff by reason of dirt and filth accumulated thereon" (11 February 1916). Poverty is no more tolerable in the country than elsewhere. Villages, whether Welsh or English, are commonly the abodes of gossips, of hypocrites and malevolent bullies; places to be visited of necessity, usually for family reasons. "I know the awfulness of village life," he assures his readers (30 June 1916).

To judge by its postbag, *Ideas* enjoyed a healthy circulation in Wales. Maybe the editor favoured Welsh correspondents, or that his manner attracted his compatriots – he freely used Welsh idioms when addressing them. On one occasion the contact turned sour. The Welsh phrase of thanks, "diolch yn fawr i ti", appeared misspelt in his column and from Treherbert, Denbigh and Clydach came letters of rebuke. Evans might easily have made light of it by simply apologising for a typographical error. Instead, he wrote:

> Gather you together then this night: one from Treherbert shall hold a lighted candle against my face so that the light falls thereon, and all you whose anger is hot shall walk up close to me, in the manner of those who go in procession, and I will not demure on the occasions that the one from Denbigh and the woman of Clydach mock

at my lamentation. Now that I have humbled myself, do you concern yourselves no
more about that Welsh phrase, for even if you do I shall take no notice. (9 June 1916)

With its hints of the ceffyl pren, the response seems out of all proportion. A nerve has
clearly been touched. Did Evans sense in the Welsh rebukes a serious desire to wound?
Readers must have been perplexed.

Though it must have been obvious, the editor's nationality is never openly declared.
Evans comes closest to doing so when a Jewish reader complains of the many jokes
directed at her race. A Fleet Street Welshman could readily sympathize.

> It is so that I belong to a people against whom there are, I would say, a million and a
> half jokes: and every joke makes me feel uncomfortable. That is, every joke is a
> slander. We all like to hear this and that said to another's discredit; never to our own.
> I laugh at Irishisms, and squirm at —, but I will not tell you. I glorify the gods in
> hymns that humour is not evidence against a man or people. So, therefore, I bear
> with grinning accusations because I know that he who laughs first does not laugh
> last. The Jews have borne much, and I think that when West is East, their triumphal
> psalms will make the earth ring, even as a blacksmith's anvil. (30 March 1917)

Outside the editorial pages, some Welsh content came from friends back home.
Besides D.L. Evans, the *Carmarthen Journal's* editor Lewis Giles, contributed. Though
he shared Caradoc's antipathy towards the Welsh Nonconformist establishment, and
publicly defended *My People*, his *Ideas* pieces on west Wales are kindly. As we have seen,
south Wales received attention largely through sympathetic notices on the miners' cause;
and resting from short stories, Edwin Pugh saluted the enduring heroism of Ferndale
colliers, more than two hundred of whom, men and boys, lost their lives in the horrendous
pit explosions of the late 1860s. In "All-conquering Welshman" (26 January 1917), *Ideas*
took up the forward march of the London Welsh consequent upon Lloyd George's pre-
miership. It catalogued Welsh successes in government, business and industry, in medicine
and law, the church and sport. "Even Fleet Street, hitherto the classic preserve of the
Scot, is beginning to capitulate to the hustling Cymro."

No particular line on Nonconformity is discernible. An article by Albert E. Thomas,
"Nonconformists Won't Enlist" (11 June 1915), suggesting that middle-class Nonconformists were too proud to fight, raised a storm of criticism. Evans had predicted as
much and reminded readers that a contributor's views weren't necessarily those of the
editor. The disclaimer failed to shield him; "some defenders of Nonconformity are
possessed of amazingly unprintable vocabulary", he reports (2 July 1915). The charge
resurfaced when the editor of the *Rhyl Journal* provided a Sunday parade sheet showing
Nonconformists outnumbered three to one by Churchmen, at which point Evans commissioned a series of articles on Christianity and the war from the Revd T. Rhondda
Williams. Williams had left Wales to become (via Bradford) the celebrated minister of
Union Street Congregational Chapel, Brighton. He too had had a book banned by a
Welsh public library and his brand of ethical socialism markedly appealed to Evans.

Like other popular weeklies, *Ideas* relied on a regular supply of short stories and serialised novels. At first Evans sought to raise standards. Between 15 January and 19 November 1915 he reprinted ten Guy de Maupassant stories (four more followed in 1916); Alphonse Daudet and Maxim Gorky were also introduced. No British author of comparable stature appeared. Evans printed Edgar Wallace and Edwin Pugh, the latter desperately poor and unwell. Thomas Burke he first published in 1915; barely scraping a living as an author, Burke had approached *Ideas* eager for any kind of job. "Write to the proprietor that this is a rotten paper and you'll get mine," said Evans,[9] thus beginning another close, if brief, Fleet Street friendship. The bulk of fiction in *Ideas* is undistinguished stuff that Evans duly puffed. His praise for Edwin Pugh on the other hand – "one of the best living short-story writers" – reflects a genuine admiration; Pugh's appeal to the Royal Literary Fund Evans readily supported by letter.

From his reading of scores of submissions, Evans offered guidance to those hoping for a spot in *Ideas*. "I give careful consideration to stories from beginners, for the reason that I was a beginner once," he declared (5 May 1916);

> And though even now I may be amateurish, I want to say that most beginners fail because they write about people and incidents of which they know nothing.... If you will write stories, write of men and incidents you know. There is plenty of material around you. Do not endeavour to be bookish. The best literature is that which is written sincerely and without affectation. If you do not move among dukes, do not write about them; if you have only an outsider's knowledge of shop life, do not write about it. Amen.

As for suitable models, "I know of only two books that will help one to write – especially to write fiction," he replies to 'S.R.', like his one-time self "a draper's assistant, living in, wanting to write fiction";

> They are the Bible and "The Pilgrim's Progress". In the Bible you get the most perfectly told tales in the world – Joseph and his Brethren, the Prodigal Son, the Woman who was taken in Adultery, etc. The person who can write a story half as good as a Bible story has fame and fortune at the end of his finger tips. I wish I could. For style – clear and simple and vivid – John Bunyan is the next best. Study these two books, S.R., the best and cheapest in the world. (29 September 1916)

Edith Nepean, writer of popular romance, provides a rare glimpse of Caradoc in his basement den at Temple Chambers.[10] Then a young Llandudno woman in her twenties, she had approached *Ideas* with her first attempt at a serial. The paper, having asked to meet her, demanded so many alterations in her work that she rose to leave the premises in tears. Then a man called her back with the words, "'We have a wild Welsh editor chained up, he wants to meet you.' Reluctantly I followed him, and I found myself at last in an office facing a tall, dark-haired, dark-eyed man, wearing a coat with fringed sleeves, and with a black cat in his arms." Edith mentioned her Welsh serial:

> "Let me see it," he said in a soft, persuasive musical voice. I handed over the manuscript and watched with a beating heart as he placed the cat on the floor. Then he lit a pipe, placed my manuscript on his desk, sat down and read it. At what seemed the end of 100 years he smiled and said: "I will give you £80 for this!"

Edith's *Gwyneth of the Welsh Hills* showed the influence of *My People*, which must have made Caradoc's task of judging "the best thing that has come out of Wales" all the more pleasurable. Its success when serialised in *Ideas* (March-June 1917) led to its reissue one year later in book form, Nepean's first published novel. Despite the Evans link, *Gwyneth of the Welsh Hills* bore a dedication "by special permission" to David Lloyd George. The press in Wales quickly spotted the *My People* similarity, forcing Evans to allay suspicions that he was now writing as "Edith Nepean".

Serialisation of Nepean gave him a chance to comment on Welsh fiction. "I know a great deal about Welsh arts and for long I have been amazed that this imaginative people have produced only two novelists of distinction – Allen Raine and Daniel Owen" (30 March 1917). The high estimation of Allen Raine (the prudently chosen pen name of Anne Adaliza Puddicombe) may come as something of a shock, but as an author himself and an editor seeking fiction for a mass-market weekly, Evans had a healthy respect for a novelist selling upwards of 200,000 copies a title. She was one of the very few able to make a living from book-writing. Yet outside his editorial office Evans had made his own contribution to Welsh arts, a book which would seemed to have "destroyed the sandcastle dynasty of Allen Raine".[11]

My People: "Banned, Burned Book of War"

1915

Early in 1913 Caradoc Evans revived his literary ambitions and began to shape the material that would soon appear as *My People*; so began the great productive period of a writer who at thirty-six might be counted a late beginner. His return to fiction can be traced to conversations with Duncan Davies, the "very argumentative" union official he'd come to know at Whiteley's. At the Evanses' East Sheen home, mostly over Sunday tea, the two Welsh exiles swapped tales of their Cardiganshire neighbourhoods, material ripe enough, so it seemed, for fictional reworking. Evans had for years stored away local characters and incidents, many gathered on his summer holiday at Rhydlewis. His nephew Howell Evans speaks of him willingly helping in the neighbours' haymaking; "With his coat off and his sleeves rolled up and a pitchfork in his hand, he would work all day, listening meanwhile to their conversation and watching for quaint phrases and ideas for short stories."[1] Village shops, like farms, were great places for story-telling, for catching up on local gossip, and Evans spent long hours at "Dan Teilwr's", a cosy workshop on the road to the school and a popular meeting place (the tailor Dan Davies shared Caradoc's liking for the stage). Another favourite gathering place was Rhydlewis Shop, the general store (and onetime post office) distinctively constructed out of painted corrugated iron. A local resident remembered how on Saturday evenings, when the shop stayed open till 10pm, she "often saw groups of men having a chat over the week's events congregated there, & buying their supply of tobacco for themselves and peppermints for their wives".[2] She particularly recalled Caradoc's eagerness for news of the Revd John Green, in her eyes "a Great Dictator who ex-communicated members of his congregation if he found that they had partaken of any intoxicating drink". Twrgwyn's pastor for near forty years, Green was "undoubtedly a fanatic" – "coming out of eternity to throw fire on the earth", his obituarist put it – and "when Caradoc was home he used to ask us about him and his latest exploits".

From earliest childhood, within Lanlas Uchaf's walls, Caradoc had absorbed tales of folk around, their characters and their exploits, all vividly brought to life by his mother. It was a talent Mali Evans never lost. "Many times have I sat with him in the kitchen of his mother's farm, near to Cardigan Bay, listening to her stories," wrote Edith Nepean;[3] Caradoc attributed to his mother any storytelling gift he possessed. Life was full of stories waiting to be written, Evans assured a London writing circle, and authors should take their material from persons and events around them. It is not advice he followed precisely. He felt the power of the past, preferring to write out of memory, his own and other people's.

Recalling the gestation of the extraordinary first stories, Duncan Davies has Evans initially pondering a treatment akin to J.M. Barrie's *Auld Licht Idylls* (1888), a founding text of the Scottish "Kailyard" (cabbage patch) school. What emerged in April 1915 could not have been further removed from Celtic pastoral nostalgia. A picture-postcard view of Welsh rural society, in the manner of the Scottish idyllists, might have commanded a popular readership – the wholesome south Cardiganshire novels of Allen Raine still sold in their tens of thousands – but Wales, so Evans believed, had been failed by her writers. "Stories" were readily come by; he would tell the truth that lay behind them. At last in his middle thirties, felt he had something to say, and the confidence and courage to say it. Moreover, he had found what mattered most – a distinctive personal voice.

A précis of his feelings, of the convictions driving his fiction, appeared in a newspaper letter of 24 January 1913, a statement altogether more striking than anything previously from his pen. Almost three years before *My People*, it heralds an immediately recognisable Caradoc Evans, the apostate reviled in Wales and by the Welsh abroad. Its context was the laboured passage through parliament of the Welsh Church Bill, the act that finally secured the disestablishment of the Anglican Church in Wales. For the ultra-Conservative *Daily Express* it provided an opportunity to rail against politicised Welsh Nonconformity whose ministry, so the paper claimed, swarmed with "big working lads" anxious to mount the ladder climbed by the chancellor of the exchequer. "The Lloyd Georgeite pastor now prides himself on being able to introduce his party's propaganda into every known form of religious worship or instruction." Styling himself "a Welsh-speaking Welshman cradled in Welsh Nonconformity", Evans more than agreed. His letter to the *Daily Express*, headed "In Darkest Wales: Politics Masquerading as Religion" and signed "David Caradoc Evans", maintained that Wales was "darkest" because of religious tyranny:

> At every turn the Welsh peasantry are bled for funds to provide their pastors with salaries and to throw up unwanted chapels. In 99 cases out of every hundred the preacher is the wealthiest man in the community. And yet there had never been a creature who holds himself more aloof from his flock than the pastor. He visits the poor and the aged when in need of funds; never else.

In art, literature and drama Wales lagged behind other countries because "All along the line Welsh Nonconformity has sternly vetoed everything in the nature of artistic enterprise." In a country gripped by a priest-caste, religion functioned as the tool of politics; Sunday after Sunday congregations were hectored by ministers ("messengers of darkness… wordy and frothy") whose instruction was, "Vote for my man or you will be eternally condemned." Evans's compatriots were hard materialists, lacking in ideals and independence of thought; which is why his letter welcomed disestablishment. The Mother Church had missed her mission in Wales. Disestablished and reawakened, she would mount a challenge to Nonconformity and so help rekindle the spiritual life of the nation.

One week later the letter appeared in *The Welshman*, a Carmarthen weekly acting as a counterweight to the Tory *Carmarthen Journal*. The paper acknowledged some degree of truth in the arguments it advanced though it was "truth caricatured", and all the more painful when coming from the mouth of a Welshman. By the end of the year the *Glamorgan Free Press* too had picked up on Evans's letter.[4] This was merely the beginning: within three years his every London move would be watched and reported in Wales.

Duncan Davies was the first to set eyes on the *My People* stories, well aware of the challenges they had posed. "I remember referring to the language difficulty. To write in ordinary English would destroy the effect. Caradoc pondered over this matter for 2 or 3 weeks and evolved the idea of a basis of Old Testament diction, and shortly afterwards he handed me 'the rat story'".[5] Biblical English lends Evans's narratives an air of authoritative proclamation: a direct and simple prose suggestive of myth or parable. In Evans's hands it gains a satiric edge, used against those who would commandeer biblical style and precept for their own selfish purposes. Chapel ministers and deacons had made the Bible their "hateful weapon"; Evans would turn that weapon against them, impersonating what he opposes. Within the narrative his dialogue shocks, a compound of translation from the Welsh, aggressive mistranslation, and a strangely distorted English. To present his world in "ordinary English" would not suffice, and such bold refashioning of language perhaps came more readily to a native Welsh speaker. "Foreigners write good English because they do not know English," he jotted in his notebook; writing in a foreign language inevitably made one a stylist. He handled "the thin language" (English) free of built-in notions of propriety and his idiolect has no parallel, in or outside literature. The mistranslations caused massive offence in Wales – "white shirts" for gynau gwynion (not "white robes" or "heavenly raiments"); "Big Man" or "Great Male" for "Gwr Mawr or "Bod Mawr" (not "Great Being" or "Almighty God"). His defence was that his dialogue sought to convey what went on inside a speaker's head, the thoughts and feelings behind the spoken words. The Aberystwyth academic George Green has him explaining:

> I knew very well what Bod Mawr means in the dictionary or to a Welsh scholar. But I knew very well what it means to the man I am writing about. He is quite incapable of thinking of a great being. A white robe means to him his Sunday shirt, complete with celluloid collar. I am trying to represent that man's mind and how it works. If he does not really say "Big Man", he thinks it, and his imagination will go no farther. It is what he ought to say if he were telling the truth about his thoughts, which is what I am trying to do.

As for literary influences, Evans told the Welsh playwright D.T. Davies that while writing *My People* "he was confining his reading then to the five Books of Moses" [the first five books of the Bible] and that he would have nothing to do with any word that did not appear in Dr Johnson's *Dictionary*. Whimsical and eccentric perhaps," thought Davies, "but significant for all that. The artist in the man had realized the need for discipline."[6] (Evans did indeed urge daily study of "Todd" [H.J. Todd's edition of Johnson's *Dictionary*], his own copy of the 1827 second edition a prized possession read for instruction and pleasure.) Besides the Bible, Evans placed *Pilgrim's Progress* as an indispensable literary model, admired in part no doubt for its marrying of biblical prose and a racy vernacular. We know too that Evans was reading J.M. Synge at this time.

> Inspired by Synge, Caradoc Evans set out to devise for himself a parallel style. He
> had to face a more difficult problem. Synge was a romantic discoverer of the folk
> and could write in delighted wonder. But Caradoc Evans was himself of the folk and,
> in expressing his own violent reactions in an objective form, had a harder mental
> discipline.

The words are Austin Clarke's, the Irish poet who worked beside Caradoc in the 1920s
and insisted that he'd been influenced by Synge – "he told me this himself".[7]

More than one editor rejected "A Father in Sion" and "Be This Her Memorial" prior to
their appearance as "Two Welsh Studies" in the *English Review* of April 1915. Acceptance
by Austin Harrison (editor-in-chief) and Norman Douglas (literary editor) more than
compensated for previous disappointments. Under Harrison and Douglas the *English
Review*, a substantial monthly strong in politics and current affairs, still had literary
cachet. Its great days under Ford Madox Ford might have passed but the new regime
carried on publishing established names while continuing to welcome the work of virtual
unknowns. "Harrison knew what he wanted, and what he didn't, and was never bemused
by a name," so Thomas Burke believed; "A solid, handsome journal, with fine blue cover
and handsome black type," said Jesse Chambers of the outlet that had given the young
D.H. Lawrence his break, and which in 1913 he still considered an appropriate place
for his fiction. The joy of Caradoc and Duncan Davies at seeing "Two Welsh Studies"
among its contents echoed the "wild excitement" of Lawrence and Chambers at the
appearance in its pages four years earlier of Lawrence's first poems. Here was Caradoc
Evans side by side with Max Beerbohm, Norman Douglas, Edward Thomas and H.G.
Wells. Yet apprehension tinged his delight. Knowing that his "Studies" would provoke a
reaction, he had hesitated over how he should sign himself; in fact it took some persuading
by the journalist Sydney Moseley for him not to shelter behind the *nom de plume* that
had served him in the past. The proper course was to reveal oneself openly and take the
consequences, Moseley counselled; "always better to be criticised than ignored". Evans
dashed away in time to use his real name in the *Review*.[8]

It is difficult to imagine two more brilliant offerings by an unknown writer than
the Evans stories of April 1915. Judged by the highest standards, they evoke admiration,
a response widely accorded them in England with their republication in *My People*. In
Wales things were rather different: just 5,000 words from an obscure London journalist
in a highbrow monthly yet within days they sparked editorial outrage in four Welsh
newspapers. It would be truer to say that the catalyst was less the stories than Evans's
comments about them delivered to the London evening *Star*. This would become the
pattern: Welsh critics responding not so much to the fiction – did they ever bother to
read it? – as to the author's insistence that his stories were founded on fact. Evans's *Star*
interview repeated the charges made in January 1913, that Wales had "no real national
life... no folk lore, not a single folk-dance, and no art", and this largely because "the
hand of the Nonconformist minister is heavier upon the people than that of the priest
in Ireland". As for fiction in Wales, novelists there had "written stories which would

have applied equally well to any part of the world if the geographical names had been altered". Evans sought to interpret national life from within, a mission he compared with George Douglas Brown's, the Ayrshire novelist whose *The House with the Green Shutters* (1901) challenged the cosy picture of rural Scotland presented by the Kailyard school. Wales had its own Kailyard fiction, "the pretty-pretty novels which are so dear to my race". These must be challenged, since "Wales will never find a new national life until she sees herself as she is." He would hold up the mirror to his compatriots, "and by displaying their weaknesses do something to stimulate the great revitalisation for which all patriotic Welshmen are looking." Evans mapped out his literary path. There would follow *The Children of Isaac*, a "grim and bitter" first novel (it was never written) and, at some future stage, a full presentment of the pains of "living in", the system from whose horrors he'd escaped (it arrived in 1930, the outstanding *Nothing to Pay*).

A *South Wales Echo* exchange brought Evans more fully to notice in Wales, and with his *Star* interview reproduced in the *Cambria Daily Leader* (Swansea), the *South Wales Daily News* (Cardiff) and the *Carmarthen Journal*, he quickly became embroiled on four fronts. So began his long, uncompromising battle with Welsh critics. His opponents, he insisted, were, like himself, "creatures of the dark days of Nonconformity", but whereas they propounded "an educated and independent peasantry", he saw one "cowered by the lash of Nonconformity". "There is no Wales," he told a startled *South Wales Echo* (15 April 1915), "she has been slain by the Nonconformist minister; there is no spiritual vision… all that is left is a mongrel people, possessed of a mongrel's vitality." The force of his challenge aroused "the normally genial" *Echo* (as Evans dubbed it). He was letting the side down ("this is the kind of judgement of Wales… he is putting before English readers"), and besmirching Nonconformist youths, those "knights and heroes of Gwalia's fair land" at the very time they were marching to war. The charge of treachery, stinging at this time, was to reappear, as was Evans's defence – that his love of Wales embraced a right to criticize her. "Gwalia's fair land" was a vision of the past; the Welsh nowadays had been robbed of aspiration and initiative, of the arts, and of literature – save for the "foolish mouthings" of preachers (*South Wales Daily News*, 21 April 1915):

> And responsible for this state of affairs is Nonconformity – a body without imagination and vision, a body which breaks down beliefs and traditions and all lovely things, and builds in their places hard materialism and avarice and hatred… the villain of the piece is the Welsh Nonconformist minister. He stalks over the land like an evil spirit; his garments typify the blackness of a nation in travail, and in the light of his eyes there is no redemption.

At this kind of talk readers stirred and (in Evans's phrase) much "picturesque virulency" ensued. Nonconformity's gifts to the people were celebrated, especially the value it placed on education and its role in preserving the language (in response to which Evans cited Cardiganshire chapels where service orders was printed in English and sermons delivered "half in bad Welsh and half in atrocious English"). He was reminded, too, that the lordly ministers of his imagination managed on £80 a year, contributed by their congregations. "The wives and daughters of these 'tyrants' are too often afraid to buy a much-needed new hat because some farmer's daughter is sure to say that her father's money paid for the finery."

This latter point – that chapel power had passed from minister to diaconate – was taken up by J.D. Williams at the *Cambria Daily Leader*, prompting Evans to a fuller statement of his case. A powerful amalgam of personal instance and passionate counter-charge, his letter to the *Leader* (24 April 1915) begins by drawing a distinction between rural and industrial Wales. His stories dealt with rural life, not with the large industrial centres where, he conceded, chapel life might well be more democratic:

> But the head of the peasant chapel is the man of the pulpit, whose power, supported by the Nonconformist body, is as strong as that of the Biblical Judges of Israel. He may not be a strong man himself, but he is strong in the sense that he knows he has the impregnable wall of his religious organisation at the back of him. In such cir-cumstances a weak man becomes a cowardly-strong man. Generations of his kind have subdued the people over whom he rules: a people who believe the voice of God has called him to rule over them. He lives in the best house of the land of his chapel, he possesses more riches than any of his congregation, he makes opinion and destroys illusions… The people are in constant terror of him. As a small boy, rather than meet our ruler on the road, I used to creep into a field and hide behind a hedge until he was passed out of hearing. Why? Because I was instructed that the preacher's face was like God's – relentless and remorseless.

The Welsh child is taught that all fiction is godless (fairy stories and folk tales included); the Bible is drummed in until it sickens. "That was my experience. I had to discover the literature of the Bible for myself some three years ago. The preacher gives the people the religion of the Old Testament; like the Russian priest in one of Tolstoy's works, his purpose in life is to keep Jesus away from his flock." To the charge that he fed the English repellent portraits of Wales, he pleaded that a balance needed redressing:

> The English are nursed with the idea that Wales is the land of song and poetry, where the inhabitants live in constant harmony with one another, where men's minds are for ever tuned to thoughts of God. All that is a sorry illusion. Wales is a land of mediocre singers, a land in the villages of which all are related, yet no one loves his neighbour, a land in which all is greed and avarice, and no one loves his God.

The *Cambria Daily Leader* exchange exhibited a degree of mutual respect. Evans confessed to liking J.D. Williams, a knowledgeable editor who wrote well.[9] For his part, Williams (described by Winifred Coombe Tennant as "a most interesting man – strange blend of modernist under the drug of Calvinistic Methodism!")[10] admitted that there was room for criticism in Wales, for satire and occasionally the lash, but thought Evans's immoderate onslaughts undermined his case. Had he "dealt in love and calmness with the weaknesses and faults of his own people, he would have done useful work". This said, Williams as newspaper editor publicized Evans's letter with talk of "a brilliant Welsh author" and "his wonderful studies of Welsh life". He printed a photograph also – a severe, studious Caradoc, full-face with pince-nez.

Once in a while a voice spoke up in support of Evans. "Of course he does not mean that all Welshmen are greedy," wrote a Llansamlet reader; "the vices of greed and avarice are inherent, the inevitable results of our absurd social system… they are conspicuous in every country." This line of thinking characterized *Llais Llafur*, the Swansea valley socialist weekly that offered Evans qualified backing. Its editor D. J. Rees acknowledged a "brilliant" polemicist, even if habitual over-statement left him wholly exposed. As it was, he had faced only coarse abuse and "a poverty of argument almost beyond tears". It confirmed that Welsh vitality had passed from Nonconformist Liberalism and its nationalist wing into the Labour movement. "When our pastors, and those in sympathy with them, shed the belief that dislike of the Anglican Church and misty rhetoric about 'feudal tyrants' are expressions of a robust religious faith, they will be in the high road to their former power. Until then things will go from bad to worse."

Evans's anchorage in the *English Review* seemed secure when three months later, in July 1915, it published two further "Welsh Studies", his stories "The Devil in Eden" and "A Just Man in Sodom". That they should appear cheek by jowl with Maxim Gorky struck the *Carmarthen Journal* as apt, since both were distinctly national writers who wrote of the poor and wretched in a style stripped of ornament. As a body, Welsh Anglican Tories took to Caradoc Evans – unlike chapel-going socialists, they spoke across a religious as well as political divide – and the *Carmarthen Journal*, their west Wales mouthpiece, offered unequivocal praise; uniquely for a Welsh publication, it tried, without success, to reprint a story or two. Still, it had prominently published the author's own defence of his work. In his letter of 23 April, Evans began by wryly alluding to the Christian charity of his critics: whatever their differing standpoints, they agreed that "in a nicely conducted community I would, a handkerchief drawn over my eyes, have been placed against a blank wall long ago". His stories were fiction – "so far as I know none of the incidents I have related has ever happened" – but no less "real" for that, since they embodied truths about a particular phase of Welsh life. "My quarrel is not with religion," Evans's letter proceeds:

> it is with the promoters of what is known as Nonconformity, a strong, powerful body who recognises no law except that of its own making, who has substituted God for the black-coated figures that oppress the people and drain them of their substance, who has succeeded in fashioning a large majority of Welsh peasants into creatures without stamina and without soul. This has gone on for generations… A pillar has been raised between them and Him and the engraving on that pillar is "Nonconformity". What do you expect from such a people? You get immorality and hatred and avarice… You know all this to be true, and you know of incidents more remorselessly true than anything I have written about in my stories.

From April onwards Evans's name crops up in the *Carmarthen Journal*. It was a compliment to the author, wrote Lewis Giles the editor, that his stories – brief fragments implying much – should so have moved the Welsh. Nonconformity had become a repressive creed, a religion of feeling, divorced from Christian practice; and from *Y Geninen*, a Welsh-language quarterly, the *Journal* translated an article practically admitting as much:

> Extreme sectarianism inevitably produces a bigoted, revengeful and wholly unchristian spirit. One of the direct effects of the sectarian spirit… is the lamentable rivalry in erecting chapels where they are not needed… These chapels are built on borrowed money, and the resources and energies of members are strained to meet these financial liabilities, leaving no room or means for real Christian work.

The chapelgoer is led to believe that so long as he contributes to the various funds the exercise of faith can be neglected.[11] "How can a working man, with a weekly wage of, say, 24/-, support a wife and a family and meet the endless demands for contributions?"

The *Geninen* article underlined from an inward Nonconformist position much of Evans's thinking, and enforces the view that for many in Wales his crime lay not so much in what he said as in his choice of language for saying it. The Welsh-language press could accommodate unflattering opinion of Wales safe from alien eyes, but to wash dirty linen in public, to expose national defects before the gloating English, was misguided and unforgivable. It was a point graphically made by H. Lloyd Jones in a *Carmarthen Journal* letter (17 September 1915). Having first hailed Evans as "a great reformer" deserving of serious attention, he sensed the damage that might follow from his powerfully imaginative "studies" of Welsh rural life. "If the *English Review* was circulated in Wales alone no harm would be done," but "how can one reform Wales by demonstrating its faults to the English whose opinion of Wales is already ridiculously low?" Evans provided ammunition for the arrogant Englishman who "over his pint of beer in his squalid, dingy gin-shops treats his neighbours with a lengthy dissertation upon the barbarians who live somewhere on the other side of the Severn". He must step back and choose between the Bible and the so-called "realism" of French yellow-back novels. "Does he desire the utmost contempt of his countrymen? Does he desire his name to be handed down as a byword for treason? It is easily done…" The questions were uncannily prescient. Evans was alienating himself completely from the bulk of his compatriots and, as he himself predicted, their hatred would pursue him beyond the grave.[12]

The four "Studies" in the *English Review* were drawn from a bank of stories that Evans hoped might form a book. Austin Harrison gave encouragement, alerting Stanley Unwin to a collection guaranteed to lift Allen & Unwin's profile sensationally (the firm that had come into being on the day World War I was declared), but "Unwin proved unwilling to antagonize Nonconformist Liberals."[13] Unwin explained the background:

> We were offered, probably at the instigation of Austin Harrison… three manuscripts we wanted to accept… but which represented too startling a departure from the then character of our publications…. It must be remembered that the attitude towards books was much more squeamish and puritanical in 1914 than it has been since 1918.

The three books I recall were George Moore's *The Brook Kerith*, Caradoc Evans's *My People*, and Thomas Burke's *Limehouse Nights*.[14]

How Evans found a more sympathetic publisher is not exactly known. W.H. Davies might have played a part. Evans came to know him at a time when Davies was contracted to Andrew Melrose, head of a minor London house, for a prose work on Wales. Whatever the initial contact, Evans must have been highly grateful. Short-story collections, of any stripe, were notoriously bad sellers, the then literary agent Michael Joseph remarking how established authors, with novel sales of thirty thousand, might struggle to reach five thousand with their volumes of stories. And these were books that could be risked; a first collection by a barely known author came close to publishing suicide. Furthermore, publishers instinctively shied away from any material that might possibly give offence; their timidity, more than the law, cramped artistic expression. As it happened, Andrew Melrose was just the man to appreciate *My People*. A Scottish Presbyterian (with a Sunday School Union background), he recognised its kinship with *The House with the Green Shutters*, George Douglas Brown's powerful antidote to the Scottish Kailyard. It was Melrose who urged that Brown's manuscript be expanded into a full-scale novel, though he declined to publish it himself, believing (this in 1901) that the book would be better served by a larger, more established, company. Within a year Brown had died; he passed away at the Melroses' Highgate home with Andrew Melrose bitterly regretting not having become his publisher. The two had been companions with similar expectations of literature. "There can be no real literature that is wholly without essential religion," wrote Melrose, and (Brown to Melrose), "The damning fault of most of the books I have read is that nothing in them seems to leap at you from out of the pages. They are talky-talky, vapid... but most books, and certainly all books of the kind we want, should be pregnant and packed."

When, fourteen years later, a second professional journalist offered another vital manuscript, "pregnant and packed" with plenty leaping out of the pages, Melrose understood its Celtic provenance and the author's line of defence. "When... I asked him [Caradoc Evans] if Welsh life and character contained nothing more beautiful than that startling and mordant collection of sketches, he replied, 'Oh yes, but it is the ugly side of Welsh peasant life that I know most about.'" This time Melrose agreed to publish, though not without safeguards: he would prepare a book-jacket note explaining that though the content might give offence *My People* was justified on grounds of its fidelity to Welsh rural life and the author's reforming intention.

The fifteen stories of *My People*, many cast as concentrated life histories, are all variously interrelated, the strength of the collection deriving in part from its tight geographical framework and further binding devices of character, action and theme. "My people" are "the peasantry of west Wales" (as the subtitle elaborates), more particularly the inhabitants of a small, settled community, his fictional Manteg. Once again Evans draws on Rhydlewis, largely at the time of his childhood, a village "in the parish of Troedfawr" (Troedyraur), fixed by consistent references to Aberystwyth, Cardigan, Carmarthen and "Castellybryn"

(Newcastle Emlyn). At Rhydlewis the Ceri valley is a fertile sweep of meadowland, bounded by high moorland to the east and south, while north and westward are gentler cultivated hills. Manteg is locked away in a shallow bowl: this would have been Caradoc's perspective as he walked up and down the hillside between school and his childhood home. Lanlas sits on an eastwards rise; the desolate moorland above, scarred by quarry and gravel pit and explored by Caradoc as a boy, is a presence in *My People*. Local topography underpins the stories – names of local farms heavily mark the fictional choices – and Evans took pains to get these details right.

Besides specific locations, *My People* alludes to events, customs and superstitions associated with the locality: Dydd Iau Mawr ("Big Thursday", the village seaside outing on the second Thursday in August); the hiring fairs and other markers of the farming year; the courtship rituals (stories regularly concern the getting of a wife); the figure of the go-between or marriage factotum; the unscrupulous itinerant book-canvasser (Evans's "Seller of Bibles"); the portents of death, including phantom funerals. As handled by Evans, they make for an unflattering view of the community, and in broaching incendiary issues (money worship, social hypocrisy, physical brutality, the particular abuse of women) in a similar dispassionate manner, he inevitably provoked a backlash – how could he simply be reporting the facts? The question of the veracity of *My People*, of the literal truth of key incidents, is a minefield. Local research will reveal the model for Nanni, or for Sadrach Danyrefail. The horrifying details of his wife's confinement we accommodate within our understanding of the story – while accepting that hospital records from late nineteenth-century Cardiganshire document a treatment of those judged insane much akin to that afforded Achsah.[15]

For all his talk of pulpit rulers devilishly stalking the land, Evans did not exclusively concentrate on the chapel and its failings. *My People* has a social dimension not always acknowledged. Ministers feature less than one might suppose, being aloof, detached presences working often through subaltern henchmen (and often, so one senses, in the power of these deacons). In five stories only is the presence of a minister crucial; in two they are barely mentioned, and in eight they are absent altogether. Repeatedly Evans calls his ministers "rulers" or "judges", and their sonorous hyphenated surnames mark their social superiority. Dress too distinguishes them (frock-coats, kid gloves, varnished walking sticks) and their manner altogether befits the enormous prestige Welsh society conferred upon them. Bern-Davydd's familiarity with God, so awesome to his flock, greatly amuses Caradoc. Whatever their wish for deification, he and his kind are all-too-human, their origins of the people, their domestic trials much as their neighbours'. Wives are difficult ("Come into the cowshed, sinners bach," Bryn-Bevan invites a chapel deputation, "the mistress has been washing the flags"), and offspring a cause of anxiety. Bern-Davydd family problems occupy "The Redeemer". At fifty-two, the inadequate Lamech prepares to follow his father into the ministry, while younger son Adam, "imbued with little understanding", languishes in Shop Pugh Tailor, threatening to sink yet further by "going low for a female". A minister's son, whatever his prospects and however strong the need of an heir, must not stoop to "a workhouse brat".

"The Talent Thou Gavest" considers the making of a Sion minister: his pulpit call, his period of alienation, his subsequent return to the faith. Child of a widowed mother impoverished by the chapel, young Eben initially thrives, being possessed of those qualities making for pulpit success: an easy emotionalism, a concern for the next world (as opposed to the iniquities of this), and a more than nodding acquaintance with the Almighty. Evans's ministers have "singing eloquence", a capacity to beguile through rhythmical oratory and theatrical displays of emotion. Assayed by spiritual doubt, Eben abandons chapel magniloquence for the everyday prose of social concern; he must preach "the real religion" against the hypocrisy and injustice around him. His new approach wins no applause, indeed is judged atheistical. Evans knew that response, for Nonconformity in great part held that socialism was an atheistical creed potentially damaging to society. The Roberts Shop Grocer incident reflects a further social truth, that a servant girl sexually exploited by a superior stood no chance in a court of law: she would be dismissed as a scheming temptress ("Poor Roberts bach was sorely tempted, and he is forgiven. And has he not sent the bad bitch about her business?").[16] Money suppresses conscience, as Ben Shop Draper understands, and Eben makes peace with his community. "I have found the true light", he announces – the light that blinds.

The notion of Welsh classlessness, assiduously fostered by Liberal-Nonconformity, barely survives a glance at south Cardiganshire around the turn of the century. In an exclusively agricultural community, size of holding is paramount. Farms of a hundred acres were considerable places, their occupants persons of standing; with a hundred and fifty acres a farmer might do a minimum of manual work, his time being taken up by farm management and marketing. As little as thirty-five acres could mean virtual self-sufficiency, but of the 203 occupied houses in Troedyraur parish in 1901, no fewer than 157 had less than thirty acres. The very smallest holdings were often in the charge of widows (Caradoc's mother, we remember, worked a mere ten). All of these 157 households were in some measure dependent on the forty-six others. Work debts bound cottagers to farmers and in this finely graded hierarchy farmers of substance naturally enjoyed the highest social ranking. War only increased their dominance. Welsh farmers, it was widely felt, were profiteering during wartime, paying starvation wages, manning military tribunals so as to keep their sons at home, and threatening with military service farm labourers brave enough to press for better conditions. Evans aimed for accuracy in his description of farms. Accounts of acreage, inventories of animals – Sadrach Danyrefail's "stock of good cattle and a hundred acres"; Silas Penlon's "nearly one hundred acres" and "ten cows and ten pigs and three horses" – are not there for rural colour: they are marks of status.

Cottagers are likewise ranked by land possessed and type of dwelling. Simon and Beca ("The Way of the Earth") subsist on ten marginal acres above Penrhos, "their peat-thatched cottage under the edge of the moor", while Madlen ("The Glory that was Sion's") brings to Twm "two pigs, a cow and a heifer, several heads of poultry, and Tybach, the stone-walled cottage that is beyond the School-house". The cottagers suffer double exploitation, being inferiors both of the farmers and the tradesmen and community

professionals. The shopkeepers and local teacher constitute a small petit-bourgeois presence, often identified with the farmers and minister but not totally accepted by them.
They are largely figures of amused contempt, the tradesmen grasping for every ounce
of profit, and "that old blockhead" Lloyd Schoolin a lightweight among chapel elders
and ineffectual at his job. "The Way of the Earth" movingly delineates the exploitation
of society's weakest as William Jenkins, a bankrupt shopkeeper, schemes for the savings
of Simon and Beca. The elderly couple live their lives by the only rules they know. "Shop
General, Castellybryn" is "a godly man and one of substance", and they pray that his
substance may be settled on their daughter. Inevitably they are outwitted, and there is
pathos in the old man's pleading at the moment of defeat:

> Simon shivered. He was parting with his life. It was his life and Beca's life. She had
> made it, turning over the heather, and wringing it penny by penny from the stubborn
> earth. He, too, had helped her. He had served his neighbours, and thieved from them.
> He wept.
>   "He asks too much," he cried. "Too much."

"He had served his neighbours, and thieved from them." The author's gaze is steady; he
knows these beaten-down creatures, moving from birth to death in an unforgiving landscape. The way of the earth is not mysteriously determined. As Beca understands, "it is
the way of mortal flesh".

Worldly success and godliness are one and the same to Manteg. Material prosperity
is a sign of God's favour. The Calvinistic message is writ large across the land: "a godly
man and one of substance"; "the strongest farmer in the parish of Troedfawr, and the
saintliest man in the Big Seat in Capel Sion"; "Behold now, this man Evan is among the
wisest in the Capel. And there's rich he is." Wealthy farmers were chosen as deacons
and, together with the minister, comprised the governing body of the chapel. If farmers
were elected as deacons, tradesmen and senior craftsmen might be appointed teachers
in the Sunday school or singing class. Smallholders and cottagers, however dutiful their
membership and exemplary their lives, could rarely aspire to office. The same was true
of women, of whatever rank: "Apart from Sunday school work and 'young people's'
activities the contribution of women was virtually limited to reciting a few verses when
asked to do so. Women who did become prominent were extremely few in number and
were regarded as oddities."[17]

Manteg has its rebels. In "A Just Man in Sodom" a harmless simpleton with leanings
towards the pulpit becomes a disordered would-be prophet exiled on the moor. Pedr
functions as some kind of social critic, castigating adulterous Sion and its thieving from
widow and orphan. Yet he can only make sense of this wrongdoing in primitively religious
terms. "The Glory that was Sion's" allows a humble cottager one rare victory. The
reprobate Twm Tybach frustrates the chapel, whose concern is its public showing against
the heathen Church – with how many it can claim as its own, no matter their quality of
faith. The story also stands apart stylistically, drawing in tone and incident on the
apprentice piece "Taffy at Home" (1908) and preserving touches of "fine writing" that

Evans came to abjure. The approach had decidedly changed by the time of "Lamentations" and the persons of "the light men", the wild boys of the inn who humiliate Evan Rhiw by draping him in skin from a buried horse, having previously carried him into a stable and "laid him in a manger". Luke's words, juxtaposed with what strike as elements of pre-Christian ritual, hint at unbiddable forces abroad. "The light men" bring to mind that chasm in Welsh society between the godly and the worldly. The elect remain apart, shunning worldly pleasure, and with alcohol a crucial touchstone, the polarization centred ultimately on the presence of a public house. In south Wales Evans had for the first time encountered a muted religious scepticism and could claim the pubs there as centres of rational debate; beer and bar-room conversation lessened the social divisions. In rural Wales the chapels strove to shut the pubs (or at least to curtail their hours). Dissent there, when it came, took the form of a religious emotionalism yet more damaging. He would brilliantly fix the inmates of his rural compounds, prisoners and jailors alike: "As they were born; so will they live. They are victims of a base religion. They have been whipped into something more destructive than unbelief."[18]

Story after story finds men and women brutally opposed. Women are deep vessels of sin and men's God-given right is to govern them. The ideal wife is a servant, as Joshua explains ("The Woman Who Sowed Iniquity"): "But then Priscila is content to stand where the little Big King has placed her — an angel ministering to me and my children." That her role is divinely sanctioned is a matter of some satisfaction in an agricultural community where the labouring capacity of a female guarantees a productive farm. It is a point rammed home by Deio to his wavering son Tomos ("A Heifer Without Blemish"): "You need a woman to look after the land, and the cattle, and your milk man. And after you." Evans's stories frequently revolve around the search for a suitable partner, and in the attendant manoeuvrings women play their part. The consequences are usually dire – murder, madness, abandonment – though a Martha might succeed, the "stranger woman" who comes to rule at Danyrefail ("A Father in Sion"). Sadrach's "gift from the Big Man" supplants Achsah, his older wife. If men want women as workhorses, they also want them sexually; but as sex is evil, so must women be. Sex is always illicit, a male's succumbing to temptation. When men fall they counsel secrecy, which turns sex into a snare for women to achieve their goals.

In "A Bundle of Life" male ego destroys all family feeling, and ultimately the man himself. Silas Penlon rightly senses in son-in-law Abram ("the chief singing man in Capel Sion") a challenge to his alpha-male status. Their social ranking is nicely conveyed: Silas's contempt for "a man of nothing" and his "foolish singing class" sits easily with a farmer of substance. Both are active Sionites, and Abram's recognition of the biblical quotation by which Silas drives his slave-wife Nansi affords a brief harmony between them. Then Abram starts to issue Nansi's orders: a "new King" is emerging, one who will demand the complete abasement of his father-in-law and the casting-out of a stepson. "Take you this brat of sin with you now, little people … for he is not of my bowels."

Hannah and Matilda ("Lamentations"), Shan ("The Blast of God"), the servant girl Lissi ("The Redeemer"), all are defenceless women variously abused. Incest between

Evan Rhiw and his daughter Matilda lies at the heart of "Lamentations", although the matter is barely mentioned, the narrator's reticence mirroring the community's. Following his encounter with "the light men", Evan returns to a troubled Matilda, who meets his bizarre appearance with her own puzzling words: "Jesus bach, if the sons of men wear the habit of horses the daughters of God must go naked." The reference is to Genesis 6,2 ("the sons of God saw the daughters of men that they were fair"), a passage treating of an unnatural sexual union that must incur divine reprobation. "Lamentations" stands justice on its head: the chapel elder Evan gains absolution while "the adder" Matilda, abused to breaking point, is roped and led away to the madhouse at Carmarthen.

Not all *My People's* women are made to suffer in silence. There are spirited, rebellious younger ones like Sara Jane ("The Way of the Earth"), a working girl emboldened by her looks, and Esther in "Greater than Love", on a village trip to the seaside. They are dangerous forces in Sion, the greatest challenge to the way men see themselves, and thus to be obliterated. Betti suffers two-pronged abuse, from her husband and her brother ("The Woman who Sowed Iniquity"). Her story moves in classic *My People* fashion from a quiet, measured opening to a violence-laden end. Evans's parents are discernible in the characters of Betti and Gwylim, while the relationship between Betti and Joshua carries much of Caradoc's interpretation of matters between Mary Powell and brother Joshua. Betti is finally beaten down – "the Lord will administer the rod of correction on this slut" – though not before some formidable resistance. A tangle of public piety and steely self-interest, Joshua stands with Sadrach Danyrefail as an archetypal man of Sion. Both are word-obsessed – Gwylim, savage husband of Betti, is also a "talkist" – a characteristic amusingly pointed in the contrast between the Almighty's matey parlance ("Well-well, Josh bach, very terrible is this about the wench Betti") and Joshua's grave pomposities:

> Joshua leaned his body against the dresser, and drew his clog from his right foot and removed the dirt that had gathered on the sole between the iron rims; and he closed his mouth so that the projecting birth-tooth in the middle of it clawed his lower lip.
> "The Big Man brought my feet here, Betti fach," he remarked at last.

Physical repugnance mirrors ugliness of character, the dirt on Joshua's clogs reminding Betti that for all his god-like assumptions her brother's feet are of clay.

In Dinah we encounter *My People's* most immediately impressive female and her story "The Devil in Eden", in which Manteg outwits a fallen angel, demonstrates the lure of fantasy and folktale for Evans from the start. Interestingly, he returned to this story at the time of *Taffy* (1924) when he recast it as a one-act play, "A Devil on the Hearth: A Realistic Fantasy of the Welsh Peasantry". His choice of subtitle is a good one and would not have been far out of place had it prefaced *My People* as a whole. "The Devil in Eden" pivots on Dinah's responses to Michael, her knowing directness contrasting with her father's responses, all mediated through biblical quotation. Michael too quotes the Book, but this man is more than his words. "Dinah rested her elbows on her stockinged knees, and she settled her eyes on the sleeping stranger – a muscular figure with tanned, hairy skin showing under his buttonless shirt." She has her designs on Michael, who fully understands. She perhaps is Evans's New Woman, but a manifestation of a traditional Welsh ideal – "shrewd in the marketplace, devout in chapel and frantic in bed", as Alun Richards puts it[19] – the kind who in the later fiction increasingly gain the victory.

Yet the images that haunt are those of victimised women in stories of mythic dimension, above all Nanni. Duped by a Bible salesman, she sacrifices herself in her "mud-walled, straw-thatched cottage" infested by rats. She has survived on poor relief (3/9d a week, the sum is mentioned thrice), for which she is obliged to labour and from which a tithe must be given towards "the treasury of the chapel". Elements of her belief, of her far-back habit of mind, invade the opening of "Be This Her Memorial":

> Mice and rats, as it is said, frequent neither churches nor poor men's homes. The story I have to tell you about Nanni – the Nanni who was hustled on her way to prayer-meeting by the Bad Man, who saw the phantom mourners bearing away Twm Tybach's coffin, who saw the Spirit Hounds and heard their moanings two days before Isaac Penparc took wing – the story I have to tell you contradicts that theory.

The erupting parenthesis cuts across the measured tone of the narrator, preparing us for so much more.

The widow's life of sacrifice is of a piece with Manteg's have-nots – the hovels of the poor are all houses of sacrifice – but Nanni's supreme sacrifice takes on a different dimension. Its potency disturbs even Sadrach Danyrefail and his minister Bryn-Bevan. Her story might sound beyond time and place, to the lasting shame of those who made her condition possible. She needs a memorial and Evans will be her bard. The "this" of the story's title is both Nanni's sacrifice and the story that forever proclaims it; Matthew 26,13 comes to mind: "Verily I say unto you, wheresoever this gospel shall be preached in the whole world, there shall also this, that this woman hath done, be told for a memorial of her." The woman of Bethany anointed Jesus, recognising the Messiah; Bryn-Bevan is Nanni's Messiah: "in her search for God she fell down and worshipped at the feet of a god". Never again would Evans break authorial cover in the way he does for Nanni; he works through pervasive irony, never openly commenting on the action, whatever the provocation. Opinion enough flows from his Sionite narrator, whose understanding – "the Lord comforts his children", in summary – is always a part of the tale.

The local basis for "Be This Her Memorial" seems to be as follows.[20] The Revd David Adams left Hawen in August 1888, when Caradoc was nine years old. To mark his departure, chapel members organised a collection from which they bought a £25 watch for Adams and a £10 watch for his wife. These were large amounts – in 1885 the weekly wage of a farm labourer in south Wales was 14/6d – and one can imagine the pressure upon Hawen members to contribute. One of their number, an aged widow living close by Lanlas Uchaf, though unable to attend the chapel, had struggled hard to put by a sovereign for the collection. Not wishing to disappoint the old woman, Adams went to her cottage, graciously accepted her gift, and returned it quietly to her daughter as he departed. In "Self-portrait" Evans gave a bluntly different version. "At the time of his leaving us Davydd Thomas [i.e., Adams] worked a money collection for himself and an old woman roasted rats and ate them to save a pound for the collection." That she scrimped, maybe dangerously, is very probable, and rumours of her meagre diet might well have circulated. When directly approached on the subject Evans variously asserted and denied the veracity of the roasted rats.

With its disciplined intensity and a narrative detachment admitting of real pathos and drama, "A Father in Sion" is classic Caradoc Evans, down to the shocking last sentence. In considering Sadrach Danyrefail, a prosperous farmer-deacon who in pursuit of private self-gratification and public esteem destroys his family, Evans touches a central concern: the nature and relationship within a community of religion and the social order. In capel-centric Manteg public esteem is furthered through self-pronounced religious justification and mechanical obedience to the externals of faith. In contrast to the women around him, Sadrach is a psychological and emotional void. For him, language is less a means of self-expression than a weapon for forcing others; cunningly he commandeers a moral vocabulary ("Christian", "disgrace", "respectable") and employs it to suppress and control. Having through portentous invocations and enjoinders established authority over his children, he incarcerates their mother in a harness loft, her circumstances appallingly conveyed in a vision of the broken older woman being exercised animal-like at night. Having pronounced her mad, he drives her into madness. "A Father in Sion" must stand as Evans's most brilliant rendition of his conviction that religion had become a vicious, repressive force essentially because it furnished an exploitable moral rhetoric and mythology (of Palaces, White Shirts and Fiery Pools). Rightly the story stands at the opening of Evans's first collection.

Rhydlewis villagers would have recognised Sadrach as a local farmer who as a matter of fact did keep indoors his supposedly mad wife. They thought his behaviour acceptable in that it spared the poor woman the horrors of Carmarthen asylum. As in the story, this farmer indeed brought in a younger woman to help run the farm – she turned out to be an excellent helpmate, if bossy towards the children.

Evans displayed the practitioner's reluctance to discourse on method. He simply likened himself to the neutral photographer, one who refused to step outside his pictures to apportion praise or blame. His nearest approach to a literary defence of *My People* came in 1924 when, nine years after having stressed the factual components of the book, he challenged his newspaper critics:

> Where have I said that my work was about Rhydlewis? Where have I said that my tale about the old woman and the rats is true? I do not know a person, or act, or deed, or incident that will give me enough matter to make a story... Why find fault because I write in the most engaging way I know? Is the builder blamed because he builds well?

Facts and truth are different; events taking hold of the writer must be shaped and adjusted to attain dramatic truth. He reflected also that, "It does not matter what an author sees in his work, it is what the public sees in it." Presumably with his consent, his publisher set about devising a marketing strategy for *My People* that would direct the public's response.

My People: Public Reaction

1915-16

A ndrew Melrose took on *My People* cautiously. Much in the stories disturbed him and he viewed with distaste the controversies they would almost certainly provoke. To justify publishing the book, he insisted it first be issued in a particular physical format. As a writer, Evans's instinct was for the shortest of short stories. He aimed at 2000-2500 words, which meant that the fifteen in the collection presented a finished text of 35,000 words at most. With an ingenuity becoming the makers of Victorian three-deckers Melrose fashioned from this a substantial crown octavo volume of 276 pages. Text-page dimensions helped: a narrow "measure" with generous margins, and running headlines placed between rules so that the first text line proper began well down the page. Evans's liking for short paragraphs, and for telling a story through dialogue, further bulked out the text, but even at an average of 150 words per page, one might have expected a volume of around 230 pages. The printers found 46 more, largely by prefacing each story with its own part-title leaf. In all, 276 pages on thick text paper produced a handsome volume bound in maroon half-cloth with gold lettering on spine and front cover. The text typography also registers, a modified Scotch Roman particularly emphasizing capitals; and capitalisation clearly carries meaning (the earlier *English Review* printings have less of them). In settings like "School of the Sabbath", "House of the Poor" and "House of the Mad" it helps capture the monumental, intimidating aspects of these institutions. Capitals cluster around Evans's chapel and its minister and deacons: "Terrible Temple", "Meeting for Praying", "Judge of Sion", "First Men", "Father in Sion". Undoubtedly Melrose delivered a weighty, imposing artefact, highly designed with no skimping on space or materials. It elevates this short-story collection – its words lie like jewels on the page.

But Melrose went further. He would publish the book on condition that it be sold at a distinctive price and with a "carefully worded jacket". The original price of *My People* is a feature now utterly lost on us, although "5/-" on the spine would have struck the first purchasers as unusual. Of the three hundred or so works of fiction published in October and November 1915, the *Bookseller* lists no other selling at this price. Six-shilling novels predominate, with sizeable amounts of cheaper fiction at 3/6d, 2/6d and less. Prices categorize fiction and were highlighted in advertisements. They are linked to physical format and, in a rough and ready way, implied something about content. Six-shilling novels – bland fodder for circulating libraries – might be bought by anyone in the certainty that they gave no offence. Its five-shilling price was a signal that *My People* did not fit this category. The *Globe* took the point, congratulating Melrose on "lifting the book out of the ruck of six-shilling novels".

If Melrose priced the collection deliberately, he doubtless held views on its title. "My people" is a recurring Old Testament phrase ("The prophets prophesy falsely, and the priests bear rule by their means; and my people love to have it so...", Jeremiah 5,31) and Evans may have taken it from there – though he spoke of "the homely eighteenth chapter of Genesis" (in which Abraham pleads with God to spare Sodom) as a spur to writing his stories. But the title is loaded in other ways: besides fixing a subject matter, it underlined the claim to authenticity. Here is a man on home ground, "a Welsh-speaking Welshman, cradled in Welsh Nonconformity". And who are "my people"? "The peasantry of West Wales" in the words of the subtitle. ("My people" also implies "my kinsfolk": one is reminded of Caradoc's response to those who accused him of tarring the Welsh at large in his fictional portraits. He did not intend them to stand for the Welsh; they were some of his relatives.)[1]

Above all, a remarkable dust jacket gave Melrose a platform to justify his association with the book. Author and title are completely banished from their natural front-cover spot, to be replaced by seventy bold prefatory words:

> These stories of the Welsh peasantry, by one of themselves, are not meat for babes. The justification for the author's realistic pictures of peasant life, as he knows it, is the obvious sincerity of his aim, which is to portray that he may make ashamed. A well-known man of letters and critic has expressed the opinion that "My People" is "the best literature that has, so far, come out of Wales."

The jacket's "realistic pictures" satisfied Evans – he considered himself a realist in as much as he faced grim fact – and predictably inflamed the Welsh.

Appearing in early November 1915, *My People* became for the *Globe*, "easily the literary sensation of the moment". Evans spoke of more than ninety reviews and some forty can be readily traced. Overwhelmingly favourable, they ensured that, by the modest standards of short stories, the collection sold well (three reprints in as many months). The *Evening Standard* hailed "a strong, notable book"; "each story... a triumph of art" (*Bystander*); "the power of the thing is altogether undeniable. For page after page Mr Evans holds you, as the Ancient Mariner held the Wedding Guest" (*Punch*). The stories won praise for their formal mastery ("not a single comment or superfluous word mars their tense directness") and their haunting personal style. Caradoc Evans was *sui generis* ("we know of nothing to put beside these merciless, sardonic silhouettes") though comparisons were nonetheless made – with Gorky, Zola and Maupassant, with the English moral satirists. The *Westminster Gazette* spoke tellingly of the influence of the Bible: "Mr Evans neither falters nor stoops. Some right instinct impelled him to use a prose that derives directly from the language of the Old Testament; and this instrument gives a deeper barb to his satire and majesty to his drama." The *Daily Herald* judged *My People* "the most poignant satire since Swift", though Swift penned no work "so cold, so detached and uncondemning, so void of praise and blame". Here was another Evans hallmark: a quiet dispassion, a freedom from extraneous moralizing, the suppression of all emotional and moral rhetoric. There is indeed an Augustan quality in Evans, a prose of lapidary beauty born of outrage and disgust. The *Daily Herald* had no doubt that he had drawn "a picture of the life he has known... and the incredible, the inescapable impression one has is that it is largely true."

Inevitably reviewers speculated on the factual basis of the book or took up the wider issue of literary "realism". For Norman Douglas, Evans was a realist employing non-realistic techniques. "The book stands apart," he suggested in the *English Review*:

> Realism has an eye for detail; pokes its nose into this and that; luxuriates. What Mr Evans tells us in his archaic language is too stark and austere to be realistic. He does not gloat or pry. He conveys, rather, a sense of elemental things – the coldness, the indifference of rocks and waters. He moves above his subject.

"Realism is an artistic method," expounded the young John Middleton Murry in the *Daily News*; Caradoc Evans hated passionately, and had "the power to control his hatred by an artistic method". His stories showed a "splendid sureness... not one of them offends, because beneath them all is the convincing passion of the thing deeply felt or keenly seen. One never has a tremor of apprehension concerning the writer's vision, or any suspicion that he himself has evoked the ugliness which he portrays." This said, Murry foresaw the storm about to break in Wales, and got a taste of it when one Welsh reader complained that newspaper praise such as his was a greater crime than the book itself. Murry backed away: his praise was not to be taken as an endorsement of Evans's views of the Welsh; he had spoken of the peasantry of the book, not the peasantry of West Wales – and, "To admit that Mr Evans's view is inspired by hatred is to announce that it is one-sided."

Two further responses stand out. Caradoc's pal Edwin Pugh welcomed *My People* in the Christmas issue of *The Bookman*. Under the heading "A Book of Novels", he stressed the extreme concentration of the prose: "each line is packed with significance... There is not a tale in the book but contains the essence of a tragedy or an epic, or at least a novel." He remarked on the humour in the book, an ingredient surprisingly lost on many. Another old companion Edward Wright wanted to contribute a piece on the book for the *Evening News* but the paper already had splendid copy by way of Arthur Machen's interview with Caradoc (12 November). Once more the author denied having invented the harsh facts of Cardiganshire life. He lacked the capacity to do so: "We have no imagination left in West Wales because no one will give us two pence for it, and we only value the things that will bring money."

By and large, critics in England favoured literary readings. Evans presented a world wider than Wales where puritan vices were lashed in a prose like no other, and somehow he had found the means to convince the reader that what he said was true. Such Metropolitan detachment proved next to impossible in Wales where attention stayed fixed on the book's non-literary dimensions. Evans thought this no bad thing: "If I had not made a mwstwr [commotion] in Wales I should have failed in the object I had in view – that of breaking down the power of Welsh Liberal Nonconformity."

Welsh reaction to *My People* proved unremittingly, incandescently, hostile. No book before or since, has remotely provoked such hatred. *My People* in the context of Wales was an act of cultural terrorism, assailing popular notions of the rural Welsh as a classless, democratic people, blessed by enlightened leadership, safe in an earthly paradise. Praise from English reviewers simply fuelled Welsh loathing of the book, as did Evans's high sense of mission, something soon exhibited in the correspondence columns of the *Western Mail* where, with prophet-like fervour, he confronted his critics on the social message of his art. The *Western Mail*, having denounced a "squalid, repellent" collection, "false and miserably misleading", became the major battleground. Tory in its politics, the paper nonetheless posed as Wales's national daily and enjoyed good sales in the south. Its editor William Davies strove to foster a sense of Welshness among a readership that he saw as increasingly disparate and exposed to Anglicization. Any attack on Welsh Wales was intolerable. So he thundered editorially against Evans while granting him a platform for his undoubted polemical gift. Here is one Evans defence against the charges voiced in the paper and attempts to ban his book:

> My book is not unclean; it is an unsavoury book, for the people with whom it deals are very wicked, and they have learnt all manner of evil devices from their pastors. They are pagans, and they worship gods. Their rulers are artful and cunning; they weep in the public places; they dot their "i's" with blood and shape their "t's" into crucifixes. Yet their hearts are lustful and cruel. They have taken away the glory from Sion, and the house is a place of intrigue for Radicals. They have prospered above any of their congregation, and their abodes are the mansions of the land. They command offerings in the name of God, and fatten thereon. They see on all sides of them peasants – whose bodies are crooked from toil, and whose souls are sterile – labouring all the light hours to keep them in comfort. They make mischief in families, and cry aloud the name of the widow who fails in her dole to the capel. They say to the congregation: "People bach, we are the Big Man's photographs." They close the door of the public houses and open the gates of Sion at a later hour for prayer-meetings, and I know of dreadful things that have befallen servant girls at the hands of praying men on the road home from the chapel. I spoke of one such case to a religious man in West Wales last August. This what he said to me: "Dear me, now, she is only an old girl of a servant.
>
> Wales would be brighter and more Christianlike if every chapel were burnt to the ground and a public house raised on the ashes thereof.[2]

The public at large came to know Caradoc Evans through his overheated exchanges in newspaper correspondence columns. Writing soon after Caradoc's death, J.B. Priestley reflected on the longer-term consequences of this. The newspaper fuss about his stories,

> though it might have given him a welcome bit of limelight at the time, really did him far more harm than good, because it seemed to limit his appeal as a genuine artist – and I think he was a genuine artist – and tended to give his work an air of the journalistic stunt. For this, I imagine, he paid rather heavily afterwards.[3]

As it happened, the *Western Mail* was temperate compared with other Welsh journals. The level of abuse still startles, directed at Evans's writing, his ugly face and dirty mind, his grasping, treacherous disposition – he was a man foully on the make, feeding filthy gobbets to the eager English. Melrose's blurb (fully quoted by the *Western Mail*) became all that was necessary to read. As for that opinion of a "well-known man of letters",[4] that the book was the best literature that had come out of Wales, this was the ignorant outsider's viewpoint, a gleeful move by one of the English to applaud a production so patently anti-Welsh. Hadn't the English recently gloated over Arthur Tyssilio Johnson's *The Perfidious Welshman* (1910) and T. W. H. Crosland's *Taffy Was a Welshman* (1912)?

Evans remained composed. In fact, he grew in confidence, convinced he had found his target. He quoted Galatians 4.16, "Am I therefore become your enemy, because I tell you the truth?" The gales of wrath amounted to little – something that did not surprise him; as he told Bangor students nine years later: "If one speaks against us we denude the hedges for sticks with which to beat him. We stand before our accusers not with the rapier of reason or the shield of belief but with foolish phrases on our lips and mud pies in our hand." Indeed, none of Evans's critics attempted any serious account of Welsh Nonconformity's real achievements. Steeped in Liberal-Nonconformist mytholo-gies, they clung to their vision of a Welsh country heaven, one spared the loss of language and religion, the class conflict and social evils that marred the industrial south. The Church had kept Wales in darkness (so Evans was reminded), and Nonconformist blood had been shed to let in the light. That these freedom fighters, the ministers, farmers, lawyers and tradesmen who drove the squire from the land, should in turn have oppressed the peasantry was nonsense: victims cannot victimise. On the contrary, through its democratic, chapel-based culture Wales had gained more than its share of the great and the good – great preachers, great poets, great politicians – drawn from all walks of life. Evans would have none of this. Victims should always be feared; the last people to look to for social compassion were those who had recently escaped from the lack of it. (As Auden succinctly puts it, "Many a sore bottom finds / A sorer one to kick.")

A task for Evans in these exchanges was to locate a better Wales, one beyond the reach of the minister and chapel-bred politician. Liberal-Nonconformity, he believed, had but temporarily consumed the nation and its end was now in sight; in the politically radicalised coalfields and the seaboard towns of the south, he sensed a new Wales stirring. In the meantime he would hack at the Liberal-Nonconformist establishment. Confident of national support, that establishment branded him a traitor, defiling the nation at large. Outrage and anger were variously expressed: a brick through his East Sheen window, pulpit denunciation of his lies, rumoured burnings of *My People*, and real attempts to suppress it.

Carrying one of the few uncomplimentary English reviews, the *Birmingham Post* thought the author's bias "palpably political". This, of course, was true, and in Wales *My People* was politically persecuted. Attempts to suppress the book began soon after publication. Of the four great national subscription libraries, Boots and W. H. Smith preferred to exclude it from their lists altogether, while the Times and Mudie's restricted its circulation. This was no small matter: subscription libraries accounted for a sizeable portion of the fiction market and such was their collective purchasing power (far outweighing that of the public libraries) that they exerted significant influence on the content and nature of fiction. Austin Harrison had no doubts that the ban was "due to one of the periodical waves of prudery which afflict the gentlemen who control the circulation of books. There are many other evidences of the currency of such sentiment just at present." The libraries had got cold feet following the successful prosecution of *The Rainbow* on grounds of obscenity and they shied away from handling another controversial title that some newspapers had, however fancifully, linked with Lawrence's novel.

The subscription libraries' stance encouraged more forceful action in Wales. On 10 January 1916 the Cardiff police raided Wyman's bookshop, threatening to seize all copies of *My People* on grounds that remain obscure; press reports talk of a warrant in connection with the 1857 Obscene Publications Act, although a successful prosecution under this act must have seemed unlikely. Evans immediately suggested that David Williams, Chief Constable of Cardiff, was moving on the promptings of others. Before Christmas, Williams had read *My People* uncomplainingly but now had changed his mind, claiming, "I was for twenty years at Scotland Yard, and I read most of the suppressed books, and *My People* is the worst book I've ever read."[5] Politics lay behind the volte-face. "In attacking Welsh Nonconformity you attack Welsh Liberalism," Caradoc insisted; "they are one and the same thing. Every chapel in Wales has its committee-room in the interests of Welsh politics. There is not a single paper outside Wales which has stated that the book is immoral."[6] Cardiff booksellers were being cowed into not stocking *My People*.

Against this unofficial censorship Evans hit back: "Mr Williams may take it from me that he will not suppress my voice in a hurry". He would bring the matter to court and, if necessary, to the House of Lords, "to prove that the police have neither the powers nor the rights to instruct the people as to what they should read."[7] A reluctant Andrew Melrose had earlier entered the fray with comments to the *Western Mail* (22 November 1915). "Realism" remained his defence. His edition had fully prepared readers for what was in store. "I devised a jacket which warned… that the contents were 'strong meat'; and I published the book at the distinctive price of 5s. to mark it from the ordinary 6s. novel. Such were the conditions under which I published *My People*, and I can only say that if the decision were to be taken again it would not be altered."[8] An additional letter to the *Mail* (16 December 1915) made clear that he as publisher had no complaint against the libraries and never talked of their "banning" *My People*. Two libraries had simply chosen not to put the book on their lists whereas the Times and Mudie's had ordered it several times but not "given it free course". It was his duty, however, to refute the charge that *My People* was "unclean"; regarding its references to incest: "Read the records of the Society for the Prevention of Cruelty to Children. There you will find that a large part of the work of the Society is in Wales, in connection with a certain form of vice – always a vice of undercivilisation."

Melrose next approached the Society of Authors and some prominent writers as well. H.G. Wells, for one, responded sympathetically, thanking the Cardiff police for bringing to his attention "some very strange and wonderful work". He judged *My People* "very finely done" and would do what he could in support of it. (Privately, he confided that Galsworthy, Gosse or Barrie might be better witnesses than the author of *Ann Veronica*, a novel blacklisted by Boots and "banned" by various public libraries.) Others rallied to Evans's defence, some offering financial assistance. At that point it wasn't needed: "I have made enough money out of *My People* to take action".[9] The action was to lobby Welsh members of parliament – only to find that whatever their private feelings none dared publicly support him. It was left to Colonel Arthur Lynch, Nationalist MP for West Clare, to take up Evans's case.[10] Lynch appealed to the Welsh love of liberty and free speech, "without which they would not have won the great victory of the disestablishment of the Welsh church." Caradoc Evans was "a man of genius and a true artist" who "paints what he sees". There was more truth in his peasantry than in "the comic-opera type tossing hay in silk stockings for West End audiences".

A case against the police now lay in the hands of the solicitors, who advised that since the police had actually seized no copies of *My People*, court action against them was well-nigh impossible. Evans now approached the Society of Authors (which he had wisely joined) asking whether it might not bring to general notice the unfairness of police action in this matter. "I am careless as to whether the Society upholds or condemns *My People*," he wrote to the secretary Herbert Thring, "but I am anxious that the public should be informed of my endeavours to vindicate my name."[11] Alerted by Andrew Melrose, the Society had taken notice of developments but could do little unless a case was brought to court.

In one last public airing of the subject, Evans crystallized his grievances.[12] The Cardiff police could apparently publicise their desire to proceed against a book, at whatever cost to an author's reputation, and then withdraw when the situation suited them. An author, so it seemed, had no means of redress:

> Naturally I want justice for myself and for my book, but a much more vital issue is involved. My book is not obscene, but in it I do exercise the undoubted right of the critic to pass judgement on the manners and customs of his time. That my judgement is severe is beside the point; yet that is the real cause of the police interference... I have done what I could. I am prepared to stand my trial. I am prepared to say that there is no obscene phrase or suggestion in my book. But I am not prepared to be accused, tried, and convicted by a Cardiff policeman, whose actions are protected by his position.

In light of all this, the English periodicals re-appraised the book, confirming their original high estimates in a second wave of notices. In Wales, however, the charge of pornography stuck. "Its apparent lack of pornographic intent has succeeded in getting printed things that have never been printed before, except in the literature of deliberate pornography," opined the *Welsh Outlook* (March 1916), a recently founded monthly under the honorary editorship of Thomas Jones who, by the end of the year, would be assisting Lloyd George in London. The ridiculous charge of pornography substantiates the view that Welsh Liberals were moving against Caradoc. In December 1915 *Town Talk* had speculated that Lloyd George, working through the Board of Control, might have been behind attempts to ban the book and in a review of Machen's *The Great Return*, Evans directly named Lloyd George as suppressor ("Mr George is Welsh Nonconformity").[13]

"We take leave to say that there is not a Welshman living of any literary note who will commend the narrative, and not a critic of standing who will dare sign his name to an approving estimate of *My People*." The *Western Mail's* lordly pronouncement proved to be largely true, and in Wales from this point on Evans's name became a byword for treason. But as in April 1915 (following his stories in the *English Review*), there again came approving words from the political opponents of Liberalism – on the left and the right. The socialist *Labour Voice* (previously *Llais Llafur*) hailed a new force in Welsh letters. Evans "can observe; he can write; he will be realistic though the heavens fall; and he has a sympathy as cordial as his touch is sure".[14] *My People* was "by a long way the best book that any Welshman of our day has written." (Allen Raine, whose name others reverently evoked as the true chronicler of rural Wales, is dismissed for her "mushy sentimentality".) The paper's review, headed "A Welsh Hogarth", was the work of W.H. Stevenson, an ex-miner educated at Ruskin College and prominent in Labour politics. Formerly a journalist with the Swansea Valley weekly, Stevenson had joined the *Daily Herald*, the national mouthpiece of the labour movement, and must have been behind the editorial that the *Herald* ran on the attempted banning of *My People*. It asserted Evans's complete sincerity and the love-loathing that marked his work. "For first and last… he is a Welshman who passionately loves his people, and passionately hates the horror and hypocrisy of the evil things in their midst."

Such a response, one should add, was far from representative of Welsh labour at large. Evans polarised positions. At Cwmavon, older chapel men urged the banning of the book from the Tinplaters' Institute library, while younger ones held altogether different views of "Comrade Caradoc Evans" (so the *Merthyr Pioneer* reported). Old-style Mabonite Lib-Labism pursued a moderate, reformist programme, one which harnessed Welshness and religion; as when the socialist novelist Joseph Keating lambasted Evans in a *Western Mail* panegyric on his Valleys people. There he linked their shining virtues – their radicalism, respect for education and culture, their love of family, community and place – to their passionate devotion to religion. "Wales is a garden of chapels and churches built chiefly out of the earnings of labourers… the earnestness of a people may be accurately measured when they stint their bodies to satisfy their souls."[15]

The *Carmarthen Journal* – unlike the bulk of its readers – remained entirely supportive of Caradoc. Even his much-maligned dialogue won praise in the paper's *My People* review: "he has succeeded, to a remarkable degree, in expressing the tone and spirit, as well as the meaning, of the terms employed in the vernacular of these districts. There is absolutely no ground for doubting the author's intimate knowledge of his subject."[16] The reviewer's condemnation of Welsh Calvinism rivals the author's. It was "a narrow, bigoted and

A Cubist Caradoc Evans

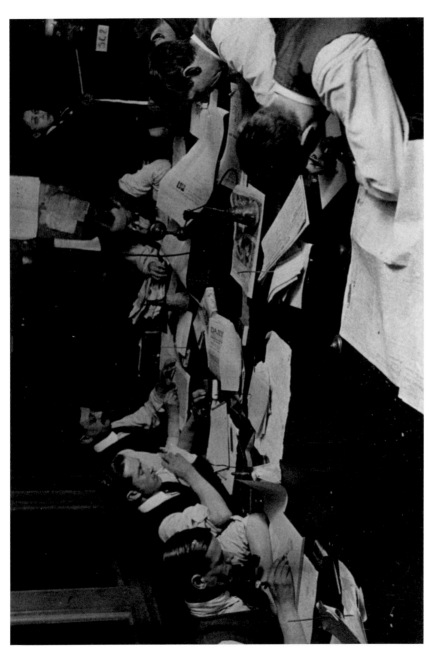

Caradoc (front left) at the *Daily Mirror* subs table, where he worked 1917-23

Evans in his Fleet Street prime, with T.P. O'Connor (centre) and Arthur Machen (left)

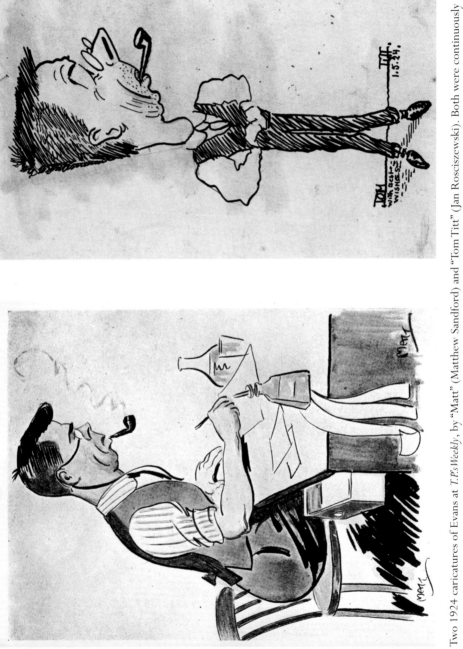

Two 1924 caricatures of Evans at *T.P.'s Weekly*, by "Matt" (Matthew Sandford) and "Tom Titt" (Jan Rosciszewski). Both were continuously engaged by papers and periodicals, Matt's sketches being a feature of *T.P.'s Weekly*

Marguerite and Armiger Barclay at "Old Roses", Sudbury 1914. They had married in
1911

Walter and "Marguerite Lovell" with Nicholas her son and Cupid

Marguerite soon after marriage to Armiger Barclay, with her adored cocker spaniel Cupid

At Evan Walters' Belsize Park studio, c. 1930: Caradoc, Marguerite, Erna Meinel (artist and friend of Walters), Evan Walters

Evans as he appeared in *Current Literature* (August 1930). *Inset*: The journalist Glyn Roberts. Recognising Caradoc from the Current Literature photograph ("great nose, glaring eyes and vast black hat"), he introduced himself and in the little time left him promoted Caradoc enthusiastically

vicious creed, as taught for generations by an ignorant and incompetent ministry".
Ministers are judged by their ability to stir up crude emotion: "if a man is moved to
tears he feels the glow of satisfaction and believes himself one of the 'elect'... but his
life during the week is thereby not altered one whit". Nor was this brand of the faith
confined to rural outposts; the same anti-Christian spirit permeated all Nonconformist
Wales. Here spoke militant Anglicanism (almost certainly the manager-editor Lewis
Giles), determined to applaud any disenchanted sectarian. The *Journal*, having failed to
land a story, did reprint (25 February 1916) Evans's review of Machen's *The Great Return*
and, departing from normal practice, displayed four large block advertisements for
another *My People* reprint.

The *Journal* seems not to have elicited Rhydlewis's reaction to the stunning emergence
of one of their own. What slender evidence we have suggests that the village, while
liking the man, took little notice of his writing. When they did, it was to condemn.
Thomas Owen, writing from Rhydlewis as "one who knew him well", assured the *Western
Mail* that "he [Caradoc] was generous and kind to his widowed mother and failing brother,
jolly company, and perfectly natural in every way. He was, however, absolutely irresponsible
and probably did not expect anyone to take his books seriously."[17] David L. Evans claimed
a special relationship with Caradoc based on their childhood together: "On Sundays we
shared the same pew in the chapel, and throughout the whole of our school years we
continued almost as closely knit as twins." He remained on friendly terms with Caradoc,
as did Lewis Giles (for whom he worked at the *Carmarthen Journal*) but as a writer
Caradoc had fallen victim to publishers' "insatiable demands for the gruesome, even
though it be as preposterous and weird as the story of the old woman's roasted rat".[18]

Within the family, there was initial pride at Caradoc's literary success. Even Uncle
Joshua wished to join in, so Evans confided (*Ideas*, 3 November 1916):

> I know of one who was dead in the minds of his well-to-do relatives for many years.
> When he accomplished something which none of them had been able to accomplish,
> and as his fame was sounded abroad, the people who had despised him came around
> him and said they were glad to call him a friend. But the man's spirit was up and he
> despised them.

The question of Dr Powell's opinion of *My People* surfaced in the *Western Mail* (29
December 1915), when the Revd T. Eynon Davies quoted part of a letter that Dr Powell
had sent him: "Yes, certainly you may mention... my utter disapproval of the whole
book." Evans's reply (6 January 1916) simply pointed out that his uncle's statement
"does not tally with the sentiments of a letter which Dr Powell sent me after the book
was published".

Capel Sion

1916-17

The battles and brawling at home did not stem the creative flow. By summer 1916 Evans had placed six new stories in the periodicals, two in the *English Review* ("The Word" preceded the first instalment of Conrad's *The Shadow Line* in the July issue) and four more in *New Witness*, Cecil Chesterton's left-leaning weekly strong on political corruption, "the Achilles heel of Liberalism". Evans was convinced of his mission; he had found his subject matter and the medium that served it best. Violently original in content and style, *My People* proved how potent, how substantial, a short-story collection could be, particularly where component pieces reinforce each other in a convincing consistent whole. Remarkably, too, *My People* paid its way, running to a fourth impression in February 1916. A second collection, hard on the heels of the first, must have seemed a fair commercial prospect and accordingly nine more stories joined the six already published to complete *Capel Sion*.

All its stories date from 1916, the blackest year of the war, one which began with compulsory conscription and ended with Asquith's fall as Prime Minister – between came carnage on the Western Front culminating in the Somme offensive. The war only hardened Evans's convictions; far from destroying any melioristic illusions – Whiggish notions of social progress, Enlightenment ideals of man's perfectibility – it was expressive of something central in our human makeup. Though set in a pre-war period, *Capel Sion* tones with a contemporary reality in its depiction of a warring unto death over land and possessions, the protagonists intimate enemies who babble of god and religion. But, "You cannot dish Christian ethics into the Devil's decanter. We are the vessels of the Devil's poison."[1] It is sinfulness that makes us human.

Evans's villagers are tethered to the chapel, locked in a prison of the mind erected over generations by preachers, politicians, and preaching publishers. Their god is the god of Sion, or more immediately, the Big Man's son on earth. To the Ruler of the Pulpit they make their sacrifices, for he is the community's protector – "Your horses will rot and a plague of worms will eat your sheep. Lightning will burn your bellies and crops… What will you do without me?" – and the arbiter of individual lives. Insistently, Evans portrays debased religion as a weapon of social control, used to bludgeon, disgrace and humiliate, and always in the service of the powerful, the monied farmers chosen to be chapel deacons. The minister calls them blessed, and their prosperity is a sign of God's favour: witness Amos Penparc, "whose riches were above any other man on the floor of Sion, and whose piety was established" ("The Pillars of Sion"); or Griffi Wernddu, "cheapened in the eyes of Sion" by his material fall: "none bid him pray or to bear testimony in the Seiat; and to another was given his place in the Big Seat and also his office" ("A Sacrifice Unto Sion"). No nonsense here about rich men and eyes of needles, or of the meek inheriting the earth.

The Revd Davydd Bern-Davydd makes his entrance by way of a sermon on the widow of Nain, a biblical story exemplifying Christ's compassion for the poor but, in Bern-Davydd's hands, one more means of ensuring that even the "religious little widow" gives of her mite. "The Word" wickedly suggests how the chapel shapes community thinking; social distinctions are reinforced, as is the crucial identification of wealth and status with individual moral worth. Sion's ruler retains the outward attributes manifested in *My People*: the lordliness, the vanity, the easy familiarity with the Almighty (to whom he is still "Bern bach"), the theatricality and ready emotionalism so beloved by his con-gregation ("to weep to the tune of the Respected gives religious delight"). Nor has his verbal zest deserted him. "The Comforter" finds him in full spate, no less comically deceiving even at the grave of his wife. Half in love with his ministers, Evans palpably relishes Bern. "The Word" tempts him into personal asides. He appears under his nickname: "Shall that be said of you, Dai Lanlas, after the report that Eynon Daviss made about you?" asks Bern; "A dirty black you was, man, to jeer at Capel Sion." (The Revd T. Eynon Davies was an outspoken opponent of *My People*.) Bern meets some improbable pulpit challengers, notably Dan Groesfford, the club-footed farm labourer who breaks his hire to answer the call of the ministry ("The Acts of Dan"). He has the cant, the empty eloquence and, more importantly, the money at his disposal. Its source is Sali Blaenpant, the enigmatic "stranger woman" who arrives unannounced at the village in her horse-drawn cart. Bern scents danger – and opportunity.

"Grasping is the Ruler of the Pulpit. Always asking he is, Pedr bach, for yellow money. There's a boy he is for his pocket." The words are Pedr's, the half-mad would-be prophet who descends from the moor to preach the sins of Sion ("Calvary"). As in *My People*, he is ribbed and humoured until his truths become too barbed. But he knows Bern's essence, his need to exploit every turn of event for his own material gain. Others take their cue from the master. "All for me, and the rest for my brother" is the sum of their ethical code – except that precious little brotherly love is in evidence. Indeed, the family remains the site of savage conflict, both between and within generations. (The nearest we approach to family affection is the doting regard of mothers for their ungrateful, inadequate sons – the religious charlatan Dan sends his "Satan of a Mam" to the local Poor House.) As ever in Caradoc Evans, men and women are viciously opposed, with men overwhelmingly the oppressors, although mothers might inflict upon daughters-in-law the wrongs they themselves have endured. Capel Sion's males exhibit a puritan horror of sex. Periodically stormed by lust, "My flesh is clean" they proclaim; and when events tell unambiguously against them, the chapel is ever at hand to assure them that they "fell by an old female". Women are always the initiators, "Satan's daughters" who break down their menfolk's defences then oppress them with the burden of their sin.

Such is Hannah Harelip ("Redemption"), a farm servant made pregnant by her employer Evan Rhos; which is an inconvenience for Evan as he closes in on a wealthy wife and decidedly troublesome when Hannah threatens him with the law. It is a futile gesture, as Evans's narrator makes plain: "Hannah was told that it is against God's will for a servant to charge her master, that God does not permit them who sit in the loft of Sion to murmur against them who sit on the floor and in the high places". Ellen Pugh is another made pregnant by a praying man ("A Mighty Man in Sion"), though here the forces are more evenly matched. Ellen at twenty-six is "strong and… proud of her chastity" whereas Lias Carpenter is a hollow Sionite propped up by his minister. He dries his trousers before Ellen's fire, and at the unignorable outcome of their coupling – "She drew in her clothes, and as her size increased she eased them; her contrivings did not withhold her state" – he furiously turns against her. Ellen determines to fight back, but can she survive without Sion when the Chapel is law and life?

If servant girls are fair sexual prey, women of means are wife-material, to be captured for their money and set to work on the farm. Evans is eloquent on the fate of such women: thus Betti, wife of Griffi Wernddu, who bore eight children and "laboured until the members of her body were without feeling" ("A Sacrifice Unto Sion"); or the dying Leisha, her marriage one long vicious sham, struggling "to trim the land which gave her little and robbed her of herself" ("A Keeper of the Doors"). Both have husbands lost to religion, a condition familiar enough to the superintendent of the Carmarthen Joint Lunatic Asylum ("religious emotion… is more apt to cause mental breakdown, and more apt to tinge mental disorder than other factors", he reported in 1905). Money worship, not a discomforting eschatology, drives Dennis Glasgoed insane ("The Tree of Knowledge"). His fevered imaginings coalesce around a supposedly wasteful wife and her likely collusion with his enemies – "Sorrowful is this. All are in array against me" – and all must be made to pay.

Two stories featuring Amos Penparc form a continuous narrative ("Sons of Their Father" and "Judges"), while Amos's rivalry with John Tyhen features in "The Day of Judgment", an uncollected story of 1917 written as a sequel to "Judges".[2] These three related pieces might well be fragments of the novel Evans planned to write: he had provisionally entitled it "The Children of Essec" (or "Isaac") – which is what indeed are Amos, Daniel, Ruth and John Tyhen ("the child of his wanton days"). "Sons of Their Father" finds them at the dying Essec's bedside seeking word of their inheritance. Amos stands apart, choosing to speak religiously, but "an awful stealer is Amos", as John Tyhen rightly divines. The later stories have the two confronting each other over the meadow, with Amos supported – outwardly – by his minister. John's resistance is stubborn and savage but the chapel breaks him down. He acknowledges Bern-Davydd's dominion; he comes to love Big Brother. Interestingly, in *Capel Sion* the minister regularly outwits his deacons, whereas in *My People* it is (we sense) the deacons who ultimately wield the power. This said, "The Pillars of Sion" shows Amos as a monster of evil, planning the seduction of the mentally disabled Silah Penlon. Here is a classic Evans configuration: a chapel elder in alliance with his minister bending a superstitious flock, and an outcast female reduced to animal status. Once again a widow is reviled, a frightened mother fighting to resist the community's view of her "mad bitch" daughter, "the Big Man's curse" (repeatedly in this collection disability and illness are seen by Sionites as marks of God's disfavour). It is difficult not to think that driving this staggering story was Evans's feelings for his own widowed mother and her severely handicapped son, his brother Josi.

Though overshadowed by *My People*, *Capel Sion* has its own distinction. It is a darker, more claustrophobic collection. We rarely move beyond the unnamed village (recognisably Manteg), which is itself less broadly realised: the working world rarely breaks in and the natural world is present only in the animal curses flung between characters. These characters are fewer in number, with schoolteacher, shopkeeper and craftsman, the village reprobates and gossips, reduced to walk-on parts (the absence of children almost goes without saying: Welsh childhood-and-countryside heaven was a state unknown to Evans). More telling is the lack of positive female presences, those resourceful younger women, shrewd, robust, intuitive, and aware of their own desirability, who offer in *My People* some challenges to the men. Ellen ("A Mighty Man in Sion"), Ann ("The Deliverer") and Sali ("The Acts of Dan") touch upon the type but, while marked off from the menfolk, they are diminished as agents of change. The reduced social canvass throws Bern-Davydd into relief; he and the workings of the chapel remain the collection's focus.

Capel Sion quietly refines Evans's literary methods – a stricter authorial reticence, a more prominent Sionite narrator – and takes greater risks with dialogue (occasionally to the point of self-parody: "Three Men From Horeb" buckles under the weight of mannerism). Yet mostly *Capel Sion* carries that sense of perfection deriving from Evans's genius for fashioning stories that completely embody his themes. Objective commentary and extraneous description alike become unnecessary; what we need to know about the characters we learn from their own words and actions. This was the first rule of his art – "A novelist should neither praise nor blame. That's the preacher's job. His job is to tell the story". To the American critic H.L. Mencken, this absence of praise and blame was the Caradoc Evans hallmark, and one which meant that his characters, repellent though they might be, were depicted from a viewpoint of no superior scorn or indignation; "Somehow, Evans gets into his portraits a sense of their helplessness." This was surely his intention; however bleak the vision, there is compassion for the most defenceless and an understanding of others, the "half-slaves, half-tyrants" whose tragedy is their helplessness.

For this second collection Melrose built upon the marketing strategy already in place for its author, one which stressed the "realism" of the stories and their value as social documents. On the front of its cream glazed dust-jacket runs the following description:

> Another contribution to the complete study of the Welsh peasantry with which Mr Evans made such a brilliant beginning in "My People." This book settles the anxious question of the author's staying power. Not one of the chapters is below the level of his former book; in the publishers' opinion a few are actually higher than his first amazing performance.

These sentences remarkably suppress any reference to *Capel Sion* as fiction. The stories are "chapters" of a "book", a companion to *My People*, the collections together presented as "contribution[s] to the complete study of the Welsh peasantry" (Melrose united them further through identical binding and text typography). The author's portrait, centrally placed on the jacket front, is of a piece with this approach. Caradoc faces his readers full-on, a serious young man with pince-nez and wearing a starched wing collar: a stern headmaster or a scholar perhaps? A carefully chosen photograph of the author was standard in a marketing strategy, and Evans spoke of pride taken by authors in their images "on the underground and in the lifts". For a 1919 reprint of *My People* Melrose would fashion a further image of his author. What did he have to work upon? "A mild-mannered, mild-voiced young man of quiet and ordinary demeanour... and a very soft Welsh accent" (the *Globe*); "a gaunt, saturnine man with a dark yet merry eye, and absolutely no sense of humour" (*Sunday Herald*). In a manner belying this latter charge, Evans recalled the occasion:

> Some time ago my publisher was preparing a cheap edition of one of my books, and one day he said to me, rather sorrowfully but quite gentlemanly: "What is the matter with your face?" I answered "It is God's" "Not a bit like Him," he said. He took me himself into a shop in the Strand and posed me himself. The result was a striking portrait of an angel in a tweed suit."[3]

The 1919 frontispiece portrait eschews any hint of the writer as iconoclast. Here wasn't Caradoc Evans with horns, as his compatriots would have wished, but a student tied to his spectacles, too absorbed in a book to face the camera. Angelic he is, with light shining down upon him and his sturdy tweed suit (the sensible, gentlemanly choice). Beneath the photograph is the author's reproduced signature and the single word "Sincerely". Duncan Davies records that "even when his first book was received with such a chorus of praise from critics of the highest standard, Caradoc never lost his head, though the reception was, of course, gratifying to him. Out of business he generally wore tweed suits, and in the London street a stranger would probably take him for a young countryman in town for a sight-seeing holiday."[4]

All was not harmony between author and publisher. For all its commercial possibilities, and the critical praise Evans had gathered, Melrose felt uncomfortable with *Capel Sion*. "And Caradoc Evans," he wrote privately after publication, "his new book is uglier than his last physically & I am secretly saying 'no more'... No, I am going back to my normal line... I do not like ugly art and the macabre has not any real admiration from me."[5] Given his experience with this author, Melrose initially backed away from a second explosive collection. He hated unsavoury publicity. He hated too – so Evans maintained – parting with more money. Money, it seems, was a perpetual issue between this publisher and his authors. Caradoc made around a thousand pounds from *My People* but "in driblets", since Melrose could never be persuaded to part with any substantial advance of royalties. "Andrew loved and knew good stuff, but he loved money more. He was a good Presbyterian and it is well known that his kind are often thrown out of heaven for neglecting to pay their pew rents."[6] (Among the "good stuff" forfeited were books by Norman Douglas, Mary Webb, the bestselling Michael Arlen and, so Evans suggested, George Douglas Brown.)

Capel Sion went on sale in December 1916; "it is not precisely Christmas reading," observed the *Daily Mirror* on Christmas Eve. In a much publicised interview beforehand, Hannen Swaffer suggested that the sordidness of Maxim Gorky's narratives of the Russian underworld were as nothing compared to *Capel Sion*, which "flayed whole parishes alive".[7] He pressed Evans on the sources of his stories and was given examples of the kind of departure from fact. "Redemption" recounted an actual happening, "except that the girl refused to be enticed over the well"; "The Widow's Mite" was "true concerning the woman and the man. The cow is an invention"; and "The Deliverer" accorded with the facts except – this a revealing deviation – "that the woman [Ann] did not die ... In real life the woman, recovering, became a perfect vixen." "I have not written a word that is not true," concluded Evans, without making plain, as elsewhere he had been at pains to do, that fiction is always "built on the foundation of the author's imagination". From the very beginning Evans dealt freely in fantasy, creating a personal universe from his own deepest instinct regarding the ways of the world. It preserves the potency of his stories which, since they deal as much in types as with individuals, hardly seem to date. That certain events never happened did not make them less true; "you know incidents more remorselessly true than anything I have written about in my stories," he taunted his critics. And such incidents have more recently surfaced in studies of nineteenth-century rural Wales, particularly those concerning the treatment of women and the exploitation of the agricultural poor. So much more "remorselessly true" do they appear that, faced with the "greed and heartlessness" of Welsh farmers at this time, Evans can now "seem guilty not so much of malice and as of understating his case".[8] Reading a story such as "Redemption" with a knowledge of the horrendous sexual abuse suffered by female servants on west Wales farms (and their total lack of redress in law) surely compels admiration for Evans as a courageous reporter on native conditions. Andrew Melrose was right: the books *did* have value as social documents. Of course, there were other sides to the picture, but only one that this author could make believable. He chose stories that answered his sense of the world as a place which while professing to value human charity, humility, sincerity and compassion actually rewarded the cruel and the overbearing, the avaricious and self-righteous. It was a disturbing vision, and one which he was repeatedly urged to soften. In time, in part, he would do so, but not in 1916.

English reviews of *Capel Sion* largely reiterated the points made about *My People*. The author had refused to broaden his canvas, to move outside the lines of bare narrative and skeletal dialogue. "He gives us no description of nature, and none of that windy, sounding eloquence which is such a snare to the Welsh mind" (the *Nation*, 13 January 1917). A lead review in the *Westminster Gazette* (9 December 1916) applauded this verbal restraint: "Digressive as some of its pages may appear at first, there is not a wasted word in any of them. No comment, no explanation is vouchsafed. Each epistle is set down starkly in the bones of its horror." The *Daily Mirror* – the paper he soon would join – judged the book "instinct with real power and remorseless insight". Evans's satiric purpose, his deliberately partial portraiture, was readily understood ("Hogarth's moral pictures" were invoked), but the *Yorkshire Post*, for one, thought the agony had been piled on too insistently. Evans's art was a selective one; the stories could not be presented as a rounded social picture. The Liberal *Manchester Guardian* (11 January 1917) more than agreed: his "course, brutish creatures bear about as much resemblance to the peasantry of Wales as an epileptic or cancerous colony bears to the normal human community." Other reviewers favoured readings that universalised the book's concerns. Evans castigated soulless Puritanism, and with such bearing upon evangelical America that H.L. Mencken professed himself willing to donate a hundred copies of *Capel Sion* to the YMCA. The *English Review*, justly claiming to be the discoverer of this remarkable author, offered *Capel Sion* unqualified praise. "As the very spirit of the macabre and cast in a strange, haunting personal style, Evans's stories have established themselves as part of the English literary canon." The reviewer makes two further basic points, that these stories stagger the reader and never make for easy reading, and that Evans speaks directly to Wales; he writes as a passionate insider, with stories "of the race, of the soil, of the blood". (The *Sunday Herald* saw an archetypal Welshman, "hammering at Mount Sion with the weapons of the Old Testament".)

How different were things in Wales! What the *English Review* considered high art, the *Welsh Outlook* thought "the literature of the sewer". Frankly, Evans wished for more: "He is manifestly disappointed that Cardiff police have not seized it, as they did *My People*," confided Melrose.[9] At least the *Western Mail* measured up, lambasting an author who had genius of sorts but, having lived in a "moral sewer", deliberately used it "to bespatter his own countrymen with filth". Evans replied with characteristic bravura (20 December 1916). *Capel Sion* was more or less a true record of what he had seen and heard and experienced:

> In my youthful days West Wales was "a moral sewer". As it was, so it is even unto this day. The creed preached from the pulpit is that God can be hoodwinked and cheated, provided you do not cease in your offerings to the pulpit. The widow can be robbed, and the righteous mocked and driven to death. The man in the pulpit is King, and his orderings are as wicked as the orderings of the King of Prussia.

Insistently he rejected another charge, that the stories were "gross in tone, in content and in effect", as the *Western Mail* had accused. "Nothing I have ever written is gross in intention. No English reviewer, and I have been reviewed by many, has charged me with that offence, and it is significant that the charge should have come from Wales."

Prominently placed on the editorial page, Evans's letter elicited a response from the editor William Davies, who could not withdraw the charge that Evans's books were "gross in intention" (and who, in debunking *Capel Sion's* style, hit on the arresting phrase "clotted idiocies" – it would resurface more than once). Evans fired back (26 December 1916) revealing a little more of his artistic approach. But first, the charge of grossness had to be refuted. Evans rode oceans of abuse, but as with the charge that *My People* was pornographic, this accusation he could not let pass. "You repeat that my books are 'gross in tone, in intent and effect'. You are wrong." Delivered of that, he turned to his style: "In the rendering of the idiom you must also create atmosphere. If the Bible or Tolstoy or Maupassant were done into straight English none of us would get any nearer to the life and conditions with which those authors deal." His far from straight English was essential in creating his fictional world.

As books change their meaning with their readers so the timing of a book's publication can affect the way it is read. Evans struck at the very moment when Welsh national pride had reached a peak: one week after Lloyd George, having ousted Asquith over the conduct of the war, became prime minister. Laying down *Capel Sion*, Asquith is supposed to have remarked, "I believe every word of it"; the collection, we know, sent Margot Asquith "into raptures". These were heady times for the Welsh, as Evans acidly recognised. "We hate the English as one hates a fool. God made him our servant and for one glorious period appointed Mr Lloyd George to govern this foolish tribe. Yet we ape the Englishman. It is the desire of our lives to speak English like the Englishman."[10] (Evans's own accent was thickly Welsh). Prime Minister Lloyd George shone as the apotheosis of the nation, a military hero who had sprung from a people of courage. In contrast, Caradoc Evans continued to indict that nation precisely at the moment when its leaders were calling for the supreme sacrifice on its behalf. *Western Mail* correspondents bluntly accused him of shirking his duty in time of war.

The *Western Mail* controversy drew in Caradoc's old headmaster, John Crowther, retired and living in Cardiff. The paper (17 January 1917) had seized on an unflattering reference to Evans in Crowther's talk, "The Welsh Novelist", given before the Newport Welsh Society. In it, Crowther returned across the years (as he had done in his poetry) to the bliss of south Cardiganshire past and the work of the schoolboy-turned-writer he taught there:

> I look forward to the time when my old pupil will give us something infinitely better, and, while condemning things of which all good men disapprove, will make the saintly men and gentle women that some of us have met in the land of "My People" live again, though only in the pages of the novel. A district which has given Wales Dafydd and Ebenezer Morris ("Morrisiad Mawr Iesu", said Eben Fardd), Griffiths (Hawen), and O.R. Owen (Glandwr) as preachers of the front rank, Ioan Cunllo, Rhys Dyfed, Gwnionydd, and other lesser lights among the bards, and Emlyn Evans and Dafydd Sciencyn Morgan as two of "the sweet singers of Wales", deserves a better fate than to be traduced by one of its own sons.

Within a week Caradoc came back, first with a differing estimate of Crowther's roll-call of worthies:

> He [Crowther] names five saints and they were all rulers of the pulpit, and they left nothing after them to hint that they were in the "front rank" anywhere except in West Wales. When a Welsh Nonconformist minister looks for a hero with which to adorn his stupid sermons he usually finds two: himself and a brother preacher.

Rhys Lewis typified Welsh mediocrity. The much admired novel of Daniel Owen "has no form, it is loosely constructed, its humour is commonplace and it is extremely dull." The letter's last paragraph compacts crucial issues relating to Caradoc Evans, ones debated at the outset of his publishing career and in contention ever since. It is a calm summation of his position.

> Mr Crowther will not pause to inquire why I have written as I have written. If I fashioned nice false novels about Wales I might gather enough wealth in three years to enable me to retire. I have no desire to become notorious; no one has. I have no wish for fame. I write because I believe the cesspools of West Wales should be stirred up, because I want to see my people freed from religious tyranny, because I love my country so much that I would exhibit her sores that they may be healed.

More understanding might have been expected of Crowther, who well knew Caradoc's background and had expressed his own dismay (semi-privately) at the ways of the neighbourhood.

These impassioned, often lengthy, exchanges prompts the question of Evans's relationship with the *Western Mail* and its editor William Davies. As a Fleet Street journalist (still at *Ideas* during these turbulent months), Evans knew how important were newspapers as platforms for his views. He took press letters seriously (as he did his interviews), often preparing typed copy in advance. His relationship with the *Mail* intrigues, for however fiercely he and William Davies might clash, they maintained a surprising mutual respect. Evans's tributes to the paper occurred at the peak of their battle. Surveying coverage of the coalfield strike of 1916 Evans writes, "And with the exception of one newspaper – the Tory Cardiff *Western Mail* – I do not know one widely spread organ which will give the men's views with any degree of truth."[11] (The "Tory" reference is significant: Liberal papers showed little sympathy for the miners.) As in politics, so in literature: the *Western Mail* was crucial to Welsh cultural health. Evans said so more than once, and on the occasion of the paper's jubilee (1 May 1919) he paid his most fulsome tribute (a wicked one also, making its point in a way that disarmed editorial criticism). His published letter recalls how much the paper had meant to the young Cardiff shop assistant who surreptitiously read its "Wales Day by Day" column ("the most entrancing feature in daily journalism") behind the flannelette counter at Howells. Nor had its appeal diminished:

> I declare that I now prefer you a month old than most newspapers of the moment. I like you for your love of Wales. You are the spirit of what Wales ought to be – strong, courageous, daring, valiant, just. In a country which is lorded by preacher-politicians, who instruct our people in the dark, evil manner of thinking, you are the only pulpit and platform from which men can proclaim the ideals of their heart.
>
> In Wales you are the one newspaper – the one institution which urges on the study of Welsh art, literature, drama, folklore, and of the Welsh language.
>
> So I sit at my machine, tapping; Congratulations on your fiftieth birthday. May your works prosper, and may the coming years multiply the fruit of your sowing and make you "young and lusty as an eagle".

Beneath the blarney lies sincere admiration for a paper which, though adrift from Welsh popular sentiment on fundamental issues, could nonetheless open its columns to opposing viewpoints. ("Opposition is true Friendship", Evans might have agreed.). Informally, Caradoc approached William Davies in an effort to publicize W.H. Davies, the Newport poet whom he had recently met. "Write him up," urged Davies; and an editor who vilified *My People* and *Capel Sion*, to the point of reprinting Ivor John's *Welsh Outlook* paroxysms, at the same time granted Evans space for an "absorbingly interesting" piece on W.H. Davies.

W.H. Davies interested Caradoc. Newport-born, of mixed Cornish and Welsh descent, Davies at twenty-two abandoned his trade of picture-framing, resolving never to become a wage slave. ("I have never worked in my life," he touchily explained, "That's what your friends do for you!") How such a man survived, through tramping, begging and poetry, became the stuff of story, from the appearance of his very first book, a poetry paperback whose imprint named the Southwark doss-house which was then his address. Having paid the printing costs of *The Soul's Destroyer* (1905), he set about the matter of sales by posting copies to prominent people with an invitation to buy. A gift to journalists – he'd lost a foot after jumping a train in Ontario, accompanied by Three-fingered Jack – Davies quickly found fame as the "tramp poet", a label challenged by "super-tramp" when, three years later, his autobiography appeared. Wittily prefaced by George Bernard Shaw (who also suggested the title), the book became an instant minor classic. Shaw was only one of Davies's patrons and protectors. A small private income cushioned his tramping days, while a Civil List pension brought comparative comfort in later years. (Edward Thomas arranged the pension, having previously paid the rent on Davies's Sevenoaks cottage.)

It was in 1914, when Davies moved from Sevenoaks into London, that Evans first met him. He had found a room above a shop in a street off Pall Mall: "It was not much of a room or much of a street," judged Evans, "But he liked the high-sounding address."[12] The two met there from time to time, Evans describing how, because of the coal shortage in wartime London, Davies had neatly stacked a ton of peat against the wall of his room. His savings he kept under the mattress, and "One afternoon I found him counting money and putting portions of it aside to send to some needy relations. 'And my bust by Epstein is in Newport Free Library,' he said whimsically." On evening jaunts Caradoc and friends occasionally met up with the fruitful poet ("he writes a poem as other men shave," remarked Tommy Burke, one of the circle). A meal at a pub in the Tottenham Court Road turned out unexpectedly. Norman Douglas and Evans were entertaining Davies and Edwin Pugh. During the meal Pugh, "a short brown-bearded mouse who pretended to be a savage rat", boasted about his fights with Whitechapel toughs, whereupon Davies responded with his boxing-booth experiences in America:

> By and by they two disappeared and they were away such a long time that Douglas and I went to look for them. They were in the gents' toilet and had been boxing. Davies said it would not be fair to throw a man with one lung through a lavatory door. Pugh said it would not be fair to stick the head of a one-leg man in a lavatory pan.

The early death of his father, and the loss of his mother through remarriage, led to Davies being raised by his paternal grandparents, a sociable, hard-drinking publican and his puritanical Baptist wife. Caradoc saw both sides of this upbringing in the metropolitan Davies, with a striving for respectability becoming uppermost. His success in classy circles – he excelled at charity readings – made him aspire to the middle-class prejudices he himself had endured. He "grew ashamed of his low-down company", thought Evans. He certainly exhibited the vanity of his calling:

> In common with poets he hated criticism and loved praise. He was sore people on the streets did not say as he passed by: "That's W.H. Davies the poet." He tried to make effective entrances to the Café Royal lounge, and no one remarked them for he was an ordinary-looking little man, but when he saw the willow-tree entrances of the pseudo poets and actors he gave up trying. He was not gifted in showmanship.

For Caradoc, Davies remained one of the great English poets. "There was wonder in his eyes, and he would gaze into a brook as if it were the first brook he had ever seen and he put this feeling into his verse." Evans's *Western Mail* piece points to other dimensions in Davies's early work: "Such is this Welsh poet who sings of the heart of the drunkard and the soul of little children, of the temptation of nature and the aspiration of lost women."[13] For all the popularity of "Leisure", it is the poems of social realism that have best survived. In 1922 Davies left London with Helen Payne (whom he married), having sold Caradoc a set of Synge that had once belonged to Shaw. He took with him a gift copy of *My People* bearing one of its author's rare inscriptions in Welsh.

Caradoc's success as a writer led to some fiction reviewing. In *New Witness* he welcomed Arthur Machen's *The Great Return* (1915) and Mary Webb's *The Golden Arrow* (1916). *My People* had much impressed Machen and Evans wrote generously of *The Great Return*, an account of remarkable occurrences at Llantrisant, including a manifestation of the Holy Grail. The book embodied a vision of Wales transformed, a land still essentially Christian but rid of chapels and preachers. That the Welsh, of all people, should arrive at such a state staggers the reviewer: "*The Great Return* is a rare dream, and nothing that is in it will come to pass."[14] In his notice of Webb's *The Golden Arrow* (headed "Chapel Prussianism") Evans seems close to reviewing himself, and his account of the "half-slaves, half-tyrants" of Webb's Welsh-border country perfectly encapsulates his understanding of his own doomed Manteg creations, prisoners of their own upbringing and their community's historical past:

> The tragedy of these creatures whom Mary Webb analyses with such uncommon insight, is their helplessness and hopelessness. One feels that they will never escape from bondage. As they were born, so will they live. They are the victims of a base religion. They have been whipped into something more destructive than unbelief. They can babble about charity while they think out devices to hurt their neighbours, and prattle about chapel when none of them knows God or is wishful of knowing Him. Their chapels are political hell places. Their ethical code is the ethical code of the ruler of the chapel: all for me and the rest for my brother. Their god is the god

preached in Sion, and he can be cheated as easily as a rich farmer ruins a servant or
a preacher robs a widow.[15]

The book he hailed as a masterpiece, apart from its happy ending, a romantic gesture
unworthy of its author.

The 1917 review of *The Golden Arrow* would prompt a friendship between the two
writers when Webb came to live in London in 1921. Later Evans portrayed her as a
woman in strikingly honest fashion; he had no doubts about her literary greatness and
said so at the time of her death (aged forty-six) in October 1927. Six months later,
Stanley Baldwin's glowing references to her at a Royal Literary Fund dinner began the
rush towards wider recognition.

One favour that Evans did her was to pass on one or two of her articles to Horace
Thoroughgood at the *Star* (the London evening newspaper) where they appeared immediately. "Then Mary wrote to me that she had enough verse (she said poetry) to make a
book: would I speak to a publisher? I spoke to Andrew Melrose, the only publisher I
knew." The parenthetical "she said poetry" is revealing. Evans felt happier with "verse";
"poetry" he distrusted – the name and what it conjured up. As an editor at the receiving
end, he regrets the spate of war poetry – "heaps of the stuff… swilled out by the
bucketful" – and implores readers of *Ideas* to send no more: "if the war lasted ten years
I have enough poems to carry me through" (17 September 1915). Relenting sufficiently
to publish the verses of a thirteen-year-old, he added, "I am not printing them in order
to encourage poets, of whom there are too many on this earth. Always my advice to
young poets is: unless you are looking forward to a dishonourable old age, don't write
poetry" (3 September 1915). Evans's lack of feeling for poetry can be seen as another
reaction against his early background. Welsh bards had killed his pleasure in the medium.
School and chapel recitations, the round of eisteddfodau, local poets of dubious distinction
– all had combined to raise doubts about the worth of the medium. He pleads with
readers of *Ideas*:

> My dear, good friends, have mercy on me, and do not send me any more "original
> pieces of poetry"… if you only knew how sick and tired my soul is of verses, I feel
> sure you would desist. I am not a bard, and I hate bardic devices, though I belong to
> a race whose every Doctor of Divinity (USA) and every Dreadful Drunkard thinks
> himself a man cunning and subtle with words. (26 November 1915)

Evans's few essays on other writers say much about himself; he wrote as a memoirist,
always from personal knowledge and enthusiasm. He was drawn to individuals with
whom he had something in common, writers from unorthodox backgrounds struggling
to establish themselves. Thomas Burke fell into this category, though nailing facts about
this self-proclaimed "son of London" is not easy. One Burke enthusiast describes *The
Wind and the Rain*, the professedly autobiographical volume that Caradoc reviewed in
1923, as a near fictional excursion "four or five times removed from the truth".[16] We
know that Burke, like Evans, did a stint compiling encyclopaedias under Hammerton

and as a would-be contributor to *Ideas* met its editor in early 1915. Reptilian in look and manner, he entered Caradoc's den so quietly that,

> I did not know he was there until I raised my eyes and saw a narrow strip of a figure. I saw a black-and-white line: black clothes, white face, and thick black hair shining as if it had been pasted down on a dummy head... While we talked he did not leave his place by the door. He seemed to have made up his mind that a trap had been set for him and that he must tread warily if he were to keep his ankles from the catch. He talked in phrases rather than in sentences, the phrases issuing at thin lips in soft, low tones.[17]

Burke too had first awoken to "the blaze and dazzle of literature" through the pages of *T.P.'s Weekly*. The paper paid a guinea for one of his stories, a fortnight's wages for the city office boy. "He had shaken the tree of prayer and a little fruit had fallen to the ground." He was tired of the City, of being "a soulless organism – the Boy". He would try to live as a writer.

Evans suggested Andrew Melrose as a possible publisher for Burke's *Limehouse Nights*, the controversial collection turned down by Stanley Unwin and written, so its author confessed, with "the peculiar assurance of a man who knows nothing of what he is writing or talking about". Melrose shied away in horror. As Evans remembered, "He had read it before, but he read it again, and when he was at the end he climbed to the summit of his Presbyterian pinnacle and spoke as follows: 'I'll have nothing to do with books about white girls and Chinks.'"[18] In September 1916 *Limehouse Nights* appeared under the imprint of Grant Richards and dedicated to Caradoc Evans. Two months later the Cardiff Libraries Committee banned it – on the strength of the dedication, so the dedicatee surmised.[19] Three years later Evans returned the compliment, offering his own London collection *My Neighbours*, "to my friend Thomas Burke of 'Limehouse Nights'".

Slim on worthwhile fiction, *Ideas* skimped on book reviews as well. Evans occasionally noticed books, a number of which inevitably had to do with the war. What caught his eye in *The German Emperor: As Shown by His Public Utterances* (1915) was "the 'me-and-God' type of phrase". The Emperor talked of entering "with implicit confidence upon this duty to which God has called me". The tone was all too familiar to a cradle Congregationalist; here was another who claimed to walk with God. Books by acquaintances caught his eye, as with Sydney Moseley's *The Truth about the Dardanelles* (1916). In his published diary the much-travelled Moseley records a conversation about it:

> Jan 19. 1917. At the Press Club. Lunched with Newman Flower (the Cassell's publisher) and got him to join the Club. Met Caradoc Evans, author of *My People* and *Capel Zion* [sic]. He came on with me to West Kensington, and told me he had bought my book. "Splendidly written," he said... "Do you know why? Because you are Eastern – the style is Eastern. No hard-boiled Englishman could have written it." Couldn't help feeling pleased, for Caradoc's own books have caused a furore.[20]

Five months after meeting Moseley Evans lost his job at *Ideas*. His fall can actually be traced way back to the time of his appointment. On 15 June 1915 the London papers reported the deportation, with her single trunk and tiny bag, of Madame Bertha Trost, a fifty-eight-year-old German subject and notable Mayfair socialite. Conspicuous in dress and coiffure, Trost had for years ostensibly carried out a business as antiques dealer and "beauty specialist" at Clifford Street. Behind this exterior lay other activities – gambling and prostitution included – which drew in a clientele of wealth and influence. From such customers Trost picked up information of civil and military importance and passed it to German Intelligence. Though deported as "an undesirable alien living as a rogue and a vagabond", her real vocation was well known, "but she carried it out with such consummate astuteness as to make her conviction almost impossible. . . . She evidently got wind of the impending action of the authorities, for she had arranged to marry a British subject. . . which would have rendered her immune from deportation."[21]

All this seems worlds away from Evans and *Ideas* but in March 1916 the paper took up this sex-and-spy scandal, publishing an account of Trost's activities followed by revelations of her former employees. Making the most of a scoop, Evans trumpeted the articles. He writes of "exalted persons who made her [Trost's] stay in England secure and kept her aloof from police interference", and of blind eyes turned to her crimes:

> War came, and Bertha was still allowed to remain in England, and was at large. Then something happened and she was deported; she was deported for doing something for which she should have been shot. . . Why [she] was allowed to live among us for so many years passes any sensible man's comprehension; perhaps when the war is over and accounts come to be settled, someone in authority shall be made to explain. (5 May 1916).

Evans refused to drop the accusation of a cover-up. He speaks of "evil in the heart of London's fashionable Mayfair", of strange friendships in "frowsty Bohemia where men of the great world meet women of the half-world". In April 1917 *Ideas* published further revelations, these concerning another vice and spy ring presided over by a Madame Palma, close friend of Bertha Trost. Once again, with talk of "misguided high-place folk" and "politicians and women of fashion" (6 April 1917), Evans sought to bring out the dimension of establishment treachery.

Now things began to go wrong for him. As a consequence of the articles, libel action brewed – much to Hulton's displeasure. Evans's 6 April column confided that he was putting up with a "grave inconvenience" and for a month his voice fell silent. He returned on 4 May, with a bitterness that startled readers:

> Many of you have written to me; some saying in this sort: Where is the Editor bloke? What has become of him? Is he a slacker? If he is, he ought to be sacked.
>
> That is the consolation I shall find in death – that somebody will grieve and weep for me. In death I shall also overcome even my enemies: I shall carry my hatred into eternity, my enemy shall brood and become angry that my spirit is beyond his spite.

Somewhere in Austria Bertha Trost was railing against *Ideas*, and "if she were in England now, well, there is no telling what would happen to the Editor". But the action against *Ideas* was brought not, of course, by Trost but by a former British associate. Hulton became apprehensive, having recently fought, and lost, another libel action. So he settled out of court at a cost of one thousand pounds and handed Caradoc his cards. It could not have been a surprise. Here was rich man's justice, the only kind there was. As he wrote on the eve of dismissal, "the rich shall be as gods, and they shall do no wrong, for the laws will be in their keeping" (4 May 1917).

The dismissal shook him more than battles fought back home. Being out of work was worrying, even though prospects in Fleet Street were good, given the wartime shortage of journalists. One imagines it was the loss of this particular job, and the circumstances of his departure, that pained him. Prior to their falling-out, he had rubbed along with the tetchy Hulton, finding the rhythm and routines of a weekly conducive enough for writing – a fortnight before his dismissal one *My Neighbours* story appeared in print. A fellow journalist, meeting proprietor and editor together, congratulated Evans on his success at *Ideas* and asked how he managed to relax. "In his spare time he tries to do a little work for the firm," Hulton dryly interjected.[22] However incongruous the notion of the author of *My People* behind a desk at *Ideas*, Evans enjoyed the work and fashioned his weekly editorial slot in an attractively personal way.

The 15 June 1917 issue was this last. Here he reflects on those like himself and the bulk of his readers who get by on native intelligence, comparing their lot with those whose privileged upbringing ensures them a comfortable, settled career:

> I do not know whom to envy most – the youth who goes up to Oxford or Cambridge, or the youth who as early as possible leaves school and goes out to work. I envy the first because a university education will keep him prosperous during the rest of his days; I envy the second because he has to exist on the wits that God gave him; of the two I am persuaded that the second is the man who matters more. At the end of your term at a village school, the surprising thing is that you are able to read and write. Still you can read and write, and at the game of life beat your university competitor.

For all his professional success and literary recognition, Evans remained insistent on his peasant roots. The draper's assistant might have lamented lost educational opportunities but the working journalist had found a good home in Fleet Street, among companionable others using the wits God gave them.

The rallying note was a prelude to one more editor's leave-taking, this a "ripeness is all" meditation affectionately signed as a Welshman:

> The last bit. I am glad. Birth and death provide the two great joys of life. Few believe that there is any joy in the end of anything; we all would believe it if we had the right vision of life. We are blind. Good-night is better than good-morning; we have earned our rest, and we are glad to seek our couch. And as sleep has no terror for us, so should death have no fear for us. No one dies before his end has come. The machinery

of the world is important in the scheme of the world, and when a bit of machinery is scrapped you can be sure that it has ceased its usefulness. If one piece were scrapped before the period of its usefulness was over, the world would be out of joint. So, in the words and tongue of a man I met in a country lane on a dark night, "Nos da, boys bach."

"Bright and Lively and Humble": a *Mirror* Man

1917-23

Despite his troubles at *Ideas*, Evans in 1917 published four more fine stories, two in the *Westminster Gazette* and another in *Everyman*. It was the trusted *English Review*, however, that in February carried "The Day of Judgment", the first of this new batch and a striking sequel to *Capel Sion's* "Judges". The *Review* stuck by Caradoc Evans. Norman Douglas had departed in 1916 (as a cost-cutting measure) but the journal's practice of promoting new authors continued, as did its hospitality towards foreign literature in translation. In 1917 it serialised Gorky's autobiography and the February issue saw Caradoc still rubbing shoulders with *The Shadow Line*. He owed much to the *English Review*: besides printing nine of his 'studies', it favourably reviewed his books and openly took the credit for having brought his talent to light. Austin Harrison accepted controversy as intrinsic to his editorial mission, believing that British cultural life had "several closed doors which ought to be forced".[1] In Caradoc he met a kindred spirit.[2]

Another Evans enthusiast well placed in London literary life was Naomi Royde-Smith. Part-Welsh, greatly accomplished, the muse of Walter de la Mare, she worked as literary editor of the *Westminster Gazette*, an evening newspaper whose influence far out-reached its sales. Its uncrowded columns offered a distinguished arts coverage that on Saturdays commanded the first three pages. Royde-Smith had hailed *My People* and *Capel Sion*, seeing the makings of "a very great writer... a satirist of his own people unmatched in English literature since Swift". She afforded her readers a glimpse of this greatness when she splashed "A Widow Woman" across the front page of the *Saturday Westminster* (2 June 1917). The story maps the fate of the humble, self-sacrificing Mali, a woman who dares to pray that her son be "as large as Bern-Davydd". A second front-page story, "Treasure and Trouble" (15 September) has a victimised farmer driven to suicide by the brutal greed of his brother, a noise in Bern-Davydd's chapel. Evans's creativity was invariably triggered by real-life events, in this case the hanging at Rhydlewis he first mentioned in his essay "The Welsh Miner" (December 1916). It pointed the depths of docility and passive suffering that religious government could induce. (An independent local witness, while not mentioning that the farmers were brothers, confirmed the factual basis of this story – her mother's brother had found the farmer hanging. She agreed that in farming disputes, mostly over water, chapel factions might well back claimants.).

In the month of "Treasure and Trouble", *Everyman* published Evans's "An Offender in Sion", a story that agitated the correspondence columns for weeks. This politico-literary weekly, largely financed by the publisher J.M. Dent, was edited by its founder

Charles Sarolea from his home in Edinburgh. A Belgian-born professor of French, Sarolea
had come to learn of Evans through Mrs Cecil Chesterton. Having entered Fleet Street
in her teens (as Ada Jones), she now served as *Everyman's* London correspondent but
Evans's work she knew from *New Witness* where she acted as assistant editor. *Everyman's*
welcome for *Capel Sion* had been guarded ("frankly, we do not quite know what to make
of the book"), and as recently as February 1917 an *Everyman* reviewer had coupled Evans
with James Joyce in an attack on *Portrait of the Artist as a Young Man* (headed "A Study in
Garbage"). "An astonishingly powerful and extraordinarily dirty study," the critic declared,
from a "clever" novelist who "would be really at his best in a treatise on drains". In all,
"Mr Joyce is an Irish edition of Mr Caradoc Evans"[4] Writing *Everyman's* literary column
(as "Roderick Random"), Ada Chesterton came out in support of Caradoc: "I had the
privilege of seeing his first stories before they were published, and they took my breath
away. Really original work always does that... I was not certain whether I liked the
work or hated it. Therefore I knew that I had knocked up against a great man."[5] "An
Offender in Sion" once more takes up the case of a defenceless widow callously mistreated
by a relative. Rachel knows that for all his religious posturing her brother-in-law Ianto
intends her harm. The "pig-wife from Shire Pembroke" faces an imposing alliance of
rich farmer ("a name above many in Capel Sion") and auctioneer "skilful in these things"
– that is, in robbing the weak of "all that was in the land and on the land". Rachel, gun
at the ready, is not intimidated.

If Sarolea wanted a reaction, he certainly got one, and an English audience now
savoured the kind of cultural rumpus that livened the letters pages of the *Western Mail*.
A Swansea reader spoke of *Everyman* as stained by a verbal morass packed with linguistic
fraud. The author's "atrocities" matched those of Houston Stewart Chamberlain, Wagner's
English-born son-in-law, whose racial theories led him to side with Germany in the
1914-18 war. Evans's reply (2 November 1917) typified his approach in such exchanges,
one that reaffirmed his own position (usually with a leavening of banter) rather than
give weight to his critics by actually addressing their points. Still adamant that Nonconformity thrives on "hypocrisy, brutality, lust", he alludes to religious leaders (wisely left
unnamed though – it is implied – personally known to him) whose avarice is unappeasable;
they hate their sisters, cheat their brothers, ruin young girls, condone incest among
their congregations and sometimes practise it themselves. The charges reach a blasphemous
crescendo: "We are as Welsh Nonconformity has made us. Not until the last chapel is a
cowhouse and the last black-coated worker of abomination is hanged shall we set forth
on our march to the light."

At this an old adversary stirred. The Revd Arthur Sturdy, the Pontypridd curate
who had preached against the traitor Evans from the pulpit on St David's Day 1916,
now rose to defend Welsh country folk, "the rugged Puritans among whom Mr Evans
and I spent our childhood days" (9 November 1917). In lauding their superior morals,
their happy ignorance of "great cities wickedly refined", Sturdy, though a Churchman,
perfectly exemplified the Welsh Liberal-Nonconformist position. Regarding high ille-
gitimacy rates in rural Wales, he urged a proper perspective:

> A lustful peasant may be implicated in illegitimacy because in the innocence of his
> carnal heart he allows nature to take its course, but illegitimacy, undesirable as it is,
> is infinitely better than the social scourge of prostitution and its attendant diseases
> and evils caused by the gilded town-dweller.

Setting the rugged peasant and "the innocence of his carnal heart" against the gilded
town dweller was the ploy of another inveterate Evans antagonist, the Revd T. Eynon
Davies, who headed his London column for *Y Tyst* (a Welsh Congregationalist weekly),
"Notes from the Great Babylon".

The *Everyman* correspondence concludes with a letter of surpassing fury (30 November
1917). Beneath its insults and threats ("we know how to deal with this renegade in
Wales"), Penry Jones makes two interlocking observations that help explain Evans's
reception among the Welsh. We have encountered them before. The Welsh belief is "that
English literary journals and English men of letters have accepted this farrago of filth
and debased verbal coinage… as a true portrayal of Welsh life and the Welsh language";
and all this "at a time when Welshmen are dying side by side with their English, Scotch
and Irish comrades in Flanders".

The *Everyman* clash spilled over into the *Western Mail*, prompting one more frontal
riposte from Caradoc, this in response to an outraged deacon at Llanfaches, the first
dissenting outpost in Wales:[6]

> Sir – Mr G.N.W. Thomas is angry. He declares that I am not worthy to be either a
> Nonconformist or a Churchman. I am a Nonconformist. But I am not a Welsh Non-
> conformist.
>
> He assumes that my saying about a cowhouse is a jest. Hence he shakes his fountain
> pen and writes, rebuking me, "there is no wit in his statement." Cowhouses are one
> of the signs of a nation's prosperity and industry: chapels are the signs of poverty
> and perfidy.
>
> Mr Thomas admits that a Welshman may be unjust – a circumstance due, he imag-
> ines, to misapprehension. That is what a thief said when he was caught with his hand
> in another man's pocket.
>
> A Welsh Nonconformist preacher does not hate intolerance; he thrives on it.
> Because he feigns teetotalism abroad and gets drunk within closed doors, he shuts
> down public houses; because he sees more gain for himself in Liberalism than Toryism,
> he makes of his chapel a Liberal committee room; because he magnifies himself
> greater than his congregation, he has come to believe that he is greater than God.
> He has bullied the peasant people into putting up ugly chapels on hillsides and in
> valleys, and has set himself up in the pulpits thereof and proclaimed himself ruler of
> the people. He is the hangman of our liberties and the enemy of God.
>
> I am, &c., Caradoc Evans
>
> 26 Thornton-road, East Sheen, Surrey.

Here are some favoured polemical ingredients: a deflecting humour; the political hits;
direct assertion buttressed (so one senses) by personal knowledge; rhetoric intensifying

the attack, moving towards a memorable climax. There's no arguing with Caradoc Evans.

Commenting on this *Everyman* set-to, Ada Chesterton mentions Evans's change of jobs. Having "preached weekly to a congregation of over a million", he had moved to the *Daily Mirror*. Fleet Street looked after its own; ex-editors of popular weeklies were fair bets for openings on dailies.[7] This particular move returned Caradoc to the Northcliffe fold as one of a half-dozen well-paid sub-editors on a paper largely known for its photojournalistic scoops. (Of the *Daily Mail* and the *Mirror*, Lord Salisbury remarked that Harmsworth had invented a paper for those who could read but not think, and another for those who could see but not read.) By 1917 Northcliffe had surrendered control to his brother Lord Rothermere, believing that ownership of the *Mirror* sat uneasily with his proprietorship of the *Mail* and *The Times*. Evans's stay with the paper (1917-1923) took in the crusading editorship of Alexander Campbell, though under Rothermere the paper drifted erratically rightwards, initially gaining readers (by 1921 it was outselling all other dailies), then beginning to shed them.

Caradoc's post had its taxing disciplines, as he was fond of repeating. In the professional rivalry between dailies and weeklies, he ostensibly backed the former. Journalists on the dailies are "bright and lively and humble" whereas literary journalists are "solemn and ponderous and sonorous and count style greater than matter".[8] As for novelists, none he knew could hold down a newspaper job for a week. Working constantly to deadlines, making judgments at speed: this marked off daily journalism. "There is no profession, trade or business in the world where so many decisions, involving so great a responsibility, have to be made at such a pace," thought Gerald Gould, one of Evans's Fleet Street circle (he joined the *Daily Herald* from a Merton fellowship). "The news pours in, like a thousand streams in spate, from every continent and every ocean; it comes from reporters, news agencies, special correspondents, by hand, by post, by wire and air: it foams in flimsies, tingles through telephones, ticks on tapes."[9] The "monstrous accumulation, heap on heap" passes from the news editor to the chief sub-editor who gives out the stories for writing up, or toning down, by his team of subs. "Splash, lead, fill – the kind of heading, the kind of treatment – all must be settled in a race against the clock." Caradoc's nephew Howell Evans, a London journalist himself, believed that newspaper subbing – the writing up or toning down of the prose of others – did not come easily to his uncle. "You have to have no style at all, just the shortest cut to say anything. By the time he reached the *Mirror* Caradoc's style was too formed and coloured."[10] He confirms, however, that Evans took great pains over headlines (as he did over the titles of his stories) and would scan other papers for ideas.

Working on the *Mirror* through the long unnatural night bound Evans yet more tightly to Fleet Street. From these years come snapshots of him in the company of fellow journalists, most of them literary men on the dailies or weeklies (one or two dubbed "alcoholic stylists" or "men of the glowing pad"). Here and there he used his connections, as when Edward Garnett, working as a publisher's reader at the end of the war, contemplated moving into literary journalism. Evans at least could confirm an opening:

Dear Garnett
The "Daily Herald" is seeking a literary editor.
The "Herald" office is in Gough Street & the man to see is Gerald Gould.
 So much, as they say in the War Office, for your information.
    Sincerely,
    Caradoc Evans

This undated letter, typical in its brevity, hints at the prickliness that tested colleagues. Although a regular in Fleet Street haunts, Evans lacked the social ease of many of his companions. He had a name for being "difficult" and a habit of sending conversation awry. "He was a man of moods, and these controlled him," Annie Rees decided; he could explode unpredictably: "a volcano capped with ice", as Edward Wright so beautifully captured him (in October 1917). Wright pinpointed his old friend's "foreignness", both of appearance and thought. "Tall, gaunt of face, with high cheek bones and eyes usually half closed, Mr Caradoc Evans looks a strange kind of alien, and is what he looks. D. G. Rossetti and Joseph Conrad show scarcely a more foreign cast of mind."[11] To *Everyman* (26 October 1917), he appeared a "stern-looking man – the very type of Puritan before Puritans turned teetotal and grew flabby". Gerald Cumberland, a reluctant admirer, met a distinctly out-of-sorts Caradoc drinking with Tommy Pope in the Cheshire Cheese. The one-time music critic of *The Times* (real name Charles F. Kenyon), Cumberland could not warm to him.

> Evans himself is soft-spoken, shy, a little nervous. Who would guess that beneath that rather uncouth exterior there dwells a mind both subtle and delicate. His ugly, interesting face is blind as a thick mask: I mean it gives you nothing, no single clue… Evans is dour, repressed and utterly without the graces that attract even moderate liking. It was, then, curious to see these two men together, Evans staring rather owlishly over his glass, and Pope, with his rapid eyes and gentle mischievous voice, creating an atmosphere that seemed to exclude the unhappy Welshman who, silent and at sea, sipped his uncomfortable drink.[12]

Pope commented on the truth of this picture of Caradoc, who himself indeed admitted his lack of social polish and far from appealing looks. "An ugly man," thought Annie Rees, "almost as ugly as Josi", a judgement not really borne out by photographs (to Tommy Pope he resembled Eamon de Valera). But while testimonies to his courtesy and forbearance as editor are plentiful, it is true that unless loosened by drink Evans could be inhibited and uncommunicative with strangers. He liked to see himself as a commoner, one impervious to false glamour, to hollow social style and etiquette. Outside Fleet Street circles and informal gatherings of the Welsh, London society was never his milieu.

The *Mirror* years were largely ones of unsung work around the subbing table, making prose more intelligible, more readable, through small, significant alterations. The odd assignment came his way. He was asked to interview the ever-controversial Augustus John who at the time, as Hannen Swaffer recalled, was threatening either to join or leave the Royal Academy ("more or less a habit of his"). The date must have been April

1921, when John, not without misgiving, accepted a long imminent invitation to become an associate. (He would resign from the Academy in 1938 over its refusal to accept Wyndham Lewis's portrait of T.S. Eliot.) In preparation for the interview Evans turned to Swaffer, himself an ex-*Mirror* man acquainted with John. Swaffer met Caradoc at the Cock Tavern, the narrowest pub in Fleet Street, where they remained rooted till closing time. An unsteady Caradoc needed helping into a taxi. "Where do you want to go?" Swaffer asked. Out of nowhere came the reply, "Look out, Swaff! God's got you!"[13] Swaffer saw no sense in the words, a reversion to "the weird phrases and ideas" of chapel days, so he guessed; yet, flung out of a departing taxi, they lodged in the memory. Soon afterwards Swaffer looked to spiritualism.

The meeting with Augustus John turned out to be the first of a number. Evans suggested a break in Wales, where he would introduce the susceptible academician to some of the loveliest girls in the world. John felt Caradoc's regard for his "beautiful country" – "like God, he chastised those he loved" – and understood his need to return there from time to time: work on the *Daily Mirror* was "miserable employment" for someone with his gifts. The offer of a trip to Wales was never taken up and the two men drifted apart. But John's admiration of Evans's fiction only increased and, whatever the personal animus at the back of his unflattering comparison of Dylan Thomas with Caradoc Evans as interpreters of Welsh life (John had come to blows with Thomas over Caitlin), he couched it in terms which could be defended, judging Evans the "far more conscientious historian".[14]

Nephew Howell happily recalled Caradoc's summer visits home. Besides helping his mother in her tasks around the house, he spent a few days with Howell's parents (his sister Sarah and her husband Thomas Evans) at Dyffryn Bern, their farm at Tresaith. This now celebrated uncle from Fleet Street struck his young nephew as odd because,

> he always wore a broad-brimmed black hat, and a pair of black-rimmed, cockle-shell glasses dangled at the end of some sort of black string-like material on his chest. I once asked him what they were for, and he promptly replied, with a chuckle and that indescribably shrewd twinkle in his eyes: "What these? They're just for swank!"[15]

Having encouraged Howell and brother Dai in their scrapping, he would hand them a pound of sweets and ask, on point of leaving, "Well, boys bach, what would you like for Christmas?"

> It was always a steam engine, a motor car, or a meccano – and we always got them. He never troubled with shoddy presents, and the steam engines and motor cars were always beautiful working models – something to make a small boy jump with joy for weeks.

It seems clear that for the most part Caradoc returned to Wales alone; few make mention of Rose his wife, who found little charm in a Cardiganshire smallholding and seemingly resented her husband's slavish attention to his mother. "He was unfortunate in his first wife, Rose Evans. To me she seemed quite indifferent to the old lady." So wrote Annie Rees,[16] recalling one particular stay when Mali became incapacitated, having spilled boiling water on her foot. Though the Evanses's holiday had a week to run, Rose left for London at once, dreading further confinement at dreary Lanlas cottage.

The four stories of 1917, bidding farewell to Manteg, mark the end of Evans's most productive years, ones yielding two published collections and much that would make up a third. He remained a short-story writer but sought to widen his scope. While output temporarily slackened – "Earthbred" and "Joseph's House" are the only separately published stories of 1918-19 – the newspapers skirmishes continued. With the appearance of *Gwyneth of the Welsh Hills*, Edith Nepean's first novel (previously serialised in *Ideas*), the *Western Mail* (29 March 1918) asked if Evans had helped in the writing – the "silly jargon" and "idiotic inanities" suggested so. If not, then Nepean was an Evans disciple in all but his love of the obscene. After clarifying his involvement with a book he admired, Evans's reply (23 March 1918) touched on the question of Welsh dialogue, citing Ben Jonson's "The Honour of Wales" as exhibiting something akin to his own "idiotic inanities". Brushing aside his reviewer, the *Western Mail*'s editor appended a response to an ill-judged cultural flourish. Jonson's Welsh peasant talk bore not the slightest resemblance to Evans's "inane jargon":

> Jonson's characters are Welshmen struggling to express themselves in English and encountering difficulties of idiom and pronunciation. Mr Caradoc Evans pretends to give equivalent values for phrases and sentences used by Welsh peasants when speaking their own language and the result is the grotesque lingual hash we find in his books.

For once Evans came off badly in an exchange. Jonson's regional foray is part of the tradition of rendering Welsh pronunciation largely by misspelling English words whereas Evans was attempting something altogether different: the remaking of direct speech so as to suggest a character's mindset. (The *Western Mail* dimly recognised this.)

Later editions of *Gwyneth* saw Caradoc joining Lloyd George as dedicatee, doubtless for his continuing support of Nepean, whether out of literary appreciation, personal friendship, or the opportunity her novels gave him to strike at major targets. His short review of *Welsh Love* (*New Witness*, 21 November 1919) opens with talk of "the black-coated band of Welsh parliamentary intriguers who take off their hats every time the Prime Minister's name is mentioned", and ends by commending Nepean's book to "anyone who takes the slightest interest in the composition of the present House of Commons". It was a foretaste of what soon would follow in *My Neighbours*, Evans's third collection.

My Neighbours

1918-20

Of the six post-*Capel Sion* stories separately published in periodicals, "The Day of Judgement" and "An Offender in Sion" were omitted from *My Neighbours* and not reprinted during the author's lifetime.[1] Two later stories, written for the *English Review*, find Evans moving away from Wales. "Earthbred" (March 1918) is set entirely in London, though his city exiles scheme over a dairy business as they might over a farm back home, using pretence and evasion to gauge or falsify its market worth; the story proceeds almost entirely through dialogue, of the oblique, distrustful kind perfected in *Capel Sion*. "Joseph's House" (August 1919) shows Evans at his very best – "the beautiful clear-cut simplicity of the story is a joy," Rhys Davies wrote to Gwyn Jones. Evans fully inhabits the consciousness of his characters, their peculiar precepts and pieties, their occasional loving deceits. There is pathos in their trapped condition, and an affecting reciprocal tenderness between Madlen and Joseph her son as they meet the inevitable. "There's silly, dear people, to covet houses! Only a smallish bit of house we want." Madlen's words allude to Penlan cottage, to Joseph's burial spot, to the coffin London colleagues deem his only proper purchase.

Who's Who for 1919 signalled Evans's public arrival. His entry confirmed his address as 26 Thornton Road, East Sheen (close to Richmond) and "walking in London" as his favoured recreation; he might have added "and writing about the London Welsh", for the basilisk gaze had fallen on his metropolitan compatriots and co-religionists. Some were honoured names, thriving in the commercial kingdom. "Moreover, people, look you at John Lewis. Study his marble gravestone in the burial ground of Capel Sion: 'His name is John Newton-Lewis; Paris House, London, his address. From his big shop in Putney, Home they brought him by railway.'" Numbering some forty thousand, the London Welsh were present in most businesses and professions, though thickest in drapery, the dairy trade and domestic service. Evans's own Cardiganshire countryfolk had cornered the milk rounds, in the suburbs and in the city; they sold their pints and butter-pats the length of Fleet Street. "They work terribly hard, and see next to nothing of the rich, fruity, cosmopolitan life that flows past their door" (the words are Glyn Roberts's, another Cardiganshire journalist working in London), "they are living in the future, the future when they will retire to Wales, solid, respectable and successful... There is something grand in their singleness of purpose – something."[2] They had brought Wales with them, banding together to live a life in some ways as Welsh as that lived in Wales. Their paper, the *London Welshman*, reveals both sides of an inward-looking community, a touchy defensiveness, alert to the smallest slight (army discrimination against Welsh officers?), and a calendar of self-celebration – concerts, rallies, eisteddfodau, Cymm-rodorion and St David's Day festivities. There were intellectual circles too, notably the Friday evening salon of Mary Ellis, wife of Ellis Jones Griffith, the Anglesey Liberal MP. "There is all the difference," reflected the writer Llewelyn Wyn Griffith, "between discussing cultural issues in a cold chapel vestry, and a gathering such as this, which contributed to our social awareness as well as our knowledge of the arts."[3] Fleet Street sharpened Evans's social awareness – not least of Liberal MPs – while for literary company he had Arthur Machen and fellow journalists in the pubs off Ludgate Circus. "When we meet in taverns we fall to quarrelling about Welsh pronunciation," wrote Machen in June 1919; "the Saxons about us think the strange words must be German and look at us suspiciously, and on one occasion, an *Evening News* colleague, who was sitting with Caradoc and myself, called out in a loud voice: 'Intern them all!'"[4]

If Evans enjoyed the conviviality of the pub, so he did his "sermon-tasting": chapel going as much as drapery gave him bearings on the London Welsh. He savoured the toothsome dramatics of Welsh pulpit giants, Ben's models at College Carmarthen ("According to the Pattern"): "now he was Pharaoh wincing under the plagues, now he was the Prodigal son hungering at the pig's trough, now he was the widow of Nain rejoicing at the recovery of her son, now he was a parson in Nineveh squirming under the tongue of Jonah." His delight in the manner of preachers, whom on other grounds he would condemn, understandably intrigued Arthur Machen. Machen's "very turbulent, highly entertaining" companion joined him one evening, following a narrow escape in the suburbs where a famous preacher was performing. "It was lucky I thought of it beforehand and had a couple of pints or he would have got me," Caradoc explained.[5]

Evans plants his fictional neighbours in his own London patch, "Thornton East" . This, and some dominant presences, helps integrate a collection lacking *Capel Sion's* tight focus. Evans opts for a broader perspective, embracing community leaders (a preacher-politician, a prosperous draper – "there's boys for you") and those at the bottom of the pile. Ministers figure sparingly, though if *My Neighbours* has a physical centre, it is Eylwin Jones's Kingsend Tabernacle – the "funny little Welsh chapel" rejected by Gwen Enos-Harries for a "Thornton Vale" English equivalent. (Evans here has Sheen Vale Con-gregational Church in mind, a stone's throw from Thornton Road and sometime in the care of H. Elwyn Thomas, whose Barrie-inspired Welsh novels gave point to his sermons on "Novel Reading – help or hindrance to the higher life?".)[6] In *I Take This City* (1933), his sparkling first impressions of London, the young Glyn Roberts depicts the queues for Sunday evening services at the larger London Welsh chapels (King's Cross, Charing Cross, Jewin in the City); two hours later the crowds spill out for pavement chat, kid gloves and black bowlers much in evidence. These chapels, big or small (some thirty-four in all – Evans gave an *Ideas* reader a guinea for listing them), "stand for everything which signifies anything to the draper and the dairyman – home, religion, friendship, the language, music. Within their means and within reason, they will contribute lavishly to the upkeep and smartening of their houses of worship, which are usually glistening and varnished to the nth degree."

"Home, religion, friendship, the language", these are themes in *My Neighbours*. Home is Wales – a good country to come from but not much of a place to live in, as the saying went. The Welsh worship Home from afar, and like Jacob Griffith ("Profit and Glory"), they visit it as lordly almoners. "Summer by summer he went to Wales and remained there two weeks; and he gave a packet of tea or coffee to every widow who worshipped in the capel, and a feast of tea and currant bread and caraway-seed cake to the little children of the capel." Back in London, his sister Annie, now Miss Witton-Griffiths, dons a hat of osprey feathers, her hair piled fashionably high, the "birth stain" on her cheek symbolically whitened. For all their nationalist protestations, his London-Welsh are culturally confused, despising the ungodly English yet aping their social ways. They puff up their surnames ("the hyphen is the mark of our ambition"), regally christen their houses ("Windsor" in the case of Mrs Enos-Harries), forsake their native language for "classier" English. Evans makes play with the shift between languages as characters align themselves socially or bargain over possessions. "Are you Welsh?" asks Evan of the woman whose shop he covets. "That's what people say," she replies.

As for religion, here is one of the faithful at prayer, believing that his hour has come ("Like Brothers").

> Not fitting that you leave the daughter fach alone. Short in the leg you made her. There's a set-back. Her mother perished; and did I complain? An orphan will the pitiful wench be. Who will care for the shop? And the repairing workman? Steal the leather he will. A fuss will be about shop Richmond. Paid have I the rent for one year in advance. Serious will the loss be. Be not of two thinks. Send Lisha to breathe breathings into my inside – in the belly where the heart is. Forgive me that I go to the Capel English. Go there I do for the trade. Generous am I in the collections. Ask the preacher. Take some one else to sit in my chair in the Palace. Amen. Amen and amen... Allow me to live for a year – two years – and a grand communion set will I give to the Welsh capel in Shirland Road. Individual cups. Silver-plated, Sheffield make. Ann shall send quickly for the price-list.

Evans more gently exposes a particular religious consciousness. His drapers and dairymen adhere to a code that secures their entry into Heaven, that paradise of pulpits, bible-thumping prophets and slap-up chapel teas glimpsed in two of the stories. "We must all cross Jordan," sighs Simon Griffiths ("Profit and Glory"); till then, let profit-and-glory Calvinism prevail. The moral imperative is to thrive and prosper: it's good to be rich; the rich are good. Hugh Evans ("Lost Treasure") loses his money together with his sanity, and thus all standing within the chapel ("grief... was in the crease of his garments"). Then he triumphs as a hard-nosed capitalist, running up cheap fashions on sweated labour. Money speeds his return to the fold, as it uplifts John Daniel, another Carmarthen apprentice: "Watch him on the platform on the Day of David the Saint. And all, dear me, out of J.D.'s Ritfit three-and-sixpence gents' tunic shirts."

By contrast, caretakers Tim and Martha, Kingsend's general dogsbodies, are the lowest of the low – in everyone's eyes, and their own ("Unanswered Prayers"). "Charitable are Welsh to Welsh," declares Tim, in what might stand as an ironic epigraph for the entire collection. He and Martha meet death outside the chapel they adore, a quick release from the humiliations heaped upon them by "boys tidy" of this Tabernacle, the exploitative Reverend Jones and the heartless Enoch Harries. Their servant daughter Winnie stirs a fateful jealousy in her mistress, though not before confronting Mrs Enos-Harries with a courage absent in others. She is jailed on a trumped-up charge brought by "Mishtress Harries", and there is fine emotional delicacy in Evans's handling of the old couple's anguished reactions. Elsewhere, greed of wealth transcends all family ties as, once again, husbands and wives, brothers and sisters, parents and children, are locked in hideous combat. To paraphrase Hitchcock, Evans brings murder back into the family, where it belongs. One compelling domestic drama, "Love and Hate", charts the slow poisoning of sisterly love as Olwen seeks to do right by her sister Lizzie and by her own daughter Jennie, a spoilt-brat shop assistant with a know-all cockney partner.

The stories set during wartime evoke little sense of the times; no jaunty patriotism, no gathering despair, no gloom of wartime London. Living and working in London, Evans could scarcely have ignored the war. In 1917 the military had camped in Richmond Park, billeting troops in private houses close to his. At Sheen Vale chapel, harvest services were abandoned because of air raids. Air raids are mentioned in *My Neighbours* (one kills Tim and Martha), but in a language that removes all sense of immediacy. As editor of the mass-market *Ideas*, Evans had regularly commented on wartime conditions – in essence, how at home the poorest were forced to bear the heaviest burdens – but in his fiction the war is a marginal event. His characters go about their money-making too engaged in personal battles to bother about the national struggle. "St David and the Prophets" marks the attitude of the wealthy Welsh. "You left on your own accord, didn't you?" asks William Hughes-Jones, big draper and chapel deacon, of a soldier home from the front. "I never take back a hand that leave on their own." In wartime, as in peace, class divisions are unsuppressed, and the chapel reinforces them. So a minister greets returning servicemen with talk of civilian sacrifices; the Somme is as nothing compared with the sufferings of a deacon: "Happier still we are to welcome Mister Hughes-Jones to the Big Seat. In the valley of the shadow has Mister Hughes-Jones been. Earnestly we prayed for our dear religious leader."

Satire feeds on specific targets, on a group, an occupation, or individuals. Evans names living persons. The Reverend Eynon Davies, his old *Western Mail* adversary, is given the lordship of Walham Green, while behind Ben Lloyd looms the most celebrated London Welshman of all, the Prime Minister David Lloyd George. The Welsh practically deified him – at Rhyl he was introduced as the greatest man since Christ. Here was the dream incarnate, the personification of nationhood and faith. At least, of his representative quality Evans had no doubt: "Mr George is Welsh Nonconformity," he declared in 1916, still smarting from the attempted ban on *My People*. "I hear his silver voice holding spell-bound hundreds of people; I see his majestic forehead and his auburn locks and the strands of his silken moustache." A fortune-teller describes Ben Lloyd to a panting Gwen Enos-Harries in phrases that conjure up Lloyd George at his zenith ("For Better"). Evans wasn't so star-struck; indeed, in "According to the Pattern" he dropped his tone of detached neutrality to treat of one fiercely determined Welshman and his calculated assault on the city, a preacher with political ambitions who advances through guile, flattery and grandiloquence, deeming such advancement a mark of God's favour.

> He bound himself to Welsh politicians and engaged himself in public affairs, and soon he was an idol to the multitude of people, who were sensible only to his well-sung words, and who did not know that his utterances veiled his own avarice and that of his masters. All that he did was for profit, and yet he could not win enough.

The key to this extraordinary character lay in the Wales that bred him. "According to the Pattern" has Ben learning from the ministers, progressing through religious cunning, pulpit fire-and-brimstone, and onslaughts against Anglican priestcraft. A breath-taking sentence on Ben's father conveys the status of women in his community. A father of seven daughters by a (nameless) first wife, Abel marries well a second time. Yet, "Even if Abel had land, money, and honour, his vessel of contentment was not filled until his wife went into her deathbed and gave him a son." Here is hallmark Caradoc Evans: deep disgust controlled in gravely beautiful prose.

Besides mimicking his "well-sung words",[7] Ben's speeches closely mirror Lloyd George's Welsh concerns (tithe, temperance, disestablishment, home rule). But it's the anti-unionism which stands out. Ben is the lost leader, the one-time champion of the shop workers' cause who is bought over by the big Welsh drapers. Now "Fiery Taffy" mocks their struggle. "Only recently a few shop-assistants – a handful of counter-jumpers – tried to shake the integrity of our commerce. But their white cuffs held back their aarms, and the white collars choked their aambitions." Contemplating parliamentary moves that will crush the unions, Ben dreams of drapers secure in their citadels, enjoying a servile labour force bridled by religious education. If union advances, dramatic in south Wales, troubled a Liberal Prime Minister, for Evans the coalfield communities held promise of a national regeneration. He had said as much in 1916, when publicly supporting Welsh miners in their demands for higher wages. It wasn't a popular view, Lloyd George having proclaimed a wartime strike in the coal mines "unthinkable – quite unthinkable".

As for Ben's nationalist affirmations ("Dear Wales... the land that is our heritage not by Act of Parliament but by Act of God", "Cymru fydd – Wales for the Welsh – is here", "How sorry I am for any one who are not Welsh"), it needed no marked reorientation (as Evans saw it) for a Liberal leader set on furthering his political career to indulge in the rhetoric of home rule, since nationalism was in the possession of those who, for all their talk of Welsh culture and the superior moral standards that flowed from it, were at heart social reactionaries, craving British respectability. Thus Ben marries English money and in his final deranged imaginings bends the knee before the English monarch. Interestingly, Ben the unprincipled opportunist, at once manipulator and puppet, accords with much in John Maynard Keynes's notorious portrait of the prime minister, a weathervane politician ("Lloyd George is rooted in nothing... he is an instrument and a player at the same time which plays on the company and is played on them too... a vampire and a medium in one").

Evans characteristically blends horror with humour, and the black comedy of *My Neighbours* reaches a peak with Ben. Caradoc clearly delights in him, in his verbal gusto and eye for the main chance. This man could talk his way out of hell; as he does in "The Two Apostles" where he bypasses the divine rigmarole for measuring individual worth. This eschatological fantasy shows Judgement Day derailed as the Welsh are called to account. In words, not deeds, do they trust, and this skittish piece confirms other constants in Evans's dissection of nation: the chapel's alliance with the secularly powerful, their joint oppression of the weak, a raging sectarianism, and the unassailable spirit of the Elect inexorably bound for Heaven: "'Ready am I, God bach,' Towy exclaimed, stretching his hairy arms. 'Take me.'" It was the author's enjoyment of his characters that struck the *TLS*; "though it is not desirable that every realist should be solemn," its reviewer concluded, "every performer in literature… has to be serious, in the sense that he has to state events as he sees them; and this Mr Evans does."

The "realist" label was ever contentious when applied to Caradoc Evans, and particularly so in Wales where critics argued that if realism meant a sense of proportion and believable natural speech, then Caradoc was never a realist. But fictional realism has other dimensions, not least a willingness to face uncomfortable social facts. *My Neighbours* touches on these in its many references to drapery. Like Joseph ("Joseph's House"), he was put to drapery at fourteen, in the belief that here was a respectable haven for less robust country lads. In truth they entered a death trap, largely through "living-in" and its disease-spreading dormitories. In theory, one could live out by getting married, but as this usually prompted dismissal, marriages were commonly kept secret (a shop girl might take off her ring when returning to barracks). Men grew old living-in, the shop their only home, and their personal relationships coarsened. P.C. Hoffman, like Duncan Davies a trade union activist, tells of older assistants with money seeking out prostitutes; "Some caught disease in that way, and we would hear all about that, too." They might end up selling matches, laces and newspapers, their shabby respectable clothes and genteel mien proclaiming them no ordinary tramps.[8] Rhys Hopkins in "The Lantern Bearer" mirrors the type.

By autumn 1919 Evans had assembled the contents of *My Neighbours* for November publication: almost certainly fifteen stories, the number that served for both *My People* and *Capel Sion*. At this point, his publisher Andrew Melrose took fright at two of the pieces, "Wisdom" and "The Lantern Bearer". The latter's title brings to mind *The Light of the World*, Holman Hunt's immensely popular painting, a night scene lit by Christ's lantern, our guide in darkest places. A monstrous false religion, cloaking giant hypocrisies, infects the Kingsend store ruled by Enoch Harries. Robbed of a share in the business by this sinister buffoon, Rhys Hopkins becomes the lantern bearer, an overseer patrolling staff quarters on his prurient nightly rounds; so begins a lust-driven downward spiral ending in vagrancy and religious delusion. Throughout Rhys holds to the man who would destroy him – "Full of eloquence he is and plentiful blessings he has had" – and in a loft above the premises seeks the essence of his master's sanctity: "he heard Harries praying, and he saw the words of the prayer coming through the floor in the shape of a spider's thread. The thread floated this way and that before it cleaved to the walls and roof of the garret." As for Melrose's reaction, it was probably the diseased sexuality that most disturbed the sixty-year-old Presbyterian: Hopkins haunting the women's room, fingering their discarded garments; gathering venereal blisters "at the mouths of dark alleys" – "I strongly advise the deletion of this story," he wrote to the author.

Melrose's grounds for rejecting "Wisdom" are far less clear, for here Evans strides familiar terrain:

> In his thirty-fifth year David Rees engaged himself to marry Ada Morris. That was when his housekeeper expressed to him her sorrow that at a certain month childbirth would tarnish her glory, whence her name would be as evil as a thirty-pounds with a latch key shop girl.
>
> "Miss Shones fach," David whispered, "don't you be so loud."

A Welsh "merchant prince" in need of an heir; the consequent pressures on an aging man ("youth should begat; old age should frolic, inasmuch as it begets only weaklings"); a bastard son secreted in Wales; male disregard of women (prized for dowries or as broodmares, else dangerous provokers of lust) – these are more familiar ingredients worked with trenchancy and wit. David Rees seeks reconciliation with his "boy chance", though only when assured of the young man's "wisdom", his canny way with money.

For whatever reason, "Wisdom" touched a nerve – "Is this story necessary?" Melrose scrawled across the typescript – and Evans was not so committed to it, or to "The Lantern Bearer", as to ensure their retention. A seasoned editor himself, he knew that these were decisions for publishers who, like editors, were the distributors, backing their judgements in the marketplace, the forum that counts; authors were the "lowly manufacturers". Melrose's disquiet extended to the Ben Lloyd stories and, shy of possible libel action, he insisted that references to Ben's parliamentary career be excised through last-minute cancel leaves. In all, difficulties with the makeup considerably delayed *My Neighbours*. Shorn of a couple of stories,[9] bearing signs of hasty proofing, and with its "1919" title-page still intact, the book finally appeared in March 1920 – mischievously close to St David's Day.

Though not extensively noticed, *My Neighbours* gathered good reviews in England, allowing Melrose to quickly design an eye-catching advertisement appending quotes from various papers. The *Bookman* neatly précised Evans's literary strengths: a fierce economy of prose, which packs a whole life-history into a single story; an absence of external comment, lending the narrative its stark, ironic appeal (the Old Testament debt was evident); and a playwright's approach to dialogue: "he depicts his characters solely by means of their conversation; and this conversation is always illuminating and dramatic." Praising its "devastating skill", *Punch* reported that the book had prompted threats of personal violence – "if I were the writer, I should purchase a bulldog," the reviewer signed off. Such sensationalist publicity, commonly generated by Evans, perturbed the *Nation*, since it allowed fiction of moral weight to be dismissed as "a sardonic kind of joke"; the writer's motives might be misunderstood, his assaults thought lacking in substance.

The *Western Mail* cried "literary filth", "lewdness" and "obscenity", then more calmly voiced the commonest Welsh objection (shared by those who, like the historian R.T. Jenkins, did not contest the factual basis of the stories) that the language talked in the book turned the characters into idiots. Evans came back in due course, attack his preferred defence. "Your reviewer complains that the London Welsh characters in *My Neighbours* are stark idiots," begins his reply (22 March 1920):

> They are not. Idiocy is not the mark of Welsh Nonconformity. The mark is that of the knave, and the people of whom I have written are gutter knaves, who, when you turn your hose on them, howl out that of all people on earth there is none so clean.
>
> Consider them. Consider the Welsh Member of Parliament and his exploits: Summon him before you, and when you have examined him and uncovered his trickery, and wiped your feet on his garments, give him a pound note and he will depart blessing you. Dangle before him a golden carrot and he will trot merrily to hell.[10]

Alone among Welsh papers the *Carmarthen Journal* once more spoke up for Evans. "We consider that in Mr Caradoc Evans Wales has found her literary genius," ran the paper's front-page review, though it added the qualification, again one common in Wales, that however salutary his writings in his homeland, "the danger is that they may so influence the contempt of neighbouring nations as to set up a very serious handicap against Welsh national advancement". Evans knew the argument, that his books gave ammunition to the contemptuous English, and countered always by insisting that he cared enough for his country to tell the truth about her. It was a truth applicable in America where, as if to give weight to the *Carmarthen Journal's* further contention that what this author was really exposing were the "phases of humbug and hypocrisy that are found in every nation", the critic H.L. Mencken again seized on Evans's relevance to a home-grown protestant fundamentalism. "Is this great and proud Republic incapable of producing an Evans?" he asked in the *Smart Set* (August 1920).

What Mencken had particularly in mind was the scalding essay that prefaced the American *My Neighbors* (May 1920). It was this edition that Caradoc gave to Tom Powell, son of Dr Joshua, in response to his cousin's expressed interest in the book. Caradoc's accompanying letter, following its truthful opening confession, neatly describes the gift:

> Dear Tom
>
> I should have answered your note sooner. Do please forgive me: I am the world's worst letter writer.
>
> I am grieved that I have not a copy of the English edition of "My Neighbours" to send you. But here is a copy of the American edition; the arrangement of the contents is different from that produced in London and the text differs here and there. It also contains an additional chapter...
>
> Yours very sincerely
>
> Caradoc Evans

The "additional chapter" is the prefatory essay "The Welsh People" designed to make clear the attitudes that underpin the fiction. Subdued irony mingles with unbridled assertion as Evans voices again his obsessions, more particularly how ministers batten on an already impoverished countryside:

> White cabbages and new potatoes, eggs and measures of corn, milk and butter and money we give to the preacher. We trim our few acres until our shoulders are crutched and the soil is in the crevices of our flesh that his estate shall be a glory unto God. We make for him a house which is as a mansion set amid hovels and for the building thereof the widow must set aside portions of her weekly old age pension. These things and many more we do, for forgiveness of sin is obtained by sacrifice. Such folk as hold back their offerings have their names proclaimed in the pulpit.[11]

Evans primes an already inflammatory piece with references to interbreeding and incest, generalizing from the example of "Shon Porth" – who "asks the Big Man to destroy his pregnant sister into whose bed Satan has enticed him" – to talk of "our villages and countryside... populated with the children of cousins who have married cousins and of women who have played the harlot with their brothers". Incest is a matter not directly broached in *My Neighbours* (though hinted at in "Love and Hate") and when in a new spirit of rapprochement Evans came to revise "The Welsh People" for publication in Britain he deleted his references to it.

Mencken, who had praised the earlier collections, turned to *My Neighbors* in an essay published one year later.[12] Read "The Welsh People" and you will, he suggested, be instantly reminded of the Georgia and Carolina Methodists. Their religious thought was the same:

> There is the same naïve belief in an anthropomorphic creator... the same submission to an ignorant and impudent sacerdotal tyranny... the same sharp contrast between doctrinal orthodoxy and private ethics... The most booming piety, in the South, is not incompatible with the theory that lynching is a benign institution. Two generations ago it was not incompatible with an ardent belief in slavery.

Unsurprisingly, Mencken's essay produced a ferocious reaction in the South, and as he recalled, "I was belaboured for months, and even years afterward in a very extravagant manner."[13] His opinion of the southern farmer didn't help – "No more grasping, selfish and dishonest mammal... is known to students of the Anthropoidea." Mencken consoled himself with the thought that his attack played some part in the revival of Southern letters that followed.

My Neighbours brought to a close Evans's glory years, ones that heaped upon him excessive praise and blame and established him for some as a genuine literary original. Once read, his stories are not easily forgotten; in the words of Thomas Burke, the dedicatee of *My Neighbours*, "They are, as all work should be, like nothing else. So was their author."

Taffy: Novel and Play

1920-23

A gainst the odds, Caradoc's stories had sold remarkably well – six printings of *My People* by 1919. In America, too, a modest market seemed to be opening up. The anthologist Edward O'Brien chose "Greater than Love" for *The Great Modern English Stories* (New York, 1919), introducing Caradoc Evans as the most promising writer in his selection (it was Evans's first anthology appearance). There were rumours of an American lecture tour. "I have no doubt that he would get an audience at, say, Scranton, Pa., but I shouldn't care to be his chairman," remarked a *Llais Llafur / Labour Voice* correspondent (10 January 1920), conscious of the Welsh immigrant community in Pennsylvania's anthracite field. Evans too lacked enthusiasm for the project. He professed a tiredness with controversy. He needed a change in direction, a more tranquil literary path.

Ideas for a larger work had been playing in his mind, including a treatment of shop life "bitterly socialistic in feeling and realistic in intention".[1] By 1920 a novel was becoming a career necessity, if only because a novel invariably enhanced the price of a writer's stories. Against this had to be set the effort that went into novel-writing: what for Evans, practised over two thousand words, was a trek over forty times as long; and one that might end with a rejection slip or else derisory sales. Any novel selling over two thousand copies could be deemed a success, thought Michael Joseph (then an agent) in 1925; and fortunate was a first novel with royalties of £50. Not that money bothered Caradoc unduly since he enjoyed a regular journalist's income, but, as he soon discovered, a novel left little time for other writing. For three years he fell silent. Then in summer 1922 came rumours of a full-length book, containing "no bitterness – or at any rate with a comedy element in it."[2] Provisionally entitled *Taffy*, the book was not the projected drapery novel but a lighter, more leisurely excursion through familiar west Wales terrain, developing the strain of comic fantasy conspicuous in *My Neighbours*. The novella *Taffy*, which sadly was never brought to publishable form,[3] is a tale of warring capellers, and of Marged and Ester, two capable younger women set on furthering their fathers' fortunes and their own marriage prospects. In Marged, daughter of the rebellious chapel elder Twmi, Evans impressively advances his ideal of Welsh womanhood. She is shrewd, robust, sensual: the kind of clear-eyed female to whom he was always drawn. True to comedy, the story ends in all-round reconciliation and an improbable double wedding – though not before the barriers to good neighbourliness and a loving union have been fully ventilated.

"The journeyings of the Welsh peasant are short: the man who lives in the heart of his parish is often a stranger at the boundary stone. Our world is the straggling village where we abide…" If the tone of *Taffy* is lighter, the social analysis remains unchanged: "Most of the people of Sion are of the same seed… they are governed by the same capel-made laws, which permit cousins to wed cousins, fathers to lie with their daughters, and children to be born out of wedlock." As the chapel conditions ways of living, so it commands the historical past. "Gwilym Hiraethog, Williams Pantycelyn, Howell Harris, Eynon Davies, Davydd Llwyd George": the Nonconformist lineage adorns vestry walls, while grey headstones in the graveyard commemorate chapel worthies such as Owen and John. Both "glorified the Big Man", in John's case "while driving his wife to Asylum Carmarthen", in Owen's "though his sister made him go with her". In the reassuring words of the narrator, "Their memorials give strength to the living and promise the righteous a perpetual name on the highway."

If the ironic thrusts hit home, they are not sustained by a narrative of commensurate power. No Shadrach Danyrefail imposes, no Bern-Davydd stalks the land. Instead, we have Ben Woodenleg, a broken-down preacher desperately recycling his sermons, disguising staleness of content by fervour of delivery (his "zealous fury… parted the leaves of ten Bibles in Capel Morfa"). With doctrinal positions long established – the Word explained a century ago by "Davydd Charles from Bala" – the preacher's challenge is to enact some striking pulpit drama. Here Ben believes he has the edge over his pulpit rival Spurgeon Evans, a college-trained slip.[4] Indeed, he is positively marked for office, for,

> it is well-known that in the old days God called His preachers from the coal mine and the plough and the threshing machine. Those who were shy of hearing He maimed so that they were more easily pressed into His service. He hurled a piece of coal upon Ben's leg, thus forcing the man into the pulpit.

Whatever their background, Sion's ministers patrol the parish, cajoling money from the weak and the strong, trusting that the Big Man "will not let one of them be cast down, but will give them the flesh of fowl and white cabbages and bread and butter and a feather bed and a pulpit from which to govern the people". Otherwise, a minister stays aloof from his flock – though "if one has the ticks, he goes to her with the clippers and the powder" (that "her" is nicely chosen: Sion's backsliders are usually women). Matters are different with chapel elders, and *Taffy* makes plain the interdependence of ministers and deacons. Ben might stoop before his deacon-employer – "Shacob spoke no word. He beckoned with his finger, and Ben felt as if he were a bundle of reeds about to be cut down by a sickle" – yet both know that a thriving chapel depends on a charismatic minister. The deacons bear the brunt of Evans's ridicule, a village petite bourgeoisie of artisans and shopkeepers driven by vanity and greed. The new Capel Split owes more to personal jealousies (and an excess of zinc roofing) than to any doctrinal difference. Hatred of the heathen Church alone unites the capellers; they set aside their warring to turn and face the Anti-Christ. A Resurrection miracle will seal their triumph, trans-forming Capel Sion into the Big Man's image, "the walls His frock coat, the two long, narrow windows His eyes, the roof His hair; the double door shall swing cross-wise and will be His lips which will utter judgement."

Evans had previously milked the grim humour of a man not allowed to die before his chapel's new burial ground can receive him, but *Taffy* plays on another facet of the Welsh way of death: the peculiar gaiety it releases – that "solemn, joyous moment" when the great misfortune falls on someone else. The death of others sharpens our own sense of life; thus,

> We do not ignore death, nor put the thought of him from our mind; we stand at the roadside and show him the way to this or that house, and we delight in attending to the many ceremonies that are due to him. Death is our enemy when his sting is aimed at us.

Death robs us of the things we love, and "Sion's love is of fields and ditches and hen lofts." What then of human love? There is sex enough in Sion, about which our narrator counsels. "The man who has sinned with a woman must strengthen his wit that he does not fall into her hands; he must trail his gaze on the floor lest he is caught in the trap she has laid for him." The fool Abel Powell, a trainee minister, fatally ignores this advice; he stoops to marrying a pregnant servant girl, even though his college principal urges that he foist paternity on someone outside the capel – such people are steeped in pollution. As our narrator laments, "Man will behave foolishly for a woman, though he is commanded to cut off even his right hand if it offends him." The Sionites understand how in consequence God has dealt with Abel and his low-bred choice; how, denied the prosperity of the Elect, they must "cast their sweat on eight acres of sandy soil above Morfa".

Outside his spokesman-of-Sion persona, Evans in his novella speaks directly of the sufferings of women, "crushed to the glazen dullness of cows by submissive giving, child-bearing, and continuous toil... you know a Welsh woman is never allowed to tire, not by day or night, before her man." Yet *Taffy* is refreshingly free of victimized women; on the contrary, we meet a range of high-spirited females harnessing their sexuality, some in dubious ways. Shan Gingerbread discreetly offers her body, and is well rewarded for her tact. Not for her the widow's burdens of wool-gathering, slaving at a neighbour's harvest, or planting out a meagre potato patch. Shan is striking creation, with supernatural powers ("of her bread it is said that no woman who ate a piece that had been carried under a man's armpit could withhold herself"). A quality of folk tale, of fabulous pastoral bawdy, colours whole stretches of *Taffy*. The communal occasion of harvesting triggers a summer wantonness, upon which "the old brown woman" (shades of *My People's* prurient, gossipy Bertha Daviss) provides a risqué commentary, first sparked by Spurgeon's gift to Marged of his precious sermon pencil: "Marged turned and lifted up her skirt and she put the pencil in the wide calico pocket which hung from her waist." Spurgeon, the young minister, comes to Marged by way of Ester, Josi Stonemason's daughter, whose transient physical allure is caught in the image of her breasts falling to the string of her bodice, like "cats being taken in a sack to be drowned". Ester has a line in fevered gossip:

"tales of strange Peggi, who liked her tom-cat better than her infant and… let her infant perish in hunger so that her cat might suckle her", and of Big Konet ("not the handiwork of the Lord"), a woman to the cattle dealers of Carmarthen but a man to the women of Cwmamman (where he worked in the pits).

From the moment of his arrival, Spurgeon Evans strikes Marged and Ester as a more than handsome catch, and in a reversal of sexual strategy, Spurgeon uses his personal magnetism, his winning way with women, as a means to advance. Neither lust nor love must deflect him from gaining Sion's pulpit (Ester perplexedly wonders "why a man of so many words did not throw her upon the floor and ravish her"). But Spurgeon bargains without Marged, as do all Sion's men. More than their match in cunning, she becomes their moral scourge. Yet she understands the deep necessity of Sion – "Sion, whose other name is life". Religion binds the community; the Capel is law and life; there can be no safety without it (only the lonely sinner is stoned, she reminds her dissident father, "like the windows of an empty house"). Chapel religion stirs the sweetest emotions and guides uneasy longings. Languorously stretched on her bed, recalling the "hot music" of Spurgeon's "song-sermons" and prayers, Marged confesses that "life without Sion is very drab". Once joined with Spurgeon, she will come to direct a chapel reborn.

In her attitude and opinions we detect something of a realignment in Evans's own thinking. The psychic roots of Nonconformity, its reordering of the emotional life, he would explore in *Nothing to Pay*, but the bedrock need of chapel and its imperviousness to criticism were realities freshly brought home to him. "Foolish is the man who kindles his anger against life, for though the flame rage never so hard it cannot scorch even the down on life's garment… sooner will Big Pistyll [spring] go dry than Sion falls." The passage inevitably prompts reflection on Evans's reforming endeavours and the doubts he harboured about the capacity of his or anyone's writings to bring about change. Though his literary disposition was cast, and though throughout the Twenties he remained embroiled in controversy, he was facing up to the pointlessness of railing against human nature as expressed in the ways of Wales. He would lighten the tone, indulge his characters as much as condemn them, and look for once on the bright side.

For whatever reason, work on *Taffy* was abandoned. There might have been problems with plotting, with achieving a satisfactory pitch and tone, since for all its imaginative daring, the novella somehow fails to cohere. Still, a narrative core was salvageable, and late in 1922 Evans began to recast it as a play. Friends had persuaded him to do so, he told the *Daily Sketch* (22 February 1923), and much of the writing he had undertaken on his regular train journey between Mortlake and Waterloo, or else in a Fleet Street pub during evening breaks from the *Daily Mirror*. A little sherry eased the labour: "I like sherry. It makes me feel a diawl [devil] of a fellow." He needed fortification, for though he enjoyed the theatre and possessed a playwright's instinct for dialogue, his "play of Welsh village life in three acts" did not come easily and he was never convinced of its worth. "Do you think it funny?" he asked at an early rehearsal, waving a dog-eared script; "I don't." It was as if he'd written the piece fifty times before any actor set eyes on it.[5]

For theatre presentation Evans jettisoned the novel's more arresting elements; he wanted an accessible piece that would hold a popular audience. So he chose the business of warring deacons, the preaching match for Sion's pulpit, and the competing strategies of Ester and Marged. "Taffy" the play becomes more clearly the love story of Spurgeon and Marged, a hero and a heroine who become partners romantically and in their resolve for religious reform.

A matinee performance of *Taffy* was the brainchild of H. Dennis Bradley (1878-1934). Essayist, satirist and wit, he enjoyed another life as director of Pope and Bradley, civil and military tailors. It was Bradley's unconventional style of advertising that first caught public attention: his pungent mini-essays mixed sharp-edged social comment with praise of his Bond Street clothes. Bradley dramatized all his viewpoints, and his strong opinions on the conduct of the war brought him to Caradoc's notice. "The wickedest, the most damnable traitor to the country is the food profiteer," Bradley raged; "even with higher wages, the poor can barely get enough to eat, and prices have been allowed to soar to such a scandalous extent that the wives and children of our soldiers, the men for whom we at home are trustees, are robbed and starved."[6] His words might have been lifted from an *Ideas* editorial column, and Bradley was indeed encouraged to write for Evans's weekly. But he cannily turned instead to the columns of the national press, printing forthright pieces at his own expense in the knowledge that, classed as advertising copy, they would mostly bypass the censor.

In politics he and Evans were opposites – Bradley feared socialism – but other bonds united them. "An idealist, although he loves to call himself a cynic," said Evans of Bradley, the reformer with passion enough to press his views against the weight of the times. It was his quasi-religious mission that Evans emphasized in the forward he provided for Bradley's third book, *Adam and Eve* (1923). Again, Evans's picture of a fierce Old Testament prophet might be taken as another self-portrait:

> Maybe he sat for years in his room near the sky, his eyes, like God's, on the street below; and the voice of God came to him, firing him with the command: "Tell the House of Israel of their sins, and the House of Jacob of their transgressions."
>
> This he does and with amazing courage and impudence – the courage and impudence that are conceived in belief. No prophet has bade people turn from their naughty ways with more scorn than that which Dennis Bradley lashes cant, humbug, and civilisation, and no Solomon has spoken more profoundly about woman.

"Mr Bradley knows her more completely than any living writer," ran Evans's earlier preface to *The Eternal Masquerade* (1922), where Bradley spoke of the abyss between men and women as the result of man in his "arrogant weakness" failing to comprehend the nature of woman. Man conjures up an idol of glass, "and assumes the power to crush it into fragments with his feet of clay":

> But woman is an individual. She disdains a category... She has seen the ghastly chaos man has made by his savage policy of destruction. And in the future, with the maternal

instinct of her sex, she will enter the arena to preserve the civilisation for which she
is responsible and save man from himself.

   And when woman's sphere of action is developed, man may arrive at the truth
of sex. For woman – understanding man's weaknesses, smiling at his sentimentality
and loving his passion, loathing his viciousness and revelling in his adoration – knows
his incapacity to bear the burden of truth and has fed him only on the transparent
lies he has hitherto craved.

Evans too looked to women for direction, for the way to a better future – their qualities
might help achieve so much – only to be disappointed by the actuality: how women,
"revelling in adoration", lay waste their gifts.

   As to West End drama, Bradley's taste and judgments made him open to Evans's
approach. The English favoured anaemia and artificiality whereas his Irish compatriots
– Bradley was a Galway man – painted life in all its vivid emotion; Synge made one fall
in love again with the theatre. And Evans had Irish qualities; his *Taffy* deserved a showing.
A playwright himself, and something of an impresario (he had sponsored productions
of Rabindranath Tagore), Bradley agreed to finance a top-flight production of *Taffy* as a
single charity performance in aid of the Actors' Association. He managed a casting *coup*
by enlisting Edith Evans at a time when, in the words of her biographer J.C. Trewin,
she was "scattering gold all over the place". Many thought her Welsh – she was not –
but Bradley judged her the perfect Marged and around her he and his producer Miles
Malleson assembled a strong, sympathetic cast that included (as Ester) Hannah Jones,
daughter-in-law of the composer Joseph Parry. Malleson, author of radical pamphlets
and a stream of "plays with a purpose", was also an actor-producer whose familiarity
with Shakespeare comedy gave him a line on *Taffy*.

   The charity matinee of *Taffy* (26 February 1923) drew to the Prince of Wales
theatre an audience no less brilliant than the cast. H.G. Wells took a box; Mrs Lloyd
George sat in the stalls, a little in front of Margot Asquith; Berta Ruck and Augustus
John looked on from the dress circle, John having made it known how enormously he
admired Caradoc Evans. Author-friends arrived in support – Mary Webb, Edwin Pugh,
Edith Nepean (who had designed Edith Evans's dresses) – as did fellow journalists
Hannen Swaffer and T.W.H. Crosland. More than thirty critics covered the occasion,
including W.A. Darlington of the *Telegraph* and James Agate, bright new star of the
Saturday Review. The theatre was filled to capacity, even the standing areas; "the reputation
of Mr Caradoc Evans as a satirist of his own people unmatched in English literature
since Swift, drew intellectual and artistic London in serried ranks," reported the *Westminster Gazette*.[7] But not all had come to praise, as one scrutinizer of the play had
anticipated. "I do not think it is the business of the Lord Chamberlain to interfere with
a Welshman's attacks on certain of his compatriots and their attitude to religion," judged
the censor George S. Street in recommending a licence for *Taffy*; "The play can hardly
be expected to make a popular appeal: so far as it is known to them it will naturally
be resented by the sort of Welshmen pilloried, but I do not think they are entitled to
prevent its appearance."[8]

The press caught wind of trouble and, sure enough, soon after lunch on the Monday afternoon a boisterous London-Welsh contingent, with students to the fore, had crowded the gallery determined to make their protest. As the orchestra concluded its all-Welsh medley and curtain rose on the white-washed walls of Capel Sion a rumpus broke out; and each of the play's three acts closed to a chorus of catcalls. Between times (so the *Sunday Express* reported) "whenever the author got one home on the jaw", the gallery "booed in a melodious manner". Cries of "shame" and "rubbish" greeted Spurgeon's big Act III speech, though applause from the stalls countered abuse from the gods. Occasionally, the audience came together in approval (at Marged's denunciation of the greed and chicanery of the deacons, most notably) and at her every entrance Edith Evans calmed the tumult. She had been instrumental, it was afterwards agreed, in keeping the occasion largely within the bounds of good humour. Nevertheless, the final curtain descended to shouts of "traitor!" and chants of "We want Ca-ra-doc!"

> It was a jeer, but they shouted it as though they wanted the author's blood. Caradoc Evans took his call courageously; he looked singularly unperturbed, as the applause of the many well-known people in the front failed to drown the yelling from the gods. "Who won the war? Lloyd George!" shouted somebody else. "Three cheers for Lloyd George!"[9]

Hannen Swaffer thought he saw Mrs Lloyd George crying, while behind her Mrs Asquith's behaviour struck Beverley Baxter as eminently discreet ("she was probably thinking of a Liberal reunion").[10] Backstage, an excited Mary Webb rushed to congratulate Caradoc; her companion Edwin Pugh thought it might have been the first time she had seen a properly produced play; she nibbled chocolate throughout and relished her interval tea. Obligingly, Caradoc introduced her to the cast.[11]

Following a single theatrical performance Evans awoke a minor celebrity. "I was greatly moved by it," wrote Augustus John next morning, "it was beautifully acted and in every way a success."[12] Margot Asquith likewise thanked the author for a most enjoyable play ("tho' I think the 1st act was a little long"), and invited him to lunch at Bedford Square.[13] On 3 March he spontaneously became the guest of honour at a dinner of the Savage Club (a Bohemian fraternity with a fair sprinkling of writers and journalists); a Welsh evening (close to St David's Day), it turned into a celebration of the author of *Taffy*. Within a short time the "Big Head" phrase, used of the chapel deacons, gained new currency in the language – all proof that a play puts an author on the map as readily as any novel. Words unexceptional on the page can catch fire in a crowded auditorium – witness the comedy of the scheming deacons, often tedious to read, but played to continuous chuckles. Not only words strike home. James Agate eloquently instanced Twmi in Act 2 rising slowly from his sick bed to move across the room:

> There was visible, palpable irony in the monstrous spectacle – a mountain of flesh voiding his spiritual rheum in patriarchal accent and gesture, a petitioner of Heaven,

cloaked mightily in wide-flung blankets like a terrifying figure of Blake, offering a
negligible soul. There was theatre here, something you could see and touch, something
which the printed page must have denied.[14]

Agate thought *Taffy* too homiletic for commercial success, a viewpoint shared by the
English Review, whose critic nonetheless praised the play as an antidote to the trash that
since the war had blighted the West End stage. "We saw live men. We heard live words.
We left more alive than when we entered the theatre."[15] As for Edith Evans, "the masterful
and passionate personality of the girl [Marged] flowed from her with an intensity that
dominated the stage". Gallery wrath had no impact: "she rode the whirlwind and directed
the storm".[16]

"There is a chapel on every road in Wales," Marged warns Spurgeon, who innocently
believes that by abandoning Sion he can escape all that the chapel stands for. English
roads are likewise marked, reflected the *Nation* (3 March 1923), as are roads throughout
the world where men and women live in community. *Taffy*, like all good satire, had a
more than local application. Understandably, critics in Wales could not agree. "Everything
we hold in reverence, and all that we have ever felt to be sacred, are burlesqued, ridiculed
and mocked," wrote one *Western Mail* correspondent; "To use our preachers – the finest
in the world – deacons, and *yr hen dadau* [the founding fathers], as objects of amusement
to a London crowd is beyond disgust," thought another. Much was made of the fashionable
audience, "prominent society people and… prominent writers, male and female. The
cream of England might be said to have been in the theatre, and they were all 'taken
in'."[17] In all, *Taffy* lent extra fervour to the 1923 St David's Day celebrations. At Cardiff,
Wil Ifan saw the play as "riding on English race hatred",[18] while J.R. Llewellyn, president
of the Barry Cymmrodorion Society, was reminded of the bill to flood the Ceiriog
Valley.[19]

Within days Evans had issued his response, an article in the *Sunday Express* (4 March
1923) requiring an editorial distancing the paper from the article's viewpoints. The
piece reworks Evans's polemical preface "The Welsh People" (in the American *My
Neighbors*) with all incest references deleted. In essence it confirmed the conviction that
"We are what we have been made by our preachers and politicians":

> Jealous of his trust, the preacher has made rules for the salvation of our bodies and
> souls. Temptations such as art, drama, dancing, and the study of folklore he has
> removed from our way. Those are vanities, which make men puffed up and collections
> small. Look you, the preacher asks, do they not cost money? Are they not time
> wasters? My capel needs your money, boys bach, that the light – the grand, spiritual
> light – shall shine in the pulpit.
>
>   That is the lamp which burns throughout Wales, from Criccieth to Cardigan Bay.
> It keeps our feet from Church door and public house, and guides us to the polling
> booth where we record our votes as the preacher has commanded us. Be the season
> never so hard and be men and women never so hungry, its flame does not wane and
> the oil in its vessel must never run low…"[20]

The "Criccieth to Cardigan Bay" reference alludes to the shrinking domain of his Liberal opponents – in the November 1922 election Liberals lost disastrously to Labour in the industrial south. Yet if *Taffy* reflects Evans's optimism at a Welsh political awakening, it was becoming increasingly clear that his brand of radicalism, with its post-*Taffy* talk of fewer chapels and better schools (more cowsheds even), struck no chord with incoming parliamentarians, some of whom were lay preachers and temperance devotees. Morgan Jones (Labour MP for Caerphilly) denounced "the liar of Wales" whose work was "vile and vicious, sordid and silly". He assured *Llais Llafur / Labour Voice* that Evans's outpourings, however intended, were proving harmful to Wales ("in parliamentary circles this [is] quite noticeable").

The Evans abuse continued. The *Western Mail* and *South Wales Daily News* printed compendia of adverse criticism (culled from overwhelmingly favourable national notices) and both ran long articles by the Revd Arthur Sturdy, an inveterate Evans stalker.[21] There is something fascinating in Sturdy's relentless pursuit. Now vicar of Ton Pentre, he recalled how to his childhood eyes the hills of Lampeter "were holding up the roof of heaven" and (in lines that could have been John Crowther's) his native Cardiganshire "A home where exiled angels might forebear / Awhile to moan for paradise." This Cardiganshire, as Sturdy elaborates, seems not a world away from the Evans country. Daily warfare against unyielding mountain land encouraged a religion "tinctured with morbidity", drawing more from the calamities of the Old Testament than the glad tidings of the New. Yes, its Puritanism told grievously against Welsh art, drama and music but (Sturdy insists), "I can appreciate the rugged nobility of the Puritan", a quality conspicuously lacking in Evans's "miasmal progeny". Sturdy accepts the author's sincerity of purpose but not his aesthetic premise. "It is one of the functions of literature and the stage not to depict life but to provide a means of escape from life as we know it." He recognised a kind of twisted patriotism, one that speaks proudly of "my people" while fouling its own nest.

Closer still to home, first leader in the *Cardigan and Tivy-Side Advertiser* (2 March 1923) suggested "A Tragedy of a Welsh Pervert" as a suitable sub-title for *Taffy* and its "freaks exhibited for the delectation of a London crowd". The paper published the condemnation of Captain Ernest Evans, the local Liberal MP (before the Manchester Welsh Society) and some hostile letters, one of them assuring readers, "– and I am in a position to know – that the nearest approach to "intellectuals" among whom Caradoc Evans has any standing are those who constitute the lower levels of "Bohemia" and the modern equivalents of Grub Street". But for concentrated abuse, the American-Welsh took some beating, their Pittsburgh mouthpiece, the *Druid* (15 April 1923), suggesting that Evans could be taught a wholesome lesson by the Ku Klux Klan. And should he ever contemplate an American tour, there were "enough Welshmen in the anthracite region to make it so hot for him that he will conclude that he has eventually reached the place for which he is destined".[22]

Meanwhile, lunch with the Asquiths at Bedford Square (6 March) had proved a gloomy affair, Evans finding it difficult to wrestle any booze from the former prime minister ("Asquith drank a bottle of port all to himself… I might as well not have been there"). Back in Rhydlewis it fuelled the rumour that Herbert Asquith had financed *Taffy*, counting any denigration of the Welsh as injurious to Lloyd George Coalition Liberals. As for the other ex-prime minister, he assuredly loathed Caradoc Evans. Reviewing events at the Prince of Wales for the *Sunday Express* (4 March), its managing editor Beverley Baxter recalled how over dinner at the time of *My People* Lloyd George made plain his opinion of Evans. "Pride of race belongs to the lowest savage. This man is a renegade."

"The Best-Hated Man in Wales"

1923-25

B ehind the glare of *Taffy*, Evans's career in Fleet Street took another major turn. By summer 1923 he had left the *Mirror* and daily journalism for the more leisurely world of the weeklies. The move came through Cassell's, a substantial publishing enterprise with editorial offices at 9 La Belle Sauvage Yard on Ludgate Hill. Newman Flower worked as a literary editor there, overseeing the book-publishing programme. He had joined the firm originally to bolster its profitable periodicals business, and it was with a new journal in mind that he recruited Caradoc Evans. *Cassell's Weekly* owed its existence to a chance remark at a cricket match involving some London-based writers and critics. Wasn't there room, one of them asked, for an informal weekly that would show the literary world off-duty?[1] Flower sensed an opening and in March 1923 launched his middle-brow literary magazine. Early issues promised well. Arnold Bennett, Edmund Blunden, Liam O'Flaherty and Rebecca West all featured as contributors, Bennett (on character-drawing) prompting a response from Virginia Woolf in T.S. Eliot's *Criterion*. Ernest Newman covered music; Middleton Murry wrote on Hardy, Catherine Carswell on D.H. Lawrence, while Lorenzo himself in Taos supplied his impressions of New Mexico. Some Oscar Wilde letters were unearthed.

By August, Flower's name had vanished from the masthead as a new editor was eased into place. Improbable though it seemed, T.P. O'Connor, veteran journalist and parliamentarian, founder-editor of the *Star* (the London evening newspaper), was eager, even at eighty, to direct a literary journal once again. He set his sights on a revived *T.P.'s Weekly*, the penny paper he had launched some twenty years previously and which during its lifetime (1902-16) achieved a circulation of 100,000. Over the years "Tay Pay" had become something of an institution, father of the House of Commons where he'd sat since 1880, mostly as Nationalist representative of Liverpool's Irish population. O'Connor wedded politics and journalism, and it was the accomplished journalist that Evans most admired. "How many book-writers can turn out anything half as good as T.P. O'Connor's obituary notices in the *Daily Telegraph* And T.P. reels them off without a note or work of reference."[2] Yet his business judgements were shaky, an admitted weakness that drew him into partnership with Cassell's. He would edit a re-titled *T.P. and Cassell's Weekly* but with the continued backing of the publishers. This arrangement suited T.P. who, in Evans's opinion, "never had enough money all at once to start a parish magazine. Besides, it would be against his policy to put money into any newspaper he edited."[3] With an August date for change-over less than a week away, Flower invited five of Cassell's staff to help put together the first issue of the re-styled paper. Evans was among them –

"thrown at"T.P. (so he saw it) by a man "disappointed I was not public school or university".

In the board room at La Belle Sauvage the newly deputed staff awaited T.P.'s arrival. It was after lunch when he showed, a moment that stayed with Evans because,

> We all did an unusual thing. We rose. A working journalist does not let respect interfere with the job he is doing. "Sit down, bhoys," said T.P., sitting at the end of the table. He always said bhoys and filum and laddo to prove he was a simple Irishman. He sat down for about an hour and pretended to be editor and took snuff. His snuff-box was constantly in and out of his waistcoat pocket. I was a thrifty person and deplored the snuff he wasted on his moustache, chin, and waistcoat; and when he left his bit of table was brown with snuff.

As T.P.'s pretence of editorship became even thinner – the first Labour government had made him a Privy Counsellor – so the role of acting editor quietly devolved to Caradoc. It was a natural development, given his interests and background, and one that suited him well. He warmed particularly to Tay Pay. As he told the *Sunday Express* (drapery-store memories stirring),

> I am glad because when I meet my editor I do not tremble in the fear that something like the judgement of God may fell me at any moment. Rather to feel joyous, for always am I greeted thus: "Good morning, Caradoc, my boy. I am glad to see you."[4]

The move into literary journalism might be supposed to have landed Evans within more congenial Fleet Street circles but this was not wholly the case. He knew the petty jealousies, the tittle-tattle and back-biting, surrounding men like Hilaire Belloc, G.K. Chesterton and J.C. Squire. It was a world of shifting alliances and ill-disguised animosities. The Irish poet Austin Clarke, later to join Evans on *T.P.'s Weekly*, judged Jack Squire, long-time editor of the resolutely anti-modernist *London Mercury*, the most powerful literary figure in Fleet Street. Each day Squire took lunch at Poppin's, the Red Lion in Poppin's Court, a discreet little pub in a tiny alley running north of Fleet Street at the Ludgate Circus end:

> He stood in the corner by the counter there, munching ham sandwiches, his tipple beside him. Among the constant writers and critics who surrounded him were Edward Shanks, Edmund Blunden, J.B. Priestley, "Tommy" Pope, John Freeman, Alan Porter, Edward Davidson, J.M. Turner and H.M. Tomlinson. Stocky, red-farmer-faced Hilaire Belloc arrived at times, looking down contemptuously on all newcomers. Here was the most influential coterie in London and it was known jocosely to those who feared it as the Squirearchy. Its leader ... assumed the manner and opinions of John Bull himself...[5]

Clarke does not mention J.B. Morton, another Fleet Street character, about to succeed Wyndham Lewis as Beachcomber of the *Daily Express*. Evans seems to have fallen out with him, unsurprisingly so if Reginald Pound's description is to be believed: "He is Harrow and Oxford and often behaves like Borstal and Parkhurst."[6]

But if Morton could be difficult, so too could Evans. A grim personality, Sewell Stokes confirmed, remarking how in conversation Evans's "bright eyes, set in a rugged face, stare relentlessly at the speaker. It seems that they follow all that is being said and are only waiting for the opportunity to destroy it."[7] Stokes felt that the man had become embittered, distrustful of anyone who would be his friend. Yet, "I have seen him stop in the street, and hunt through his pockets to find coppers for a small boy who was begging from him and whenever he is doing what he feels to be important writing he has his dog curled up at his feet. Almost as if he found true companionship with those with whom he could not quarrel." The writer Con O'Leary, yet another Irishman on the staff of *T.P.s Weekly*, believed Stokes had penetrated to "the wistfulness and charm of manner" behind the craggy Welsh exterior.[8] He congratulated the young essayist – Stokes was just twenty-one and had included a vignette of Evans in his book *Personal Glimpses* (1924) – on his "affectionate insight into the very heart of a man of genius who all his life has had to stand alone". Evans was an acquired taste, with but one or two close friendships.

Closest at this time must have been Arthur Machen. The two Welshmen had known each other since 1912, when Evans was advancing in journalism and Machen, fifteen years his senior, worked as an *Evening News* reporter. Machen was a Celt in his own terms, an identification which shaped his religious and artistic outlook and conferred a sense of personal apartness strange in so sociable a man. (To a Portuguese acquaintance, Luis Marques, he recommended Welsh for its salutary effects on the mind: "Why not learn Welsh and enter a territory wholly strange and wonderful?") A devotee of the lost Celtic Church, Machen shared something of Evans's attitude to Welsh Nonconformity. He recognized the *farceur* in Evans, but had publicized *My People* and was "very far from saying that his violent attack is void of foundation".[9] In turn, Caradoc admired Arthur Machen, both as a person and a writer. Much in their backgrounds united them. Lack of money drove Machen out of education, and he too had struggled alone in London, subsisting as a publisher's clerk and a children's tutor. His flight into journalism came late, beyond an age when he could romanticize the profession. Fleet Street was "not really a nice street", its routines inimical to his habits as author: whatever the deprivations of the earlier London years, he had the conditions for writing – solitude and silence, preferably in the waste hours of the night. Leaving book-writing for journalism was like moving from eternity into time: a quota of words to be hammered out in a room with a half-dozen others (each with a telephone) and always with one eye on the clock. Yet perhaps his finest book, the autobiographical *Far Off Things* (1922), was written as a newspaper serial, and critics have rightly remarked the benefits of disciplined journalism on a style prone to over-elaboration. Evans would continually argue that the Fleet Street English of his day was sounder than that of most novelists ("it is simpler and more lucid and less hackneyed"), and it follows that he praised Machen's best writing for its journalistic strengths. "Look at H. G. Wells and Arthur Machen and Gorki and Tolstoy and Maupassant: they read like inspired reporting."[10]

Yet the two of them drifted apart. In February 1924 Machen tried to broker a deal over Evans's manuscripts, assuring the bookseller and minor publisher Harry Spurr (of Spurr & Swift) that Caradoc had kept everything. Evans lost interest in the negotiations, as he did in Machen's weekly gathering of writers and journalists at a wine lodge under Ludgate Viaduct. "It is ill to despise friends," Machen admonished him (2 May 1924), "and he who neglects them despises them. You know we meet every Saturday at Sherriffs at 2 pm, but you have not been there since Dydd Dewi Sant."[11] Three weeks later he was discounting Evans's excuses: "And such nonsense about Morton! He has not been near the place for a month & is a Belloc man not a Squire man, and I believe will now be out of town every weekend." But Evans dropped by the wayside and out of Machen's life – to the older man's genuine regret. "Caradoc and I were always the best of friends," he wrote to Evans's widow; "Emphatically, we got on together. I remember a man saying, that when I would hesitate, and remark 'I don't think I should care to do that at all', a word from Caradoc would immediately produce smiling assent. I am sure that was quite true. He was a rare fellow."[12]

The pattern of broken friendships became familiar. Evans never could sustain them, and others who enjoyed his company – Duncan Davies, W.H. Davies, Thomas Burke – found contact puzzlingly terminated. No one could come too close. Duncan Davies wondered whether he'd given offence, Machen's letters got no reply, and Evans inexplicably failed to get in touch with W.H. Davies when, briefly, he became the poet's close neighbour in a village near Stroud. Not that Evans's regard for these former friends diminished; indeed, Machen was the only living writer whom the drama critic Raymond Marriott ever heard him praise unreservedly. He admired Machen's integrity, his devotion to literature ("the passage into paradise"), his commitment to the truth of his vision.

If he accepted Machen's mysticism, he warmed appreciably to H. Dennis Bradley's study of spiritualism, an enthusiasm shared by many at the time, including Hannen Swaffer, the fearless *People* columnist and another drinking companion. Evans thought Dennis Bradley a "commonsense spiritualist" who pursued his psychical research in the belief that it would bring hope and comfort to countless ordinary folk. Bradley persuaded him to join in the séances arranged for George Valiantine, an American medium brought to England at the beginning of 1924. During a five-week spell Valiantine held sittings with some fifty influential people – writers, editors (Austin Harrison among them), artists, doctors, scientists – usually in parties of eight invited to Dorincourt, the Bradleys' home in Kingston Vale. There on three occasions Caradoc and Rose Evans met Valiantine – each time with startling results. On 3 February Evans inspected the medium's ectoplasm, pronouncing it a slimy, frothy bladder "into which you could dig a finger but through which you could not pierce".[13] At a sitting ten days later the deceased Edward Wright, Evans's earliest Fleet Street workmate, came through to Caradoc and Rose, claiming to have attended the matinée performance of *Taffy* and complimenting Miles Malleson (present at this sitting) on a fine production. February 27 produced a yet more spectacular exchange, one which stunned the company (it included Newman Flower, another with spiritualist leanings). A voice, described by Evans as struggling up through the floor between his feet, spoke directly in front of his face. It was the voice of his father and it spoke to him in Welsh.[14] Their exchange made the *Western Mail*, as it did more specialist outlets. All students of metapsychics are familiar with it, wrote Ernest Bozzano in his *Polyglot Mediumship (Xenoglossy)* (1932), because it stood as incontrovertible evidence of "xenoglossy" – the ability to speak a language without prior contact with or study of it. Valiantine had lived continuously in the United States and knew no word of Welsh.[15]

Other extraordinary sessions followed. In July 1924 a quiet dinner party at the Bradleys turned into another sitting. First the table began to levitate, "pushing itself against Mr Evans's chest, and raising itself supernormally, eventually rest[ing] on his head". Once more Edward Wright came through; as he did at the end of September when Caradoc and Rose were again at Doricourt. This time he was followed by Freda, the spirit of a lively young girl who sat on Evans's lap and repeatedly kissed him on the cheek. It appears to have been Evans's last sitting, though friends like Swaffer, his atheism crumbling, kept up attendance, as did Radclyffe Hall, Lady Una Troubridge, and others of the Society of Psychical Research. How seriously did Evans take all this? Caught up in the fashionable taste for spiritualism, he had mingled with believers at the Albert Hall, yet "I might have been a bit bosky [tipsy]", he confessed, alluding to his evenings with Bradley; "I wouldn't like to give evidence about it." He returned to events at Dorincourt, privately, in his journal, at a time when his second wife Marguerite was mourning her mother's death:

> Last night we talked of life after death, survival of personality; the Bradley sittings and my own experiences when I said that I heard my father speak to me in Welsh and a spirit came and sat upon my knee and kissed me with its kisses and I felt its moist breath that could only be the breath of life upon my cheek. If it was the breath of life it was not a spirit. After these many years I cannot with truth say that I am so convinced. I cannot trick her [Marguerite] in the face of such sorrow. A man's voice addressed me in Welsh. That much is true, but I would not recognize my father's voice. He died when I was a very young child. It is possible there was a fraud – and not necessarily with Bradley's knowledge. Bradley was credulous.

Evans mentions that a grateful Bradley gave him £100 for knocking one of his books into shape (*The Wisdom of the Gods*), and around this time he had a say in another manuscript when, after reading for Andrew Melrose *Little Calvary (Calvaria Fach)*, "a romance of Welsh life", he recommended publication and a sizeable advance for its author Sydney Griffith. When the novel appeared in October 1924 it carried an unusual preface expressing the publisher's delight at having at last been able to provide an antidote to *My People*. The basis of Evans's approval can only be surmised – *John O'London's* thought the story "Celtic and nebulous … the strong beautiful character of Mam shines through like a sunshaft" – but more than once he applauded Welsh fiction that was diametrically opposed to his own. Introduced to Griffith in Melrose's dark-panelled Covent Garden office, he opened the conversation in Welsh. Griffith confessed that though living in Cardigan he was actually a settler from England. Had he known that, he would have advised a smaller advance, Evans joked.[16]

In the immediate post-*Taffy* period Evans did a little writing of his own, producing a playful piece for Tommy Pope, who like Caradoc, found himself running a journal nominally edited by another. The Catholic monthly *Illustrated Review* was launched in July 1923 under Hilaire Belloc's editorship, with Pope serving as deputy. Despite encouraging sales, Belloc soon lost interest in the paper (though not in the salary), leaving Pope to assemble three subsequent issues. For July Evans submitted "The Coffin", a beguiling exercise in fantasy revolving around the widow Ann who, having married Captain Shacob, "fattened wondrously; her flesh almost choking her, she was wont in hot weather to throw up her hands and scream that she was dying". Taking her at her word, Shacob negotiates a deal with Lloyd the carpenter whereby Shacob will pay for the coffin the day after her death. But Ann refuses to die, and as she increases in bulk so her coffin has repeatedly to be enlarged, in time becoming a handy play-pen for her grandchildren. "There are no fires and damnation here," said one delighted critic, "death meets life and they nod and walk together." "The Coffin" gained instant recognition, being chosen by Edward J. O'Brien and John Cournos for their *Best Short Stories of 1924* (together with work by L.P. Hartley, Katherine Mansfield, Somerset Maugham, T.F. Powys and Dorothy Richardson). A similar black humour enlivened "Children and News" (*Cassell's Weekly*, 19 May 1923), a contemporaneous sketch cast as autobiography – and revealing of the impulses that first drew Evans to journalism – but memorable for Sam Postman's delivery of letters to Cardiganshire cottages with a knitting-needle pierced through his hat. "His son Abel often companied him on his journeys to unseal the envelopes with the needle and to be instructed in the several ways that Sam dressed up his black and doleful news." But tragedy befalls postman Sam: accused of withholding a postal order and "thinking out a religious answer he drove the needle with which he was fidgeting far into his head".

Evans's creative energies had largely gone to reshaping *Taffy* prior to its publication in book form. A printed edition of the play might have seemed commercially risky but "that epic matinée" (as Berta Ruck described it) had raised a storm of publicity which Melrose thought he might exploit. He made the most of *Taffy: A Play of Welsh Village Life*, published in March 1924. Cased in Oxford blue, its 86 pages bulk large, the last two devoted to praise from 26 theatre critics. A prefatory note explains that the play as printed is "slightly different" from the version staged at the Prince of Wales. This is something of an understatement. Whatever its social success, Evans had come to feel that *Taffy* was artistically flawed, and he seized on a printed version as a chance to put things right.

Taffy, one might mention, was not the only play of Welsh village life before the public at this time. For a decade or more Welsh drama had enjoyed a renaissance, evidenced in a mushrooming of amateur companies and the emergence of a group of Welsh playwrights treating of native subjects. Talk of a Welsh National Theatre was in the air, especially in the circle of Lord Howard de Walden, a sympathetic north Wales patron who nourished hopes of a bilingual company with a repertoire of Welsh plays (he had backed such a venture in 1913). Irish parallels (and the achievements of the

Abbey Theatre) were inevitably invoked as English-language plays by J.O. Francis and Richard Hughes gained performances within and outside Wales. Barely down from Oxford but emerging as an organisational focus for a new theatrical flowering, Hughes insisted that the dramatic strength of Wales lay in its little companies, from which, via regional groupings, the stars of a National Theatre would naturally arise. Meanwhile London blandishments must be resisted. Was not J.O. Francis's *The Dark Little People* hopelessly mangled by an English company in 1923? In a survey for the *Review of Reviews*, Hughes pointedly ignored *Taffy*, choosing instead to slate *My People* as a "cold-blooded and wilful trading on English ignorance, prompted by personal dislike of his fellow-countrymen, and having at most only local application to one or two valleys". Evans's response (June-July 1924) was predictable: "I do not hate my people. I like them well enough to criticize them. I hope my play 'Taffy' proves this."[17]

Like Hughes, Evans was sounded for his views on Welsh drama.[18] He agreed that the Welsh were naturally talented, though with a fatal tendency to overact and neglect good teamwork. Addressing a Saturday afternoon gathering at the University of London (24 May 1924), Evans amusingly elaborated on his compatriots' dramatic gifts. Theatricality was a distinctively Welsh attribute: the propensity to take the word for the deed, to assume the mantle of the poet, the prophet or the politician. "Our whole life is a stage play. We do not reveal ourselves on our own hearths or on our deathbeds, or even to ourselves…We have acted so long that we have lost ourselves and are wearing the misty skin of someone that never was… We are the real play-boys of the Western World."[19] Evans's talk made *The Times* of 26 May, the day the *Western Mail* provided some lengthy extracts. They proved to be but an appetizer for a more provocative airing of another favourite Evans theme. In the *Western Mail* (2 June 1924) came "A Tilt at the Eisteddfod", an 800-word essay that would prompt the paper's most strenuous effort to dethrone "our most brilliant but misguided countryman". The Eisteddfod, Evans wrote, appeals "to our apishness, to our love of play-acting":

> Therefore our little bards and little singers; and nearly everybody in Wales is one or the other. And often both imagine that by taking part in these clowning and crowning ceremonies they are big bards and singers. But, alas for their vanity! Having won their prizes they scurry home to their pulpits and shops and are heard of no more beyond their own villages.

The petit-bourgeois basis of Welsh cultural life, the association of literature with competitions and cash prizes, the easy assumption of greatness ("one cannot be a bard merely by putting on druidical robes… great art is born of misery and pain"), these were worries shared by others within the ranks of Welsh writers, but an attack from the author of *My People* on their "clowning and crowning ceremonies" was altogether different. And how Evans had taken to his task:

> The National Eisteddfod is an ill-managed circus. There is no spiritual profit to be got out of it. It feeds the conceit of its promoters (who are mostly political agents)

and the money tills of the proprietors of hotels, boarding houses and public-houses.
But it does give us the opportunity of hearing the sound of our own voices and lauding
ourselves to the uttermost. And a self-lauder is one to whom no praise is due.

A predictable correspondence followed, interesting for a letter from the surviving
brother of Allen Raine remarking that the well-loved novelist, though not ignorant of
Welsh faults and failings, had "preferred culling the flowers at the river banks to stirring
the mud at the bottom".[20]

This was as nothing compared with what the *Western Mail* had in store. Its editor
William Davies was taken by Evans's cultural analysis but disturbed by its sardonic
expression in the nationally circulating dailies – and the London press eagerly seized
on whatever Evans had to say about Wales.[21] Davies would not stand by and see his
country debased in the eyes of others. Evans must be exposed as a wholly unreliable
witness. For this task he selected John Tudor Jones (the poet and editor John Eilian), an
Anglesey man, Oxford-educated, and at the start of his journalistic career. Davies
suggested that he spend a week in Rhydlewis preparing what would be the most comprehensive assault on Evans that the *Mail* had ever launched. Jones's earlier pieces for
the newspaper are sprinkled with Evans references: how a nationalist in a Cardiff
bookstore expressed horror at his attempt to buy *My People*; and how R.J. Berry, dramatist
and Congregationalist minister, had been far more sympathetic, denying that Evans was
simply after the money ("somebody must have oppressed him rather severely in some
way or other"). One might add that in 1922 Berry published "The Wrath of Hosea", a
rendition of the first stanza of "Mary had a Little Lamb" in the style of Caradoc Evans.[22]
The 1920s produced at least three parodies of Caradoc Evans and Berry's has some nice
touches. Evans wrote to congratulate him – like a village cricketer being praised by a
Test player, Berry flatteringly replied.[23]

The *Western Mail* was beyond such pleasantry. It trumpeted J.T. Jones on Rhydlewis
– Evans's people as they really are, not as in the pages of *My People*. Ostensibly on
holiday, Jones had moved quietly among them, photographing haymakers, enjoying
local dramatics, questioning an extra-mural lecturer who conducted classes in the
village. His true mission became apparent only when four linked articles appeared in
the *Western Mail* (17, 18, 19 and 22 July 1924), each prominently positioned on the
editorial page.

Jones reached Henllan station on a cheerless July evening. "Rain was falling mer-
cilessly when I alighted from the train, and I had to complete the remainder of the
journey in a Ford car. I shall not forget very soon the journey in that rolling and
pitching motor car along those dented and narrow rain-swept roads." Arriving at the
village he finds no room at the inn; indeed, he finds no inn; anyone requiring strong
drink has to walk two miles for it. "Few do this," says Jones, "for the people are sober
and self-respecting. Mr. Caradoc Evans himself when at home, so I was told, is one of
the few that sometimes tramp two miles." In place of the pub is a YMCA hut – "from
which, by the way, even young ladies are not completely barred" – a venue for public
meetings, concerts, plays, lectures and evening classes. Here are "a people to whom

culture is very life". "They hunger and thirst after education," agreed Ifan ab Owen Edwards (son of O.M. Edwards and founder of the Welsh League of Youth), who held extra-mural classes there. The villagers "live 'the religion of the helping hand' with all their hearts and souls," Jones concluded, for they have been guided by men "of noble character, of highest intellectual attainments, and of qualities in every way outstanding". Caradoc's minister and his schoolteacher, for instance: "Mr. Adams and Mr. Crowther… A great respect for them still remains in the district." As for the author, "the strong, silent men of Rhydlewis regard him as beneath contempt… Only one thing perplexes me now, and that is how such a pervert as Mr. Caradoc Evans can ever have risen from among such people."

The assault sent Wales into raptures. For *Seren Cymru* and *Y Darian* it was a necessary demolition job, since Evans was providing "a feast for the English, who love to live on filth".[24] J. Dyfnallt Owen, poet and Congregationalist minister, expressed his "deepest appreciation" of the *Western Mail's* service to Wales: J.T. Jones's articles were the first coherent answer to Caradoc Evans "based on a thorough knowledge of Welsh life". John Crowther likewise gave thanks: Evans's characters existed "only in the perverted imagination of the author". One of Evans's relations offered a less fevered response. From Broniwan, Rhydlewis, David Powell writes that his cousin's books "pictured with tenfold exaggeration some remarkable characters, perhaps known to him years ago in the days of his youth, while Mr. Jones was content with a few passing glances"; had Jones made a closer study, he might have discovered things less agreeable to write about, and thereby "done us good service". Most locals cared not one whit whether Evans likened them to beasts of the forest, or Jones to angels from heaven. As for Caradoc's books, Rhydlewis thought them "a huge joke".[25]

Evans responded with relish, first explaining to *The People*, a popular Sunday newspaper, that the nearest Rhydlewis pub was indeed two miles away – through the fields.[26] It was less by road.

> I go there by the road; the villagers creep by the hedges in the fields and they do their drinking in the small pigsty or cow house at the back of the inn… I drink in the inn because of the peaceful company I find there. If I wanted a riot I would get a heap of it at chapel. Perhaps I would join the night gang, the chief purpose of the members of which is to uproot their enemies' apple trees, smash windows, and coat doors with dung or coal tar. Last August the enemy was one of the two preachers in Rhydlewis.

The *People* interview set the tone for his *Western Mail* reply (28 July), which begins with Jones's arrival at the village:

> On a rainy night the people of Rhydlewis heard the sound of a motor-car on the Henllan road, whereupon some moved to their doors and some stood at their windows, all stretching their necks, widening their nostrils, and opening their eyes; and when the car was upon them and they beheld a stranger within, these words issued at their lips: "Who is the boy bach? And what shall we say he wants?"

> The boy bach said his name was J.T. Jones, his home was Anglesey, and his errand
> was to proclaim Rhydlewis the most godly village in the world, and to show up
> Caradoc Evans as a liar, an idiot, and a pervert. Then he said: "Take me to a public-
> house. Even your champion must rest his weary head."

The absurdity of the boy bach's errand, of a twenty-one-year-old grasping the truth of
Rhydlewis on a one-week visit, is sustained throughout the piece. As always, Evans the
polemicist seizes on significant detail, here the fact that Jones was told that the nearest
pub was two miles away, not along the open road but by the villagers' furtive route.
"We Welsh are the pattern which all people should follow. No other people knows God
more completely... We know God cannot watch us in the dark nor see us in strange
places, and he is not acquainted with the uncommon paths. God is the God of the
daylight, the God of the yellow cornfield..."

Y Darian, Seren Cymru, Dyfnallt Owen and John Crowther, all are wittily dispatched
in a second response, but what arrests in Evans's letter of 12 August is his voicing of a
moral imperative against which all criticism is futile:

> Why all this fuss? I am as God made me, and in that condition I shall remain, despite
> the religious curses of Welsh Nonconformity. I do that which my hand is set to do. I
> cannot imagine myself in Mr. Dyfnallt Owen's pulpit any more than I can image Mr.
> Owen writing "Taffy". People who do not know me, people who think they know
> me, people who find delight in hating me, and people who believe they can do better
> than God, say: "He is doing it for advertisement," and "He is doing it for money." I
> do it for neither: I do it because I have got to do it.
>
> What purpose is there in blackguarding and reviling me? Why find fault because
> I write in the most engaging way I know? Is the builder blamed because he builds
> well?

If there was a lovely side to Welsh rural life, someone should try to reveal it. "He will
find in the *Western Mail* a friend – indeed, the only newspaper friend he will find in
Wales."

As if to demonstrate this hospitality, the paper printed a favourable notice of *Taffy*
(the book), contributed by W.J. Gruffydd, Professor of Welsh at Cardiff, editor of the
newly founded cultural quarterly *Y Llenor*, and a determinedly outspoken individual. He
was not ashamed to admit that he had thoroughly enjoyed reading the play and he
regretted not having been privileged to see it performed on the stage. Evans's works
were not essays in realism; they created their own universe, "lit by a sun other than
ours, filled by a deadly air in which normal human beings cannot live". Close on Gruffydd,
and again in the *Western Mail*, came a lengthy well-argued piece by the playwright D.T.
Davies, champion of the Welsh-language theatre movement and, like W.J. Gruffydd, a
man not uncritical of Welsh Nonconformity. Surveying Evans's achievement, he felt
convinced that "We have no one in Wales, with the possible exception of Kate Roberts,
who has treated the short story so adequately as a literary form."[27] As to the "misrepre-
sentations", the truth about Rhydlewis had little to do with the value of the fiction.

"Criticism, a hundred years hence, will be interested in Rhydlewis chiefly as the birthplace of Caradoc Evans, and to the extent that it will shed light on the personality of the author and his work." Evans had been goaded to the point of madness by aspects of Welsh social and religious life. "He has not examined them carefully; he has not understood them. Still he has responded ferociously, blindly and almost obscurely to their stimulus." Taking all the issues of life into account, Davies had to come down on the side of Puritanism and Nonconformity, while accepting that Nonconformist life had "atrophied the aesthetic sense" in many Welsh men and women. "The divorce of the practice and appreciation of art from Welsh life is being realized increasingly. We are becoming more conscious of the attendant void in our spiritual life." Regarding Evans's much criticized idioms, "Considered separately, many of them are absurd and ungainly...Yet a vigorous style is attained, marked by a sense of balance and rhythm, a staggering directness now and then, and, above all, the severest economy." Presciently, Davies sensed a danger: that Caradoc would "attribute his success to the unusual character of his phraseology rather than to his innate gifts as a storyteller"; he was "unnecessarily handicapping himself with the mode which he affects at present." This said, the humour in *Taffy* suggested that he was now in the process of acquiring a truer view of life.

By coincidence, D.T. Davies's essay appeared the morning after Evans's review in the *Cardigan and Tivy-Side Advertiser* (29 August 1924) of two of Davies's plays. On his fortnight's annual holiday Evans had joined some 250 others at the village production of *Y Dieithryn* and *Y Pwyllgor* ("The Stranger" and "The Committee"). "Members of the Rhydlewis Company can act," wrote Caradoc, "but they must remember that the actor finds his characters on the plains of reality and not in the wastes of fiction magazines." The lead actors both succeeded and failed: "succeeded in getting their goods well over the footlights and failed to help the three other members of the cast to do so. Team work is essential in all plays." Still, the performers were better than the plays; *Y Dieithryn*, in particular, struck him as "a sackful of wordy pretentiousness".

Back in London at the end of summer, Evans resumed his public speaking, somewhat surprisingly perhaps, for the Welsh dramatic gift had eluded him. He cut no figure at the podium, his shy, reticent manner being quite at odds with his explosive material. His voice, low and husky, was barely audible from a distance, and his Welsh accent was the strongest Berta Ruck had ever heard from an educated man – "or come to that, from any man. Caradoc was the only person I'd heard pronounce the word 'buns' (he handed them at tea) as 'bunce'."[28] On Friday 7 November, he stood to address the Literary and Debating Society of University College, Bangor. He spoke of a nation ground down by cold-hearted religiosity, of the poisoned spiritual inheritance of people such as himself, born into rural Wales.

> I write down our condition to the tyranny of the preachers and the Liberal politicians. They have not only robbed us and given us a god of their own likeness – a god who imparts neither charity nor love – but they have dominated us for so many generations that they have fashioned our mind. They have built a wall about us. Within that wall

> – within the Nonconformist compound – we are born and spend our days in captivity.
> There are men who can break from any prison and our captors – our leaders – are
> the prison breakers.[29]

Wales had no place for dissent, or for rational discussion. The Irish and the Scots were
encouraged by societies and the press, but "if you want a platform in Wales, you must
buy one in a chapel, and even then you cannot say what you like. If you want a thing
printed you must submit it to some Liberal Nonconformist newspaper." The only exceptions were *Y Llenor* – which could stand side by side with the best English reviews – and
the *Western Mail*, "a very great newspaper which has done more for literature and art in
Wales than all the National Eisteddfodau". The Eisteddfod was "a horrid witness to our
famine-stricken mind", rewarding "the masters of the commonplace". Dublin, whatever
its turmoils, produced more poets of worth than the whole of Wales for all its bardic
show. "The Eisteddfod is our national conjuring trick. We shake the hat, and therefrom
comes a great mass of singers and bards, artists and dramatists…The Eisteddfod magician
has not yet produced a live rabbit." Creative literature lived not by cash handouts but
by "bought bread and cheese" and its reward was the sum of satisfaction it gave to "the
soul of the artist" in the fashioning of it.

As hard on Welsh literature – "Does the young man hide a copy of *Rhys Lewis* in his
desk or behind his counter?" – as on Welsh moral failing – "and in accusing my people I
accuse myself" – Evans nonetheless at Bangor offered grounds for optimism. Chapel
congregations were discontented, divided, and quarrelsome. The 150 who made up the
six Sunday services at Rhydlewis's two chapels were comfortably outnumbered last
August by the audience for D.T. Davies's plays. People are tiring of politicised religion
preached with mock dramatics. Nonconformity and Liberalism had nothing to do with
religion and social progress; they were a wrangle designed to keep Wales in subjugation.
"But we are not dead," Evans insisted;

> We have intellect. It is in the coalpits, in the universities, and in the fields. The signs
> are clear that we are awakening. We have a group of writers and a group of politicians
> who are marching along; they are not faint of heart; they are marching with dignity
> and majesty and with great purpose. They and those who will come after them will
> create a new Wales or a Wales for the Welsh.

His vision of a reborn Wales failed to quell the students, who were further incensed
by his refusal to answer questions about the message of his books (these were *fiction*, he
reminded them). The ensuing commotion prevented any vote of thanks and Evans, for
his safety, was bundled out of the hall. One witness, I.B. Griffith, recalling the speaker's
"unruly hair, hatchet face, and a voice that made no music", explained how difficult it
had been to absorb what was said on account of the continuous heckling; Griffith himself
threw whitewash at Caradoc as he made his way from the building.[30] He emerged on
Penrallt Road but pickets were watching all exits and a crowd soon surrounded him.
He remained unperturbed, calmly smoking a cigarette amid the demonstrators until

two Society officials guided him down Glanrafon Hill as far as the Deanery. Here the students charged in numbers and (in the words of the *Western Mail*) "did a most curious thing. They hoisted Mr. Evans on their shoulders and walked with him to his hotel, at the same time booing and singing the Welsh national anthem." Curious indeed. One is reminded of the *ceffyl pren*, the act of public humiliation visited upon Caradoc's father, but in the raising aloft of the speaker, it is difficult not to see a gesture of admiration for someone with the courage to stand his ground. They found something thrilling and invigorating in his anger and defiance. (Dylan Thomas reports Aberystwyth's similarly ambivalent reaction – "the university students love Caradoc and pelt him with stones whenever he goes out".) At the entrance to the Castle Hotel, where Evans was booked for the night, he was lowered to the ground. He offered a few more remarks, about Wales's future lying with its universities, then turned and made for the bar.

There two dissatisfied students tracked him down, T. Ceiriog Williams (later a headmaster and Daniel Owen enthusiast) and the writer T. Rowland Hughes, intent on an interview for the College magazine. They refused the drink he offered them, at which point he wished them goodnight, "declaring that he had had nothing to eat since morning".[31] The following day Evans reflected on his Bangor welcome. It was what one expected of Wales, where "they don't want to hear the truth", though the female students, he conceded, had been noticeably more attentive ("they have a better sense of fair play"). More than sixty years later, Ceiriog Williams defended the students' behaviour, insisting that only after the lecture, when Evans refused any questions on his writings, did the rumpus actually begin.[32] He provided some background to the event. "The years when I was at Bangor, 1921-25, saw the awakening of the Welsh spirit – not violent but aware that something should be done. There were some spirited ex-servicemen from the First World War at college, one being the father of Dr Geraint Gruffydd, and he was an ardent Welshman.[33] The invitation to Caradoc Evans to come to the Literary and Debating Society was the reaction of English students to those who were proclaiming their Welshness."[34]

At the end of November Evans travelled to Cambridge for another university engagement. He had promised to address the Heretics Club, a radical intellectual circle founded in 1909 with the intention of encouraging total freedom of thought. The Club was accustomed to more distinguished names (six months previously Virginia Woolf had memorably lectured on modern fiction – "On or about December 1910 human character changed," she revealed to her audience) – and the source of Caradoc's invitation remains a puzzle. The philosopher R.B. Braithwaite acted as chairman for a Sunday evening (30 November) that, unusually, had not been publicly advertised. Nevertheless, Welsh undergraduates arrived in numbers, many brandishing leeks. As at Bangor, Evans battled on through his text against a barrage of noise which Braithwaite attempted to quell by threats of summoning the police. Then one student got to the piano, struck up "Land of My Fathers", and brought the Heretics' evening to a riotous close. Outside Welsh students shouted their abuse as a substantial police escort saw the speaker back to his hotel.

Reporting the demonstration, the *Western Mail* could offer nothing on the content of the talk except that it constituted "a slashing attack on Liberalism and Nonconformity".[35] A fair assumption, one might have thought, though this time they were wrong. Under the title "Spirits in Trousers", Evans had actually provided some knock-about, sceptical reflections on his spiritualist sessions with the Bradleys at Dorincourt. When passing over into the spirit world Evans looked forward to meeting one or two who had caused him pain:

> There was a Welsh preacher of my boyhood who sneered at me, and a Welsh farmer who set his dog upon me, and a Welsh praying man who kicked me into a heap because I laughed at his bandy legs; there was a man who said I had a face like a concertina, and there was a card sharper who swindled me of the money that was to take me on holiday and caused me to spend that holiday in Kensington Gardens.

He had even composed a small parting prayer for the leaving of this earthly life: "Bury me lightly that the small rain shall reach my face, and the fluttering of the butterfly shall not escape my ear." The words (echoing Oscar Wilde's at his sister's grave) seem strangely at odds with the man and his reputation, though they came to serve as his epitaph. At the close of 1924 he might more truthfully have chosen "the best-hated man in Wales", a handy nomination first used by Sewell Stokes in September of the year[36] and straightway widely adopted – not least by the recipient himself.

The speaking engagements continued into the new year. As an author and Fleet Street editor regularly in the news, he was asked to address the Publicity Club of London (9 February 1925) and the 23 March meeting of the London Writer Circle, held in the hall of the Institute of Journalists. For the first engagement he spun a few witty remarks on the ingrained vanity of authors, warning his audience that their professional talents would be redundant in Wales, where every man was his own publicity agent. A Welshman "wears his virtues like a soldier wears his medals" – and "I favour this method of publicity," Evans confessed.[37] For a crowded meeting of the London Writer Circle he delivered some "Advice to Young Authors" on getting started in fiction. Characteristically terse and epigrammatical, the talk provides a rare instance of Evans reflecting on his own approach.[38] Authors must look at the world around them, at persons and events known best, then press the truth of their vision, however unpalatable and dissident it might seem. "We can only record a little of what we see and hear. The lie of today is the truth of tomorrow. Thus the novelist should convince himself that his story is true before he begins to write it; in that manner he will be able to tell his story as if he were telling the truth." As for the initial choice of material, that was a matter of personal temperament and disposition. Regarding himself:

> I like stories that are gloomy, morose and bitter, for I feel the author is chronicling the horrid sins of his enemies. An angry man is nearer to himself than a happy man…
> Love – the love we profess and write about – is a poor handmaid. The Fury never leaves us; she abides with us for ever; she harshens the mellowness of our dying days. Love falls at the first stumbling block, and while she companied with us, we found her as insipid as milk and less interesting than a billiard ball.

By harnessing "the Fury" Evans believe he had brought upon his head "such a heap of abuse as would smother a sensitive Englishman". "The repute of the man who defrauds servant maids with pictorial Bibles is fairer among the Welsh than is mine," he famously proceeded. Yet he remained undeterred. Authorship was a passion, and for those born with the spirit of writing in their blood there could be no turning away. "We cannot despise this spirit, nor will it allow itself to be despised. Nothing can wither it and its fruits live after death."

Evans tempered the afflatus with some words on the fiction industry. Short stories relied on the magazines, and magazine editors make plain the kind of work they are seeking: "Listen to the counsel of editors, remembering always that they are the distributors and you only the lowly manufacturers... It is better to discover the secret of the things the magazines print than to stand forlornly in the by-ways of poverty shouting: 'My art is not for sale.'" Success does not come easily; first stories should be laid out, their eyes covered with pennies and their bodies draped with shrouds, and "when the author has found he has about fifty corpses in the drawer, he will awake to the knowledge that he is possessed of the spirit that even grief and disappointment cannot quench." Parting from his audience, a group of young men and women not socially dissimilar to those he'd known at the Workingman's College, he sounded a proletarian blast. Literature need not be a university preserve. The country was full of promising writers – in the coal mines, factories and shops, in the armed services, in offices and on the land. "The gift of writing is the monopoly of no one class. It is universal."

An abbreviated version of the talk appeared in the *Writer* (April 1925), "the only Monthly devoted to the interests of the coming journalist and author" its banner heading proclaimed.[39] One author long since arrived – indeed about to receive the Nobel Prize for literature – published in America a book that would soon trouble Evans. Nominally the work of Archibald Henderson, *Table-Talk of G.B.S.* had been compiled from Bernard Shaw's written responses to questions prepared by Henderson, his biographer. The ensuing "dialogues" Shaw extensively edited and in May he read proof for the British edition (published 11 June). Here a passage on literature and science has Henderson enquire, "If both realistic and romantic fiction are perverting and demoralizing the youth of today, are not greater watchfulness on the part of parents and a more rigid control on the part of publishers and legal authorities clearly desired?" To which Shaw replies, "A reaction against the pornographic novel seems already to be setting in. Caradoc Evans's *My People* and D.H. Lawrence's *The Rainbow* were suppressed after publication in England, for example..." This could not be allowed to pass. *My People* might have been suppressed, and in Wales suffered the charge of pornography, but Evans in 1916 had vigorously challenged this libel and now he did so again. Shaw accepted responsibility for the passage – after all he had passed final proof – and from his own pocket paid £100 in an out-of-court settlement, a further £20 going on a "dignified apology" in the press.[40] By mid-August *Table-Talk* was reissued with a cancel leaf that managed a superior swipe: "A reaction against the pornographic novel seems already to be setting in. I will name no names, as I do not want to suggest that all the authors objected to have corrupt motives: indeed I am sure that the only ones whose names would mean anything to you took a sincere artistic interest in their indiscretions."

Evans admired the younger Shaw, the vigorous social radical and brilliant platform orator – "No rebel sparked more splendidly than Mr. Shaw about 1887 [the year of *An Unsocial Socialist*]. His words blasted the trees in Hyde Park and his breath threw down railings" – and during the *Table-Talk* kerfuffle Shaw contributed to *T.P.'s Weekly*. "Bernard Shaw is very clever indeed and he might have been a genius if there was not so much chaff left in his brain bin," mused Evans in 1933.[41]

Taffy at the Royalty, "An Early Closing Show"

1925

The printed edition of *Taffy* allowed a major reconstruction of what Evans had come to regard as a seriously imperfect play. "There was no coherency in it, and no joining up of the story. The psychology of the two leading characters failed to convince: "I knew why Spurgeon changed his mind, falling from a bad man to a decent man [but] I did not make it clear to the audience."[1] Accordingly, a revised Act 1 develops Marged as a radicalizing force, a process continued in Act 2 where Spurgeon correspondingly becomes a fitter object of her regard and less a young man on the make. Marged's clarity of vision is underscored by one new speech in Act 3 which has her powerfully rebuking the Big Heads for betraying their religious inheritance:

> Your prayers will build you nothing. You are men of speech and your sorrow is dry. You have no regard for the first Capel Sion that was Bensha's mud-walled hut on the moor. Every night a candle burnt at the window to guide the folk who came on the narrow path to read the Beybile in Welsh or to seek Bensha to go and read the Beybile to the dying. And however black and stormy the night no one lost his way or went in vain. The Sion that you want to pull down was built by love. Short is the fame of love. After their day's work women brought timber down the hill and over the valley to make this Sion. And in the night men opened gravel pits and brought up stones from the quarry by the light of a flaming fire of twigs and furze. All worked in the sure belief of another God than the God of the English-speaking parson who shot calves and lambs for sport and whose horses trod the corn and tore the hedges. Their love and their sacrifices are nothing to you. Do not the moments of their labour taunt you with shame? You pule and you whine and pluck your garments like a man waiting for a feast for which he has made no provision.

Marged's exchanges with Spurgeon lie at the heart of the play, imbued with fresh warmth and feeling, and the revised third act introduced the most quoted lines in *Taffy*, Marged's lyric outburst at Spurgeon's declaration of love.

> I have hated you. And loved you. O love made noises in my heart. It stilled the rill of the morning milk as it fell into the pitcher, and at night it chased away the white moss of slumber from my eyes. It stirred the woman within me.

The love scene took reviewers by surprise, though its romance and tenderness are salted at the close when Rhys Shop, a chapel Big Head, quietly releases his hens to gobble up the rice he had earlier sold – at exorbitant prices – to the wedding guests. Overall, Evans's stance seemed clearer. "He loves Wales with the divine love that chasteneth," the *Review of Reviews* believed.[2] Evans presented signed copies of *Taffy* to W.A. Darlington, drama critic of the *Daily Telegraph*, and to Clement Shorter, founder-editor of the *Sphere*; he hoped Shorter would like the play and "will tell me even if you don't".

Taffy as revised for publication was first heard at Stockport on 11 October 1924 in a performance that opened the Stockport Garrick Society's repertory season. An outstanding amateur company with roots in the town's Unitarian Church, the Garrick had a history of presenting challenging works (by such as Ibsen and Shaw) judged too risky for the professional stage. "There is a compelling satirical fury about the comedy, and it finds expression in crisp, forceful, and curiously flavoured diction," wrote the *Manchester Guardian* (13 October); "Not the least of the shocks the author administers is to make his poltroons bend torrents of finely imaginative and figurative talk into channels utterly mean and base." The *Guardian* critic would have liked such talk in the mouths of actors who were Welsh.

By summer 1925 a London revival was confirmed, in a production booked first for a fortnight at the Q theatre (Jack de Leon's venture in Chiswick designed to try out new plays), then for a limited West End run. Encouraged by this fresh exposure, Evans set about yet further revisions, putting in the finishing touches during his summer break in Rhydlewis. An experienced cast was recruited, with Joan Maude and Tristan Rawson as Marged and Spurgeon. Milton Rosmer took charge of production, collaborating in rehearsal with the author to achieve a tighter, less homiletic, third act.[3] Prior to the Chiswick opening Evans created some headline-grabbing publicity by explaining the play's revisions and offering to tour it through Wales; he was prepared to receive the bricks ("and Welshmen are fond of throwing bricks," he added, with his shattered East Sheen window in mind). He hoped his compatriots in London would at least have the courtesy to listen to his case. "I poke no fun at the Welsh because I like the Welsh too much," he told a *Western Mail* reporter.

The first night of *Taffy* at the Q (8 September) was a predominantly Welsh affair.[4] The orchestra played Welsh airs as a celebrity audience filed in: Welsh parliamentarians, the secretary of the Welsh Church Commission, the High Sheriff of Cardiganshire, and the novelist Edith Nepean. Along came T.P. O'Connor too, eulogizing the production before the curtain rose. Evans seemed nervous: that morning he had heard of a possible demonstration and wondered about the wisdom of sitting among the audience. Bruce Winstone (playing Twmi) suggested a nearby pub, but three hours' drinking might have been dangerous so Evans settled instead for a little room backstage. He had a Welsh bible for company – his wife Rose had suggested that he carry it with him, knowing that in moments of stress he habitually turned to his bible – and while his countrymen were "bellowing like lustful bulls – they lusted for my blood," Evans, as Rose had predicted, fortified himself with "the only Welsh possession that I truly love".[5] As it transpired, *Taffy* met with enthusiasm, cheers drowning the boos, and in answer to repeated calls the author appeared on stage. Smilingly he addressed the house:

> On behalf of everyone connected with the production of this play I thank you for
> your kind reception. I am grateful particularly to my fellow countrymen for their
> kindness in leaving their little businesses to come here to witness the truth of the
> portrayal of the three Big Heads and Ben Watkins. (Shouts of "Liar!") We have been
> behaving ourselves as riotously as men and women do at Welsh prayer meetings
> ("Liar!" again, and "Why don't you produce the play in Wales?") and having done so,
> let us depart tonight as men and women depart from Welsh prayer meetings – with
> new sins in our hearts.

Depart they did, and policemen waiting in readiness were quietly stood down.

Rosmer's production pleased most critics and the cast had clearly enjoyed it, even
if Twmi's accent swung alarmingly between Bradford and Belgravia. Ivor Brown in the
Manchester Guardian (9 September) thought that "the hero and heroine who turn away
from Capel Zion's darkness to the light that is in honest labour are too long-winded to
be good company. It is the knaves who take the tricks in Mr. Evans's game, and these
gargoyles of pious fraud were presented with a riotous sense of mischief." The *Observer*
(13 September) saw these gargoyles as "intensified from life…. Hideous as they are,
their very vividness makes them authentic." Joan Maude was good enough as Marged,
although she lacked the "serene assurance and power" that Edith Evans had brought to
the part in 1923. Passion marked the *Western Mail's* response. No man was doing Wales
more harm than Caradoc Evans, yet "he can produce more effect in one line than most
craftsmen of the present day can produce in twenty," and the revised third act was "easily
the greatest of Mr Caradoc Evans's achievements".[6]

Following its fortnight at Chiswick (8-19 September), the production moved to
the West End for a three-week run at the Royalty. The text still troubled the author who
tightened the last act yet again. His modifications, though not extensive, are significant
in that they come at the climax of the play. Out went Spurgeon's passionate indictment
("I abhor the righteousness of the capel…") recycling bits from Evans's polemical pieces
and instead we have more positive sentences from Spurgeon as he turns his back on the
dreadful chapel:

> But this Sion is only a bit of Wales. There are in Wales other Sions, where men are
> not lost in the multitude of their own virtues. Oh, yes, there are fair hearts in the
> land in which dwell neither greed, nor hate, nor pomp, nor deceit… I tune my spirit
> to the eternal song, and my feet shall company youths and maids in whose minds are
> stored the streaming glories of our past… Yes, I'll pant after the lowly, and cause
> them to stiffen with the pride of an ancient people.

Such eager hope, the trust of a young man shedding his preacher's garb for the clothes
of an honest labourer, echoed Evans's rallying call at Bangor. The unexpected burst of
optimism naturally provoked some questioning. "In Allen Raine, Edith Nepean and
Lloyd George," Evans elaborated in the *Western Mail*, "you have only one side of Wales
shown. No country can prosper on conditions of the Kailyard. The dung heaps must
be seen and the causes must be removed. I have been trying to remove them."[7] Now

there was cause for hope, for Evans sensed "a new outlook, a new ideal and a new aspiration" abroad in the nation. But the language of hope came less easily than the blasts
of condemnation – "a snarler is more honest than a smiler" – and from drafts of his
Bangor speech one sees the difficulty he had in avoiding the bathetic ("very soon we
shall be at the dawn of the flowery freshness of the new morning" he sensibly scrubbed).
But why this rush of optimism? That the Liberal-Nonconformist ascendancy was but a
phase in Welsh national life was a viewpoint he steadily maintained, and his appeal to
"the streaming glories of our past" recalls his letters of a decade previously. Nonconformist
theocracy was an evil aberration that like "an army of occupation has killed more spirits
than any famine". But the chapels were emptying, the priests were losing their grip, as
congregations came to realize that "Liberal-Nonconformity is not Christianity; it is a
wrangle to get people into Parliament and so preserve the vested interests of Nonconformist capitalists."

Evans is tantalizingly vague on those who might be hastening the new order. He
would have applauded the political realignment of the early 1920s, the electoral collapse
of Liberalism as the idealistic young turned heavily to Labour, even if many of the first-
time Labour MPs elected were cast from the same chapel mould as their defeated
opponents. Politicized labour had brought to the south Wales coalfield an unprecedented
share of prosperity, at least until 1924. As Evans put it, "The men in the pits and the
men in the fields are straining at their tethering cords"; less so the men in the fields,
though a flash of rural radicalism lit the immediate post-war years – "the one short
interlude in history when farm labourers exercised some form of influence over their
lives," writes David Pretty; "The striking farm worker of 1919 presented an image that
would have seemed unthinkable only a few years earlier."[8] The Labour Party briefly
became the beneficiary of this new found political awareness, for whatever its radical
beginnings, Liberal-Nonconformity now seemed unable to find compassion for the
plight of the rural poor – for that one turned to clergyman of the reviled Anglican
church. In speaking of a group of writers intent on creating "a new Wales, or a Wales
for the Welsh", Evans could only have had in mind W. J. Gruffydd and *Y Llenor*, a journal
he more than once found opportunity to applaud. Gruffydd, too, was seen as a traducer
of his nation, particularly hard on Nonconformity as it had degenerated ("a pale shadow
of the old way of life, the hollow trunk on which the leaves are all withered and which
all manner of vile fungi flourish"). A satirical piece in *Y Llenor* (1923) – cast as the
obituary of a self-made Caernarfon worthy – conjures up Caradoc Evans in substance
and tone.[9]

The early 1920s saw a confluence of reforming currents, not least in education (one
of Evans's more widely shared concerns), and if by 1925 the first Labour prime minister
had fallen and the south Wales coalfield begun its bitter downward spiral, it was still
possible for Welsh intellectuals to talk of a new beginning. W. J. Gruffydd pointed the
direction for the reawakened consciousness that Evans had rightly detected. It lay not
in place-seeking politicians at Westminster, whatever their party labels. In a piece on
Caradoc Evans, Gruffydd wrote, "Today the younger generation, as represented by Mr

Saunders Lewis and Mr [Ambrose] Bebb, has definitely dissociated itself from all the party cries of British politics, and seeks to save its soul by fostering a spirit that will not look to England and English movements for its inspiration."[10] An element in this recreated Wales would be a genuine pride in the national language, concern for which has too often been "only a portion of the tribute which our public men paid to a formal orthodoxy". Evans's lectures and journalism illustrate how much his thinking at this point overlapped with Gruffydd's, even on the matter of language:

> The Welsh boast of their language. Yet the first care of many of the town Welsh is to keep their children from learning it. I know Cardiganshire Welsh parents who will neither allow Welsh to be spoken at home or their children to be taught it. Even in Welsh Sunday schools in such places as Carmarthen and Llanelly and Carnarvon and Colwyn Bay English is the spoken language. Though we hate the English we imitate them...
>
> I do not say that the Welsh language is of commercial use, but it fits the shape of our tongue; and it is priggish to forget it as it is to forget one's mother. And if it is worth the while of English and Jewish parliamentary candidates to learn phrases of it for the purposes of electioneering,[11] it is worth our while to keep it green. Our language is our inheritance. It is not a vote catching dodge.[12]

Evans long lamented the national sense of inferiority, a condition shaping reaction to his writings ("whatever will the English think"), and he vigorously returned to it in 1925. Evans contrasted the achievements of the Irish (and the Scots) with the dismal record of Wales. Cardiff was Welsh only on the map of Wales, readers of the *Sunday Express* were assured.[13] There was harmony there – the harmony of master and servant:

> The people of other nations have fought for their own with sharp-edged stones in their hands and with stubborn songs on their lips. The Cardiff Welsh have opened their doors to the invader, saying "Come you in, boys bach, and rest you here; show us the way and we will follow you."

Though sounding like a man ripe for Plaid Cymru, formed in the very month of this article (August 1925), Evans was far from treading the nationalist path. Nationalist political sentiment he associated with Lloyd George's early careerist moves, and any new party of Wales would simply be a mask for social conservatism and inevitably one more "stairway to money-for-nothing jobs". One finds no firm party allegiance amid the brilliance and burlesque of his polemics. Instinctively a man of the left, his position is best defined in terms of his opponents. Nonconformist Liberals were the enemy.

On Monday 21 September, *Taffy* opened at the Royalty before a packed and largely appreciative house. Coming forward at the end of the play, Evans faced a degree of bar-racking but, as at Chiswick, a lively first night had passed off without serious incident. Caradoc and Dennis Eadie, the actor-manager who brought the play to the West End, were quietly satisfied: the revisions had made their mark and a syndicate come forward with ideas for an American production. There was even talk of a tour of Wales with the all-Welsh cast Evans wanted. The evening, too, held one particular personal pleasure – the appearance of Duncan Davies. Since leaving drapery, Evans's old Lampeter pal had found employment in Fleet Street, on the circulation side at Hulton's, a job frequently taking him into the provinces. From time to time in London he dropped in on Caradoc at *Ideas* and the *Daily Mirror*, and they still occasionally met over Sunday tea at East Sheen. Backstage at the Royalty, they chatted warmly; Davies was leaving London for good but felt sure that he and Caradoc would meet up from time to time. This was not to be – and through no fault of Davies's.

Nothing in the first night at the Royalty, or in the two subsequent performances, could have suggested what might happen on Thursday, 24 September. The unprecedented scenes that evening swelled the Caradoc Evans legend.[14] Word of likely trouble went out among the London Welsh (milkmen and shop workers especially) and by the time of the evening performance a crowd had gathered outside the theatre chanting the author's name. Arriving by taxi, Evans passed through the throng unnoticed, despite his much-photographed face and disreputable black hat. Inside the theatre, full to capacity, the excitement was palpable but the first act passed off with no major disturbance. Then, at the lowering of the curtain, some in the audience struck up the Welsh national anthem, a signal for serious protesting. Booing, whistling and cries of "Judas, Judas" disrupted the second act; twice the curtain had to be lowered for leading lady Joan Maude to appeal for calm. The third act, it was obvious, would produce some sort of crisis, but against a barrage of noise the players embarked upon it. Once more the curtain came down, allowing Jack de Leon and Tristan Rawson (playing Spurgeon) to ask for a decent hearing – the kind that London gave to any play. The jeering and catcalls subsided, though not for long, and with the curtain lowered yet again Jack de Leon urged the demonstrators at least to wait for Spurgeon's closing speech – they might possibly approve of the play's final sentiments. Again the noise subsided, but far from converting the critics, Spurgeon's declaration of hope whipped them up anew. At which point the drama passed from the stage to the auditorium, where summoned policemen moved among the noisiest protestors. With dialogue scarcely audible and people struggling to leave, house lights were raised on a scene of widespread disorder. Scuffling inevitably broke out as half-a-dozen people, flanked by cheering supporters, were marched off to Marlborough Street police station.

Out of sight during the performance, Evans afterwards talked in the foyer and outside the theatre. He regretted the police arrests: "I complain about Welshmen being thin-skinned, and I want to be more tolerant myself than they are."[15] He put a brave face on the evening. The cast had shown courage under fire in managing to complete the play – only at the very close had some cutting been necessary. The exhibition must have been pre-arranged, "an early closing show". A spokesman for the protesters agreed: the Thursday half-holiday for shops had given the London Welsh a chance to show their disgust, not simply at the play, but at Caradoc Evans in every guise, and the harm he was doing to Wales. Describing the disturbance, the *Daily Mail* had the trouble-makers "swept out of the theatre on an alcoholic tide". Drink had played its part, as one arrested dairyman made plain in a statement before the magistrate – a nice little drama in itself:

> When I entered the theatre everybody was singing, so I lifted up my voice in the general chorus. Then I was thrown out and somebody pushed me against the constable, and I clutched him before I knew he was a policeman. He let me go, but I fell down and somebody fell on top of me and got me by the throat, and when I came to, the same policeman had me again, and the police doctor said I was drunk in a dim light.[16]

For being drunk and disorderly he and two others were each fined twelve shillings, a sum promptly raised by supporters.

The newspapers made much of the evening. During the war a play or two had prompted protests, but this was the first time a London theatre performance had actually been brought to a halt; and the scenes had been ugly enough to bring in the police. The *Nation* stood aside from the brouhaha. The playwright had shown that in Wales, as elsewhere, a measure of godly cant hides a deal of meanness and greed. He had said so with liveliness and wit. Nevertheless, "It appears that Mr Evans is wrong to suppose that Welshmen are as bad as Zola's Frenchmen in *La Terre*, or as Ibsen's countrymen in *An Enemy of the People*, or as Mr Theodore Powys's Englishmen, and he cannot make amends by having his young leads as impeccably pure and idealistic as your best American." The behaviour in the pit was regrettable – it served to confirm the playwright's indictment of his people – and the *Nation* trusted that the management would still stand by its production of the play. This indeed it did, until the end of the scheduled run (10 October) and the hope of calmer Celtic waters – a revival of *The Playboy of the Western World*.

With the passage of time *Taffy* seems, at least on the page, an innocuous Welsh comedy with a few happy touches. For all its success on the stage, and despite the many tinkerings, Evans was never truly satisfied with it. It was writing against the grain: a play for popular consumption, mixing indictment and idealism and providing the requisite happy ending. This said, *Taffy* took its author out of his solitary writing den into the world of theatre, where he regularly attended rehearsals and collaborated with stage professionals on modifications to his text. And *Taffy*, freed from print, can still come to life, as subsequent revivals showed.

If Evans abandoned playwriting (save for "A Devil on the Hearth", his unperformed, unpublished reworking of "The Devil in Eden"), his interest in theatre remained. In the ranks of its unsung professionals he found much to admire, and regret. A piece for the *Sunday Express*, printed while *Taffy* was running, laments the condition of these workaday actors "drilled into downtroddeness".[17] In crooked passages and dark dressing rooms, they "lift their eyes in adoration when the money-man passes by". Yet the best actors were the unknown actors, not the £150-a-week darlings of the gallery clubs "whose only attractive possession is their bodies". Drama was kept alive by intelligent men and women who never talk about "art" but who so love their calling that they work for next to nothing sooner than not work at all. It is their blessing and their curse. "The stage is for youth and old age; there is no place in it for plain faces and middle-age wrinkles."

The lambasting of *Taffy* continued. The president of the London Welsh Literary and Musical Societies' Union spoke of sacred altars dragged through the mud for the benefit of an English public "in which the animal instinct is supreme"; Ivor Novello, gushing about native talent ("I do not think there is anything more beautiful than Welsh drama, poetry and ballads"), thought the whole play's attitude "one of unpleasantness", while the high sheriff of Merioneth contented himself with Caradoc's "face like a concertina" jibe (his full remark was that if the face was an index to the soul, Caradoc's ought to be a concertina).[18] Once again W. J. Gruffydd came to the defence, remarking (in *T.P.'s Weekly*) how dangerous it was for any Welshman to speak of Caradoc Evans except in terms of execration.[19] Scathingly he referred to those who having lost all the respect and trust of their fellow countrymen – "unfrocked ministers, fraudulent financiers and discredited politicians" – suddenly recapture public esteem through "one great act of atonement", their vilification of Caradoc Evans. Gruffydd would not join them. He had welcomed *Taffy* in book form and was yet more admiring of the revisions. The moral failings it castigated were symptoms of a decayed puritanism, itself but a phase in the life of the nation, as Evans was right to insist. He was also right to divine a new mood abroad in Wales and, Gruffydd added, "if all Welshmen were to agree in thinking thus, our very hopes would create the substance".[20]

A little earlier John Crowther, Caradoc's old schoolmaster, had penned his remi-niscences of the schoolboy at Rhydlewis. He recalled the author of *Taffy* struggling with the intricacies of English composition. Years later, in the summer of 1912, he and Caradoc had wandered the seashore at Llangrannog, discussing English literature; and though he might have criticized his pupil in the past, now "there is no one, believing as I do that the genuine stuff is in him, who more desires his success than I do".[21] In the event, Evans published nothing of consequence for the next five years. His interest in the short story exhausted, he knew he wasn't a dramatist, or a novelist, or so it seemed.

There were signs of a writing journalist in four pieces composed at this time for the *Sunday Express*. "The Captive Welsh" (16 August 1925) has been mentioned, an attack on Cardiff and Swansea, "two ugly Welsh sisters which hate each other with sisterly bit-terness". Swansea gets off lightly, "ashamed of her sloping face, into which are dug channels of drab roads, and on which are set houses like the jagged teeth in an old cockle-woman's mouth". Cardiff gets the roasting, a town lost to incomers through the hollowness and hypocrisy of the natives. Their type appears nightmarishly, as a David Adams *doppelganger*:

> I was in the buffet of an hotel in St Mary's Street… when there entered a man; a tall, high cheek-boned man, who was clad in a frock coat and a black straw hat, and who wore a red beard. He asked for a double whisky and a small soda, and having gulped the drink he looked around him. His gaze fell on me, whereupon he called up a teetotal look into his face and address the company thus: "I have searched for Satan, and I find him where I expected to find him." Then he fled, forgetting in his holy fear to pay that which was due.

Boyhood memories colour Caradoc's subsequent pieces, less confrontational perhaps (the first had drawn responses from civic leaders in Cardiff and Swansea), though venomous enough towards the Hawen elect. Pondering the Welsh bible, a copy of which had helped him through his agonies at the Q, Evans recalled (13 September 1925) how it had become "a hateful weapon" used for crushing the peasants. On the eve of his departure to Carmarthen, the young lad was presented with a copy on behalf of the congregation by Adams's successor at Hawen (J.J. Jones), "a fat impudent man, whose face was like the body of a hedgehog, but whose eyes had none of those of the hedgehog's gentleness. He scattered evil wheresoever he went, treading it into the earth with his heavy, flat feet. The village is still reaping that which he sowed." Yet that bible, despite its provenance, became a precious treasure, "for in its pages I found God, other than the God of Welsh Nonconformity".

"My Preachers" (*Sunday Express*, 25 October) took a more relaxed, irreverent, view of his religious growth. "I am a sermon-taster and, like all sermon-tasters, every soul-licking sermon causes me to say to myself: 'What a bad boy bach, dear me, you are for sure.'" The cosy thrills of chapel were encountered first as schoolboy, enthralled by pulpit actors who made every sermon a drama. In the days before theatres and cinemas, the churches and chapels were places of entertainment; and so they remain in Wales. The English cannot preach, being "afraid to open their mouths". There were exceptions, like the great Congregationalist Dr Joseph Parker, the Northumberland quarryman ("He blasted rocks and the stones he fashioned into anthems"); and the Revd R.J. Campbell whose "white accusing chin attracted the Puritan in my soul" and whose "bright eyes hypnotized to the City Temple thousands of maids and middle-aged spinsters". With the decline of the sermon came the decline in chapel attendance, a state of affairs suggesting that tragic actors should once more be enlisted. "There is no need to believe in God to be a good preacher," and a good preacher, loose liver or no, remains the heart of a chapel, supplying the succour that "refreshes the soul and fortifies man in his pilgrimage". Evans would keep up sermon-tasting, "proud [to] belong to a people whose god is a preacher and whose heaven is a chapel."

Before the end of 1925 Evans had fulfilled one or two more speaking engagements, in October discoursing on "The Welshman as Playgoer" before the Gallery First Nighters Club in Maiden Lane and a month later addressing a luncheon of the British Motion Pictures Advertisers' Society. Knockabout performances drawing on common material, they leave an impression of a man fast becoming the prisoner of his reputation, deliberately acting up to it, saying the things expected of him. The October talk opens promisingly, with allusions to the time of the meeting (a Sunday evening) and the actor who played the rogue minister in *Taffy*: "This evening I would rather be in a yellow-varnished pew in Capel Sion, listening to the song-like eloquence of the Rev Fewless Llewellyn, and putting in his collection- plate a white-washed farthing for a sixpence, than face members of the Gallery First Nighters' Club."[22] Again, Evans lays stress on the incorrigible the-atricality of the Welshman and the fit-up world he inhabits:

> The earth is his stage and the lime is his sun. From cradle to grave, his life is made
> up of speeches, gestures and grimaces. Whether he is perched on a tree scaring the
> crows from his small wheatfield, or on his knees in the Big Seat, or in the pulpit wal-
> loping the devil from the neighbourhood, or threshing the hedges, he is always acting.

And events at the Royalty Theatre gave him fresh cause to lament the Welsh incapacity
for self-criticism. "No one knows how sick he is until he sees his tongue in a mirror. So
with the Welsh"; and when they see their sickness in the mirror of the stage they
wretchedly blame the author of the mirror. "We imagine that in killing the author we
cure our ills."

Editing *T.P.'s Weekly*

1926-29

For his remaining years in journalism Evans flourished in a job that properly matched his talents, the *de facto* editorship of a literary tabloid engaging a general readership. Thomas Burke felt certain that his friend had at last found a fitting home, and within a quarter of Fleet Street generously peopled by Celts. *T.P.'s Weekly*[1] itself became something of a literary Murphia, with O'Connor as father-figure. Evans thought him the greatest journalist he had ever known (sixty years in the business!) and a writer of no mean accomplishment. Yet at heart T.P. remained the "cultivated peasant", frugal in tastes and habits; "in common with most writing peasants," added Evans, "he knew men better than nature." On T.P.'s death in November 1929, a little after his eighty-first birthday, Caradoc's spontaneous tribute served as an epitaph for Hamilton Fyfe's 1934 biography of O'Connor. "He was a kind man, loving mercy and hating injustice. He often told me that he would not die before the workers were paid more than a living wage, before poor children were given better educational facilities, and before capital punishment was abolished."[2]

Working alongside Evans was the novelist Con O'Leary (1887-1958). Educated at University College, Cork, and with the drawling accent of that town, he had been brought to London by O'Connor (whose memoirs he was ghosting) from the post of editor of the *Manchester Guardian's* weekly digest. He became a pervasive presence at *T.P.'s* through his articles, stories and reviews. He was a Melrose author too, having published a volume of Irish sketches under the title *An Exile's Bundle* (1923). Sometime later, probably in 1927, he and Evans were joined by another Irishman, Austin Clarke (1896-1974), a poet, playwright and novelist, and one-time lecturer at University College Dublin. A fiction critic on the *Nation* and occasional *T.P.'s* contributor, by degrees Clarke became a full-time employee on the paper, keeping a look-out for shaky grammar – here his MA in English was an asset – as well as helping O'Leary cobble together columns nominally written by the ailing O'Conner. "Caradoc kept to the scissors and the paste pot, while Con and I tore a new biography or literary history in two, read hastily for anecdotes, interesting details, started to type the article, meeting somewhere in the middle...".[3] As for Evans in his office on press days, Tommy Burke thought it a sight worth paying to see: "Flames, lightning and whirls of paper were about, and somewhere in the core of that chaos was Caradoc. Then, abruptly, the storm would subside; the last page was sent away, and Caradoc would step out as though nothing had happened."[4] Caradoc's colleagues were his drinking companions, the mercurial, kind-hearted O'Leary and the wistful, contemplative Clarke. Both were steeped in matters Irish, and Evans warmed to their positive patriotism; as he did to their clever habit of pinning upon themselves the more lovable failings of their race, for fear the English would label them with more serious faults – a trick they shared with the Scots but one that eluded the Welsh.

On a fattish salary of £500 a year, and the owner of a substantial new house nearer Richmond (he and Rose purchased 468 Upper Richmond Road in 1925), Caradoc was now enjoying what by Fleet Street standards were privileged working conditions. The sixty-year-old Arthur Machen, a veteran of daily journalism, looked with envy on the leisurely rhythms of the weeklies, where "none knew what hurry meant". Besides, literary editors had tangible power through the funds at their disposal and their ability to advance careers. Fleet Street pubs saw much sycophancy and hobnobbing as the freelancers courted their gods. The silent, decorous company listening to Hilaire Belloc pontificating at the Red Lion in Poppin's Court reminded Evans of nothing so much as a gathering of divinity students before the chairman of the Congregational Union. "Presently Belloc went and several of the company turned to me and said: 'What are you drinking?' and 'What your paper wants is a page of book reviews.'"[5]

Being pestered by would-be contributors was an occupational hazard; Fleet Street was stuffed with amateurs searching for openings and much needed cash. "There is an abundance of fruit on the tree of amateurism": Evans's own words might have echoed in his mind as he returned to the Belle Sauvage, although it wasn't only amateurs who looked to literary journalism. Rebecca West rejoiced in her "incredible arrangement" with *T.P.'sWeekly* "by which I write whenever I like on whatever I like for vast sums"; and Dilys Powell confessed the "great blow to me (and my finances) when the magazine closed down".[6] Journalism was a writer's bread and butter and *T.P.'sWeekly* paid well. "In my present state, I feel I never want to write another book", wrote D.H. Lawrence, an occasional *T.P.'s* contributor, in October 1927. "What's the good! I can eke out a living on stories and little articles, that don't cost a tithe of the output a book costs. Why write novels any more!"[7] The Twenties proved a golden decade for big-name authors with a flair for popular journalism. In February 1929 Evans offered Compton Mackenzie fifteen guineas for 1,500 words on "What's Wrong with Modern Woman?", at a time when Arnold Bennett commanded £70 for a weekly piece in the *Evening Standard*.[8]

Closest to *T.P.'sWeekly* in spirit was the other literary tabloid, the longstanding *John O'London'sWeekly*, edited from 1924 to 1928 by George Blake, a journalist in his thirties who would later take control of the *Strand Magazine*. Blake spoke of *John O'London's* as serving up literature and art to a mass public "according to T.P. O'Connor's recipe". Such a journal might outline Gibbon's *Decline and Fall* in fifteen hundred words. Did this serve as an incentive or a substitute? Blake knew all sides of the argument and believed that on balance such periodicals were a force for good. In the words of Sidney Dark, Blake's predecessor at *John O'London's*: "We realised that there is a large public interested in books, that has little knowledge and is anxious for advice, information and guidance, but has no appetite for high-brow criticism."[9] Elucidation, not criticism, was the policy, with an emphasis on older, established texts. Likewise, when presenting fiction "I found it good policy to reprint first-rate non-copyright stories; they were unfamiliar to the majority of our readers."

Unashamedly book-driven and backward looking, with no intrusive political agenda, *T.P.'sWeekly* spelled out literature's sovereign mission. "It interprets man to man, race to race, creed to creed, and to understand the point of view of others is the beginning of wisdom, and the beginning of the end of quarrels that arise from mutual ignorance."To some extent, this ethos resonated with the more politicised adult education movement and in its first Edwardian manifestation the paper instigated a chain of literary discussion groups. O'Connor resurrected the idea in 1924 with his *T.P.'s* London Literary Circle; it met with fair success and similar circles were established outside London. Such groups were good publicity and one more means of consolidating a readership (*John O'London's* chose to sponsor a series of weekly lectures). More immediate props to circulation were the cash-prize competitions that speckled the pages: literary crosswords, missing-word competitions, and nominations for the best single line of poetry ("I saw eternity the other night" a popular choice). T.P. O'Connor would speak of his almost personal affection for his readers, his spiritual association with them even, and the paper's active postbag goes some way to corroborating this.[10] The didactic touch is evident in a series like "T.P.'sTraining in Literature' (with Virginia Woolf and Arthur Quiller-Couch as contributors) and the literary course conducted by J.B. Priestley. Overall, the emphasis lay on arresting articles (prosiness and dullness taboo) with a high biographical content – "in journalism as in life it is the personal that interests mankind". So readers were given more intimate snapshots of their authors – wives on writing husbands (EdwardThomas, Conrad, Dostoevsky); a brother's memories of Chekhov, a son's of Dickens; Henry James through the eyes of his typist. An early scoop, close to home, was a vignette of Wilde at the *Woman's World*, a Cassell's magazine he briefly edited. His assistant Arthur Fish recalled how Oscar's dress and manner lit up the dingy Belle Sauvage. "In winter a long fur-lined coat with heavy fur collar and cuffs; in summer a pale-grey frock-coat suit, and always a silk hat of super-glossiness. On his cheerful days there would be a button hole of Parma violets."[11] Still valuable in *T.P.'s* pages are the many autobiographical essays, especially the long running series "In the Days of My Youth", which attracted a wealth of celebrities, literary and otherwise. (Hugh Walpole's autobiography, too, was serialized, as was Margot Asquith's.)

The journal published a spread of fiction, with H.E. Bates, Arnold Bennett, D.H. Lawrence, Rose Macaulay, Kathleen Mansfield, R.H. Mottram, Liam O'Flaherty, Hugh Walpole, Alec Waugh and Thornton Wilder notable in the lists. Much trumpeted serialised novels included those by Hardy, Somerset Maugham and the immensely popular Warwick Deeping – a literary history distributed gratis marked the start of his *Sorrell and Son* (1927). Evans always welcomed Thomas Burke ("writing stories which editors glory in") and looked favourably on Edwin Pugh, another reliable journeyman whose early work had so impressed him. As for poetry, *T.P.'sWeekly* generally reprinted famous poems rather than risking new ones. One exception catches the eye: some posthumous verses by Mary Webb. She had been a prose contributor and Evans's lone advocacy of her novels was a matter of in-house pride. Among the essayists and reviewers some bigger names are present: Belloc, Bennett, Priestley and Wells, together with Rose Macaulay and Rebecca West (the latter a witty, fearless contributor). J.B. Priestley became a mainstay and, together with H.G. Wells, most readily captured the spirit of the magazine and its lower middle-class readership. "H.G. Wells won't take any nonsense from editors or publishers," Caradoc had observed, "but they've got to print him because he is the only thinking writing Englishman".[12] Among the reviews what surprises is the occasional hospitality towards work by D.H. Lawrence, James Joyce and Virginia Woolf. Faber & Faber indeed applauded *T.P.'s Weekly* as the first to welcome "Anna Livia Plurabelle", while Lawrence paid ready tribute to its stand on *Lady Chatterley's Lover*. "What a rag of a paper, *T.P.'s!*" he mocked on 12 July 1928, amused perhaps by the conjunction in the current issue (7 July) of his "Laura Philippine" sketch, an Aldous Huxley lead essay, and a readers' postbag on the question, "Is God good?" Two months later *T.P.'s Weekly* had this to say of *Lady Chatterley's Lover*: "Mr Lawrence has carried realism to a pitch seldom aspired to in the whole history of literature. And the result is a fine novel, bold and – stark is the only word to describe it."[13] Lawrence could not hide his delight: " – imagine *T.P.'s* coming out so bravely!" Doubtless here, as with Joyce, the reviewer's taste well outran his middle-brow readers', but the paper's favourable estimate genuinely heartened Lawrence, who alerted others to it.

Evans's hand is usually discernible behind the Welsh material in *T.P.'s Weekly*. Always disposed to help his friends, he found room for Arthur Machen and W.H. Davies, as he did for Edith Nepean, both her stories and her articles.[14] Besides Nepean, Evans printed Berta Ruck who, "gypsyish – lavatory chains in her ears and beads", irritated him at the office by dragging in her secretary. He also promoted Dilys Powell. "Caradoc and his assistant [Con O'Leary] used to lecture me about making my writing a bit more lively; they tried to turn me into a real journalist"; and to some effect for Powell came to ghost a few T.P. articles.[15] The Welsh journalist Evelyn Lewis was another beneficiary. She produced a thousand words on Dic Aberdaron (the eccentric polyglot traveller) and on Lampeter College, articles that Caradoc claimed to have read "with deep interest and enjoyment". Among other Welsh contributions are pieces on Geraint Goodwin and the playwright D.T. Davies; J.O. Francis on Welsh drama and the London Welsh; A.J. Cook on his early disillusionment with religion in Wales; and an article on Congregationalism by T. Rhondda Williams, the dissident minister whom Evans had accommodated in *Ideas*. Eye-catching too is some Wil Ifan poetry and a characteristically trenchant "In the Days of My Youth" from W.J. Gruffydd. "Wales must rid itself of what I must call that degrading concept of popular politics as a personal and commercial enterprise," he wrote in March 1927.

Evans stayed content in Fleet Street. The trials that beset other editors – pursuing and rejecting contributors, the dull business of copy-editing, the repetitive production routines – he accepted without complaint. He knew the world outside and never could forget the disciplines of drapery. Further back lay the grinding labours of his Cardiganshire farming community. He took his nephew Howell Evans, a comparatively prosperous farm son, and in 1928 found him a job with the *Cambrian News*, the Aberystwyth weekly managed by Henry Read whom Evans had known from Read's long editorship of the *South Wales Daily News*. (It was said of Read, an avid teetotaller, that he could smell beer down the end of a telephone.). One never quite knows how to take Caradoc's rhapsodies on journalism, the profession and the medium, for which he made the wildest claims. We know that its romance first struck him at Cardiff and that in large part he was educated through the popular press, by *Reynolds's Newspaper*, the socialist *Clarion*, his very own *T.P.'s Weekly* (in its pre-war manifestation). Nor would he ever allow anyone to forget the *Western Mail*, repeatedly stressing how crucial it was to the cultural health of Wales. Yet Sir William Davies cut no commanding figure. Glyn Roberts, a young Welsh journalist embarking on what was to be a tragically short career, describes an ordinary little white-haired man with "a mannerism of licking his thumb suddenly every now and then. The cuffs of a woollen sweater showed under his coat sleeves."[16] These were Evans's sort of people, not the artistic types. "Men and women who follow the arts fancy themselves greatly; they ride high over the folk who with hands and brains keep the nation going. They company only with their kind and... their church is the club of self-worship." The journalist, on the other hand, "doesn't care a damn for your bank balance, your family, or your university".[17]

It was the comradeship of Fleet Street that Evans valued. For the American Frank Morley, London manager of a New York publisher, it was the most clubbable of streets, where "You could stagger from Monday morning to Saturday night, wandering continuously from one group of discussers to another."[18] Evans was a smoker and drinker, an habitué of legendary watering holes like Shirreff's, a wine lodge beneath the railway thunder of Ludgate Viaduct, the Rainbow in the Strand, and Poppin's (the Red Lion in Poppin's Court, also known as the Compositors' Arms) with its "deep settees and quiet red lights over the only bar, where everybody stood and drank together".[19] The *T.P.'s* gang took daily lunch at Shirreff's, their bacon-and-eggs and toasted ham sandwiches washed down by pints of beer paid for from the stream of books arriving at the office for review; when sufficient had accumulated, they were taken by taxi-load to be sold in the Charing Cross Road. But lunchtime beer dulled the senses and at Austin Clarke's suggestion draught champagne was tried instead. "Soon we were drinking a couple of bottles a day, in the underground cellar, later bombed, at the corner of Ludgate Circus. The exhilaration was pleasant and the effects of dimness disappeared rapidly."[20] Clarke adds that, "Every Friday evening there was a pleasant custom: girl typists and secretaries sat in the wine-cellar with a bottle of excellent Burgundy and a plate of biscuits on the small tables before them."

The journalists' weekly celebration took place on Thursday evening at Henekey's, High Holborn, the day the two literary weeklies went to press and Robert Lynd submitted his Friday article for the *Daily News*. "We counted our week's work done and ourselves free to meet and drink (in strictest moderation) and talk shop," so remembered George Blake.[21] He gives a partial list of those congregating at Henekey's: "Lynd, Caradoc Evans, Con O'Leary, Larry Morrow [with Blake at *John O'London's*], Frank Morley, Frank Whitaker

[*Musical Times*], J.B. Morton ["Beachcomber" of the *Daily Express*], George Malcolm Thomson [*Evening Standard*, *Daily Express*] and Negley Farson [American journalist and author]... not a true-blue Londoner among them!" Caradoc loved the tavern spirit – "the same lads in the same place at the same time" – where his nationality distinguished him. T.P. O'Connor observed "the laughing philosopher" at times give way to "an excited, vehement, angry Welshman consumed by what he regards as a high mission among his people". His colleague Austin Clarke remembered,

> a burly peasant and native speaker of Welsh who frequently sang hymns with his com-patriots at closing time. He had a strange vocabulary of four-letter compounds which affrighted strangers, and a habit of greeting all contributors with ambiguous questions such as "When did you last bury your rhubarb?" The embarrassed caller was aware dimly of the obscene implications of the Colliery phrases.[22]

The Welsh singing hymns at closing times brings to mind a comment by James Agate, that Evans would not disown Sir Hugh in *The Merry Wives of Windsor* for his "if I be drunk, I'll be drunk with those that have the fear of God."[23] (The lines are actually Slender's.) Reginald Pound, features editor of the *Daily Express*, placed Caradoc among a dwindling band of Fleet Street personalities, "characters" of the feather of J.B. Morton, Arthur Machen, T.W.H. Crosland and Hannen Swaffer. Pound had been warned that Evans could be prickly, but meeting him over sherry he was pleasantly surprised: "Vigorous, untrained mind, suggesting lazy competence," Pound recorded in his diary; "Evans likes to spend his energy talking to someone who can talk back. I've taken to him and I don't know why, as he showed no enthusiasm for me...."[24] Pound labelled him a "professional enemy", while Tommy Pope argued that "a man of such force of character and of such determined convictions can hardly fail to make enemies. But he remains one of the most arresting personalities of our time."[25] Tommy Burke agreed:

> He [Evans] is a lean figure, dark of hair and visage, and heavily lined. He has the smouldering gloom of his race that flashes now and then into nervous heat. He goes about with spurts and dashes, bursting into a place and bursting out before you know he has been there... He talks in cascades, words tumbling over each other, precisely the opposite to the caustic manner of his work; words, too, that cause people in trains and buses to look aghast.[26]

Yet he was popular among his friends, "One of the most genial and companionable of men", in Tommy Pope's opinion.

As for physical appearance, it is George Blake's description that most accords with photographs of Evans in the Twenties. "Imagine first a hollow, strong face, the mouth large, the eyes small and piercing, beneath a black felt hat, of which the turned-down brim keeps even the high cheek-bones of the creature in shadow."[27] (The felt hat marked his profession – no journalist sported a bowler.) Blake gives an example of Evans's arresting talk, "invariably violent and violently phrased":

> I always remember a terribly moving story he told me once of an old Welsh peasant
> setting out to meet at Holyhead a son who had prospered in the States. He was a
> poor man and he had to walk all the way, and the road to Holyhead was one of those
> smooth, straight, oppressive highroads we have built for our motorists; and, according
> to Caradoc, "there was this poor old man, trudging that great *arrogant* road." I have
> italicised the epithet, because, even if I have told the story ill, I shall never forget the
> intensely dramatic effect of the word as Evans used it. Stevenson would have lifted
> his hat to the Welshman for the singular justness of the phrase.

Evans sayings lodged in the memory, although his supposed farewell to London – "Death
is but a door. Should I, a Celt with an immortal soul, get out at Tooting Bec?" – must
remain among the apocrypha.[28] The verbal ticks are accredited. He earned the nickname
"Old Bloke" through his favourite term of address ("listen, Old Bloke"), and Reginald
Pound noted his habit of ending every sentence with "don't you know" ("a lovely mahn,
Arthur Machen; a lovely mahn. Oh, yes, a lovely mahn, don't you know").

   Evans's hours outside office and home were not entirely spent boozing with chums.
Mary Webb became an unlikely companion after she moved to London in 1921. Their
friendship began some time earlier when, in a note from her Shropshire cottage, she
thanked him for his review of her first novel, *The Golden Arrow* (1916), in which he'd
applauded her grasp of the Welsh border farm folk among whom she lived – in his
words, "a sorry, pathetic crowd of half-awakened children aspiring vainly after they
know not what".[29] A correspondence followed (it has not survived) in which Webb
described her cottage near Shrewsbury and the productive garden she worked. Week
after week, she wheeled a barrow to Shrewsbury market where she stood for hours
selling her vegetables at a stall. "She made her own clothes, gardened, house-worked,
and tended her chickens. I am sure she would not kill a chicken or consent to one being
killed. She sent me a dozen eggs in a new egg-box."[30]

   Mary and her husband Henry moved to London in 1921, partly for the sake of their
careers, his in teaching, hers in literature and journalism. Caradoc describes first meeting
her outside the *English Review's* new offices in Garrick Street. Disfigured by Graves' disease,
she was not as he had expected. He met "a spindly earthy little woman… Her feet were
biggish, her fingers were thin and trembly and long and like a sewing woman's, her nose
was hooked, her neck was goitred, and her eyes were brilliant bulging glass marbles." Her
voice struck him too, "the deep musical voice of the Welsh people", for she had Welsh
blood in her and claimed her characters were Welsh. She was house hunting, and she
hinted at relatives who did not want her in London at all. "They're afraid I'll live near
them and shame them." (They were Henry's sister and her lawyer husband.) Mary Webb
and Evans met often; "Sometimes we sat in the Embankment Gardens, sometimes we
strolled round and about Fleet Street, sometimes we drank tea (mine very strong, hers
very weak and without milk or sugar) in a tea-shop." She talked mostly of her work. "I
asked her how she managed to write books, as she had a household to look after. She said
that whenever inspiration came to her she would leave the humdrum task on hand – wash-
ing-up, and so on – and there and then sit down and write the chapter or two that was

on her mind."[31] She thought more of her verse than her novels "You have no idea how hard I work over a poem…. But stories – well, they just come to me and I write them without thinking and often I'm surprised at what I've written, so strange it reads." Evans praised her novels emphatically and bolstered her as a woman. "Once she dropped her handkerchief and I picked it up; and her eyes told me I had done a most unusual thing for her. After that she dropped her handkerchief frequently, and she would stand at doors that I should open them for her."

While she was still in Shropshire, Caradoc's literary contacts had been a little help. Two of her nature articles were published in the *Star* and Andrew Melrose agreed to take a volume of her verse provided she wanted no advance of royalties and gave him first option on her next three novels. "He used to say that a poet who asked for a royalty account was not a poet. Mary had nothing to do with him." On her behalf, Caradoc went to see St. John Adcock of the *Bookman* about a short-story anthology he (Adcock) was supervising. "The best loved man in Fleet Street", so Evans said (and Adcock greatly helped Webb with *Bookman* reviewing), but he and Evans clashed when Adcock took exception to Webb's "Caer Cariad", a story Evans had asked of her with Adcock's collection in mind. Mary reports that the two men "had words", Evans withdrawing his own contribution and other stories he had gathered.[32]

"Mary Webb Shropshire" stuck out in High Bohemia, an eccentric among the Bright Young People and the older, fashionably cosmopolitan, women novelists. At the London literary parties she liked to attend,

> She always arrived late … and made a sort of leading actress entrance. She delighted in the gaze of people. A filmy material would hide her goitre, a subdued frock would hang on her stoopy shoulders, and she would walk across the floor like a courageous, vain, wise little gnome. Third-rate women novelists would eye her and third-rate women novelists are spitevenoms, and in fear that some of their underhand saying should reach her, I would say in a loud and Welshy voice:
>
> "I like your dress, Mary. Paris."
>
> "Isn't it pretty? It took me three days to make."

Mindful of her appearance, Webb more than once showed Caradoc photographic proofs of herself. She would reject, then destroy, those she thought "too literary", "too spinsterish", "too plain" or "too stiff". She chose "the pretty one" – herself in profile with a piece of chiffon over the goitre.

"Have you children?" she once asked him. "Thank God, no," Caradoc replied. "I'd love a baby. I'd love several," she confessed. The childless Webbs lived in leafy Hampstead (close to Edwin Pugh), but Mary found no true happiness there, or anywhere else in London. Her marriage began to disintegrate as her husband grew ever closer to one of his young students. Evans is silent on this, though he writes of her becoming more discontented and desperate about money. He had regularly given her work, book reviewing for *T.P.'s Weekly*, and in spring 1926 he commissioned fifteen hundred words on the literature of the Book of Common Prayer. She seemed particularly anxious and disturbed;

having delivered the manuscript, she telephoned every half hour with changes to words and phrases, worried the printer for a morning as her piece went to press, and at the last moment asked that the ten guineas fee be doubled. "Mary, you're too greedy to live," said Evans:

> I was and am very sorry I said that. Sometime after she took herself into the country to die. She died, and no one seemed to care that she was dead.
>
> All her life she had wished for riches, fame, applause, admiration, babies and pretty dresses, and she got none of them. She is the heroine of a fairy story with a sad ending.

In his frank, unemotional way, Evans brought out the pathos of her situation. That she had found no fame or applause truly puzzled him, for he placed her with the best of novelists ("great, almost as great as Hardy"). Yet when in October 1927 she died in a Sussex nursing home, his *T.P.'s Weekly* obituary was, according to Webb's biographer, the "sole tribute".[33] Such perverse neglect made him angry. Three years later he wrote, "Many of the people who move in high places and whose shouts strike the imaginings of the public knew she was great but they held the secret until her burning mind and suffering body had ceased to care."[34]

Evans's literary output during these years shrivelled almost to nothing (although he quietly chipped away at a novel). Even so, these fallow years did not remove him from public attention. Out of the blue, he became the centre of yet another Welsh storm when in February 1927 the International Confederation of Students published (in London) *The Handbook of Student Travel (in Europe)*, a reference work designed to supplement the standard tourist guides. As an appendix, it carried a list of books on European countries "recommended to students as being likely to throw some light on general conditions in, and the mentality of, the States and peoples". In the case of Wales, one title alone made the list – *My People*. "This is either a deliberate insult, a sorry hoax, or a case of stupid ignorance," hollered the *Western Mail* (23 February); distribution of the *Handbook* must be stopped immediately and copies withdrawn from circulation (six hundred were on their way to the United States). The *Handbook's* editor apologized profusely but his offer to rectify matters in a second edition was spurned by the *Mail*. The current edition must be withdrawn, "and we hope the students of Wales will insist on its being withdrawn'.

Caradoc could hardly resist a few words to his favourite newspaper (and greatest organ of publicity). *My People* indeed was the only good book to have come out of Wales, he told a *Western Mail* interviewer (24 February), and while it pleased him that the NUS shared this opinion, he would rather his book be taken up by younger members of the Nonconformist churches in Wales. A vain hope, of course, since the Welsh did not buy books, "even as pieces of learned furniture". As for those copies bound for America, their impact would be as negligible as that of the five thousand copies of *My People* sold in the United States. "The Americans are interested in Wales only as an idyllic sort of

State where everybody is happy and where the church bells ring in chorus on Sunday morning." Unsurprisingly, Evans's interview stoked up further anger, and the *Mail* could justly speak of the "deluge of response" in support of its insistence that the *Handbook* be withdrawn from circulation. Under "An Insult to Wales" (a well-worn headline in this paper), it photographed the student presidents of the four Welsh university colleges and reported that following their meeting at Cardiff, J.E. Meredith (Bangor) had left for London to place Welsh student demands before the NUS. The NUS now backed down, agreeing to replace *My People* with a list of books submitted by the Welsh Students Representative Council. The *Western Mail's* rage was unappeased: such changes would apply to a new edition – what about those copies already in circulation and the hundreds shipped to America?

The controversy took an interesting turn as readers nominated books truly representative of Wales. A "strong dose" of Allen Raine was advocated, together with *Rhys Lewis* (1885), Daniel Owen's second novel (poorly translated into English), and *Change*, J.O. Francis's Glamorganshire play of 1913. Away from imaginative literature, O.M. Edwards's *Wales* found particular favour, although one Cardigan Anglican minister resented its "sectarian standpoint and anti-church sentiments" (published histories of Wales were "polemical tracts" and Daniel Owen a depicter of "the gloomy and fatalistic mentality produced by a Calvinistic religion"). Then on 23 March Evans at last found a champion: for Duncan Davies the characters in the books of his friend were faithful portraits of personalities existing in rural Wales ("making due allowances for literary treatment"):

> The respected Josiah Bryn-Bevan is the prototype of many ministers from Welsh pulpits, and as for Shadrach Danyrefail, why, I met him in a lane near Lampeter less than a year ago. To sum up, then, if a book be selected on the matter of Welsh mentality and characteristics, I can think of no better than *My People* – in fact, I can think of no other.

Davies's solitary stand brought a response from Idwal Jones, playwright, humourist and extra-mural studies lecturer, who had amusingly parodied Evans in a bilingual sketch performed at University College Aberystwyth in February 1926. The occasion, a Saturday evening, lived in the memory of Aberystwyth alumni. Jones's skit, "My Piffle", has a sophisticated Welsh family act as rural primitives for the benefit of a visiting English lady novelist whose notions of Wales have obviously been gathered from *Taffy*. Jones now properly argued that, treated as an imaginative work "brought into being by the stimulus of certain traits to be found in the rural areas of Wales", *My People* was something of which Wales could feel proud; but "regard it as a sane guide-book for the foreigner in his study of Wales and you end up by being ridiculous". (One might mention that in March 1926 Caradoc published in *T.P.'s Weekly* Idwal Jones on bilingualism in Welsh rural schools.) The *Handbook* correspondence rattled on, almost to the end of April and Cardiff City's wondrous defeat of Arsenal in the FA Cup final. By which time the NUS had promised that efforts would be made to withdraw its *Handbook* from circulation; any copies awaiting distribution would carry an amended bibliography, comprising O.M.

Edwards's *Short History of Wales*, J.O. Francis's *Change*, and Professor Alfred E. Zimmern's *My Impressions of Wales*.[35] *My People* would naturally be dropped, a demotion little troubling its author – on 7 April the *Western Mail* was advertising another reissue of the detestable book.

Cardiff's epic Cup Final victory drew a good piece from Evans for the *Sunday Express* ("When Wales Wins", 1 May 1927), some passages gaining currency in Wales when W. J. Gruffydd reprinted them in *Y Llenor*:

> We are the sportive children of the soil. Everything in our lives is a contest. We choose our preachers by contest; our prayer meetings are competition matches in words; our eisteddfodau are flooded arenas, on the face of which float little bits of knowledge and money prizes; even if the glory is temporary, the money is useful. I have heard it said that we are bad losers. That is not so. Our skin is tender. Defeat irritates us into majesty.

Unlike Gruffydd, the *Western Mail* lost no chance to bring down Evans. In November 1928 it dragged him into a barney over Evelyn Waugh's *Decline and Fall*, its correspondent suggesting that *My People* lay behind Waugh's "Welsh" dialogue and his knowledge of Wales. Waugh protested at the blind assumption that an author must be in agreement with the remarks of all his characters ("This is the sort of trouble that really vexes authors in their contacts with their less intelligent readers"). As it happened, he entirely sympathised with Dr Fagan's diatribe against the Welsh.

Evans had more of a part in another Welsh scandal of the time, this one concerning the Welsh-language poet Dewi Emrys, the bardic name of David Emrys James, a journalist and former Congregationalist minister. While appreciative of Evans's talent, Emrys had privately confided that he felt his compatriot "permitted the artistic to be stained by a veniality that is only worthy of the huckster in the market place".[36] This was in 1926, the year he won the bardic crown at the Swansea National Eisteddfod. By spring 1927 his crown was in pawn and Emrys himself a huckster in the marketplace, hawking his verses outside the London Welsh chapels he had once commanded as a minister. Now he was down and out, sleeping rough on the Embankment or in the crypt of St Martin-in-the-Fields. James's waywardness, his drinking, his profligacy and rebelliousness, became common knowledge; less so the connection with Evans, though it seems it was Evans who persuaded him to publicize his story in the *Sunday Express*. Annie Rees, who knew both writers, gives her account of events:

> I know Caradoc financed him, but alas gave him drinks too in some club in London and in this inebriated state conducted an interview and published it in the London Press. Emrys would never have dreamed of such statements in his right mind... and Emrys had to bear the brunt of the attack.

That Evans had a hand in the *Sunday Express* interview (24 April 1927) is certain. He had strong contacts within the paper, and if the story told is Emrys's, the opinions are decidedly Caradoc's. Pulling from his pocket a pipe, some manuscript poems, a book on trout fishing, a volume of Greek verse and sixpence, the mendicant poet contrasts his present situation – lodging in a Salvation Army hostel – with his pre-war glory days as minister at Finsbury Park, when he enjoyed a salary of £500 pounds a year and a congregation likewise numbered in hundreds. He lost his living through offending those who "worship the God of their own grossness" and because of some forthright views. One of these, voiced at a shocked temperance gathering, was that "the curse of this country was not drunkenness but bad beer – beer so full of chemicals that it turns men into beasts." Following army service, Emrys had drifted with the current, coming eventually to rest among the outcasts on the Embankment. There he discovered more Christians than in all the chapels of Wales. "Any fool poet can be Crown Bard of Wales because genius is low in Wales. Its narrow godless Nonconformity stagnates and narrows the whole national outlook and mentality – how can genius be born in such a mire?" As an instance of narrow godlessness he relates how on account of his shabby dress he was refused admittance to a Cymmrodorion Society meeting where Stanley Baldwin was guest of honour. Outside Cardiff's City Hall he had stood in the cold and rain until the doorkeeper gave him a shilling for a night's shelter over a fried fish shop.

As Annie Rees observed, Emrys suffered for his outburst. Straightway reprinting his interview, the *South Wales Daily News* rounded on him. "It is not Mr James who has the right to impeach Wales," its leader intoned ("Still Another Defamer", 27 April),

> It is Wales who should impeach Mr James…. She sent him forth with all the gifts she had to give. By his own prodigality he has wasted them and abused them. He has brought dishonour to Wales and her institutions. He has shown himself a coward in face of the facts of life. He has smirched the standard of his nation, of his calling, of his culture, and by his own life has made them a mock and a scorn. Is this a Welsh poet, patriot and preacher? Rightly she rejects him.

And, the newspaper cleverly asked, how come Mr James got soaked outside City Hall on a night that was fine and dry?

Caradoc's speaking engagements continued. In November 1926 he addressed the Tomorrow Club, a forerunner of PEN. Under John Galsworthy's presidency, it brought together at Long Acre writers from different cultures and different generations, older established authors and their *enfants terribles*. Evans's informal talk had the catch-all title, "People – and Things", and though lacking a coherent thread, it offered a little autobiography and some fine obiter dicta.[37] Rejected by his Board School, he had made his way in the world with a smattering talent. Now at forty-seven he'd become "a bit of a novelist, a bit of a journalist, a bit of a playwright; a bit of a puritan, a bit of an atheist, a bit of a pagan", the product of his social background and a particular family history. Most of all, he had inherited a religion bounded by time and place. Rich Welshmen did not pray; they had learnt the lesson of the times, that "Poor saints are out of date. Poor saints laboured in vain, and their wisdom is in the strong room of oblivion." In Swiftian spirit, Evans hammered out the joyful wisdom. "It is nobler to die rich than poor", and since riches are what we most desire in life, the Cross of Gold, not the Crown of Thorns, is a truer Christian symbol. "New Testament maxims make bankrupts"; "The precept that should be engraved on every heart is: 'If your religion interferes with your business, chuck your religion.'" Evans's address also provocatively compared the Welsh, the English and the Scots. It was the Scots who most fully exploited the art of self-valuation, and thus were the most praised of peoples. Yet at home they told the truth. By contrast, the Welsh could nowhere confront their weaknesses. "The most horrid spectre is the spectre of our own sins. All that we ask is that the rest of the world believes that we are as sanctimonious as our spoken sentiments and as holy as we look in our photographs." The great provoker of the Welsh acknowledged one further abiding truth, that "There are two subjects that are privileged from jest: the Holy Scriptures and the Welsh people."

As has been shown, Evans's every utterance on Wales and its language made the press back home. Though he spoke Welsh readily enough, and occasionally used it for book inscriptions,[38] he shared the prevailing assumption that it was the language of a dying world, "very beautiful, but commercially and in a literary sense it is done for. It belongs to the little people, fairy people – Tylwyth Teg!"[39] Evans turned more fully to the language in a piece for the *Sunday Times*[40]. It begins with some references to the "little languages" that nobody wants. The Scot – "the wisest man on earth" – had "cast his language into the soaring mists of his highlands", regarding it as an encumbrance, "a profitless heirloom". The Irishman, "with the despair of the exile, gave a burlesque of his language to the comedians of America and Europe, though the Irish child has to learn it for two hours a day in his school, but his parents think him a bit of an *omadhaun* [foolish boy] if he brings too much home to tea." But Welsh was still alive, and most on show on Sundays among the London exiles:

> We may try to conceal our accent during the six unholy days of the week in our traffic with the English, but on the Sabbath we are mindful of the tongue in which Adam rebuked Eve and in which the Prophets nagged the bad men of Egypt. I know of no Welsh home in London in which family worship is not conducted in Welsh; I know of no Welsh milkman who on Sundays does not measure his milk with the words of a hymn on his lips.

Back in Wales, the Nonconformists were fighting to save the language:

> In many districts the enthusiasts have insisted upon Welsh-speaking schoolmasters and upon daily lessons in the language; they have brought trouble without end to motorists by placing up road signs in Welsh.... I am afraid that this compulsion is a sign that Welsh is ill. There is no reason, other than that of sentiment, why it should recover. The English are in Wales, with their shops and professions. The Carnegie Library has its representatives travelling up and down the country with their bags of English books. The English newspapers go into the most remote villages. The vernacular press in Wales is deader than our slain mutton.

Evans's hope was that his language would survive in London as long as he continued to live there. "I hope so, for at the proper time every Sabbath evening I rise and go forth to join my countrymen in Hyde Park, where we disturb the slothful loungers with our Welsh hymn tunes."

Early in 1929 *T.P.'s Weekly* ran into difficulties. Behind the scenes, several organisational changes had occurred, beginning with the closure of the printing works adjoining Cassell's editorial offices, a consequence of the growing unrest among printers that culminated in the strike of 1926. Fleet Street proprietors began transferring printing to Watford, from whose cheaper presses messenger boys travelled twice daily to pick up copy. Then in May 1927 the Berry Brothers, owners of Cassell's, moved the firm's periodicals into Amalgamated Press, another of their publishing concerns (Cassell's once more becoming a private company). Under Amalgamated ownership, the paper first moved premises (to an upper floor of Fleetway House, Farringdon Street, in July 1927), then changed its name, dropping the Cassell's connection to become, from September 1927, simply *T.P.'s Weekly*. Next Austin Clarke, exhausted by the pains and pleasures of the job, fled to Dublin, only to succumb to a "rustic plea" by telegram from his distracted editor: "Come back. More money. Caradoc." (Clarke had already been making around £1,000 a year in Fleet Street.) By May 1929 there were signs of a paper in trouble – it had shrunk from 32 to 28 pages – but its demise was nonetheless unexpected and sudden. "I announce with regret that this is the last number which will appear of 'T.P's Weekly'," wrote O'Connor in the 2 November issue. For a long time he had struggled against ill health and fatigue and now it had become impossible for him to keep up publication. The proprietors had accordingly received his letter of resignation. His *Sunday Times* articles would continue "but *T.P.'s Weekly* will be no more". With that, the paper folded and a fortnight later O'Connor was dead. The cessation of a journal that was T.P.'s only in name (towards the end he rarely left his house) perplexed and dismayed the staff. The paper had suffered no dramatic decline in readership, but within Amalgamated Press a claimed circulation of some 72,000 copies was judged not sufficient enough.

Enter Marguerite

1928-30

E vans had a way with women. He encouraged them to talk and he listened to what they said, a refreshing experience for those accustomed to "domestic half-attention" (as Professor Gwyn Jones observed, meeting Caradoc in the 1940s). During his years at La Belle Sauvage Evans conducted a semi-secret life, though his affairs were known to colleagues since they usually began at *T.P.'s Weekly*. The editor's office was fertile ground – literary ladies came to meet him there as potential or actual contributors. Teresa Hooley, a poet of Irish ancestry, first arrived in September 1924. Aged thirty-six (nine years Evans's junior), she had answered his request to see her regarding some poems of hers he had taken. Soon they were in love, or so Hooley believed, but they never became lovers "in the accepted sense". Married and with a baby, she was terrified where such an escalation might lead. It helped that she lived in Derbyshire, that their affair relied upon letters and her occasional trips to London. On one such outing, Caradoc introduced her to Con O'Leary. "Look at her, Con. She's beautiful. Doesn't drink, doesn't smoke, doesn't whore. A good result, indeed."[1] Teresa was Caradoc's ideal, far removed from the "modern girl" of the 1920s, from the flappers and Bright Young People – "the modern girl can make a bottle of brandy blush," he tut-tutted. Hooley had sensitivity and intelligence beyond the ordinary. "I remember him saying once: 'two women in my life have made me think – you and Marie Lloyd!'"

Casting back over their relationship – it petered out in 1926 – Hooley thought Caradoc had been very good to her. He gave her a chance in poetry, taught her "to hate clichés and the poetic fallacy, and to cultivate originality". In this she never really succeeded, though *Songs for All Seasons* (Cape, 1927), her first post-Evans collection, at least struck the *TLS* as "less open than its predecessors to the charge of prettiness"; it conveyed "a sense of pain at the heart of beauty and the suffering and sacrifice that life exacts". A poem to Caradoc begins the collection – "All that I have or am / To you belongs" – but he's an unnamed dedicatee. Other Evans poems in Hooley's collections (besides "Epitaph for a Welsh Novelist") suggest the man and the spell he cast.[2]

> "Rock Flowers" (closing lines)
> "Out of the strong the sweet,"
> High on the open mountain
> Where the storms and great rains beat,
> In the cleft of a grim, scarred boulder,
> Flowers of burning hue

Glowed 'neath the changing heavens,
Like love in the soul of you.

  "The Realist"
On the sandy downs beside the sea
She found a feather, silver and black –
Silver as salmon, black as jet,
Blown from a gull's or a magpie's back.
"Look!" she cried with a swift delight,
"The loveliest thing this evening yet –
A plume of faery, sable and white,
A flutter of pierrot mystery,
Oh look!" He nodded a careless head –
"Just do to clean my pipe," he said.

  "Traitor"
Last night I dreamed of you,
You, whom I thrust from all my thoughts by day.
You looked, you spoke as you were wont to do
Before you went away.
Ah, sick am I to know
That still, despite the bitter guard I keep
O'er those locked memories of long ago
I am betrayed by sleep.

It might have been "the Celt in us both which was the co-magnet," Hooley suggested;
"Anyhow, I'll never forget him." She died, aged eighty-five, at Derby in 1973, her poetry
all but forgotten. Kingsley Amis anthologised "The Realist" – "in its unusual way a masterpiece" – speculating of the couple in the poem that "the poor sod may even be married
to her".[3] But, as Hooley came to learn, Evans married "his Countess".

"His Countess" was Marguerite Barclay, a writer of popular romance published under
the pen names "Countess Barcynska" and "Oliver Sandys". She entered Caradoc's life in
October 1928 – and through the door of his *T.P.'s* office. While he stayed utterly silent
on this and his every affair, Marguerite left three reports of their first encounter, all
slightly different and none wholly accurate. She broadly sets out events in her Oliver
Sandys autobiography *Full and Frank: The Private Life of a Woman Novelist* (1941). Her
estranged husband Armiger Barclay, a restless part-time journalist, had wrongly claimed
in *T.P.'s Weekly* that he was "Countess Barcynska" and thus sole author of *The Honeypot*
(1916), a comparatively successful novel on the world of musical comedy. Marguerite,
shocked and angry, made known her feelings to Winifred ("Biddy") Johnson, her friendly
editor at *Woman's Weekly*. As it happened, Johnson's office was a floor below Caradoc's at
Amalgamated Press and she reported Marguerite's displeasure. Through Johnson, he in
turn invited Marguerite to submit an article which would rebut her husband's claim.
This she did, and when proof copy of her rejoinder seemed slow in reaching her, she

took herself from Kingsbury, the northwest London dormitory suburb where she lived, to deliver a commissioned script to Johnson and to check on her *T.P.'s* submission. Evans already knew a little about her, and what she looked like, having published some flattering photographs of her the year before: pictures of a woman nearing forty, stylishly dressed, sensuous of face, with soft eyes and bow-lipped mouth.

She entered *T.P.'s* premises. "There were two large rooms leading to the editor's room, which was the smallest of the three; and whereas most of the rooms in the building were lavishly furnished this had no more in it than a plain table, two hard chairs and a cupboard of review books." As for meeting the editor, "It was as if a shutter clicked down on the whole of the rest of my life." Handing her the proof of her rejoinder-article, he invited her to make any changes overnight and return it to him promptly in the morning. He escorted her to the lift.

She appeared next day on the stroke of ten. "The morning was cold. An entire scuttleful of coal had been thrown on the fire which was all but out... The window was wide open and the man [Evans], his coat off, was in a bright yellow shirt. He had shaggy goat's hair and violent features and the eyes of a squirrel" ("shrewd, penetrating, deep-set", she elaborated). He offered her some books from the cupboard, in particular the love letters of Abelard and Eloise. It was a gift with the fly-leaf inscription: "These lovely letters for Marguerite from Caradoc". He turned to her personal life. What were her origins? ("The man always comes to that derivative question in meeting a stranger.") And her marital state? She was married to Armiger Barclay but signed herself "Mrs W.P. Lovell". He mentioned that Winifred Johnson had told him that she (Marguerite) had a young son and "you're devoted to him and you don't go to cocktail parties, or smoke, or drink beer, and your only vice is mother-love". Marguerite talked of her daily routine, the mornings spent writing and her afternoon drives in the car. Evans boldly suggested future drives – in the mountains of Wales, perhaps? He took her hand, pressed her ring into her finger, and with the help of Isaiah, unburdened himself. "I love you. You know I do. I adore you. I adored you the moment you came into the room like the Queen of Sheba, and I said to myself O who is this that cometh from Edom..."

Five years later, in her biography *Caradoc Evans* (1946), Marguerite intensified the drama and romance. This man had swept her away. "As soon as I was in his presence I knew that this was my hour and my man whatever was to come afterwards." He sees her to the lift, notes down her telephone number and rings her at midnight from a kiosk outside a pub in Richmond, there rhapsodizing until past one in the morning. So began their almost daily meetings and his late-night boozy phone calls. Come 1957, and her third account (in *The Miracle Stone of Wales*), she has Caradoc seizing her hand and "pressing a heavy gold nugget ring I was wearing deep into my finger; so deeply that it hurt." Pain, she soon discovered, was the price of being with him. "He stormed his way into my heart exactly as he had stormed his way through life. There was no calm in him." Once again, she repeats the story that "A year later I was married to the man." In fact they would not marry until May 1933, four-and-a-half years later.

One stumbling block to union was that both were already married; to complicate matters, Marguerite for years had been living with another man, while Evans, besides a wife, had a sparky mistress on his heels. Her presence is hinted at in Marguerite's second account, when, in his office, their mutual declarations of love are interrupted by a ringing telephone and "a woman's thin voice" speaking down the line. "A contributor and a damn nuisance," Caradoc covered up, "I don't want to see anyone but you ever again." Taking him at his word, Marguerite regularly appeared on the premises, her presence announced by her wafting perfume. In his *A Penny in the Clouds* Austin Clarke recollected that "Whenever Mille Fleurs drifted into the inner office in which Con and I were typing... we knew that Caradoc's new mistress, a popular novelist in a large fur coat, was sitting by his desk." But the "damn nuisance" would not go away. She challenged him at work. "Once we heard voices raised. The door banged. His older mistress had found out, and when she seized the telephone receiver to ring up her rival, the alarmed Editor had snipped the wire with the scissors. He came in afterwards to us, with a dismal expression. How could he explain to the engineering staff the mystery of the cut wire?" Clarke portrays a man of heightened sexual appetite:

> Despite the fact that he had to meet the amative demands of a large woman and a small one, Caradoc remained unsatisfied. His great wish was to have carnal knowledge of a woman doctor. Articles on medicine and home treatment were a feature of the periodical. In turn, attractive women doctors sat in his office, with tempting gun-metal-coloured stockings but all of them kept their elegant legs crossed.

"I cannot say whether Alma was my greatest stroke of luck or my greatest misfortune," said Franz Werfel, third husband of Gustav Mahler's widow. The Evanses, husband and wife, might have said much the same of each other through the years of their tempestuous marriage. Caradoc wrote almost nothing about their private life. Marguerite, in her autobiographical writings, more than hints at its darker side though perhaps in her fiction she comes closer to the truth. Both were complex, volatile characters with unusual, difficult pasts.

Marguerite Jervis was born "under fire" (as she puts it) on 7 October 1886 at Henzada, lower Burma, the eldest child of Florence and Henry Jervis. Regimental surgeon with the 7th Bombay Infantry, Henry Pruce Jervis married Florence Mary Chapman at St Thomas Cathedral, Bombay, in December 1884; he was 29, she just 18. Soon afterwards Jervis took part in the third Anglo-Burmese war (1885), a conflict that secured the British annexation of Burma. Back in India, on the plains at Raipur, he ruled his house in military style – servants lined up on the veranda for a weekly pay parade. His little daughter spent her first seven years in India, a delicate, highly imaginative child. Christened Marguerite Florence Laura, she was always Daisy to her family, save for her father who, disappointed she wasn't a boy, took to calling her Jack. This remote, unloving man, with a young wife made weak by childbearing (five babies died in infancy), shaped Marguerite's emotional development. Fortunately, she had "Aunty Tots" by her side, her mother's sterling older sister, at least until the age of seven when she was packed off to school in England. There she trod the cheerless path of countless "orphans of the Raj", children separated from parents and suffering small private schools like the one near Radlett run by "two educated gentlewomen (daughters of an Army officer)" who took in Marguerite at eleven.

In November 1902 Henry Jervis retired, aged forty-seven, on an army colonel's pension and settled with his family at Southampton as a physician and general surgeon. Marguerite, now an attractive teenager (despite her "sparrow-legs"), won a crowd of admirers. Two marriage proposals ensued, offers that her mother, who had married young herself, thought well worth consideration. But in the words of Marguerite's auto-biography, "I was strenuously opposed to marriage – the backwater oblivion where one spent the rest of one's life as Mrs Someone." Her horror was "of living ordinarily and then dying and being buried without having done a thing by which I could be remembered. Just a name on a gravestone." She wanted the independence that springs from an own personal income. "I wanted to earn things for myself and never be dependent on a man. This independence is one of the few resolutions I have kept. I see no reason why the bond of marriage, specially if there be no children, should compel a man to keep a woman into perpetuity." Radical stuff, predictably infuriating her father, who again was far from impressed when in 1905 his eighteen-year-old daughter got a story and poem in print and enlisted at Beerbohm Tree's newly founded Academy of Dramatic Art on London's Gower Street. Only modestly successful at stage school, she turned more seri-ously to writing stories ("trash" in her father's eyes) and looked to openings in journalism – a Modern Girl on the surface but instinctively conservative beneath.

An Anglo-Indian restlessness propelled the Jervises next to Reigate where they found a house big enough to accommodate Marguerite and her two younger brothers, Charles and Edmund. Reigate proved a turning-point. Just as she was developing an identity of her own through acting and writing fiction, her parents urged her to marry a rich young suitor whose sole interest seemed to be hunting. In revolt, she sought the company of a much older man of Polish-Jewish background, an aloof, enigmatic character, married but separated from his wife and lodging alone in Reigate. Known as Armiger Barclay – the forename means "one who is entitled to bear heraldic arms" – he had been born Bernard Armiger Barczinsky in Durham in 1858, of a father who, so Armiger said, was a naturalized Polish count (his title most likely conferred in Czarist Poland). Having spent a childhood on the continent, Armiger returned to a changeful career in England: part-owner of a racing stud, provincial theatre manager, master at a Jewish boys' school founded by his father. By the time of Reigate he was a published novelist but wholly reliant on journalism. He was attractive after a fashion, an Edwardian mix of clubman and country gentleman, his grizzled beard smartly trimmed in the continental manner. He described himself as a votary of all forms of sport, "riding, hunting, shooting, yachting", who otherwise took his exercise in motor cars and taxis. For Marguerite his literary side had huge appeal and for a couple of years she and Armiger would sometimes write in tandem.

Her early publishing history takes some untangling on account of her many pen names. She speaks of writing short stories first in order to "get slick" and her name on magazine covers. She mentions periodicals such as *Answers* ("the Popular Journal for Home and Train") and *Modern Society*,[4] as well as *Sievier's Monthly* (1909) and the *Winning Post Annual* (1905-23), two titles managed by Robert S. Sievier. A dashing chancer with a background in racing, Bob Sievier excited Marguerite ("a real man", she thought). She became sub-editor of *Sievier's Monthly* and contributed extensively to both his magazines, writing as "Olive Bree" and "Oliver Sandys" (the surnames deriving from her mother's Cornish family), and occasionally as "Armiger Barclay".[5]

In 1910 Armiger and Caroline his wife were divorced, opening the way for his marriage to Marguerite at Aylesbury on 17 July 1911. She was twenty-four, he fifty-three (though admitting to fifty). Starved of paternal love, she had chosen a surrogate father no less cold and severe than the Colonel. As for Henry Jervis, he disowned his daughter: how could she marry a man just two years younger than himself – and a Polish Jew at that! The newlyweds were soon in difficulties. Marguerite paints herself, not very convincingly, as "frightened and innocent" at this time, insisting that Armiger had assured her that "marriage with him would be a sort of father & daughter arrangement... Father & daughter – ye gods!"[6] He had appealed to her literary ambitions; as well as father-daughter, theirs would be a master-pupil relationship. Installed in their honeymoon home at Bierton, a village north of Aylesbury, Mrs Barclay settled to writing. Armiger stressed the importance of discipline, of sticking to office hours rather than waiting for the "mood". She was eternally grateful: "Office hours is very sound advice and I have kept to that rule of Armiger's throughout my working life."[7] Regarding his own role in their cottage industry, it was, so Marguerite alleged, strictly editorial, and in his regard for the accidentals of a text he could have been Mrs Albert Forrester, bestselling novelist in a Somerset Maugham story, who discovered the comic possibilities of the semi-colon. Marguerite had written a story:

> Armiger read it and approved it. Then he got a bottle of red ink, knocked off a few commas and put some in and changed a few into semi-colons, knocked off a few quotation marks and broke up a few paragraphs.
>
> The next morning he typed it and then brought it to me to read.
>
> The title page gave me a jerk: the author of my story was Armiger Barclay. He noted my look of surprise.
>
> "I left your name out," he explained, "because *The World* will take almost anything I write at three guineas a thousand."
>
> I had the parachute sensation.[8]

Abandoning her parents' circles – safe-income people with pensions or private means – Marguerite gave herself wholly to authorship. It was her duty to be productive and she maintained an enviable output (including one story in the *English Review*), all this despite their frequent house moves caused by Armiger's quarrelling with landlords. From Bierton they went south to Bushey Heath, another place of fields and farms, where they found a Jacobean property (fit setting for Armiger's antiques). Marguerite cherished no hope of a child by a man she did not sleep with and who had no fondness for children.

Instead, she lavished her affection on a black spaniel puppy named Cupid – until her increasingly resentful husband insisted that the creature must go. Cupid became the pet of young Monica Dunbar, destined to be one of Marguerite's confidantes and our major external witness to her life before Caradoc. Monica's parents, Malcolm and Helen ("Nell") Dunbar, living nearby at Edgware, happily took in the little dog. "Poor Marguerite, longing for a child and even deprived of her dog, became ill and we were asked to return Cupid, which we gladly did and so gained the friendship of a life time."[9]

In July 1914, a month before war began, the Dunbars photographed Armiger and Marguerite in the garden of Old Roses at Twinstead, near Sudbury, yet another delightful old house they had come upon. Marguerite gushed to Nell of how she would redesign it. "Grey is a lovely colour for showing off china. But for myself I almost prefer a very delicate shade of green – it is almost a grey green. We have this in our drawing room here with rose Persian carpet & it looks rather well."[10] War put a damper on things, particularly for Marguerite who had "relations galore all mixed up in this". Still, Armiger assured her that the fighting would be over in about six weeks and would be decided on land; "He doesn't think the Germans will come forth at sea."[11] Old Roses had charm in plenty, but Marguerite never truly felt happy there. How could she? "A young girl with an old man she didn't love and a spaniel she did love but which he did not want her to keep because its black hairs shed themselves on the rose-pink carpet."[12] In September 1914 the Barclays abandoned Old Roses for Sudbury.

If all they could find in Sudbury was a "semi-detached atrocity", the place had its attractions. Here a new man entered Marguerite's life, a Captain Walter Preston Lovell, "doing army organizing work" and quartered nearby. A bachelor of forty, handsome, reserved and lonely, Lovell became friendly with the Barclays sometime in 1915, dropping in on them most evenings after work. Then on 13 January 1916 Marguerite gave birth to a son, her only child, registered at Sudbury as Nicholas C.G.A. Barczinsky. Speculation predictably began concerning the child's paternity. Could Walter Lovell be the father? The Dunbars thought this impossible: one look at Nick would convince any doubter that he could only be Armiger's son. The resemblance was lost on Marguerite's doctor, who thought the boy a living image of his mother. Certainly, Nicholas in later years showed his mother's facial features. He spoke little, and unreliably, about his family and his past, though he did confide to an intimate that Armiger was not his biological father – nor was Walter Lovell. His mother had taken another lover, unsurprisingly a military man (named Parry and possibly Irish) whom Nicholas met from time to time and got along with quite well.[13] It is worth noting that in 1931, a year after Armiger's death, Marguerite put him [Armiger] into her novel *A Woman of Experience*, where a man of forty marries a girl of seventeen (and Marguerite would wrongly state that she herself had married at seventeen), then proceeds to claim the success of the books she writes. She mothers an illegitimate child and walks away from her marriage.

Shortly after Nicholas's birth, with a wife too tired to capitalize on the success of *The Honeypot*, her novel of the stage, Armiger worried about finances. He had insisted on an upward move to the Manor House at Melbourn, south of Cambridge. There

Marguerite wrote to Nell Dunbar, "I'm really rather happy – very happy where he [Nick] is concerned. As for the other [Armiger], well it remains as it was. I'm sorry for the third person though [Walter]. It must be very hard for him because he cares & is all alone. Still, it's best as it is. I have my darling little one to think of first & foremost."[14] The Manor House, "very large and old with a lovely garden", stretched their resources alarmingly and one solution, so it struck Armiger, was for Marguerite to return with Nick to Sudbury and keep house for Walter Lovell, who had since taken a furnished property there. "I have often thought what was in Armiger's mind at this time," Marguerite writes in *Full and Frank*; "Did he imagine the golden-egg laying goose he had married had lost her fertility and therefore the best thing to be done was to get rid of her and should it by any chance start laying again he could easily reclaim her?" Strange as it struck outsiders, she and the baby would indeed join Lovell at Sudbury; and poor Cupid again would be given away. One might add that Armiger's equanimity in face of Walter Lovell, and the wish to be rid of Marguerite, could have had something to do with his closeness to another woman, perhaps the mistress who came into reckoning shortly after his death. The "full and frank" Marguerite is silent on this.

Walter Lovell was at ease in the Jervises' world. A military man with service in India (his country of birth), he knew the British "Anglo-Indian" crowd. Monica Dunbar thought him "a kind and gentle character", "a very delightful man, rather in the style of David Niven".[15] In 1917 he transferred to Ipswich, distinctly a come-down for Marguerite: "[It] is full of officers & soldiers & house accommodation is terrible. We have a <u>dreadful</u> little villa… with 1d in the slot gas machine & everything to match." Besides, there were servant problems. "I have a brute at £30 p.a.! She's been with me 7 months, is stone deaf & eats like a rhinoceros."[16] She now adopted Walter's name, styling herself either Daisy or Marguerite Lovell; Walter joined the family in calling her Daisy but Armiger's preference for Marguerite was increasingly becoming her own. As for "Mrs Lovell", this was, as Monica Dunbar understood, an acceptable response to a difficult position. "Socially, divorced women, certainly in middle class circles, were not regarded with favour in those pre-1920 days. Marguerite's whole career as author depended upon the editors of women's magazines having a good opinion of her, as well as not disgracing her parents by what was then regarded as "living in sin", and I think it is also clear that having made a "deal" with Armiger over the Countess Barcynska books, divorce proceedings were out of the question."[17]

The Armiger "deal" was a consequence of her return to productive authorship and it centred on the rights to "Countess Barcynska". In no circumstance, Armiger warned, was Marguerite to use for literary or private purposes his family name Barcynsky or its feminine form Barcynska. Countess Hélène Barcynska was *his* pen name and published books that carried it were consequently his property. A compromise was reached: since theirs had been collaborative undertaking (however marginal Armiger's contribution), husband and wife would each receive a half-share of the income generated by Barcynska titles. This Marguerite accepted, believing she had wrung out an important concession: that in the event of her husband's death, or his ceasing to write, the literary name and income would naturally lapse to her. Under this agreement the "collaboration" continued. Marguerite sent her stuff to Armiger who passed it on to literary editors, notably to Biddy Johnson at *Woman's Weekly*.

With the ending of war, Walter Lovell resigned his army commission and became over time Marguerite's literary secretary. She quickly hit her stride, in 1919 earning "exactly £1040" by her pen.[18] Things got even better when, still chafing at the half-share in novels that "in truth and essence" were hers, she looked beyond Barcynska to her other pen names. Passing over Olive Bree (it smacked of cheese, as Armiger said), she settled on Oliver Sandys for *The Garment of Gold*, published in 1921. At this new move Armiger became alarmed and aggressive, insisting that Marguerite straightway renounce "Oliver Sandys", a name more associated with her stories, and stay with him as "Countess Barcynska" for the novels. Big money was at stake – two Barcynska novels had raised £1,600 in film rights. Marguerite held firm, leaving Armiger to join a band of British tax exiles living on the Côte D'Azur. Marguerite cemented her relationship with Biddy Johnson and Amalgamated Press, agreeing a five-year contract for four *Woman's Weekly* serials a year, at a thumping £500 each. These serials, partly rewritten, would then be released in book form, in succession of cheaper editions. From 1922 onwards Marguerite duly averaged four novels a year – two Countess Barcynska titles and two by Oliver Sandys – almost all published by Hurst & Blackett. Film rights swelled the coffers. (Her novel *The Pleasure Garden* won a place in cinema history: it signalled Alfred Hitchcock's directorial debut when filmed in 1925.) All in all, she enjoyed the fruits of her success: the luxury of a chauffeured car, and high-end clothes and millinery from Jays of Regent Street, one of London's most elegant dressmakers, patronised by royalty and the stage.

From late 1920 she, Walter and Nick had been living in Southbourne, at the back of Bournemouth, a spot attractive to Marguerite's parents who in turn moved to nearby New Milton. There in February 1927 Henry Jervis died of a massive stroke. Marguerite's relationship with her father had been intense and ambivalent. She recognised the military man's rigidity of mind and that he ruled by fear both his staff and family, crushing any signs of independence. She had begun at a disadvantage, having been born a girl, though neither to her nor his sons did he show much paternal affection. Her imaginativeness and bookishness meant nothing to him and her marriage to Armiger Barclay sealed the alienation ("henceforth I was dead to him forever"). At Nicholas's birth he yielded so far as to send a note of congratulation, a letter "bedewed with glad tears and kept under my pillow", says Marguerite in *Full and Frank*. "Oh I did long for my father to love me!" Having courageously resisted him, she went on craving his love and approval. At his death she believed this was given her; henceforth she would love her father's memory as deeply as she loved him in life. His framed officer's commission and his dress sword became her household holy relics.

Only in her final years would Marguerite come to live on her own. She had a horror of the solitary state. "I wouldn't be left alone for <u>worlds</u> myself," she confessed to Nell Dunbar while unhappily married to Armiger,[19] and she recalled her childhood terror of being lost and alone. She needed the security of a dominant man, whatever his imperfections – and her writing career suggests that she thrived under such men. Walter Lovell, though an army officer, was not of this kind. In their early years, "baby-bound and cradle worshipping", she found him a suitable companion, if lacking the artistic dimension. By the time she met Caradoc she was feeling "an inner emptiness". Having swapped Southbourne for Kingsbury to be closer to Fleet Street contacts (her widowed mother was now in Brighton where her sons were schoolmasters), she became increasingly unsettled, even about work. Serial writing, though splendidly paid, was starting to pall, and converting serials into books was now a chore: "My book public was growing and my true joy was in writing novels in which the characters behaved not so much according to formula but as if they themselves were working out the plot." This joy she conveyed in a Kingsbury letter to Nell Dunbar: "always busy – writing books & films & simply adore it".[20] Then in September 1928 Armiger (living in Menton) came forward in *T.P.'s Weekly* as the authentic Countess Barcynska, describing his writing methods and the constant need to guard against copyright infringement. His article provoked Marguerite's response and her fateful first meeting with Caradoc.

Evans might have stormed his way into her heart, but Marguerite's guilt over Walter was real and acute. A companion of ten years or more, he had helped in her writing career, taking on office duties, filing correspondence, keeping accounts, and generally managing her affairs; and he shared the considerable burden of bringing up young Nick, a delicate, difficult, ridiculously pampered young lad educated at home by an endless succession of tutors. Marguerite resisted Caradoc's charge that Walter was simply a money-hunter, the lonely boarding-house soldier short of a decent pension who had met a breadwinner "scratching on a goldmine with her pen".[21] Her confusion deepened as Caradoc's behaviour, often erratic, veered worryingly out of control. These were tur-bulent times for him, on both personal and professional fronts. He needed to find a new publisher, since Andrew Melrose had sold up to Hutchinson's in 1927 (a year before his death); then to get a new agent after Andrew Dakers retired (Evans moved to A.D. Peters). More troubling was the collapse of *T.P.'s Weekly*, for this almost certainly spelled the end of his career in journalism. A fifty-year-old literary editor stood little chance of landing a suitable berth in Fleet Street at a time when prospects had worsened for journalists of every stripe.

Losing his job in November 1929 did not immediately threaten Evans's finances. The year's gratuity he received on leaving meant more money in the bank than at any time before. But he was at a loose end, passing hours in drinking haunts. At home, Rose urged that he look for another job as quickly as possible, and "Rose was right economically, of course." Caradoc's words come via Marguerite in her later biography of her husband. There she has him elaborating on the first Mrs Caradoc Evans:

> Rose and I weren't getting on. I was to blame... that I hadn't made her happy for
> the past years on account of our divergencies. I daresay she resented my Fleet Street
> friends and the hours I spent with them... I don't blame her for anything that went
> wrong between us. It was just inevitable. Rose always did her best for me and never

interrupted me when I was working. She knew what my work meant to me although it meant nothing to her. I might as well have written in Chinese, but she let me alone. She didn't care about my literary friends. I wanted to bring Mary Webb home to tea once and she wouldn't receive her. That led to an argument. I told her I had run across a woman who was going to be truly great. I was excited about it. She didn't understand the reason for my excitement.

Rose Evans survives in a few passing references (none of them directly Caradoc's) that cast her as a straightforward, unaffected woman out of her element both in her husband's London circles and among his family in Wales. From time to time in the early days she had holidayed at Rhydlewis, finding little to like in the village. "A very selfish person" who never understood her husband, insisted Annie Rees. By the time of the Evanses' divorce, selfishness and lack of understanding were all Marguerite could see in Rose, a greedy cockney sparrow unable to follow the great Welsh eagle in its flight; "she hated his beautiful work and said he wrote dirty books." In time, in sorrow, she would look more kindly on Rose.

Marguerite's public writings are discreet on Caradoc's behaviour after he lost his job. Privately she hints at his disorder, fuelled by excessive drinking ("my divine hobby"), his destructive womanizing and towering rages. Duncan Davies had noticed the change, attributing it in part to the dubious new company Evans kept – this, and the emotional turmoil at thoughts of leaving London. He and Evans loved the great city, and Davies remembered his own real suffering at having to move away, in his case to Cardiff. Nevertheless, "I realize that the best thing that could have happened to Caradoc was the leaving of Fleet St and its tragic dangers. On those occasions when I met him in his later days in London, chiefly at The Cock Tavern or the [Cheshire] Cheese, it was obvious that he was mixing with a Bohemian crowd of the type which had brought thousands of brilliant men to ruin."[22] Davies named Joe Simpson and Jimmy Pryde, two men who, along with the *Sunday Express* journalist Nathaniel Gubbins, were among the more colourful of Caradoc's new drinking pals.

A professional humorist, for whom the world was intolerable without a glass in the hand, Nat Gubbins turned in a highly successful weekly column of satirical fantasy. Drinking with Gubbins made Evans late for one liaison with Marguerite and forced a revealing half-apology. "You ticked me off and I said unkind things to you. I provoked you and went on provoking and could not stop myself. You looked so beautiful. It pleased me to make you cry."[23] Pryde and Simpson were artists of Scottish background and both were on the rocks around this time. Caradoc had tried to help Simpson by taking his etched caricatures for *T.P.'s Weekly* – "he got very difficult – wanted more than we could pay him" – and buying a few prints for himself (Simpson specialised in sporting subjects and characterful portraits). Marguerite warmed more to the tall and handsome James Ferrier Pryde, a gifted, spendthrift artist in his sixties, living alone in a cheerless flat with no money even for a fire. Following one dismal Sunday visit, during which Marguerite made Pryde's bed, she and Evans sent him a ton of coal.[24] Even so, they would carelessly neglect him at Christmas 1930. Pryde had nowhere to go; plenty of friends to stand him a drink but none to invite him home. Marguerite had freed herself of Walter for Christmas Day, as Caradoc had of Rose, and the two agreed to meet Pryde later on for dinner at the Adelphi. As the day unfolded Jimmy was forgotten. Caradoc "in erratic mood" took Marguerite back to the Richmond hotel he had booked but she left to be home with Walter by nine. Two hours later Caradoc arrived at the Adelphi where Jimmy had been waiting since seven. "He pretended not to mind – took it very well and wasn't even offended – but he minded like hell. I've been sorry about that Christmas for every Christmas after."[25] Lacking a woman to look after him, Jimmy could not cope – and neither could Caradoc, Marguerite was convinced.

Drink got the better of Caradoc one time at the Ivy, a Covent Garden haunt of theatre folk. In September 1930, shortly after his success with *Nothing to Pay*, he buttonholed a mildly amused Lytton Strachey. Writing to Roger Senhouse, Strachey recounted how Evans had "apostrophised" him in Anglo-Welsh for three quarters of an hour. "'Truly to God' was one of his favourite phrases – 'Truly to God, Mr Strachey, you can write English – English – you know what I mean – you *know* – yes, Mr Strachey, English, truly to God!'" Marguerite, "a vast highly coloured woman in the Spanish style", had rescued him, then taken them all in her car to Gordon Square where Strachey lived. There he thankfully managed to escape.[26]

By 1930 Caradoc had made friends with the young Welsh artist Evan Walters. Born in 1893 at Mynydd-Bach in the parish of Llangyfelach, near Swansea, Walters by the 1920s had gained two active champions: Mrs Winifred Coombe-Tennant was a generous patron and Augustus John an influential admirer. Having awarded him a prize at the 1926 Swansea National Eisteddfod, John hailed Walters as an artist "essentially and profoundly Welsh" who "would assuredly make a great name for himself". His words seemed to have come true in November 1927, and with John's help. Unable to meet a commitment to show at a Mayfair gallery, John recommended Walters in his stead. The ensuing exhibition, his first in London, proved a notable success. *The Times* welcomed Walters unreservedly, as it did his second one-man show (June 1930). It wasn't the celebrity portraits (Lloyd George, Gerald Balfour) that impressed – they lacked depth of observation – but rather his rendering of "types" and typical events ("The Washerwoman", "The Hewer", "Feeding Time", "The Friday Bath"). His was a "whole-fisted" portrayal of the landscape and people of Llangyfelach, the mining village where he still spent much of his time.

Augustus John's review of the exhibition, an extended essay in *Vogue* (11 January 1928), advanced the view of Walters as an instinctive artist who, if not wholly self-taught, had escaped "the false academic attitude so fatal to most young talents". He had likewise survived the stultifying environment of Wales, where the paintings that find acceptance were of the "nightgown school of scriptural subjects, the anecdotal banality of coloured supplements, or landscapes of impossible prettiness." Prettiness and sentimentality were qualities demanded above all. John's applause for the rebel Walters mirrors his regard for Caradoc Evans, and the artist's approach to his subject matter – Walters displayed "an unimpassioned realism and leaves the spectator to supply his own emotional constructions" – again brings Evans to mind. John applauds the "saturation" in Walters. "He possesses his country so completely that the mere presentation of a scene carries with it all the possible emotional associations without its being necessary for them to be emphasised, or even explicitly stated."

Caradoc got to know Walters in the wake of the 1927 exhibition. Through Walters he met Sean O'Casey, recently married and settled in London, and Walters in particular became a valued London friend. Marguerite, too, liked a man whose Welsh country background resembled Caradoc's. She thought the two uncannily alike in their good points and their bad; both could be perfect companions but also cruel and mad. Winifred Coombe Tennant's observations on Walters, whom she knew over thirty years, bear witness to this.[27] She first met, in 1920, a "young dark typical Welshman… very intelligent and pleasant" who soon became "a strange and wondrous being, capable of cruelty and roughness, yet intensely sensitive. He is full of undisciplined power!" For Coombe-Tennant, he remained "a fine painter", but "a man of bad temper, and a bully" – this after Walters had kicked out the wife he had married just five months previously.

Towards the end of 1930, Walters persuaded both Caradoc and Marguerite to sit for him at his studio in Belsize Park. He had hopes that his Caradoc portrait would be shown at Swansea's Glynn Vivian Gallery. After all, Walters was a local artist and his subject a notable author born not too far away. He had dramatically misjudged. In paint as in print, Caradoc Evans remained unwelcome in his homeland, and in institutional Wales above all.

A Cubist Caradoc Evans

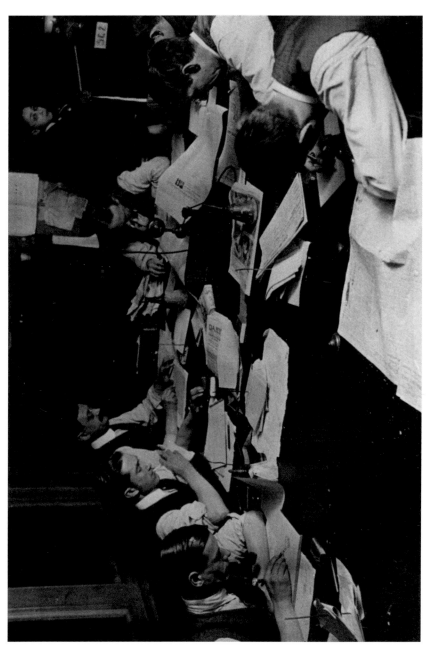

Caradoc (front left) at the *Daily Mirror* subs table, where he worked 1917-23

Evans in his Fleet Street prime, with T.P. O'Connor (centre) and Arthur Machen (left)

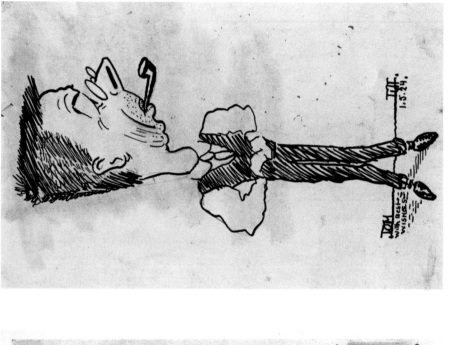

Two 1924 caricatures of Evans at *T.P.'s Weekly*, by "Matt" (Matthew Sandford) and "Tom Titt" (Jan Rosciszewski). Both were continuously engaged by papers and periodicals, Matt's sketches being a feature of *T.P.'s Weekly*

Marguerite and Armiger Barclay at "Old Roses", Sudbury 1914. They had married in 1911

Walter and "Marguerite Lovell" with Nicholas her son and Cupid

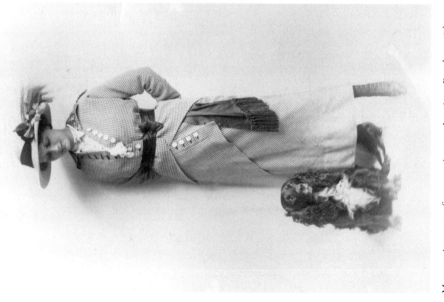

Marguerite soon after marriage to Armiger Barclay, with her adored cocker spaniel Cupid

At Evan Walters' Belsize Park studio, c. 1930: Caradoc, Marguerite, Erna Meinel (artist and friend of Walters), Evan Walters

Evans as he appeared in *Current Literature* (August 1930). *Inset*: The journalist Glyn Roberts. Recognising Caradoc from the Current Literature photograph ("great nose, glaring eyes and vast black hat"), he introduced himself and in the little time left him promoted Caradoc enthusiastically

Nothing to Pay

1930

Before the turn of the decade, the long promised novel had sufficiently progressed for Evans to seek a new publisher. He did so with notable success. On 19 March 1930 a contract was signed with the newly restructured Faber & Faber for a work entitled *Nothing to Pay*; the advance was £175, substantial for a first novel. Though its pre-eminence in literary publishing dates from later in the Thirties, the Faber publishing house had (as Faber & Gwyer) since 1925 enjoyed a rising prestige, its chairman Geoffrey Faber having appointed T.S. Eliot as full-time literary editor and member of the board. Eliot was the star Faber author, followed by Ezra Pound, Herbert Read, Walter de la Mare, and Siegfried Sassoon, whose *Memoirs of a Fox-Hunting Man* proved a money-spinner. (W.H. Auden joined the list with *Poems*, published in September 1930, three weeks after *Nothing to Pay*.) Acceptance of *Nothing to Pay* came through another director, the Baltimore Rhodes scholar Frank Morley, appointed in 1929 to the reconstituted firm to advise on manuscripts and, as the chairman put it, "bring grist to the mill". Evans had occasionally met Morley across the tables of Henekey's and the Wellington, two haunts of Fleet Street's more convivial bookmen. Morley admired Caradoc Evans, both for his work on *T.P.'s Weekly* – the paper had been the first to welcome Faber's promotion of James Joyce[1]– and for his gifts as a writer. He took *Nothing to Pay* when it was only three-quarter finished, as Evans explained to Herbert M. Vaughan, but on condition that it was finished in time for the return to America of a New York publisher. "I finished it," he added.[2]

Morley believed that the novel, combined with reprints of *My People* and *Capel Sion*, could revitalize Evans's writing career. The reprints, designed along the lines of Cape's eye-catching Sarn edition of Mary Webb, were crucial to his strategy. "Panting to be able to start the ball rolling", Morley urged quick copyright clearance from Hutchinson (who had bought up Andrew Melrose): "I want to hear about the previous books just as quickly as possible for the campaign on *Nothing to Pay* has got to be thoroughly worked out and the sooner I can get started the better are the prospects all round."[3] As it transpired, protracted wrangling over payment for the reprints forced Morley to proceed with *Nothing to Pay* on its own. He did so enthusiastically enough, and in the W.W. Norton Company secured a progressive American publisher. Norton at first found the book unapproachable "for concentrated savagery" and thought that it would benefit from a new first chapter. Evans promptly obliged, offering an alternative opening to Morley also. In the event, the new chapter (on Bensha, the wedding bidder) came to stand at the beginning of the Norton edition and was incorporated as chapter two of the published Faber text.[4]

Simultaneously, Evans provided both Faber and Norton with promotional copy for their dust jackets and for a projected "Booksellers' Guide to Caradoc Evans". He showed an editor's interest in design, approaching Morley as friend and equal. The two saw eye-to-eye on colour: "A green cover will look dam [sic] fine," agreed Evans when touching on another matter, whether the "paragraph of praise" should appear on the back or front of the dust jacket. As he saw it, the complimentary assessments of his work he had gathered, from Thomas Burke, Arthur Machen, H.L. Mencken, J.B. Priestley and Hugh Walpole, would have more impact if placed on the front, where such names "will make the literary editor open his eyes with wonder" and favourably dispose reviewers.[5] (If used, Machen should not be cut, he warned, "for cutting his stuff kindles the devil that is within him".) In the end, Faber put "the praise" on the back while Norton preferred the front, understandably leading there with Mencken's opinion that "Evans has developed a new form of fiction." Another Norton decision pleased the author: the giving of prominence (via both inside jacket flaps) to Thomas Burke's sketch of Evans's brave beginnings, the shop assistant who out of sheer poverty wrote stories on glove box paper. As for an author photograph, neither publisher chose to include one – "thank goodness", said Caradoc.

Evans was now fifty-one, late to be publishing a first novel, and his previous stabs at the form suggest a real difficulty in treading "the hard dry road of eighty to a hundred thousand words… the end so far away from the beginning". In speaking of *Nothing to Pay* as containing "stories within the story" the Faber blurb acknowledged that it was not built on traditional lines.[6] Instead we have largely free-standing chapters, episodes in the protagonist's unfolding history, his passage from childhood to an early death. Hannen Swaffer claimed that he it was (with Zola's *The Ladies' Paradise* in mind) who urged that Caradoc write "a novel about a Welsh draper's assistant who comes to London and becomes a kind of William Whiteley"; his friend was ideally equipped, knowing "both the small side of the drapery trade and the emporium side".[7] As early as December 1916 Evans had promised a full-length drapery novel but would first write about shop life in his 1920 collection centred on the London Welsh. "According to the Pattern" and "Joseph's House" are perhaps the most compelling stories in *My Neighbours*. Both have the scope of a novel and in various ways they foreshadow *Nothing to Pay*, the book, so it seems, that Evans was destined to write; one that would show "the ways of the town, of men and women" and "the motives that excite humanity".

In language often of poetic intensity, *Nothing to Pay* considers the myths and reality of commercial success as exemplified in the career of Amos Morgan, a Cardiganshire draper's assistant. Its inter-related concerns had long possessed the author: Welsh Non-conformity as it was and had become; emotional stultification induced by money-worship; the hell of family, a cauldron of resentment and bitterness. For Evans, the deepest lunacies reside within the patriarchal family, where collective shortcomings are amplified intolerably; husbands and wives, parents and children, all become tormenting alter egos, recognizing in each other failings overlooked in themselves. Allied to this is a belief in ancestral inheritance, that the life of the individual is partly programmed by those who have gone before. As he put it in 1926: "I think that man is occupied by the army of his ancestors, the mad and bad, the wastrel and miser, the moral and immoral, the fair and foul. They are all in him from his first carnal conception…"[8]

The opening chapters sketch Amos Morgan's family background. His people helped transform Pont Ceri (a veiled Rhydlewis). Great-grandfather Bensha, the extravagantly garbed *gwahoddwr* or wedding bidder, belongs to its mythic past, to the world of folk-belief, of mermen and flying serpents, "lewd songs" and "carnal jests", out of which arises a quality of religious fervour previously unknown. The land is God's (the valley mist "like the white smoke of God's nostrils") but nowhere is seen God's house. The parish church is deeply alien – on Sunday morning young men play football against its walls, with "Parson… on a tombstone shouting the orders of the game". Bensha, waving his garlanded bidder's staff into the Sign of the Cross, resolves on a purifying mission. From the mud-and-stone cottage on the moor (historically identified with the *ty unnos*, or "one-night house" built in defiance of the lord of the manor) he will preach the true gospel. Evans here draws on the heroic phase of Welsh Nonconformity, grounded in opposition to Anglicanism. Capel Moriah was built through the skills and sacrifice of local men and women "hungry for spiritual refreshment and in the certainty of a God other than the God of the jocose Parson". That idealism he sees as betrayed, and with profoundest consequences for his people.

As it happens, Evans here forgoes the fierce anti-clericalism of his earlier fiction (Moriah's minster is a lightweight, surrounded by tradesmen-deacons, not the menacing farmers of substance who govern Manteg.) The Ceri canvass broadens outwards socially and backwards historically to sketch the community's sustaining values. The approach is through wild rural fantasy laced with dark humour, leaving the fuller indictment of Nonconformity – Ceri's bequest to one of its number – for later in the book.

Ianto Morgan, father of Amos, has all the marks of a man from the Evans country: word-obsessed, given to violence, exploitative of women, at war with his kin. (That he is pathologically mean goes without saying.) The verbal spray he turns on Catti, longing for re-admittance to Moriah's "incantating eloquence". She gets samples enough from this suitor: "The rain, Catti fach, is falling. It's beating on your roof as if the Big Man was beating His fingers on the dome of the universe bidding creation awake." Catti melts before him – "Amen! Don't stop! Amen! Go on, man bach!" – and becomes the slaving wife whose industry saves Tyrhos from Ianto's bad husbandry. Yet, "She was contented; at night her spirit was never too broken to feast on Ianto's bedside eloquence or her body too wearisome to be stirred by the sounding lashes and sweetening honey of the perfect prayer."

A masterly eighth chapter has Ianto journeying with Amos to Holyhead, there to welcome home a long-lost brother. "Abel Robber", as Pont Ceri knew him, had sought a better life in America and had now returned, so it was rumoured, an "Abel Millionaire". The north Wales Evans pictures is bleaker and more baleful even than his home Cardi-ganshire patch. "Rabbits and dogs squealed in the teeth of traps, disturbed ewes bleated to their lambs, crows croaked dismal salutation to the morning." Ianto interprets the passing landscape: "Mountains heaving in divine anger and torrents yelling horror down the clefts of awesome rocks witnessed the Lord's way with sin; well timbered nants and green meadows, fat kine and fruitful gardens, and farmhouses and chapels witnessed the Lord's goodness to those who believe in Him." Little evidence of prosperity presents itself; father and son trudge through a pitiful land with a past of futile suffering:

> They were on the arrogant Holyhead Road, passing between low hedges and wire fences, by crooked villages and straying sheep, by trees which looked like tramping hunchbacks and fields which shamelessly flaunted their sterility. Short dark people in black clothes, the hopelessness of impotency in their gait, were shuffling to their chapels; chapels which are memorials to the ages of toilers who cast their sweat upon the desolation around them.[9]

Ianto's wild encounters are with folk variously disturbed, out of whom he wheedles a few pence, chanting hymns and peddling cards bearing brief scriptural texts. Lust of money drives him on through the night to greet a rich returning brother. "Far is America," he intones, "but not land or sea can divide the love of brothers." Entering Holyhead he catches sight of Abel, broken and destitute, leaning against a wall. The rejection is immediate and absolute:

> Ianto lifted his eyes to the smoke that was rising straightly from the chimneys of the houses, and he said:
>   "There will be heat."
> Then he and his son turned their faces to the South.

Back at Pont Ceri, Ianto's breath-taking lies cannot appease the villagers. He must philosophize with the hammer. Advancing menacingly "with long, high steps", his hammer on the slant, he invites his neighbours to claim back their "mean little presents", their fawning gifts to "Abel Millionaire". His triumph is short-lived; denied Abel's wealth, his world turns stale and unprofitable. But the young Amos's future is decided. It's drapery not farming for him.

"Washed of the smell of stable, earth and manure, and the sweat and breath of animals", the country boy arrives in small-town Carmarthen. There he and fellow apprentice Slim Jones trail a member of a touring theatre company into a local pub, Slim in high excitement: "A parcel of sparks is the actress. What ho! Tidy one for a stroll in the fields. Preachers say that an actress is a deep well of sin. Diawl! Her breasts are like a bladder of lard, and as tightly packed." Yet it is Amos who gets to stroll with Florence Larney through the fields along the river. The older woman's "hungry laugh" provokes "no riot in his eyes", but primed by "the violent ardour and the gentle warmth of the pulpit spirit", he gives in to her. "When the two arose the youth's face was as grey as that of the water and the woman's bosom as placid."

Another woman watches over Amos. Miss Sara Owen typifies religiously respectable Carmarthen. In her family home hang portraits of Nonconformist worthies and of Jesus reading a Welsh biblical commentary; "a small round table had on it a very big Bible and on the Bible was a silk hat; on a harmonium was a worn hymn book and a book of Band of Hope songs." The hat belongs to Sara's "fianzay" Eben Lewis, "this being the Eben whose bardic name Pembroke glorified the shire of his birth" (for Evans he will be an irresistible source of comedy). We see him outside the Red Cow, hymning beside Miss Griffiths, the butcher's daughter, who trills "like a wounded bird on its death flight". "In the darkness and loneliness of country roads", Eben has taught her how "to imbue her songs with love of Jesus". There is quiet dignity in Sara's passing of Eben's engagement ring to the now pregnant Miss Griffiths so that her shame might be lessened ("Eben only lent it to me"). Sara Owen understands the lure of Florence Larney and seeks to protect "the pensive one". On the surface, she succeeds; displaying traits the years will deepen, Amos "clearly and honestly" denies all knowledge of the actress and shuns disreputable Slim, the nearest he has to a friend.

The depiction of Manchester House brings to the book a new dimension of documentary realism: descriptions of stock, details of pay, of commission and fines, and standard drapery slang – all indicate an author at home in the world of shops. "Boss" is a haunting figure, engaging customers passing by, "leading them by the arm into the shop, and returning them again to the pavement". Almost blind, he takes in all that allows him to prosper; emotionally unencumbered (he is unmarried), he stays apart from politics and sectarian strife. Amos judges him an exemplar, though Boss's rules for success have not deadened his sympathy for others. Even Miss Owen takes pleasure in the goods she sells ("very chick", "ultra splendid"). Only their profit concerns the pensive one.

By degrees Amos moves eastwards to Barry where at Commerce House, their shop-cum-brothel, the Picton Reeses feed off dockland lusts. As the temporary loss of a lover dulls Annie Rees's appetite for trade, so her drunkard husband Picton ("in sobriety he was an offence") takes up with Florence Larney. Such curious couplings little interest Amos. His one intimate encounter with Mrs Rees – "her tongue was active and its text was love" – echoes the riverbank moment with Florence. In the perfumed warmth of her bedroom he succumbs, eyes glistening "beneath their cold lashes". He is quickly satisfied. Money not sex propels him, first to Cardiff then onward to London, the drapers' metropolitan Mecca.

The Cardiff pages draw on Caradoc's time at the St Mary Street store of James Howell. "Sam Samson", an indelible portrait of its founder, evokes some of the novel's finest writing. Even in hagiography James Howell emerges as a forbidding, dictatorial character and this much is evident from Sam's first entry:

> On a sudden the shop-walkers quickened their movements and became more servile to customers and more exact to assistants, and assistants increased their readiness and deepened their smiles. A short, broad man had come to the well. His frock coat and square-crown hat were grey; his face was as grey as the stone he had digged in his youth in Carmarthenshire quarries, his eyes were as fiery as those of the ferrets which delivered rabbits into his boyish hands, and his wide nostrils had the power of the man who has conquered by terror and lives by terrorism.

"Hey, mister!"

His words sounded like the cracks of whips on a frosty morning.

Amos is duly inspired; he craves to be one of Sam's kingdom, to fight for his place in a system driven by fear. Sam is the master they all must serve, in and out of hours – precious spare time they spend harvesting hay on his farm or working in the hotel he owns. One fine forensic passage deserves quoting at length.[10] In it Evans probes the background of those among whom he worked at Cardiff, people of rural stock forced south to coastal towns and coalfield communities in search of a decent living. At Sam's they become more enslaved, stripped of ambition and hope – all save his Amos Morgan:

> He [Amos] was one of the two hundred or so young men and women who had been drawn in Sam's from the shires of Carmarthen and Cardigan and Pembroke; they were the children of small holders who had skimped and borrowed to call a few acres of land their own, and despite their sufferings and cheatings they could not pay the interest on their borrowings, for there was no profit in their labour; and they who had demanded that God's land should be for the toiler and not for the squire or rector found their holds passing to lawyers and shopkeepers and politicians, these being the lenders whose hearts were stiffer than those of squires and rectors. They vowed that their children should not tread the barren hills and the sterile valleys, and that they should prosecute a calling at which their shirts were drenched by neither rain nor sweat.
>
> Most of the elders had worked at Sam's since their youth and every morning they were qualmish with the fear that the day would bring them a moment's notice. How could they offer their bodies in the market place, bodies from which the spirit of courage had flown? The only market they knew was Sam's. The only god they knew was Sam.
>
> The women curtsied and madamed and waddled about the showrooms like puppets whose clocks are running down, and the men smirked and whiffed and strutted like aged husbands wheeling the carriages of their young wives' babies begotten of lovers, but their curtsies and smirks inflamed the haughty contempt of lady shoppers.
>
> Burns carpets said:
>
> "In all life's nooks there is no creature more cruel and callous than the lady who goes shopping."
>
> But if Amos humbled himself his imagination was in a far place, and in that place there was a store which was bigger than Sam's and a man who was more despotic than Sam, and the store was his and he was the man.

The "socialistic" Burns alone is a critic. From Amos he gets grudging respect but no support. Amos is the boss's man, disdainful of the Union and its protests against working conditions, mumbling punitive shop rules "as one rehearsing a prayer". His eyes are set on London, though "The big London drapers are like God; they call many but choose few."

With the London chapters, shop owners' hypocrisy emerges more strongly. "Living-in" they justify on moral grounds: young men and women (women especially) need protection from the perils of the street. Perils in plenty await assistants (women especially) chosen for the Kentish Town Bon Marché. Its owner John Hampton-John presides over a swamp of spite and jealousy, of public humiliation and sexual exploitation. Yet he is of the "Apostolic Troop" at Holborn's Welsh Tabernacle. His store has its pre-breakfast daily service, he recruits through the *Nonconformist World*, and preys on females appointed. One such person resides in the background, the malign Miss Sanders, once "a crisp haired, agile heeled Fen woman, the wiles of whose sharp mind and the use of whose virile body were at his [Hampton's] call". Pregnancy demands swift action. "At a time that she discovered her state she did not murmur against him, but went for a while to the house of a woman who lived in the neighbourhood, and thereafter to a secret place; and when she came back her hip was crippled and she was no longer desirable in any man's sight." Hampton's erstwhile Indispensable, demoted from mistress to housekeeper, is a gothic presence in the store. "She did not give over the symbol of her trade: her scissors always hung at her lame side, striking the floor as she moved about the corridors or the kitchen or her little sitting-room. At night she sat at her window, her body bunched like a bluebottle tied in a spider's web, working for Hampton by mind or hand."

Two Cornish assistants work at Bon Marché, Drake and Gwen Bartlett, whom Drake has known all her life; "a very nice young lady", so he thinks, who "ought to be somewhere stylish". In turn Gwen becomes an Indispensable, "consorting with none of her fellows, haw-hawing in the elegant English fashion, and laundering and drying her pretty underclothing at Miss Sanders fire." When she too falls pregnant the housekeeper takes her in, her comforter – and destroyer. At Paddington station Drake and Amos despatch Gwen's body back to Cornwall, clear of the city fog that chokes Drake's words of compassion, a "doomful" pea-souper through which the two shuffle warily, "like bears through a trap strewn thicket".

"Rest on me," says Drake as Amos succumbs to a fit of tubercular coughing. Something in the doltish Welshman has moved him, as it did Gwen Bartlett. Amos reciprocates characteristically, with indifference or, in the case of Gwen, with a sharp surge of the lust that drives him to a "draggled wretch" on Primrose Hill. In chapel, he had thrilled to the feel of Gwen's body against his scraggy thigh as the preacher proclaimed that money is the reward of godliness. Towards the end of the novel a love-mongering sermon from Eben Pembroke (his career rebuilt in America) brings an entire Welsh congregation to a peak. But sex is a "fault of the senses", a momentary craving to be assuaged at minimum cost. The chapel has given him strength. He examines himself and finds that he is good:

> Thinking only of his business, taking not another's burden for his own, going upon no unprofitable errand, prosecuting no idle entertainment, above all believing in the God who never fails His children in the Tabernacle.... Thereby was he strengthened: from Tabernacle comes peace to your house, custom to your shop, and money to your pocket; from Tabernacle comes immunity from the faults of your senses.

For Amos, avarice and piety walk hand in hand. He remains the dreariest of misers, his money of the quietest kind, an end in itself not a means. "The only things that bring ineffable contentment are those for which there is nothing to pay; all others breed regret." Constant work, cold opportunism, the obliteration of all sentiment and self-respect, these are his weapons for living, these and adherence to chapel Law.

In the novel's final third the south Wales characters reappear, Florence Larney and Picton Rees, Slim Jones, Sara Owen and Miss Griffiths, the Carmarthen butcher's daughter made pregnant by Eben Pembroke. Welcoming though they are, Amos keeps his distance, his thoughts on a shop with "Amos Kentish-Morgan" displayed above it and patterned on the linoleum floor. Dismissed from a Holborn store on grounds of health, he turns to property, the consequent upturn in his fortunes taking in the outbreak of war (the book's sole reference to a public event). He casts an eye over those around him and their struggles to survive. "How the wicked and the waster prosper," he concludes. Justice must be restored. So he pretends not to know Slim Jones who is threatened by a hostile crowd mistaking a Welshman for a German; and Tabernacle's news of Slim's death in uniform positively uplifts him – a business nuisance has been removed. One sermon text resounds during the encounter that grants Amos full schadenfreude. A penniless Drake begs for a life-saving two-pound loan. "I haven't any money at all," Amos assures him, "Not one coin." At which, "He felt as if he were the heir of the sun's gold. 'The Lord maketh alive.'" (The text is the first book of Samuel 2:6-7: "The Lord killeth, and maketh alive.... The Lord maketh poor, and maketh rich: he bringeth low, and lifteth up.") His bedrock beliefs have put him beyond the reach of common humanity. He knows no better; we might call him sincere, innocent even, for it is to a quality of childlike innocence that Florence Larney, kind-hearted and courageous to the last, responds when she rounds on the wretched consumptive: "You blithering angel face!... If your neck wasn't so lean and scraggy, I'd twist it and put your head on the doorstep as a lesson."

There are two marriages within the close Welsh circle – and one parting of ways. Picton Rees, kicked out when Amos buys their Soho hotel, returns to Annie his wife. "Better the lumpy mattress of marriage than the feather bed of sin," he decides. Slim Jones marries Miss Griffiths and in the short time left him proves a tender husband. Following their wedding feast – "pork pies, buns, plum cake, and tea and coffee" – Slim takes Amos and a half-dozen others to the Holborn Empire music hall. Amos too gets married, but on a Sunday, "trade being slack on that day". Marriage has much to recommend it – "a wife needs no salary, she does not defraud her husband, she is always at her husband's call; for a wife there is nothing to pay" – and his choice of Sara Owen, "a oner for saving", appears to make sense. But, "They were too much alike to make good company. Both were close. They separated the grain from the chaff, but they did not throw away the chaff." Sara's meagre body holds no attraction ("and in love she was a martyr"), unlike the local publican's wife – "full and rosy-red and loud and blooming". Amos's wealth elevates him at Tabernacle ("A. Kent-Morgan" – "How a boy bach with nothing got on!"), but if "cooing eloquence" from the pulpit still arouses, religion itself begins to pall. It's all around him at home, in Sara's old harmonium and her pictures of preachers and Jesus. Religious symbols are saddening; "religion is a preparation for death."

The desolation and disorder intensify as Amos's story draws to a close. If Evans cannot condemn him – landscape, family and upbringing has made him what he is – he denies him the means of redemption. Inevitably, he dies as he lived; there can be no deathbed repentance. The great death scene has him on his sickbed attended by the publican's kind-hearted wife. With "the horrid gaiety of the doomed man", he clutches at her ("his long fingers seethed with desire") while his own wife Sara broods in the shop. As his mind breaks up he briefly inhabits "a high sunlit plain" before slipping into a valley, "a land through which man groped alone". Muddled memories crowd in, and visions of earthly mansions, his shops where ex-prisoners stand behind counters ("for the wage of a punished man is low and he never errs again") and "the honey of his women" is free. He cannot escape the conviction that "Miss Happiness is Miss Money" despite the dim awareness that "her hiding place is among the secret recesses beyond the horizon, that the quest of her has no end."

Reflecting on his time as a shop assistant, "the most unhappy, hopeless period of my life", H.G. Wells had this to say at the 1931 annual conference of the Shop Assistants Union:

> ... there are a great many writers who were formerly shop assistants. The curious thing is that not one of them, with one brilliant exception, has written about the shop and what it means to be a shop assistant. There is one, who is too little esteemed, who has done the thing with a certain brutal thoroughness, and he tells a great deal of truth. That is Caradoc Evans in his book *Nothing to Pay*.... It is an extraordinarily good book, and has in it all the slang and technical stuff of a pretty bad shop.[11]

The compliment would have pleased Caradoc. *Nothing to Pay* was his exposé of a drapery underworld seldom documented, in or outside fiction. Trade union reformers bemoaned the difficulty of gathering adequate information about conditions of service, even though from the beginning of the twentieth century shop workers numbered at least a million. Their assumed social superiority, their wish (in frock-coat and silk hat) to preserve a respectable middle-class front, made them reluctant to speak out. Yet their working conditions and wages were such as no skilled artisan would endure. Joseph Hallsworth and Rhys J. Davies, in their *The Working Life of Shop Assistants* (1910), constructed the grim factual picture; *Nothing to Pay* renders it with graphic immediacy.

If Amos Morgan's consumption has its symbolic side, it arises from his occupation, one urged upon him by Catti who repeats Caradoc's grandmother's counsel, "In the shop... the coat is ever dry. And the little feet are never wet." Shop work was thought a suitable haven for delicate sons; the facts speak otherwise. Unbelievably long hours (up to 80-odd a week), dismal food, bodies packed together in unhygienic living quarters, all took a dreadful toll. The death toll from tuberculosis among living-in shop assistants exceeded rates for quarrymen and coalminers. There are regular reminders of Amos's worsening condition: the blood-soiled handkerchiefs; the narrowing body, "like a tall stalk and his cheeks like roses painted on a china vessel"; "Your ribs are thin enough to sharpen a pencil on," says the military doctor when Amos tries to enlist. "Get a job in the open if you want to live a few more months," he adds (reversing Catti's advice).

"One went down to dust at 7 or 7.30, and got out of the shop in the evening at 8.30 or 9," remembered H.G. Wells; "You were let off one day a week at 5 o'clock." *Nothing to Pay* quotes similar hours, and salaries with the usual qualifiers: "thirty and spiffs [commission]"; £25 "and his eating and lodging". Sam's men sleep six or seven together in rooms they cannot stand up in, and "the week-day dinner hour was only fifteen minutes and dinner always mutton and potatoes". At Fowler's food improves ("beef and beer") but hygiene is appalling. Shops had squalid sanitation: no bathrooms, no hot water, primitive lavatories, infestations of rats and fleas and bed bugs. At Fowler's an outbreak of illness, stemming from contaminated drains, leads to deaths that are quickly hushed up. Evans precisely records the ensuing improvements (for a staff numbered in hundreds): "The drains were cleaned. Two bathrooms, each with hot and cold water, were built, one for the women and one for the men. A closet was added to the two in the women's sleeping quarters and also to the two in the men's. The closets in the basements were cleared of their foulness and peepholes were made in the doors so that offenders could be marked and docketed."

At Cardiff "Sam gave spiffs and took away spiffs." He took away through multiple rules, the breaking of which rendered the culprit liable to a fine. Rules festooned the walls of drapery stores. Sam's has its legendary eighty-nine, which Amos religiously digests in his fifth-floor bedroom:

> He read that no one shall enter his bedroom in business hours, take a swop line without signing a shop-walker, go to the lavatory without signing a shop-walker, cheek a customer or buyer or shop-walker, lose a leaf from a check book, sleep out without a permit from Mr Samson, enter the premises after eleven o'clock at night. The breaking of these rules and over seventy others was punished by fines of from threepence to five shillings and were taken away from spiffs, it being unlawful to take them from salaries.

More than once Evans mentions the "three shillings a month... taken from every salary for the services of a doctor, a library, and a boot cleaner", money that found its way into Sam's pocket.

Terms of hire specified dismissal at a moment's notice. Six assistants are sacked at Cardiff in five months; at Hampton-John's they come and go with the seasons – Drake, at eighteen months, is the longest serving employee. P.C. Hoffman, an officer of the Shop Assistants' Union (and another activist at Whiteleys), comments, "End of season sacking was common throughout the drapery trade, and the flood of unemployment, with the terror involved, kept the shop workers in that state of servility considered necessary to discipline them." Ruthless employers dismissed worn-out staff at will, knowing that outside younger men and women were fighting to get in. *Nothing to Pay* is particularly eloquent on the plight of the ageing shop worker and the competition they faced: "seasoners with the timorous jaws of ancient horses and maids and youths panting for the race". Splay-footed Miss Johnson accepts that "shop life is for the young and slippy. Customers think you must be young to know the latest fashions." At fifty-five, her cheeks "crimpled like seaweed in the sun", she stands no chance of a berth. The engager at Fowler's, surveying the daily queue of "cribbers" (assistants seeking work), dismisses every man and woman who appears to be over forty, and every man not attired in the regulation uniform of frock coat and silk hat.

So sustained an assault on the bosses implies no ready sympathy for the workers. Caradoc Evans has no heroes (the *Saturday Review* thought him "about as sentimental as a table of logarithms"). His shop assistants are creatures of low cunning, twisted emotionally and lacking in backbone. "Endurance of affronts makes the perfect draper," Amos reflects; "he could adore the tongue that scolded him and kiss the foot that kicked him." Wells understood such sycophancy. There was no dole for an assistant suddenly dismissed: "You swam for as long as you could and then, if you could not scramble into some sort of shop, down you went to absolute destitution, the streets and beggary."[12]

Wells had famously written about shop life in *Kipps* (1905), recording the drudgery, the petty rules and punitive fines, the cold overcrowded bedrooms, the inflamed ankles and sore feet of assistants vying in obsequiousness. "I tell you we're in a blessed drain-pipe, and we've got to crawl along it till we die," says the apprentice Minton. Kipps becomes restlessly aware of the downside of his occupation and is further distanced from Amos by a healthy romantic love life that makes drapery bearable. As Kipps is essentially likeable and easily identified with, so Wells's portrait of the shop owner lacks the savagery of Evans's depictions. Shalford at Folkestone is a task master dedicated to "Fishency" and "System" but without the sadism, lust and hypocrisy of the London-Welsh despots. Though the church's position is hinted at (a "large, fat, sun-red clergyman" reminds Kipps "to do his duty in that state of life into which it has pleased God to call him"), the link between religion and the commercial ethic is not pursued; class attitudes to work and money interest the author more. "Mr Wells knows what he is writing about, for he began life behind a drapery counter," said Evans of *Kipps*. Wells praised *Nothing to Pay* in much the same way. "Caradoc Evans, like myself, has been a draper, and the scene he draws of a draper's existence in the meaner shops of London is, I know, true in all substantial particulars."

Wells believed that *Nothing to Pay* "was badly treated by the critics and did not get a proper run", doubtless because reviewers minimized the drapery context. Few English critics, however, denied that the novel had substance, style and impact. "A book that is like no other," rightly said the *Daily News*; "words in Mr Evans's hands take on primitive significance and brightness". "The corrosive etching is done with remarkable power" (*TLS*); "Many of our novelist nowadays square their jaws in an awful determination to appear 'powerful': Caradoc Evans succeeds in being powerful simply and without effort" (*Everyman*); "a terrible picture, yet so deftly limned that it commands attention" (*Sunday Times*). Harold Nicolson, little interested in the subject field, made *Nothing to Pay* one of his novels for Christmas 1930; the book, "sly, observant, admirably constructed", was redeemed by an "entrancing sardonic humour". In America, the *Saturday Review of Literature* contrasted the novel's serious concerns and the trivial preoccupations of more "sophisticated" writers. Evans's characters are fighting for their very lives and Amos "has cultivated avarice as the best means of keeping himself fit and steady for this battle as it goes on in the lower middle classes and lower". The reviewer saw Swift's Yahoos in these appalling presentments of human nature, and "It is not taking Dean Swift's name in vain to say so."

Discussion inevitably touched on the nature of the novel's realism. The *National Review* was quite decided. The whole book was "superbly written in a condensed style, in which every piece of description, every piece of character-drawing tells". But,

> *Nothing to Pay* is not a realistic book; it is a fantasy – a fantasy of evil... You cannot
> call a work where the magnifying-glass is brought to bear on certain aspects while
> other are ignored, realistic... The book is a savage sardonic exposure of the miserly
> life; Amos in this book can rank with Harpagon or Balzac's skinflint.

V.S. Pritchett (*Spectator*) agreed on the novel's mode: "It is fantasy that Mr Evans, with considerable and scalding art, emits. Mr Evans is no more a realist than Mr T.F. Powys. One accepts neither Mr Powys on Dorsetshire nor Mr Evans on Wales.... there is a wild sardonic humour about Mr Evans's hatred, something which whips the narrative off realism's earth."

Less enthusiastic English reviewers stressed the demands the novel's gallery of unattractive characters made on the reader ("people like a book in proportion as they can like the people in it"), its bitter censoriousness ("a spark of sympathy would be as strange as an iceberg in the Sahara, and as welcome"), and the disconcerting nature of the prose. Speaking of this prose, the *Saturday Review* thought that few authors using the English language had been less English in manner than Evans – "Conrad seems a typical John Bull by comparison". Michael Sadleir's verdict (in the *Listener*) was that *Nothing to Pay* was a book that could not be ignored by students of fiction, "but it is hardly of a kind to entertain the general reader, because entertainment is not within the intention of the novelist." In fact, Evans's first novel achieved a modest success. Initial interest was high and within a month a second impression (2000 copies) was called for.

English reviews, by and large, got the measure of the book's relationship to Wales. In the words of the *National Review*, "It is a bitter mordant satire, not on the Welsh alone, for the things of which he writes, though clothed in Welsh detail, are really universal." *John O'London's* wrote that the book "compels attention by the author's own intensity, which has moulded a style and has driven him to create a rugged barren world and to people it with lost souls whom, for need of a name, he calls the Welsh.... It is not a transcription from life but the comments of genius upon life. He required that kind of world for artistic reasons."

Such talk cut no ice in Wales. On publication day (28 August), the *Western Mail* launched a frontal assault on Judas Evans. Artistically, the book could be counted "his most successful accomplishment" yet at base it was "a synthesis of everything he has heard or seen or imagined detrimental to his country." For this pandering to English taste, "he will receive his pieces of silver". *Nothing to Pay* was "filth masquerading as truth", abounding in "lewd imagery and frank obscenity". An accompanying editorial urged its suppression: "It is called 'realism' in the jargon of the modern school. We prefer to call it filth. *Nothing to Pay* is a dirty book and we are surprised at its publication." An ensuing correspondence revealed how correctly the paper had gauged national feeling. Evans should be publicly horsewhipped and his book burnt and banned – could not a Welsh MP raise the matter in the House? Meantime an appeal might be made to booksellers to cease its sale voluntarily. Cardiff City Library took the hint, making *Nothing to Pay* available upon request and for reference only. As to the future, the Welsh press must totally ignore Caradoc Evans and leave the job of reviewing him to "those poor, misguided souls who still regard us as a nation of loin-clothed aborigines". The conviction that the English gloat on things anti-Welsh remained unshaken: "While thus he writes, English people slap their knees with delight."

Whatever the provocation from his homeland, Evans kept silent. He had much on his mind, most pressingly his deteriorating relationship with Frank Morley. *Nothing to Pay* turned out to be his first and last Faber book. From the outset he had wrangled with Morley over money, mostly about advances for his earlier books. Morley set out the company's understanding, which was that *Nothing to Pay* should appear more or less simultaneously with a reprint of *My People*; *Capel Sion* would follow next and, depending on sales, *My Neighbours* after that. These reprints, in a high-end format priced at five shillings, would capture a new market for Evans, one more advantageous to him than that which cheaper reprints might bring. As for reprint royalties, Morley could run to a nominal £10 advance per volume until sales justified more; it was his understanding that Evans had initially been willing to offer his previous books on straight royalty with no advance – which was why the *Nothing to Pay* advance had been so generous. To Morley's surprise and dismay, Caradoc had chosen to pull out of the reprints contract, so forfeiting the chance to see his back catalogue in print again along with his first novel. In a letter of 6 June 1930 Evans set out – forthrightly – his own reading of events:

> Dear Morley,
> In the beginning you were not keen on the immediate publication of my former works. I mentioned the matter when I was signing the *Nothing to Pay* contract and the tenor of your answer was that it depended on the reception of *Nothing to Pay*. So that's that, my lad. Also: I should be a fool to agree to terms which are more meagre than those I got for my first book and to a clause which can prevent *My Neighbours* from ever being published. Here is another bit: I could have had two hundred and fifty pounds in advance of royalties for *Nothing to Pay*. But I do not repent of my bargain with you; that bargain was made because I like the Faber imprint and after much meditation…
> Always Sincerely,
> Caradoc

Relations between the two men, centred solely on the novel, stayed amicable. Caradoc presented Morley with a typescript by Percy Brown, a newspaper cameraman. He thought Brown's text had possibilities and if Faber thought so too he would put it into book shape "and for nothing to pay".[13] In 1934 the company duly published *Round the Corner*, dealing with Brown's war experiences as an unofficial photographer in Belgium and France.

Neither Morley nor Evans wholly gave up on a deal over reprints. Evans broached the matter through a fresh proposal from his agent, the firm of A.D. Peters. He would settle for a royalty advance of £100 on his three short-story collections and of £250 for his next Faber book. Morley came back, offering a £60 advance for the reprints and £200 for the next novel (provided they approved the script). This Evans flatly refused; two other firms (so he claimed) had offered him more, and much as he regretted looking elsewhere, he was left with no choice. "All my journalistic life I have been counselled to keep my work precious, but you know that accepting good advice usually means accepting less money."[14] Dismayed again, Morley declared that the terms he had given Peters were the best that could be offered blind; this said, there might still be room for compromise: "our relations have been so friendly and our respect for you... so real, that I feel this ought to be the subject of a discussion".[15] Caradoc remained adamant. His last letter on the matter, dated 28 November 1930, runs:

> Dear Morley
> Goodness knows I never wanted to wander away from Faber & Faber. Since early September I have tried to discuss terms with your firm for my next book and since April any reprints. I failed. Then I saw Peters and a final offer was made to him in my behalf. So there is nothing more to discuss.
>   I have arranged for the publication of my reprints and the sums that I receive for them is nearly double Faber's offer.
>   Always sincerely
>   Caradoc Evans

The truth of the second paragraph cannot be established (and no reprints ever appeared), although Evans did indeed approach another publisher while still bargaining with Faber, an act so offensive to Peters, who was using every means to persuade him to stay with Faber, that he washed his hands of Evans entirely. "I know nothing about his arrangements or plans for the future," he wrote to Morley, "In fact, I have no official concerns with his affairs."[16] One might guess that the publisher approached was Allen Lane of Bodley Head, a bachelor drinker and a popular habitué of Shireff's. According to J.E. Morpurgo, "even after he [Lane] had taken more than his fair share of alcohol, he was forever on the alert for a hint that might be elaborated into an addition to the Bodley Head list".[17] Caradoc, we know, gave him a copy of *Nothing to Pay* signed "in admiration".

Evans's defection from Faber & Faber must be counted a disaster. He turned his back on what seemed set to be an outstanding literary publishing house, one of whose directors, a friendly admirer, was eager to promote his work. To have had landed on the

Faber list almost his entire output up to that point would have positioned him perfectly at a critical juncture, the moment when he became no longer the working journalist writing part time but a fully professional author. "Riotously inadequate", was Evans's description of the proffered terms. Doubtless Morley could have stumped up more – Faber's bestowed cachet not cash, it would come to be said – but Eliot had brought Morley to the firm to supply some business savvy – something that Faber & Gwyer for all its growing kudos conspicuously lacked (Morley had looked after money matters at the *Criterion*, Eliot's literary journal). Caradoc had never much bothered about royalties before. In the past, of course, he had enjoyed a steady Fleet Street income whereas now he would have to depend on whatever his writings might bring. Marguerite was a daily reminder of the rewards of fiction writing, and had more than once upbraided him for underselling himself. (He would end up at her publishers, but with scripts poles apart from hers.) Now he had lost a prestigious publisher and yet another literary agent; it was all of a piece with the disarray that marked his closing time in London. Erratic and aggressive, blind to his own best interests, he had acted impulsively with little thought of the consequences. This said, one has to question whether Evans's next novel would have measured up to Morley's expectations, for the £200 advance he offered remained conditional on Faber's approval of the text. The novel in waiting found its publishers, and much trouble it brought them.

Leaving London

1930-31

T he publication of *Nothing to Pay* gave Tommy Pope the chance to write on a good Fleet
Street friend. He repeated what Caradoc had told him about his early years, how the
family's impoverished circumstances laid them open to "every known form of humiliation
and ignominy"; Evans would never forget the agonizing experiences of childhood which,
even now, he could only recall with bitterness. Others knew of his Cardiganshire background,
as they did of his drapery torments and fearful start in Fleet Street, but only Pope reported
Caradoc's "itch to write" that made itself felt at Board school. "He has himself told me that
one of his earliest recollections is that of standing on a raised road looking down on a river
with a pencil and a sheet of paper in his hand trying to write something – something; he
did not know what."

An arresting picture of Evans accompanied Pope's piece in *Current Literature* (August
1930), a photograph that crossed the mind of Glyn Roberts in Woolworth's on the
Strand. A twenty-year-old Welshman recently arrived in London, Roberts thought he
recognized at the stationery counter "the great nose, glaring eyes and vast black hat" of
the author of *Nothing to Pay*. Though Raymond Marriott, Roberts's companion that day,
had his doubts, they approached him. "He looked annoyed, but said kindly: 'Yes, I am
Caradoc Evans. But who are you?'"[1] Learning of their hopes in journalism, he warmed
appreciably, even inviting them as he turned to leave to visit him "anytime" the following
weekend. No meeting transpired – he had forgotten to give an address. A week later
they chanced on Evans again, this time in a bar off the Strand; he had waited in for them
"all day Sunday" and, deciding that they were not coming, had gone to chapel. "There is
always something new in chapels to amuse or scare," he said. Glyn Roberts worked on
the Strand, a civil servant in Somerset House, having thrown up university at Aberystwyth.
Now he contemplated a further change. He wished to be a full-time journalist and with
a few published pieces behind him (one in the *Daily Express*) he was trawling Fleet Street
for likely openings. Caradoc urged caution. "Keep at your job," he wrote to Roberts (5
October 1930), "and write stories and poems and articles and make sketches [Roberts
drew political cartoons], and the hour may come when your position will justify you in
abandoning it. That is sound counsel."[2] Roberts's hour would come surprisingly quickly,
and with some effect on Caradoc; in 1933 he began for the *Western Mail* a series of combative articles on the so-named "Anglo-Welsh", their first exposure in Wales as a literary
group (he'd already promoted them in one or two English periodicals).

Roberts's pal at Woolworth's was a jobbing drama critic predominantly writing for
the *Stage*, a weekly that became the theatre profession's shop window. Raymond Marriott

met Caradoc on and off through the Thirties and into the Forties and left a perceptive account of him. He confirms the Evans of the *Current Literature* photograph – "those compelling eyes, with their fire and look of scalpel-sharp penetration" – a man who talked quietly and quickly in a strong Welsh accent but "for the most part… wished to question, brood and watch".[3] If no one ever seemed to bore him, he favoured "argumentative people with minds of their own, the more unorthodox the better". He mocked the literary establishment and had no time for book reviewers, insisting that not one of them was honest. "He often protested vigorously that he loathed 'art and artists', and it is true that he knew, or cared for personally, very few writers." Friends like Evan Walters and Sean O'Casey he spoke of affectionately, "considering them apart from the intellectual crowd which he never tired of ridiculing. On the other hand, Fleet Street people had a fascination for him, and whenever I saw him after he had left London for good, the first thing he asked for was the latest newspaper gossip." No wonder that Marriott got nothing from Evans concerning his own fiction and little about any other writer, apart from unreserved praise of Machen and admiration for Mary Webb.[4] As for Rhys Davies, a short-story writer beginning to make his name, Evans thought him a feeble imitator of himself.

Marriott again was not alone in detecting a certain pose in Evans's violent opinionating and never could be sure when he truly meant what he said. Tone of voice was important. "It was easier to gauge the sincerity of his feelings: the emotion that lay behind his hates and enthusiasms was always deep and sincere, even when one doubted that the words he spoke conveyed his considered intellectual conviction." George Blake (of *John O'London's Weekly*) speaks of Caradoc – "a poet frustrated" – pretending to hate many individuals and institutions, "but that, perhaps, is because the dream of his adolescence, of any sensitive boy's adolescence, could not be fulfilled". In Fleet Street pubs "he would come among us and curse this, that, and the other in language magnificently strong. One seemed to be living for a time against what I can only describe as a Wagnerian background. And then, when the group had thinned to two or three, the poetry in Caradoc would break through in flashes that were sometimes blinding."[5] Marriott saw most sides of Evans's character, the "fury of hatred", the "courtesy, gentle manners and a certain simplicity", the intense understanding and sympathy when human problems and difficulties were concerned. On the aggressive part of his nature ("which could be frightening"), Marriott acutely observes, "It had a subtle cruelty that awed as well as mystified. One thought of him sometimes as an uncommonly sensitive person who had determined to become insensitive and had only half succeeded."

Besides *Nothing to Pay*, Evans in 1930 published three short pieces, two in the *Daily Express* and a lively contribution to a book on Fleet Street. He had now entered his fifties, the point in life (so he'd been told) that marked the beginning of wisdom, "the age when the rebel throws down his arms". But not Caradoc Evans. In April 1930 he gladly launched a "Some of Our Rebels" series for the *Daily Express*. Under the sub-heading "Things that Anger Me", he picked out three "stumbling blocks to my well-being".[6]

Religion is laid aside for the scourge of tuberculosis, a problem with a peculiarly Welsh dimension. Evans quotes official figures on the grip of the disease in Wales, a consequence of the damp, unventilated "slums hidden under the charming faces of many of the old Welsh towns" and of slovenly farming practice in the rural counties. The "child of Welsh peasants" expands:

> Farmers' living houses are built on slopes below cowsheds, from which liquid manure streams and makes pools before doorsteps. Cowsheds are badly aired, if aired at all, and life is spent in and out of them. Animals known to be tubercular are kept in store, and in the last stages of their decline they are killed and sold among neighbours. Walls of sheds are thick with the refuse of ages, and udders are never cleaned or floors washed with water.

Wales did in fact head the lists of TB mortality, the situation being worse in rural areas. Preventative action by local authorities was greater in the urban areas, where "social duty came before concern for the financial protection of ratepayers".[7] Caradoc puts his own spin on rural failure: money ("dry money") and energy were taken up in campaigns to regulate the drinks trade, and "the prohibitionists have their agents in pulpit, council chamber, and on the magisterial bench". Local authorities were heedless of the welfare of people, and of animals.

Over animal cruelty "the Fury" most certainly never left him. Evans gives painful examples, of a dog kicked to death for losing a race (its owner was let off) and a man who wrenched a pony's tongue from its roots (he was fined five shillings). "Men may ill-treat children and animals to the best of their diabolical ingenuity. Few are brought to account, and fewer are convicted." In fact, "It is safer to violate a girl or to burgle a house than it is to break a 'dry' law." Then out of the blue, in a passage decrying the treatment of horses at Continental slaughterhouses, comes the assertion, "Woman could end this unholy traffic but woman does not walk in the way of pity and compassion."

Women puzzled Evans, as he thought they did all men. Though lacking in political cunningness, women were by nature an elevating influence and their powers of persuasion could be a matchless force for good. "Women could stop cruelty to children and animals and they could abolish our degrading prison system and our Biblical system of revengeful punishment by hanging. There is not an evil they could not end. War they could end, but rather they encourage war and enlist themselves as kissing recruiting officers..."[8] Their failure to meet his expectations provokes some extravagant misogynistic rants. He seems to have forgotten Dennis Bradley, whom he praised for his understanding of women as shown in *The Eternal Masquerade* (for which Evans had provided a preface). Marguerite thought Caradoc's wounding remarks on women were his vengeful response to the humiliations of his shop days, when fashionable ladies sat in chairs – assistants were made to stand and wear a smile – and insolently commanded him, "and made [him] pull down bales and bales of stuff from the highest shelves, and then didn't buy." She believed he never got over his shop days – he hated calling women "madam".

The literary and Society women Evans met at London gatherings were worlds away from the women he knew back home (and from those who peopled his fiction). The "bright young things" of the 1920s were dedicated party-goers. The younger women among them, the fashionable gamine "flappers" with their page-boy haircuts, took to smoking and drinking, and dancing to new syncopated rhythms in a way that decidedly shocked. Flirtatious and reckless, they seemingly lived for the moment, with little concern for the world at large and no sense of social duty. Evans refused to see them as harmless followers of transient fashion; dedicated pleasure-seekers, frivolous and irresponsible, they were symptoms of something larger, and he loathed them. He loathed even more the older "sophisticated" socialites, picturing the woman of fifty (often a romantic novelist) dancing in the arms of her gigolo or swaying to the jazz of "coloured" musicians. He wondered how upper-class women ever got men to marry them. "They know next to nothing about household management, other than that their husbands pay the bills; they know nothing about household economies, other than that servants must be under-paid and under-fed; they know nothing about household obligations, other than they must comport themselves like figures moulded with Dresden clay; they know nothing about children, other than they kill their unborn with noxious drugs."[9] (Through her triumphs over adversity, Mary Webb shone in comparison.)

His second newspaper piece, "So Don't Blame London" (*Daily Express*, 8 September 1930), is a love letter to the city where he had lived and worked for thirty-odd years. More surprisingly, it extols the suburbs. Friend Machen found wonder among them, glimpses of the eternal beauty hidden beneath the crust of commonplace things: "There are certain parts of Clapton from which it is possible, on sunny days, to see the pleasant hills of Beulah, though topographical experts might possibly assure you that is was only Epping Forest."[10] Evans hymns sheer suburban ordinariness, suburban villas and their carefully tended gardens; "Lovers of flowers do not walk in evil ways, their ways are the ways of peace." He welcomes the peacefulness and privacy, the suburban gift of anonymity after village nosiness and backbiting. He admires the ordinary Londoner's tolerance and slowness to anger; he bears his woes uncomplainingly, "braying not his troubles like members of the professions." Evans had been led to expect something different. He had expected Vice, for most preachers have stock sermons on London "and they prove that each of its streets dips down to hell". Vice there certainly was (trafficking in women and drugs; gambling casinos and night clubs) though it is largely in the hands of foreigners and kept alive by those "coming amongst us from town, village and hamlet" – "the good man who hankers after naughtiness", "the chaste wife who loves to go gay". So the ordinary honest, industrious Londoner is blackened with others' misdeeds. Caradoc's panegyric begged the question put by one *Daily Express* Welsh reader, "Why could Caradoc not be as fair to Wales?"

In a hangover from "Things that Anger Me", his London goodbye manages at one point to fuse disgust at casinos, the romantic novelists who frequent them, and sickening animal cruelty. The evil view of London is not confined to chapel sermons, Evans writes; it is present "in the works of middle-aged women novelists who seek happiness in

Continental casinos and find thrills in the blood of slaughtered pigeons at Monte Carlo".
At the shooting range attached to Monte Carlo's casino trapped live pigeons, crippled
through the clipping of their tail feathers, were blown to pieces by the gentry and nobility
of Europe, with betting on the number they could destroy without a miss.

Evans's last piece of 1930, a leave-taking of Fleet Street, sadly became a farewell.
Tommy Pope had asked him to contribute to an essay-collection he was editing, one
that would reveal something of life behind the scenes of the great newspaper world. In
September 1930 Pope penned a short introduction to *The Book of Fleet Street* and in
November the volume appeared (its frontispiece reproducing "Amongst the Nerves of
the World", C.R.W. Nevinson's dynamic painting of Fleet Street). Between times Tommy
Pope died, aged fifty-five, an immensely popular figure who like so many working journalists left no lasting testimony in book form of the knowledge and wit that delighted
his friends. Marguerite had met him at *T.P.'s Weekly*, "a sandy-greying little man... with
a pile of books up to his chin" – Caradoc had helped him through the bad days with
plenty of reviewing work.

Evans's *Book of Fleet Street* essay was the "bundle of memories" its title promised:
scary tales of his start in journalism and sharp sketches of Andrew Melrose, Mary Webb
and T.P. O'Connor. It reinforced the feeling pervading Pope's collection, that whatever
the trials of Fleet Street, however testing its internecine wars, those who work or have
worked there remain profoundly attached to it. The spirit of Fleet Street unites them
(it was said Pope carried its essence about him). Edward Shanks, a Cambridge man
taken on by the *Daily Mail*, instances "the undying feud between the reporter and the
sub-editor, both of whom, however, unite in regarding the persons who write the leaders,
the gossip columns, and the theatrical and musical criticism, as pampered and all but
useless passengers in a ship of which they constitute the effective crew."[11] Yet all drink
happily together in some favoured journalists' bar; professional attitudes made no
difference to personal relationships. Likewise political attitudes; should any of their
number face unemployment through newspaper amalgamation or closure, "All Fleet
Street, whether its cabbage patch be Tory, Liberal or Labour, come together at these
junctures and sympathize and scheme for the benefit of the stricken men."[12]

This had been Evans's world, a place of myth and legend, frequently sentimentalized
but more convincingly captured by another of his Fleet Street acquaintances, the *Manchester
Guardian's* London editor James Bone. In his *The London Perambulator* (1925) Bone describes
the "short, shabby street" they knew so well, to the east bounded by Ludgate Hill and
St Paul's, and to the west by Temple Bar, where Fleet Street meets the Strand. Running
off Fleet Street to the south narrow twisting alleys sloped down to the Embankment
while the northern hinterland, a mass of courts and passages, was home to the printing
trade. There Dr Johnson had his house, from which he compiled his Dictionary, Caradoc's
beloved book of words. In the constricted avenues off Fleet Street most publishing took
place. "It is fascinating, it is dumbfounding, to study all the names on the house fronts
and on the boards at the foot of the narrow stairs. All interests seem to be concentrated
here." Bone mentions *The Church Worker*, *The Methodist Recorder*, *The Catholic Herald* among

religious titles; *The Racehorse*, *The Poultry World*, *The Beekeeper* for bird and animal lovers; *The Licensed Victuallers' Review*, *The Baker* and *Automobile Engineer* as some of the trade journals. On Fleet Street itself publishing largely gave way to banks and insurance offices, to eating houses, tea shops, tobacconists, cheap tailors, chemists, tourist agents, stationers, bag shops, a post office and one bookshop. As for the fabled taverns, in the main they were found along tight passages that held the steam of sausages and mash. The immaculately attired James Bone was a nightly visitor who stuck to a small whisky-and-soda – "even the whisky-and-soda looked immaculate".[13]

Fleet Street was its own little village and the one part of the City with a night life, thanks to the journalists and printers (compositors, readers and machine men) and the distribution men with their vans and motorcycles. "Never was there such a place for gossip", a patch where most were known by sight and often by nickname (Caradoc's "Old Bloke"). Fleet Street denizens may have looked unexceptional but they worked at Nevinson's nerve centre where power, fame and fortune sat. This short shabby street "dictates to Parliament, to the Church, to the people.... The greatest generals and admirals quail before it. The Throne is not unmoved by its praise. It can make wars, though it cannot make peace. In short, it's capable of almost anything." ("It cannot yet make all people think alike, but it can make them think about a like subject.") Printing presses might no longer resound in newspaper offices but once heard in youth, so Bone believed, "the terrific pulse of the news" would not be forgotten by a Fleet Street man till his own pulse ran down. He could have had Caradoc Evans in mind.

But besides his working life Evans also had a domestic life and Fleet Street's irregular hours accentuated their disconnection. Journalists usually lived an innocent double life, a professional circle developing around lunchtimes in pubs and end-of-the-week celebrations. Caradoc's double life was hardly innocent. After a time in marriage, he took to coming home late at night and not telling Rose where he'd been. There were tiffs because she did not trust him and increasingly had cause not to trust him. Besides hankering after London "naughtiness", he was conducting a full-blown affair with Marguerite. In October 1930 he told Glyn Roberts that he'd been away from home for some time and would be going away again for a few days more. It is likely that the first of these absences was because of a visit to Wales with Marguerite. She, her brother and Caradoc took a short summer holiday at Aberystwyth; she wanted son Nick in the party but he flatly refused to go with them or even to meet Caradoc. "You can never trust a Welshman," Walter Lovell had told him.[14] Nonetheless, the holiday proved "perfect".

Shortly before, in July, Armiger Barclay died in exile on the Côte D'Azur. Marguerite claimed some forewarning of this, recounting a dream in which her husband appeared before her. "I was reading in bed and I was constrained to lift my eyes from my book in a way a spider constrains me to lift my eyes to it."[15] Afterwards she learned from a newspaper announcement that Armiger had died in Menton on the day of the night of her dream. With his death came her freedom to remarry but an unforeseen problem as well. A mistress of Armiger's surfaced, together with an incomplete "Barcynska" novel, the mistress strongly believing that Armiger's share of the Countess Barcynska earnings now would pass to her. Aside from this conflict over copyright, which was eventually resolved in Marguerite's favour, David Higham (then working for the literary agents Curtis, Brown) was invited to complete the Barcynska novel for publication by Hutchinson. This he did, and for the fifteen thousand more words needed to bring it up to Walter Hutchinson's required 80,000, Higham earned £15 – "at that moment very welcome".[16] Marguerite nowhere mentions this book or Armiger's mistress.

In late 1930 Marguerite and Caradoc sat for Evan Walters at Belsize Park. In the portrait of Caradoc (38 x 30 ins.) earthy colours predominate. He wears a brown three-piece lounge suit, a soft collared shirt and brown tie. He sits on a wooden chair, a wall hanging behind him. His look is direct, relaxed (pipe raised in hand), his expression thoughtful and assured. There is little hint of "the scourge of the Welsh", none of London bohemia, more perhaps of the country schoolmaster. Gwyn Jones, who knew Evans well, thought the portrait caught him to perfection. The Marguerite portrait (30 x 40 ins.) is in striking contrast. Set against a plain background, she comfortably reclines on what looks like a chaise longue. She is stylishly dressed, with a wide-brimmed hat of flamboyant red, roped pearls, a salmon dress with modesty piece across an ample bosom, and a black outer garment. A fox fur rests across her shoulders and her left hand, with conspicuous display ring, holds what appears to be a scarf. She avoids our gaze, happy in her own thoughts; her look is smilingly alert: high arched eyebrows, open lively eyes and fashionable cupid-bow lips. Her make-up seems heavy, reinforcing the theatrical impact. Marguerite much attracted Walters (he would later propose marriage) and he brings out her sensuous appeal.

Quietly set aside in his studio, Evan Walters's portrait of Caradoc suddenly sparked Welsh newspaper headlines when Swansea's Glynn Vivian Gallery flatly turned down the artist's offer of the picture on temporary loan. There was no point in the town's Art Galleries Committee even seeing the painting. Its subject was enough. The motion to reject, passionately moved by the chairman David Davies, proprietor-editor of the *South Wales Daily Post* and a force in the town, won a substantial majority. Reporting the decision, the Swansea weekly *Herald of Wales* confessed, in a leader headed "Patriotism and Art", to feeling uncomfortable at the ban of a portrait of "the most powerful Welsh writer of his day" by "the most prominent Swansea artist of his times". The "violent animosity" towards Evans expressed by the committee – and widely evident in Wales – was a tribute to the "bite" of his writings. An Evan Walters admirer, the *Herald*'s editor J.D. Williams had a sneaking regard for Evans as well and found things to admire in *Nothing to Pay*: the novel showed less extreme caricature and "more fidelity to life in depicting people who, however noxious, have their counterparts. His study of shop life in London is painful, but terrible convincing" (24 January). A week later, on 31 January, the *Herald* reproduced the painting, the first picture of a portrait which (the paper reminded its readers) the Swansea committee had rejected sight unseen. Next came a letter from Caradoc (7 February), speaking of a loan "refused with angry joy" and a chairman who believed that he (Caradoc) lived by "throwing filth at his country". David

Davies had promised not to enter the Glynn Vivian as long as the picture was there.
Evans's response was characteristic: "It is so that those who look in vain for me in paint
will be consoled and lifted up with the sight of Mr D. Davies in the flesh." But against
the committee's decision, endorsed with "Pauline fervency" by Swansea's mayor and
other local worthies, were the many distinguished critics who praised Evan Walters the
artist. As for this specific picture, Evans thought it captured him as he was; "and in
banning the portrait the committee refuse to allow lovers of Wales to look at my likeness
and to spit through their teeth upon the face thereof." The committee's action proved
the accuracy of some of his own pen portraits of the Welsh.

Reflecting on this episode before a 1948 gathering of the Scottish PEN, Dylan
Thomas drew a similar conclusion.[17] Serving as cub reporter, he had attended the very
meeting at which the offer of the portrait was discussed. In the chair was "Dai Davies,
the proprietor of the newspaper for which I doodled":[18]

> "About this picture of Caradoc Evans now," he said. "Caradoc Evans is a liar. He says
> that Welshmen are narrow-minded hypocrites. I throw that lie in his teeth. We are
> not hypocrites. We are not narrow-minded. We'll show him. I refuse to have his
> portrait hung in our gallery."

Although the feelings of the Swansea committee were widely known, no formal
notification of refusal reached Walters. Left in ignorance for a couple of months, he
withdrew his offer in disgust. The Glynn Vivian seemed the natural resting place for this
painting but he would now approach the National Museum of Wales. "Will Cardiff have
what was refused by Swansea?" asked the *Western Mail*, over a report of the fresh loan
offer from Walters (3 December 1931). The *Mail* reproduced the portrait, a reproduction
that sufficed for the Museum, which in turn refused the painting, and on grounds that
it trusted would dampen controversy. "Since the Museum possesses an excellent and
recent example of your work in portraiture," wrote the Museum's director Dr Cyril
Fox to Walters, "it does not need the example offered by you on loan." Predicable
applause resounded from such as the *Western Mail* (in a leader), the Cardiff Cymmrodorian
Society, and the recorder of Welsh National Eisteddfod. Walters turned angry. The
National Museum might have a fine building but its art collection was appalling; it might
be used to Welsh artists lying down at its decisions but he was made of sterner stuff; he
"had lived too hard a life and experienced too great a struggle to accept such treatment
from laymen" (*Western Mail*, 25, 29 January 1932). He would look beyond Wales. Within
a week the Oldham Art Gallery and Museum invited him to show the picture in its 1932
spring exhibition. "Oldham has been a good friend to me," he assured the *Western Mail*
(1 February 1932).

Two months later in Wales the story took a startling turn with reports that, of all
bodies, the Arts and Crafts committee of Port Talbot's National Eisteddfod had agreed
to accept the portrait for its August loan exhibition.[19] Evan Walters quite naturally had
been invited, along with other prominent Welsh artists, to submit a work for this
Eisteddfod. Responding artists did not normally specify their works, only provide details

of physical size. But in replying Walters had said that he would send his Caradoc Evans portrait – if it was returned in time from Stockport, where it was going after Oldham. In mentioning this controversial piece, he had mischievously challenged Port Talbot to take what Swansea and Cardiff had declined. And Port Talbot had requested a picture from him, which Swansea and Cardiff had not. What now should the Committee do? Could they possibly ask him, a major Welsh artist, to nominate another piece – anything but Caradoc Evans! – or must they submit to his choice? The Committee was reminded that in Swansea and Cardiff the artistic community would gladly have welcomed this picture: it was local council prejudice that led to rejection. Here was Port Talbot's chance to show itself free of such small-mindedness. Despite strong voices against, a motion to accept the portrait was carried by nine votes to two. At the very least, the work would be a positive attraction during Eisteddfod week, though the excitement and controversy surrounding it might entail special insurance cover. Controversy was certainly guaranteed, and it grew with the feeling that the Eisteddfod had been bounced into its decision. The rumpus took an alarming turn with news in May of an anonymous letter addressed to the "Chief of Police, Port Talbot" threatening that should the picture be hung on Eisteddfod walls nothing on earth would prevent its destruction. "Don't rouse young Wales, and remember Carnarvon!" the letter warned (a reference to the tearing down by Nationalists of the Union Jack from the tower of Caernarfon Castle a short time before, on St David's Day).[20] At this, the Arts and Crafts Committee sought a way of reversing its decision without appearing to have succumbed to naked threats of violence. The Finance Committee rode to the rescue: the insurance premium for the picture was beyond its means; rejection of this particular painting was a financial imperative, but any other Walters picture would be welcomed.[21]

The saga of the portrait stretched from January 1931 to May 1932, during which time Evans published nothing apart from his letter to the *Herald of Wales*. And next to nothing was heard of him, save that he was going to Gloucestershire "with his publisher". He went in April 1931, but with Marguerite. They had rented a black-and-white cottage below a hilltop market town; Evans gave Faber the address: "Spring Cottage, Minchinhampton, Nr. Stroud". In *Full and Frank* Marguerite describes the parting from Walter Lovell (he is "Leslie" in her autobiography). At least they parted amicably:

> The years we spent together were as kind and gentle as he could make them. It was not his fault that his interests were not mine, that he could not follow me in my wild-duck zigzag flights. My mind and my outlook were too strange for the man who had known only outdoor girls and the daughters of Army officers and ICS [Indian Civil Service] types. My people were Army, but I am not according to the pattern that slips into retirement to Cheltenham, Winchester, Bath... His favourite reading was S.M. Crockett's *The Lilac Sunbonnet* [a Kailyard novel of the 1890s], his favourite journal the *Field*, to which he contributed some very informative articles on birds and fish.

She recalls his words at their leave-taking, how he ran down the steps of Suncrete, the house they rented in Kingsbury, to say "I hope you will be happy, old girl.... Well, if you are not – if anything goes wrong, you know what to do. I'll be waiting." Both she and Walter had misgivings. Their breakup might be deeply damaging, she knew she would be wildly unhappy at times, and an impassioned last minute appeal from Walter might yet have turned her. But he shut the car door, walked quickly back to the house, and the chauffeur drove her away.

What surprises in this account is Marguerite's failure to mention Nicholas, the impact the break from Walter had on her son, and her own heavy guilt at having failed him at a time when he badly needed her (in "the hobbledehoy years between fifteen and sixteen"). She was robbing him of the man he knew as father for one who might have little time for him and with whom she frequently quarrelled. She had failed her son because she had been swept off her feet by "a cyclone of a literary genius". Putting her own feelings first, she had caught up and taken him away from Rose, his perfectly pleasant wife. As ever, Caradoc's side of the story is untold, at least by him. Marguerite offers more in her Caradoc biography and recurrently in her fiction. She never wholly believed that his arguments with Rose were over Mary Webb and his other literary friends. Literary friends were not the problem. But that he reflected fondly on Rose during flare-ups with Marguerite is not in doubt. "I wish to God I'd never left her," Marguerite ventriloquizes again. "What the hell made me discontented with a good woman who kept my house unduly clean and cooked my food and gave me peace when I didn't deserve food or peace."[22] In 1931, in Gloucestershire, a new troubled household would need to take shape. No, this would not be retirement in Cheltenham. In fact, Nick refused point blank to leave with Marguerite. If she threw in her lot with Caradoc, he would stay and live with Walter. Her duty was to Walter and Nick. "I forsook my duty. My duty became Caradoc – Caradoc before all else. And so we ran away.[23]

Wasps

1931-33

Bound for the Cotswolds, Marguerite picked up Caradoc in her car. For luggage he had nothing but books, the indispensable ones: Dr Johnson's *Dictionary* (Todd's three-volumes), dictionaries of quotations, *Chambers Encyclopaedia*, his Bible and his typewriter. "He had packed no clothes. He had his old mackintosh and his shaving tackle. He was in a high, schoolboyish mood – not grown-up at all."[1] The mood changed abruptly when he confessed to having left his wife without a word of goodbye. As far as Rose knew, he was leaving for a spell in the country with his publisher. Marguerite was appalled. "It wasn't fair – not to face up," she told him; which prompted a savage outburst against her own amicable relationship with Walter – "a soldier and a gentleman without any brains, of course". It reduced Marguerite to tears.

The choice of Gloucestershire had much to do with Marguerite's wish to remove Caradoc from London, from his wife and his drinking pals. It was Caradoc who had found Spring Cottage, through a newspaper advertisement. The property belonged to a tea-planter married to a French wife. They were going to Ceylon for a look over their estates and wanted tenants to mind the property in their absence. The rent was cheap, though tenants would need to pay the wages of Suzette the maid and Tom the gardener. Caradoc took an instant dislike to Tom, a windbag – and another ex-soldier – who he sensed was having an affair with the maid (which indeed he was, and Suzette was pregnant). But set in a lovely garden, Spring Cottage otherwise pleased. Caradoc straightway chose his work room, the smallest, least comfortable available, before strolling with Marguerite up the hill to Minchampton. They found a pub there and Caradoc dived in, telling Marguerite – who did not drink – to wait outside. Tired of waiting, she walked back home. A pattern had been set. Marguerite elaborates:

> I had feared in London he drank too much for his health – or good work. It was the one reason why I made up my mind I would never live in London with him. Maybe it was a foolish, mistaken idea, but I thought I had a mission in life to make him more temperate if I could – gradually. A drinking man cannot do the finest work of which he is capable and I was so very anxious that he should do more work – the best and finest that was in him, for whatever else I did not know about Caradoc, I was sure of his flashes of genius. I even dared to think that his love for me might make some difference and turn him from writing on sordid themes, but I did not succeed until his last six short stories, written without bitterness.

"Beer and me – beer is me," Caradoc proclaimed. There were periods "on the wagon", broken by wild drinking spasms that saw him utterly beyond reason, "a megalomaniac – as near as could be". Dislike of Tom finally drove him from the pub – Tom drank there too – so he ordered a cask of beer for home, which he kept under lock and key.

One small service Tom did provide was to fetch home a creature Evans would adore, a dog named Jock. Of some terrier mix (perhaps a dash of fox terrier), Jock came at eighteen months through a local paper advertising a Sealyham; "We can't go wrong with a Sealyham," Caradoc affirmed. Sent to pick up the dog, Tom returned way past the time expected. "I couldn't get him along any quicker. He stopped to fight on the way with every dog he saw and once went after a rabbit and I lost him altogether." Jock had begun as he meant to go on – and Caradoc could not have been happier. He took pride in Jock's fighting abilities, that he'd never taken a licking and never avoided a scrap. "He goes straight into it." Jock's virtues were constantly extolled. "Jock's a gentleman – a perfect gentleman. Ho yes, Jock's a nobleman, he's better than I am by a long chalk. He's miles above me." Evans would stand by Jock, as he would other dogs that joined the family, through all their many troubles. "He had that extraordinary sense of obligation with regard to animals. It was not nearly so strong when it came to humans." W.H. Davies was a case in point. He had come to live at Nailsworth, a short journey away by car, and he wrote inviting his friend to call upon him and his wife. "I did not go and only God knows why," Evans lamely commented.

The stay at Spring Cottage lasted no more than four months. Matters between Caradoc and Tom worsened so much that Tom, his behaviour with the maid exposed, was finally sacked. Tom's wife next abandoned him, taking the children with her. Caradoc expressed no regret whatsoever at the wreckage of a home. Tom's wife was well rid of him, as were the children. Marguerite had little regard for him – he was a braggart, with "something foxish about him" – but Caradoc's contemptuous reference to him as "the soldier" annoyed her. He used the same designation for Walter Lovell and sometimes she was uncertain which one of them he was abusing. His mounting hatred of Walter seemed totally without foundation, but similar rantings surrounded anyone else whom he felt Marguerite had some special regard or affection for, man or woman. "This was such a pity and it was so unnecessary," she writes, "for he governed my life and I would not have had it otherwise. He was the only person who had ever governed me. His ascendancy over me was absolute and complete." As, at base, was hers over him; the household's sole breadwinner, she was keeper of the purse. Within their tortured relationship was a sado-masochistic streak. Both held the whip-hand, and both took verbal lashings.

From Spring Cottage the pair moved eastward to the market village of Fairford and "an unfurnished old Cotswold house with a Roman wall around it". Here a fresh issue concerned them. On 4 September 1931 Rose Evans petitioned for divorce on the grounds of her husband's frequent adultery with "Marguerite Florence Laura Barczinsky, an authoress", citing their stay at the Great Western Hotel in Paddington a month before. On 1 January 1932 she filed for alimony and on 27 May was granted a decree nisi in an

undefended suit. During their married life (so she claimed) there had been trouble
because of her husband's association with women. In April 1931 he had told her he was
going away for three months to Gloucestershire with his publisher. Later she found that
this was not so. Evans was ordered to pay Rose £30 and a like sum in costs. Early in
June he lodged £30 in court but by the end of the month his bill had risen to £132, an
amount regarded as discharging all liability for alimony up to the January date of the
Chancery order. Thereafter payment would be at the rate of £3 per week. Whatever
rate was set would have been beyond Caradoc whose income had fallen to nothing.

   He had work in hand, however. In their 1932 spring list Hurst & Blackett announced
Evans's forthcoming new novel *Wasps* and newspaper reports also mentioned *Gangrene*,
another novel on the stocks in which the Gloucestershire peasantry would supplant the
Welsh as butt of the author's satire. The *Western Mail* (23 February 1932) coaxed a few
words from Caradoc:

> The people living in some of the Gloucestershire villages are so simple: more doltish
> in fact than I have ever struck before. They are badly educated too. There is no fun
> in Gloucestershire. I am amongst the farmer type of people a lot of the time, and I
> never hear them joking. They simply have no sense of humour. The villagers are not
> hospitable like the Welsh peasants; rather are they like the Cornish folk [Marguerite's
> people]. You can be a stranger there for years and always looked upon with suspicion.
> I have not seen a pretty girl since I came to Gloucestershire. There are some very
> pretty girls in South Wales, but the prettiest in the world – and the healthiest – are
> in London.

   A letter of this period survives from Evans to Evelyn Lewes, an author-journalist
he knew slightly, in response to her request that he read and comment upon a story by
"Miss Powell Price". He replies from the Fairford house – temporarily renamed "Rhydlewis"
– gladly offering to give an opinion on the story. "But my opinion is not worth anything
in the magazine market. No one's is except the editor's and two editors of the same
mind are rare."[2] He reports that he has just finished a book [*Wasps*] and is working on
another, "and I would work ever so fast if I were not engaged in a quarrel with my
landlord." Evelyn Lewes's letter additionally mentions Elizabeth Inglis-Jones, whom
Caradoc confesses not to have met although he found her book "considerable and should
have received much more attention". Perhaps her publishers concentrated their sales-
manship too much on Wales; the Welsh people do not buy books." (The book in question
would have been *Crumbling Pageant*, Inglis-Jones's second novel, set in Cardiganshire and
published by Constable.) Evans signs off hoping Miss Lewes is happy, "and if you are
journalising I know you are happy". Marguerite makes no reference to landlord quarrels.
The couple had trouble enough when *Wasps*, scheduled for spring publication, failed to
materialize. Just when is the next book coming? asked Glyn Roberts in December; it
was nowhere to be seen – and neither was its author.[3] Was the roaring Fleet Street
taverner now a Gloucester country mouse?[4]

   Trips to Rhydlewis continued, now with Marguerite who describes first meeting

Caradoc's mother (and his younger brother, the semi-paralyzed, semi-speechless Josi).
They drove from London to Wales without a break, so eager was Caradoc to reach Rhydlewis. On the rutty approach to Lanlas Caradoc pointed out one or two landmarks
featuring in his stories (notably Nanni's cottage). Leaving the chauffeured car, the couple
walked the narrow garden path to the porch of Lanlas, Caradoc calling out "Mam" as
they entered. Once inside the cottage, Marguerite saw "a little woman with a grey shawl
over her shoulders, low clogs on her feet, sitting by the fire. Her white hair framed
strong features that became strangely soft as she turned her face to the door looking
for her son who had found fame."[5] Approaching her nervously with a "Here we are,
Mam. This is Marguerite!" Caradoc began, "She wants to hear all about the preachers
you are going to have at your funeral." It was an old family joke: Mali Evans liked to
talk about her funeral. At eighty-four, bent and frail, she still baked her own bread and
for this occasion had prepared a welcoming tea: "boiled eggs, bread and butter, apple
tart on a plate, jam, cakes and cream". Marguerite much enjoyed her first Welsh cottage
tea. She witnessed something else that she came to feel was characteristically Welsh,
the "beautifully undemonstrative" greeting of mother and son.

> The Welsh people do not show their family affection for one another by endearment
> or caress. They do not kiss.[6] Of their deepest feelings they do not speak. The man
> does not remember being kissed by his mother, but his regard for her was the strongest
> thing in him, and if she did not like me something would happen to the quality of
> his regard for me, for if she did not find me to be the right measure by her standard
> I would fall short of his. She was never wrong. He claims she was never wrong in
> her judgment of people.

Mali admired Marguerite's clothes, touched and fingered her dress, wishing to know
its cost ("the more expensive, the better," whispered Caradoc). She asked about Nick
and said he must come with them next time. They left with the news that they intended
to live in Aberystwyth quite soon, and when they did, they would see her frequently,
once a week at least. Photographs of this visit survive. Marguerite reproduced one in
her biography of Caradoc. Dated 1932, it shows just him and his mother standing outside
Lanlas. (Marguerite cut herself out of this picture.)

It was Marguerite who found Caradoc new publishers, a downward slide from Faber.
Hurst & Blackett were a highly professional enterprise shifting books by the hundreds
of thousands. They satisfied a popular market, mostly through domestic drama and
romance fiction aimed at a female readership. Marguerite was the classic Hurst & Blackett
author, producing a dependable product under more than one pen name, doubtless to
avoid the impression of a single author saturating the market: subscription libraries had
limits to the number of titles they would take from any one author. In Hurst & Blackett's
1932 Spring List *Wasps* sits awkwardly alongside two of Marguerite's novels, though the
publishers did their best to distinguish "one of the most important novelists – both as
storyteller and stylist – of modern times".

With publication set for June, advanced copies were distributed, their dust jackets displaying commendations from Harold Nicolson, Frank Swinnerton and Sylvia Lynd within a wasp pattern of black and orange-yellow bands. (The title-page bore no year of publication; "We can't sell books with dates in them," Walter Hutchinson insisted.) The *Western Mail* received a copy and, mindful of Evans's recent divorce, drew attention to the novel's dedication "To Countess Hélène Marguerite Barcynska"[7]. It was "an amazing book, packed with potted wisdom, fantastic characters, and incredible incidents," and would appear in less than a fortnight. But *Wasps* never appeared, at least under Hurst & Blackett's imprint. Almost immediately the book was withdrawn from circulation. Another pre-publication copy had fallen into the hands of one particular writer of popular romance who, despite the routine disclaimer, "all the incidents and characters of this tale are entirely fictitious", saw herself libelled therein and promptly threatened legal action unless she were entirely written out of the story. The novel represented more than a year's continuous work and was all set for publication. The libel charge Evans emphatically denied: "I have never libelled anyone in my books," he assured Raymond Marriott; "Anyway," he added cloudily, "truth in art is never libellous or malicious. But there you are…" The moment remained with Marriott as the only time he remembered Evans ever having used the word "art" other than in a scornful sense. Already embroiled in one libel lawsuit, Hurst & Blackett dared not risk another. Publication had to be delayed and the offending passages removed. Evans took the rejection quietly. He had no option but to agree to the rewriting. Pressing one more advance copy into Marriott's hands, he urged that he keep it at all costs – a rare witness to the text as he had wished it.

Though nowhere specifically recorded, it seems to have been common knowledge that the offended novelist was Edith Nepean, who saw herself slightingly portrayed in the character of Dame Edith Shawle.

> This was Edith: a stocky woman of about the age of fifty whose eyes were like sloes, whose short legs were like logs of unhewn timber, whose feet bulged under scarlet shoes, and whose dress was scarlet and young womanish.
> "I'm the novelist," she said.

Evans elaborates fantastically on her appearance – "she parted her wide lips and her teeth were like rows of pigmy huts at the mouth of a giant's cave" – but just as wounding is the character examination. Though she poses as a moral guardian, Dame Edith's fiction shamelessly feeds off the prostitute's world and she herself takes a continental tour "sampling the gigolos of all nations". In the manner of her gushing heroines, showy, sentimental and titillating, she writes home describing her travels:

> Bella darling – Bucharest is the Paris and Monte Carlo and Berlin of the Near East rolled into one. French is spoken here in the army and racing circles and I'm learning it. I'm the guest of a Colonel in the Rumanian Army and he introduces me as his little English pal…. Yesterday I had a headache and I opened Nicolesco's tunic and

laid my weary little head on his chest and my heart beat madly and the stream rushed joyously on its way and the sun streamed its happy rays all over me as I lay panting on the grass, feeling tumultuously happy. Oh, how I do adore him. He calls me Draguta Mea! His military duties take it out of him so and he gets tired very soon – too soon. I'm dying to be home with Chris and immediately I am I shall go to Madrid. Why don't you come…

Dame Edith is a composite portrait – Marguerite is partly drawn upon – but one understands why Nepean should have been so incensed. Much of the detail suggests her: the name of course, her age (Nepean was forty-six in 1932), the honorific "Dame" (she married into the gentry), the consciously "modern" outlook on life (she was an authority on women's fashion), and the Carpathians reference; a noted continental traveller, Nepean settled for a while in Transylvania to write on Tzigan life. What puzzles is the warm relationship Evans had always enjoyed with Nepean. He was the first to publish her work, and continued to do so while at *T.P.'s Weekly*. Furthermore, he had received her as a friend at Rhydlewis ("many times in his mother's lifetime have I sat with him in the kitchen… listening to her stories"). In late 1930 he put Clifford Evans in touch with Nepean (at that time writing for *Picture Show*), through whom the young Welsh actor met some influential people in film.[8] Nevertheless, whatever the degree of discord over *Wasps*, the two writers bridged their differences and Nepean's obituary notice on Caradoc was to be wholly affectionate, fully acknowledging the debt she owed him for launching her literary career.

During autumn 1932 Evans set about expunging Dame Edith from *Wasps*. She becomes Ernie Brown, a "flabby-mouthed, fiddle-voiced, robin-chested" homosexual passionately interested in the welfare of younger men.[9] By the end of the year Caradoc had redrafted, taking the opportunity to revise certain sections substantially. In the meantime, Hurst & Blackett had suffered staff changes, Rodney St John Richard having resigned the management to start his own publishing company in conjunction with Ashley Cowan. His new firm, Rich & Cowan, had in mind a broader list, strong on naval and sea books (both directors were ex-naval officers) but with a showing in sociology, politics and drama. Andrew Dakers next joined the firm as literary adviser with responsibility for fiction and biography. Among his commissioned biographies was one of Arthur Machen by John Gawsworth (the pen name of Fytton Armstrong), a book which had its beginnings in a pub conversation between Gawsworth and Caradoc Evans. When talk turned to Arthur Machen, the teenage bibliophile Gawsworth knew he had met an admirer whose devotion matched his own.

"It isn't Machen writing, it's God writing through him," said Caradoc Evans, vehemently bringing down his fist to prove his point so heavily upon a table in the private bar of the Black Horse, Mortlake, that every bottle and glass in the room chimed – though, in discord – before relapsing shivering back into silence. So complete was Evans' assurance, so convincing his belief, that although his pronouncement was not taken altogether literally by his listener on that grey Autumn day in October 1930, it emboldened him to continue with his collecting where Machen material was concerned.

He was already a confirmed Machenian, was the listener who was myself. But of that moment, it is to be confessed, this book was born.[10]

Dakers actually turned down Gawsworth's *The Life of Arthur Machen* (it would not be published until 2005) but nothing deflected him from Caradoc Evans, a writer he had represented as literary agent and now wished to publish. Hurst & Blackett were accordingly persuaded to forego their existing contract and on 4 May 1933 *Wasps* finally appeared in print, a year later than originally scheduled, heavily revised in places, and under the new Rich & Cowan imprint.[11]

Still dedicated to "Countess Hélène Marguerite Barcynska", the Rich & Cowan *Wasps* is an extravaganza of shifting, clashing tones. Playful irony gives way to knockabout farce, much of it savagely ludicrous in cartoon fashion: as when Sam Policeman's wife suffocates her husband by driving "the snout of a mackerel far into his mouth" while he lies snoring beside her (Sam had planned to use the fish in some form of punishment for her infidelity). More than any Evans novel, *Wasps* employs a folk-tale idiom to carry its messages, most of all the philosophical John Honeybone's conviction that man is irremediably flawed:

> There are in man four wasps that masquerade in other names: faith by which we are robbed, hope by which we are tortured, and charity by which we are demeaned. The fourth goes by its right name – greed. Families will stand together to devour their enemies and when they have won they will set about to devour one another for the possession of as small a thing as a spade and the conqueror will by and by devour himself. Greed is our controlling wasp and by it shall mankind perish.

The chief vehicles for this lesson are a Tenby-born brother and sister, David and Bella Lloyd, who while contriving to fleece outsiders (in London and Wales) privately scheme against each other. Evans once again seizes the chance to guy particular aspects of Lloyd George's early career. David Lloyd, "relighting the gospel of Liberalism in Red Ford", makes a political martyr out of Bill Blake, a vagrant womanizer arrested for poaching rabbits from local estates. "In and about Gelert his song was that William Blake's liberty was the nation's liberty and his jail the nation's jail. By evening a train of men and women attended him and acclaimed him the masterful gander who would drive into their pens the gentry turkey-cocks." No drab bird himself, David Lloyd takes on the Tory churchmen. Caradoc covers favourite ground with this new Lloyd George double: his vaunted nationalism (a "Welsh out-and-outer"); his radical posturing (the socialist mouther turns Tory stooge); above all, his theatrical sense of self and accompanying addiction to words ("the magic of sound can conquer truth").

At David Lloyd's core lies dynamic materialism; "money begats labour and out of labour comes happiness and money," so runs the precept, though his moneymaking schemes prove fruitless. A butt for most of the story, he gains some gravity towards the end. His materialism, we come to realize, is as natural to him as breathing; it gives him his grip on the world. Separately, he and Bella scheme for John Honeybone's wealth; Honeybone is ailing, but still lovingly served by Martha, his housekeeper. Now it dawns on Lloyd that Honeybone might not sign the will that he (Lloyd) has secretly redrafted.

> He had brightened John Honeybone with cheer, had sent his sister Bella to tend him, and had stopped the red-eyed virgin Martha from weeping upon him in death. Honeybone had no kin, and if he died intestate there would be brabblings without end; Bella was not wedded to him, and if she were the inheritor the money would remain in her pocket for all time; Martha was neither wife nor mistress and she who has no place on a man's gravestone has none in his will.

That last bitter aphorism encapsulates one more lesson of *Wasps*, that marriage is the surest conduit of money. In Kensington David Lloyd pursues Alice Sandman, her expectation (marriage plus bed and board) matched by his (marriage and money). Her physical allure ("she was in her thirty-fifth year, the age at which woman is fully ripened") is lost on a man who avoids distracting emotional entanglements – "He had no doings with woman, beyond offering marriage to three women."

Bella's story, her attempt to gain the Marriage Mint, provides unremitting exposure of the sexual battlefield, where men are made vulnerable through a lust that at some point will evaporate. Thus Bella's Welsh lover perversely spurns her the moment she becomes a widow ("When a wife loses her husband she is cast off by her lover. Pugh was the salt in Kingdom's commerce with Bella and Pugh was dead and therefore she was without flavour. He had had his fill of her and he would put her from him."). In London the factory owner Joseph Marlowe tires of her, but his freedom comes at a cost: having "burnt his commonsense in lust", he must settle a house upon her. With all her setbacks, Bella knows that although "an easy woman is without esteem and that a woman should consider her body as a merchant his wares", all women must tread Harlotry Road to reach their Marriage Mint. One looks hard for a happy marriage in *Wasps*, though there is some suggestion that manifest quarrellings and violence may not tell the whole story (and what is said of one Cardiganshire gentry couple – that "the bitter tune of their private incivility was not that of the love by which they held each other" – well applied to Caradoc's own row-addicted life with Marguerite). Nonetheless, it is revealing that prior to Bella insinuating her way into Lovesnest, John Honeybone, unmarried and celibate, lived happily there with Martha in a father-daughter relationship.

Bella's path of "sober harlotry" takes her to London and Whittle Way, a place of discreet prostitution soon to be annexed by one Herbert Manland. He is the Patriarch of St Amor's, the Bayswater temple of worship with sidelines in property and perfumed vice (in the Hurst & Blackett original the temple was named Penetralia). The St Amor's section of the novel opens up a strange hinterland of religiosity, sensuality and decadence.

> The frailness of human nature was the strong foundation of St Amor's. Of all joys the greatest comes by the flesh. Man is reckless in its pursuit, but woman loves to deny it and consents to be aroused only by some rigmarole that she can name religious

rite. Many of the calls of the flesh are below the depth of common understanding:
St Amor's ministered unto every call.

Manland puts it more snappily: "All men are pagans from the waist down – and ladies
too." Evans had found in Nonconformity an intense mingling of religion and sex and the
readiness of men and women to submit to self-professed Messiahs. St Amor's sanctifies
sex in an aesthetic of camp theatricality – "most effective", enthuses Ernie – and suffused
throughout with the spirit of the Song of Solomon: "blow upon my garden, that the spices
thereof may flow out. Let my beloved come into his garden, and eat of his pleasant fruits."[12]

St Amor's conjures up the Victorian Free Love movement and more specifically the
Agapemone or Abode of Love, Henry James Prince's religious community at Spaxton,
Somerset, but with roots in Evans's part of Wales. In 1836 the young Henry James Prince
came to study at St David College, Lampeter, a newly founded institution for the training
of Anglican clergy. There his manly passions were sublimated in religious ecstasy, aided
by the Song of Solomon, the book that become favourite reading for the Lampeter
Brethren, a group of fellow theological students gathered around Prince. Two of their
number succeeded him in English livings (impropriety having cost Prince both), with
the Revd Lewis Price following him to Spaxton at the foot of the Quantocks. There the
free church built by Prince for a prosperous devotee became the centre of the Agapemone,
the religious community which Prince (now "the Beloved") had been inspired to found
and which he guarded closely. The Abode of Love attracted numbers, more than a
thousand in the 1850s, a time of dramatic change in the practices of the community.
On a sofa in view of the congregation Prince copulated with one of his followers. God
did not deny the flesh, and as a vehicle for the Holy Ghost, the Beloved must need experience that sexual union which as an ordained clergyman he had properly denied himself.

In the late 1880s, following a wave of wealthy new converts, the Revd J.H. Smyth-
Pigott visited Spaxton and became the sect's pastor in Clapton, east London, his lean,
handsome, much photographed face coming to identify the movement ("that self-satisfaction
oddly combined with spiritual fastidiousness so frequently in the faces of successful
preachers", notes an Agapemone's historian).[13] In 1896 an expensive new Agapemonite
church, known as the Ark of the New Covenant, was opened near Clapton Common
and on Prince's death (in 1899) Smyth-Pigott assumed the mantle of Beloved, then pronounced himself the Messiah. His doings at Clapton gave rise to extensive, lurid publicity
– talk of hordes of adoring women kissing the feet of the master – and ultimately closed
the Ark. Smyth-Piggott returned to Spaxton, accompanied by his aging wife and a younger
devotee, the Spiritual Bride of the Lamb. "There is no such thing as marriage among us.
We are all brothers and sisters in the Spirit." Smyth-Pigott's defence of life at Spaxton
convinced no one and he was eventually unfrocked for immorality.

Evans would have been aware of the Clapton church on first coming to London – it
promised a field day for secularists like G. W. Foote – as he would twenty-five years later
when in 1927 the newspapers, recording Smyth-Piggott's death, raked over the scandals
of a closed religious community. In *Wasps*, St Amor's suffers similarly: "Patriarch's Beauty
Choir. Sensational Orgies in a London 'Church'" – such headlines drive out John Manland

(latter metamorphosed as Cyril of Forest Gate). The parallels between St Amor's and the foundations of Prince and Smyth-Piggott are altogether striking, not least in the social composition of their respective devotees. The Patriarch speaks of shining his arc lamp on "snobbish sanctimonious silly old London town", and his rank theatrical High Anglicanism draws in titled roués, snobbish tradesfolk, literary pretenders and others of frowsty bohemia.

In the Welsh context, too, Evans charts new social terrain, that of the minor gentry, a group markedly absent from his previous fiction though not entirely unknown to him from his own Rhydlewis background (where the Lloyds of Bronwydd were a conspicuous and largely beneficent presence). We enter *Wasps* by way of Rhys Pugh, vicar of St Michael's at Red Ford, north of Castle Edward (a thinly veiled Aberystwyth), "the fifth Pugh to stand up in his church for God, squire and landowner". A character largely seen through the eyes of the villagers, he is a linchpin in their chapel demonology. And Evans is on their side. The upper echelons of Cardiganshire society are wholly blighted, physically, mentally, emotionally and morally. Dan Kingdom of Old Roses surveys his dismal, degraded kind, "the clay-cold men and fever-eyed women of the gentry";

> many of them were the unsound children of unions between cousins and some of more abominable unions. The women were faithless and those who loved not one another made love-toys of chauffeur-gardeners and handy-men and clergymen, but they were sensible of their duty to the Church and to their high estate and chose no lover from the lowly ranks of chapellers; the men were faithful because they were weaklings and because they drank themselves into silliness, and they gambled away their land to buy motor-cars and follow hounds and they hoped to recover it with prize-money in a sweep. Both the men and women were prideful and arrogant, though their mansions were set upon a wilderness.

Such intensity of feeling rarely surfaces in *Wasps*, which prefers to deal in fantasy and indulgent comic satire. The old Liberal-Nonconformist targets are given a rest, though Evans cannot resist a David Lloyd, or Archdruid Ap Reuben presiding over the Eisteddfod circus at Castle Edward. Ap Reuben, it goes without saying, is a faker and a rogue, "sneak[ing] from his task of unfolding the streaming glories of his nation in the great marquee to find Bella". Caradoc delights in this Welsh cultural idol ("I'm a Celt to my last trouser button") and his verbal magic.

The Eisteddfod episode stands out, as does the chapter that follows, a near detachable grisly fairy tale concerning Lias Tailor Methodist, the dwarf whose daughter Fanny falls pregnant by Bill Blake. She craves a rabbit to eat, and three of Blake's gleaming teeth: Lias satisfies her first desire, passing off cooked kitten as rabbit, then turns to the challenge of Blake's teeth.

Wasps won fair reviews, and at least it got reviews, more than it would have done had Hurst & Blackett published it. With some 15,000 new books issued each year, newspaper silence would have been lethal, but Rich & Cowan, though a small company, was causing a stir, the *Bookseller* contending (3 November 1933) that rarely had a new publishing firm "progressed with such rapidity into a stable position". The firm had expectations of *Wasps* and fashioned block advertisements for the two most productive national papers, the *Sunday Times* and the *Observer*. Impressive copy lay at hand, thanks to Francis Isles in *Time and Tide*: "Exhilarating, extremely amusing, almost libellously provocative, totally mad, and altogether delightful.... I read it with joy. *Wasps* is a book which cannot be described. It must be read." And reading it "was like being ferociously butted by a large woolly sheep". The book had an "insane zest", and on that score alone was worth six dozen of the "thin-blooded examinations of anaemic nonentities' souls which seem to constitute half of the dismal fiction of today". Isles acknowledged its unreality but by taking it all as fantasy he enjoyed it as much as it deserved. The *New Statesman*'s Peter Quennell approached the book in similar spirit. *Wasps* was "a disconcerting, top-heavy, fantastic book... packed with Rabelaisian and frankly ludicrous incident" – and a trifle long-winded for English tastes.

Others saw a more serious work: "a dreadful satire on lust, pretence and greed" with no moments of relief; yet one had to read on, or so thought the *Sunday Times*; "a truly terrible book, and not one to be incautiously recommended". The *TLS* was frankly repelled by the novel's nihilistic vision; and "Satire that holds no higher ideal than the thing it condemns is a serpent that bites its own tail and with deadly venom." Granting that Evans was clever and often witty in his irony, the *TLS* nonetheless wearied at the narrow range of mannerisms and interest. Edwin Muir felt much the same. He doubted that Evans could truly be called a satirist, "For a satirist must always have in his mind an ideal of normal humanity, so that by contrast with it vice should show in its full deformity" (*Listener*, 17 May); Evans had "abundant energy, an admirable turn for curt insulting portraiture, a humour as disrespectful to humanity as a blow in the face. These are gifts such as not many writers are given, yet when one has read the book it is hard to say what one takes away from it except the spectacle of a talented writer in a first-rate fury." Gerald Gould in the *Observer* pondered Evans's marketability: "With a larger tolerance, a deeper understanding of life, and a less provocative style, Mr. Evans could immensely increase his appeal. Is it to be presumed that he does not care to? For that he is an artist of considerable power, and the potentialities of considerable sympathy, is clear. He has, anyway, so well succeeded in impressing his personality that his following is assured."

Gould found the novel difficult going, with its idiom coming close to stifling the storytelling. In support, one might mention the parade of obsolete or dialect words ("coggery", "covin", "cribbled", "fleered", "fuffed", "maffled", "quobbed", "sloomy", "stam", "wambled") and perhaps the "potted wisdom", the maxims that stud pages. Many are powerfully expressive of Caradoc's sentiments in important areas: "None knows better than the poor that of all the blessings the greatest is money"; "Music is the goddess of Welsh chapel religion and creed her handmaid. She tunes the preacher to prophetic pitch..."; "The passion of a surfeited lover never burns again"; "A woman spreads her troubles as the honeysuckle its tendrils"; "Selfishness is the beginning of child worship and sorrow is its reward"; and the previously quoted, "She who has no place on a man's gravestone has none in his will."

Gould's belief that Evans had a following was seemingly borne out by the immediate reprinting of *Wasps* (and a Faber's reissue of *Nothing to Pay* in August 1933). Indeed, Rich & Cowan were emboldened enough to advertise *Wasps* in the *Western Mail*, a week after the paper's reviewer F.J. Mathias had dismissed the book as "spiteful nonsense... too hopelessly mechanical to be anything but stupid... funeral sermons are travestied; death-beds are mocked; at the National Eisteddfod the Archdruid ap Reuben behaves like a blasphemous rake" (4 May 1933). In Evans's Wales, "sin is triumphant, honour a myth, sex a snare, and ideals delusions". The country did not exist outside the author's imagination. Other Welsh critics shared Mathias's revulsion. "A non-stop sewer tour," reported J.C. Griffith Jones; "a libel on life and upon men, on Englishmen and Welshmen alike. When I had waded through the 288 pages of filth I opened all the windows in my room and drank in the clean night air with a sigh of relief."[14] At least there were no attempts in Wales to limit the novel's circulation; in the Irish Free State *Wasps* joined *Nothing to Pay* on the list of banned books – Austin Clarke much resented not being able to read it.

By the time *Wasps* appeared, Caradoc and Marguerite were married and living in Aberystwyth. Divorce being a two-stage process, the decree nisi of 27 May 1932 became absolute on 27 February 1933. From that day onwards Caradoc was bound to pay Rose Evans £156 per annum by weekly instalments of £3. (He had also been ordered to pay an additional £41.14.10 in petitioner's costs.) Within a month he had remarried. On 22 March 1933, at Maidenhead Register Office, David Caradoc Evans and Marguerite Florence Laura Barczinsky (yet another variation of her name) became husband and wife. He gave his age as 51 (he was 54), she put hers as 43 (she was 46). It was a quiet ceremony, in the presence of relations sworn to secrecy. Not until June did their marriage become public knowledge, through a front-page story in the London evening *Star*. The scoop stemmed from a reporter having noticed Marguerite's dedication of *Under the Big Top* – a Countess Barcynska novel published in May – "To My Husband Caradoc Evans". The *Star* could also reveal that the Countess and the novelist named Oliver Sandys were one and the same person. None of this was news in Aberystwyth, where Caradoc and Marguerite Evans were already making themselves known; or indeed to Glyn Roberts, who informed the *Star* that he'd noticed the *Big Top* dedication in the copy that Marguerite had given him. "Miserable incompetent" as he was, he had failed to recognize a front-page story.[15] If Roberts missed out on the marriage, he picked up on a Hurst & Blackett announcement that "the pen name of Countess Barcynska is the sole property of Mrs Caradoc Evans, and that anybody attempting to issue any work under that pen name will be infringing copyright."[16] In all, 1933 was a good year for Roberts, the time when with missionary fervour he began to promote Caradoc and other Welsh writers in English. Caradoc's first letter on returning to Wales was probably written to Roberts; dated 12 April 1933, it provided one more new address, 17 Queen's Road, Aberystwyth.

Return to Wales

1933-34

T rue to his promise, Caradoc moved to Aberystwyth so that he might be near his mother for whatever time she had left. Mali's health had worsened; she was now fully dependant on her capable young granddaughter Lil, child of Caradoc's sister Sarah (and sister of Howell). Aberystwyth was the obvious place to live: within an hour's drive of Rhydlewis and a spot Marguerite liked from the start. She took to its kindly people, to the rural peace and the sea. It was a town like no other; within five minutes, one could be away into unspoilt countryside.[1] "Properly it is a town, but overgrown village better describes it, for though it has few characteristics of a town it has all those of a village. If the man was out and I wanted to find him I had no more to do than ask almost the first person I met..."[2] English seaside resorts were always trying to improve themselves, "make themselves like bits of Hammersmith Broadway, but Aberystwyth has no self-improvement ideas. It is as unchangeable as the rock from the feet of which rises its tall slim houses." In one of those tall slim houses – 17 Queen's Road – the Evanses found rooms, this within a month of their marriage. Belatedly honeymooning at Maidenhead, the pair confirmed to the press that they would indeed live in Wales, finish the books they were working on, and perhaps collaborate on others. Marguerite had a book with a theatrical background and Caradoc's next novel (tentatively entitled *The Lift*) might in time appear as a play, as it was meant to be originally.[3]

Marguerite's theatre passion sprang from an escapist childhood, a time when the stage seemed a realistic route from an oppressive home life, the semi-militaristic regime insisted upon by her father. Now settled at Aberystwyth, she would take to the stage again. In December 1933 she hired the Bath Street Forum for a dramatization of her novel *Chappy – That's All*. She gave the occasion an extra theatrical twist when, revealing a form of spiritualism that chimed with her Christian faith, she placed on a front row seat a sheaf of chrysanthemums in memory of her beloved aunt Tots. While Marguerite had been writing *Chappy*, Tots lay gravely ill in a nursing home. "I am absolutely convinced that my aunt sat… watching the dramatized version of the book she laughed and sobbed over when dying."[4] As for the nature of the play, it was Marguerite's "fairy tale for grown-ups", and the Forum audience received it with bouquets and gifts – although the vampish quality she brought to the role of an unscrupulous society sophisticate raised a few local eyebrows. Nor, so it seemed, was *Chappy* an isolated happening: town-talk held that Marguerite had further productions in mind. A maverick Queen's Road neighbour, one Frederick Warburton, caught wind of the rumours and sensed a chance to make money. Professing distinguished theatrical lineage, he knocked on

Aberystwyth doors with the story that he himself had taken the Parish Hall for a season of London plays. Would residents care to subscribe to his venture – as Mr Caradoc Evans the author had done? Warburton's prosecution followed and on 6 December 1933 Evans appeared in court as a witness. He confirmed that the defendant had called on him, enquiring whether it was true that he was going to form a repertory company; he replied that he was not. When Warburton next claimed to be the godson of the great actor-manager Sir Frank Benson, "I saw that he was one of the many Englishmen who think Aberystwyth is a town of 'twps'." Evans smelt a crook and gave nothing towards his "fool scheme". For having obtained money by false pretences, Warburton received two months' hard labour.[5]

Besides "Olive Bree" on *Chappy*'s cast list was a "Nicholas Sandys".[6] Marguerite had persuaded her son to re-join her after two years' separation. During the stay in Gloucestershire she corresponded with him and with Walter Lovell, her erstwhile partner. Walter still wished to be with her; Nick, most stubbornly, did not. "It was the absence of Nickie that was breaking my heart. I cried in secret and I cried in my sleep. This troubled him [Caradoc] very greatly for he wanted Nickie to join us for my sake."[7] With their Aberystwyth base secured, Marguerite coaxed her son to try living with her again and to make his peace with Caradoc. He came "unwillingly, angrily, resentfully" but Caradoc soon won him over, largely through talk of books and the authors he personally knew. Aware of the teenager's curiosity about black magic, Caradoc gave him books by Arthur Machen, Montague Summers and Aleister Crowley. They fell on fertile ground. Nick's interest in the occult grew steadily until in middle years he became a practising white magic devotee. But at eighteen, in Aberystwyth, there needed to be career plans and, like his mother before him, Nick looked to the theatre, or possibly film. He preferred to be known as Nicholas Sandys, both on and off the stage.

With accommodation at Queen's Road barely adequate for a family of three, the Evanses set their sights on larger premises across the road at Queen's Square House. After protracted negotiations with the Longley family, this handsome corner dwelling, with its railings and flowerbeds and grass in the front, became their home in the spring of 1934 at a rent of £95 per annum (the Longleys retaining a flat there with a separate entrance). Alas, the Evanses rather overdid the housewarming: thick smoke and sparks issuing from the Queen's Square chimney landed Caradoc a 5/6d fine for letting it be set on fire.[8] Marguerite claimed that at their request Henry Longley had converted three houses into one.[9]

> Anyway, so that we might not interrupt each other, Caradoc and I did our writing in rooms as far away from each other as the accommodation would allow. So the kitchen was in the middle of the house. Caradoc's writing-room led out of the kitchen and the drawing-room, a beautiful room he was very proud of, and loved to show to visitors because of the antiques and treasures I collected. My writing room was at the very top of the third house.

Both had books to complete and Marguerite in particular needed to regain her productivity – the new household depended on it. Upheavals following departure from London had been a distraction – just two published novels in 1932 – and arriving at Aberystwyth she sensed for the first time ever something close to writer's block (a condition she would rectify in her own distinctive way). Cast by Hurst & Blackett as "England's best-loved woman novelist", she kept her target of four books a year. Her Barcynska novels she felt had greater sophistication and broader themes than her Oliver Sandys productions, but their purpose was essentially the same, to lift the spirits; "for ever since I started to write as a little girl I always had in mind sick or sad people for my public, whose need was to be taken out of themselves and cheered, not shocked or horrified."[10] Perhaps stronger on characterization than on plot, with some freshness of background detail, her novels embraced a sunny vision of life; "personally, I'm all for the happy ending".[11] She drove her pen relentlessly with little sense of herself as an artist: she was happily the popular novelist ("sales exceed 1,000,000 copies", her publishers claimed). If she had a regret, it was that her fiction served no reformist cause. "Reforms can be brought about by fiction," as Dickens proved. "He is supreme. He keeps his tandem in hand. He never loses his story interest in his passion to right a wrong."[12]

Nevertheless, one admirer would come to see Marguerite in the early 1950s as on the verge of introducing something new in novel writing. The astrologer Edward Lyndoe, a former Aberystwyth resident who turned in a weekly horoscope for the Sunday *People*, wrote to encourage the intermingling in her fiction of real people (their permission granted) with characters of her own creation. She found the suggestion tempting and in her next Barcynska novel *Sunset is Dawn* (1953), based on her theatre venture in Aberystwyth, she, Caradoc and others, openly appear as themselves. In truth, throughout her career she had drawn on people around her for fictional characters, often thinly disguised. From the moment she met him, Caradoc frequented her pages as the type of temperamental genius.

In Barcynska's *Exit Renee* (1934), written in the flush of marriage, he appears as Lewis Ford (directly derived from "Rhydlewis") and she as Olive Bree (her stage name). The novel takes the form of a diary kept by the heroine Renee Dove who, following the break-up of a relationship, journeys to Wales. At Morfa (clearly Aberystwyth) she is urged by an "E.C. Holborn" ("Holborn" is a Queen's Road house name and "E.C." the London postcode of Holborn district) to meet Lewis Ford and his novelist-wife Olive Bree. Renee has read some Lewis Ford ("The beauty of his prose is like purple over sores. The purple he draws aside to reveal the moral cancer of his country as he sees it and mankind as a whole"), and she knows that Olive Bree writes "nice books. Typists read them, and clergymen and bookmakers and old ladies." At a country fair Renee spots them. "A craggy-faced man in tweeds and a shabby black sombrero hat... Lewis Ford shot at me a penetrating look from under his deep-set eyes – smallish half-lidded eyes with a peculiar gleam in them, the gleam of the fey. His wife was beside him." Olive Bree's personality, so Renee gathers, is exactly the opposite of her husband's. "She is an exotic-looking creature with the tiniest hand and feet that I have ever seen on a well-proportioned woman"; "You're in love with Lewis Ford, aren't you?" Renee says to Olive. "Dear, I worship him – just worship."

Now follows the story of their love, seriously different from Marguerite's supposedly factual accounts:

> Lewis had a wife [Olive explains] who got left behind when he became famous.... She tried to make chains for him. They lived in the misery of the utterly incompatible. I don't blame her entirely. Very likely she had thought she was marrying a respectable underling who would live with her in a red-brick villa, and when he changed into a zebra she was startled and annoyed.... I had a toy soldier husband, who lived on my wits – not his. His pastime was playing tennis, while I wrote, and his conversation was on sport – trout-fishing and shooting birds. Lewis and I had a total of thirty-five years of endurance between us – Lewis twenty-two, Olive fourteen not out. The big drill that was to break up our matrimonial macadam did not start to work until I walked into his Fleet Street office.

Olive proceeds: "One day I received an illiterate letter from his wife, commanding me to break off the disgusting intrigue I was carrying on with her husband... or she would take us both into court. She had enough evidence." Furtively, Lewis plans his getaway, filling each day a bag with the books he could not live without and deposited them in an empty room he has secretly hired. There they are crated up and addressed to a stone retreat in Gloucestershire. "Lewis's wife became a fury scorned. She refused point-blank to apply for the decree absolute until she had screwed three-quarters of his income as alimony and bargained for his house, his investments and everything that she could turn into cash. He threw it all into the curving fingers of greed to place a wedding-ring on mine."

Olive's own pitched battle was even grimmer, because hers was a fight for a child not for property. "I have a son", Olive goes on, "and the toy soldier refused to give him up, and I had no peace in my soul, even though I was with Lewis. I was torn in two. The battle lasted a year, and I won it. A Chancery Judge gave me the custody of my boy. We are all three together now and the storm is over.... The greedy London sparrow can't peck at us now, and the soldier has no more shot." Eighteen-year-old Nick is introduced ("Olive Bree's son Teddy – dark and handsome, and with his mother's charm, destined for the stage") and terrier Jock scraps away victoriously. As for the difficult negotiations to secure Queen's Square House, Olive holds that the landlord, hating her husband's books, "made out an impossible lease in order to drive Lewis out of Morfa". Moved by all she has heard, Renee suggests that Olive puts it in a life of Lewis Ford ("someone will when he's dead"). To which Olive teasingly replies, "I couldn't do it in cold print. I may disguise it in a novel one day."

Marguerite's writings, in whatever genre, present problems for an Evans biographer. Her three volumes of autobiography are all valuable, as is her book on her husband; they are intimate and revealing yet only moderately accurate on fact. Caradoc frequently appears in her later fiction and while what she tells of him there mostly accords with her 'cold print' record, there are interesting, sometimes startling, differences. Of course, fiction affords such licence – novelists are never on oath – but we sense that on certain issues the fiction is more believable, that the truth has indeed been disguised in a novel. This said, it must also be recognised that, as with her biographical volumes, her fictional renditions do not present a consistent picture. In Barcynska's *Sweetbriar Lane* (1938) Walter Lovell is something of a hero and, as we have seen, Rose Evans appears in a far more favourable light.

The remark in *Exit Renee*, that his landlord wished to drive Lewis Ford out of Morfa, raises the question of Evans's reputation at this time and Aberystwyth's perception of the new arrivals. Caradoc's every move still fascinated the press in Wales. Twists in the tale of the Evan Walters portrait were fully reported, as was a book-burning episode in Barry. Soon after the Evanses came to Aberystwyth, J.R. Llewellyn, Chairman of Barry Council seized a copy of *Taffy* from a library borrower and threw it on a Council cart bound for the refuse incinerator. Councillor Llewellyn was forced to make good the loss, since only the book selection committee could decide the suitability of particular titles ("otherwise we would have no library at all"). Interviewed afterwards, Llewellyn said: "It was my great joy to consign that infernal volume to the ashes of Hades. If I am obliged to pay the market value of the volume, I will do so, but replace it, never, never, never." The incident made the *Western Mail* (9 May 1933), and the national Sunday *Observer*, all in the month when Llewellyn's wife was crowned Barry's temperance queen and, as one newspaper reader noted, the Nazis were burning books.

Caradoc at Aberystwyth found three exceptional friends. The astrologer Edward Lyndoe was more a sparring partner, the two arguing fiercely over politics. Evans upbraided Lyndoe for his constant criticism of Russia and, for all his astral foresight, being unable to see that war was certain to come – Evans could smell its approach. Its advent failed to shake Lyndoe's anti-communism – "He should shut up about the Russians... What right has he to criticize Stalin" – but Lyndoe's affection endured. "What a man!" he wrote to Marguerite following Caradoc's death, "And what a woman to risk life with such a Niagara of a genius."

Meetings were more tranquil with Sarnicol (Thomas Jacob Thomas), a Treharris grammar school headmaster who for a while ran the Welsh column in the *Merthyr Express*. Ill health brought him prematurely to Aberystwyth where, at Laura Place, he and his wife found an imposing Georgian town house, soon with an entrance hall "distinguished by its old oak Welsh dresser and jugs and the great carved impressive Bardic chair which Sarnicol had won".[13] The cadaverous poet and epigrammatist immediately warmed to Caradoc, assuring the *Western Mail* (on the evidence of passages in *Wasps*) that Caradoc was "nothing less than a true poet", and a man who in his heart of hearts loved Wales and her people.[14] He noted an affinity with Huw Menai: embittered by early experience, both writers had struggled hard for recognition, but whereas "Caradoc has won through brilliantly; Huw is still in the thick of the fight." Sarnicol sensed the wider implications of Evans's work; reading him, inevitably "You have in mind not Wales but the world;

not the Welshman but Everyman." By refusing to explain his writings Evans had allowed himself to be profoundly misunderstood. Besides literature, the two discussed religion. An intellectual agnostic, Sarnicol attended chapel largely for his wife's sake. He too was a sermon-taster, without Caradoc's relish for pulpit theatricals. Inevitably, Marguerite compared their marriages. Sarnicol's disposition was peaceful and it seemed he never quarrelled with his trim young-looking wife, "a diligently good, religious, Christian little lady" who supported him to the hilt (and whose interests did not touch Marguerite's). The Evanses, on the other hand, had arguments every day, "Fierce ones – arguments and squabbles!"[15]

Caradoc fascinated Dr George Green, an educational psychologist and university lecturer. Green would see him walking the promenade, alone or with Marguerite and Nick:

> There was something incongruous in the wide-brimmed hat of soft black felt that he wore, which combined in a fantastic fashion the Evangelical preacher and the Fleet Street journalist. He wore soft collars, often vivid in colour – I remember them mainly as bright green or brighter red – with ties that were carelessly knotted and usually the worse for wear. His trousers were generally of thickish tweed, the rough, hairy kind that never presses well and assumes, after a day or two of wear, a shapelessness that is permanent. The coats he preferred were sports coats of loudly checked tweed, and he preferred them old.[16]

Evans looked what he felt himself to be, a pilgrim in a foreign land, naturally drawn to the stream of misfits the town attracted, people with whom he could talk and drink. Green thought him too easily taken in. "He spent hours listening to the fantasies of half-crazed people under the impression that he was hearing stories of real injuries inflicted on helpless victims." A common feeling of being outsiders drove Caradoc and such people together.

Green first called upon the Evanses one evening in 1934. "A maid took my card, and showed me into a drawing-room furnished with pieces which had obviously been collected by someone with a taste for unusual and beautiful things." (Not Caradoc, he rightly surmised.) Green had come to seek advice on a script he was preparing for the town's historical pageant, scheduled for the coming July (a considerable undertaking involving some thirty-five Cardiganshire schools). Both Evanses responded positively: Caradoc on the wording of the script, the sound and rhythm of the phrases; Marguerite on the actors, their costumes, groupings and movements. From that day on, a closeness developed between George Green and the two of them, Marguerite counting George "our greatest Aberystwyth friend". She liked his style, his distinctive dress: he wore no hat or overcoat, and what he did wear distanced him further from Aberystwyth men. George liked colour, his taste readily evident in a fetching array of shirts.

He talked a lot with Caradoc, and to some effect. "George knows a lot more about me than you think," Marguerite has Caradoc saying. The disconnection between the man, "so transparently simple, so free of hypocrisy, so generous, so embarrassingly grateful for any thoughtful act", and the artist, "the creator of the savage, cruel people who come to life in his books", intrigued the psychologist Green. "I once asked him about the people in his books. I cannot now recall the precise form in which I put the question, but I can remember his reply. 'Welshmen?' he replied. 'I didn't mean them to be taken for Welshmen. They are some of my relations.'"[17] In fragments, over time, Green learned about these relations, about his mother's poverty and pain and the close relative who "had taken advantage of her simplicity and trust to rob her of everything". Evans grew up "often meeting this man, well-to-do, respected, unctuous and patronizing and contrasting his prosperity with his mother's poverty and want." Green could not vouch for the facts of this story but that Evans believed it completely he did not doubt. It provided the template for much that occurs in the black and white fiction. "What Caradoc hates he treats cruelly, flaying it with bitter words and savage ridicule. He mocks as he flogs." Caradoc knew pity. "He felt the suffering of man, woman, horse, dog or bird as if it were his own. But he did not understand that the people he ridiculed mocked and scourged were deserving of pity too..." (One might argue that an encompassing pity is implicit in Evans's fiction. All in his rural compound are victims, the inmates and their keepers.)

"Dr George Green (author & producer of the Aberystwyth & Cardiganshire peace pageant)" appears in a gallery of Aberystwyth celebrities drawn by the cartoonist Matt Sandford. The lantern-jawed Sarnicol also features, looking worryingly gaunt and gloomy. The whole Evans family are present (all conspicuously behatted): pipe-smoking Caradoc, Marguerite, her drop earrings glittering (the sole woman among twenty-two men), and "film actor" Nick Sandys beneath an extravagant black fedora. The date would be 1935 (possibly 1936), the time of Marguerite's greatest local prominence.[18]

Not everyone in Aberystwyth looked admiringly on Evans. Jack Griffith was perplexed by George Green's whitewashing of his character. Griffith too wrote short fiction and was pleasantly surprised when L.A.G. Strong confirmed Caradoc's flattering estimate of one of his stories and published it in *Lovat Dickson's Magazine*. It was a story about a horse killed in a coalmine. "'Good God, Jack!' he [Caradoc] exclaimed, 'This is a classic already! You should have been earning your living with your pen for the past five years!' He read it again, then added: 'Soak yourself in the Russians. Read all you can of them. Soak yourself in the Russians!'"[19] Griffith thought Caradoc flattered only when it suited him and "could be crushingly rude to the insignificant and the helpless". He instanced Caradoc's courtroom performance in the Frederick Warburton case – his "being witty at the unfortunate creature's expense, sneering at his mentality and claiming to have summed up the man's character in a few minutes".[20] Shortly before, Griffith witnessed Caradoc Evans bawling out the manager of W.H. Smith because *Wasps* wasn't adequately displayed. "Seeing that one half of the window had been given to him, and the other half to Mrs Evans for her latest Oliver Sandys book, there was little the manager could have done short of spreading copies over the pavement outside. Caradoc, of course, as he often did, was showing off." He was surely something of a show-off when it came to matters of dress, his patterned suit and black broad-brimmed trilby setting him apart from the town's clerical greys. Whether calling in shops, feeding gulls from bread-filled bags (he fed the donkeys in summer too), or quietly sitting on a prom bench with Sarnicol, he was aware of the figure he cut, and he played up to it. Marguerite likewise stood out; an over-dressed, over-made up, theatrical figure in a dowdy little town, she was not particularly liked.

In 1934 Caradoc's mother died. His arrival at Aberystwyth had noticeably cheered her spirits, but on 17 July 1934 she passed away aged eighty-six. Four days later, on Saturday 21 July, Mali got the funeral she wanted, one of the largest in the locality. Three ministers officiated: John Green (Twrgwyn) at the house, Stanley Jenkins (Hawen) at the chapel, and John Phillips (Newcastle Emlyn) at the graveside, this trio accompanied by D.D. John (Penbryn) and T. Tegwyn Davies (Aberporth).[21] Mary Evans was buried in the ground of Twrgwyn, the Methodist hillside chapel where her brother Joshua also lay. Reports of the funeral put Caradoc among the chief mourners but he failed to appear in person. Annie Rees was not the only one shocked by this and she turned to Sarnicol ("his bosom friend") for an explanation. "He had very definite reasons," came the reply.[22] Caradoc's nephew Howell Evans assures us that within the family his absence provoked little comment.[23] Caradoc was baffling and unbalanced, "not conventional in any sense". Indeed, he was absent seven months later when Howell's mother died, aged sixty-one. Caradoc's second sister Sarah (Mrs Thomas Evans) was always his favourite, "a good wife and a good mother", Marguerite has him say of her; "She worked like hell. She worked because she liked it – anything to do with the farm."[24] Sarah's funeral took place in February 1935. Caradoc arrived on the day but remained seated in the car outside the austerely beautiful St Michael's Church at Penbryn. (Her grave, with its towering headstone inscribed in English, lies next to Allen Raine's.) It was Howell's belief that as with Caradoc's mother, so with his sister – on both occasions Caradoc was too distressed, too afraid of his emotions. ("He was a man of moods and these *controlled* him," echoed Annie Rees.)

Marguerite never doubted her husband's deep love for his mother, whose photograph he kept in his spectacle case. "When his mother died he was too upset to go to her funeral. He was genuinely ill and I sat with him in his writing-room all that afternoon – not talking, just with him. Neither did he talk. He was beyond words or tears. We went to her grave a few days afterwards, he and I." Gazing down upon it, he said, "Do you know, I never knew until now what a little woman she must have been. I always thought she was tall."[25] They went straight home in the car, "for the man cannot bear to express his sorrow in public, least of all to his relations".[26] A letter survives from Evans, written in response to a note of condolence from Wil Ifan.[27] It reads:

> Dear Mr Evans,
> Thank you very much for your kind message.
> Mother was good & all who knew her are sorry that she is dead.
> Yours very sincerely
> Caradoc Evans

A month later Annie Rees met Caradoc at the Neath National Eisteddfod. He seemed still very cut up about his mother's death but was making provision for Josi. The local postman James Davies and his wife would look after him at Lanlas. "Caradoc's care of his brother is something to see & marvel," Annie Rees told Anthony Davies. "When I was a child I knew he paid a man to shave him & cut his hair. Throughout the long years he saw to his care & comfort to the smallest detail. Still sees to him, I mean he has seen to his welfare in case of his death." (In fact, it was Caradoc's sister Mary who took on most of the expense of looking after Josi, up to her death in 1943.)

At a personal level Caradoc could be charm itself. "Of course I remember you quite well and more I remember your beautiful work in *The Poacher*."[28] He is writing to May Hopkins (30 June 1933), part of a brother and sister act, Ted and May Hopkins, music hall and theatre comedians who specialised in Welsh character sketches. He had once called backstage at the London Coliseum after seeing their Poacher sketch and May Hopkins now was writing to ask if he had any comic sketch or Welsh play that they might use. The longest of long shots, one imagines, but Caradoc lets her down gently. "I have a play in mind and when it is finished I will surely think of you. If I do get an idea for a sketch I will write to you." The following year, on 20 September 1934, he acknowledged an inscribed copy of *Ffansi'r Ffin*, sent him by Revd J. Seymour Rees. "I never read Welsh fiction or fiction about Wales, but I will read yours with pleasure & I am sure with interest." He appears to have read Glyn Jones's early story, "Eden Tree", seemingly sent him by the author. "I like it enormously," Caradoc replies. "It is a strange piece of work and treated with unusual cleverness. If you continue in the manner of it, you will find an audience, small but worthy. Not for several years have I read anything half so brilliant from a newcomer. You are an artist, you are a very fine artist." Glyn Jones had already detected what Marguerite would confirm, that praise with a strong dose of flattery was Caradoc's habitual mode. "I think it came out of his desire to make people pleased with themselves in order to make them like him. This may not sound kind, but it is true."[29]

Evans's letter to Glyn Jones, dated 14 February 1935, makes no mention of Jones's visit to Queen's Square House some three or four months previously and in the company of Dylan Thomas. Glyn Jones first met Thomas earlier in 1934, having driven from Cardiff to Swansea where Dylan was living with his parents.[30] Jones at twenty-nine taught at a school in Cardiff; Dylan, ten years his junior, confessed, "On the economic level, I have no function." Both were published poets and in his first letter to Glyn (March 1934), Dylan mentioned his attempt "to form an anthology of English poems and stories written by contemporary Welshmen". Top of his list might well have been "the great Caradoc Evans", the Welsh *enfant terrible* who, even in oils, had panicked the Swansea Art Galleries Committee in schoolboy Dylan's presence. Dylan was an out-and-out fan – Gwen Watkins recounts his reading aloud Caradoc's stories, "doing all the characters, like [*Our Mutual Friend*'s] Sloppy with the Police-news, 'in different voices'".[31] Glyn had reservations. "He [Caradoc] was regarded in Wales as the enemy of everything people of my upbringing and generation had been taught to revere, a blasphemer and a mocker, a derider of our religion, one who by the distortions of his paraphrasings and his wilful mistranslations had made our language and ourselves appear ridiculous and contemptible in the eyes of the world outside Wales." Yet despite all that was urged against him, Glyn read Evans's stories "almost always with curiosity and respect, often with considerable admiration".[32] Glyn it was who set up the visit, having received a warm invitation from Caradoc. "I shall be delighted to see you & your friend. Come to tea & give me two days' notice," ran his Queen's Square House reply, a letter dated 16 October 1934 "written in a minute and rather spiky script in the central two or three square inches of a large sheet of writing paper which had a list of Caradoc's books printed down the side." Glyn and Dylan travelled to Aberystwyth in Glyn's Austin 7 car one Saturday, on 20 October perhaps, or maybe the following Saturday (Dylan's twentieth birthday). Given the absence of documentary evidence, and the faulty memories of those involved, doubt surrounds the precise date of the visit and some events of that Saturday evening, but the strange Queen's Square setting stayed vividly in Glyn Jones's mind:

> On the day of our visit Dylan and I were shown into a spacious drawing-room furnished with splendid antiques of varying periods and styles, the sort of place that, although roomy, seems overcrowded with too many exotic ornaments and large vases of fancy grass, and Buddhas, and icons with scarlet lamps burning under them, and too many damask curtains. Caradoc was sitting in the middle of this profusion, in the process of being interviewed by a local newspaper man. Mrs Evans was also present, looking like an ex-actress, or what I thought an ex-actress would look like: that is, her face was very much made up, she wore unusual and highly-coloured clothing and a good deal of conspicuous jewellery, including shoulder-length ear droppers. Her welcome to us, two complete strangers, was extremely cordial.[33]

It struck Jones that most of the anger in Caradoc's exchanges with his interviewer was simulated – outrage and strong opinion made for good copy and good publicity – for with the reporter's swift departure "Caradoc's manner changed immediately, and he turned upon us the full blaze of his blarneying charm. His courtesy, simplicity and gentle manners have been remarked upon by many who knew him." Caradoc in the flesh transfixed the noticeably handsome Glyn Jones; indeed, Jones's physical description of his host brings to mind some of Caradoc's own fictional depictions:

> He was not by any means a good-looking man. He had a large ill-shaped nose and a too-long upper lip, and his face was at once very bony and flabby, with thin hanging skin. His lower lip pouted, and the hood-like lids, which he often slid forward and held down over his eyes, were of reptilian thinness. Mrs Evans talks in one of her books about his "shaggy goat's hair", and that is a perfect description of the coarse, wiry, dirty-grey covering rising thick and upright on top of his head. In conversation he was a great encourager, a concentrated and smiling listener, an enthusiastic nodder and agree-er.

Surprisingly, in view of such luminous preliminary detail, Jones's memory faltered when it came to the ensuing conversation. He could recall little "apart from the goodwill of it". Marguerite offered her own brief accounts.[34] She has Caradoc surprised on a summer morning by "two young fellows" whom the housemaid had ushered into the drawing-room, one of them a poet. A nervous Dylan is encouraged to read his poetry (*18 Poems* would be published in a matter of weeks), to take his typewritten half-sheets to the end of the room and to stand up and shout. "My wife will tell you if you can elocute. She was an actress.... Dylan took up his position. He started in a low key. He mumbled. Then, as he gained confidence, an organ filled the room. 'Tree-mendous!' said Caradoc. 'Mind you,' he added truthfully, turning to me, 'I don't know what it means. I don't know what Sibelius means, but I like his sounds." Alone with Marguerite, Caradoc confided some misgivings about the poetry, how it might be no more than a display of wordy gymnastics. "Good heavens girl! What was his meaning! I know what he was about, though. It's just occurred to me. He's looked up some abstruse, erotic word in the dictionary that no one else knows and built up a sort of Heath Robinson-in-words edifice around it. He may get away with it, God knows. I hope he doesn't though, for the sake of poetry."[35]

Dylan's one reference to meeting Caradoc occurs in the long undated letter to Pamela Hansford Johnson, assigned to October 1934 in *The Collected Letters*. A cock-a-hoop Dylan enthuses:

> Last week-end I spent in Aberystwyth with Caradoc Evans. He's a great fellow. We made a tour of the pubs in the evening, drinking to the eternal damnation of the Almighty & the soon-to-be-hoped-for destruction of the tin Bethels. The university students love Caradoc, & pelt him with stones whenever he goes out.

No mention is made of Glyn Jones, and of that Saturday evening Glyn only recalls that in their Aberystwyth hotel bedroom he recounted the story of Dr William Price, Llantrisant. Dylan, totally engrossed, burnt cigarette holes in his bed sheet and "began a Lucky Jim-like manoeuvring to try to conceal them". When faced with the striking discrepancies in these various accounts, Glyn, while repeating that he remembered little of what passed in the drawing-room that day, raised the possibility that Dylan may in his letter be describing a second visit to Aberystwyth.[36] Dylan did in fact visit Caradoc again, though this was some time later, not in October 1934.

In the wake of "the famous Caradoc expedition", Dylan Thomas wrote to Bert Trick from London (December 1934): "This bloody land is full of Welshmen, and, day by day as I feast my eyes upon their mean and ungenerous countenances, I feel more like Caradoc whose books are, in a small circle at least, becoming a highbrow success owing to my uninterrupted praise of them."[37] As it happened, Caradoc had another young Welsh champion in London. Glyn Roberts had arrived there in 1930 as a twenty-year-old civil servant and having read *Nothing to Pay* (and met its author) became an advocate of Caradoc and of other Welsh authors who wrote in English. Now working for the

Daily Express, he prepared a *Bookman* article boldly the entitled "The Welsh School of Writers" (completed in 1932, it appeared a year later). It claimed that a number of Welsh men and women, while forming no detached or compact group, were beginning to impress as writers. Roberts led off with Caradoc Evans but gave space to Rhys Davies, Richard Hughes, W.H. Davies and others. He sounded a combative note: the Welsh writers he most admired had emerged in the teeth of a native culture lauding "pedagogues and pedlars of the platitude", so that any English-language writer of Wales would almost certainly have to contend with parochial prejudice, if not abysmal misunderstanding and streams of childish abuse. Little wonder that those who had surmounted it should be strong personalities with something urgent to say.

In April 1933 Roberts turned exclusively to Evans in a piece for the *Saturday Review*. He recounted the author's past trials, how he sweated blood to produce his early sketches, this before the masterly *My People*, over which James Joyce enthused. Caradoc appreciated Roberts's piece: "To say the truth, it is extremely well done," he wrote from Aberystwyth (12 April 1933). Duly encouraged, Roberts turned in the *Daily Dispatch* to consider Caradoc in the context of Wales. His compatriots should not worry. Evans had done their reputation no harm among people whose opinion they need care about; besides, "Self criticism is a great deal more beneficial than continuous mutual back-scratching." Evans was "a very fierce and very sincere patriot. I know this to be true." Decidedly a man of the left, Roberts nonetheless found room for Saunders Lewis and the "band of intelligent and energetic men, mostly young men" behind him. Wales had not yet rallied to their Nationalist cause, "but most great movements have sprung from a band of young theorists grouped round a table."

Snippets in Roberts's articles suggest his closeness to Evans. *Wasps* he has read before its general release (through the pre-publication copy given to Raymond Marriott), and Roberts learns that the Evanses intend to collaborate on a book or two. He can also vouch for Caradoc's love of country ("I know this to be true"). Curiously, he mentions in passing James Joyce's enthusiasm for *My People*. That Joyce admired Caradoc Evans was said here and there at the time though nowhere, so it seems, did Joyce express any opinion of Evans. (The two, of course, had been linked – "Mr James Joyce is an Irish edition of Mr Caradoc Evans" – by the anonymous reviewer of *A Portrait of the Artist* in *Everyman* (23 February 1927). But Roberts is more precise, citing *My People* specifically, and that Joyce knew this collection, at least in part, is clear from one of the *Finnegans Wake* notebooks at Buffalo.[38] Compiled in 1924, notebook VI.B.14 shows some forty or more words and phrases taken down by Joyce from the first four stories of *My People*. A few of these found their way into the published text of *Finnegans Wake*. Joyce might have learnt of Evans from the *Everyman* review. By what word-of-mouth means Roberts learnt of Joyce's interest in *My People* is not known. Perhaps from Caradoc himself, quoting Frank Morley? As we have seen, Caradoc had been close to Morley at Faber's during 1929 and 1930 (the time of *Nothing to Pay*) when Morley had personal contact with Joyce, both in England (in summer 1929) and in Paris (where Morley and T.S. Eliot spent late sessions in Joyce's company).[39]

Roberts's great achievement was his part-autobiographical account of a young Welshman's storming of London. Full of ringing opinion, *I Take This City* (July 1933) is pungent
and provocative. If the occasionally cocksure author rushes too readily to condemn, his
book has a verve and sparkle that still makes it readable. Here he is on Aberaeron, his
home at the end of the 1920s (when Glyn Jones thought Cardiff "a vast cultural landscape
of nothing and nobody"):

> Nothing ever happens except the thin stream of tiny incident and gossip which no
> one would notice were it not the whole life of the place. The streets are deserted.
> The church, with a capacity of several hundreds, is elated if thirty attend a service.
> The harbour, a large capacious pretentious affair, has never justified its construction,
> nor is it likely to. A ship creeps awkwardly in about once every three months. There
> is no cinema. There is just a Hall of Memory to the local men killed in the war; there
> the lads of the village get together to play billiards at night, and do not bother to
> remove their hats. Defeatism and melancholy pervade the atmosphere.

Against all local wisdom, Roberts left his university course at Aberystwyth after just
a year. "I know exactly how you feel," said the Professor of Welsh Literature (presumably
T. Gwynn Jones), "You want to be up and doing. But it doesn't pay. Stay here and get your
degree first." Sound advice, one might have thought, but Roberts saw things differently.
Wales was a degree-mad country, where everyone wanted a label to attach to their name.
He surveyed his fellow students, most of whom came of poor families either from the
mining and industrial south or from the farms and small shops elsewhere in Wales. They
were preparing for the climax of their lives, their final degree examination:

> Everything tends to confirm their belief that it is the big crisis of their careers. They
> are at that point pigeon-holed and judged. A man who got a second is, for all time, a
> better man than he who took merely a third. To take a first is the greatest achievement
> (apart from the miraculous double first, which falls only to men like gods) open to
> man, if he be a Welshman. From then on his whole life must of necessity be… a
> journey downwards, a drawn-out anticlimax. He has achieved what he was born to
> attempt; he has succeeded, and behold the label. His education is complete; he usually
> says so himself.

Within a year Roberts was up and running in London, a qualified Estate civil servant at
Somerset House yet planning to ditch job security for the hectic instability of Fleet
Street – this at the height of the Great Depression. The boldness that brought him to
Fleet Street allows him confident judgments on those fields best known to him from
not quite three years of journalism: Fleet Street itself, theatre, film, and "the book
racket". Inevitably, he writes of London, its face and spirit:

> It stretches and flops for miles, casually and 'samishly'. Its unremarkableness makes
> it remarkable. It is a city of abounding life, yet it often strikes you as somnolent and
> apathetic. It is very English, and yet packed with foreigners. Although it naturally

has its hundreds of freaks and oddities and perverts and geniuses, its proportion of
abnormal people is, I should say, low. The tendency in London, a very powerful tendency, is to conform; its population is a mediocracy. Thomas Burke, after much
thought, told me that the big thing about London is its *indifference*.

In separate chapters Roberts asks "What is typically English?", contemplates the
sub-species of Londoner ("destitute of traditions, memories, heritage of any kind,...
[the Cockney] is the weakest, wateriest, least picturesque and colourful of all who live
on these islands. He won't survive as a type much longer"), and turns his spotlight on
"my people". Roberts understands that every Welshman in London believes "there is
damnable, relentless and unreasoning prejudice against him and his race outside Wales.
It colours his whole outlook on life, his attitude towards strangers, his disposal of his
leisure, everything. So deep-rooted a conviction must be considered seriously, if only
for its effects." Personally, he is relaxed about his nationality. "It is good fun being Welsh...
When all the platitudes and ancient gibes are done, it does make you different. People
remember you. If they know any place or person in Wales, they tell you of it, and a
bond of union of sorts is at once struck. Being Welsh has always helped me in my work,
so far as it has made any difference any way, and my pronounced Welsh accent seems an
asset." He quotes "a very great artist" to close: "Caradoc Evans has called his people the
dead-fruit of Europe. It is a good phrase, but I bet he doesn't really believe it. The Welsh
are very much alive; but they're living the wrong life." He flatteringly refers to Evans
elsewhere in his text and matches Evans's estimate of the intellectual superiority of
Welsh rural folk over their English counterparts by quoting Sabine Baring-Gould approvingly:

> The Welsh of the labourer and small farmer class are brighter, quicker, keener than
> those occupying the same position in Saxon England.... He reads more, above all,
> he thinks more. He leads an inner life of thought and feeling; he is more impulsive
> and more sensitive. He is more susceptible to culture, more appreciative of what is
> poetical and beautiful, and does not find in buffoonery the supreme delight of life.[40]

A presentation copy of *I Take This City* prompted Caradoc's sincere congratulations.
He had read it "from first to last; and I wish it were twice as long. It is the ablest, brightest,
and most entertaining first book I have ever read, and certainly the most courageous"
(16 July 1933). These words were sensibly seized upon by Jarrolds in their publicity for
the book and gave the *Morning Post* its "Caradoc Minimus" heading for a review. A further
appreciative letter, together with a print of the Evan Walters portrait, arrived from
Aberystwyth as Roberts produced three new articles for the *Western Mail* on Richard
Hughes, W.H. Davies and Rhys Davies (August-October 1933). "I hope you are well
and making money," Caradoc writes. Sadly, Roberts in his Soho garret "stacked with
books, magazines, rejected articles, files, clothes, cricket shirts, running-shorts, boxes
full of old letters and assorted scraps of paper", was "as much a starving author as anyone
ever was" – and disturbingly far from well.

It was Roberts who broke the news that Caradoc and his wife were to join forces and produce three books together. Their first, most valuable, collaboration was the brief epistolary novel *I Loved a Fairy* (October 1933). All its letters are composed by a forty-two-year-old Scottish editor of a bogus Fleet Street periodical, a vanity paper kept afloat by wealthy minor celebrities whose effusions it publishes. The first letter is dated 23 July 1922, the rest being mostly written over the next five months. They chart the unnamed editor's doomed love for "Miss Fairy", the seventeen-year-old Marguerite Jervis, anxious to make a name for herself, on the stage or as a writer. By the end of the year she has married a man of her own age and background. A short postscript advances the action seven years. Against his better judgment, the editor too has married and is living with his wife in a large Georgian house in Richmond. When he advertises a flat within it for rent, Fairy answers the advertisement. They meet in Richmond Park. She now has two children but – like the editor – is caught in a loveless marriage. They plan no further meeting. Duty compels that they stick to their course, lying on the beds they have made.

The book is a remarkable autobiographical mix. We have Marguerite's meeting with Caradoc, with its immediate stunning consequences, and her deep-down need for an older man. The father-daughter relationship with the editor (in some ways presented as ideal) conjures up Armiger Barclay, and, of course, her father Colonel Jervis. Sex is the worm in the bud, always to be distrusted. There are passing allusions to Walter Lovell and to Caradoc's first wife Rose. Though Countess Barcynska is named as author, the book draws much on Caradoc's ideas and attitudes and here and there incorporates his published words. Whatever the nature of their collaboration, *I Loved a Fairy* presents Evans on a range of topics (most memorably on journalism and literature) and has been drawn upon for this study.[41]

In April 1934 *This Way to Heaven* appeared, Caradoc's new novel ("for my wife Marguerite") whose working title had been *The Lift*. It is set in an ill-defined London; more particularly, a down-at-heel Hammersmith between the 1880s and World War I. We begin at Hope Home, an offshoot of Temple Congregationalist Church and a refuge for charity children – "male brands plucked from the burning bodies of women in jail". At fourteen they find themselves in local businesses where thanks to their training tools, the Bible and the birch, they will stay ever "duteous to their masters". The progress of two such boys, Ben Tugard and Jasper Sowell, provides the overarching narrative for an otherwise fragmented novel cast in eighty-one brief chapters. Ben and Jasper stand out at Hope Home: Ben for his animality and Jasper for his wisdom – "he's cute with figures", his first employer confirms. Both accumulate wealth, Ben through every vice, Jasper through a strange mixture of vice and virtue. For Jasper, a Temple worshipper at one point jailed for theft, counts his thieving no wrong since it was undertaken on Ben's behalf. "He had been appointed Ben's keeper and given a sack to carry Ben's sins and for the fullness of that sack he would be rewarded with a yellow seat in heaven and for its emptiness a gridiron in hell." He will further Ben's worldly ascent, knowing that the "higher man advances, the greater the number of his sins".

Around the two protagonists swirl a cast of variously unlovable characters. Simon Moreland, Jewish banker and property owner, has contrived to become the secretary-treasurer of Temple. He gives Ben his first job, explaining – as he robs him of a shilling – that the way to heaven is "kindness to your employer". Moreland uses handsome Tobias Harley as bait to land more banking customers (and himself lands in jail for false book-keeping). Another local employer, Peter Grinley, lacks what most he craves – a son to carry on his warehouse business. His young wife provides a child but sadly it's a girl, fathered by another man. Seduced from militant atheism by the "rich odours of the Hebrew Bible", Grinley finds a god to rage at. His religious dementia deepens to the point of suicide when, also for want of a child, his daughter Ruth embraces death by drowning. From Temple womenfolk sewing and knitting in the vestry, she had learned that "woman is born in sin and walks with shame". Denied in love, marriage and moth-erhood, she too turns mad.

> She was at her patching and she called upon Tobias [her husband] to sing a song to which she listened as composedly as if she were not out of her senses, and she put by her patchwork and said quietly: 'That's baby'. She went to her room and drew up the lid of the timbered coffin-shaped bath-tub and she saw her child under the water and she entered into the water, and drew down upon her the lid.

Ruth's biological father is none other than Temple's shepherd, the eye-catching Rev-erend Daniel. "Trimly packed was the trunk of John Daniel, comely the countenance, rugged the features, lovely the hair of silver and grey and brown, and perfectly moulded the limbs." Little wonder that Mrs Grinley is smitten. He stands apart from Evans's run of ministers, "the good pastor whose mind was a commonplace book that has a word which sweetens every joy and lightens every ill." He grants his suicide daughter a full Christian burial despite the protests of chapel deacons worried at the thought of rising to heaven with "loonies". Voice of sweet reasonableness, he has little in common with Tobias Harley, the dashing blue-ribboner fighting the demon drink among Hammersmith's down-and-outs. Tobias too has looks, and Daniel's way with words, but employs his assets cunningly. "No rascal lover was he…. His delight was in himself and his concern was for himself, and like all climbers to whatsoever heaven, he was thoughtless of those who fell that he might stand." At his side is Fishy Brown, a Dickensian peg-legged preacher with a stock of "oly books", melodramatizing sermons for the tattered wretches down at Gospel Hall. The one-time fish porter proves an adept fisher of men – and of women. "His talks and songs gained the good opinion of simple women and his banner call to sinners brought forth sportsmen who likened his pitch to a warren, the women to rabbits, and they themselves to men with guns."

Mary Grey, stage-obsessed and skilled in recitation, moves among the Hammersmith temperance warriors. "Though she was the cold mistress of her mind and heart, her artifices kindled heat in her hearers and exalted their spirit, be her matter from Shakespeare or Fishy Brown." Shakespeare is Mary's god; her desire, to play all his leading female roles. Though her looks bespeak her character – "her face was a dusky cloud and her eyes were dusky torches and her nose was a ruthless crag and her hair was a mantlet upon her shoulders" – she provides what rich men want in return for financing her theatre ventures. As Mary St Martin she snares a string of backers, offering herself eventually to Ben Tugard, now master of the Dome departmental store. He is tempted – "the price was *Othello*" – but Mary is over fifty and Ben craves "fresh goods".

Working openly as a prostitute, the widow Ada Bright (briefly Ben Tugard's landlady) knows the plight of older women in the marketplace. Beginners and the young are preferred and amateurs constant competitors. *This Way to Heaven* alludes to the loose ways of shop girls, and to housewives and their tally-men. Ada's neighbour explains:

> If there's anything I want and we're a bit short of money, he [her husband] doesn't mind me getting it from my tallyman and pay as I can. There are two or three about most days. You'll see them if you stand in the window. That's what I do and my man knows I'm at home like. Between two and before the kids come home from school is the time. My husband trusts me, you see, and he knows I'll never bring disgrace on his family. Once you get your husband's trust, you're all right.

Ada is suddenly murdered, though not before Buller Bright, her son by Ben Tugard, has embarked on a career in journalism (a significant move in the story).

By this stage a "growt-headed clodderer... drenched in lust", Ben walks his way to hell and in a closing scene reminiscent of "Saint David and the Prophets" (*My Neighbours*) the others are discovered in a peculiar half-world, a kind of arboreal holding ground for either heaven or hell. There a kindly Inspector of Weights must assess them for moral worth. Cannot they remain where they are? Simon Moreland asks. This is impossible; they are in a land of stage scenery where, much like the world they have left, "the only real thing is the light of hell running in streams". Young Buller Bright requests that he first be allowed to marry his girlfriend. "You've got to go to hell for that," he's told, "It's part of the punishment." But the Inspector offers some advice as they approach the weighing platform. "Fill your mind with the choicest and nicest thought you can think of about other people. A kind saying, even if it is not meant, is heavier than a million straight talks." John Daniel "crawled with fine sayings and there's no doubt that he comforted hundreds of people with them. He went up in a flash." As did Fishy Brown, "and if ever there was a hypocrite, he was one." ("Cheering comfort does not lose its colour whether it comes from piety or hypocrisy," we have already learned.) Sensing their lack of kind thoughts, that for them faith, not deeds, ensures salvation – the Inspector suggests that they take the option of being weighed all together not singly. One of them might be worth all the rest. So it proves. Buller's professional passion saves them. A journey to hell: it's the scoop of his life and "Where there's a story there's Bright Buller.... It's my paper, you see, and I can't let it down. I've got to be loyal." (In a *Western Mail* interview Evans said that *This Way to Heaven* concerned the qualities that led you there, "religion, sacrifice and loyalty".)

In April 1934 came a few high-profile notices – Evans still had standing in literary Fleet Street – though these were hardly favourable. For Edwin Muir the novel's gallery of characters resembled Victorian woodcuts expressing but "a single idea or lust" (*Listener*, 2 May). The *TLS* went further: Evans's men and women were "wooden, spasmodic puppets who jerk and jump their ways hugger mugger from eccentric incident to incredible sequel…" (10 May). The *Western Mail* (19 April) proved surprisingly charitable, rightly remarking the extraordinary vividness of individual scenes. The reviewer, Frederick J. Mathias, had softened since his "filth masquerading as truth" notices of *Nothing to Pay* and *Wasps* (it was possibly the last review of this Cardiff schoolmaster; Mathias died a little later). He conceded that Evans's hatred of hypocrisy was sincere and justified, and thought it "a pity that a talented man should turn an attitude into a pose and allow a feeling to become an obsession".

Fantasy, fable, nightmarish morality, *This Way to Heaven* perplexes. The rush of events, incident strung haphazardly to incident, tells against the reader, for action-packed through it is, and with conventionally arresting ingredients (sex and religion, suicide and murder, cut-throat business rivalry), the novel lacks dramatic tension and narrative drive – almost to the point of unreadableness. It is as if style alone will suffice, a mixture of "semi-biblical chant" (H.E. Bates's phrase) and a highly literary demotic, the whole perversely unidiomatic and doused with archaisms, neologisms and slang.[42] *This Way to Heaven* has little of *Wasps*' gaiety and most of its faults, its fluency impeded by the continuous glossing of events. Readers meet a barrage of "sayings" (many none too pithy) spawned in various minds. "In proverb-wise mood" Joseph Grinley proves unstoppable:

> Bibles are not meant to be read. That's why they're so atrociously printed. If they were read there would be a slump in church stock. Their ugly covers frighten children and soft-wits to death. There's no article of furniture more difficult to get rid of than a Bible. If you use it as packing-paper you might just as well drown yourself. You've got to be well-to-do to be an atheist. If you burn it – well, a chap would sooner burn his mother than his Bible which he can't read and wouldn't if he could.

Some sentences hit home immediately: "Old men do not order their affairs by any philosophy. They are full of contrarieties, building as if they should never die and planning as if they should die tomorrow." Others prompt only head-scratching: "Whosoever dwells in the hogcote of sloth and corruption neither embroiders the fleshmonger's trade nor weaves it into an entertaining fable." One or two lie close to Caradoc's heart: "The mind is the burial ground of ancestors and the awakening is the beginning of thought", and "A mother will betray a city for her son's gain" – a reflection surely stemming from Marguerite's fixation on Nick.

In fairness, Evans provides another memorable opening. Hope Home is stunningly introduced by way of its "pale matron" Margaret Tallflower and her peculiar attachment to Ben. The boy stirs her sexually, her longing only assuaged through canings administered privately as Ben lies "stomach-wise" on her bed ("sometimes she spread oil on his stripes"). She is drawing out evil thoughts. The daughter of a Shropshire rectory, as a young girl she too had been stripped and whipped by her father for lusting after men. The way to heaven was the virgin's way, her mother had agreed. Later snapshots capture something of Hammersmith's preaching missions and the drapery world of the Dome; noteworthy enough in this novel, they are tepid rehashings of ingredients better handled by Evans elsewhere. "What then has happened to him?" asked H.E. Bates in the *Spectator* (26 April), wondering, "not so much how Mr. Evans gained his reputation as how he will sustain it".

Yet the person mattering most thought the book easily the author's best. In a letter to Evans from his Rich & Cowan office, Andrew Dakers showered it with praise:

> I have known the types you deal with – only in London and the suburbs – and the truth of your stripping delineations of their characters struck me as absolute. Your capacity to concentrate on the inner quality of their hypocrisy and spiritual malformations, while leaving with the reader the illusion that they also pass as normal human beings, is one which I do not know of any other writer possessing in an equal degree.

The matron of the school was "a creation of astonishing power – but every character is a perfect etching", and "Of the actual writing, I can only say that nowhere out of parts of the Bible could one find anything so vigorous, compressed and telling." The ending was the book's only flaw. "I was simply defeated to know how the characters had died, or whether they were in the ordinary sense dead at all."[43] Dakers hoped for a wider public than that reached by *Wasps*: "In the new novel you have remained within better comprehended limits, among people, all of whom can be appreciated by the man-in-the-street." His hopes went unrealised; *This Way to Heaven* sold badly.

Rogues & Vagabonds

1934-36

With a restless son eager for a stage career, Marguerite pondered again the possibility of a theatre company playing in the town. Caradoc might think it a "fool scheme" but Aberystwyth struck her as a place that could support a limited season of English plays; it had regular summer visitors and a body of students during terms. A venue, too, was at hand, the recently opened Municipal Hall (later the King's Hall) situated on the seafront. She was not some crazy amateur walking into disaster: she had a theatre background and a number of professional contacts. Despite more than one approach, no agreement with the Hall could be reached. This might have spelt the end of an improbable mission but, stung by the town's rejection, Marguerite came up with a bold new strategy. With the proceeds of a book advance, she would still found a repertory company that would take full-time to the road, putting on plays in Cardiganshire villages and small-town public halls. Each venue would be visited once a week on the same night with a different play. On 18 April 1935 the *Stage* reported that "Marguerite Florence Laura Caradoc Evans... carrying on business under the name of Oliver Sandys (Countess Barcynska)" was applying to Cardiganshire County Council for registration under the 1925 Theatrical Employers Act. A licence duly granted, Marguerite set about recruiting her company and planning a practicable itinerary for a summer season beginning in the third week of June. To a highly sympathetic local press she explained that she would be taking into the countryside a succession of English-language plays, most of them recent West End hits. She respected the Welsh drama movement thriving locally – indeed, had sat through numerous chapel-vestry and welfare-hall performances, with her husband acting as translator. The enthusiasm she witnessed prompted the thought that these same audiences might for a change like to see English plays performed by English actors to professional standards. (She let slip Caradoc's main criticism of local amateurs: that they lacked good teamwork, and invariably placed their tables centre-stage – "always bang in the centre!")[1] For the touring route of her company, officially The Rogues & Vagabonds Repertory Players, Marguerite settled on a circuit within a thirty-mile radius of Aberystwyth (where all her artists would be billeted) and taking in, wherever possible, seaside villages favoured by summer visitors. The company would travel out by charabanc and the scenery go by lorry. To the north, Borth, Talybont and Machynlleth were chosen; to the south, Lampeter, Aberporth and New Quay. She praised the out-of-town venues, offering "contracts that would suit any fair dealing theatrical solicitor" (unlike the Municipal Hall).[2] Little, alas, could be done about seating – wooden kitchen chairs in the stalls, long wooden benches in the pit.

In London Marguerite and Caradoc interviewed applicants drawn by her *Stage* advertisements. These notices stayed in the memory: an old-style Tory lady (improbably
married to a rebel socialist), she sought artists of "definite ability, education, and good
social standing",[3] as if recalling the less polished types she'd met at drama school. She
understood that Aberystwyth was a town where theatrical people were thought "smudgy".
This image needed countering; she encouraged her recruits to attend local places of
worship and to shun the pubs, the ladies especially – "ladies who are seen in pubs are
not ladies in Wales". She was lucky in her appointments: the seasoned repertory actor
who could double as producer or business manager, set designer, stage carpenter or
electrician; and in the gifted quartet of young women she brought to Aberystwyth. She
placed a premium on youth, for youth more readily coped with the strains of a play a
week.

Recruitment completed and rehearsals underway, in the second week of May Marguerite staged herself at Queen's Square House for a *Cambrian News* reporter. He found
her "sitting in her chapel study, working at her latest novel. On the walls were hanging
crucifixes and sacred pictures, and on a table in an alcove a lamp burned before a figure
of the Madonna and Child.[4] She spoke of the risks in taking to the road; there would be
no profit – high transport costs made that unlikely – but should her expenses be covered
she would consider extending the season. Crosville buses had agreed to run special
services to all the halls on her route. Surrounding her, the reporter noted, were photographs of the Rogues & Vagabonds and posters announcing their imminent arrival.

These were the posters plastered along the roads of the surrounding countryside.
Taking charge of publicity, Caradoc had commissioned bills of various size simply stating
"The Rogues & Vagabonds are coming". "We all went forth in the car, long distances of
thirty, forty miles with a bucket of paste and a brush and he [Caradoc] and the chauffeur
would paste the rocks, gate-posts, telegraph-poles and even the wayside stones with
the eye-catching slips and strips and posters. He even borrowed ladders and pasted the
roofs of derelict shepherd's huts or any uninhabited building that could be seen from
the roadside."[5] The posters aroused curiosity – and eventually the law. "Countess Fined"
ran a *Cambrian News* headline (9 August 1935) – she was "Countess Barcynska" to the
press and others in the town; the title sat naturally on a woman of style and means –
over a report of her appearance at Tywyn, on 2 August 1935, on a charge of "having
caused to be exhibited certain playbills, so as to injuriously affect the view or rural
scenery from Towyn, Aberdovey and Pennal highway in contravention of the byelaws of
Merioneth County Council". Two Trefechan men actually did the posting but were absent
from court, having pleaded guilty by letter. The company's regular bill-poster must have
hired these men for this job, so Marguerite explained, adding that they would not have
known the county byelaws. Yet she most surely did, as the policeman in court made
plain. On 26 May, she and her husband had stopped their car to ask him about Merioneth's
billposting rules. He had told them it was strictly prohibited. "They are undoubtedly a
great disfigurement," sighed Lord Atkins, on vacation at his Aberdyfi home but presiding
on the Bench that day. He fined Marguerite £2 and the men 10 shillings each. "After

handing the clerk three £1 notes to cover her own fine and those of the men, Countess Barcynska, with a smile to the Bench, left the Court."

With the season's opening fixed for Monday 24 June 1935, Marguerite threw a cocktail party the Wednesday before to introduce her Rogues & Vagabonds. At Aberystwyth's Queen's Hotel the press gathered in numbers, drawn by the prospect of words from Caradoc, who rarely failed reporters. He did not disappoint. "I have nothing to do with this venture of sending English plays into rural Wales," he began not quite truthfully, "into places which have never before seen English plays performed by professional companies. The idea is my wife's; the money is hers; and if there are losses, they will be hers also."[6] Conscious of nationalist sniping at an unabashedly English initiative, he continued:

> For years Wales has been calling for a national dramatic movement and there is plenty of money in national pockets to found such a movement. But while national tongues are loose, national pockets are tight. You cannot build a drama by shouting about its need. Art is not built on speech, but on endeavour, and it is fostered by money. Dramatic enthusiasm and dramatic ability are in Wales. There is no country in Europe that contains so many born actors as Wales, and no country that has contributed less to the stage.

For the Welshman shows his dramatic talent in other fields, preferring "against the insecurity of the stage, the security of the pulpit, and a glimpse of the promised land of politics, which ends at another national theatre, the House of Commons". Drama in Wales was "neither an art nor a profession" but "the belauded handmaid of the chapels. Belauded handmaids remain handmaids until they totter lonely to their graves" – which was what would happen to Welsh drama unless Welsh nationalists commercialised it. He ended with an extravagant dismissal of the warnings given to his wife, that Welsh villagers could not possibly appreciate Noël Coward's sophisticated wit. Nowhere in England had he found such a high intellect among the ordinary people as in Wales:

> The brightest Shropshire lad is a lout beside a second-rate Welsh youth. The Englishman speaks only one language and he speaks it wretchedly. The Welsh speak two, and if they speak their own most abominably, they speak English superbly. We may speak it with a sing-song, but the man who can sing a language in ordinary talk, knows it.

His fanciful final assertion, that "The Welsh are the keepers of the English language", must have been fuelled by having heard Dylan Thomas read aloud at Queen's Square House ("an organ filled the room").

Marguerite's Queen's Hotel speech, if she gave one, went unrecorded; Caradoc's made the papers, there provoking the criticism that it underestimated how far Welsh-language drama had freed itself of the pulpit and also overlooked the English companies occasionally travelling through rural Wales. From Idwal Jones, academic, playwright and satirist, came the sharpest attack. He saw the whole Rogues & Vagabonds project as patronising. "We, unsophisticated folk of Lampeter, Aberporth, &c" begins his heavily ironical *Western Mail* letter (26 June 1935), "already owe a deep debt of gratitude to Mr Caradoc Evans for his charming rural studies of the people whom apparently he now desires to educate, and I, for one, desire to express my appreciation of this salutary attempt to wean the benighted people of Aberporth and other Welsh villages from their preoccupation with the affairs of the chapel, the Sunday School, Welsh literature, and the Eisteddfod, by giving them a right sense of values through the medium of Noel Coward's plays, portraying, as they do, life in the more erotic circles of the West End of London." Marguerite might have responded that she was seeking not to educate but to entertain, and with the kind of fare most likely to fill her venues and thus minimize her losses. Likewise, Idwal Jones misunderstood her intentions when ridiculing "the very original idea of fostering Welsh drama by performing English plays in the villages of Cardiganshire". It was a love of theatre, rather than Welsh drama, that she sought to foster; the Welsh, she felt, were more drama-loving than theatre-minded, and "The interest in the theatre has to be built up into a habit."[7]

For her first production she chose *The Marquis*, a lesser known play of Noël Coward's, because "I wanted to make a direct appeal to the Welsh aesthetic taste – the craving for colour." She had a sense of what "goes" before a theatre audience and her glittering well-dressed show – a costume comedy set in an eighteenth-century French chateau – delivered the desired theatrical blast. The hired costumes were those of the London production and the design and detail of the set owed much to the salon of Marguerite's friend, Princess Elsa of Liechtenstein (so the press was told).[8] The play opened at Talybont (24 June), moving next to Machynlleth (on a night of torrential rain and thunder), thence to Borth, Lampeter, Aberporth and New Quay. At Borth a packed house gave Marguerite a rousing welcome; at Aberporth and New Quay many attending knew Caradoc personally and hoped to see him on stage; he stayed seated in the audience, flanked by a few old school pals. The warmth of reception at every venue surprised and delighted the actors, as it surely did Marguerite. "I was told that I was a fool to launch such a venture; even my husband disagreed with me," she confessed at New Quay, yet her first week had paid its way – which was more than could be said of the Municipal Hall which had seemingly lost over £1,300 in nine months' trading.[9]

Yet there were setbacks as first Talybont, then Machynlleth, withdrew from the circuit. At Talybont there appears to have been a falling out over a proposed hike in hall fee. As for Machynlleth, where attendances had been low, Marguerite was told that as a centre of Welsh-language amateur drama the town had no great appetite for the "West End Artists, West End Production" her company promised. A hastily rearranged schedule saw a second night at Borth fill Talybont's spot and Aberdyfi eagerly taking Machynlleth's place. From the start Marguerite might have chosen Aberdyfi – much favoured by the Merioneth smart set – had the travelling distance not been so great. From mid-July, the new five-venue weekly schedule took effect: Aberdyfi (Monday), Borth (Tuesday and Wednesday), Lampeter (Thursday), Aberporth (Friday) and New Quay (Saturday). The performance time remained at 8.15 pm and admission prices at 2/4d (reserved), and 1/6d or 1/- (unreserved).

Following three West End successes – Sutton Vane's fantasy-drama *Outward Bound*, Edward Percy's *If Four Walls Told* (turning on malicious village gossip) and Anthony Kimmins's drawing-room comedy *While Parents Sleep* – Marguerite risked a play of her own. Set in a hotel in hell, *Hell Freezes* was her satire on English society. "Hell is what you make it," she elaborated, "and most of us experience it on earth. After all, there can be no greater Hell than that of bitter remorse... In my play I send to hell a fox-hunting, bibulous, brainless English aristocrat" – a type she knew too well.[10] *Hell Freezes* opened on Monday 22 July at the Pavilion, Aberdyfi, "to a crowded house which seemed to contain half the county families of Merioneth".[11] Marguerite took the final curtain in response to calls for the author, but the speech she left to her husband. "The play is a family affair," Caradoc claimed; "The idea came from Nick Sandys and the play came from my wife. I filled the fountain pen, sharpened pencils, and tapped the keys of the typewriting machine."[12] After the show, artists and friends enjoyed a champagne party (the kind of occasion that left poor Harry Daniel, their chauffeur, sitting outside sometimes till two in the morning).[13]

A *Western Mail* letter (27 July), rebuking Marguerite for the play's "luxuriant" picture of Hell, prompted by way of an interview a summary of her personal credo. The fox-hunting peer and his companions were all products of a luxurious and parasitical existence. "In my play they continue in the after-life much as they existed in life; and this..., is my considered view of what happens immediately after death." She may have made the devil "too nice", but she did not actually believe in the devil:

> I believe only in the supreme power of good and the one great beneficent life force which we know as God. I believe we become one with the God who for a little while gave us the ineffable gift of life and personality, a gift so holy and mysterious and awful that to sustain it we must spend half of the short span in a condition of sleep. I believe in everything the Church teaches, except the devil and eternal punishment. If I believed in eternal punishment, I could not believe in good. I believe that we are punished by our own actions for everything we do which violates God's one great law – the law of love – and in being punished we are also forgiven. I believe that if we continue to live a life of retrogression we shall in the end die as the grass dies. The vital spark which was God in us is extinguished. The spark was not strong enough or the mechanism was faulty.

Five weeks on, the company remained in the black. Demand for seats had justified the extra night at Borth: people were travelling in hundreds from Aberystwyth, residents and tourists alike, many still asking why the Rogues & Vagabonds never played in town – "and always my answer is the comic contract offered me by the Municipal Hall". The next seven weeks, to the season's close, saw three outstanding presentations: Noël Coward's *Hay Fever*, Ivor Novello's *Fresh Fields*, and J.B. Priestley's *Laburnum Grove*. Marguerite's Welsh endeavours had not gone unnoticed in London, where "Managers, knowing that I was taking the theatre into a new country, gave me reduced terms for plays and some allowed me to put on plays that were still running in London."[14] Coward and Novello gave their plays at 6%, while J.B. Priestley (an early Caradoc Evans defender) sanctioned *Laburnum Grove* without a prepaid fee. Marguerite took note of the teachers and clergymen among her audiences – they fondly imagined that exposure to English plays might stem the advance of American cinema slang – and the amateur-drama enthusiasts present (many of them teachers) whose interest was in lighting and stage effects and small-stage presentation.

The quality of performance is difficult to assess. The local press habitually praised, but London journalists too, taking summer breaks in Wales, found much to admire. One attending *The Late Christopher Bean* at Aberdyfi (Emlyn Williams's adaptation of a French comedy) thought the production "point for point... every bit as good as that I saw at the St James' Theatre."[15] Another, having missed Benn Levy's *Mrs Moonlight* in London, "caught up with an excellent production in a West Wales village hall"; it confirmed what others had told him, that Countess Barcynska had "done a great deal to brighten up village life in West Wales".[16] A valuable insider's view comes from Violet Luckham.[17] As Violet Lamb she had joined the Rogues & Vagabonds at the very beginning (lodging at Bryn-y-Mor, the farm above Bryn-y-Mor Terrace). She confirmed how well the company was received on the summer circuit, invariably playing to full houses. Criticism came from Caradoc, who would stand in the wings, or sit in the hall, and afterwards voice his "acid remarks". Further critiques came the following morning when chauffeur Danny did the rounds in the brand-new Riley, delivering the Countess's bits of advice to individuals. One note to Violet would never be forgotten: "Play hysterically – all out!" it ran.[18]

Violet Lamb gained her first lead in *Peg o' My Heart*, a massively popular romantic comedy. Its Aberdyfi performance on 19 August 1935 was a gala occasion, spiced by the appearance on stage of the Evanses' dog Jock and Peko his chum. At the curtain a member of the audience gave the canine performers two large bones, each tied with blue ribbon. For the rest of the cast came a supper party hosted by Colonel D.J. and Mrs Ward of Bodalog, their other guests a mix of local notables and distinguished visitors. Those listed by the *Cambrian News* (23 August 1935) include the Hon. Mrs Shelley (whose father Lord Atkin three weeks before had fined Marguerite for bill-posting), Viscount and Viscountess Ratendone (he the former Governor General of Canada), Lady Spilsbury (wife of Sir Bernard, the pathologist), J.S. Crooke (Birmingham MP), Gwendoline Brogden (singer and actress), and Mrs Alison and Miss Isabella Rieben (Aberdyfi's celebrated golfers).

Before the season's close the company risked darker fare, in J.B. Priestley's *Dangerous Corner*, before signing off in September with Somerset Maugham's *Caroline*, a comedy whose moral (so one critic thought) was that happiness is longing rather than fulfilment; everything – particularly woman – is the more desirable for being unobtainable. However interpreted, the play delighted Aberdyfi, where the final curtain saw roses and carnations raining on Marguerite.[19] Aberporth's effusive farewell prompted some ribbing in the

Western Mail (17 September 1935), aimed both at the company and press reports of its doings. The *Mail's* column, "In Town This Week", is signed "By a Lady of St James's" who has spent the weekend in Wales. She speaks of crowds gathered at the Village Hall, Aberporth, to watch the arrival of the audience. The more prominent among them are noted (including Caradoc's cousin Dr Tom Powell, JP), together with their show of gratitude. "At the conclusion, all members of the company were presented with boxes of cigarettes and chocolates. Countess Barcynska appeared upon the stage. She wore a black dress under a black taffeta coat and a wide-brimmed black hat trimmed with white gardenias. A decorative turquoise necklace was matched by the Countess's earrings, and she was presented with a bouquet of pink carnations." Nor was such gratitude misplaced, since "Countess Barcynska has done a great deal for those members of her audiences. She has brought romance and glamour into their workaday lives. It is grand to think of young men getting back from the cornfields, changing into their Sunday best, and setting forth for the village hall to enjoy the witty epigrams of Mr Noël Coward or the cynical remarks of Mr Somerset Maugham." Shades of Idwal Jones!

Marguerite looked back on a great twelve weeks, an exhilarating experience for everyone, above all because of the enthusiasm shown wherever they went. Her company deserved all the credit. She had chosen young men and women whose life and soul was the theatre. "They all work together for a common cause – the cause of the flesh and blood stage."[20] Hours were rigid, rehearsals taking place in the mornings and early afternoons given over to more work on parts. Late afternoons meant "charabanc pilgrimages" to the five circuit centres. "The winding up-and-down road to New Quay on summer afternoons and late on summer nights, the sweet smelling Vale of Aeron to Lampeter, the stern and romantic Dovey Valley to Aberdovey: is it surprising that they were in the right key to give their best to their audiences?"[21] Violet Lamb fondly evoked these golden days of repertory; Marguerite's theatrical background might have been limited, but she had understanding and genuine artistic feeling. She created an excellent atmosphere for rehearsals in her Queen's Square drawing room. "I am an actress first," she would claim, "though I left the stage at seventeen after the glory of playing in Shakespeare in London with my idol Ellen Terry, in her last season at His Majesty's."[22] She loved the feel of an audience, even if only of one; thus her reading to Caradoc every day a chapter of the book she was writing. (A novelist lacked this "feel"; she had only a trickle of letters telling her she had "done it again" or not.) Violet found Marguerite thoughtful and generous by nature, making sure, for instance, that food and drink awaited the players at each venue – pork pies, sandwiches, cakes and drinks – "for acting on an empty stomach isn't easy".[23]

Another factor in the company's success, so Marguerite insisted (with her opponents in mind), was her refusal to label it a "movement". "The trouble about so-called movements is that they so seldom move. I did not attempt to educate dramatically a people who have the finest sense of the theatre in the world. I merely set out to provide them with fare I was practically certain they had the discrimination to appreciate. I wanted to entertain with the best I could give those who live in remote places and who cannot travel afar."[24] This remained her response to critics of her whole "London plays for rural Wales" adventure: those who believed that this torch-bearing mission, overseen as it was by a "Countess" gushing patronising praise on her audiences, cast the Welsh as benighted provincials.

Marguerite's "London plays", it should be said, were repertory favourites everywhere. A recent London show had distinct crowd-pulling cachet, so that "During the twenties and thirties many reps came to rely heavily upon well-tried popular West End hits irrespective of the worth or variety they contributed to the season."[25] Only Birmingham, Oxford and Cambridge risked any adventurousness in programming. The Anglo-Welsh writer Rhys Davies disdained the "rather rubbishy" plays the Rogues & Vagabonds put on – while conceding that performances were "sleek, well-brushed", "not bad at all"[26] – but repertory was not a theatre for intellectuals, or one with overtly educational aims. If it had a mission, it was to serve a local community or region and to provide a counter-attraction to the cinema, whose onward march accelerated rapidly with the advent of "talkies" – by Marguerite's time, Aberystwyth boasted three thriving picture houses. She championed living theatre: for the price of a cinema ticket she could offer flesh-and-blood artists, not cold images on a silver screen.

The season over, Marguerite found herself almost £150 in pocket ("not a colossal reward", though this mattered little). From the book advance that initially comprised her theatrical banking account, £300 had been spent before any curtain went up. Salary costs were large (she paid the going rate of £4-£6 a week), transport took some £30 a week, and hall hire worked out at roughly £2 a performance. Costume hire from Nathan's, the leading theatrical costumiers, swelled production costs, as did procuring second-hand scenery from Birmingham and London. Nevertheless, the season had paid its way and Marguerite could barely contain herself: "It was a venture of love and youth and spring, and we hitched our charabanc and our lorry to a star. The star has smiled on us. The star has danced."[27]

The star was rural Cardiganshire ("my husband's county") and the dance was set to continue, this time in Aberystwyth. On 13 September 1935 the *Cambrian News* announced that, in a matter of weeks, the Rogues & Vagabonds would enjoy its own town base in Queen's Road – not at the Municipal Hall, as the Countess made clear. "I will leave the Management Committee to dramatize and stage themselves at the expense of the ratepayers. If I fail, the ratepayers of Aberystwyth will not have to pay for my losses." Once again she met with doubters, who reminded her that summer seasons were short and that in winter nobody goes out at night, especially when it rains and blows as it does in Aberystwyth. Wasn't it better to pull out at this point, in a blaze of popularity?[28] Wise counsel, one might have thought, but Marguerite was lost to such reasoning; to quote the old theatrical rallying cry – and the title of a book she'd embarked upon, her Rogues & Vagabonds novel – "the show must go on".

In a break from preparations for her season in town, Marguerite, together with Caradoc, accepted an invitation to attend the opening at the Glynn Vivian Gallery of an exhibition of works by former students of the Swansea School of Art. Among exhibits was the Evan Walters portrait "The Countess Barcynska" (marked "n.f.s."). Evan's patron Winifred Coombe Tennant, who opened the exhibition on 11 October, left her diary account of a happy occasion: "Tremendous ceremony, and, thank God, I made a very good speech. Once on my feet the art of speaking came back to me. Caradoc Evans, the writer, who was there greatly praised me – a man not given to praise.... I took Caradoc to see Evan Walters' picture of Zanga [Alexander Coombe-Tennant], over which he was enthusiastic. It all went off wonderfully well and I enjoyed it." Caradoc and Marguerite figure prominently among the guests at the opening in a picture taken of the occasion.[29]

Back in Aberystwyth, the Rogues & Vagabonds reassembled, though without the four female mainstays, whom Marguerite sadly had to let go, accepting that for their careers they needed to be nearer London. The company had its sights on 23 October 1935, when a production of *Little Women* would launch the new Queen's Road theatre venue. With another book advance, plus £150, Marguerite had rapidly managed to convert a wooden garage, set in the hollow of a quarry behind the Queen's Hotel, into a small, intimate theatre.[30] Unprepossessing from the outside ("a long, low shed in a quarry", in Rhys Davies's words), it was fitted with comfortable seating – old gold tip-up bucket chairs obtained from London's Steinway Hall for £120. "It isn't enough to stage the best plays and engage the best actors," Marguerite stressed to the *Cambrian News* (18 October 1935): "You must have a stage to set off your actors and your plays, and my stage is fitted with a proscenium which is gorgeously painted and is fitted with the latest German lighting devices. I have not forgotten the comfort of my audience. My two-and-four and one-and-six penny stalls are identical with the stalls of a West End theatre. It is useless to put on a good play if your audience cannot witness it in comfort." She had in mind the degree of luxury achieved within "picture palaces", the quality of seating in particular. Props, too, bespoke quality: her Worcester tea service, silver tray, and old oak coffer taken from Queen's Square House (all to be ruined by rough handling on the stage).

Though no photographs of her Quarry Theatre have survived, we have a few descriptions. It was a hit between the eyes. The walls, panelled with beaverboards, were painted in Welsh colours – green and yellow – with crimson dragons set in daffodil-yellow panels. The proscenium arch (its curtains of green velvet) displayed a Welsh mountain panorama and the motto "The Best for Wales". Altogether, "the most artistic and luxurious little theatre this side of London", pronounced the *Cambrian News* (18 October 1935), eagerly using the Quarry as a stick to beat the troubled Municipal Hall (at this point shedding staff on financial grounds).

Buoyed by good-luck messages from C.B. Cochrane, Noel Coward, Edith Evans, Cedric Hardwicke, Ivor Novello and others (some were framed in the foyer), Marguerite could not have been happier. She placed the opening of her own theatre alongside the birth of Nick as "the two things that thrilled me most in my life".[31] The Quarry was her temple made with hands, whose magic would light the flame of theatre in the town. The magic decidedly worked on the essayist Evelyn Lewes, whom Marguerite had earlier invited to tea ("we will talk about books"). Lewes swooned at the Quarry's "really comfortable seats, agreeable lighting, the artistic colouring of the walls around us, the thick carpet where gentle-mannered attendants tread so softly, the well chosen melodies of the overture, and even the dainty appearance of the programmes. The founding of this little theatre adds lustre to Aberystwyth, and restores one of the chief attractions it possessed in the last century."[32] Marguerite's wish was for true theatre devotees, as opposed to those who dutifully turned out for a local production almost as an act of charity. "I have no use for that pernicious form of ticket-selling which takes the form of door-to-door and shop-to-shop blackmail. You cannot build a business by begging people to support you. You must give them something worthy of their support without your asking. I try to blend art with commerce and I refuse to believe that the two are divorced."[33]

Comedy, the staple of repertory and commercial theatre everywhere, bulked large in the Quarry's opening season (October 1935-February 1936), and repeats of successes again drew crowds, the *Cambrian News* reporting "bursting audiences" on a December Friday and Saturday for *The Late Christopher Bean*. The Quarry's seating capacity is unknown but no more than a hundred or so seems a fair guess.[34] Performances began at 8.30 pm and seat prices remained at 2/4d (reserved) and 1/6d and 1/- (unreserved) – the unreserved in line with cinema prices (as Marguerite liked to stress). Christmas called for something special, in this case *Alice in Wonderland*: deliberately not a conventional pantomime, which in Marguerite's eyes was "just a number of music-hall turns thrown into a sort of skeleton".[35] Sticking strictly to the Lewis Carroll story, her *Alice* moved on from the Quarry for successive evenings at Aberaeron, Lampeter, Machynlleth and Talybont. With the turn of the year, and a dip in Aberystwyth attendances, the company incorporated Aberaeron and Lampeter into a revised weekly schedule and accommodated at the Quarry on Saturdays an extra early evening show so that those living out of town could catch their buses home. The new arrangements remained in place until late February when a leading lady's illness brought the season abruptly to a close.

With the promise of a return in spring, the company took a break. Marguerite looked back on the trials of winter: the tempestuous weather; the competition from whist drives and dances, as well as the cinema; the distraction of elections, both local and general (the latter in November 1935). Yet Quarry attendances held up, or so one gathers, for on 6 April 1936 the Quarry duly re-opened, embarking on its new spring season with the abandoned production of *Full House*, Ivor Novello's comedy obtained by special permission while it ran at the Haymarket. For the next six weeks the company played twice nightly at Aberystwyth (Monday, Friday and Saturday), moving out in the middle of the week to Lampeter, Aberaeron and Borth. Besides more Coward and Novello, Patrick Hamilton's psychological thriller *Rope* was offered, and, by way of contrast, *Lady Precious Stream*, the adaptation of a Chinese classic that began a three-year London run in November 1934.

In April came unexpected recognition of the Countess and her company in the shape of a *News Chronicle* article by J. Kitchener Davies. An early Plaid Cymru member, the Cardiganshire-born Davies was a Rhondda schoolmaster, author of the notorious mining valley drama *Cwm Glo*, and a serious theatre activist. Not, so one might imagine, a man with much time for West End stage escapism. Yet he acknowledged the company's success (similar ventures had failed, even in Cardiff); production was "completely meritorious", and costumes, sets, lighting and properties all "adequate and satisfying". He understood the difficulties surrounding the choice of plays, where "The promoter has to decide between box-office security and less thrilling, but more solid, theatrical fare... Perhaps our teacher-ridden amateur movement cannot help but turn the playhouse into a school for taste, and so burden audiences with plays that are considered good for them." Countess Barcynska had backed her artistic policy with money of her own and the fruits were there to see. "The sooner the drama in Wales is divorced from philanthropic ends, and its promotion is considered as a business undertaking, the more robust will be its growth." A conclusion that echoed Caradoc's at the Queen's Hotel the year before.

With the arrival of summer visitors, the company felt able to return full time to Aberystwyth. To keep up Quarry attendances, Marguerite took the major step of offering two different plays a week (with the programme change on Thursdays). Though trusted repeats eased the actors' burden (*Fresh Fields*, *Lady Precious Stream*, *Hay Fever*, *Outward Bound*, *Rookery Nook*, *The Two Mrs Carrolls*), this new regime caused resentment, and from one company newcomer in particular. Early in 1936 Philip Yorke (best known as the last squire of Erddig Hall, Wrexham) joined the Rogues & Vagabonds from a strong background in repertory. "Our dear and incomparable Philip", wrote Marguerite of a popular son of the gentry, a kind, entertaining eccentric – he bathed in the sea on the coldest days – and natural curtain speaker. (Caradoc, for all the publicity he aroused and enjoyed, was still uncomfortable before an audience, his low voice scarcely audible at a distance.) Marguerite recollected her clash with Yorke, conceding that he had been right about the new two-plays-a-week regime: packing in so many words each week made acting a grind and led to more fluffing and drying.[36]

Through summer the Quarry stayed busy. Marguerite turned to her box-office winners, five plays by Noël Coward and three by Ivor Novello – among the latter *Symphony in Two Flats*, whose brief New York run Novello made light of: "We opened in a heat wave and closed in a heat wave... unfortunately, it was the same heat wave." Marguerite managed to land Rodney Ackland's *After October* (set in arty Hampstead) while it successfully played at the Aldwych. "It may well be said that theatrical history is being made in Wales when Countess Barcynska makes it possible to see in Aberystwyth a London play in a two-and-fourpenny stall at the Quarry Theatre," waxed the *Cambrian News* (31 July 1936). Two productions aroused more local curiosity. In June, Nick Sandys took the lead in Bram Stoker's *Dracula*, a role fitting well with the dark satanic image he cultivated (his broad-brimmed soft black hat was a constant); and on August bank holiday Monday the company revived Caradoc Evans's *Taffy*, the "play of Welsh village life" that some ten years earlier had sparked a London theatre riot. The play, so Marguerite told the *Cambrian*

News, was an idyll and an indictment; an indictment of hypocrisy, not of religion. The Rogues & Vagabonds production played up the lyricism and love interest and lessened the satirical sting. Marguerite claimed to have removed but one line only, the final line of the play in which, after a chapel wedding, the miserly Rhys Shop urges his hens to gobble up the scattered rice he had earlier sold the guests. Marguerite ended it instead with the line before, the words of Spurgeon the preacher as he declares his love for sweetheart Marged, "God has put a new wick in the sun." Having opened at Aberystwyth, *Taffy* toured Borth, Aberporth and Llandrindod Wells, at each sold-out venue provoking no murmur of dissent. Its reception only confirmed Marguerite's thinking on the 1925 brouhaha: the Welsh audience at the Royalty theatre wasn't truly itself; "the Welshman in his own country is a gentleman" but in London is liable "to be infected with the mob spirit of cockney hooliganism".[37] Caradoc himself had a walk-on part in this *Taffy*, as a white-bearded chapel member, and nephew Howell Evans reviewed the play for the *Western Mail*, where he now worked.[38]

As summer ended and holidaymakers departed, Quarry attendances slumped alarmingly and an Aberystwyth resident felt compelled to voice his fears. The theatre company in Queen's Road was struggling on with very little encouragement, he told the *Cambrian News* (23 October 1936):

> To an actor it must be disheartening to play to a half-empty house. I have yet to discover any disadvantage at the Quarry. The plays are well produced, the acting is easily up to the best repertory standard; the seating is very comfortable, the hall is warm and the prices are reasonable. All that is missing is a crowd of steady supporters. It would be a lasting reproach if we lost the only repertory theatre in Wales.

By chance, his letter appeared in the week of Somerset Maugham's *Rain*, a drama set in soggy Pago Pago (in American Samoa); at one point rain beats down on the roof of a shed where a crowd has gathered – an experience familiar enough to the thirty or so nightly Quarry regulars as Aberystwyth's winter took hold. The roof suffered badly in the gales and started to leak. "The landlord had it patched and patched, but people kept on watching the play under their umbrellas."[39] Rain water rushed down the north-end slope of Queen's Road, "as if on purpose to stop people coming to the theatre, but I never heard that it held at bay any of the faithful". Actors, too, took the weather in their stride, mopping up water that found a way from the quarry face into the dressing rooms under the stage.

Faced with such difficulties in town, the Rogues & Vagabonds took once more to the road, performing at Borth, Aberaeron, Aberporth, and again, Llandrindod Wells. At the Quarry they managed till Christmas, this time playing safe with a traditional *Cinderella* starring a splendid illuminated stage-coach. Marguerite never saw it, being confined to her sick bed. Illness spared her a sadder sight, the notice board announcing the closure of her Quarry, the theatre she so desperately wished to hand over to Nick as a going-concern.

From Birmingham came a letter of dismay: "I personally have enjoyed the performances of Countess Barcynska's company, with their intimate and friendly atmosphere, far more than my visits to theatres in Birmingham, and I know that my preference is shared by many other holidaymakers. If there is insufficient support in the winter months, surely it would be better to close the theatre for a short season than to carry on at a loss."[40] This strategy was the obvious one, but the Quarry had closed for good. The old gold chairs were sold to a cinema and the curtains, cables and fittings, the dozens of bulbs and decorations, were left where they were. (The great gale of January 1938, which battered Victoria Terrace and threw waves high over houses on the front, was thought to have swept out to sea the theatre remains.)

Marguerite put her Quarry losses at £1,300, the heavy downward dip beginning in autumn 1936. "In the summer-time we were packed out, but in winter I lost money week after week and I had to pay the artists out of book-earnings instead of box-office takings. I was losing very badly."[41] Just why she persisted through winter remains a matter of conjecture. Did it fill an emotional need? Could she not, a warm-hearted woman naturally drawn to the young, bear to say goodbye to artists who had become her friends? One of her favourites, Violet Luckham, confirmed the comradeship among them in the early, touring days and how the company left its mark on all who performed in it; those who took a chance on Aberystwyth and the Countess there made friends for life. Violet's further comment, that one or two of the younger actresses felt they might have been chosen as potential girlfriends for Nick, points to another dimension: what Marguerite's company meant to her son. Among its members there was agreement that Nick – who lacked any kind of training, motherly possessiveness having kept him from drama school – was poor on the stage. Yet his worshipping mother saw makings of a competent professional, either in theatre or film. Had the company, sinking and subsidised to the tune of £50 a week in salaries alone, become a stage-nursery to give young Nick a start-off without too many bumps and knocks? This became Caradoc's settled conviction, and blood-red quarrels ensued.

Some notes Evans made soon after the Rogues & Vagabonds folded reveal his jaundiced view of actors. At the drama academies "girls become frolicsome kittens and boys lisping girls". Repertory women he found more manageable because they did remain women; the men, full of self-love, were "jealous, spiteful, cattish, disloyal and treacherous.... Dispraise them at a rehearsal and they throw fits and throw cushions and kick furniture and send the critic slanderous anonymous postcards." In the journal he kept between 1939 and 1944 he calls them "jackals", chief of whom might have been Bry Ferguson, the Quarry's last stage manager who cost the company £5 a week in props. Here indeed was "a realist". "He provided real eggs, real bacon, real haddock, real everything for stage food. He would have provided champagne if he could at the woman's expense. The woman smiled. She wrote another book to pay them all." If publicly Evans distanced himself from the company and its policies, he participated – more or less willingly – in many of its day-to-day activities. "But he worked, my goodness, how he worked!" insisted

Marguerite. He shifted scenery, scrubbed down and helped paint fresh "flats", and took charge of the curtain – pulling it "very often disgracefully, so that it stuck and the artists remained visible as far as their waists until he jerked it up or down again." Marguerite praises him, too, for quelling the occasional insurrection, the kind arising among stage people, "whose magnified pettinesses and jealousies assume such an undue proportion in little 'reps'".[42] She gladly left "the spouting and the sacking" to him. But what surprises more, because it contradicts what she said at the time, is her later assertion that Caradoc gave birth to the very notion of the Rogues & Vagabonds. Noting the audience's enthusiasm at one local amateur dramatic performance, he seemingly turned to Marguerite with, "Look, see, they're starving for real plays, not home-made dramas of their own. How would it be to show them how it's done? Spend your advance money on your latest book and give Wales a repertory company – a 'pro' show, and mind you, it's got to be first class. Make your slogan, 'The Best for Wales'." "So it was," Marguerite swears, "that Countess Barcynska's repertory company of English players was inaugurated."[43]

It seems likely that at the outset, realizing that Marguerite was not to be dissuaded from her repertory adventure, he supported her as best he could. The first summer season had been a success, even turning a profit. Later, when profit vanished, he still participated though urging that Marguerite cast off her theatre madness. As losses grew serious, so his rage intensified. All to no avail, "The place was such a joy to me that I would not admit even to myself that I was very tired. I just went on and on and on. Not even the man could stop me: I am as God made me. I went on and on and on till I dropped."[44] She would have no lasting regrets. On the contrary, "Those years before the war that I spent in Aberystwyth, married to Caradoc, were, taking it all in all, the most fulfilled and certainly the busiest in my life."[45]

Aberystwyth Gadfly

1936-37

T he two-year theatre extravagance cost the family dear. Besides robbing the exchequer of some £1300, the Rogues & Vagabonds invaded writing time with consequences for earnings. A related problem had arisen soon after arrival in Wales. Suddenly, Marguerite began to "stick": her mind unaccountably emptied and her pen refused to work. Caradoc tried consoling her – "Sometimes it takes me a whole morning to write a sentence. Come out for a walk and feed the seagulls" – but for the first time ever Marguerite was suffering writers' block. A domestic dispute had occurred shortly before, a falling-out with Kate their ancient cook, who refused to bake jacket potatoes on Sundays. It was a sin, she said. On Caradoc's instructions, Marguerite sent her packing. "No good shall come to this house," Kate whispered to the housemaid as she left Queen's Square; she would pay the Evanses back. Some small revenge came swiftly – "when we went to bed [we] found a pile of muddy potatoes in their jackets between the sheets!"[1]

Still unable to get on with her writing, Marguerite took up Caradoc's half-serious suggestion that they visit "Old Griff" on Pumlumon (Plynlymon), a notable *dyn hysbys*, a wizard or wise man, one of a number living around Llangurig. "Yes, there is a fairy land in Wales," claimed Evans, aware of the country's venerable tradition of folk magic; "There are still wise men, magicians and superstitious villagers. Perhaps I am superstitious, perhaps I really do believe in the little people."[2] In addition to their healing gifts, such *dynion hysbys* were thought able to counter witchcraft, and it was to lift spells cast on cattle by evil wishers that their services were most requested. Marguerite left two accounts of first meeting Old Griff. As usual, there are discrepancies and a vagueness as to date – elements of more than one visit are perhaps incorporated into what is presented as the initial encounter – but Marguerite is at least consistent in describing the kingly conjuror. "What a magnificent old man he was in both appearance and presence; tall, burly, upstanding, clean-shaven, white-haired, blue benign-eyed, dressed in an old tweed coat (Welsh tweed), Welsh flannel shirt open at a pillar-like bronzed neck."[3] Most probably Griff was Evan Griffiths of the variously recorded Pantybenni, Pantbenny or Pantybenau, a farm dwelling in a dingle below Pumlumon pass. (His photograph is hidden away on the National Museum of Wales website.)[4] Born in 1854, Griff would have been seventy-eight or seventy-nine when the Evanses knew him (1933-34). At their initial meeting Caradoc first talked (in Welsh) about Griff's sheep and sheepdogs and the pony he rode on the mountain, before broaching the business of Marguerite's inability to work. "The wise man fell into a silence, looking at me," she writes. "Then he took me into another room. He brought out from a drawer a very large old book printed in old characters and crowded with strange astrological symbols. He looked into the book and then up at the clock and seemed to make a calculation."[5] Someone had been wishing her ill but Griff had bent the evil wish. She would be working very quickly now, he assured her. Indeed, she would. Back in Queen's Square House, she wrote a full-length novel in a month. A friendship with Griffiths developed (he is "Jim" in her first account) and Marguerite drove more than once to Pumlumon to talk with him.

This earlier account, published in *Full and Frank* (1941), makes no mention of Griff's "miracle stone", the subject of Marguerite's short book *The Miracle Stone of Wales* (1957), where again she tells the story of the recalcitrant cook, of her writer's block and the trip to Pumlumon in hope of a cure.[6] This time Griff brings out no astrological book; instead, on entering Griff's cottage, her eyes straightway caught "a translucent blue stone that was set on one side of the hearth. It was roughly hewn, with many facets and looked like a lump of glass or quartz. I had never seen any stone of such colour before. Green of the sea in the depths of it mingled with the predominant sapphire blue." On subsequent visits Marguerite noticed how Griff, sitting in his high-backed chair by the side of the chimney piece, would rest his fingers lightly on the stone. Weighing some sixteen pounds, it had been in his family for hundreds of years, possibly brought from Palestine by one of his ancestors. They called it Y Garreg Ddedwydd (translated as The Happiness Stone) and believed in its beneficence, that it could help anyone in trouble, distress or sickness, or with a deeply earnest wish – "if God willed". (One should mention that descendants of Griff, interviewed much later, remembered the stone as a doorstop.)[7]

Shortly before he died, Griff insisted that Marguerite become the keeper of the stone. One day she would know what to do with it. So the Happiness Stone, the healing stone, came to rest in Marguerite's writing room, on an antique French cabinet and – significantly – beneath her prized painting of the Madonna and Child. "If you live in Wales long enough, specially amongst the mountains, and if you become one with the people, you will understand how the supernatural is a commonplace, accepted and believed in. It is in a compartment entirely separate from religion; but if one delved deep enough one might find a common beginning."[8] Griff died soon after, in December 1934 aged eighty: "had a bad spill off his pony on the mountain and he wasn't found for hours," was the story in town. True to form, Caradoc did not attend the fittingly grand funeral but a week or so later drove with Marguerite to Llangurig, to Griff's grave at St Curig's church. (Griff's full legacy would not be realized until the 1950s, when a new male companion would join the widowed Marguerite in accepting the Stone's supernatural powers. She believed the wise old man of the mountains had put a white magic spell upon her. In time, it would fall on her son.)

Marguerite's writing fluency decidedly returned; four books a year became the norm with Aberystwyth joking that the Countess could write two books simultaneously, one with her left hand, one with her right. Caradoc, too, livened his snail's pace. He set about another novel for Andrew Dakers, confidently listing its appearance ("1935") in his *Who's Who* entry for 1936. But *Mother's Marvel* was rejected, on grounds that remain obscure. Marguerite takes up the story:

> He had no money and there were liabilities that were weighing on him. He had written a full-length 80,000-word book called *Mrs Shore's Magic Cake* [the original title of *Mother's Marvel*]. It was a commissioned book, but the publishers concerned had refused to print or pay for it on the score that it was dangerous and pornographic. It must have been a frightful blow to him, but he never said a word. He went quietly to his room after he had read the rejection letter and put the typescript away finally in a drawer. And in a drawer, unpublished, it is still put away, as fine a piece of writing as anything he ever did.[9]

Marguerite adds a footnote claiming that, "The firm at that time was on the verge of bankruptcy." Rich & Cowan might well have been ailing – it was one of a string of imprints swallowed up by Walter Hutchinson (then allowed to function independently) – but at no point in mid-1930s did the company stop publishing. Coincidentally, in 1953 two further explanations were advanced. In her novel *Sunset is Dawn*, Marguerite has Caradoc reporting his publishers' belief that the book was "too porcupinous" ("bristling with libels", he elucidates), while in London the bookseller William Griffiths told a group of librarians that "Caradog Evans found no difficulty in publishing his books until in *This Way to Heaven* he treated the Cockney character in the same way as he had the Welsh. He was rewarded by the loss of his publisher." Griffiths, then managing the Welsh department of Foyle's bookshop on the Charing Cross Road, implied an intimate knowledge of the author – "Many were the hours I spent chatting with him, always in Welsh."[10] The simplest explanation would be that the novel was rejected on purely commercial grounds, that Rich & Cowan, dismayed by poor sales for *This Way to Heaven*, baulked at the financial risk. Though hardly pornographic, the book has its share of unsavoury material (murder, prostitution, masochism, aggressive circumcision, a touch of incest), and it might well have been thought "porcupinous" (Caradoc spoke of it as "banned"). A small firm like Rich & Cowan would have lacked the resources to defend any libel action and publishers, whatever their standing, were generally more cautious in these matters than the law. Circumstances had clearly changed by 1949 when, five years after Caradoc's death, Rich & Cowan published *Mother's Marvel* at Marguerite's request.

A novel in fifty-one brief chapters, *Mother's Marvel* opens in 1900 at the Kew grocery shop of the unmarried, unappealing Kitty Shore. Thirty years old, she lives with an occasional lodger, the hunchback Griff. Though not blood relatives, the two have grown up as brother and sister. Temperamentally they are polar opposites: whereas Griff loses his job as a bus conductor for giving children free rides, Kitty "made no woman speak her name with envy, any man write her name on his heart, or any child seek kindness in her eyes". Between them, they concoct a patented food, a blend of corn flour, potato flour and yeast with seemingly miraculous properties (in part an aid to sexual performance). Sales of Mother's Marvel take off so spectacularly that factory production is called for. Kitty wants rid of Griff but knows that he is necessary, both for their booming business and to father the child she craves (this, despite her horror of sex: "She was a virgin born for immaculate conception and she was cold and chaste and scornful of human frailty and abhorred the bed in which she had to be defiled.") Baby Peter duly appears, his "mother's little marvel". Kitty will share him with no man, least of all his father. "In that circle of white light where stand the fathers of men", Griff is deaf to her ceaseless abuse.

The outbreak of war brings a slump in sales of the cereal. Freed of their soldier-husbands, wives "found that change was more provocative than any such stuff as Marvel". The ever-resourceful Griff keeps the business afloat – their "stuff" now proclaimed "Ladies Friend", a deterrent, not a boost, to motherhood. Compassionate as well as resourceful, Griff bolsters young Millie, a wife mistreated by her husband, the shell-shocked landlord of a local pub. Until she became pregnant herself, Millie had nursed young Peter and foreseen his dismal future. Shielded by foolish mother-love, he would gain no foothold in reality. Cinema would seduce him, a world of illusions and dreams.

A murder in the vicinity panics a move by Kitty to Madam Ax's guest house for ladies. There spinsters and widows flatter Peter in his film-star ambitions and Madam herself spots an opening for Tony her teenage son. Her fanciful notion of his marrying Kitty actually comes about ("he had the looks men hate and women love… sinewy body, skin as sooty as his kinked hair, and black eyes of melancholy violence"). But a match rich in promise proves barren and Madam Ax in fury rounds on Kitty Shore, a mother who can be milked through a son to whom nothing is denied. Indeed, Kitty gifts Peter the factory and her £60,000 life savings. The factory becomes Shore's Studios and Peter a god to the fawning actors surrounding him. Back on the scene, his shoulders botched by quack surgery, Griff takes on the role of Studio guardian; where others circle for pickings, he will quietly look after Kitty and defend what's left of her interests.

The second half of the novel moves into the largely Jewish world of Soho cinema. There Peter is continuously bled ("money has no meaning for this child-man"). Eve Adam, a star-struck eighteen-year-old getting by through "sheltered harlotry", marks the "simp with cash and a studio" as easy prey. She introduces Peter to Lam Arch – "a couple of cissies", taunts Eve. Of dubious sexuality, Jewish but passing for Christian, Lam has his place in the Wardour Street cinema chain, a provider of unpolished film scripts.[11] Work on one such script – "six foolscap sheets of unbroken twaddle" – begins in Peter's studio, a film with parts for Eve and for her rival Miriam, a "very beautiful" Hackney Jew whom Lam has counselled in Christian ways.

Kitty recognizes Eve as the woman who will rob her of her son, and Eve duly marries Peter. But Kitty bides her time; she has kept her son from his father and will take him from his wife. "He had gone on a play-pleasure journey", but would return. Kitty easily buys off Eve who has already joined forces with Tony, Madam Ax's son. The sight of her new partner Tony dallying with Miriam stirs murderous thoughts in Eve. She alerts Miriam's mother to her daughter's "misdoing" – with startling consequences. Miriam's mother, "her fatness clothed most voluptuously", tracks her daughter to Tony's lodgings.

Outside, "heating her rage, Eve heard a long loud scream and she followed the sound of it to Tony's room and just as she was about to beat the door of the house, the Jewess came out, and giving her a portion of flesh, said: 'Here's your bit of Christian flesh.'" The vengeful circumcision becomes the pivot of a new scenario touted by Eve before Ben Gott, a heroically masochistic Hollywood director; she finds him, sparsely clad, staked out in his hotel bedroom. Lam is no longer around, the second player in Soho cinema whom Eve has permanently despatched (the first she heaved into the Thames at Kew).

Peter's exploitation of Kitty goes on, but "All sons come back to their mother on their way to the earth", is Griff's belief; and, as Eve admits, "the cripple stood apart from the rest" with "sight that travelled long distance and pierced thick walls".

Evans in *Mother's Marvel* once more abandons Wales for a London of the early 1900s. No character is overtly Welsh (though there's a Welsh dimension to Griff) and no chapels or ministers are present. The setting moves from Kew to Wardour Street, Soho cradle of the British film industry. The business naturally interested the editor of a literary weekly whose proprietor T.P. O'Connor, through all the years Evans knew him, successfully presided over the British Board of Film Censors, an organisation set up voluntarily to forestall any enforced government censorship – and "controversy over film censorship was never far from the surface of British public life".[12] Cinema interested Marguerite too; as a novelist she had gained substantially from film rights while accepting that the spread of the picture-house posed challenges for her beloved theatre.

Mother's Marvel displays the chaotic relationship between trade's main players: the producers, the distributors (or renters), and the exhibitors (or cinema owners). The Soho in which they operate, often with overlapping roles, is a place of wheeler-dealing, all thoughts on money-making, none on filmic art. Wardour Street optimism is unshakeable since (in the words of Eve), "The maddest miracle is possible in the fantastic world of the cinema." Jews were heavily represented in the British branch of the industry, as financiers, film producers and cinema owners (the Ostrer brothers, the Hyams, the Bernsteins, Oscar Deutsch), and Jews in *Mother's Marvel* are portrayed much as in *This Way to Heaven* – "flashy fakes", in Lam Ach's words. For Guy Bernard, Jewish boss of ninety-odd picture palaces, "the people in the cinema industry, both Jews and Christians, were a tribe brought together by fortune and divided into suckers and sucked, and they were all his fodder."

Jews come to the fore in *This Way to Heaven* when Buller Bright gets caught up in a journalistic spat over how best to handle a local disturbance involving Jewish theatre promoters. The banker Simon Moreland is present in the novel from the start: "His was the wisdom of a people who raised the ancient tales of persecution and God's chosen children and world-wide ramble, the humility of a people who thrive by the jibe and scorn of Christian, the dexterity of a people whose fingers are more skilled than the fabled fires of the alchemists, and the subtlety of a people who fit themselves into every condition and who rule every land in which they sojourn." In novels so comprehensively misanthropic, derogatory comments on Jews seem unexceptional and no reviewer remarked on them. Evans doubtless shared the casual racism of his day, as did Marguerite (in their war over literary income, she saw her first husband's Jewishness as truly revealing itself) but the Jews had qualities that Evans admired and believed the Welsh could learn from.

For immediate pertinent context, one might look again at *I Take This City*, the work of a gifted son of a cultured mid-Wales family[13] and a book Evans mightily praised. Germane to *Mother's Marvel* is Glyn Roberts's account of a cinema trade show (he wrote for cinema papers):

> It is at the Trade Show of a picture that you realize to what extent the cinema game has been monopolized by the Hebrew....Hundreds of bulky men and bulkier women, squat, glossy and hoarse, barge in. They greet one another with rich fat beams and cannot talk without mauling one another heavily. They grip one another very firmly by the arm, and lean close to exchange intimacies. They are superficially cynical, but profoundly romantic in practice. They revel in their own films, wallow in the melodrama and gape, jump and clap at the thrills. If you laugh loud and long at heart-tugging melodrama – as once I did – they honestly believe you have been "placed" there by a rival company to wreck the show.

"Even the Wardour Street mahatmas who are not Jewish look as if they ought to be," Roberts goes on, "Working in the street has that effect." "Aristocratic" Jews and intellectuals are another matter:

> England has its share of them, like every other country in Europe; nearly everything that is worth preserving owes its existence to their efforts and their money. They are handsome, polite and likeable; witty, intuitive and wise. In the Law, in Medicine, in the City, they have distinguished themselves, and in Music, the Theatre, Literature and Art. To catalogue the Jews who have attained greatness in various spheres would be to produce a list astounding when one thinks of the fewness of the Jews. Most of the greatest interpretative musicians have been Jews. Nearly all Germany's great writers today are Jews.

London had always been good to the Jews, and good Jews ("of which there have been many") have been good to London. "So the colony has flourished."

For anyone privy to the Evans household, *Mother's Marvel's* central dynamic is the Kitty-Peter relationship, a reflection surely of Marguerite's worship of Nick. Various remarks in the novel could be Caradoc's warnings to his wife: "Spoilt children grow into monsters as often as not"; "When you go, he'll be left for good and all"; "He'll never cry for you, so long as he lives." (Nick in later years carried not one item belonging to his mother: no book, no letter, no photograph.) Most remarkably, the observations on Peter – "the young man was not concerned with any person or thing other than himself and his camera"; "he who lives alone must suffer alone" – would be echoed twenty years later by a desperate Marguerite when writing about Nick. The novel's spleen against actors inevitably brings to mind the Rogues & Vagabonds as Evans came to see them:

> The actors were as worthless as the cigarette ends which encircled their feet at the
> bar of the Bird. Each was paid a pound at the end of the every day and none of them
> was thankful or grateful, but after their kind they all competed with one another in
> making fun of Peter and his mother and when they had spent their jibes and sneers,
> they separated into two's and three's and back-bited [sic] one another. Where there
> are actors there is treachery.

It might surprise that Marguerite should seek to persuade Andrew Dakers to issue a
once rejected book with so much unflattering content. But Caradoc says nothing in
Mother's Marvel bearing on her handling of Nick that he had not said many times to her
face. Each was well aware of the other one's writing and how they appeared within it.
Marguerite never doubted her husband's genius and desperately wished to believe that
his work had not suffered by their leaving of London; indeed, that *Mother's Marvel* was
"as fine a piece of writing as anything he ever did".

The 1949 Rich & Cowan edition, hurriedly proofed at some cost to clarity, aroused
minimal interest. Lionel Hale in the *Observer* (28 August) dismissed a "somewhat slimy
satire", its humour "both grinning and grubby". The *TLS* (2 September) attempted a
summary of the plot, picked out Griff's patient love for Kitty, and characterized Peter
their son as "an uneducated pauper incapable of earning a living". The novel was remarkable
chiefly as "the last work of an author whose considerable talents were often sadly misused".
In Wales, Pennar Davies agreed. The novel was marred by "a childishly crude and painfully
self-conscious sensationalism" and could serve as "a warning to every artist who is
tempted to cultivate his reputation rather than his art".[14]

Nothing to Pay is by some distance the best of Evans's novels. *Mother's Marvel* amplifies
the failings of *This Way to Heaven*. It has next to no narrative tension, characters barely
recognisable as everyday human beings, and beneath the phantasmagorical surface action
a hollowness that robs the book of emotional appeal. Evans's ceaseless misanthropy,
however much it reflects the way he saw the world, simply wearies the reader. This said,
Mother's Marvel has its moments ("a true poet writing in prose", ran the Dakers blurb)
and comes closest to gripping attention in its early treatment of Kitty – her need of a
child and the snaring of Griff. Once again, too, Evans intrigues by his handling of low-
key prostitution, Adam's "sheltered harlotry":

> What did her make-up bring her? The small money of little men who loved their
> wives not less that they consorted with a harlot. There were sombre regulars and
> one was like the other: "How much? Times are bad, you know. What's your reduced
> sale price? Sure you're all right?" Her make-up ended and she stood at her window.
> Her eyes were large and round and in them was the petrified glint of the harlot. Men
> and women dawdled for the public-houses to open. The women were plain and the
> men solemn. Whether the business of Sunday be in church or tavern, it is prosecuted
> soberly and sombrely. There is a market for a virtuous woman, be she never so plain.

Following the rejection of *Mother's Marvel*, Caradoc set about an Aberystwyth novel but
no book of his would appear before the short-story collection *Pilgrims in a Foreign Land*

(1942), fully eight years after *ThisWay to Heaven*.Yet he remained in the news, sometimes
with the help of others. "Have we been doing Mr Caradoc Evans a grave injustice?" asked
Huw Menai in the *Western Mail* (8 April 1935).The grim Rhondda poet had relayed two
instances of Cardiganshire meanness. Inevitably, he received a reply that – almost as
inevitably – brought up Caradoc Evans's savage raids on Welsh idiom. It was what Huw
Menai wanted. "To find fault with him [Evans], nay, even revile him, for only having,
with a little artistic licence, given a too literal translation of certain Welsh sayings, and
at the same time studiously ignore his main attack on the life of Cardiganshire, and
perhaps on the life of Wales as a whole, is in a way to admit that his graver charges are
irrefutable." The exchanges continued, Menai asserting that he could, if challenged,
write "an indictment of Welsh life in the form of a cold, bare recital of ugly and terrible
facts – not imaginings, but facts stamped on the mind and heart by the brutal heel of
bitter experience – that would make the writings of Mr Caradoc Evans appear tame
poetry by comparison."[15] Caradoc saw no need to intervene; the ex-socialist political
agitator could well look after himself.

In August 1935 Evans cast a baleful eye over a favourite sight, the National Eisteddfod,
if in an unexpected place. "A Nation of Penny Whistlers" ran the headline of his front-
page article in the Saturday supplement of Glasgow's *Evening News* (an accompanying
photograph showed the "Druids' Circle" assembled at the castle in Caernarfon, host
town for the Eisteddfod that year).Welsh nationalists were there in force, having accepted
advertisers' objections to their request that the entire Eisteddfod programme be printed
in Welsh – "Even the Nationalists are reasonable in money matters," noted Evans.[16] However, English was barred from the platform; which made it difficult for Sir Michael
Assheton-Smith, Caernarfon's colourful mayor – awkward words were spelt out pho-
netically for him. Caradoc's solid criticisms were ones he had voiced before, that without
cash prizes there would be no competitions, "and competitive greed is an abomination
and murders artistic endeavour".The Eisteddfod needed a rebirth or it would die, since
it had no relevance in the real world of arts and crafts. "It is the institution of a nation
of penny whistlers." Cash, crown or chair, "The highest award it can give you will take
you not as far as the Welsh border." If others echoed Evans's strictures (none so stridently
in public) it was far from the sole perspective among Welsh writers in English. A fortnight
later Geraint Goodwin met Caradoc's assertion that the Eisteddfod lacked artistic
credibility – that "cash or crown or chair takes the winner nowhere" – by pointing out
that this was not strictly true, but even if it were, it did not matter.[17] John Ceiriog
Hughes (Ceiriog) "the most sublime lyric poet Wales has produced", in Evans's sense
"got nowhere". He never saw the need to; was he therefore to be judged a failure? As
for cash rewards to the winners, "If Mr Caradoc Evans knew of the pennies collected
in chapel vestries throughout the winter, of choirs travelling all night because they could
not afford hotel expenses, of the scraping and sacrifices that have made possible the bulk
of competitors, he would not have laid so strong an emphasis on the cash prizes."

Evans's Scottish blast made the *Western Mail's* Eisteddfod supplement, in particular
his charge that Welsh choirs were mentally lazy: "I do not suppose that there is a choir

in Wales with a repertory of more than a dozen pieces." Again, similar charges had come from others – Sir Walford Davies thought that while the powers of Welsh choirs were great, "their discrimination was small, and the chief danger was the unthinking acceptance of trashy music." Evans had devilishly signed off his piece with the suggestion that to raise Eisteddfod standards "a couple of Jews and a couple of Scots" should be placed in control. A year later, the Eisteddfod committee responded with an equally extraordinary suggestion, that Caradoc Evans himself should join a judging panel.

The astounding news of Evans's appointment as a Welsh novel adjudicator for the 1937 National Eisteddfod at Machynlleth – at Port Talbot not even his portrait could be admitted – was announced in *Western Mail* (9 July 1936) under the headline, "Gorsedd furious with the dishonour". The Machynlleth committee had reached its decision following stormy meetings and strong opposition from the Gorsedd, or bardic circle ("between them and committee members there were heated exchanges and hard words"). The offer was "a gesture of peace towards the most outspoken critic of Wales". Evans accepted the invitation, if in little spirit of reconciliation. "There was no unanimous call for me," he told the *Western Mail*. The Gorsedd's objections were that he could not read Welsh and that his wife "dotes on English plays". "My wife loves Wales," Caradoc confirmed, "but what right has an English person to love Wales? Love of Wales is the monopoly of the Welsh." Still, he would not relinquish the appointment: "I do not say that I am the best man in Wales for the job, but I am among the few honest people capable of such a job."[18] An accompanying *Western Mail* leader spoke of Machynlleth's audacity in appointing Caradoc to judge the Welsh novel competition. Such a challenge to the power of the Gorsedd ensured a lively battle (and probable victory for the "bardic veto"), but at least it would bring to prominence "the backward and neglected art of novel-writing in Wales".[19]

One measured response followed, an article by the classicist Gilbert Norwood telling of Socrates before his judges explaining that he had been sent to stir up the Athenians as a gadfly stings into activity a noble but sluggish horse. "I believe he would have greeted Mr Caradoc Evans as a brother gadfly." The degree of wisdom and truth in Evans's strictures was important, but no more important than the manner in which the public reacts to them; and "Wales has shown herself alive and vigorous, entirely conscious of the criticism and prepared with spirit to defend herself." The contrast with England excited. "Writer after writer hurls ferocious satire at the English, and with what result? They devour the books with relish, roll the burning insults on their tongue, turning up their eyes in an ecstasy of connoisseurship, and cry like Macbeth, 'Stay, you imperfect speakers, tell me more.'"[20] Relish for these onslaughts was easily explained: they are deemed to apply to others, never to oneself. It proved that the English were not a nation at all, "but a collection of cliques, parties, classes".[21]

As the date of the Machynlleth Eisteddfod drew nearer, eight adjudicators resigned from the literary panel in protest at the growing Anglicization of the festival. They instanced the appearance of Winston Churchill and Lord Londonderry (the pro-German "Londonderry Herr") among the galaxy of presidents. Evans's appointment was not specifically raised, although Thomas Parry, then in the Welsh Department at Bangor, privately conceded that it played a part in his thinking (and Londonderry's appointment turned his stomach).[22] Caradoc courted dismissal: it was idle, he told reporters, to expect Eisteddfod novels to reach any English standard so long as Welsh fiction remained the province of Nonconformist ministers – a class who imagined they had a monopoly of Welsh letters. Wales had talent enough but no non-political platforms on which to display it. Evans hoped that examples of such talent, from "a poor man who cannot afford to pay and can write", would come his way – for if the standard of work submitted was no better than in the past he would make no award. "My job is to lift the National Eisteddfod a stage higher than it is."[23] He never got the chance; by March 1937, the Eisteddfod committee had dispensed with his services. Nevertheless, he would be paid in accordance with the terms on which he was engaged. Resigning nationalist adjudicators would now have no cause to blame the Machynlleth committee for bringing anti-Welsh influences to bear on competitions. To Evans it was confirmation that the Eisteddfod did not welcome judges who spoke the truth. "What it wants is praise for this and that piece of work as being the greatest ever."[24] Every year one heard about a new Welsh Dickens or Scott, "and that is the end of it, unless the author publishes his work at his own expense".

Throughout his time in Aberystwyth, Caradoc sounded off to reporters. He was easily caught at Rogues & Vagabonds performances and, in 1935, at a local eisteddfod where he adjudicated the short-speech competition. He had words to say about Aberystwyth town planners, that they thought more of a bandstand than they did of housing, more of municipal halls than of town sanitation; "Goodness knows what money is sunk and irretrievably lost on these things."[25] In August 1935 he upbraided David Evans for talking "village poetry stuff" about Welsh village girls at a Nationalist Party summer school. Aberystwyth's professor of German seemed to think, "that our Welsh girls are the frail, light-headed *twps* of the Western World. If he were talking about Gloucestershire villages, where the girls are as beautiful as they are dense, there would be some justification for his remarks." Welsh girls were quite different. "I know no woman more wide awake, more sensible of her presentation and more nimble witted regarding her future than the Welsh maid. She knows her mind at fifteen and keeps alarmingly chaste until she finds her choice in money, with a bit of love to make way." Cultured Englishmen get nowhere with her. "Like the Jewess, the Welsh girl casts her love among her own people, and like the Jewess, she prefers cash to kisses."[26]

Two targets emerged more strongly: Welsh nationalists and broadcasting in Wales. BBC Welsh regional programmes were atrocious; Wales could do much better – "we are not a nation of papwits" – though the Welsh voice did not come across particularly well: "Something happens between the 'mike' and the listener which robbed it of its beauty."[27] There were exceptions, Lloyd George and the Revd Philip Jones of Porthcawl. "Mr Lloyd George's voice is comparable with the loveliness of the little hills and valleys of Wales. Mr Philip Jones's celebrated cough is a song." (Caradoc's delight in Philip Jones is unsurprising, *The Oxford Companion to the Literature of Wales* listing among his attributes, "his delicious Glamorgan dialect, his agile word-play, his charmed wit and ease of utterance".) Would Caradoc himself wish to broadcast? The BBC was considering a series of debates on Nationalism in Wales, Scotland and Ireland. In Wales, Saunders Lewis would most likely present the nationalist case and Caradoc might possibly be his opponent. Evans was not interested. He had "no wish to enter into a squabble with a party which seems to believe that words build memorials. As far as I know, the Nationalists have done nothing for Wales but talk and write Welsh books which inoffensive schoolchildren have got to read."[28] In any case, he thought any invitation from the BBC most unlikely. "I have never been asked to broadcast. I am about the only Welshman who has never offered himself to broadcast. I think I am about the only living Welshman who has never pestered Members of Parliament for their support to obtain a BBC job."

Out of the blue, in December 1936 an invitation arrived from Broadcasting House, Cardiff. Would Evans be prepared to participate in "Points of View", described in the *Radio Times* as "a series of talks by literary men who have in their published writings shown a very individual attitude towards life and literature. All of them will be writers who have displayed a keen interest in Wales and all things Welsh." Evans replied positively, but did he get to choose his own subject? And what would be the fee? He asked one further question, "Does your Director know the sort of stuff I am likely to give?" The response from Cardiff (31 December) suggested 8 February for the talk, which would be of twenty minutes (7.30-7.50 p.m.) and be broadcast from the new Aberystwyth studio. As to content, "We should like you to feel free to choose your own theme." The fee for this kind of broadcast would be about £8.8.0. The concluding paragraph ran: "Our Director, of course cannot guess what kind of material you are likely to include in your talk, but he will certainly be very interested to see your script when it comes to hand." On 8 January 1937 Evans confirmed the 8 February date. His talk would be some 2500 words and its title would follow shortly. The *Radio Times* told listeners what was in store. "Caradoc Evans, author of 'My People', will speak... about Welsh Nonconformity and the Welsh arts – oratory, music, and drama. He will also point out what these arts owe to Nonconformity." On 28 January the BBC received what it called "the first draft" of Evans's script and straightway wrote to tell him that it was unacceptable. He had not abided by the brief outlined in the 31 December letter, that he speak "from the standpoint of a writer, especially dealing with literature to a great extent as your material" ("feel free to choose your own theme" was quietly passed over). However, the Corporation would give "full consideration" to any further script he cared to submit. The BBC's letter was left unanswered. The following week, on 3 February, extracts from the talk appeared in the *Western Mail*, together with a leader justifying the paper's decision to accept what the broadcasters turned down.

An internal BBC memorandum (headed "Caradoc Evans Refuses to Broadcast") described how the Talks assistant had shown Evans's script to the Welsh regional director, Rhys Hopkin Morris; the public relations officer also read it and "the general feeling was that the sentiments expressed in it would outrage Welsh listeners. His [Evans's] comments on the ministry, the drama, trade and morality in Wales, were very offensive. We felt that it was not a sincere expression of a point of view, and that… he had not fulfilled his part of the contract." His talk was blatantly a publicity stunt and that the *Western Mail* should print extracts (over one and a half columns) surprised them. Meanwhile, the young Cardiff academic Gwyn Jones, "author of *Richard Savage*", had agreed to fill the vacant 8 February spot.

The *Western Mail* supplied more detail. "We have not banned the talk," Owen Parry told the paper (he was the BBC's programmes director at Cardiff); "We sent the manuscript back to Mr Evans for certain emendations which we decided to suggest." No reply had been received. Interviewed at home by the *Western Mail*, Caradoc spoke of his "very beautiful" manuscript, "more of an idyll than a criticism". His impishness gave the paper its editorial line. It sensed what Raymond Marriott had grasped, that Evans's ferocious opinionating did not necessarily spring from deep feelings but was designed to provoke a response. The actor was reprising his role, seeking new ways of saying cruel things, "and if we did not believe that most of his performances were staged with his tongue in his cheek we should find him quite intolerable." As it was – and here the paper's perceptions differed from those of the instinctively more cautious BBC – the people whom he once upset would now dismiss him with a shrug, "What else could Caradoc do or say?" In a *Manchester Guardian* interview (4 February) Evans took the BBC rejection more seriously. He had never felt himself capable of providing "the pots of white paint that they seem to require for Welsh programmes":

> I think that my views are more constructive than the fulsome and washy flattery that is broadcast about Wales and the Welsh. We cannot possibly be as good as these talks would lead us to believe, but unhappily we are inclined to believe that we are and therefore that there is nothing left for us to do but to remain in that heavenly state. Such flattery is destructive to any aims and ambitions that we may own. The purpose of broadcasting is that of a newspaper – that is, to provide its listeners with views of all kinds, provided these views are reasonable, sensible, and constructive.

No emendations to his text would be made. "So far as I am concerned, the ether will not hear my voice on Monday night."

The "idyll" (or at least the truncated version printed in the *Western Mail*) is something of a mishmash, a string of loosely connected assertions, some sharp, some silly, almost all sardonic, on familiar topics.[29] Welsh women alone escape a mauling – those nimble witted village girls are now women, "wise, capricious, fickle, hasty-tempered, forgiving, and loving; they make good wives, sacrificing mothers, and hospitable housekeepers." On Welsh religious life, on the Eisteddfod, on Welsh music, literature and drama, on nationalist mock-heroics, he remained his mischievously caricaturing self. Chapel religion was "the national art of Wales" from which spring "all our little arts". Welsh religious art is homely. "We do not paint pictures of a God no Welshman knows and of angels no Welshman has seen and call them sacred art. Our art is simple and intimate and real. The walls of our dwellings are solemn with photographs of chapel preachers and chapel politicians and our cemeteries are the prettiest man-made places in Wales." And if chapel life is in decline ("the pulpit stairs are rickety"), the Nonconformist hold on the press and literature has yet to be broken. Arthur Machen was Wales's only man of letters (largely unrecognized by his people), "Otherwise we have not a novelist or poet, writing in English or Welsh about Welsh life, who contributes one pennyworth to literature or thought."

Nationalism was yet another art "grown on the chapel floor". Evans dubbed its followers "the Shadrachs, Meshachs, and Abednegos of our capellers: boys bach who scream for a fiery oven because they know there isn't one." (This, three months after the Penyberth pyrotechnics, the attempted firing of the RAF bombing school.) "Welsh Nationalism is exhibitionism, and exhibitionism is not patriotism." As for the National Eisteddfod, Caradoc once more bewails cash prizes and what was expected of adjudicators: "The judge who places our standard the highest in the world we applaud and invest with Gorsedd membership; and the judge who places us a degree lower we hiss and hoot." (The airing yet again of such views gave the Machynlleth committee no option but to sack him.) He ends his talk with a patriotic flourish. The Welsh should look less to England and more to the Jew and Scot. "Our nationalistic protestations are false and a cloak for our inferiority complex," an inferiority confessed in talk of "Welsh Melbas, Welsh Carusos, Welsh Irvings, Welsh Dickenses... and so on". Let the Jew and the Scot (who had made Cardiff great) come among us "to teach us the meaning of Nationalism... and to knock into our heads the truth that a good Welshman is better than an imitation Englishman."

Prior to the polemical onslaughts are hints of a writer at work. Evans's talk opens promisingly with a vision of his seaboard town:

> I live at Aberystwyth, the Methodist bonfire which sprawls on the instep of an arrogant hill and which lightens the darkness of both land and sea.
>
> Of the Free Churches, whose mother is Nonconformity, Methodism is the most important, and, therefore, this is a very good town to live in. We have no public baths, because it is well known that very frivolous thoughts rise in the steam of bath water. The dun ruins of the castle that the First Edward built on a hill which looks out to sea, we have beautified with an imitation Druidical circle of stones and a war memorial worthy of any master of bridal-cake sculpture. Our teetotal pledge is a £25,000 theatre-dance-banqueting hall, which we bar against such riff-raffs as cannot dance or confer or feast without strong drink. This pledge costs us 5d in the £ on the rates. For most of the year it is closed, staring seaward like some forlorn tailor-made woman with nowhere to go and nothing to do.
>
> Satan creeps in to the holiest of places. English men and women stain our summer Sabbaths with the most naked bathing this side of a South Sea island. But our Big Heads are not asleep, not even in the heat of a summery Sabbath afternoon; and from the height of the promenade they pour scorn below upon the infidels who sunbathe on the beach or gallivant in the sea. Satan brought the chain-store to steal our profits. By this every trade has suffered save one, this being the trade of coffin-making.

While his script lay with the BBC, Evans mentioned having written 5,000 words of a new novel to be called *The Holy City*. He had in mind a vitriolic debunking of his home town Aberystwyth (telling of "chapel intrigue, of mean pride, of soul-killing gossip") but under his wife's influence the bitter had been abandoned for the beautiful – or perhaps merely postponed. The novel was never completed, or if it was, never published (and no manuscript has come to light).

The *Western Mail's* belief that readers would take the script in their stride was seemingly borne out by the very few letters it provoked. The paper judged that people were more preoccupied with a published report on the Gresford colliery disaster, with this and Wales's home loss to Scotland at rugby. Nonetheless, on 6 February 1937 (the Saturday of that "dreadful defeat"), a letter from Gwilym Davies appeared. Baptist minister turned peace activist and League of Nations champion, Davies counted himself among the many who felt no bitterness towards "our social Trotsky" – he had written some truthful things about Wales – but "his persistent acting of the clumsy iconoclast" was a waste of literary talent. More in hurt than anger, the Rhondda novelist Jack Jones faced Evans's contemptuous dismissal of Welsh writers in English. The work they had done so far may not be worth much to Wales, to literature, or to thought, but it had to be done by someone; it was a necessary breaking of the ground for a school of writers who might one day equal the Irish. In the meantime, the Anglo-Welsh stood between "the hypercritical and the lingual purists". A Welsh periodical dismisses them as "lost to Wales" and our "gadfly" Caradoc Evans thinks it no loss at all.[30]

"Caradoc Breaks Loose Again", cried the *Western Mail* when releasing the BBC talk. It would be the last time he did so. In a matter of months, he would leave Aberystwyth for London and withdraw from public debate – though not from the public eye.

Ruislip and Broadstairs: Gathering Storms

1937-39

T he Evanses left Aberystwyth in June 1937 – under cover of darkness, so town gossip went. For Caradoc in particular, life had suddenly turned for the worse. On 10 May he found himself in court facing a committal order for non-payment of maintenance to his first wife Rose (described as "destitute" now). In defence Evans simply stated that he had no money to offer, his royalties having dwindled to nothing; every penny previously earned had gone to Rose. However, two new books were in the pipeline, one of which might appear in November. He had gained no advance on either of them. A painful cross-examination began: "You are now living in a huge house in Queen's Square?" – "My wife pays the rent"; "You have a car and a chauffeur?" – "No, my wife has"; "Does your wife make you any allowance?" – "She lends me money." The Judge intervened, looking more towards November and the promise of some payment by Evans. Rose's solicitor reminded him that similar promises made in the past had all proved barren. The questioning resumed: about Evans's "banned" novel (*Mother's Marvel*), his Fleet Street earnings, his appointment as Eisteddfod adjudicator (no fee as yet forthcoming), his secretarial work for his present wife's theatre company ("the only thing I did was to look at the plays"). A man of the defendant's talent, faced with his obligations, should surely seek regular employment. The Judge was not so certain; while acknowledging the difficulties the case presented, he accepted that professional authors depended on their books for their livelihood. Evans had not been guilty of contempt of court by not making payments under order. He could not pay if he did not have the means. The case was adjourned until December, by which time the defendant's finances should have improved.

The local *Cambrian News* (14 May) and *Welsh Gazette* (13 May) naturally reported the case, as did the *Western Mail* and *Manchester Guardian*. The *Mail's* account was briefer than might have been expected – it appeared on 12 May, George VI's coronation day – but such humiliating exposure understandably distressed the family. Marguerite was appalled, the more so since they all were suffering through Caradoc's mulish refusal to accept from her, as a gift or a loan, the £72 immediately owing to Rose. The sum was trivial compared with her Rogues & Vagabonds losses yet Caradoc stubbornly insisted that his troubles were his own and he alone must face them. Face them he did as they worsened, though in London not in Wales.

Before they left Aberystwyth two intriguing encounters occurred, both barely reported, and barely believable. Gwyn Jones learnt of one after coming to live in the town. He was told that Rose Evans had turned up at Aberystwyth (presumably in connection with the court case) and chancing to meet Caradoc outside the railway station had promptly felled him with her handbag – "before an audience of taxi-drivers well-versed in strict metres and local charges," Jones embellished his retelling of the tale.[1] He is our sole authority for the handbagging incident, as is Marguerite for Dylan Thomas's second Queen's Square visit in early 1937.[2] The now established poet seemed as boyish and diffident as in October 1934 but once again produced an inspired reading. "Get yourself heard," Caradoc urged, "heard as well as read. You will be more read if you are heard." He thought Dylan should to try his hand at a play; Dylan answered by quoting *Taffy*, Marged's confession to Spurgeon: "I have hated you. And loved you. O love made noises in my heart. It stilled the rill of the morning milk as it fell into the pitcher, and at night it chased away the white moss of slumber from my eyes. It stirred the woman within me." A mildly embarrassed Caradoc felt the need to apologize for this rare lyrical outburst, deeming it the product of three swift sherries. He warned against "the spirit in the bottle": "I am mad enough without that, and so are you, perhaps." The visit ended with Dylan being prevailed upon to make a secret wish on Marguerite's Miracle Stone, housed in her upstairs workroom. A single wish was permitted but Dylan gave himself three – "They are all joined together, three in one, like the Trinity." (The Evanses would learn what they were when they happened to meet Dylan in wartime.) Marguerite puts no date on this second visit. It could have been shortly after 9 February 1937, the date of Dylan's letter to his agent David Higham proposing a visit to Caradoc in connection with a projected book on Wales; or it might have been April 1937 – we know that Dylan was in Machynlleth at this time.

A move away from Aberystwyth suited all the family. Caradoc could have lived eternally in Fleet Street among the drinking men, and Nick, no longer a boy, looked to London as the place where the play he had written stood some chance of production and so boost his prospects of work. Marguerite lived happily enough in Wales but she enjoyed her dealings with editorial people and London would bring her within touching distance of Jean Mitchell at Hurst & Blackett and the redoubtable Mrs Webb at Hutchinson.[3] The choice of Ruislip was Marguerite's – she had lived in nearby Kingsbury, another north-western suburb – and having found the "pretty-pretty" Corner House, half-timber and half-brick, in Ruislip's better Kingsend district ("a few dignified tree-shaded residential streets with fancy houses of every design… all set in smiling flowery gardens") she impetuously signed a five-year lease.[4] But Ruislip disappointed. It wasn't bustling enough for Caradoc, and Marguerite could no longer cope with dormitory suburbs. "The one-man shop has been elbowed out by the chain-shop companies. The pavements are always crowded with girl-mothers carrying shopping baskets and wheeling collapsible prams."[5] No, not Marguerite's cup of tea.

Nick flourished most. His play *The Jade Claw* – the story of an Indian prince who can transform himself into a marauding beast of prey – was put on at the Portfolio (5 October), Fay and Viola Compton's artistic little enterprise behind Baker Street, with Nick as the sinister prince. The *Stage* (7 October) thought the play "flamboyant and crude" but with some occasional excitement, "especially when the stage is plunged into darkness and the growls of a panther may be heard from outside". Touching on the "the psychic forces of the East", the piece seemed designed to show the power of white magic in counteracting black. As for Nick, he was "apt to overdo the prince's silky tones". On the second night Caradoc fell down a hole backstage and broke his ankle. "He was in agony but wouldn't let on until we got home," Marguerite reported to Glyn Roberts; "Now he will have to be hopping on one leg for several weeks."[6] Marguerite had invited Roberts to see *The Jade Claw* in the hope that he might further Nick's career; the once regular contributor of Welsh articles to the *Western Mail* was now a film critic. In fact, Nick's play won a radio broadcast (directed by Felix Felton) and a request from Margate's Theatre Royal to put on a production with Nick in his original part.

Caradoc's court appearance made plain how low his stock had sunk: no book in print, no royalties, and the prospect of literary oblivion for another once well-known name. Yet Evans had his admirers, Welsh and English, and as if to raise his spirits, in 1937 they came forward in numbers. The year was a particularly good one for the so-named "Anglo-Welsh",[7] with books from Rhys Davies, Geraint Goodwin, Wyn Griffith, David Jones, Glyn Jones, Jack Jones, Lewis Jones, Goronwy Rees and Ernest Rhys, together with *Welsh Short Stories*, a landmark Faber anthology in a category of fiction increasingly associated with Wales. The anthology included Caradoc's "The Way of the Earth", praised as "powerful and affecting" by Frank Swinnerton in the *Observer* ("that pince-nezed pussy-cat, but he's a clean penman," Caradoc told Edward Lyndoe.)[8] More significantly, the year saw the advent of Keidrych Rhys's *Wales*, a little quarterly of "creative work by the younger progressive Welsh writers". Caradoc received a complimentary copy of the initial "Summer 1937" issue, along with an invitation to contribute and a small request for help. One feature of *Wales* would be its "Bibliographies of Modern Welsh Authors" and Rhys wanted Evans to front the series. His brief bibliography duly appeared in the second number (prefaced by biographical notes), while issue 3 (Autumn 1937) printed sentences from Caradoc's letter of thanks for the opening number: "I like its note and its courage. It is easily the best thing that has come out of Wales. It is nice to look at a list of contributors without a 'Parch'."[9]

At first an affair of individuals, Anglo-Welsh literature developed its groupings, the earliest with Dylan Thomas as linchpin, the Swansea wunderkind whose *18 Poems* (1934) had thrilled and mystified. Both he and Glyn Jones nursed hopes of a new periodical serving young Welsh writers but it was the twenty-year-old Keidrych Rhys, "tall, handsome, beautifully dressed in country tweeds... and speaking disconcerting Welsh with the accent of the English public schools", who in summer 1936 knocked on Glyn Jones's Rhiwbina door and introduced himself as the founder-editor of just such a magazine.[10] He set about the enterprise with confidence (and a little private money), telling Vernon Watkins that "behind my bovine mask and tender years I might know more about Poetry than most". Rhys had a wider mission, no less than to raise the national consciousness of a new literary generation: "Though we write in English, we are rooted in Wales", his militant manifesto proclaimed. "A really grand idea" thought

Dylan – of a literary periodical, that is; he had doubts about the politics – but both he and Glyn Jones stood shoulder to shoulder with Keidrych as his combative little magazine went on sale in July 1937. All three were Caradoc enthusiasts, Dylan Thomas from the beginning and Glyn Jones on receiving Evans's letter of praise for "Eden Tree" (after which "I was prepared to listen very sympathetically to whatever was said in defence or praise of Caradoc and his work").[11] Rhys instinctively admired professionals and following a fiery taste of local banking (it involved a gun) had wished, like Caradoc, to devote himself to journalism and literature. Glyn Jones it was who suggested that complimentary copies be sent to older established authors, believing they had a place alongside Keidrych's "progressive" newcomers.

"It's about time some critic of note wrote an article dealing with the school of new Welsh writers – it's sufficiently vigorous now." So urged Rhys Davies.[12] Glyn Roberts in his journalism had given the Anglo-Welsh some profile and now Keidrych Rhys on radio offered his own brief survey. He sought something approaching a canon, an author-itative tradition of Welsh writing in English. It was pioneering work – "No one has even bothered to make even a bibliography" – and at times tough going: "boring novels to be read, most written simply for entertainment and money, which couldn't possibly stick in one's mind for a week."[13] Then in 1915 had come *My People*. "Up to then there had only been Allen Raine's popular fiction about Wales, full of stage trappings – the English idea of our origin, history, tradition…. Poor stuff, and quite despicable." By contrast, Evans's first book was "rich, strong, and though obviously bitter and of satirical bent, very true to life." It was unequivocally *new*, "the first expression of the life and ways of thinking of a nation hitherto without expression in the outside world."

The Gollancz novelist Gwyn Jones also broadcast on the Anglo-Welsh and, like Kei-drych Rhys, deemed *My People* a fundamental text and turning-point. In Jones's later words, "For good (or if you prefer, for bad) he [Caradoc] destroyed the dynasty of Allen Raine and the Maid of Cefn Ydfa, and sank it in the sea."[14] Jones, one should make clear, stood quite deliberately outside the circle of *Wales*; a lecturer in Old English and Scan-dinavian literature at Cardiff, he had his own very different ideas on the kind of journal *Wales* needed. Yet both he and Keidrych Rhys remained extraordinarily committed to the notion of an Anglo-Welsh literature, and if they disagreed over its purposes and direction, both acknowledged Caradoc Evans as a founding father (one who a few months before had comprehensively dismissed his offspring). For Gwyn Jones, as for Rhys, Caradoc Evans had a two-fold significance: first, in the excellence of his writing at its best, and secondly, in his acts of literary heroism and work of liberation: "before most of us set pen to paper he had fought savagely and successfully against philistinism, Welsh provincialism, and the hopelessly inhibited standards of what little Anglo-Welsh literature there was."[15] It saddened Rhys that "a man of genius like Caradoc Evans, who had suffered so much to produce his first book, should have been so scandalously treated."[16] Caradoc was ever a flashpoint for strong emotion: a traducer whose savage lies set the Anglo-Welsh on a path of misrepresentation, or a great reforming satirist, the pattern of artistic survival in face of petty parochialism. His polemics had fallen on receptive ears. "What spoils Wales is Nonconformity, out of which nothing good comes," Keidrych wrote to Edgell Rickword, editor of the *Left Review*; "That's why I think Caradoc Evans is a genius. All our BBC officials are sons of notorious third rate trashy poet-preachers." Idris Davies went further, believing that "one of Wales's greatest needs is [the] eradication of Christianity within its borders. The real Wales, like the real Ireland, has been hidden behind the dirty veils of theology."[17] Gwyn Jones the scholar-novelist was naturally more measured: "the well-meaning moralist is the emasculator of art," he told radio listeners; Nonconformity's decline had been one pre-requisite for the emergence of the Anglo-Welsh.[18]

Caradoc's commendatory letter to *Wales* mentions no single contribution, praising instead the magazine's overall "note and courage". He warmed to its warrior temperament and caught echoes of himself – his insistence on the cultural superiority of common Welsh folk over their English counterparts, and his talk of the Welsh as keepers of the English language – in the remarkable paragraphs prefacing Keidrych's invitation to subscribers:

> There is actually no such thing as "English" culture: a few individuals may be highly cultured, but the people as a whole are crass[19] .... We publish this journal in English so that it may spread far beyond the frontiers of Wales, and because we realise the beauty of the English language better than the English themselves, who have so shamefully misused it.

Such sentiments embarrassed Glyn Jones – the *Liverpool Daily Post* found them "very amusing" – but Gwyn Jones too, when he launched his *Welsh Review* (1939), would speak of the Anglo-Welsh as promising to re-invigorate the tired body of English literature.

From the outset *Wales* met with hostility from the Welsh-language establishment. Its first issue made Iorwerth Peate seem old, very old, its modernist pretensions epitomized in Dylan Thomas, this time drunk on psychoanalysis and looking through dirty glasses on body and soul. Expert in Welsh folk life and a National Eisteddfod judge – he was one of those who resigned following Caradoc's Machynlleth appointment – Iorwerth Peate saw the whole sorry *Wales* affair summed up in the opening of Glyn Jones's poem: "This is the scene, let me unload my tongue, / Discharge perhaps some dirty water from my chest."[20] Keidrych declared that the Peate gang were doing their best to kill off *Wales*, and apparently succeeding – by late 1937 the magazine had trouble meeting bills. One of the gang, the BBC director Rhys Hopkin Morris, thought Dylan's "Prologue to an Adventure" merited prosecution; he [Morris] is "on the Religious Book Club and goes round the theological colleges", Keidrych told Edgell Rickword; he might have added that Morris also banned Caradoc Evans's radio talk earlier in the year. The uproar delighted Evans whose second letter to Keidrych (1 September 1937) heaped more praise on *Wales*:

> You have aroused the Big Heads and you and your colleagues ought to be very proud. But they are not big Big Heads; their word seldom carries to the border of their own counties. You might say it seldom goes beyond the walls of their chapels; and *Wales*

is not a sort of "Trysorfa Fach" that is hawked after chapel.[21] May your next issue
make the Big Heads madder still.

The letter excited Keidrych who passed it to Vernon Watkins, who in turn passed
it to John Pritchard, one of Swansea's Kardomah boys whose poetry *Wales* was printing.

The last of Evans's letters to Rhys (21 February 1938) seems to have been a response
to the idea of a special Caradoc Evans issue of *Wales*. "I am honoured indeed and thank
you," Evans replies, before voicing further support: "The Eisteddfod, BBC, Cymmrodorion,
etc, is the monopoly of Nonconformity and young writers with interesting and startling
opinions are naturally barred. But the young writers will win because they have real
opinions, not the ready-made capel sort. Dylan Thomas is winning." At the outset Caradoc
half-promised *Wales* a story and "Your Sin Will Find You Out" would lead off the August
1939 double issue, his best piece of writing in years.

Much would be endured in the meantime, perhaps the darkest moments Caradoc would
know. His health began to suffer, his mind as well as his body, as he started drinking
again. November passed with no new book and thus no payments to Rose. In consequence,
on 2 December he found himself once more at Aberystwyth County Court.[22] Maintenance
arrears now touched £200 and since his last court outing he had paid a mere £2 10s
(half his Machynlleth Eisteddfod fee). The promised book seemingly lay with his publishers
but was unlikely to appear before the following autumn. There remained the possibility
of a royalty advance, though not for three or four months. He was still solely dependent
on his present wife who (he confirmed under questioning) had no financial interest in
the Baker Street theatre run by Miss Fay Compton. He spoke of the utter futility of
trying to look for a job – "I am a literary journalist and there is no suitable job except
on a literary journal" – and of how the adverse publicity surrounding this case had
severely damaged him. The damage would be worse if the court acceded to Rose's
solicitor's request that, as Evans no longer lived in Aberystwyth, his case be transferred
to Uxbridge. The judge thought the request a reasonable one; the next hearing would
be in Uxbridge. Behind Caradoc's preference for Aberystwyth might have been the
feeling that he would find some courtroom sympathy there. The Welsh judge in May
had shown him more respect, more understanding of his problems as a writer, than was
likely to be forthcoming at Uxbridge.

Five days later Evans sampled Uxbridge justice, but as witness in a case brought
against Marguerite by yet another sacked cook, the spirited Winifred Bennett. She was
suing for a month's wages (£5.17.6d) in lieu of notice. She explained that Sunday 20
June, her day off, she did not arrive home until midnight. "Look at her, she's drunk,"
said the Countess, calling her a disreputable woman.[23] On Monday morning she was
ordered to leave the house by 2.30pm. "I refused, but a policeman told me to clear out,
so I went." She had been insolent to Mrs Evans with good cause, refusing to clean taps
and to sew rings on curtains because she was hired to cook not to sew. Caradoc confirmed
that since they came to Ruislip in June, Miss Bennett had often said, "Why don't you
do the taps yourself. All you do is scribble, scribble, scribble." When on Monday he had

threatened to call a policeman, she answered, "The whole force won't shift me." Judgement was given for the defendant, who did not ask for costs. The *Western Mail* reported the case; the *Cambrian News* gave Aberystwyth the gist in its headline, "Cook sues Countess. Mrs Caradoc Evans wins Case."

Evans's next court appearance was a wholly different affair. On Tuesday, 8 February 1938, at Uxbridge he learnt that arrears to Rose now amounted to £287. Once more he repeated his story, that he could find no work, that he lived on his wife, that he still had nothing to pay with. His finished book, a work of fiction but "not a thriller", would not appear before the autumn. He was asked its title. Was this necessary? he enquired. The question was not pressed. Instead, he wrote down the names of his publisher and his literary agent. Rose's solicitor questioned his industry. "While you've been writing one novel in two years, can you say how many novels your present wife has written?" He could not, and neither could he hand over rights in his new novel: it might make thousands (though he confessed that none of his books had made more than a few hundred pounds). Was he prepared to give an undertaking that he would hand over any money from this book? "I am wishful to pay," Evans answered. "It does not look as if you are really," said Judge A.H. Maxwell, losing patience. He made a committal for twenty-one days, suspended so long as Evans paid £10 a month.[24]

One would like to know which new Evans book lay waiting: *The Holy City*, one supposes, his Aberystwyth novel whose bitterness Marguerite sought to dilute; five thousand words were written, so he claimed in January 1937. If it was *The Holy City*, it seems strange that nothing more was ever heard of it and that no fragment has survived. Evans did complete a short memoir of Mary Webb for *The Colophon*, a New York quarterly for book collectors. He returned corrected proof to the editor F.B. Adams in January 1938, together with Dorothy Hickling's photograph of Webb for Adams to keep. Published in February 1938, the essay was well received, as Adams wrote to say. Evans thanked him more than two months later ("I have no excuse to offer"), at the same time posting the "Special Storm Edition" of the *Cambrian News* (15 January 1938): it would explain how "The property I left at Aberystwyth went into the sea."[25] ("The property" was the Quarry theatre whose fate the Evanses had learned of through friends in the town: the whole caboodle washed out to sea.) At the close of 1937, Caradoc also returned to Evelyn Lewes her copy of Jonathan Ceredig Davies's *Folk-lore of West and Mid-Wales* (1911). He had kept it far longer than intended, perhaps in connection with some modern folktales he had embarked upon, stories that would eventually appear as *Pilgrims in a Foreign Land* (1942).

Marguerite writes of the dreadful days as Caradoc's legal liabilities piled up, "doubling and trebling – even if they were allowed to stand over":

> The shadow of a committal order and prison loomed over him. To me he showed no sort of emotion about it all. He encased himself in a steel coat of reserve. I begged him to let me help him. I said he could pay me back any time or no time, but he simply refused.... He said the onus was on him and he would far rather go to prison and finish with it. I wrote him a cheque, several cheques. He tore them all up and

got into furies over all sorts of extraneous trifles. He couldn't help it. Within himself he was a seething mass of nerves and I was perfectly aware that the very thought of being shut up and confined in prison for his debt made him as nervous and apprehensive as a child.[26]

To take his mind off immediate worries, Marguerite revived *Taffy* at the tiny Grafton Theatre in Tottenham Road, formerly a basement cinema converted from a wine cellar. She cast a Welsh girl, Cecily Bowen of Abermule, as Marged, opposite Cecil Scott-Paton as Spurgeon (both Rogues & Vagabonds troupers who became husband and wife). Marguerite approached the play from what she called "an idealistic angle, so that the satire only ran beneath like an underground stream". As at Aberystwyth, she dispensed with conventional scenery – it struck her as too sophisticated for a play of this kind. Instead, she had cut-outs made of an apple tree and bushes for the exterior scenes and Evan Walters painted a "futuristic" apple tree, "a glorious sight".[27] Reviewing the opening night, Monday 21 February (the date of Caradoc's third letter to Keidrych Rhys, on notepaper advertising *Taffy*), the *Times* applauded the deliberate crudity of the staging. It was presented "as it might be in a remote Welsh village which disclaimed the travelling cinema and cared for drama more than its appurtenances. This is a good idea and serves incidentally to soften the satire." Marguerite covered her losses but writhed at the painful publicity:

> I was dragged into the limelight (with photograph) under the caption: "Novelist's Wife puts on play to Save Husband from Prison".... It made me furious that Caradoc, who had given so much of himself to newspapers, and so many interviews out of sheer good nature to newspapermen, should be so bruised and shot at by his very comrades, but although he felt this public discussion of his private troubles, he bore the newspapermen not the slightest ill will. All he said was: "It's their job. It's what they're out for – a story – no matter what it's about. Good God, even a newspaperman has got to earn his living."[28]

The publicity took a different turn after the St David's Day performance. Several Evan Walters paintings were hanging in the Grafton bar, among them his Caradoc Evans portrait, and as if to counter the shows of esteem from the literary Anglo-Welsh, on 1 March "An inflamed patriot, entering surreptitiously and unseen, dexterously slit the canvas over the throat." The assailant was never caught. Caradoc declined the picture when Walters offered it (repaired) as a gift. "Good God, no! I don't want to look at me. I am me with my mother's milk turned sour in me. That's bad enough." He would not let Marguerite accept either, not unless she kept it in the coal cellar, "so for years it remained in Evan's studio with its face to the wall collecting dust".[29]

Caradoc's reaction to the attack is not recorded. Did he feel as Henry James did, "very scalped and disfigured", when in May 1914 a militant suffragette took a meat cleaver to John Singer Sargent's portrait of James at the Royal Academy? Marguerite makes plain his disorder at this time. "He was drinking very heavily again. I was troubled and unhappy. The little cockle-shell of my marriage-boat was getting a fearful battering. In these days he wasn't my Caradoc at all. He was a mad dog. Half the time he didn't know what he was doing or saying."[30]

These "nightmare days and nights" are broached in the Barcynska novel *Sweetbriar Lane* (1938), where domestic flare-ups set husband Daniel off on wild jaunts into Fleet Street, hunting up old friends, drinking and wandering about all night, talking to down-and-outs and prostitutes. Arguments begin with talk of money. "Other women's husbands provide for them. You can't even provide for your former wife," taunts Florence, who "no longer saw romance in her cyclonic lover of ten years ago". She can't think what he writes about holed up in his den with his Dr Johnson's *Dictionary*. For days he sits scratching out. "It just means that you put the same words back again nine times out of ten." Counters Daniel, "But I know it's the right word when I come back to it the tenth time, don't you see." Florence does not. "I write as the words come in quick flow unless my brain is tired, and it's the only way to make money. If I shut myself up in my room and chase words through a forest of dictionaries, I might take as long as you do, and then we'd starve." The "kept-boy" warms to a dust-up. Florence spends her money on herself, not on him; he doesn't want a big house, a big car and servants, and the clothes of a debutante. "All I want is bread and cheese and an onion and a pint of beer, and a pen and ink and paper." Letters from former wife Grace ask about her alimony ("not very politely"). Florence understands how she feels. Why can't Daniel commercialize himself and write something that will please an editor. After all, "Your name alone is news." He answers as always: "I can't write what isn't in me." He has embarked on "fairy stories", and "All my fairy stories have sad endings. That's where they're different from everybody else's. They're not copies." Doubting that sad-ending fairy tales will easily find a publisher, Florence offers to "tickle them up" a bit (as Marguerite "tickled up" *The Holy City*).

The quarrels are fully played out before Florence's son Heron, a bewildered youth in a chaotic household who upbraids his mother for muddling up her life so badly. She breaks down, tears coming more readily than words – "Emotionally she could weep to order like the consummate actress she was." Daniel too wades in, suggesting she no longer loves her son, "Because he isn't your baby any more." And what was he? "A lost boy," whom Florence had simultaneously spoiled and neglected. The little cockle-shell marriage-boat was truly taking a battering. The thrill of their union had gone. "The only time I was really thrilled was when you made love to me for that one glorious fortnight before we were married." Daniel says he could make love again. "But I couldn't respond. Your terrible tempers have left me all dried up and stranded like a dead starfish on a hot beach when the tide is out." At first she thought them well suited, but they weren't. "Our constant fights and goings-off-the-deep-ends are such devastation." And after the rows, "The general prosaicness... You've gone very grey and you're so careless about your clothes, and you don't look right sometimes. You say that yourself and you mustn't mind me saying so. You can be so aggressively not a gentleman and it grates." Florence further twists the knife. "I haven't any regard for you... I'm a little sorry for you because you're so obstinate and helpless."

She hands Daniel ten pounds for tobacco and for the beer that has thickened his waist. She is set on a few tranquil weeks in Ireland with an Irish actor-companion, "the ape-actor" who Daniel suspects is having an affair with his wife. "You needn't worry about that," she assures him. "The only man I ever had an affair with was you. I may look very sexual and exotic, but I'm not." Telling Heron that his mother has gone on a motoring jaunt with "that actor idiot", Daniel offers the young fellow (who now has a girlfriend) some serious advice: "never let a woman pay for you, not even if she's your wife who began by loving you. It isn't sound. Take that from me as a piece of gospel truth. And get out of Unfortunate Street. Don't linger in it. The best woman soon tires of the man who fails."

"Caradoc Evans 'Bows to the Law'. Judge Declines to Interfere with Order. Much Wronged First Wife". So a *Western Mail* headline gave the outcome of Evans's fourth and final court appearance on the matter of alimony. On 8 February 1938, a committal order had been made against him, suspended so long as he paid £10 a month to his former wife (to whom a sum of £287 was due). He could not pay the £10, said his solicitor at Uxbridge on 8 March; only his present wife could. Last year he had earned £10-£15 and all he would have in the next two or three days was £4. He was prepared to pay this, and to meet the amount of arrears from a book he hoped to publish, when and if it might be published. Should the order stand, it meant his putting pressure on his wife to pay his debts; either that or going to prison for twenty-one days. The court saw no reason to interfere with the 8 February order. "I cannot believe that this very much wronged woman [the first Mrs Evans] should be kept out of her money by constant applications of this sort," said the judge. Interviewed by the *Western Mail* imme-diately after the hearing, Caradoc denied that he had behaved all along with an eye to publicity:

> I say, rather than my present wife should pay another penny on my behalf, I am going to prison. The funeral is mine. I shall be the corpse and the mourners and the undertaker as well. I bow to the law. All I need is a bowl of leek broth and a hunk of bread, and while I am in prison I shall still be a Welshman. I shall have only one regret. I am sorry that the daffodils will be over when I come out of prison. In the meantime, one thing I may do. I may take from my wife's car the little Welsh woman mascot – made by the last woodcarver in Wales – with me to prison. Perhaps it will be more lucky in prison than it has been to me on the outside.[31]

Caradoc never tasted prison, and we do not know why. Marguerite has this to say in her biography of her husband:

> I do not know what happened eventually about his legal trouble. Sometimes I wondered if some well-disposed person had discharged his debt for him. Certainly he was never pressed any more for what he had not got. It was the one subject he would never discuss with me. He put up a wall of "Ask no questions and you will be told no stories" around that subject and me. There was, I always felt, a mystery and an undercurrent there, but if he did not wish to tell me things of his own accord I never pressed or questioned him. He would only have hedged and hidden behind the hedge.[32]

Domestic strife seems rarely to have impeded Marguerite's creativity. She managed a novel every two or three months while at Ruislip. "There is always peace when the pen is in one's hand, even when writing is most difficult." Her routine was not to be broken: mornings kept for work with no deviation, Terrier Jock beside her, gazing up with eyes of love and listening to all her outpourings; Jock was special, the dog who had come their way when love was new. But Caradoc needed pulling out of London; its very nearness made him thirsty. He seemed bent on self-destruction and she feared some dreadful calamity (Daniel in *Sweetbriar Lane* takes his own life). Release came indirectly through theatre. Marguerite writes to Monica Dunbar in July 1938 of having to go for the night to Margate to reopen the Theatre Royal for an actor friend, though "I can't make speeches. Just dry up." Nick would be performing there, in *The Jade Claw* and as the husband in Martin Vale's *The Two Mrs Carrolls*. Margate, the Thanet seaside resort for working-class Londoners, distinctly failed to impress. One day at the hotel Jock fell thirty feet from a balcony into the garden below. The vet said it ought to have killed him, but helped to his feet, Jock wagged his tail – cause of yet more wonder for Caradoc: "By God, you're some dog, aren't you, Jock?"[33] Marguerite wrote again, this time to Monica's mother Nell: "Oh, I forgot to tell you Margate itself sickened us so that we pined for beauty & tore straight off to Wales where we spent a glorious five days." It was now September 1938, with Britain preparing for the worst: recruiting air raid wardens, opening gas mask centres in London, and planning a partial evacuation of the city's population. "Isn't this war scare awful?" Marguerite's letter concludes. "It sends one to one's knees."[34]

A short drive from Margate was Broadstairs, a quiet retreat that kept its charm even as the season closed:

> A tar-timbered jetty like some prehistoric monster basking in the sea and a bleak turreted brown-grey house. Wide shopping and residential streets suddenly becoming steep and running full speed to the jetty, where they turn narrow and humble with dark basements. Gardened esplanades with broad green swards. Large verandahed houses of the affluent (closed for the winter). Pretentious boarding-houses and guest-houses trying to look Grand Hotelish (closed for winter). The Grand Hotel itself (closed for winter).

The description is Marguerite's, from the opening of *Writing Man* (1938), her first Broad-stairs novel. The turreted brown-grey house was Bleak House, where Dickens stayed on summer holidays (it was Fort House then). He first stopped in the town a full century before and an 1837 letter to his biographer John Forster captures its beguiling unevent-fulness: "I have seen stout gentlemen looking at nothing through powerful telescopes for hours, and, when at last they saw a cloud of smoke, fancying a steamer behind it, and going home comfortable and happy." The Dickens link would have appealed, given the Evanses' near-worship of him. "He stands head and shoulders above us all," thought Marguerite, remarking "his wholesale humanity", "his zeal for truth" and a fiction that entertained "yet was capable of doing some real good".

On the Western Esplanade she came across Westbury, "a dream of a little house looking right out to sea in a lovely garden".[35] The semi-bungalow was secured on a three-year lease and in October 1938 she happily abandoned Ruislip for Broadstairs, a largely middle-class town without the waves of cheaper week-enders flooding Margate and Ramsgate in summer. In genteel Broadstairs the presence of a Countess Barcynska caused something of a stir: she was reckoned to be a Polish writer who wintered in the south of France. Frank Muir remembered from schooldays her seafront property being proudly pointed out to visitors.[36] Besides her "delightful bungalow", Marguerite had also discovered, in West Cliff Road, a "drabbish black-and-white corrugated iron structure", a small, run-down theatre crying out for refurbishment. As in Wales, so in Kent. "Nick and I have taken a dear little playhouse place which we have done up like the Quarry," she wrote to Evelyn Lewes; "We intend to open at Whitsun, but in this world state of disruption, I am hesitating."[37] Despite "the shadow and looming of war", she did indeed revive for a summer season her Rogues & Vagabonds company, encouraged by Nick (a budding romantic lead) and the availability of two Aberystwyth dependables, Nina Gerrard, a character actress, and the indispensable James Hart, her ideal producer for the repertory she had in mind. He thought little of the new school of actors and their methods of under-playing. "It's prevalent because it's easy. Our first-rate people don't do it. Gielgud, Leslie Banks, Flora Robson and Edith Evans — they throw their beams of light every moment they are on the stage."[38]

With Broadstairs hotels and landladies booked to brimming for July, August and early September, it did not look like a crisis or war and the refurbished old theatre accordingly reopened on Monday 26 June 1939 with *George and Margaret*, Gerald Savory's comedy, playing to a full house. "No expense has been spared in bringing the Playhouse up to date," reported the *Stage* (29 June); "it has been entirely redecorated in duck-egg green and silver, new seating accommodation has been provided and the stage has been fitted with the latest system of lighting." Ivor Novello, Edith Evans, Robert Donat and others had sent their greetings and good wishes for the venture's success. With fresh flowers prettifying the foyer and Marguerite's lacquer trays, antique vases and Staffordshire china perched on ledges around the walls, the Playhouse quickly became popular, Ramsgate and Margate running special buses for theatregoers. The musical director's wish to school the public in classical music seemed questionable; Marguerite liked his interval choices but "at the end [it] should be popular — *Boomps-a-Daisey*, for instance after *God Save the King*… the public must go away light-hearted — especially after *The Two Mrs Carrolls* with all the tension and suffering in it."[39] Monica Dunbar enjoyed *The Two Mrs Carrolls*, particularly Nick's performance (Caradoc too was impressed) and remarked how the three of them, "Caradoc, Marguerite and Nick all seemed so happy."

Though Marguerite told Evelyn Lewes that she felt "quite alien in England now", as indeed did Nick — "We gave our hearts to Wales" — she agreed that life had improved at "awfully nice" Broadstairs.[40] The London worst was behind them; their little marriage-boat would survive the tempests because they were "two utterly unbalanced and

Caradoc and Marguerite at Maidenhead, "their honeymoon retreat", 22 June 1933. They had quietly married in the town three months earlier

The Evan Walters portrait of Evans, 1930. Comprehensively rejected in Wales, it was attacked when displayed in London on St David's Day 1938. The repaired canvas is now in the National Museum of Wales

"The Countess Barcynska", by Evan Walters [1930?]. Shown "n.f.s." in Swansea 1935, the portrait is also at the National Museum of Wales

Queen's Square House, Aberystwyth, the Evanses' home 1934-37. A commemorative plaque sits below a first-floor window

Caradoc outside Queen's Square House with Violet Gatcombe Evans, a freelance journalist who interviewed him for the *Western Mail*

Nick Sandys in actor's pose. Desperately wishing for a stage career, he found no regular employment in this or any field

From the jacket of Marguerite's 1936 novel based on the Rogues & Vagabonds Repertory Players, the touring company she established in 1935

Brynawelon, the Evanses' four-bedroom house on a rise at New Cross. They rented there in 1940, moving to Aberystwyth in October 1944

Terrier Jock and sheepdog Timber at Brynawelon. "Jock's a nobleman," enthused Caradoc; "he's better than I am by a long chalk. He's miles above me."

Caradoc outdoors at Brynawelon, in headgear that amazed Gwyn Jones who thought it a cut-down woman's beach hat: "It was of fine straw, red, green and yellow, brilliant and gay, and looked like an inverted beehive, but he wore it with unflinching gravity."

CARADOC EVANS
DIED
11TH JANUARY 1945
BURY ME LIGHTLY SO THAT
THE SMALL RAIN MAY REACH
MY FACE AND THE FLUTTERING
OF THE BUTTERFLY SHALL NOT
ESCAPE MY EAR.
CARADOC EVANS

Caradoc's desk-tablet gravestone in
Horeb cemetery, New Cross.
Marguerite's design incorporates the
writer's emblems and an epitaph
offered by Evans himself in 1924

Christmas 1946: Marguerite with
Timber at Penrhyncoch, two years
after Caradoc's death

incredible opposites who could not exist without each other". Her conclusion comes from *Sweetbriar Lane*, a book she thought Evelyn Lewes might like since "There are portraits there!" – as in fact there were in *Writing Man*, the Barcynska novel Lewes had just finished reading. "Yes, Evan Aberporth (my name for him!) is a portrait. Recognisable, I am afraid, but Evan doesn't mind & he is such good copy."[41] The flavour of this copy can be sampled in Aberporth's broadsides against women. (At the beginning of her *Caradoc Evans* biography she insists that she would not have put down anything that her husband did not say.)

> For a woman a king has been known to take off his crown and throw it at her feet. Go into the City and see white-faced men scurrying like ants. What for? What are they doing? Making money to satisfy women's inordinate greed and vanity. Go into the West End and look at the big shops – the jewellers', the furriers', the dressmakers', the florists'. Look at all the beauty parlours where women study how to trap men with all the artifices brought about by mudpacks and astringents and massage and violet rays. Spiders – that's what women are. They spin their webs out of their bodies – mesh of the senses – and poor men can't keep away from the web.

"Take it from me," Aberporth counsels a younger writer, "Most men are sick of their wives." He expects his own wife, the novelist Daisy Bell, to one day up and leave him. It was inevitable: "Because no woman can put up with me all the time. I'm awful to live with…. I say cruel things that hurt and stab and watch the effect. The fonder I am of someone the more I've got to hurt. I'm an intellectual sadist."

Daisy looks more kindly on men: "Most… are satisfied with affection and home comforts and a certain amount of love if it isn't too possessive." She looked for something more, for a happiness that did not exist, that no man could ever give her; "I don't think peace will fall upon me until I am very old and perhaps I won't live to enjoy it." Made-up and stylishly dressed, Daisy understands how others might perceive her – "She looks as if she's been a go-er with the men and still could be" – but insists that once only did she commit adultery, when the whirlwind struck Aberporth and herself. "We met too late. It was all a muddle-up before the divorce. And I took you from another woman. And I shouldn't have. And I'm sorry. I've always wanted to tell her that.." But once you had stepped out you had never to look back. "It's as bad as looking down when one is mountain-climbing, and life is one long mountain-climb." So Marguerite walked out daily with Caradoc, arm-in-arm along the esplanade or on the beach at low tide, he slashing inanimate objects with his stick– chalk cliffs, the side of a boat, an ancient stone archway…. A psychologist might pick on that," she has him say.[42] On his own he strode out regularly to the Captain Digby, a cliff-top pub overlooking Kingsgate Bay.

In *Calm Waters* (1940), more or less the story of the Broadstairs Playhouse, Marguerite again portrays herself and Caradoc, she as "Maggy Alban", he as "Lewis Morris". Within their household two predictable issues spark the fiercest conflict: Maggy's son Jon and her careless way with money (the two are often linked). Lewis makes all too plain his dislike of his stepson, a lad who got on his nerves with nothing of interest to say. "He

has been worshipped from the cradle and he can't understand why I don't worship him."
Lewis's own upbringing was so different:

> I had my heart broken before I was his age. I never had a mother to fuss over me.
> She turned me out to earn my own living when I was fourteen. I was pitchforked
> from a country village to a big town and no one cared what happened to me. It made
> me write a book. You can't achieve without you suffer. I want the boy to achieve.

He understands that it's not Jon's fault that his mother loves him so. "It makes it all the
worse. He doesn't want all that adoration and I could do with it. I can't hurt her, so I
hurt her through him. I do it deliberately." Maggy responds in kind ("there was a lot of
the actress in her"): "I hate my husband. I never knew I had such hate in me. He's killed
my love stone dead. He killed it with the stones he hurled at Jon." Outsiders with some
knowledge of their marriage find it difficult to apportion blame. "Actually she is most
to blame. He is a flame of a man and a poet. She probably let him think that he was her
sun, moon and stars, and perhaps he was for a short while – and then he found out that
Jon was her son, moon and stars. That must be a bit upsetting to any man who is fond
of a woman and most of all to an egoist."

When it comes to money Maggy fully concedes her carelessness. She spends on
fashionable clothes – those more than a season old have "a destructive effect one one's
poise" – and Jon has a wardrobe filled with Bond Street tailored suits. ("I glory in my
shabbiness," Lewis claims.) As for housekeeping, Maggy gives the servants free rein. If
she spent her time supervising and asking suspicious questions, how could she manage
to write so much? Her income has always more than matched her expenditure. But
reviving the Broadstairs Playhouse was extravagance on the grand scale and Lewis is
bitterly opposed. His wife would once again become prey for the scheming adventurers
who answer advertisements in the *Stage*. All this outlay so that Jon the would-be actor
should have a new nursery to play in.

One new Isle of Thanet acquaintance lightened weekends at home. George Bullock,
biographer of Marie Corelli and Raymond Marriott's younger partner, lived not far
from Broadstairs and when Marriott came to stay he took Bullock to meet the much
talked about Welsh author. "My first remembrance of Caradoc Evans is of a tall, bony-
looking man with grey upstanding hair who, after he had been in the room only a short
time, began attacking me for not liking the Welsh. His wife was speaking to me about
one of his books when he sharply interrupted her with: 'He doesn't like my books. He's
only interested in highbrows.'"[43] On learning that Bullock had come to London with
just £5 in his pocket Evans's attitude softened – "But Good God, man! You've done well.
You're a hell of a success! Why didn't you tell me all this before?" – though a mutual
wariness prevented real friendship. Nevertheless, over the next few months Bullock
saw quite a lot of the Evanses, staying with them over night and learning more about
Caradoc. His impressions mirror Marriott's. The sweeping pronouncements – "What's
the matter with journalism? It's a grand profession! All the best writers are journalists"
– were those of a man who liked argument for its own sake, exaggerating wildly in

order to provoke. Glyn Roberts's name came up, the young Welsh journalist who had recently died.[44] Caradoc pronounced him a genius. Bullock knew Glyn Roberts, thought him well informed, politically educated and a writer of excellent newspaper articles. "To call anyone like him a genius was absurd. But it was never any use to oppose Caradoc when he had made up his mind to support a statement, and after a time I stopped trying." Thus he let pass Caradoc's assertion that he wrote solely for money and had no interest in art.

"Easily, his favourite topic of conversation was Fleet Street and the personalities connected with it." Behind the lauding of journalism, Bullock sensed Caradoc's nostalgia for a world he had left, for the days of *T.P's Weekly* above all. He learned too that when it came to animal cruelty Evans was quite beyond argument and pretence. Somewhere Evans had read that Emily Brontë in a fit of anger had beaten her dog close to death. "He burst forth in passionate denunciation of her whole works. No writer who could ill-treat an animal was worth reading." Someone pointed out the common discrepancy between an artist's life and their works. "But nothing we had to say would move him... a writer who would beat a defenceless dog was incapable of creating anything of value." In the end the argument became so heated that the subject had to be dropped. "In his passionate self, and the demoniac force with which he attacked things or people who annoyed him", he brought D.H. Lawrence to mind. "He seemed at times to inhabit a different universe from that of most men – an intenser world where everything glowed and burned more fiercely."

Bullock lost touch with Caradoc when the Evanses moved back to Wales. Marriott and Bullock, both conscientious objectors, would later join Rhys Davies in London, in the homosexual court surrounding the damaged and doomed Anna Kavan. Davies had long known Marriott and did not share his liking of Caradoc. In June 1939 Davies mentioned a Foyle's Welsh literary luncheon he had been unable to attend; "your friend Caradoc Evans" was there, he pointedly wrote to Marriott. In fact, Evans too had failed to show, even though due to respond to "The Art and Literature of Wales" toast. Wil Ifan took his place, remarking how impossible it was to deal with such an important subject in the eight minutes allotted – "although Mr Caradoc Evans, had he been here, would have said it was too much."[45]

By the end of the war George Bullock was physically and mentally unwell (he moved to Porthcawl for the sake of his health), but in March 1948 on Welsh radio he spoke affectionately of Caradoc: "his simplicity as a human being; his kindness, courtesy and gentle manners; the graceful way he gave thanks for any small services; his readiness always to be of help." As an example of this helpfulness, he mentioned his Marie Corelli biography. Evans had found among his old Fleet Street papers "three priceless illustrations" for Bullock to reproduce. The book was ready for publishing when Bertha Vyver, with whom Corelli shared a lifelong romantic friendship, refused him permission to quote letters and passages from the novelist's books. She had heard that the biography was not wholly laudatory. At his wits end, Bullock telephoned Broadstairs for advice. "Flatter her," Caradoc answered at once. "Tell her that you think her friend was a wonderful writer and that you are going to say so in your book.... Writers love flattery – all writers. It's their weak point." Bullock did as he was told and by return came a letter from Vyver saying that he could quote whatever he liked. Bullock's *Marie Corelli: The Life and Death of a Best-Seller* appeared in 1940; "She comes out of it all absurd, but unconquerable and very far from being contemptible," said the *Times*.

At Broadstairs Evans continued crafting grisly fairy tales. "I only see bits of them," complained Marguerite, "he likes to hug his work like a dog his bone." In *Writing Man* she elaborates. He [Evan Aberporth] had been at them for over a year, getting slower and slower. Words for him were gods. The waste-paper basket bore witness: "Three words on a sheet thrown away. A sentence. Thrown away. A page with more scratchings than words. Thrown away." A dustbin crammed to the top with all he had thrown away caused the dustman to ask their cook "if I was a mental gentleman who plays with paper". "Perhaps I am," Aberporth reflects. Talk of his "genius" cut no ice. "Genius be damned. I'm a workman. A painstaking workman who isn't in love with his job." His wife was the genius, her words ceaselessly flowing. She computed their total number – by now in the millions ("the noughts are a bit confusing") – as she habitually counted the words of every chapter as she wrote them. "It makes me feel I'm getting on." It served a practical purpose as well, given Walter Hutchinson's absolute insistence that all his novels be of 80,000 words, just one of his stipulations when it came to publishing books. He banned the printing of the year of publication, and had the entire season's catalogue bound in at the end of every book.[46] By subscribing to Hutchinson's belief that books were commodities like any other, Marguerite had prospered. They were "not frightfully rich at present", a new car having just been paid for and rents settled for the three properties they had on their hands.

Reviving the old Broadstairs Playhouse struck Evans as another huge financial risk. Besides, he detested the back-stage bickering and endless theatre shoptalk. Even so, he plunged into everyday theatricals, just as he did at Aberystwyth. "He became more normal in his behaviour, though not nearly normal all the same," wrote Marguerite; "The war scare had him taut and on a string." She mentions his worries concerning an usherette, an English girl who had worked as a dancer in Germany and had met Adolf Hitler there. She thought him a gentle creature, not like his "shouting pictures"; "Before Hitler came into power she said it wasn't safe for a woman to be in the streets at night alone because of the Jews' dreadful behaviour. But now everything is changed, and everywhere he is building and re-creating a new Germany."[47] Caradoc smelt a potential fifth column: thousands of girls in theatre and restaurants spreading propaganda about this nice fellow Hitler and the good he's done in Germany. "Why, we'd have a very respectable army of sympathizers." Marguerite should have a word with her. (In fact within the town at this time were active members of the British Union of Fascists.)

On Saturday 19 August, the Rogues & Vagabonds assembled at the theatre for morning rehearsal. Caradoc was absent. For five years he had talked of war – war and conscription – and could no longer take the strained, edgy atmosphere. Any act against Polish independence would find Britain immediately fighting on her side and Germany's non-aggression pact with the Soviet Union looked certain to be confirmed. Sick with apprehension, the little company debated whether or not to open that night. They had billed a sure-fire winner for their next production, Emlyn Williams's *Night Must Fall*. Advance bookings had been steady, and then stopped dead. What should they do? In the event, Marguerite's mind was made up for her: the Playhouse must close, on ARP orders (Air Raid Precautions).[48] "Came the shrieking siren of war," Marguerite would write to Nell Dunbar; "Theatre closed down by the police, the scared sad little company disbanded. Nickie completely broken down."[49] Frank Muir caught sight of the Countess, "a sad-looking, rouged old lady in a large and floppy straw hat" buying dressed crab (the "old lady" was fifty-two). The Evanses packed up with the rest, but where next to go? Marguerite could not possibly stay in Broadstairs – "where every road leads to the Play-house" – so accompanied by Nick and Jack Berrangé, a young actor who could drive, she motored to Charing, near Ashford, for a night with two old friends, a husband-and-wife dance duo who had built a log cabin in the woods.

For the first time we have Caradoc's picture of events to set beside his wife's. For whatever reason, at Broadstairs he chose to keep a journal. Most entries are undated but it opens at this point:

> PANDEMONIUM. The great pack-up. In the woman's theatre here in Broadstairs the curtains are drawn over the stage. I drew them. The jackals have slunk back to London with their last payrolls (unearned) since the ARP closed us down.
>
> *Night Must Fall* the last play. It was to have been a bumper week. All bookings cancelled.
>
> The woman downcast.
>
> Is it because she says goodbye to peace or goodbye to the jackals?

Peggy Cooper (stage manageress) and James Hart (producer) were no jackals; of Hart he writes: "I like him. He is about 65; agile. He is not afraid to take off his coat and sweat changing scenes with me to help him while the jackals look on. My taste for actors is gone." He records Marguerite's departure:

> The woman has gone off into the blue with Jack Berrangé and Nick.
>
> I packed them off. Jack was driving. The first time he has driven in England. He is a South African. Juvenile lead; tall and blond. He calls the woman his second mother. She puts her wings over him.
>
> I packed them off as I felt she must get away from me. I am too much for her. I am too much for myself.
>
> Chamberlain screamed on the wireless when he foreshadowed war. It was horrid. So is it horrid that the woman is not here. I miss her company and I do not know where on earth to find her.
>
> God knows where they went off to or what made me make them go.

During her night in the woods Marguerite got things clear. Be close to the earth, her Charing friends had said; the closer is Nature, the closer is God. "Earth and the mountains

—Wales. It must be Wales." Whatever her troubles and anxieties, there were books to write; "The talent God gave me was to be my blessing." Caradoc did not demur. "He would not have urged Wales or given me advice. He never does advise in big things. Whatever decisions I make are on my head and his are on his head."[50] Returning to Broadstairs in the morning, Marguerite passed the keeping of Westbury temporarily to her gardener; he could take all the kitchen produce in return for cutting the lawns. She telegrammed Margaret Roberts enquiring about likely accommodation (one of the Roberts family of Aberystwyth brewers, she lived at Abermâd mansion, Llanfarian). The reply was swift: "Come at once all of you don't delay have found rooms on farm near Aberystwyth."

Brynawelon: "That Private Madhouse"

1939-43

Returning to Wales again through its "incomparable mountains", Marguerite saw sights long cherished: men and women turning into chapel, a young couple driving slowly along in a cart, a gypsy party cooking on the roadside, long-tailed sheep scattered over hillsides and a shepherd on a mountain pony, his dog following behind. Evan Griffiths sprang to mind, the wise old man who "spelled white", casting out evil for so many. At Llangurig churchyard she stopped to pray at his grave – Caradoc waited with Nick in the car – before Pumlumon pass and the descent towards Cardigan Bay. At the wheel was Eric Andrews, business manager of the Rogues & Vagabonds.

Settling at Abermâd farm, four miles south of Aberystwyth, the romanticist soon turned realist. "The farm was not comfortable. Welsh farm houses are not built for comfort, and why should they be?" asked Marguerite; they were places of perpetual toil. Standing tall on the Llanfarian to Llanilar road, Abermâd (now Nant-rhwydd) looked prosperous and "modern", but draughts pieced the red-brick building, cooking was on paraffin stoves, and bath taps gave out trickles of cold water and "an inexhaustible supply of dead flies". Marguerite's "overflowing love of Wales" likewise stopped short at two favourite farmhouse dishes, cawl ("flavourless and greasy") and home-cured bacon ("salty and hard and rancid"). Armiger had taught her the subtleties of French cooking; Caradoc said "Armiger Barclay knew nothing about the food that makes men and women live long."[1]

The Evanses secured the four best rooms in the house and for four pounds a week fuel and light were thrown in, together with swedes and potatoes and the occasional services of Miss Daniels, farm-servant and general housekeeper to the widowed farmer. The hard-pressed woman did her best, showing Marguerite how to sweep and dust, lay a fire and make a bed. She sometimes called Marguerite "bach", sometimes "buggar" ("also a term of endearment in these parts", so we gather). In the absence of a functioning bath, a basin of water sufficed, Marguerite's half-hour of piecemeal washing lending "a righteous glow" to the day. Miss Daniels doubted their need of a bath since the Evanses did nothing but waste paper – and "What is the use washing places nobody can see?" Marguerite explained that her work was writing stories, "love stories". Though unmarried, Miss Daniels knew all about love – from her youth. Then there had been sweethearts and "foxing in the hay and catch me in the corn". Caradoc wasted paper in his own private room, his "church" where incense was strong tobacco. It housed two unplayable upright pianos and a large case of stuffed birds surrounding a stuffed fox. The animal exhibits disturbed him. "If he hates killing for sport, he hates more stuffing the things you have killed for house ornaments."

Writing from "Abermaid Farm" soon after the retreat to Wales, Marguerite told Nell Dunbar of what they had been through at Broadstairs ("a deserted wilderness and a dull sullen sea with three lines of ships guarding the harbour"). They had left it all standing and come to Wales, "to the great peace of nature and the hills where there is only one post a day and letters and newspapers arrive – or don't." Her concern was solely for her son. At Broadstairs as at Ruislip he had made some show of earning his own living and was now temporarily boarding at Abermâd mansion:

> Nickie is getting more like his old self – almost but not quite. The old self will never be completely restored. He is such a peace-loving person and the whole idea of war and killing revolts him.
>
> Conscription does not touch him so far. He could never, never stand it. His nerves would give way, I know. The idea of the Navy does not terrify him and he has written in to various sources to see if he can get into the RNVR [Royal Naval Volunteer Reserve]. So far no vacancies.
>
> Meanwhile I am doing everything I can to find something on the land for him to do to keep his mind tranquil and he will probably get some small holding and start off with a few sheep and chickens....
>
> Safety for myself I do not mind, but if the worst happens and my son is snatched from me, I could never live. I am dead against this settling of political scores by the lives of the innocent. I cannot see anything good can ever come out of the shedding of blood. You lost your brother. What for?[2]

Marguerite went ahead and bought thirty ewes in lamb from the farmer, maybe reckoning that Nick would gain exemption from military service on account of his work on the land. Her resilience in face of conditions utterly new to her, and through the cruellest of winters ("frozen spars like stalactites, frozen river, cascades frozen into still-ness"), surprised Caradoc. Frost and snow never bothered him; "This is the weather for me!" he called out as he set off briskly for a walk.

His journal of this period notes events and situations wholly absent from Marguerite's record. We learn that the Abermâd farmer was a Hereford man: "He is seventy, as strong as a gorilla. His shoulders have humped into a kind of platform for carrying hay to his animals. He has a son who is stone deaf through inattention to his ears in childhood. He had to work in the wet and damp when he should have been in the hands of doctors. There is no farmeress. She went Up Above long since."[3] In her place was Miss Daniels, "a gnomish little woman with gold rings in her ears. Marguerite has taken to her." Others lived at Abermâd farm:

> There are evacuees from Liverpool in the other part of the house. Now that we are here the farmer does not want them. He says they must go to the Mill House and he will put some sticks of furniture into it for them. He says he lives by doing good turns to everyone and he will behave like a true-blue Christian to these blacks. I have

seen some children about who seem to be running away from someone every time I
see them. Miss Daniels says the mother of the children is ill in bed. Who attends to
her? Answer: No one.

Marguerite hears groaning and weeping in the night. She goes to investigate. The
mother has had a miscarriage. The children are scared stiff. The mother sleeps in a
black vest. She has no nightdress. Marguerite finds her a satin one. She puts the little
girl in our bed and we sleep three. The boys shift for themselves.

Now the mother has been carted off to hospital. She will be away for a week at
least. The Mill House is rat-infested and oozes damp. They are to be transferred there
on the mother's return.

The maltreatment of Abermâd's evacuees outraged Caradoc; George Green recalled
the "endless trouble" he took to get the authorities to act against a farmer who was
charging a poor woman, an evacuee, an exorbitant rent for "a damp, ramshackle, rat-
ridden outhouse".[4]

Suddenly the Herefordshire farmer sold Abermâd to a well-to-do woman who gave
the Evanses notice to quit, this at a time when "Aberystwyth was full and everywhere
else was full – not even rooms!" In March 1940 Marguerite advertised for a house,
meanwhile negotiating for the pub at Llanilar three miles away. She had the idea that
Eric Andrews and his wife Louise Smith would live there too, acting as pub managers;
much to Caradoc's annoyance, she had kept on Eric as chauffeur until something more
suitable materialised. "He drives her car but forgets to grease it. He has a meagre body
and the face of a poet. He is no poet. He hardly ever ties his shoelaces or cleans his fin-
gernails.... She [Marguerite] thinks she is responsible for Louise, Eric and the baby.
God knows why."[5] To Caradoc's relief, the pub passed to a bona fide publican and Marguerite's advert drew a response.

A house was for rent at New Cross, a less-than-a-hamlet strung along on the Pontrhydfendigaid road five miles inland from Aberystwyth. Its Welsh name Brynawelon
(Hill of the Breezes) rang warning bells but they agreed to view it. Set on the breast of
a hill, it was a double-fronted, four-bedroom house complete with a stony acre rising
sharply behind. The house stood high above the road, from which steep steps led up to
the front door. Close by, on the seaward side, was Capel Horeb, a Calvinistic Methodist
chapel whose vestry housed the local primary school, and overlooking the chapel, at
the head of a sloping field, was a small inconspicuous burial-ground (Caradoc's "garden
of graves"). Eastward lay a shop cum post office and a pub, the New Cross Inn. Marguerite
fell for Brynawelon at once; it offered six rooms (plus kitchen, bathroom and store-
room), had been thoroughly done up (Triplex range in the kitchen, hot and cold
washbasins in the bedrooms), and had splendid views of the valley and the heads of
Pumlumon to the north. The owner thoroughly agreed (she had been in milk in London);
its situation was grand: "A chapel within a minute and the mountains all in front of you."
"What's that piece of linoleum over the letter-box for?" Caradoc asked. "Oh, just to
keep us nice and cosy in the winter, and the wind is a great rattler. The Book of Malachi
is our Sunday-school lesson this year," she quickly added.[6] The rent was £60 a year –

top price, thought Caradoc, which a Welshman would have bargained over but which Marguerite accepted unquestioningly. In April 1940 they moved into Brynawelon, Caradoc, Marguerite and Nicholas, together with Terrier Jock and a sheepdog pup rescued from Abermâd. The Evanses named him Timber because of his blue-grey timber wolf coat. Another of the litter, a bitch named Taffy would join them later (like Timber, she was prone to dreadful fits.) At Abermâd the farmer bought back Marguerite's ewes in lamb and met the £45 asking price for her maize-painted Vauxhall – "last year's model", Caradoc explained. Petrol rationing had forced its sale and henceforth the family would have to rely on the skeleton public bus service between Pontrhydfendigaid and Aberystwyth. (Caradoc rescued the hand-carved Welsh dragon from the vehicle, the little Welsh mascot he had contemplated taking to prison: "I have a fondness for it.")[7]

Despite their longish stay there, neither Marguerite nor Caradoc much liked Brynawelon. It was damp and bitterly cold in winter when gales rattled the letter-box. Rats came into the house, breeding under the hot water cistern and dying under the boards. Outside, the rocky garden was unproductive – only chives and weeds seem to grow there – but for all these disadvantages the house proved fertile enough when it came to writing. In four-and-a-half years at New Cross, Marguerite's unbounded creativity gave her readers seventeen novels (perhaps not her very best) and a winning autobiography, *Full and Frank*, that – she was thrilled to relate – sold out on publication (in November 1941). Painfully slow by comparison, Caradoc finally published his short-story collection, wrote a novella *Morgan Bible* and some memorable biographical pieces for *Wales* and the *Welsh Review*. (A further batch of stories would be brought together and published a year or so after his death.)

The writer who returned to Wales mostly belonged to the past – "the almost forgotten Caradoc Evans", a *Western Mail* reviewer called him. But "Your Sin Will Find You Out", the story long promised to Keidrych Rhys, had led off the August 1939 issue of *Wales* and from Cardiff Gwyn Jones approached him for permission to include "A Mighty Man in Sion" in *Welsh Short Stories*, a Penguin anthology he was editing. Writing from Brynawelon (3 May 1940), Caradoc gave permission and congratulated Jones on his *Welsh Review*; he thought it "extraordinarily well done" and hoped it was making money. (Sadly, the *Review* had gone under at the end of 1939.) "Famous first words", Jones annotated Caradoc's letter of response. Shortly afterwards he wrote again, this time requesting of Caradoc a brief author-biography for what would be a high-profile Christmas paperback. His great regard for Evans did not curb his editorial instinct; from the notes Evans supplied he omitted altogether "Badly educated at Rhydlewis village school" and substituted a bland "His stories of Welsh rural life resented by some" for Caradoc's "Book *My People* banned by police and burned in many public places." The resentful "some" would stir again when the Penguin volume appeared but in the meantime Jones could report his own appointment as professor of English at Aberystwyth and his imminent arrival in the town. Evans seemed genuinely interested: "I shall be delighted to see you when you come to Aberystwyth," he wrote to Jones (18 July 1940).[8]

Later in the summer the thirty-three-year-old English professor, expert in Old English and Scandinavian literature, hurried to meet a living legend and literary hero. Sarnicol had set up the visit and accompanied Jones out to New Cross. "Always the man for a gesture", Caradoc awaited them outside Brynawelon, at the head of its flight of stone steps:

> [He] gave me a grave Mid-Wales appraisal as I came thrusting up in my spring-heeled South Wales fashion. He was polite, even gracious, but wary. We went into a room whose floor was covered with a dimmed-down, ageing, but entirely sumptuous black Chinese carpet, on whose receptive pile we proceeded to circle each other like a couple of Cardiganshire corgis. Later we adjourned to the field outside, and I had my first sample of his good-humoured, well-paced, and mordantly libellous conversation. Sarnicol, looking very old-world in what used to be called a come-to-Jesus collar and glasses, played the benevolent ringmaster...[9]

A friendship developed from there, sealed (so Gwyn Jones thought) when Caradoc honoured him with his warmest sobriquet, "Old Bloke". Gwyn and Alice his wife would meet the Evanses in town, have tea with them in Brynymor Road (where the Joneses had taken rooms), and in turn journey out for afternoons at Brynawelon. Gwyn remembered particularly a visit of July 1941, "a superb day of sun and breeze... when we lay out in the garden above and behind the house, watching four hares playing near the tree line, while Caradoc discoursed with his impressive voice and enchanting intonation of his days in London". On a walk to Llanilar for dog biscuits, Caradoc extracted from Gwyn what always interested him most: details of the young man's origins and family background. "By dam, you have done well," came the predictably flattering conclusion.

Jones studied Evans minutely; how he stayed silent for long periods without ever seeming absent from the conversation. "He would sit with his head hung forward, his lids drooped like a bird's, and his short black pipe rising and falling like a little boat on his big lower lip, amused and absorbed and awaiting his moment." He arrested attention, through appearance, manner and voice:

> Not only was Caradoc a personality, he looked one. Yet he was not a big man; indeed, his chest was narrow and his shoulders, towards the end of his life at least, somewhat folded. But he had a fine head and his features were unforgettable... He had a long bony peasant's face, with a good strong nose, prominent black nostrils, and thick upstanding grey hair. Eyelids were crinkled and pink, like a parrot's. His mouth was loose and wilful, with a long upper lip after the Irish fashion, and the lower swollen and purple, with a small self-coloured lump on it; and he often carried it pouted outwards. The sides of his jaws were pink, and I never saw him when he did not look newly shaved.

Somewhat dressy himself (his style discreetly flamboyant: baggy plus-fours and horn-rimmed glasses, or military jacket in jungle green), Jones was much taken with Caradoc's get-up – always distinctive, often bizarre:

In the way of hats nothing was too fantastic. Most of them were cut-down women's hats. Once he bought a woman's hat, and in reply to expostulation: "But that's a woman's hat, Caradoc!" he crushed it down over his ears and said bluntly: "Well, it's a man's hat now!" Later he consented to have its brim pruned. It was of fine straw, red green and yellow, and after pruning the very image of a small beehive, but he wore it with Red Indian gravity. Add a green and blue tweed jacket of violent check, a white cricket sweater with red and black club colours round the neck and waist, a navy blue shirt with a sewn-on scarlet collar of Viyella, and a green tie, and you are beginning to get the picture. Add black corduroy trousers, white socks, and sun-smiting polished brown toecaps, and you complete it. I must say, he looked exactly right. Nothing about him but proclaimed with glory: I am Caradoc Evans!

As to Evans's voice, Jones thought it "distinctive and beautiful, slow, rich and musical. His accent was as Welsh as mine, and he had the odd trick of punctuating his talk with a phrase he pronounced two ways: either 'dontcher know' (that is, Mayfair) or 'doant u know' (authentic Rhydlewis)." And "He was a grand talker, especially about people and authors."[10]

For fifty years and more Jones championed Caradoc Evans, in print, on radio and at the podium (as he did other Welsh literary contemporaries, with a vigour and selflessness unusual in the creative artist). Caradoc offered little in return, on the Joneses or anyone else (save in private conversation), though his journal does record one of their afternoon visits:

Gwyn Jones and his wife Alice to tea. I do not think there is any guile in Gwyn. I do not think he would stoop to defraud even the Income Tax. He might be a Samoan. He is a fine chap. I like his smile and I like his teeth and I like his wife. I cannot pick holes in either of them. Alice is pretty. She paints her face. She paints her face richly and lavishly in the style of Evan Walters. She is not afraid of colour. When she is in the bus or in the town she wonders why people stare at her. Is not a picture meant to be stared at? She is quite homely, but I suspect she has a tongue. She has little donkey feet the same size as Marguerite's.

Caradoc's entry captures them well. The moral probity conspicuous in the later Gwyn Jones was evidently present from the start, and from the sentences on Alice one might have guessed that she and Marguerite would become good friends. Tall, stylish, theatrical, with flowing red hair and distinctive wardrobe, Alice Rees Jones took an altogether sharper view of Caradoc than did her husband, but over the next four years the couples regularly entertained each other, Alice becoming Marguerite's confidante as the Evanses' troubles worsened at home.[11]

Marital strife was but a part of this "weird and grotesque household", this "lunatic establishment" set in "the Welsh wilderness". The descriptions are Pauline Bertha Block's, the living-in general maid who came to work at Brynawelon in June 1940. Marguerite was lucky to find her; servants were scarce at this time. She might cope without a chauffeur and car but a housekeeper was essential, a necessity for the industrious, not a luxury of the indolent, for only if unencumbered by housework could she keep up the flow of fiction essential for paying the bills. Paula, as Marguerite called her ("I think it sounded more romantic when she honoured me in some of her romantic stories"), was a German-Jewish refugee, a divorcée who to escape the Nazis had joined her young son Walter in England shortly before the outbreak of war.[12] Walter was at school in Shrewsbury and Paula's brother too had fled Nazi Germany, landing a teaching post in Warwick.[13] Having registered for domestic work at an employment agency (she could think of nothing else), this diminutive thirty-seven-year-old woman found herself "kidnapped as a Maid or Servant in the true sense of the word by this bizarre looking family of three in Aberystwyth... a grey and joyless sea-side place at the time." During her twenty-one months at New Cross (June 1940-February 1942) Paula came to loathe Caradoc Evans, his "warped mentality and sinister traits in his character". Some years later, having trained as a psychiatric nurse, she judged him a "complex-burdened unhappy man... a schizophrenic at large afflicted with paranoid notions and total frustration as an artist and writer. Being the typist of his successful "writer" wife Marguerite, he often scalded her with his sarcastic tongue and she then painfully writhing under these oral lashings paid him back with hysterical outbursts and palled up with me behind his back in our combined fear of and hatred against him."

Judging by Paula's accounts, Evans's behaviour at this time bordered on the criminally insane. She claimed that he secretly opened her letters, denounced her to previous employers and hid away her suitcases to prevent her fleeing the house. His hardly credible accusation was that she had been a prostitute in Germany who had come over to England to spy and to put lighted candles in windows to guide the German bombers.

> One night he dragged me out of bed – because he found a useless little tray-cloth in the garage, which I must have shaken out by mistake while cleaning. He was convinced (or acted so) that it was sabotage and evil intention on my part. In my nervous state I burnt the toast once – he threatened to send it to the Home Secretary Herbert Morrison. He took sadistic pleasure to frighten me out of my wits. He drove his misdeeds so far as to bring me before a political tribunal in Breconshire, identifying me with Nazi activities. I had to pay quite a considerable sum for the car journey which was a blow to my financial state – since I paid nearly every hard earned penny towards my then small son's education.

At the outbreak of war all German nationals living in Britain – Jewish refugees included – were classed as "enemy aliens" and went before hastily convened tribunals to assess any security risk they might pose. Aberystwyth housed one such tribunal but Paula's took place at Brecon. Predictably, she emerged as a "friendly enemy alien" posing "no risk to national security" and placed in Category C.[14] By what steps Evans hastened Paula's appearance at Brecon is unclear, but his mad accusations, his monstrous belief that she was siding with Germany, drove her away in the end:

My friends wrote behind my back to my brother to come to Wales and "rescue" me.
He arrived – big, burly and red-haired and very worried. I am small and was at that
time <u>very</u> thin and brown-haired. What did that amiable man C.E. say? "This man is
a typical Nazi and if he could he would murder innocent English children – besides
he is <u>not</u> your brother but your lover. You do not resemble each other in any way."
After making all sorts of difficulties and intrigues they [the Evanses] released me in
the end from their clutches (servants were hard to come by during wartime –
especially in such an absurd household). Kind-hearted but cowardly Marguerite kissed
me goodbye and <u>both</u> said that I must feel heavenly now to escape from that private
Madhouse (their <u>very</u> words).

Her worried friends were the Adlers, an Aberystwyth Polish-Jewish family who kept a
hairdressing business in Pier Street and with whom she briefly stayed before joining her
brother at Warwick. (She kept in touch with the Adlers, as did Walter her son.)

   Paula fled Brynawelon in February 1942. Shortly before leaving, she began a patchy
diary: scribbled words in German written under candlelight in her bedroom at the close
of her "slave-labour" day (hooting night-owls gave a musical accompaniment). Her entries
covered just the first twelve days of January 1942 and in 1978, at Gwyn Jones's request,
she translated them into English. Her New Year's Day entry is typical (it incorporates
additional comment prompted by having to prepare a translation):

   I did rise at 6.15 a.m. Did dining room fireplace and other morning tasks. Traditional
   English breakfast 8.30 a.m. (Ingredients like bacon and eggs obtained from the black
   market.) Routine morning work. Then a mad rush upstairs to bring Nicky (or <u>Mr</u>
   Nick, as his mother never failed to call him) breakfast in bed. The room, heavily
   draped with dark curtains as safeguards from icy winds and draughts, smelt sour.
   The doting mother arrived in this hothouse of a room to inspect whether son and
   breakfast were alright. He snuggled under his bedclothes like a contented cat slobbering
   her morning milk. Well, he slobbered his porridge. Besides, I think he could not face
   so early in the morning the grimness of his step-father. After the first of the endless
   washings up I began to grapple with my enemies the fireplaces. Admittedly I was a
   hopeless stoker. When Caradoc watched me and poured out his usual diabolical
   morning sermon my spirits were dampened. The flame of anger was aroused but not
   the flame in the fire-place. So he started poking with devilish lust. A bright fire was
   soon crackling. But I thought maliciously that the poker would have been better
   employed to land in one of his ribs. Started cooking on the miserable Calor gas stove.
   After meal and tidying up I scrubbed kitchen floor to the endless music of the rattling
   old typewriter next door. One of the frequent visitors came. I made tea. Found no
   time for washing and changing. Work till 9.30 p.m. Slept badly.[15]

Paula detailed her daily tasks. Besides cooking on the miserable gas stove, she dragged
coal to "my enemies" the various grates, afterwards tending their fires. She did the
family's washing ("big pieces and sheets went to the laundry at Aberystwyth"), the
darning and the mending, and by way of rest polished the endless brass: "Brass was the
foremost obsession in this household." As for the dogs, she loathed "the greedy hounds"

whose "delicious broth" meant boiling sheep heads in hefty pan. ("The sight of their broken dead eyes and protruding teeth made me sick".) De-worming saw excrement spread across the living room floor, "an obnoxious scene in smell and sight", but "to Caradoc's honour... he himself cleaned up the mess". The Evanses indulged the creatures, their high spirits and misbehaviour:

> Marguerite pampered them with sugar and brandy on their "off day". Brandy was a rare commodity in these times of war. Still, cunning people like the Evanses got it, together with the gin or whisky so necessary for Marguerite's insomnia. They got it from a man in Aberystwyth. Caradoc could not say enough bad things about him and labelled him as "a dirty little Jew".

Paula likened Caradoc to Hitler in as much as both "had more regards and love for animals than for humans". Caradoc never listened to music on the radio "– only wartime-news and I think that he secretly indulged in all the reported Nazi cruelties and animosities and brutalities". Hearing of German atrocities in Russia (7 January 1942), he turned on Paula at breakfast: "You all should hang or be shot without exception....Your brother would murder, shoot and torture children to death, if it was in his power. He only came as a spy to England." (Paula glossed this diary entry, mentioning that her brother, a participant in the Kindertransport operation, had risked his life by returning to Germany to rescue Jewish children. (Caradoc himself in his journal recorded the suffering of Paula's father-in-law, thrown by a bunch of Nazis into Lake Constance: "When he came out he was thrown back again. Thus for about twenty times. Then he was put in a cellar and beaten.")[16]

Paula duly appeared in Marguerite's fiction, most notably as "Trudel Losch", a domestic servant in *Meadowsweet* (1942); she is present also in *Full and Frank*, Marguerite's autobiography completed in early 1941 (prior to the Brecon tribunal). Of more help to Paula was the reference Marguerite penned, a single hand-written sheet dated 22 February 1942. She explains that her general maid is leaving at her own request to be near her brother in Warwick. She praises her Continental cooking but admits that, "Domestic work under country conditions is not her strong point." On the other hand, "She could, if necessary, manage a small modern house or flat with town amenities quite well." And there are other possibilities: "In illness she is quite exceptional & would also be well qualified to attend upon an elderly or a sick person." Marguerite cannot speak too highly of her character. The mother of "an admirably brought up little boy", Paula is "absolutely honest & trustworthy. As an individual I have the highest respect for her." The reference was ill received – "as if I would have needed it!!!" and "Very patronising!" are Paula's impulsive annotations. She had done with domestic service. Marguerite's suggestion of nursing, however, might have set her thinking for Paula would spend more than twenty years as a hospital psychiatric nurse. (Her time in a Welsh "private asylum" had provided preliminary training.)

Marguerite's reference was not the last word from Brynawelon. While temporarily lodging with the Adlers, Paula received Marguerite's chatty letter (March? 1942)

explaining that her remaining belongings at New Cross would be parcelled up and
brought by bus to Aberystwyth. She learned that Margaret, her young replacement as
general maid, had settled in nicely: fires caused no trouble ("she understands the flues")
and her cooking was adequate ("the toast beautifully made!!!"). The weather having
improved, Mr Nick had come down from his room and Marguerite would be taking tea
with Mrs Powell at Nanteos and picking snowdrops there. The milder spell might tempt
Dr George Green out to New Cross again – "We miss him so", writes Marguerite.[17]
Then comes a change of tone:

> All is quiet here... but deep down I can hear the volcano rumbling & I can see the
> glow of the fire. But all the same I think it will be better. If it isn't I must be strong
> & not crumple up any more for it is no use living in such unhappiness – why should
> Mr Nick have to suffer & hear his mother insulted for no reason & without cause.

Requesting Paula's Warwick address, Marguerite offers the hand of friendship rather
awkwardly; she knew what Paula had endured at Brynawelon. "The only thing is you
were never suited to domestic service. You couldn't adapt yourself or get with practical
ways, but [Marguerite repeats] as a nurse or companion to someone you would be excellent."

Paula saved the letter but did not answer it. Three months later came a second from
Marguerite (26 May 1942), asking after Paula's news and not holding back on her own.

> Now do you remember when you were here we were going to a solicitor about my
> husband's dreadful unkindness to me, but of course I was weak & didn't, & after that
> when you were going you said that if ever I needed your testimony you would give
> it. Well, I think I have truly made up my mind that it must end or I shall be in my
> grave and it isn't fair on Mr Nick.
>
> Even with this Welsh girl here [Margaret] it is just the same, as you said it would
> be. He can't control himself at all.

Marguerite now asked for this testimony, something for a solicitor setting out Caradoc's
abusive behaviour towards his wife and stepson at Brynawelon: "Say the truth as you
know it & make it very plain." Paula (she imagined) had remained so long with the
Evanses "because your heart was kind & you saw a fellow woman in such mental suffering".
She pleads for a swift response, "by return, Paula, while I am feeling brave".

Again, Paula kept silent. She judged Marguerite "a hysterical and unbalanced woman
with a kindly disposition. But kept in harness and fear by her Husband's (if he ever was
that?) violent and schizophrenic character." She knew the pattern of their behaviour, as
her diary entries reveal (10, 12 January 1942):

> Dreadful domestic scenes. Fortunately I was no way involved this time. M fell while
> she took Timber out on a lead. He strained and toppled her over on the slippery
> garden path. Poor "innocent" – in this case anyway – C was attacked with a deluge
> of abuse and insult. So he put his hat on. (They always put hats on when there was a

quarrel. I did not know what it symbolised at the time but I have my own ideas now.)
So Caradoc disappeared with hat, stick and Timber and did not return for mealtimes.
M threatened to leave him with Nick and all her "other possessions". Nick on his
part opened up the verbal floodgates of his contempt for this "despicable man". He
sharpened his illusory knife to stab Caradoc.

They made up again and went to Aberystwyth in amiable harmony. A conspicuous
threesome in the small town of Aberystwyth. I was left alone to do my usual chores.
In desperation I threw a lump of mutton fat in the fire to bring it alive. Of course it
flared dangerously. Just when the three approached the house up the hill. Marguerite
cried hysterically, "She has set the house on fire." But the fire died down together
with her anxiety.

As anticipated, Marguerite's determination to divorce was short-lived. Her next letter,
dated 5 November 1942 (beginning, "You never write – where are you and what doing?"),
confirmed that the Evanses were still at Brynawelon and that "life has been fairly serene
lately – quiet, more content". However, her point in writing was to ask whether Paula
could possibly stand in for the housemaid Margaret who was due a fortnight's leave
(which she was willing to delay until March or April). Marguerite must have realised
how long a shot this was, as was her additional request for the name of anyone who
might possibly take on Timber. The dog "hates Mr Nick worse than ever & tries to bite
him…. He is a splendid guard." The rest of the letter mixed local gossip with affection
for Paula and no little regret at the way she had suffered under the Evanses. "We liked
you… Paula, although you didn't think so, but oh! It was so tragic when you couldn't
make toast & how you hated the sheepsheads & [skinning] the rabbits!" This time Paula
replied – for which she was heartily thanked with a jar of New Cross honey (10 December
1942). The past was all behind them, so Marguerite hoped, and "Some time when the
war is over we shall meet & you shall come & stay with us as a guest & not as a servant."

Reflecting on her diary in 1978, Paula acknowledged "an unpleasant feeling that I
glorified myself into a martyr":

> In my hopeless, unhappy state of mind I only stressed the bad things. But still there
> were some "Welsh rare and good bits" as well – even at Brynawelon. It is not in my
> character to condemn happenings and human failings outright. I have enough of them
> myself! But at this far off time I felt like a small helpless boat tossed in sea of evil
> and abuse.[18]

Among the rare and possibly good bits might have been a marriage proposal – completely
out of the blue, according to Caradoc's journal: "The servant here, a German Jewess
refugee, went for a walk yesterday and she met a man. The man said to her: 'I have five
cows, seven pigs, and so on. Will you marry me? Let me know next Sunday. You will
know me by my dog.' The suitor was George, who did the garden and odd jobs at Brynawelon. Paula liked him well enough to consider becoming his wife, since Marguerite
records overhearing her in the kitchen accepting what seemed like a marriage proposal.

Marguerite took George aside in the garden: had he asked Paula to marry him? "No fear," he smiled; "Sleep with her I said I would and let her know afterwards. But I like to live by myself. I said in fun, but she is not one for joking at all."[19] Marguerite well understood George's sexual appeal. "His longish hair and end-of-the-week unshaved beard are golden, his eyes are deep blue and his lips are tender and slightly puckish, and they go in and out and you can easily imagine panpipes in his pocket." A year after leaving Brynawelon, Paula received news of "YOUR George" (February 1943). The police had found animal skins buried in his garden and a sheep hanging up in his cottage with some of it cut into joints. "Anyway, he confessed he had stolen it & <u>apparently</u> cut it up & jointed it beautifully with a tiny pen knife & a child's saw – his only implements…. He won't confess to whom he sold his sheep or parts of it." Jailed for illegal butchering, George became a great favourite with the warders, Marguerite later reported (23 September 1943). "He <u>is</u> a nice fellow & if he did kill sheep I am sure he didn't do it for himself!"

"The rattling old typewriter" that Paula had heard on New Year's Day belonged to Marguerite. Of necessity work came first. "Pre-war contracts have been cancelled," Caradoc's journal explains; "Everything has been cut by half, take it or leave it. She does not seem to worry about that. The only thing that worries her is the slaughter of youth." Marguerite had the stricter routine, beginning at nine each morning, while Caradoc began when he felt ready, having collected his newspaper from the post office. He then retired to the long low writing room under the eaves, with its single table and typewriter, his father's framed christening card and a framed portrait of Dickens. "More austere, a man's room", thought Marguerite. She preferred an armchair downstairs (or a deckchair outside in summer) and a writing-pad on her knee. When not engaged on his own work, Caradoc helped with his wife's. He genuinely admired and praised her literary gifts and readily undertook her typing. He could help with little else. His sticking points were words – each weighed for sound and rhythm – whereas Marguerite's free-flowing sentences gave the impression of effortless ease. Her difficulties were with plotting and characters, aspects that troubled him less. But the very act of telling him about them "usually loosened my brain". *Meadowsweet*, the Sandys novel portraying Paula was one of four Marguerite published in 1942. Caradoc too at last had something to show for his years of labour on fairy tales like no others.

Finished in early summer, they came out in December 1942 as the collection *Pilgrims in a Foreign Land* – "folk-tales merging into adult fairy-stories" in the words of the Andrew Dakers blurb. Though his seventeen grim little pieces show the trappings of folk- and fairy-tale (not least some witting, wilful animals: foxes, squirrels, hares and owls), the forces at work in this fantasy world are those habitual in Evans: ruthless physical violence, greed for land and money. Men and women remain at war, the men savage and lustful, god-befuddled, prey to obsessions – and largely ineffectual. The women are more potent, more rounded individually, pragmatic and intuitive, and ready to use their bodies in life-and-death battles with men. The bloody victories are theirs. Adah beheads preacher Pilgrim (who wronged her in the past), Katrin gains her goals (a child and a husbandless farm), and Miss Fach her postmaster and her pig man; she longs for Tim Pigger's death and a return to respectable society (for "the capel never rejects a widow with a full purse").

Chapel nowhere is centre stage though it has shaped mentalities and its shadow darkens lives. In the finest story, "Your Sin Will Find You Out", Adah is broken from chapel first for her behaviour with young Joseph in the cowhouse – "not know did I that she was teaching me bad" – then for committing the "dirty sin" of bringing the law on Joseph, a preacher-to-be. The Big Man himself instructs the lad to pay no maintenance for Bet his little daughter; furthermore, the Big Man grants him straightway the means to flourish as a preacher: his mouth will be filled with bubbles and suds, "the speech of a capel prophet". But one more sin will undo him; his soft "soap religious" will dry and he be "slap-bang[ed] into Hell". For thirty years, Joseph hawks his religious medicine among the "forlorn people on hill tops". He is Pilgrim Whiskers now, on account of his fondness for a particular hymn (it was Caradoc's favourite also), one beginning, "A pilgrim in a foreign land / Both near and far I roam."[20] By chance, Pilgrim comes upon Adah, though they do not recognise one another. She is attempting, "in the heavy heat of a Sunday evening in June", to sharpen the blade of a scythe, her knees clasping the pole. With a joking reference to the grim reaper, he offers to help, easing the task by detaching the blade from the pole – a fatal move. Pilgrim is pleased with his work: "What an edge!… Fit for the crooked man!" He learns that for years Adah and daughter Bet have wandered, chapel outcasts striving for reacceptance, but wherever they rest the chapel finds out their sin "and no rest we have". That is "the law religious", Pilgrim reminds her, quoting Numbers 32:23, "your sin will find you out". Yet with the Big Man's permission – and the whole of Adah's savings – he will wash away her sin. He pictures the Heaven that awaits her:

> No land to plough, no shirt to wet or sweat, no tatoes to blight, no cows to milk on frosty mornings, no shops with short weights, no greedy landlord, no cruel tax-gatherer, no collections on Sundays, no mouthy big heads. Capel is Heaven. A yellow capel is Heaven. The Big Man made colours and he painted Capel Heaven with the brightest yellow and the others he threw into the drab old rainbow.
>   "Alelwia!" cried Adah joyously.

Bet is unconvinced. An old tramp has duped her mother, one with "lazy broad thighs" and "a hairy chest", so she sees as she pulls off his shirt wet with the rain earlier discerned "in the breasts of the far hills". She will dry it by the fire then lie on it in bed, as Adah requests: "A morning comfort is a flesh-warmed shirt." Pilgrim stirs – "A short wench fach you are, but husband high…. Smell you not a man?" Bet ignores him, climbing quietly with his shirt to the loft where she sleeps. Pilgrim's sudden sharp reprimand brings Adah into the room. She has recognised his voice and Pilgrim is on the ladder leading to their daughter's bed. The antiphonal exchange that ends the story has its own grim beauty, Pilgrim and Adah in turn beseeching the Big Man's help, he bowed low in prayer, she astride his shoulders, the blade of her scythe on his neck.

"Your Sin Will Find You Out" has the classic Evans stamp: a striking story, thematically charged, told in stripped-back prose that drives the narrative forward. First to last, it holds the attention and packs an emotional punch. It fittingly opens the collection.[21] The pity is that none of the stories that follow are of comparable quality. The further Evans enters his land of faerie – perilous, primitive and cruel – the more cluttered his narratives become, the more heavily wrought his style. "Changeable as a Woman with Child", by telling its tale more directly, generates more forward momentum and allows some emotional engagement. Katrin, Ianto (an itinerant weaver), and a knowing hare all fight for survival. "I need no man on my farm", says Katrin, and seemingly no hare as well. "A Widow With a Full Purse Needs No Husband" similarly impresses, an Aberystwyth story concerning Miss Fach, courted by a respectable postmaster and the disreputable Tim Pigger. "Cash he has and dirty it is," says the postmaster, dismissive of Tim; "Miss Fach had something to say which she did not say. It was: 'Cash is never dirty.'" Yet she possesses a further dimension, given only to angels and beasts, a gift that ensures her triumph at the story's magical end.

Pilgrims disappointed the critics. R.D. Charques in the *TLS* (5 December 1942) would have spoken for most readers when he welcomed the folk-tale elements garnishing Evans's treatment of his accustomed subject matter and noted instances of verbal dexterity and ghoulish humour. "The effect, for a time, is newly disconcerting and almost piquant, despite the unvarying emphasis upon the sub-human and sinister, and despite a flow of Welsh-English that is almost painful to read. But after the second or third or fourth story the reader had very nearly had his fill." The *Manchester Guardian* (18 December), bewildered by such sentences as "This rib was fingerbreadth and there's bewitchery she was in a miff", found the collection depressing and "very often irritating". Against these, one might quote Frank Swinnerton, fabled bookman and an Evans enthusiast. Reviewing the collection for the *Observer* (27 December), he made *Pilgrims* his book of the week: "seventeen artful, poetic, ruthless episodes... rich in devilish glee. All who are not horrified will rejoice in their malignant beauty."

The *Western Mail* of course was horrified. In a particularly weak review (9 January 1943), "J.P." showed little sign of having read the book. His words echo the *Western Mail* of 1915: "Thousands of Cardiganshire men are risking their all in the war.... Yet this writer, safe from bombs, torpedoes, and shells, can contribute nothing towards Cardiganshire's war effort but these gross libels on his people." His efforts drew a rebuke from Gwyn Jones, "a fellow author" who went to town on the obligations of newspaper critics (14 January): they should think for themselves, not quote from the *Times*; they should attend to the job in hand, not waste two paragraphs out of four in showing "the nobility of their feelings"; "they should certainly read a book before talking about it, [and] they should show a reasonable maturity of mind." J.P. came back (21 January), accusing the professor of lacking "reasonable maturity" in defending a fellow author at the expense of artistic judgement. Evans's book, for all the fine writing, was "a bad job – judged by artistic standards alone – and Mr Gwyn Jones, despite his offended author's pose, should know it."

Marguerite next had her say (29 January). If her husband vilified the Welsh, he himself was Welsh to the bone: "In his heart Caradoc is a flaming Welshman, a Calvinistic Methodist who will never be able to extricate from Calvinism. The roots are too deep. He sets his stories in Wales because he knows Wales, but their appeal is universal." Her intervention let Caradoc clarify his denominational allegiance: "I am a Congregationalist and just as bad as a Methodist." Bad because:

> We chapel-goers... never envy another man's virtue, but always another man's money. We never pray for our own sins, but always for the sins of the man who drinks beer. We know there is no harm in beer, but we are jealous of the pubs because men with theological opinions go there to discuss them. People do not come to chapel because usually the biggest big head is the village Hitler and because they are weary of sermons about the Red Sea, the Prodigal Son, and locusts.[22]

As for the *Western Mail* review, whether J.P. had read the book or not, "the work brewed in him a very bad temper and in that temper he wrote about it and me....You can no more write good stuff in a temper than you can box."

One response to *Pilgrims* barely known in Britain deserves mentioning, a review by Douglas Stewart in the *Bulletin*, the Australian political and cultural weekly. Stewart, a poet and critic, was the paper's literary editor for twenty years and in its literary Red Page (28 April 1943), he applauded the collection's attempt to bring the quality of poetry into prose fiction. Evans had succeeded "partly because he creates a fantasy-world where poetic language is acceptable and also – and more importantly – because underlying his fantasy is the most ruthless realism." Likewise, beneath the comedy tragedy lies; nearly all the humour has bite. Stewart instances the squire in "Do Not Borrow Your Brother's Head", one of the Welsh gentry whose way (Evans writes) is "to slander Wales and her language and her peasants". The squire is a genuinely poetic character, a comic sight getting drunk on horseback, which he does because he knows the consequences of dismounting to drink. He is pictured at Machynlleth,

> on his filly at the door of a tavern, making a thirst with bloaters and quenching it with beer. While at this business the squire never dismounted for the reason that in drink he could not go back, and there was no person who liked him enough to give him a leg-up. He drank himself blind drunk and fell forward on the filly's neck, and he murmured: "Gee-gee, home."

"It is rich, profoundly original writing; and, resembling the universal folk-tale, the stories come far closer to the world of poetry..." Douglas Stewart's high estimate of Evans's later work matches that of another poet, the Irishman Austin Clarke.

One further remark in the *Western Mail* deserves attention since it properly brings to notice the importance of Andrew Dakers. "It is surprising that with the present paper famine it was allowed to be published," J.P. comments. The war affected publishing in unexpected ways. You could sell anything which could be called a book, remembered Leonard Woolf of Hogarth Press. Yet the reading boom could not be fully exploited because shortages of materials restricted edition sizes and the growth in new titles. Under paper rationing (introduced in February 1940) established publishers were allowed a percentage of the amount used by their firms in the twelve months before the outbreak of war. Though active in publishing for years, Dakers had set up his own publishing house as recently as 28 August 1939, having obtained sufficient paper and cloth for a small initial list. "Nothing sensational but good sound stuff," he judged. Actually, he had taken a gamble on one sensational title, a book by Leonardo Blake, an astrologer who foresaw that Hitler would be out of power, and out of life, by the summer of 1940. In a printing of 50,000, *Hitler's Last Year of Power* ("a message of hope for the world") became an immediate bestseller, so removing the danger of rapid extinction from a small new firm.[23]

In the *TLS* (31 October 1942) Dakers laid out his publishing credo. "A publisher's only function is to select books which the public either want or need," and the public would decide whether prosperity or bankruptcy would be the reward. Large "monopolist" publishers posed a danger in wartime through their use of scarce resources on long runs of "entertainment best-sellers" at the expense of their lists of new books – which were becoming increasingly hard to find. The profession at large should aim for the publication of the greatest possible number of titles "in order to keep the stream of English literature in full flood… and so defeat the tendency of war to silence the new voices which its incidence makes vocal."

From his Great Russell Street offices (close to the British Museum) he published fiction and non-fiction, with an emphasis in the latter on Christian approaches to the war and to the world that would follow it. (He was sympathetic also to spiritualism, astrology and the occult.) Perhaps *Give Christ a Chance*, a 1941 title, sums up the bulk of his non-fiction list, which boasted two books by the pacifist and socialist J. Middleton Murry (*Christocracy* and *The Betrayal of Christ by the Churches*) and Vera Brittain's pacifist *Humiliation with Honour*. Dakers too weighed in with *The Big Ben Minute*, his plea for a minute of concerted prayer for victory over "the forces of moral and spiritual decay that even now threaten to destroy our Free World from within".[24]

Among his novelists Jack Lindsay stands out, both his popular historical fiction and his *We Shall Return* (a communist treatment of Dunkirk). Dakers knew Caradoc's work from earlier times at Rich & Cowan and retained his admiration. Even so, *Pilgrims in a Foreign Land* posed real commercial risks. Wartime anthologies of short stories were common enough – here the Anglo-Welsh benefitted greatly – but these were multi-author collections; single-author collections were a tougher proposition and warnings against them were legion. The firm's publicity gave figures for its better sellers and *Pilgrims* is not among them. Dakers nonetheless stuck by Evans and within a matter of months took another slim volume from him. "It pleased me much when, in his last years, he asked me to become his publisher."[25] Evans in turn spoke well of Dakers, a man as important at the end of his career as was Andrew Melrose at the start. At crucial points, in times of war, he found publishers who believed in him.

Brynawelon: The Last Phase

1943-44

With the turn of the year came news of Arthur Machen living in retirement at Amersham and worryingly short of money. As his 80th birthday approached, friends and admirers were invited to a lunch in his honour at which he would be presented with a cheque made up of donations from them all. The event was scheduled for 3 March 1943 (his birthday) at the Hungaria, a fashionable restaurant in Lower Regent Street. Caradoc received an invitation although the last contact between the two of them had been in 1930 when Machen had written admiringly of *Nothing to Pay*, believing it the best thing Evans had done. Rightly he predicted that he would get no reply from "the hên ysbryd drwg y Ceredigion" (the old evil spirit of Ceredigion).[1] Despite his long service to literature, Machen remained outside Welsh literary circles and no Welsh signature endorsed his birthday appeal. Gwyn Jones thought this a pity: "Believe me," he wrote to Colin Summerford, organiser of the appeal, "we are proud of Arthur Machen in Monmouthshire – he is not a prophet unhonoured in his own country".[2] Summerford acknowledged the lack of Welsh signatories, but "The only major Welsh writer who occurred to me was Caradoc Evans and it seemed uncertain that his name would tilt the scales in the right direction among His People."[3] This said, Summerford wanted Caradoc's presence at the lunch, even offering to pay his fare. Unfortunately, wrote Marguerite:

> The truth is he is not half so strong as he would make out & on the one occasion he has been to town since the war he was so knocked up that it just isn't advisable. In normal times the journey by train is long enough but nowadays is almost unbearable. I don't talk to him about his health because he is too nervy but his doctor told me to keep him from all sorts of strain or excitement – and he does get excited being a Welshman![4]

She sent their good wishes to "the grand veteran" and a contribution to his birthday fund. Others generously rallied around, the appeal raising £2,200 – when £1000 would have been good going.

Brynawelon through the winter had remained comparatively calm; "fairly serene", Marguerite called it, and one personal weight had been lifted. She had worried even more over servants since the extension of conscription to women aged between twenty and thirty, who were now required to undertake "war work". In May 1942 her twenty-three-year-old local help Margaret had been duly called up, at which point Marguerite approached Owen Evans, Cardiganshire's Liberal MP, in an effort to get her exempted.

In November she could report success. Her literary work had been deemed important enough in keeping up public spirits for her to carry on employing Margaret ("a good girl & nearly as noisy as the dogs but I like her very much").[5] She blessed her good fortune; Mrs Powell at Nanteos was servantless, and so was Sir George Fosset Roberts nearby. With relief she settled to more writing, as did Caradoc, his short-story collection behind him.

His longer fiction had steadily worsened since *Nothing to Pay*, leaving a sequence of stylistically overwrought novels that for all the onrush of incident remain curiously lifeless. The novella *Morgan Bible*, though airing old obsessions, has a refreshing wit and élan.[6] Completed in a matter of months and published in June 1943, this day-in-the-life (and death) tale has an acutely local setting: New Cross's Capel Horeb becomes the book's Capel Salem and Horeb's nearby chapel house the focus of much of the action. For his titular character Morgan Bible (Bible, for short), Evans summoned up the late nineteenth-century figure of the book-canvasser. Ruthless in pursuit of sales, these crooked, aggressive hawkers of dressed-up family bibles remained in folk memory long after respectable travelling booksellers had displaced them ("Be This Her Memorial" memorably introduced one). Door-to-door bible canvassers were often itinerant preachers or broken-down clergymen brought low by drink or sex. Nathaniel Morgan, we learn from a flashback, originally trained for the ministry but was one of those *Nothing to Pay* college students classed "no preachers and no prayers [but] O-rait with girls in fields". O-rait with Miss Jones in a graveyard, Bible is duly expelled and for thirty-odd years wanders the countryside peddling "religious tea". Arriving at Salem, he swaps his bogus beverage for bibles, in which new line he prospers so successfully as to become "the strong-willed chief big head in whose gift was Salem's prize".

The prize is a £100-per-annum living for Salem's minister and *Morgan Bible* charts the events of the Sunday, "this special Sunday", when three prospective incumbents are called to "preach with a view". It is Sunday 3 September 1939, special in other ways: while the village congregates in chapel, Chamberlain declares war on Germany. It is special too for Bible, the day when the past at last catches up and his coffinless end is foreseen.

Evans and his critics in Wales were (he said) all "creatures of the dark days of Nonconformity". A man of the same generation, Bible has wholly internalised this brand of the faith; above all, a God made in his own image. With his mind the Big Man's mind, what need of Christ or conscience? ("Christian?" Evans once was asked: no, he was a Nonconformist – and better than a Christian.) Directly in touch with this God, obedient to His laws (against drink and "to-doing" on Sundays), Bible is "gloriously certain of a cushion in the middle of Heaven's big seat". On earth a religious man is by definition a chapel stalwart. Sunless, grey-plastered Salem stands against the surrounding mutable world, its own "garden of graves" – blue stones, white marble, shining granite – a reproach to the valley below that forever changes its colour ("like a cheap-jack shirt in boiling water") and shelters a river that "lolls and meanders like a light wife going to visit her sponer on the sly". Even so, Bible advises Bowen B.A, "Religious capellers like to hear of the fleshpot in a sermon" – this the wisdom of one who has lived a life of sexual relish among lusty-pious country folk. His soft, tuneful lowing works a charm on Ester – "she could pass for ten years younger".

Sex and drink are the two great trials facing Salem's men. Vessels of temptation, women are God's way of testing men's hearts. Bible takes strength from biblical misogyny. A woman is "the animal which is the least of one's ribs" and "the bit and rein... keeps a wife from going astray". Evans's later fiction embodies in a universe of its own long-held positions concerning the sexes. His men still trust in language, in its power to deceive and control, while his women are shrewder, keener of eye, more emotionally unfettered. Yet they idolise the unworthy, the men who make them suffer. Miss Lewis's avowals of love are "pagan speeches" to Bible, parrying with religious blather. "Women love the men who hurt them and hate the men who make sacrifices for them," so Caradoc writes in his journal, an extreme expression of acceptance that we fall in love with persons, not with personified virtues.

Lost to human charity and common moral good, Bible looks down on Salem hypocrites; and indeed it seems not quite right to call him hypocritical. More properly he is pharisaical, in his extreme self-righteousness, his obedience to biblical Law, his conviction of a superior religiousness (it leaves him free to marry bigamously and to murder). Yet with regard to money he practices – and believes – what he preaches, unlike "the hypocrites who stand on a money purse and say they stand on dross". For him, "money is the most useful thing to gather on the way to Heaven". If sayings against drink are endless from this "only true-blue at home and abroad", there are likewise no bounds to his praise of money. Money motivates, makes everything right; money makes you holy. Aptly, it is Bible's son who delivers the full-throated "Money is God" sermon at Salem, a flattering endorsement of the wartime profiteering Evans saw around him. "God has made a war that Welsh farmers shall prosper," Gwyn Owen concludes. His words fall on one sceptical listener, the chapel deacon Tomtoot (his "toot-toot!" deriving from Brynawelon's gardener George, for whom it meant "chin up" or "never mind"). Alone among Salem's men, he is cast in a positive light, praised for his industry and go-ahead farming ways in a plain clear prose contrasting with the general idiom of the book. Smitten by Miss Lewis, Tom's cynicism evaporates. For him it must be marriage, and he seeks to win her with words recalling Spurgeon Evans in *Taffy*, one of Caradoc's few true men.

Gwyn Owen's rivals for Salem's pulpit are a sorry flockless pair. Escaped from Aberbedw (Aberystwyth) workhouse, Bowen B.A. cadges weekend board and lodgings in return for a worn-out sermon passable out of town. He has just one, "but one on the lips of a mouther can be stretched and twisted into a life of Sundays". He picks up work others spurn: "baptising or burying merry-begottens, interceding for the dying who had not drunk of the living medicine of the capel, praying and preaching at the funerals of suicides and spinster mothers". Bowen lodges in the reader's mind, as does Ester's run-down farmhouse, and other odd, arresting detail in Evans's gallery of grotesques:

grim-reaping Andrew Coffins with his nose for death; doughy Storess Penlan, who helps lift dead husband Josh – "he had boots on and a silk hat and a greatcoat" – up into the village bus so as not to waste his ticket: "There's sick is the husband-preacher, so travel softly, good you." *Morgan Bible's* realm of fantasy needs a gipsy on the moor, and Lissiann's three-legged fox, who "could run swifter on the leg that was not than on the three that were", captures the essence of fairy-tale. As does Ester's robin with its journeys to Hell, and the barbed little ballad of "a schoolin in spectacles who was killed by a mad wench he had put in the family way. How did the polisses find the murdess? The wench's likeness was on the spectacles."

Among supporting characters the enigmatic Miss Lewis stands out ("her long pale fingers like candles against her cheeks"). She is Bible's young mistress or, as he prefers, his spiritual bride. From his first Christ-like appearance – the Christ of Holman Hunt's *The Light of the World* ("a pack on his back and the light of a bicycle lamp shining on his face") – she adores him. Seeing her standing in white against Salem, "an angel on a tombstone", he senses an agent of destruction. "Life is full of mishaps and the last and worst comes from some true woman." It is Miss Lewis who upends the hearthstone that causes a fire, lit by Bible's discarded wife, to consume his entire life's savings. Henceforth it is death-in-life.

George Green recognised Caradoc's "capacity for pitying the people whom he had hitherto thought fit only to scourge. True, they needed scourging, but they were doing it to themselves throughout their lives." The *Morgan Bible* blurb mentions this quality of pity, discerning a related "grandeur" in the way in which an otherwise despicable man goes to his chosen end because "nothing blackens misfortune like money loss". Bible stands last in a line of Evans protagonists mentally unhinged by greed. They embody his monstrous despair at a world of tragicomic creatures joined in an infinite, futile pursuit – for "Enough money is more than you have."

This late caprice shows Evans close to his best. The sharp vignettes, the wicked humour, the wild prose-poetry, all keep us reading on, more so perhaps than a plot which, pitched in a fantastical mid-world, can accommodate the unlikeliest turns. Bible holds the narrative together, his puppeteer's dexterity, his frightening charm and lustful entanglements, his final psychological breakup. The narrative voice slides in and out his consciousness, mostly to voice the precepts of Capel Salem. Maxims abound, drawn from the stock of "sayings" Evans kept at hand concerning (as ever) money, women, and the Welsh ("A happy Welshman is as rare as a bee in snow", "A melancholy lover commends himself to the Welshwoman", "A Welshman seldom kisses"). That "The Welshman is an inquisitive creature, but he seldom asks direct questions" the dialogue determinedly shows.

Morgan Bible posed yet another publishing challenge. Novellas (like short-story collections) were rarely welcome in the trade and this one covering a day in the life of a Welsh village community was no comforting *Under Milk Wood*. *Morgan Bible* was the work of an author whose glories were well in the past, offered at a time when new Welsh names were gaining attention. Once more, however, Andrew Dakers produced a nicely designed little volume: at just over a hundred pages, it mirrored *Pilgrims in a Foreign Land* in its spacious text setting and two-colour typographical jacket. More than one reviewer commented on the blurb and the phrase "spiritual troglodytes" to describe the characters within. Caradoc too was taken by it; in a presentation copy to Gwyn Jones (dated 28 May 1943) he happily applied it to himself.

Review copies were widely dispatched, one improbably landing on the desk of *Y Faner* (most likely after some spadework by Gwyn Jones who enjoyed good relations with Kate Roberts, the Welsh-language newspaper's part-proprietor). Breaking a rule of not reviewing English-language books, *Y Faner* published a favourable notice by Saunders Lewis (18 June), whom Evans came to know and chat with while living at Abermâd. For Saunders Lewis, Evans was one of those writers (Joyce and Wodehouse were others) seeking to "refresh" the English language; "to create from it a personal, new and particular language, before English can be a means of artistic creation for them". Evans's own artificial language was the basis of all his work, "the language that creates the atmosphere in his novels that builds the special, consistent and detached world to which his characters belong". As a writer he strives to be "hard, manly and severe", though his nature and instincts are otherwise ("his novels are a battle against this"). And if Evans lacked in "broad, balanced humanity", he was a "skilled literary craftsman and frequently a craftsman of genius".[7] The *Western Mail* (5 June) was admiring, almost in spite of itself. "One cannot deny the quality of the prose – economical, taut, a psalmody quality, the psalmody of a Black Mass," and if it could have believed that what Evans was exploring was some universal "mental hinterland… typified in a Welsh community for the sake of verisimilitude", then *Morgan Bible* might have been acceptable. But the blurb gave the lie to this with its talk of "the queer, incredible texture of this branch of the Celtic race". "A museum piece", the paper concluded, though appealing to those with an interest in style.

The *TLS* (19 June) found the "nightmare vision of Wales and the Welsh" difficult to digest: "There is undeniable power of a kind in Mr Caradoc Evans's way of writing, but frankly it is put to repellent use." Its editor-in-waiting was altogether more admiring. This wasn't everyone's book, Alan Pryce-Jones warned *Observer* readers (9 June), "but those who like hate-filled novels will appreciate its violence, and every discriminating reader must admire its technical virtuosity and the acid flashes of humour which burn occasional holes in the dialogue." No contemporary writer resembled Evans, save maybe Ivy Compton-Burnett, "with whose hermetic world of desperate family life his own Welsh people, shut in their chapel communities, discover an unexpected kinship. Like her he creates a life more dreadful than reality, and into his crabbed elliptical prose he breathes a peculiar heat of excitement."

If mornings were for work, afternoons were for walking the dogs and for calling on neighbours, the farmers and their families and others in the community. New Cross farmers ("thinned or bent by their work, like trees the wind has shaped", so Marguerite pictured them) were invariably warm and welcoming, as were the cottagers. Neighbours' doors were always open to one man in particular, the Reverend Tom Beynon, Horeb's notable pastor since 1933. Soon after arriving in New Cross the Evanses struck up a friendship with this Calvinistic Methodist historian and editor of Howell Harris. "I like old Tom," Marguerite has Caradoc say, "He ought to have been a jockey. He can tell me things – not half the things he could tell if he likes to, of course."[8] He fed Caradoc's fascination with Welsh pulpit giants past and present. Following one afternoon tea at Brynawelon, he left behind two of his own published articles; Caradoc found them "full of interest" and wrote to tell Beynon so, waspishly adding "I wish writers in the vernacular were as lucid & economical as you are. Most of them have nothing to say & take too long to say it.... We were all delighted to see you yesterday afternoon. Do come again."[9] The fiercest critic of the religious culture that bred him, Evans never rejected religion as such and regularly joined Beynon at Horeb, apologizing when he couldn't and writing him appreciative notes. "That was a grand sermon you preached yesterday afternoon. It was witty and wise and I hope some of its wisdom will remain in the loft of this barn which is me. I like your story about the miser and a man named George."[10] Villagers remember Caradoc sitting at the back of Horeb, feet up on the pew in front, commenting occasionally on the sermon. The "sermon-taster" loved the stories ministers told to press home their messages, like the one he records in his journal.

> A man named Prys built a chapel in a theological college in North Wales in memory of his wife and among the pictures with which he decorated it is "The Light of the World". The college porter took a short-sighted woman visitor into the chapel. "I suppose that's Mrs Prys," said the woman of "The Light of the World". "No," said the porter. "It's a portrait of her brother." Preacher who told the story said that Jesus is everybody's brother.

He liked Tom Beynon's choice of words: "simple words, that always produced an effect upon him – a tranquillising effect that lasted throughout the evening".[11]

Architecturally Horeb might have been nothing, one of those stark little chapels "scowling over the landscape", as Marguerite put it. Of the Church of England herself, she often attended Horeb with her husband; in hoarse whispers he translated the gist of the sermon as it proceeded. Acoustics were poor – twice Caradoc asked whether anything could be done to improve them – and the chapel freezing in winter, too cold for Marguerite, yet within its walls she confessed, "I drew nearer to God than I had ever been." (And to her intense satisfaction, it was the "white-haired shepherd of Horeb" who would officiate at Caradoc's funeral.)

Marguerite embraced the romantic view of Wales and the Welsh – often to the point of embarrassment. She pondered her deep attachment to a land where "grandeur and beauty are so perfectly blended"; it wasn't the land of her people but a place where she felt she belonged. Sitting in the bus one day, listening to "the babbling of the women with their enormous shopping baskets" and understanding not a word they said, the answer came to her:

> It is because Wales resembles the land of my birth, especially the hill scenery whereon
> my eyes feasted after those bouts of fever, the higher and ever higher mule journey
> ascending the mountain-side, the blessed change of temperature. It was like coming
> from hell's oven to the sweet-cool of heaven. The foreign tongue might be the speech
> of India and the speech of myself with my early playmates – brown-skinned Yaseen
> and Suliman and my pretty ayah Mootima with rings on her toes…[12]

Wales a "sweet-cool heaven"? This in truth was Marguerite's thinking, a woman as ready
to see the good in people as her husband was to deny it. Caradoc confirmed: "She holds
that nothing bad can come out of Wales and that this place in Cardiganshire where we
live is the nearest on earth to God's heaven." He preferred hell's oven London. "God
never meant me to live in the country," a journal entry insists, and as with his wife, his
feelings were rooted in the past, in the green grave of Rhydlewis. His journal again: "I
hate the stillness of the evening. I am afraid of the mountains when the stars are out.
Each evening I sense some impending disaster. Of the seven evenings in the week Saturday
is the most awful. Ever since I can remember I have been afraid of the solemn seriousness
of the Sabbath eve."

Evans's remark about Marguerite and Wales was actually an aside in a *Western Mail*
interview concerning the 1942 National Eisteddfod at Cardigan. Before a University of
Wales Union audience there Gwyn Jones had given "a good rich lecture on the Anglo-
Welsh writers" (or so judged Idris Davies who was present). Jones argued that it was
not the function of literature to show a nationalistic view in all circumstances; the quality
of the literature was the fundamental question. The brutality, the sensuality, in contemporary novels about Wales might stem from the background of their writers. Turning
to Caradoc Evans, Jones cited the Tuberculosis report of 1939, an appalling indictment
of social conditions in rural Wales, more shocking than anything in Evans[13]. Such a
defence of the *enfant terrible* sparked a flare-up. The historian R. T. Jenkins could accept
Evans's factual statements but never his travesty of the Welsh people's language – nothing
like his Welsh-English dialect existed in heaven or on earth. His was the abiding objection
within Welsh-language circles, one made clear by T. Rowland Hughes in a letter to Gwyn
Jones.[14] He had read (in bed) Gwyn's defence of Caradoc in *Life and Letters Today* (September
1942) where his critics, "other than stylistic", were again referred to the 1938 inquiry
into anti-tuberculosis services in Wales and the "frightening report" that followed.
Caradoc Evans made Hughes see red, and:

> I don't think that your argument about the T.B. report is an answer to the critics of
> C.E. Let him write about T.B… or about anything he likes so long as the theme has
> basis in fact & not in his own imaginative malice. Let's take a simple instance. His
> characters refer to God as "the Big Man". I've never met anyone who has heard that
> expression & even the most ignorant of the peasants in Cardiganshire are too well
> grounded in their Bible to use such a pagan phrase. I've often heard "Y Bod Mawr"
> (the Great Being – or the Big Being, as C.E. would probably translate it). This is not
> a question of style, Gwyn, but of moral values & his stories are full of similar instances.
> But if I'm not careful, I shall start quarrelling with you!

The *Western Mail* leader (10 August 1942) took a surprising line: "On the main issue raised at Cardigan, is it not true to say that we Welsh are too sensitive to criticism? If the realists of the new school of writers help to harden us up a little no great harm need be anticipated." Caradoc took heart from this. So-called patriots couldn't stand the truth and "a man who cannot stand the truth is no patriot. He is just a nuisance and a drag on development".[15] His greatest Welshman was Dr Ernest Jones, Cardiganshire's pioneering medical officer of health;

> I cannot trace one piece of reform to the Welsh chapel.... Preachers do not even come near the skirt of the evils that are under their noses – craftiness, hypocrisy, profiteering. For them the supernatural is everything and human charity nothing. What do they preach about? Locusts, the plagues, the Red Sea, the prodigal boy bach, temptashoons. What are the temptashoons? Cinemas, cigarettes, dablen, which is beer. Not a word about farmers' wives who work three times harder than their husbands and for no wage. Not a word about dogs shut in an outhouse from Saturday night till Monday morning without a drink. Not a word about pale weak children who are denied the fruits of the earth by money-grabbing parents.

The blast comes from Evans's *Western Mail* interview (12 August) concerning the Eisteddfod lecture. The reporter found him smoking a pipe in his sparsely decorated writing room correcting final proofs of *Pilgrims in a Foreign Land* – the foreign land was Wales, Caradoc told him, and they the pilgrims. Actually, the words were before the reporter in a typescript specially prepared by Evans for the interview. The published *Western Mail* text heavily censored Caradoc's final sentences (quoted above) but retained his "bit of truth" about Gwyn Jones: "He is miles above the gang of Welsh creative writers; the rest of us do not count." Gwyn was not seduced; in fact he came to doubt that Caradoc ever read a line of any Anglo-Welsh author of the mid-1930s renaissance.

In April 1943, two months before *Morgan Bible*, Marguerite published *No Faint Heart*, a story with a local setting praised in the *Cambrian News* as "reveal[ing] the heart and under-standing of this novelist who is doing so much to cheer and uplift the reading public in these heavy days". A year later the novel's account of appalling Welsh cruelty to sheepdogs made the newspapers. Both she and Caradoc loved dogs, and Caradoc's passing references to the cruelty endured by sheepdogs – dogs hanged or kicked to death, dogs routinely left unfed – hint at a crusading concern of the Evanses. Their own three dogs were pets, not the farm creatures who suffered through the widespread rural belief that hungry dogs worked harder ("Keep your dog's belly empty or he will not work for you"). Many consequently were forced to scavenge on the rotting carcases of sheep. It was a sin, Marguerite is told, to throw bread to a dog – "more patriotic" to soak it for the pigs or the hens; a dog should look for food. Caradoc's journal mentions a woman big in the chapel ("she will weep at the mere hearing of someone's death and her voice is sweet at funeral hymns") who asked a gamekeeper to shoot her dog. He resisted, stressing how fine a dog she possessed. "If you will pay his licence and catch rabbits for to feed him I will keep him." The gamekeeper – out-of-work – killed the dog for nine pence.

Welsh mistreatment of farm dogs features early in *No Faint Heart*. Mrs Trueblue, a widow with a step-daughter and a servant helping her run her farm, sounds off willingly on dogs – "only good to help with sheep and cattle and to frighten tramps from the house". She understands that in England a great deal of fuss is made of them, "but in Wales we keep them in their place and if one comes over the doorstep he will get a hiding he won't forget"; "Dogs are no use unless you treat them hard." The novel tells that, "Lots of people still hang dogs in Wales when they don't want them. Or else they drown them. Shoot them sometimes – not often. A shot costs something and a sack is worth sixpence. A rope can be used again." This is just and proper, thinks Mrs Trueblue: "They hang men not wanted. What is good enough for a man is good enough for a dog." She strangles a dog of her own for stealing eggs – Timber, Marguerite names him; chained when not working, he could not hunt for rabbits.

No Faint Heart set off a lengthy *Western Mail* exchange begun by the secretary of the National Canine Defence League (a Welshman, as it happened). Skin-and-bone farm dogs suffered horrendously, being commonly drowned, in some parts hanged, when their working days were over (*Under Milk Wood's* Mr Ogmore remained "a proper gentleman even though he hanged his collie").[16] Marguerite contributed twice.[17] The sheepdog was simply there to work for nothing, and to work until he dies ("fortunately his life is not a very long one"). The remedy lay with the chapel, since "The Welsh farmer is not cruel; he is kindly, and if it came from his religious counsellor that his dog needs at least one good meal a day and a place on the hearth with the family on cold wintry nights, he would have a much happier dog and a more valuable dog." Caradoc refrained from writing. Instead he campaigned locally on behalf of one suffering sheepdog and continued his clandestine war against barbarous gin traps, rooting them out whenever he found them.

Neighbours thought the Evanses sentimental and irrational over dogs and their own three cosseted pets were the cause of local conflict. Three months after Paula Block left, Marguerite told her:

> Taffy went off the other day with Timber & Jock worrying sheep & lambs & we had the police here warning us they mustn't be loose. Three days after, they got loose again & two awful farmers came running with guns & said they were going to shoot them then & there. They were very excited. In the end they calmed down & went off but ever since the dogs must be on chains all day. It seems hardly worth being alive for the poor things.[18]

Caradoc held that sheep "ran like loonies for nothing at all, even without being chased", but both Timber and Taffy were unpredictable and Timber could be dangerous. Marguerite tried to find a new home for him as his hatred of Nick increased, while "poor darling Taffy" suffered a string of fits (eight in two days) that led to his death. Caradoc's journal elaborates: "I took the bus and I took Taffy with me and I patted and talked to him and Judas was my brother." A 2s 6d payment at the police station ensured that Taffy was "properly done in": "He curled up and went to sleep."[19] Timber remained a liability, attacking at will and biting Caradoc severely enough for the wound to need days of dressing by the district nurse. ("Dog eats dog!" Paula glossed the incident.) Caradoc took the blame. "I came between the dog and his bone; that was why he bit me; and I was in the wrong. When I show him my dressed wound he is very contrite and holds up his front paws." Timber remained at Marguerite's side after Caradoc's death. She watched him lying on the divan in "doggy relax", on his back with four paws in the air showing his white snow-leopardy "underneaths". "The divan is spread with a lovely hand-embroidered coverlet" – a present from George Green – "and Timber's naughty head rests on a snow leopard cushion, which matches his underneaths and completes the picture. What a pet is Timber!"[20] A dog man himself, Gwyn Jones mused more than once on Timber, "that treacherous, hysterical, lynx-coated, easily hated but much to be pitied dog of theirs, on whom they lavished such destructive affection – a special line of Marguerite's".[21]

Caradoc's journal, intermittently kept between 1939 and 1944, was (said Marguerite) "the only fragment of his personal life as recorded by himself" and concerned "people and events of the moment". It offers nothing on Evans's writings (no mention of *Morgan Bible*) and little of an intimate personal nature. He prefers looking outwards, often to indulge his *Who's Who*-listed pastime of "beholding the mote that is in my brother's eye". Inevitably the war intrudes. However distant it may have sounded in Cardiganshire, where Aberystwyth was much as in peace time (save for billeted military trainees and the many evacuees), the war impinged on the Evanses. Enemy bombing indirectly took Marguerite's mother's life when her Brighton home was destroyed – she suddenly died four weeks later – and for all the neighbourly assurances that New Cross was safe, Hitler having been a student at Aberystwyth,[22] the first bombs dropped on the county fell uncomfortably close to Brynawelon. Late on 16 August 1940 three were off-loaded two fields away from the house, New Cross being on the German flight path between northern France and Liverpool, Manchester and Chester. The story went around that Hitler was trying to make friends with Wales by attempting to bomb the man who lived at Brynawelon.

Lads in uniform were honoured at Horeb. Before he joined the RAF, Dilwyn Williams brought milk to Brynawelon and ran errands in Aberystwyth for the Evanses. Home on leave, he received a money gift at a concert in the chapel. Evans knew his family and that his father Tom, a roadman, had been badly gassed in the 1914-18 war but received no pension because his disability developed only after his discharge. Though illness had for years prevented him from working on the roads, "a kindly council" went on paying him. Dilwyn's mother did the work, selling her produce in town – "vegetables, flowers, chickens". Richard James, another airman, endured a celebratory evening at Horeb: hymns and songs from soloists and choir and speeches from just about every man present. "The champion praying man made the presentation speech, in the course of which he pretended to hand over the gift and then drew it back several times. This made the airman feel small, having to put out his hands and then draw them back; so when the gift was really made it was several seconds before he accepted it." A lieutenant in the

Fleet Air Arm, Richard James would lose his life when the *Empress of Canada* was torpedoed off the coast of Ghana in March 1943. He was twenty-three. (A Horeb commemorative plaque now sits in the graveyard above.)

Farmers who had served on the Western Front in World War I were determined that their sons should not be conscripted, and if we are to believe Caradoc, there were just two serving soldiers in the neighbourhood. "Small farms with no more than ten to fourteen acres of land find they have work for two or three sons," although before the war these sons worked away, the farmer worked for someone else and his wife kept the place going. "But who am I to write this, for if I had one son, two sons or three sons I might do the same." Marguerite was equally determined that Nick's call up be blocked. From an old army family herself and personally drawn to military men, she was utterly opposed to the war.

Evans had no cause to hold back against farmers on another wartime issue. As the editor of a penny weekly he had thundered against overpricing during World War I and once more is eloquent on the endemic profiteering around him. "In all wars the idealist fights for an imagined golden land, while the practical man gathers a golden harvest at home," he jotted down at the time. Practical farmers can't stop making money on a thriving black-market, notably in butter ("tons of butter"), eggs and rabbits. "Kind as the State is to farmers, the farmers are kinder to themselves. They charge anything for their produce." He pictures them driving to chapel on Sundays in newly bought cars ("they get petrol somehow"), "even if chapel is only half a mile distant", and thanking God for extra profits at week-night prayer meetings. Yet they run risks in charging sixpence for a cabbage (as heartless as its seller): "They are driving people to tinned vegetables and after the war they will find that people like tinned vegetables better than fresh."

Despite these accusations, and his campaigns against gin-traps and the ill-treatment of dogs, Evans readily made friends with neighbouring farmers, even lending a hand at haymaking. George Green singled out one incident as typical of the man:

> He knew that I kept a stock of flints for my lighter. In the early days of war these became very difficult to buy. Caradoc was worried because a farmer of New Cross could not get any. The man, he explained to me, used to work in the fields away from his house and liked to smoke now and then. But the man could buy neither matches nor flints. Caradoc came into Aberystwyth specially to ask me if I could spare him some, and bring them with me next time I came to Brynawelon. He would not take them himself: the gift was to be mine. I was to make it myself. In the evening we went over to the farm together, taking the farmer enough flints to last him for the next three months. Caradoc was probably the most delighted of the three of us.[23]

Writing to Paula Block in February 1949, Marguerite brought up "those sad, dreadful days when we thought you were for Germany (Mr Evans especially)". She attributed her husband's demented behaviour to the emotional stresses of war: "I am sure the war broke his health & his brain," she lamented. Nowhere was a broken brain more evident than in Evans's spy and fifth-column obsessions. The journal speaks of spy stories abroad in Aberystwyth – five spies photographing a mansion, German parachutists landing a hundred miles away – and New Cross Inn was a seat of rumours. "You get as much first-hand information that it might be the drinking place of the High Commands of England, France, and Germany." Doubtless there he mentioned the moving lights he had seen in the direction of Devil's Bridge. He tracked them with a telescope and reported them to the police but the officer at Devil's Bridge was sure that no one in the vicinity would signal to the Germans. "It has not yet occurred to the police that a fifth columnist might have come into the neighbourhood. Anyway we have had a raider over us almost every night with two exceptions, since that night."

Marguerite came to see herself as a war widow in all but name; Caradoc's trouble might have been his heart but his conduct during the war surely hastened his end. He hung on every news report, crouching over the radio often up till midnight. It was as if he wished to get into the wireless set and be nearer the core of the truth. His face was a barometer for war news, "the little vein in [his] temple throbbing with excess of emotion". Proudly patriotic, sceptical of pacifists, angry at those who might undermine national morale, he found Churchill's speeches matchlessly uplifting: "We like him because he casts out devils with energy and vigour. We like him for his sound English; every Welshman knows good English and likes it. When an eloquential preacher denounces sinners we are glad we are not sinners. When Winston Churchill denounces Germans we are glad we are not Germans. Faint hearts he strengthens and the timid man he makes into a warrior." George Green confirmed this esteem:

> For an hour or so before Mr Churchill spoke, Caradoc would be examining his wireless set, to see that everything was in order, and checking his watch, to be certain that he would miss nothing. From the beginning to the end of the speech Caradoc would sit absorbed. "Didn't he do that well?" he would ask at the end. He would go on talking for the rest of the evening about the Premier's choice of words – simple words, but exactly right. He would talk of the way the speech, apparently extempore and casual, was skilfully built up from its beginning to the peroration. He would discuss its effect upon listeners.

Green naturally drew parallels with Evans's own way with words, how hard he worked on every sentence he wrote. "He could, of course, on occasion say what he had to say in clear, simple English, in which only now and then an unusual construction appeared" – as the journal demonstrates.

At a practical level Evans threw himself into local authority salvage schemes (one plank in "the People's War"). Marguerite saw him nearly killing himself carrying heavy sacks of tins half a mile to the dump – all to no avail since no lorry ever carted the tins away. She pointed out the public's indifference: who else collected the tins and bones and other things the authorities asked them to save? He would not be deflected: "It's my bit, you see. I'll have done all I can." Salvage and thrift must combat waste. Evans's fury heightened at the sight of "waste", the luxuries, the unnecessary goods, shipped from overseas at a hellish risk to lives. "On sale in the shops I have seen toilet-paper costing 3s. 2d. a packet and made in New York. Women buy it. How many sailors and how many ships is a packet of toilet-paper worth?" Evans upbraided Marguerite over her American toothbrush; for months the very sight of it upset him, inducing feelings of war-guilt in her over a purchase carelessly made.[24]

The Evanses while at New Cross enjoyed the company of friends, one or two like George Green and Sarnicol dating back to their Aberystwyth years. Marguerite's social energy brought others into their circle, including some notable women: Margaret Powell, elderly chatelaine of Nanteos; Katherine Guthkelch, long-time warden of Alexandra Hall (the university women's hostel); Ethel Commander, with a background in Birmingham repertory; and staunch friend Ingeborg Flügel, wife of John Carl (Jack) Flügel, psychologist at University College London but war-exiled in Aberystwyth. Living at the time at Aberdyfi, Berta Ruck, a popular novelist with a Welsh-speaking grandmother, wrote to Brynawelon having read Marguerite's *Full and Frank*. She was struck by the similarities in their backgrounds. She too had been born in India of a military family, her father Captain Ruck described as "dark, distant and religious". After school in Wales came the Slade School of Art, then Fleet Street and beginnings in fiction, before her marriage to volatile literary man, the novelist Oliver Onions. Ruck left vivid impressions of the Evanses, "this most violently contrasted couple" from utterly different stock:[25]

> Their looks, to start with! He, with that face of an extraordinarily clever peasant. That lanky, loose-limbed figure on which he seemed to be wearing tramp's clothes – it was probably the way he'd *thrown* them on that gave them that effect. (A thoroughly-washed and clean-shaven tramp, which made it all the more odd).... And unpredictably emanating from all this, was the aura of *charm*. He'd that in common with his wife: both, too, had an individuality that would make strangers look twice, and ask "Who are they?"
>
> She, so *soignée*, with a faint aftermath of stage in make-up and dress. I can see it now, the little shallow black hat set on her silver-gilt hair (never tinted), her veil of big black spots thrown back from her pretty, retroussé face, the great brown appealing eyes, the full figure tapering down to her tiny feet – her small hands loaded with heavy exotic rings.

Berta lived too far away to join the group who regularly visited Brynawelon. The Flügels came more than once, as did the young historian Dr Frank Lewis. A brilliant Aberystwyth student, he recalled the first time he saw Caradoc, in summer 1932, "oblivious to the heat and the holiday makers... placidly expending his odd coppers upon the few tawdry, antiquated, automatic machines" on Aberystwyth Pier. With an MA behind him, Lewis proceeded to Oxford where within a couple of years he completed a doctoral thesis on the German church, 1225-75. He published a little in the late 1930s before suffering a chronic breakdown that left him mentally "in and out" for the rest of his life. During the war years Lewis visited the Evanses as often as he could. He found it a relief to leave the "crowded, complaining bus" at New Cross, walk a few paces in

the cold, silent darkness, then climb excitedly the "quaintly precipitous steps" of Brynawelon: one passed from "the ordinary workaday world into an enchanted room, lighted
just sufficiently by an oil lamp or two, where there was always an atmosphere of permanent
goodwill towards men."[26]

Anita Davies, a Rhydlewis girl studying at Aberystwyth, echoed his delight. Following
Marguerite's initial invitation, she visited the house either with Henry Bird in his car
(he lectured in art), or alone by bus. Marguerite liked her to make a day of it: the Lloyd
Jones bus left Aberystwyth station at 11.30 a.m. and there were buses back at 6 and 8
p.m. At Caradoc's request she played Welsh folksongs on the piano; he had known her
pianist-mother and guessed that Anita might play.[27] Brynawelon appeared "very glamorous",
full of Marguerite's antiques and religious bric-a-brac, the Buddhas and Madonnas on
tables and shelves. As for Marguerite herself, Anita confirms what struck others: the
heavy makeup (raddled cheeks, "lipstick all over the place") and legs too thin for her
body. But she was a wonderful host and it was great fun being there. She would not
forget the notice on the gate of Brynawelon inviting tramps to go to the back door and
get their pipe filled. Inevitably, Anita landed in Marguerite's fiction: she is Neeta, the
heroine of Barcynska's *Love Never Dies* (1943), where she is physically described and
given a character to live up to. The young undergraduate caught Nick's eye and the two
became friendly, so much so that through the post at College she received a proposal
of marriage – in the form of heart-shaped card with space for an answer, Yes or No.[28]
(She wisely wrote "No".)

Anita ran into one or two of the university staff at the Evanses, including George
Green, Professor Flügel and the soon to be knighted Cyril Burt. In company Caradoc
was congenial; "a great encourager, a concentrated and smiling listener, an enthusiastic
nodder and agree-er," according to Glyn Jones. Slowly he would be enticed to speak
about himself, largely through reminiscences of personalities he'd encountered during
twenty-five years in journalism: Arthur Machen, Norman Douglas, T.P. O'Connor, W.H.
Davies, Mary Webb. Fleet Street was always with him. After all, it had taken an ill-
educated shop assistant struggling with English at night school and put him in two
editorial chairs. He missed the company of like-minded men and the life of the pubs
where they gathered. He longed for "the Mile End Road on a Saturday night", Marguerite
told Herbert M. Vaughan, author of *The South Wales Squires* and another friend of the
Evanses; "Not knowing that part of the world I can't explain why!" she added.[29] A man
of private means, Vaughan devoted himself to historical and literary pursuits but, as
Frank Lewis pointed out, guests at Brynawelon were of all social and educational classes.
The protector of tramps and stray dogs remained "uninfluenced by fame or intellectual
attainments in his choice of friends".

It is Evans's nearest neighbours, not the distinguished visitors, who people his
journal: the next door conscientious objector seen "praying by the roadside or in a lonely
place"; cat-loving Mary Evans who lived with the mysterious Miss Arnold (Mary's "face
is olived and for its extraordinary nobility might have been made in Egypt); John
Umberella [sic] with his map of France marked where he might have been wounded;

gardener George ("toot-toot!") who proposed to Paula. Evans takes us to New Cross Inn for the business of buying a pint:

> Mrs Pugh who keeps the pub brings you your beer, takes your money, finds the key of her cash drawer, unlocks it, gives you the change, locks the drawer, and hides the key. Buying a beer is a big ceremony. By the time she has locked the drawer you call for more beer. Mrs. Pugh is aged 83. Yesterday she spent in bed, very weak and without appetite. The weakness must have come upon her suddenly. One day last week she was giving me her views on Capel Horeb and some of Horeb's members, especially Horeb's big heads. She hates Horeb. "Church am I, Mr Evans bach. Capel and beer do not mix."

We get snippets of country wisdom, mention of phantom funerals, of witches and the "spelling" of cattle, the folk beliefs and superstitions widespread then in Cardiganshire. Above all, there are gossipy tales picked up at the post office or on afternoon walks, stories concerning neighbours which often mirror the fiction. The reports of family feuding and conflicts over money might be seeds of a full-fledged Evans story: they prompt touches of his fictional idiom ("What blacks to defame my perished mam for a cheat"). Tramps make for two compelling tales. Common enough in the countryside, where they were thought to be shell-shocked casualties of the Western Front, tramps might be given temporary farm work. They usually left without warning, often in the early hours. One memorable pub encounter, previously assigned to the 1940s, actually belongs to an earlier period. Evans had finished a pint in a Carmarthenshire pub:

> As I was preparing to depart, the bright-eyed, skinnish, yellow-faced woman of the place said to me: "Come to the cellar and I'll show you where my dog died. Oh, he was a fighter." She lit a candle and I followed her. In the grey-hued cellar she said: "We found the old dog here on the morning of my husband's funeral. Dead. There was one wreath too many for my husband's coffin and so I laid it on the body of my dog. ""And", I asked, "whose wreath was that you cast away so lightly?" She answered: "Mine."[30]

We know from Paula Block that Evans's behaviour in company, his courtesy, gentleness and humour, hid a darker side: he could be mocking and casually cruel. Thus beside the kindly journal entry on Dilwyn Williams and family we have his teasing of John Umberella,[31] shot in the leg while fighting in France. The ribbing becomes excessive:

> Three days ago I told him that Hitler had a book with the name of every Cardiganshire soldier who fought in the last war and his name was in that book, "and when a parachutist lands at New Cross, John, he will look for you and shoot you first." That dreadful fear you see in the face of an ox on the way to the slaughter-house came into his face and immediately I felt sorry for my callousness and I was only joking.

Marguerite suffered similarly over Taffy when Caradoc without her knowledge had the dog put down. He regularly rebuked Marguerite for forgetting Taffy's worm pills whenever she went to Aberystwyth ("being a sentimentalist she cannot bear the idea of the aftermath"). Returning from town without Taffy, Caradoc explained what he had done, adding that Taffy might never have been seized with fits had Marguerite remembered the worm pills. "I am sorry I said this for I am not sure it was worms at all. He was a highly nervous dog who could not pass a car in the road without crouching in the ditch and quivering until it had gone by.... His fit trouble might have been caused by his nervous state. I have since told her this but I cannot remove the doubt I have sown. So she continues to reproach herself."

In 1944, the last full year of his life, Caradoc appeared in print again in two improbable places: *Wales* and the *Welsh Review* – both had gone under in 1939 but were now back in business. Gwyn Jones foresaw no shortage of material for either of them ("There's a positive mushroom field of contributors, and I don't doubt successive harvests from under the soil," he told Keidrych Rhys).[32] In 1943 both editors were picking in the mushroom field and while Gwyn Jones vacillated over relaunching his *Welsh Review*, Caradoc gave Keidrych Rhys a fine slice of autobiography, a "Self-Portrait" memorably outlining his pre-Fleet Street years.[33] It begins with three caustic etchings, two of his village schoolmasters and a fuller one of "Hitler's schoolin", David Adams. A belated heartfelt tribute balances these, that to Duncan Davies: "He showed me the London he loved and seemed to be part of; and there was born in me a deep and abiding love of London." In the course of a constant companionship Davies became Evans's guide and counsellor, and "what schoolins failed to do this young shop assistant from Lampeter did: educate me." It was Davies who, looking over Caradoc's fledgling Cockney stories, put him on the proper path: "You don't know what you're writing about. Tell stories about the people you know – the Welsh." A reflection on thirty years of writing about people known, the closing words of "Self-Portrait" sound the note of epitaph:

> Cant and humbug and hypocrisy and capel belong to Wales and no one writing about Wales can dodge them. I do not think my stuff has done Wales any good. It is not in me to do that. It is not in anyone.

One point about "Self-Portrait" as it appeared in *Wales* (March 1944): although David Adams is clearly alluded to, he here becomes "Davydd Thomas". Keidrych Rhys explained that "*Wales* was printed by the *Western Mail* when I lived near Carmarthen & the national daily took far too much interest in my proofs." To obviate any charge of libel, "The man's name was changed twice (at least) by telegram!"[34] (Evans in the past had openly expressed his strong dislike of Adams and the "Self-Portrait" printed two years later in Marguerite's biography of her husband names "Davydd Adams" outright.) The *South Wales Evening Post* (18 March 1944) picked up on Evans's piece: "His self-portrait... is brilliant and pitiless; he spares himself no more than his race," but "wherever Mr Evans says Wales, please read Cardiganshire". In *Reynolds's Newspaper* David Raymond addressed Caradoc's conclusion. He agreed that his "stuff" had done Wales no good, a consequence of his incompleteness as an artist; Evans was "too blinded by bitterness to see that human nature has more than one side". (It was Raymond incidentally who passed on the story of Caradoc's intervention in a Welsh Parliamentary by-election: how he turned up uninvited to support the Labour candidate much to the consternation of his agent. "The slightest whisper about the place that Caradoc was supporting the Labour man would have ruined the poor fellow's chances far more than if he had blasphemed in public on Sunday.")

By happy chance, Duncan Davies saw "Self-Portrait" in *Wales* and was delighted that Caradoc had not forgotten him.[35] "I had known Caradoc since 1899, and for several years I was in <u>daily</u> contact with him," he wrote to Marguerite soon after Caradoc's death. Davies had taken up the cudgels on Caradoc's behalf over *Pilgrims in a Foreign Land* and written again to the *Western Mail* (1 July 1943) urging that Caradoc's name be put forward for an honorary degree of the University of Wales. He provided his own commendation: "Apart from the literary merits of his books, which are beyond dispute, Caradoc Evans has done his fellow countrymen permanent service by his Voltairean castigation of the crude and vulgar anthropomorphism which has passed for religion in Wales for so many centuries."

Gwyn Jones much wanted Caradoc in his revived *Welsh Review's* first number; what he had in mind was a series (headed "Men and Women") in which Caradoc would write on those characters, the writers and journalists, he so often talked about. No less revealing of himself, the articles would be a way of coaxing some kind of autobiography out of him. On 3 January 1944 Evans submitted "the dope", an expanded piece on Mary Webb that duly appeared in the *Review's* opening issue (March 1944). Gwyn noted Caradoc's menacing rubric: "To the Printer. Do not alter anything in this article," "Printer" being a tactful spelling of "Editor". This editor had no wish to disobey. Evans's manuscript showed "his never-ending fight for perfection, and after one experiment I never again sent him a page-proof. He was indefatigable at winnowing, and could say as much in a sentence or two as any man since Swift."[36] Quirky, penetrating, spiced with the striking phrase and, as always, self-revelatory, Caradoc's "Mary Webb" dazzled Idris Davies. He had read "Self-Portrait" as well. "How fortunate both you and Keidrych Rhys are to get the great Caradoc to write such prose for you," he complimented Gwyn Jones (20 March 1944); "And what extraordinary prose it is…. Perhaps it would be very risky (for I remember I write to a Professor of English) to call it the greatest prose in English literature, but it certainly is different from any other kind of English prose I know."[37] Evans's article told Reginald Moore, founder-editor of *Modern Reading* (a short-story magazine), a lot about Mary Webb that he would never have guessed and would, he anticipated, lead to a closer study of her novels (16 March 44). Wyndham Lewis sincerely hoped not: "old Caradoc's curious urge for that dreary Webb woman" surprised him; "Baldwin ran her, which would damn anybody for a start!" (18 March).

Evans's second essay (on W.H. Davies) was the first thing Idris Davies read in the September issue, "and it could not possibly be better. O the cracking Caradoc!" he enthused (10 September 1944). Caradoc next lined up T.P. O'Connor, the veteran Irish parliamentarian who had given him his last and best job in Fleet Street. He was working on this third piece when he died.

"The Earth Gives All and Takes All"

1944-45

C aradoc's health had long been a worry but damp, draughty Brynawelon took a toll on all the family. "Caradoc has been ill almost all winter and on with an unshakeable cold. I don't think Wales agrees with him," Marguerite wrote to Herbert M. Vaughan (10 June 1942), three days after she apologised to Tom Beynon for having missed Sunday chapel – she'd "caught a chill and couldn't attend". In February 1943 influenza put her in bed for a fortnight, at a time when Nick was succumbing to asthma and Caradoc's health would keep him away from Arthur Machen's birthday lunch. In September she reported that "Mr Nick is having his usual dreadful colds",[1] a condition that worsened when winter came and "Hill of the Breezes" more than lived up to its name: "The biting and cutting Welsh wind off the mountains howled its eerie hunting song for days and nights on end."[2] She shivered through one November chapel service: Caradoc had enjoyed the sermon (despite Horeb's poor acoustic) and her complaint was only of the cold – it would mean little chapel for her during winter.[3]

December 1943 saw Caradoc in hospital; he had developed pneumonia. Simultaneously Marguerite had influenza ("feeling fairly unutterable – sick, no taste, no smell, palpitations & what not"), though she seemed more anxious about Nick and how he would cope if matters worsened. She conveyed her concerns to Alice Jones and was heartened by the response: on Sunday 5 December she thanked Alice for her assurance that if anything went wrong the Joneses would "sister & brother" him. News of Caradoc was better. Anxious to return to writing, he was asking for drafts of a story to be brought to the hospital (along with *The Times* and *Western Mail*). His condition had sufficiently improved for him to be home in a day or two – a comforting thought, even if she feared he would return the same intractable patient. His pneumonia was the consequence of ignoring medical instructions that he stay in bed for twenty-four hours with a fire in his room. The need to be careful with fuel meant no fire in the living-room below – where the wireless was fixed. Marguerite stayed at his bedside, talking and reading to him. But:

> Caradoc was restless. At midnight he suddenly made up his mind he must hear the news. I begged him not to go. I tried to stop him. That annoyed him. There was a big battle on, and he could not wait for the newspaper. Wilfully he refused to put his dressing-gown on. He hated being fussed. "My cold's gone. And I'm as warm as toast," he said. In a quarter of an hour he came back. "No news. It's just the same. I'm as cold as stone," he announced.[4]

For tuppence, he would have gone out into the chilly night, so she told the Joneses (5 December):

> In fact he threatened to do so. He will sit in his room & write in an icy temp. with the <u>stove out</u> & <u>the window wide</u>. When he gets back [from hospital] do write him a letter of good counsel to <u>take care of himself</u>. In wet or cold weather he'll go out minus coat or mack, walk miles & come back drenched – or, have a hot bath & go out afterwards! Such is my violent, beloved, never-quite-out-of-the-nursery Caradoc.

Home from hospital, Evans straightway wrote to Tom Beynon explaining his absence from Sunday service at Horeb. Arriving at the house to greet him, Beynon failed to get past Margaret the maid; her orders were that Mr Evans must be shielded from all visitors. But the Reverend Beynon was an exception – next time "just walk in without knocking", Marguerite urged him.[5]

"Mr Caradoc Evans, the Welsh novelist, who had been suffering from pneumonia, is now convalescent," reported the *Times* (16 December 1943). And so he was – for a week. The regime mapped out was "early to bed, breakfast in bed, gentle exercise, feet up and cushions", all in accordance with the hospital's insistence that what he needed most was peace and quiet for a good long while. Caradoc saw things differently: "Peace and quiet? To hell with all this fuss. I'm not in the grave yet. I'll have all the peace and quiet I want there.... I'm going out for a walk down Penywern."[6] Penywern hill (as Marguerite explained) was the "long grinding gradient" beyond New Cross that Caradoc tried to tackle again, as he had done on his "long tramps across country whatever the weather for a Sunday newspaper". Mist and rain he welcomed as the best weather for walking, but the odds were now against him and inevitably setbacks followed. "To say the truth it has been a rotten time for both Caradoc & Nick," Marguerite wrote again to the Joneses (27 February 1944); "The pneumonia has left Caradoc very groggy & he will have to go slow until the fine weather comes – doesn't walk or talk much. It takes too much out of him. And Nick has had bronchitis." When everyone was fitter, and the weather brighter, they could all meet up again. "When you see Caradoc either of you don't talk much about his health. I think he worries rather because he feels so weak & his heart troubles him. He has been so frightfully energetic all his life – just a volcano in constant eruption – and now the calm puzzles him." This was always an issue: how best to raise the matter of Evans's health and his dangerous self-neglect. He bluffed that there was nothing wrong with him, apart from a brassy "tobacco cough". He pointed out the work to be done, the jobs about the house: gathering sticks, chopping wood, shovelling coal, and walking the dogs whatever the weather.[7]

Besides his showing as memoirist, Evans continued writing stories, his latest in a different key. Marguerite had long urged him to make his work more acceptable by softening its tone, by abandoning (as she put it) "the bitter for the beautiful". At last he appeared to be listening. Seven of these late stories were gathered up and published posthumously under the title *The Earth Gives All and Takes All*. They follow a lengthy memoir of Caradoc by his long-time friend George Green. Professor Green was now in Egypt, having taken a post at the Alexandria Institute of Education following the sudden death of Sophia his wife. In correspondence with Andrew Dakers, Green suggested that the esteem and friendship that Evans had found since returning to Wales had affected the man personally and might increasingly have coloured his work. "I am sure you are right in what you say about the possibilities of his output, had he lived," Dakers replied; "Mellowness, relative in his case, is the word that distinguishes his latest writings from his earlier, perhaps more dynamic, work."[8] The Dakers blurb underscored this thinking: Evans's last stories were without question his crowning achievement "and many readers will be astonished at the mellowness and charity of attitude which they reveal. There is none of the bitterness or fierce criticism of sections of the Welsh people which were present in his earliest books; rather there is compassion and understanding." Though shaky on the Fleet Street career, George Green shows more knowledge and insight than almost anyone who had previously written on Evans but he was not Marguerite's first choice for the introduction. Naturally she hoped Gwyn Jones might provide "a critical and personal forward".[9] He seems to have declined her request, one suspects because he could not speak of the personal without describing Caradoc as he found him, a superb subject in himself and "positively empyrean" in his household setting; but one had to be cruel to do him (and his household) justice, and that would be impossible with Marguerite around.

Fronting George Green's introduction in the published collection is a brief preface by Marguerite headed – emphatically – "Without Bitterness" and picking out the title story, "The Earth Gives All and Takes All". The story begins: "A tree of wisdom grew inside a certain farmer and sayings and sayings fell from it. The farmer gave hundreds of the sayings to his neighbours and the over-freight he stored in his head." His forty-acres need a servant-wife to look after them and Silah the village schoolmistress seems a fit for the job.

> Silah schoolen was a tidy bundle and she was dressed as if every day was a Sunday. She was not tall or short, fat or thin; her cheek-bones were high and her lips were wide and her top teeth swelled from her mouth in a showy white arch.
>
> The farmer came to the threshold of schoolhouse.
>
> "Hoi-hoi," he said. "Stop the learning and come you here."
>
> Silah came to him.
>
> "Hear I do you are for auction," he said.
>
> "Who is the bidder?" asked Silah, pretending she did not know.
>
> "A farmwr well to do."
>
> "What is the bid of the farmwr well to do?"
>
> "Forty acres and livestock, dresser and coffer and press and settle and tables and chairs."
>
> "A man with no bed needs no wife."
>
> "Forget I did. A bed there is."

They marry "at the time of the rising of the bees" and settle in the farmhouse, itself a witness to the great Nonconformist legacy and here afforded a clean-cut, dignified prose:

> The house was built of mud and rubble and by the Bible in the parlour his people had lived in it for over two hundred years; and if the parlour was small it was sacred as the room where infants were baptised and dead rested. But the kitchen was large and the ceiling hooked for hams and sides of bacon and the table on the flagged floor was big enough to cure a pig on it; and everything was orderly. The floor was clean, the cases of the grandfather clock and the weather glass and the dresser and the yellow wardrobe were bright, the jugs and plates and tureens on the dresser shone, and everything was neatly arrayed on the window sill: boot polish and boot brush, cactus in a pot, two Bibles and two hymn-books of a size convenient to carry to capel, the farmer's razor and shaving brush, which was also a clothes brush, the two certificates with their faces downward.

Silah and her farmer are a common late-Caradoc coupling: he the abstracted husband lost in language, she the more knowing wife. A hired servant joins them: "The man was Ianto, and he was like a pillar of good earth and his eyes were as brown and uncomplaining as those of a willing horse." Silah and he draw closer as the preachy farmer declines. "Limper you are than a sick man's whistle," Silah tells him, catching his reflection in the wardrobe mirror as she combs her hair.

> The first year of War Number Two brought more money to the little smallholders and freeholders than they had thought there was in the world, and there was no welcome for the farmer and his sayings anywhere. No matter, no matter. He would store in his loft as many sayings as he could comfortably. The tree withered. No matter, no matter. His store would last him one year two years. Yet he was sad and his heart tumbled about in its hole. He looked into his loft and all his sayings were dry dust on the floor. Come, Oldest Brother. Before he was cut down he called Silah to him and said to her: 'Do not you now look for me in pulpit Tabernacle King David Proverbs because I will be in hole deaf and dumb. Far'well.'"

Marguerite remembers first reading this story at bed-time, Caradoc's usual time for bringing her new work. The heart tumbling about in its hole was how his own heart felt and, yes, all his thoughts and book writings now seemed dry dust on the floor. ("Life is a shell; you break it with your teeth and all you find is emptiness," he recorded among his papers). Oldest Brother would surely come, and with him a hole in the ground – "That's what I think of death." The story was still untitled – "He usually left the titling of his stories to the last and spent a great deal of time over it" – but one phrase within it appealed. He had scribbled it on the back of the typescript. "The earth gives all and takes all, and Silah and Ianto caressed and kneaded the earth and they poured their water upon its backward places." The passage occurs near the close of a story of three self-minded individuals locked in partnerships (marriage and/or work) who manoeuvre for personal gain. But scheming men and women may eventually come together, if along differing paths.

"Two things are a farmer's delight, a horse who is glad to see him and a piecess of clay to warm."Thus Silah coaxes Ianto. They are goals achieved in "Oldest Brother", where Bensha, his wife, and a knowing horse manage to work contentedly their hillside acres. In a caravan close by lives Bensha's mother whose protecting love has not always encompassed another women. Seemingly, there can be reconciliation on a Welsh mountain farm. "Oldest Brother" is perhaps the nearest Evans came to bridging realism and surrealism, to seeing fact and fantasy as one. It shows a rare warmth of feeling – towards the horse in particular (animals readily stirred his compassion). One of the better stories selected for Dakers, "Oldest Brother" had already appeared in the *Welsh Review* (June 1945), its Mabinogion touches pleasing Gwyn Jones: "Hysbys was in his prime. He was as fast as a sunbeam, and his coat was so yellow that if he were in a field of ripe corn on a sunny day you would not know which was corn, which was Hysbys, which was sunlight."

With the Evan Walters portrait of Caradoc strikingly reproduced on the jacket (and serving also as frontispiece), *The Earth Gives All and Takes All* was, at a hundred pages, another well-produced little Dakers book. The verso of its two-colour title-page gave June 1946 as publication date but it came on sale in early December (showing signs of hasty proofing). As reviewers found, its contents refined the approach of *Pilgrims in a Foreign Land*. Robert Herring at *Life and Letters* had already printed "To Keep a Rainbow White" and his literary monthly welcomed its reappearance in this new collection, "the last fruits of a narrow, personal, but nevertheless intense art which it is difficult both to place and to assess."The reviewer Robin King spoke of "parables of Wales" (their fundamental occurrences might have happened in BC or AD): "they make an immediate and extraordinary impression on the mind. But because the vision and the imagination displayed in these pieces is so personal, it is inevitable that for a time at least, they will not be read as widely as they deserve… Seldom, in the past year or so, has so good a volume of stories appeared."Austin Clarke judged similarly: he thought Evans "a remarkable and a great artist" and his later stories profoundly original achievements, proverbial in their concentration, and laced with "a wild, harsh, unlovely poetry".[10] The lack of attention given them continued to baffle him – "for they have been completely neglected". Other reviews suggested one reason. An overall softening of tone hadn't made Evans's style and idiom more accessible; the strangely spoken dialogue in particular was terser and more loaded than ever and, warned R.D. Charques in the *TLS*, "the reader needs to keep his wits about him to know what is going on" (22 March 1947). Charques, who had kept an eye on Evans for the *TLS*, hailed these last examples of a "furiously individual art".[11] Welsh reaction was scarce. Paper rationing meant a four-page *Western Mail* with minimal coverage of books. The *Welsh Review* felt justified in not reviewing it, having printed one of the stories (along with other pieces by Caradoc) as well as Gwyn Jones's lengthy obituary-essay. Ivor Lewis acknowledged the book in *Wales*, glad that those barely believable reports of a calm last phase "without bitterness" had turned out to be false. Evans must have been fooling. "Here is no painful expiation. The early harshness is tempered, certainly, but the vision is fundamentally the same, as bright, as witty, and as free of soiled sentiment as before."[12]

Returning to 1943 and Caradoc's bout of pneumonia, we find Marguerite's relations with her housemaid seriously deteriorating. On 5 December she unburdened herself to Alice Jones: "Since these troubles our little half-wit maid has been most peculiar & I've had an abusive letter from her mother asking why she had not had her usual day off – this on Caradoc's worst day! I have a feeling when she does go home she is quite capable of not returning…" This possibility had to be confronted: "Do you know of any underly domestic who would like a country post?" Margaret did indeed leave Brynawelon, though exactly when is not recorded. With no replacement in sight, the Evanses struggled on. Cooking and writing did not mix, and as he saw his wife springing up from the book in hand to baste a chicken, put on the greens or look at a pudding, Caradoc could only repeat that bread and cheese and an onion were good enough for him. By July 1944 Marguerite was confessing to Nell Dunbar, "I do not know Nell how much longer I can continue without a servant and write my books. It is one long incessant toil from morning till night."[13] What dismayed her was the sense that this was but a foretaste of the world to come. "If 'this freedom' we are fighting for is all to end in Socialism & the masses sitting on top making rude faces at the former 'gentry' will it be worthwhile? I wouldn't mind in the least being controlled by such people if only they had better manners."

Marguerite occasionally opened up to Nell Dunbar, who kept the bulk of her letters (having excised the odd embarrassing passage). Caradoc met the Dunbars in 1937 (at their home in the Chilterns) and the Dunbars visited the Evanses several times at Broadstairs. Called up at the outbreak of war, their daughter Monica became a WAAF long-distance driver prior to her commission in 1943. Initially stationed at RAF Hell's Mouth (Porth Neigwl), near Abersoch, she spent part her leave at Brynawelon (her leave pass for 5-12 May 1940 survives), for "we were good friends, all of us, and Caradoc a kind and considerate host".[14] She was sure he missed "London in danger" and was always keen for its news, but he also absorbed her accounts of Coventry and Merseyside the day after their massive bombings. "Caradoc must have had a most devastating effect on anyone who had a guilty conscience. He had such a straight and penetrating gaze – not unkind, but as if he had to know whether one meant what one said." As for Marguerite, "what a sweet generous maddening and lovable person she was… I never heard her make a catty remark all her life. She seemed eager to help others and to share whatever good fortune was hers."[15] Monica remembered "the elegant child-loving young woman – over-loving in the case of Nick – silver-spoons are not always a young man's best tools."[16] Nick she thought "quite devastatingly good looking" but being a good seven years his senior, theirs was "the casual but affectionate friendship as between a sister and younger brother".[17]

During this time she posted Caradoc two literary efforts of her own, a 1939 dog story published in a popular magazine, and an earlier published poem on the death of King George V. The great encourager excelled himself:

My dear Monica

I like your dog story. It is very properly told and the suspense is kept up to the end. Besides it is told economically with not a word too many, and that's a big thing.

Your poem is a thrill. It thrilled me. Hymn or lamentation, it is superb. I never thought you were capable of such a beautiful – such an artistic job. The form is very difficult, but you have done it and produced a thing of true feeling. Do some more is the counsel to you of

Caradoc[18]

Monica remained a great favourite of the family, as Marguerite told Nell Dunbar:

How fond we all are of her & how even <u>Caradoc</u> who "sees through" most people can find nothing to say of her but that she is unspoilt & 100 percent. It's a wonderful thing in these days when most girls – & young men – have lost their sense of values altogether. And not all the rubbing shoulders with all sorts as she has had in her service experience, has changed her poise.

My dear, I must get on with my book. My Love to you both. Ever.[19]

On leave Monica saw the Evanses at home. "Husband and wife devoted their entire mornings to writing, and now and then there would be bursts of temperament at meal times, of a superficial nature only. Caradoc had an impish streak to which his wife responded more often than not, with tears, but half of it was play."[20] One particular breakfast stuck out. There had been "a slight tiff" the evening before and Caradoc was not in the house. "Suddenly he arrived, as radiant as the spring morning outside, holding between his hands a battered old straw hat filled to the brim and overflowing with all the loveliest hedgerow and meadow flowers he could find; a profusion of scent and colour and beauty. Marguerite accepted the proffered "peace offering" with delight, and harmony was restored."[21] Monica visited Wales for the last time in or soon after 1950 and although the two corresponded frequently she never met Marguerite again. She continued to read her books and even suggested fresh themes. She knew how directly Marguerite drew on the places and people around her (the Dunbars among them), and that she "dramatized situations from fact to fiction in such a way that future readers might justifiably wonder which was which."

It was accepted that Caradoc in company remained on his best behaviour. In late summer 1944 Gwyn Jones took the writer Glyn Jones to Brynawelon (B.J. Morse, a Cardiff lecturer in Italian, accompanied them). Caradoc turned on the charm, first on Glyn ("By dam [sic], you have done well"), then on Glyn's wife when she happened to say that she was none too impressed with her name. "'Dor-Reen!' he cried, with emphasis, astonishment, and an almost voluptuous appreciation of the two syllables, 'By dam [sic], that's a fine name! Do-Reen! That's the *hell* of a fine name!'"[22] A few days later the Evanses took tea with Gwyn and Alice at Brynymor Road where Glyn and Doreen were staying. Glyn couldn't help but notice how Caradoc had changed in the ten years since he and Dylan Thomas first met him:

His clothes were as outlandish and colourful as ever; he was wearing black corduroy jacket and trousers, a magenta shirt, a cable-stitch cricket sweater and a brimless straw hat shaped like a smallish beehive. But his body at sixty-seven was old, and his face, with droop-lidded eyes and the blunt, bulby, long-nostrilled nose, seemed gnarled and scooped out, the cheekbones in particular standing forth with prominence under the thin skin.

But Evans rose to the occasion, listening to others with flattering intensity and commanding the company when, "mixing in the most comical way the accents of Aberteifi and London clubland, [he] described encounters with Frank Harris, W.H. Davies, Sean O'Casey and others." When they left Gwyn's house for a stroll, Glyn had a chance to compliment Caradoc on his work for the *Welsh Review*. "He grinned through his pipe-smoke, rugged and momentarily bright-eyed; he seemed glad that I had said that. Five months later I felt glad myself I had said it, because going to my job by train one cold winter's morning in 1945 I read in the newspaper that he was dead."[23]

Commenting years later on Huw Menai's "always inflationary" writing style, Glyn Jones recalled how Caradoc had spoken of the method he employed when revising his stories: "[It] was analogous to putting a piece of white-wood in a vice and tightening the contraption up until every inessential element, under the enormous pressure, had been squeezed right out from between the woody fibres – air, moisture, natural juices, rosin – and only the compact, quintessential iron-hard timber remained."[24] Glyn might have heard this directly from Caradoc or it might have come via Gwyn Jones. Both Joneses, one might add, thought well of Marguerite, Glyn describing her as "a fine and generous English-woman whom I always liked and admired very much, warm-hearted, merciful, tireless in her concern for the young, for outcasts and misfits, and bountiful towards her friends and dependants."[25] Gwyn judged her "warm and loving, though I fancy she did her menfolk no good".[26] Caradoc's position seemed barely sustainable: "kennelled comfortably" on the earnings of his wife yet "beleaguered by a possessive, even proprietorial love".

Through Alice his wife Gwyn knew of the goings-on at Brynawelon: Caradoc's casual cruelties, his malicious pleasure in his wife's discomfort, Marguerite's flare-ups and snap-backs, the "stormy quarrels or lightning flashes of hidden rancour". Nick's presence exacerbated tensions at home (and in company irritatingly curbed free speech). At twenty-eight he was still his mother's golden boy. Gwyn thought National Service might have been the saving of him, as would almost anything that removed him from his mother's payroll. "I rarely spent much time in his company without wanting to cry: 'Get away from here! Get a job, anywhere. Keep yourself, and keep your individuality and self-respect.'"[27] Nick became the focus of a protracted row towards the end of 1944. He had fallen for a local beauty, a daughter of Ben Samuel who sold oil around the locality. Sensing that this might be "the real thing", Marguerite apprised Alice Jones of unexpected opposition. "Now I don't object in the least because her people are not the same as my people. (The father is an oil-vendor who has given her a good education.) At any rate the family don't come into the picture as far as we are concerned, nor have they tried to. They have tried to discourage the girl if anything for this reason."[28] No, the opposition came from Caradoc: he said he found it "odd that I who have been proud of my ancestry should smile on a more lowly marriage for Nick." But smile Marguerite did. Gwyneth Samuel had given Nick an incentive and purpose; his wish was for an early marriage and a quick return to the stage. Caradoc kept up the attack, alluding to "Nick's working-class wife" without much brain and an accent that got on his nerves. This, from a man who boasted his peasant roots and never disguised his accent. "These things hurt!!" Marguerite assured her "dear little pal". Could Alice, when she came over, "say some tactful things in praise of the girl – only if you feel it genuinely. I hate to see N's beginning of happiness dashed and cavilled at. I think if he [Caradoc] sees others take a different view he will do likewise."

Evans positively warmed to what he called "a first-class row": "When he was angry he hated to be touched lest the anger melted out of him."[29] That Caradoc manufactured these quarrels largely to escape Brynawelon was the view of Ronnie Hughes, briefly a friend of Nick's. An Anglican priest in the making, Arthur Ronald Hughes first encountered Nick in pre-war Aberystwyth when he took the drunken young actor, a couple of years his junior, back to Queen's Square House. The following morning he received a gentlemanly call of thanks (this shortly after a similar call from Marguerite). He did not meet Caradoc till a few years later when Nick invited him out to Brynawelon. He anticipated a boozy affair but Nick took him quietly to a shed at the side of the house where he kept a bottle of rum. Each took a swig – "the only drink you'll get", Nick told him – correctly as it proved. A surprisingly formal tea party ensued. Hughes came to understand Caradoc's need for temporary release, life with Marguerite having (so he imagined) "the oppressiveness of the feather bed – look how she ruined Nick".[30] Hughes must have learned much from Nick,[31] who wrote only once about his stepfather. "I knew how devotedly she [Marguerite] loved him and how he adored her. Perhaps I was jealous of him. I must have been. I knew he was jealous of me. His jealousy would flare up in sudden volcanic eruptions...."[32] Nick had developed a taste in literature. "Write one good prose sentence yourself or a few lines of poetry a day," his stepfather counselled – "there's no reason why an actor shouldn't know how to read or write or spell."[33]

When things got rough at home, particularly with shouting matches over Nick, Evans found a haven at Linden Vista, Cliff Terrace, home of Miss Commander. With a shared interest in theatre, Ethel Commander came to know Marguerite but was unsympathetic towards Nick.[34] Pubs too were natural retreats, as were hotels licensed for alcohol on Sundays. Sooner than join the Conservative Club, a private club on Eastgate where Sunday drinks were served (predominantly to non-Tories), Caradoc would sign himself in as a weekend hotel guest. Gwyn Jones spoke of him during quarrels at home thrusting his slippers into his coat pocket and making for the Llanina Arms, near New Quay. Marguerite would then have to fetch him by taxi. Behind these memories lay one incident described by Marguerite in a letter to Alice Jones. In October 1944 (shortly before the family departed Brynawelon) Caradoc had flown into "a fearful rage" because Nick's girlfriend Gwyneth was coming to supper. He went off, so he said, to Aberystwyth but he actually went to New Quay. The arrangement that she later meet him at Llanina crossroads fell through – she arrived but he wasn't there – so she returned to Aberystwyth where she remained for the night, fearing his anger when he returned. Having got a lift, Evans arrived home "blind drunk" at 8.30 p.m. He was "still mad-drunk with temper" the following morning when Marguerite went out to Brynawelon with Mrs Dan Roberts (whose husband had given him the lift). "[He] Called me all the names under the sun in front of her, told her Nick had 'dodged' the Army, & was so terrible she took me away with her." Marguerite's letter hints at a possible further source of conflict – the existence of another woman. "My dear, he <u>went to New Quay</u> & met that woman there. This is established now. And he manufactured the <u>whole</u> row of Gwyneth & made the excuse of it to get himself out of the house!! <u>Did you ever?</u>" Adultery was impossible, at least on this occasion, since "he was only an hour or two in New Quay, drinking with her the whole time. She also drinks like a fish.... ALL <u>Vile</u> – that part."[35]

Marguerite opens her biography of Caradoc with marital strife at Brynawelon. A trifle might upset him, "a careless word, or no word, or even a seeming inattention he would magnify into a slight or a deliberate insult." He was primed for "a first-class row" which he might have enjoyed though his anger was real enough:

> His *daemon*, when it possessed him, troubled him most in the mornings. It brewed in him while he slept. In the early hours it would start him off banging or drumming the bed-head or his bed-table until it awoke me and I would tremble in my bed, for then I knew I was in for a trying day – or half-day. When the *daemon* jumped on his shoulder, as soon as he was out of bed I could tell it by his step. He stumped heavily then, planting his feet down. He would chant the only two lines of his war-song – husky, out of tune and all about the house:
>
> "I swung him high, I swung him low,
> I cut him down and let him go"
>
> Or words like it.... So I would know he was full of trouble which might blow up or blow away.[36]

It would be blown away by endless cups of tea and, eventually, by writing. "The *daemon* had fled. I could go on with my work. All was well again with my world and his." Evans in his blackest moods terrified Marguerite but she mentions no physical violence, not in her books or in her divorce letters to Paula Block. (Paula thought Caradoc a sadist whose lashes were strictly "oral".) One moment of physical pain occurred in the bedroom. Evans wished to read and told Marguerite that if she didn't settle down to her book he would beat her "like the tinker beats his wife". "No you won't –" she challenged; at which he played the tinker, taking hold of her wrist and bringing down his palm "hard and swiftly and often" on her finger-tips. "Does that hurt?" She assured him it did. "Then read your book and let me read." He returned to *War and Peace*.[37]

George Green noted Evans's arrogance, a defiance of those about him "carried to extremes of truculence that led him to hurt people for whom he greatly cared". Gwyn Jones concurred, telling radio listeners: "Of course, he was thoroughly malicious, and loved being the centre of a row, partly because he was an actor who dramatized himself most of his waking hours, and partly because he had a temper… I can only describe as devilish." His face reflected his contradictory nature: "it could be the most genial face in Wales: it could be quite frightening. He had a grin all his own for special occasions which put ice in your bloodstream."[38] Those occasions were mostly when he heard something to the disadvantage of those he disliked. He liked Gwyn Jones, for his calm, equable nature in particular, yet for all their friendship Jones felt "confident that one day we'd quarrel magnificently, and he'd lay my head open with the nearest fender". Thirty years later, he said as much to Paula Block, that he'd assumed Caradoc would one day lay his head open with a poker – unless I saw the storm-flag and laid his open first".[39] What could possibly have provoked such a quarrel remained unsaid. One gets the impression that over the four years they knew each other, Jones became increasingly impatient with Caradoc's self-dramatization and mischievous promotion of trouble. The scholar-academic and editor lived a wholly different life in friendly, close-knit Aberystwyth, a marvellous place for students and teachers alike in a college described by Jones as "sternly educational and research-centred". As for the re-launched *Welsh Review* (and its parallel book-publishing programme), this was the beginning of what proved an "extraordinarily enjoyable venture", one that further enhanced his standing in Welsh cultural life.[40]

Jones went out to work, climbing the eighty-seven steps to his room at Old College on the seafront (his readings from "Beowulf" would mesmerize students in the great West Classroom). The Evanses stayed at home. They lived in each other's pockets, unlike the Joneses or George and Sophia Green. Marguerite liked Sophia well enough but George was the closer friend. He might arrive on his bike in the late afternoon or early evening and stay talking at Brynawelon till nearly midnight. The Greens "never went about together everywhere", remembered Marguerite; "They each had their separate set of friends and separate life. This was their understanding." Marguerite's marriage was different: she and Caradoc never wanted a separate life; indeed, she calculated that, "In fourteen years we only missed out sharing three days."[41] Gwyn Jones confirmed that Caradoc had no real friends and little regular personal contact beyond Marguerite and Nick. They kept the outside world at bay, though at some considerable personal cost. Gwyn paints a graphic picture of them walking around Aberystwyth together, sometimes accompanied by Nick in his own picturesque attire – a grouping like no other. Caradoc surely treated Marguerite abominably but (so it struck Gwyn) at Brynawelon he had become a dog on a chain and "like that sly and treacherous but much to be pitied dog Timber of theirs", he bit the hand that fed him.[42] Destructive affection, "blood-sucking devotion", was a special line of Marguerite's.

Marguerite freely confessed her devotion – "Caradoc was King and Emperor in his home" – but however much she liked to present herself as the subservient one, it was long understood in Aberystwyth that she held the purse-strings and the casting vote. In the eyes of Ronnie Hughes, his was the impotent rage of the kept man. Further marital secrets are embedded in Marguerite's fiction, and what Evans wrote of the Cardiganshire couple in *Wasps* should also not be forgotten: that "the bitter tune of their private incivility was not that of the love by which they held each other."

The family left Brynawelon in October 1944. Without domestic help its daily upkeep was crippling and servants were impossible to come by. Evans's last journal entry records the decision to leave. It begins with a note of defiance – "It is raining today. I will go out in the rain and I will not come in until it pleases me" – wholly in keeping with his obstinate disregard of all advice on his health. He then proceeds:

> The woman has said that we must go from this place into the town. She says I am not to hew wood or break coal or carry tins to the dump. She says we are too far from amenities. It is what I have been urging all along, but now she has come to my way of thinking I don't want to go. For four years I have tried to make her mind my mind and now that I have prevailed my mind is not her mind. I want to stay here. I hope we shall be back in a fortnight. This is what I have told everyone.

The late change of heart was predictable. Evans would say how he hated wherever they happened to be, in town or country, but as soon as they had left he would wish himself back there again. Person or place, uncle's hatreds were shallow, so Howell Evans said.

Finding rooms in Aberystwyth wasn't easy. Soldiers and airmen packed the town joined by civilian strangers, the latter a dubious bunch by all accounts ("fugitives", Caradoc called them). The military having commandeered many premises, the Evanses settled for 36A North Parade, a centrally located upper-floor flat approached by three flights of stairs. It proved a tight fit for three adults and sheepdog Timber (too old for town, terrier Jock had been left at New Cross, boarded with neighbours at seven shillings a week). Fortunately, the new landlady Mrs Owen was a qualified nurse and a wayward seventeen-year-old girl in the care of Convent Sisters provided some daily help. Evans liked Aberystwyth well enough, the Free Library with its daily newspapers, the lengthy promenade for afternoon walks. The poet and children's writer T. Llew Jones remembered having occasionally seen him sitting alone on the Prom, "a grey, thin, lonely man" wearing his "rather strange hat". (Jones would never forgive him for so perversely distorting in his fiction the language of the south Cardiganshire farm folk they both knew well.)

From their time at New Cross the Evanses had once more become familiar figures in the town, an audacious trio as striking in appearance as they were ten years previously (Nick's hat and cape brought the Sandeman port advert to mind). Marguerite's theatrical clothes and make-up continued to draw attention. Descriptions of her are remarkably consistent, and largely unflattering, with the emphasis on her uneven proportions – a large body with thin "sparrow legs" – and a face painted layer over layer "like a toy soldier's". One account described her shortly before Caradoc's death as "heavily made up, blowsy, with an air of sophistication" – in all, "ugly-attractive"[43] She must have been attractive, thought Gwyn Jones, for "she never wanted for men – and women invariably disliked her!"[44] She left an indelible impression on the young son of a local grocer:

> She did not so much wear clothes as envelop herself in yards of taffeta and silk, over which hung diaphanous layers of pastel coloured chiffon. These multi-coloured draperies, like her dainty silver sandals and rings on every finger, brought to mind

some gaudy tropical bird blown off course by the wind and dumped among us dowdy
sparrows.... Meanwhile bracelets crawled sinuously up her bare arms, while beneath
her generous chin hung row upon row of shiny coloured beads. Had it not been for
a large floppy hat, black but enlivened with brooches and worn "to hide her grey
roots", claimed my mother, she might have stepped out of a painting by Alma Tadema,
part Roman matron and, with her nut-brown arms and bangles, part Nubian slave.[45]

It was in late 1944 that the Evanses in town bumped into Dylan Thomas. He had
come to live in New Quay where his strange behaviour and heavy drinking were
rumoured. Meeting him by chance, Marguerite thought "he had coarsened and his
features were thickening already". "What about those three wishes of yours?" Caradoc
asked, alluding to Dylan's private moment with Old Griff's miracle stone. "Was there
anything doing?"

Dylan removed clinging tobacco flakes from the moist loose lips between which a
cigarette had been dangling.
    "Not likely. I asked for fame, success, money."

"How, posthumously, in the fullest measure, his wish was granted, the world knows
today," Marguerite reflected in 1957.[46]

Evans came to Aberystwyth terminally ill though outwardly it little showed. The
pneumonia that struck ten months earlier had weakened him; he looked older than his
years and had lost weight but he remained as active as ever: "as volcanic and vital and
violently interested in everything – the war, things and people. People especially," Marguerite said. She believed he "understood & penetrated the depths & deviousness of
everybody he came into contact with except himself."[47] His belligerence and obstinacy
continued and, as winter took hold, his disregard of all medical advice. Marguerite
worried as he stood around in the bitter cold chatting with people in the street. With
Christmas in mind, she bought him, through a personal advert in the *Times* (no clothing
coupons required), "a really posh overcoat, unworn, with velvet-lined pockets, of lovely
warm tweed".[48] Evans professed to like it but still preferred his old threadbare coat.
You can't hang on to it any longer, she pleaded. "I will hang on to it as long as it will
hang on to me," he replied. They compromised: he would accept the present but give
her half of its £12 cost. Straightway at the local jeweller's she bought him another present,
an engraved Georgian silver watch with a lovely movement. It delighted him. He had
lost his own watch some time ago, then her father's (at Abermâd out in the snow) – a
loss on a par, he reminded her, with *her* loss of his treasured fountain pen, the one he
had written *My People* with and given her when they met. Marguerite next turned to
Christmas cards. Hers to Paula Block apologised for not being able to send any honey:
they had left the countryside for a flat in town – "no more awful paraffin & so on – gas
fires everywhere". She wondered whether Paula was still keeping house for her brother
in Warwick. "If not would you like to come to us. I think we should be much happier in

the town & you would manage better!" Wages would be thirty shillings a week. No positive response was anticipated (or received).

Caradoc's brassy cough had worsened. It sounded alarmingly as he and Marguerite walked up Brynymor Road on Christmas Day to call upon the Joneses. Alice was out with the dogs so they talked for a while with Gwyn about Caradoc's forthcoming piece on T.P. O'Connor for the *Welsh Review*. On the downhill return, "More coughing – such a spasm of it I thought he would never get his breath back."[49] It was a turning-point. Caradoc agreed to see a doctor but insisted that Marguerite should not get involved – "writing's your job, not nursing". Caradoc's doctor, Charles Burrell, arranged that a chest specialist see him and at the hospital on Monday, New Year's Day 1945 (the day after his sixty-sixth birthday), Dr J. Kenyon Davies assured him that his chest was clear. "It's your heart, my boy," he said in Welsh, "I'd like a few more photographs". His report would be sent to the doctor. A week later Dr Burrell, "a great, healthy, handsome man like a giant Teddy bear", came around with the report and its death words, "an aneurism and a pulsating mass". Caradoc would need to go slow and have treatment and rest. Husband and wife went out for a walk. It was chilly and Marguerite asked him to button up his coat. "'Why should I button up my coat? My throat isn't my heart.' And he kept his coat wide open." They fed the seagulls and visited Mr Adler, who had property in the town. He promised to tell them about any suitable flats that the military were vacating. In the evening Caradoc telephoned his nephew Dr Emrys Davies (son of his sister Mary), an ophthalmic surgeon at Croydon, to ask what an aneurism was. Emrys said he would write and fully explain. Caradoc listened to the 8 o'clock news and returned to the bedroom. His habit was to read, usually until midnight, but this night, "He was lying down, very tucked-up looking. Fragile. Tired – so tired." It would be their last night together. Believing that death was near, Evans a little before had feelingly addressed his wife in a letter she later discovered in a drawer amongst his papers. It was dated 6 January:

> My darling,
>
> For all the travail and unhappiness I have brought into your life I entreat your for-giveness. You have never failed me.
>
> When I die I would like you to arrange to rest beside me.
>
> My clothes for Josi and I know that you will care for him out of your great and loving heart.
>
> Do as you wish with my books and papers. Destroy, sell or keep. There is nothing else except the wherewithal to bury me.
>
> Caradoc Evans.[50]

The morning of 10 January found him coughing and fighting for breath. A hurriedly summoned Dr Burrell gave an injection – it was angina, a heart attack, and more might follow. At noon on that Wednesday he was admitted to the newly extended Aberystwyth and Cardiganshire General Hospital on North Road, at this time staffed by local GPs who looked after their patients. The young house surgeon Joan Jenkins was able to assure Marguerite that Caradoc's first night had been quiet and comfortable. With proper rest he might recover for a while but there could be no cure; he would have to be careful always. He lay in a little room outside the general ward. "The hospital was very full – wounded as well,"[51] wrote Marguerite. She had arrived in the morning with a clutch of that day's newspapers. It was George Green's idea that she take them; if Caradoc wasn't up to reading them, "Never mind. He's a newspaper man. He may like to touch them and know they're there." She found him exhausted, barely able to speak. Mrs Powell (Nanteos) had sent him some eggs; was there anything else he wanted? He asked for the honey linctus that Marguerite made up and his copy of Balzac's *Droll Stories*. She left early, promising to return in the afternoon. Caradoc was sleeping when she came back, so again she quickly left, leaving the honey linctus at his bedside – she had forgotten the book. The hospital rang at dusk. Mr Evans was comfortable and there was no need for her to come in the evening. Marguerite said she would bring the Balzac in the morning and "some Left books from Dr Green".

There were telephone calls at North Parade: one to the Dunbars telling that Caradoc was seriously ill and another from his nephew Emrys who planned to arrive in the morning. Then, late at night, the phone rang again, interrupting Marguerite's prayers. It was Mrs Miles Jones, the matron. Caradoc had passed away. "He died at eleven-thirty, very peacefully," she said. Five minutes before he had rung his bedside bell and told the nurse that he had a little pain. It was all over in five minutes; there was nothing anyone could do. Marguerite asked if she might speak with his nurse. She was at the matron's side.

> "Please – my husband… Did he ask for me?"
> "He said nothing – only that he had a little pain."
> "Are you sure he didn't ask for me?"
> "Quite sure. He went so quietly –"
> "Thank you."

Emrys Davies arrived the following morning. He reminisced about his days as a medical student in London and the grand time his uncle had given him on the weekends they spent together. He understood the difficulties Marguerite must have endured as his wife, the constant arguments and clash of egos. "Caradoc loved quarrels," he confirmed; "You must remember that. It was part of his makeup. If he hadn't got a good reason for an explosion he could manufacture one." He needed to live at a certain pitch. Emrys had witnessed his acting up before Rose. "I've seen him coming out of his house in Richmond looking like a thunder-cloud with a slipper sticking out of each pocket – God knows where he was off to. He probably didn't know himself." Marguerite reflected on Emrys's mother Mary, whom Caradoc had unflattering pictured in *Nothing to Pay*. She had died a year ago, when Caradoc lay in bed with the heavy cold that turned to pneumonia; Marguerite brought the telegram reporting her heart failure. With the years Caradoc's view of his sister softened, and particularly after their mother died. Mary had shown her true self in the arrangements she made for Josi. With common sense, kindness and generosity she ensured that nothing in his life would change; that he would stay on in the same house and be cared for by worthy people.

Emrys left for London that same evening. He could not stay for the funeral or indeed return for it. As the only ophthalmic surgeon for the Croydon group of hospitals, he was constantly occupied, often working throughout the night on the heavy wartime eye casualties.[52] But he comforted his aunt. How could one have wished for Caradoc to live "in constant dread and anxiety – never knowing from one day to another when the next attack will be. Alleviation, perhaps, but no possible cure, and he knowing it all the time." Evans's death certificate gives as the cause of death: "(a) Cardiac failure (b) Aneurism of Aorta". Before the advent of penicillin, late-stage syphilis (up to 40 years after the initial infection) was the most common cause of thoracic aortic aneurism. There were reasonable grounds for supposing that this was the case with Evans and evidence has come to light (from sources which cannot be named) that makes it a practical certainty. (In view of his increasingly unstable behaviour, the histrionics, mood swings and fits of paranoia, an accompanying neurosyphilis cannot be entirely ruled out – some ten percent of those with primary syphilis later develop neurosyphylis).[53]

Having lost her husband in the flesh, Marguerite soon gained the company of his spirit self. It was at her side in the morning, even before Emrys arrived. She heard Caradoc's voice instructing her, giving directions plainly in something like the Whispering Voice she had hear as a child in India. Without question, it was his voice: "the ears of my heart received it". She wrote as much to Hannen Swaffer, a solid spiritualist, who pronounced her "clairaudient – an unconscious medium possessed of the gift of being able to hear the voices of the so-called dead."[54] He would publish her letter in *Psychic News* under the heading "Caradoc Evans, though 'Dead', arranges his Funeral". Marguerite had pondered where he should be buried, his relations having left the decision to her. New Cross never occurred to her since he always maintained that he hated the country. He had asked her to save him from burial at Rhydlewis; the place that always filled him with melancholy: "A week was all I could stand." It must be Aberystwyth, she supposed, and at Caradoc's prompting she turned to John Lewis Evans who ran the furnishing warehouse on Great Darkgate Street ("Speciality: Home-made Bedroom Suites...Funerals completely furnished"). In the course of their discussion about a suitable town site for the grave she heard Caradoc's voice "almost as clear as speech" saying impatiently: "Cut it, cut it. Put me in New Cross. Finish it. Get rid of him. New Cross me." Within a couple of hours Jock's caretaker arrived from New Cross to tell her that a fortnight previously Caradoc had gone out there for a jaunt and to pay for Jock's board. In their chat he chanced to say that he'd like to be buried above Horeb. "I was up there the other day taking a look around and I thought what a wonderful spot it was."[55]

News of Caradoc's death was broadcast immediately, on radio and in the press: Gwyn Jones and Alice learned of it at Blackwood, where they spent their Christmas vacation. The *Western Mail* accorded it a second leader and sixty or more obituaries can be traced in national and local newspapers and in one or two magazines Most drew on syndicated material: "the best-hated man in Wales" was endlessly quoted, Sewell Stokes's label that stuck to him all his life, as were events like the Barry book-burning and the West End *Taffy* riot. His unknown age was remarked upon; it was a secret even to his wife (Rhydlewis folk correctly calculated it as sixty-six). Here and there former colleagues had their say. "One of the most perplexing and picturesque characters ever seen in Fleet Street," wrote an unnamed columnist in the *Newspaper World*: "At one time I knew him as well as most men, yet I knew him not at all. He wrote with bitterness but gushed with good nature.... He was as sprightly a companion as one could wish to meet in the Street and he would shower compliments right and left with a generosity that was some-times embarrassing." Newman Flower, head of Cassell's, told the London *Evening News*:

> He was an honest man: he believed everything he wrote. He liked the Welsh people – but he saw their weaknesses.... He portrayed his fellow-countrymen with the utmost gusto as mean, mercenary, greedy, selfish, perfidious, untruthful and amoral. Now you can do this sort of thing to Englishmen – and they merely laugh. But if you do it to Welshmen it brings them to boiling point. Yet Caradoc Evans seemed always to be surprised by the uproar that he caused in Wales.... Personally there was nothing embittered or malicious about him: he was friendly and unpretentious.

The *Sheffield Telegraph* offered the story of Caradoc being shaved in a Cardiff barber's shop. A customer suddenly recognised him. "Are you really Caradoc Evans?" asked the barber, waving his razor. The writer replied that he was. "Then I don't finish shaving you," said the barber. "Get out, or I may be tempted to cut your throat." And Caradoc rose from the chair, wiped his face, and went out – half-shaved. An addition to the Evans apocrypha one might suppose – sparked by the slashing of the Evan Walters portrait? – though "He told me this himself," the *Telegraph's* columnist insisted.

Later editions of Friday's *Western Mail* (12 January) reported Caradoc's death, as did Saturday's paper, side by side with its leader on a man the paper had vilified for nigh on thirty years. With its own past in mind, it reflected that "Whenever he wrote he inflamed his fellow countrymen with the result that they hardly gave themselves a chance to recognise, much less enjoy, his undoubted literary gifts.... What he did was to give new life to the short story.... As to his subject matter, discriminating Welsh readers must admit that as an artist he was at liberty to pick and choose and even to overstress in order to achieve his purpose which was caricature." Had he been born a Czech, a Hungarian or a Chinese one would have recognised the same caricatures with different names and a different background. Nevertheless:

> As a Welshman Evans's disservice lay not in the fact that he deliberately caricatured his fellow countrymen but that he unintentionally and indirectly set an example to a rising school of Welsh writers in English, who instead of standing up and looking around prefer, as it were, to bend and peer under stones. The result... is that the Welsh as characters get easily the worst treatment in English fiction of the day.

This sparked a correspondence that ran for a month or more, with contributions from Keidrych Rhys, Dewi Emrys and Duncan Davies among others. Edith Nepean described at greater length how much Evans had helped her at the start of her career. "To the end Caradoc remained faithful to his old friends, and at Christmas came an old lustre jug and a pot of honey – little did I know that the end was so near." She endorsed what others in London had said, that "Caradoc wrote bitterly of the Welsh, but if anybody said one word against his country or countrymen he was up in arms."[56]

Marguerite joined the exchange (16 February). Caradoc was not painting his countrymen in particular but drawing on them as types:

> What he was holding up to scorn and obloquy were all those unlovely traits in humanity which made him so sad and so angry at all times – hypocrisy, graft, greed, cunning, cruelty – those same sins which made Jesus so sad and so angry when He overturned the tables of the moneychangers in the temple. But what stands out of all this controversy is the one thing unassailable – that Caradoc Evans was a great stylist who has written the name of a Welshman on English literature.

She came to see that "What he was flaying so cruelly and ruthlessly was himself – all those faults and weaknesses which he knew were his faults and weaknesses and which he deplored and hated in those moments when his flashes of genius beat back upon himself and stripped him as the bark of a tree is stripped by lightning."[57] His work was both accusation and confession since (as one of his "sayings" puts it), "The only evil we see in another man is the likeness of our own evil". He had stood in his characters' shoes, known how they thought and felt. Gwyn Jones, perhaps surprisingly, kept silent. He would present a masterly memoir and critical assessment in the March issue of the *Welsh Review*; "I think your goodbye to Caradoc was fond and just," Dylan Thomas applauded. R.B. Marriott in *Wales* (Summer 1945) has already been quoted. He began with a reference to "the few, and inadequate, obituaries" of Caradoc that had appeared in the national press, nearly all of which had stated that he had become "tamed" (the *TLS* obituary had spoken of Evans's recent stories as "full of affection for Wales"). "This view is quite erroneous." He then provided a telling memoir-essay on the Evans he knew in the Thirties.

Both the *Cambrian News* and the *Welsh Gazette* published obituaries, the *Gazette* (18 January) fairly representing how Evans was received in the neighbourhood following his second homecoming: "Afterwards people learned to accept him with good natured tolerance, and during the many years he spent in Aberystwyth district he was 'just one of the people'. . . . To those who knew him closely he was always pleasant and companionable and of generous heart. Despite his often unorthodox appearance he was sociable and in conversation he was a keen and appreciative listener."

Letters of sympathy poured in, letters and telegrams from friends and family, over a hundred in all. Brother Eddie consoled Marguerite with the thought that Caradoc had been spared a long and painful illness like their father's. Brother Charlie understood that, even at this time, his "darling Daisy" would be worrying over Nick. Caradoc's relations seemingly wrote nothing, apart from Enid, Dr Emrys Davies's wife. Rhydlewis sounded through David Jones of Garnant (Carmarthenshire), for whom Caradoc Evans was always "Dai Caradog and childhood's playtime in the Vale of Ceri nearly sixty years ago"; and also through the Revd J. Seymour Rees whose wife Annie, a Rhydlewis girl, claimed close knowledge of Caradoc's family background. He mentioned having gathered all local press material concerning Caradoc with a "synopsis of his life story" in mind. Among Aberystwyth and New Cross friends, Olive Gale (of the Coliseum cinema) recalled her chats with Caradoc on London churches; the Revd R. J. Pritchard mentioned his recent attendance at Aberystwyth's Welsh Congregational Church (he had tried Tabernacle, the Calvinistic Methodist temple-fortress); and eighty-four-year-old Margaret Powell, last of the line at Nanteos, would not forget his "kindly thoughtfulness" in helping her down the stairs when she went to tea at Brynawelon: "He was one of the kindest and most sympathetic of men." She spoke of the man not the author: "I don't like his books at all abusing Welsh men!" she wrote to a friend (9 March 1942) when reporting the arrival of the Evanses at New Cross. [58]

A sense of the man emerges from other letters of condolence. "He was so sincere," wrote Nansi Powell Price:

> One always felt, here was somebody real, who kept nothing back. There are so few people like that. He used to draw one out when he talked to one. I think that was his especial charm – a sympathy & of course he was a great talker. In his writing he was a genius & a pioneer. You were so happy at the Queen's [Square] House & New Cross & that is how I shall remember him, strong & vital. You would not wish him back, so sad and tired as he was.

A few old Rogues & Vagabonds looked fondly on repertory days. Violet Lamb offered something sharper: "I shall never forget Caradoc. His was an unforgettable personality – there was a richness and vehemence about him that was almost Shakespearean. He frightened me at times & yet always I thought of him with great affection." Writers and journalists got in touch: J.B. Priestly (a *T.P's Weekly* stalwart), Raymond Marriott, George Bullock, Evelyn Lewes, Gwyn and Alice Jones, Glyn Jones, Ted Richards, Berta Ruck, Ruby M. Ayres ("He was such a great man and I always liked and admired him tremendously") and Sarnicol (with an "In Memoriam" – in Welsh). Herbert M. Vaughan talked of Caradoc having made his mark on literature – "I value much his early books which I have here with some autograph letters of his" – and D. Owen Evans, M.P. for Cardiganshire, "never had any doubt of his real affection for his countrymen. He pilloried some of us because of his hatred of sham." John Carl (Jack) Flügel spoke of his death as a great loss to English literature: "One felt that every new work he produced was an 'event'". Back in London now, the Flügels' memories of Aber were bound up inextricably with their visits to New Cross, "when you and he dispensed such very happy and delightful hospitality." Mona Maeder, to whom Marguerite fled from Broadstairs in 1939, wrote: "It was so wonderful of you to realise the greatness of Caradoc Evans & to love him when the world will need a hundred years to wake to it." She knew the cost of living with greatness (though adding, "You were unhappy long before this, I know").

Duncan Davies wrote at length, the first of a series of letters that stands as our only record of Evans's early London years. And one person unknown got in touch, a Mrs J.B. Swete of Fishguard, who felt bound to express her sympathy and her regard for Caradoc's work. "I always admired his writing, so true to life, as he had seen it, and as I have seen it.... Forgive me, a stranger. I hope you will understand."

Evans was buried on Tuesday, 16 January 1945. Relations travelled from Rhydlewis and Tresaith for a brief service at the house, among them Caradoc's niece Lil Powell (with her husband Captain David Powell) and her brother Howell, whom Caradoc had helped into journalism. Outside of family, the few invited were those Caradoc would have wished to be there, among them Medical Officer of Health Dr Ernest Jones (from time to time he dropped in for a chat at Brynawelon); the astrologer Edward Lyndoe (Caradoc's old sparring partner); Mr Tibbott the Eastgate draper (he sold Caradoc his woman's beehive-shaped straw hat – worn with "a savage dignity", said Marguerite); and Henry Read of the *Cambrian News*. "I like Read," so Marguerite has Caradoc say, "He's a genuinely good man.... He may have a bee in his bonnet about booze but the bee has cost him money, and he doesn't care about that either.... I like his conversation when he gets on to Dickens. He's a Dickens fan. He's a maniac on Dickens."[59] Two Catholic nuns joined the company – "They sit in the far corner of the room by the window, their heads bent, their faces hidden by their enormous white coifs." The Revd Tom Beynon conducted the service, reading texts that Marguerite had copied out for him on a small sheet of green paper: Ecclesiastes 11:1-7 ("Cast thy bread upon the waters...") and verses from the fourth chapter of the Song of Solomon, which Caradoc often quoted as the most beautiful of love songs:

> Until the day break, and the shadows flee away, I will get me to the mountain of myrrh, and to the hill of frankincense.
> Awake, O north wind; and come, thou south; blow upon my garden, that the spices thereof may flow out. Let my beloved come into his garden, and eat his pleasant fruits.

A short prayer, followed by the Lord's Prayer, then the party moved off to the New Cross burial ground. Marguerite stayed behind at North Parade.

With Marguerite not present, we rely on the newspaper accounts of the burial at the top of Horeb chapel's tussocky, steep sloping cemetery. A heavy mist shrouded the Ystwyth valley below and the wide mountain ranges to the north and Caradoc's favourite "small rain" fell occasionally during proceedings. His coffin was borne by local farmers and farm-hands, friends he had made while at New Cross (the *Cambrian News* named eight). Tom Beynon again officiated and though Caradoc's wish was for the simplest of services with no orations, Beynon (speaking in Welsh) did say that he had been a regular, appreciative worshipper at Horeb: after each sermon, he never failed to send a short note of thanks. Philip Jones, Porthcawl, was his favourite preacher and "Pererin wyf mewn anial dir" his favourite hymn – the congregation duly sang it at the graveside. Their number was small but representative of Evans's diverse interests. "They included nun, Presbyterian elder, college lecturer, educationist, doctor, Fleet Street and local journalist, and tradesman."[60] At Marguerite's request Gentleman Jock was also present, their canine companion of fifteen years, brought along by his carer Mary Evans, Tŷ Canol.

Later that afternoon, when the relations had departed, Marguerite went out to New Cross by car. Timber accompanied her, as did Kathleen Riche-Evans, her new Catholic friend. It was still all rain and mist. She stood at the grave for a while and "touched with my fingers the cold white pillow of rain-soaked chrysanthemums with my initial M in red tulips, and then I turned to go." In time a stone would be laid, designed by Marguerite. In desk tablet form it displayed the writer's emblems: a closed book with a quill and inkwell low at the sides. His name is given – "Caradoc Evans" – and the date of his death. For an epitaph she chose Caradoc's own words: "Bury me lightly so that the small rain may reach my face and the fluttering of the butterfly shall not escape my ear." Slightly misquoted, they are a parting prayer he offered years before for the leaving of this life. Back at North Parade she sat to compose a message of thanks to those who had sent their condolences. Printed on a small round-cornered card and signed "Oliver Sandys (Marguerite Evans)", it told the simple truth: "Thank you so much. The song and the shout and the tempest have gone out of life for me and I do not like the calm."

Postscript

On 9 May 1945 Marguerite placed on Caradoc's grave flowers of red, white and blue; she told him it was Victory Day, that the war he had followed so intently was over. She thought of him constantly, heard his voice and responded. Aberystwyth was unbearable without him so once more she was on the move, this time to a small secluded bungalow named Heddle (now Dolwen) in Penrhyncoch. There she did all she could to keep his name alive, finding outlets for unpublished stories (most notably, *The Earth Gives All and Takes All*), giving his journal to the *Welsh Review*, and looking again at publishing the novel *Mother's Marvel*. She rehabilitated his rejected Evan Walters portrait: in 1946 it went from storage in London to the National Museum of Wales – "one of Walters' main masterpieces", acknowledged Iorwerth Peate. (The Museum accepted too Walters' companion portrait of Marguerite.) Encouraged by Gwyn Jones, she set aside her bread-and-butter writing for a biography of Caradoc. Gwyn met with her at Heddle shortly after the July general election. Churchill had been defeated, Labour were in with a landslide majority, and Marguerite and Nick were appalled. But you must accept it, Gwyn insisted; what else can you do? Nick, in his handsome dressing gown (at mid-afternoon), paused for a moment then answered: "I have my revolver. If they come for me, I shall know what to do." ("Shoot Attlee, or himself!" Jones speculated; it was a line out of one of the films "the ineffable ass" admired.)[1] Mother and son had swallowed Churchill's broadcast suggestion that Labour, if it came to power, would need a "Gestapo" to enforce its socialist policies. Nick became obsessed by the country's leftward lurch. "He has just got this Labour Government on the brain!" Marguerite told Alice Jones, and he was bent on leaving for California and films. "In a way, I understand his great urge to be up and away, but I CANNOT impress on him, hard though I try, that it is absolute folly to land in any country without any definite job or definite plan."[2] Lacking an income of his own, Nick could go nowhere unless his mother paid.

Losing Aberystwyth town life engendered no regret. "My dear, I just love it here," Marguerite assured Alice Jones, "and I loathe coming into the town." Nonetheless she rallied in defence of Katherine Guthkelch, long-time warden of the seafront women's hostel. "The G" was a commanding figure whose bourgeois English background set her apart from her Welsh working-class charges. Their complaints to the *Western Mail* about inadequate food in Hall sparked a response that put them in their place. What did the young ladies of Alexandra Hall expect? Marguerite asked (31 January 1947). She had recently stayed in a London hotel where for six guineas a week (bed, breakfast and dinner) she received "unutterably bad porridge, one rasher of bacon so thin it had to be fried with the rind on, or a tablespoon of haddock, or a morsel of dried egg.... Let these young women, who nearly all of them hail from modest homes, sample what they would get at any hotel or boarding-house… for £5 to £6 a week." Blame the Labour Government for this, not Mrs Guthkelch or the College!

Meantime Marguerite had allowed herself one last theatrical fling. In 1946, with holiday visitors returning, she revived the Rogues & Vagabonds for a brief summer season. With no proper director, designer, stage manager or administrator, her post-war company was a shadow of its Thirties' self. Between mid-July and mid-August a half-dozen actors, all billeted in Penrhyncoch, put on five plays at Borth's Public Hall. Nick was much to the fore – "expected to make a great impression on the writing and theatre worlds of tomorrow", ran the programme notes optimistically. (He made a decided impression on his leading lady Barbara Miller, their whirlwind romance and engagement making the *Cambrian News*.) John Edmunds, later a television newsreader and founder-director of Aberystwyth University's drama department, writes amusingly of a shoe-string enterprise that welcomed an Ardwyn school sixth-former eager to serve as assistant stage manager and bit player. One embarrassing moment occurred at the dress rehearsal of Rose Franken's romantic comedy *Claudia*, where Claudia asks her boyfriend David, "Do you love me?" "The 'guest actor' playing David, who thought a lot of himself, remained silent for an unconscionably long time, so I helpfully hissed from my corner: 'Yes.' The guest actor looked despairingly out at the Countess and shrugged his shoulders expressively. 'John, dear,' she said kindly, 'he won't forget that line.'"

> Countess Barcynska lived up to her name: she garbed herself colourfully and made up grotesquely with a defiant gash of bright red lipstick. At rehearsals she would sit out in front with the book and a cigarette and advise Nick to cut any lines he hadn't learnt. In the prompt corner my blue pencil was rapidly worn down. There being no-one else, I was responsible for running the show: drawing the curtains, putting records on the gramophone, adjusting the lighting, creating sound effects, looking after the props, and of course prompting. The only way to effect a blackout was to use the main power switch, so, in addition to my other stresses, I had to contend with the irate billiards players in a room off the stage who didn't appreciate being periodically plunged into darkness. The most demanding play of the season was *Blithe Spirit* with its blacked-out séances; it ran for two weeks and since most of the company had left by then, I was – somehow – playing Dr Bradman.[3]

In September 1946 Marguerite's biography of Caradoc went on sale having gained a £500 advance, "amazing for an expensive book", she thought (it sold at 16 shillings). Gwyn Jones praised it in the *TLS*: "an unusual, and in many ways a remarkably successful, experiment in biography… intimate, revealing and tenderly drawn [but] not the definitive life." Austin Clarke in the *Irish Times* (28 March 1947) found it "extraordinarily vivid", though its intimacy embarrassed: "She dramatizes her husband as if he were the hero-villain of one of her novelettes." Her "sugared confection" could have no appeal for Caradoc Evans admirers and would bewilder her "shop girl" readership. As it happened, the biography ran to a reprint and two years later Marguerite's *Unbroken Thread* appeared, a journal of early days at Penrhyncoch (August 1945 to March 1946). There her conversations with Caradoc continue; they happily reminisce and she passes on the current local news. Terrier Jock had died at seventeen-and-a-half, "as perfect as a dog could be". He was buried at New Cross, his passing marked by an impressive slate headstone inscribed with a verse of Marguerite's. She asks if there are dogs in the afterlife: "Of course there are," Caradoc tells her – "Dogs, but no lamp-posts." She mentions a marriage proposal, not from George Green (as Caradoc supposed), or from Evan Walters, who declared that he wished to be with her ("he will straight away see about getting a divorce from the wife he only lived with for one day!" she told Alice Jones), but from one "R.Y.", a judge working in India. Caradoc urges that she consider it seriously.[4]

A return to fiction became necessary and despite predictable problems in recruiting domestic help, Marguerite began a run of novels inspired by Caradoc. Writing *Conjuror* (June 1950), the story of Keidrich [sic] Jones, a young Welsh magician who finds fame and fortune with the aid of his elfin cat Modus, she felt her "beloved Caradoc… very close by my shoulder, fingers over my pen". (The *South Wales Evening Post* saw in her fictional Keidrich a striking resemblance to Caradoc.) Yet the novel brought much grief. Throughout the text its protagonist is "Keidrich Jones" but, strangely, on the dust-jacket (and again in the prelims) he becomes "Keidrich Rhys", an oversight taken up by the London *Evening Standard*. It proved the trigger for the real Keidrych Rhys to begin a libel action, from which his solicitors would withdraw when it could not be shown that the name "Keidrych" was proprietary. In 1952 Marguerite reported that a change of solicitors had brought a revival of the libel charge, with Rhys now claiming that his Druid Press and the periodical *Wales* had folded because of a falling off in sales through the loss of his reputation following *Conjuror*.[5] Gwyn Jones was able to confirm that both press and periodical had gone under twenty months before the novel appeared. (Rhys's memory of the affair was rather different: "the Countess got various scrawny bitches to waylay me & urged me to sue Hutchinson & not her. I didn't bother!")[6]

By 1952 Marguerite, with Nick and Timber, had moved to Shropshire. She had come to feel that Penrhyncoch (unlike New Cross) was secretive and unfriendly, its cottage doors always closed. (In fact she had temporarily left the village for a flat in Belsize Park.) In late 1951 she was telling Gwyn Jones of a place she had found at Church Stretton. "Now, isn't this strange? – Slap bang opposite the window of my flat is a frowning rocky ridge called 'the Caradoc' [Caer Caradoc] & it is just as if I am looking at his face in stone – the very spirit of the man as expressed in Nature."[7] Before she left she would pass to Jones a quantity of Caradoc's papers, together with photographs and other oddments. He must do with them as he thought best (they eventually went to the National Library of Wales.)[8]

Marguerite's Church Stretton flat was on The Burway, the second floor of Burway House, where her home help remembered a sweet-natured woman scribbling away in her huge armchair. Nick was a different story, lounging about for hours in his dressing gown – and throwing things at his mother in fits of anger.[9] His behaviour at Penrhyncoch had given cause for concern. Following a tip-off, the police arrived at Heddle in September

1951 to investigate his possession of firearms and Marguerite's fear that lives were in danger: Nick had said he would shoot himself, and his mother (an episode quickly passed off by the couple as foolish theatricals).[10] Marguerite clung to belief in Nick's brilliance and was cheered when a diary-novel of his appeared in America. Nicholas Sandys' *Starset and Sunrise* (1951) is a farcical romp about a young girl from a Catholic approved school who ends up a movie star. Its Catholic publishers Sheed & Ward felt able to claim: "The author knows motion picture studios as well as he knows homes for delinquents – two fields of knowledge seldom mastered by one man." Nick's writing continued at Burway House but with nothing brought to completion. Advice from Marguerite might result in yet more smashing of china and meals thrown across the floor. "He is not mad," she assured Alice Jones; "His mind (<u>when</u> he will take the trouble) is quite brilliant – he thinks of ideas in flashes, but <u>never gets any further</u>, just starts <u>& never finishes</u>."[11] Consequently, "he is dreadfully lonely because he doesn't make friends, not being sufficiently interested in people for themselves for them to be interested in them."To counter this isolation, she paid for his breaks in Cornwall, London and Paris. California remained his Mecca – meantime, a big sea-fishing cruise to the West Indies would suffice. She was "down on the ground", she confessed to Alice, with unceasing trouble from Nick, money draining away, and no books written for almost a year. As if this wasn't enough, her sheepdog Timber had been put down.

Yet all was not despair: Marguerite had a boyfriend, a Captain Hewitt, married, from Minton, the hamlet near Stretton. Indeed her arrival in Shropshire had much to do with him. She claims to have met him first at Aberystwyth, in the house of a mutual friend who suggested that he might be the man to help with the Kenya background of a book she had in hand. A pioneer-settler there, Gordon Hewitt had served with the King's African Rifles in the 1914-18 War, being mentioned in despatches for services in Uganda commanding the Nandi Scouts. In his immaculate dark-grey suit, he impressed Marguerite from the start: "He was inordinately tall and massively made, six foot one or thereabouts with a soldier's bearing. The short neatly trimmed beard he wore did not give him any look of age in spite of its whiteness. He had no age." (In fact, "the eternal boy" was a year younger than she.)[12] At their first encounter he suggested they take a "sea-breather", a spin in his car to Aberdyfi, a spot he loved. Driving northward, they briefly stopped at Heddle where he spotted Marguerite's blue Happiness Stone. It transfixed him – he knew of one exactly like it, a stone with miraculous properties in a cave on the slopes of Mount Elgon. Could it be that Marguerite's Stone was the complementary half of this "magic" stone in Kenya? She told the whole story in *The Miracle Stone of Wales* (1957), and how a televised interview of April 1955 – in which she displayed the Stone and explained its background – prompted a stream of enquiries from people eager to experience its beneficent power. Many arrived in person at Aberdyfi where, so it seemed, she had straightway settled with Hewitt. For those unable to make the journey to this "little Welsh Lourdes" Marguerite sent out a postcard that had been in contact with the Stone; "Keep it intimately in bag, or wallet, and close beside you at night. Do not let other hands contact it", ran the instructions. "The poor countess was

finally running a Lucky Stone touch in Aberdovey," as Keidrych Rhys saw it.[13] He shed
no tears; the woman was a pain, tiresomely repeating that contributors to *Wales* were
all influenced by her husband, from Rhys Davies to Dylan and the rest. As Welsh correspondent of the Sunday *People* Rhys would give her little scam no publicity.

Such was Marguerite's easy-going way with facts that *The Miracle Stone* has her
moving directly from Penrhyncoch to live with "Kenya Gordon" at Panteidal Lodge, a
Norwegian-pine chalet overlooking the estuary a little short of Aberdyfi. She omits
entirely the intervening years at Burway House (during which the pair were seeking a
suitable Aberdyfi property), because "I considered the Shropshire migration of no interest
& it would lengthen the book to no purpose."[14] Another absence from her account is
son Nick, who was living in London having left Shropshire well before January 1955,
the date when Marguerite actually departed for Panteidal. Yet he was rarely out of her
thoughts. Getting away from her might have been for the best but she hated to think of
him lonely and frustrated, parked in a Bayswater hotel. She wrote to Monica Dunbar
(22 September 1955): "If he had <u>any</u> job he would feel that there was some pattern in
life. I would give my life & soul to make things right for him if I could." She was certainly
giving him her money, blindly believing that he still had the talent for a stage career or
for the production side of television or radio – "He is so <u>full</u> of ideas."[15]

Two years later she confessed to Monica that things could not be worse – she was
close to bankruptcy on account of Nick. His five years in London had cost her £600-
£700 a year while her income had fallen to less than £1000. Television and changing
taste had drastically reduced her book-buying readership; libraries still wanted the hard-
backs but the cheap-reprint market had evaporated. "Financially afflicted" herself (she'd
borrowed from the Dunbars), her first thought was still of Nick "in the ditch" in London,
not knowing what to do. To her friends it seemed incredible that Nick, through all his
years there, had found no job to sustain him but relied completely on his mother. "God
knows I have told him over & over again how ceaselessly I have been working and how
that the sands are running, but whenever I did, he only said I was driving him to suicide
& to stop my hysterical ranting."[16]

At some unspecified point Kenya Gordon – unmentioned in her letters – left Marguerite and Nick to themselves and returned to Minton. By April 1959 Marguerite too
had moved, to 51 Trinity Street, Shrewsbury, from where she relayed to Monica Dunbar
yet more dire news of Nick. Through a friendship with Lady Demetriadi (wife of Sir
Stephen, businessman and civil servant), at Christmas 1958 he had sailed to America as
the house guest of a Mrs Vincent Smith – or so he imagined. But Mrs Smith had paid
for his passage on the understanding that he would act as a domestic help. He was now
her prisoner in California, unable to exploit the Happiness Stone – which he'd brought
over with him – before "going all out for films". Utterly destitute, he sought repatriation
and on in September 1959 managed a return to England (a "journalist" on the ship's
passenger list). The Stone was left behind, seemingly in the keeping of a friendly doctor
at San Francisco who would use it for healing purposes. Despite its loss, Marguerite
was elated; she told Monica Dunbar of a "lovely little cottage" she had found some fifteen

miles from Shrewsbury. "It is a dream & Nick so pleased & happy about it – a different person. He came back a gaunt creature weighing 9 stone. Now he is a good 12!"[17]

Marguerite's "dream" was No. 1 The Ancient House, Little Stretton, a semi-detached timber-framed Tudor cottage a couple of miles from Church Stretton. Settling there in September 1960, she gave the impression of one who had known better times, a lady of standing down on her luck. If she was almost a recluse (though still "carrying on" with the Minton man), "Count Nickie" was a local character, at least in the Ragleth Inn where he drank regularly and heavily. Rumour had it that he treated his mother abominably, to the point of threatening to murder her. "Selfishness is the beginning of child worship and sorrow is its reward," wrote Caradoc in *Wasps*. Marguerite's last years were distressingly bleak. The theatrical flame flickered briefly with talk of amateur dramatics in her spacious upstairs room but nothing came of it. Despite the grant of a civil list pension for literary services, money remained a problem; she still managed a couple of novels a year but for a public that hardly existed. A letter to Gwyn Jones mentions a bad fall suffered in 1962 and how an ensuing hip operation had left her "so weak and immobile".[18] Caradoc's fate further saddened her. "Why has the Dylan Thomas vogue swallowed him up & his name as a near classic almost forgotten?" she enquired of Gwyn, reminding him of the shy young poet who thirty years before had admiringly sought out her husband.[19] Above all, she feared for Nick, "a lost soul on his own", in need of a base in London and some semblance of home surroundings. A last letter to Monica Dunbar offered thanks for the necklace and a scarf that had come as a present. She hoped they would bring her luck – "or rather luck for Nick which with his happiness is all I ask of life and of God".[20] Concern for Nick brought his close friend Sarah Clynch to The Ancient House. Dr Winnie Gooch was in attendance and she it was who explained that Marguerite was looking to Sarah to care for Nick in the years to come. "Marguerite was not too ill to speak; she just couldn't find the words."[21]

On 10 March 1964 Marguerite Florence Laura Evans died of heart failure at Shrewsbury's Copthorne Hospital. She was seventy-seven. Following an 11 a.m. service at Llanfihangel-y-Creuddyn church, she was buried beside Caradoc at New Cross on Friday 13 March. Berta Ruck joined the small group of mourners – notice was short and a heavy fall of snow covered the ground – as the Revd J.D. Jones, Horeb's officiating minister, helped carry the coffin up from the chapel to the cemetery top. Caradoc is recorded as requesting that "when our two gravestones are side by side let there be honeysuckle throwing its tendrils over the both of us." No honeysuckle was planted and no stone for Marguerite put in place. Her grave remains unmarked, a mossy plot a little below the field boundary hedge and fence.

A Shropshire newspaper reporting the funeral said that her son was "unable to attend" ("through illness", Nick later explained). He might only recently have returned from another funeral, that of Wing Commander Forest (Tommy) Yeo-Thomas, the famed SOE agent who died in Paris on 26 February. Nick admired "The White Rabbit" intensely, claiming him as a friend, and having ordered an eye-catching floral tribute he fully intended to be present at the British Embassy service. But tracking Nick's movements was never easy. Following his mother's death and the sale of The Ancient House, he lived peripatetically out of suitcases, as an indefinite house guest, a paying lodger (when funds allowed), or a caravan owner-dweller. One caravan spell in the 1970s found him in York-shire, near to Patricia and Arnold Crowther, married elders in Wiccan religion and ancient witchcraft. With "his impeccable manners and air of good breeding", Nick struck Patricia as "a gentleman in every sense of the word", someone who could talk on a range of topics, "including magic and the worship of the Old Gods, to whom he was devoted".[22] Then he suddenly upped and went, and communication ceased.

Distinctive in black opera cloak and matching fedora, Nicholas Sandys returned to Aberystwyth in November 1979. He had left the motherly care of Sarah Clynch to fend for himself in Wales. Friendly advice was forthcoming: that he should look after the whole self, his body as well as his spirit, and that meant eating properly, cutting down on expensive cigarettes, and definitely on "surfeit drinking". He was almost sixty-four and desperately awaiting an old age pension. Penury would drive him through various cheaper town bedsits out to the caravan park at New Cross, not far from Brynawelon his wartime home. Congenitally secretive about his past, he spun fabulous tales for the *Cambrian News* and others of the past as he wished it had been: birth in Poland; a promising stage career ("I may yet be another Ronald Colman!"); war service that the Official Secrets Act prevented him disclosing; a post-war spell in America script writing for MGM – work cut short by his having to return to England to nurse an ailing mother (her death bizarrely assigned to 1956).[23] Fitfully connected to the everyday world, Nick enjoyed well enough its pleasures (a glass of whisky above all), and his face-to-face charm and courtesy won him friends in Aberystwyth, most of them women. Wiccan beliefs and rituals brought some measure of calm and self-control. His "god in female form" was Isis, Egyptian goddess of the moon, and however cramped his living quarters he found space for an altar with two white candles, a chalice of sanctified water and an athame, a magical ceremonial dagger. To close friends he signed off his letters with "Blessed be" ("as we of the craft say") and a carefully drawn circled pentagram.

Nicholas left Aberystwyth in 1987. An ill-managed diabetes having put him twice in hospital, he thought it best to return to Sarah Clynch at Margate. Things did not work out well there. His health further deteriorated and "this blasted diabetic trouble" hospitalized him again. He was feeling "left wing low". But Wales remained in his heart, "the land of the Goddess" and of happier youthful days. In 1992, aged seventy-six, and now styling himself Nicholas Barcynski (the name given him at birth), he went into hospital once more, this time with a perforated stomach ulcer. He appeared to have recovered well but a few days later, on 28 May, he died.

BOOKS by Caradoc Evans

My People: Stories of the *Peasantry of West Wales*. London, Andrew Melrose, [1915]

—— new edn., London, Dobson, 1953. Introduction by Gwyn Jones

—— new edn., Bridgend, Seren Books, 1987. Introduction by John Harris

U.S. editions: New York, Duffield, 1917; New York, Boni & Liveright, 1918

Capel Sion. Melrose, [1916]

—— new edn., Seren, 2002, with two post-*Capel Sion* stories. Introduction by John Harris

My Neighbours. Melrose, 1919. Actually published 1920

—— new edn., Aberystwyth, Planet, 2005. The American text, plus two stories rejected by Andrew Melrose

U.S. edns.: New York, Harcourt, Brace & Howe, 1920. Adds Evans's polemical preface "The Welsh People", re-orders the first four stories, and displays some textual variants

Taffy: A Play of Welsh Village Life in Three Acts. Melrose, [1924]

Nothing to Pay. London Faber & Faber, 1930

—— new edn., Manchester, Carcanet, 1989. Afterword by John Harris; pbk reprint, London, Cardinal (Sphere Books), 1990

U.S. edns.: New York, Norton, 1930; New Directions, 1995, pbk reprint of Carcanet 1989 edn

Wasps. London, Rich & Cowan, [1933], the R&C edn quickly suppressed; London, Hurst & Blackett, 1933

This Way to Heaven. Rich & Cowan, 1934

Pilgrims in a Foreign Land. London, Andrew Dakers, 1942

Morgan Bible. Dakers, 1943

—— new edn., *Morgan Bible & Journal 1939-44*. Aberystwyth, Planet, 2006. Edited with an afterword by John Harris

Mother's Marvel. Dakers, [1949]

Fury Never Leaves Us: A Miscellany of Caradoc Evans, ed. John Harris. Bridgend, Poetry Wales Press, 1985. Includes an biographical introduction and the revised text of *Taffy*

Selected Stories, ed. John Harris. Manchester, Carcanet, 1993

BOOKS by Marguerite Evans

Countess Barcynska, *I Loved a Fairy*. Hurst & Blackett, [1933]

Oliver Sandys, *Full and Frank: The Private Life of a Woman Novelist*. Hurst & Blackett, [1941]; new edn., London, National Book Association, 1947 (lacking illustrations)

Oliver Sandys, *Caradoc Evans*. Hurst & Blackett, [1946]

Oliver Sandys ('Marguerite Caradoc Evans'), *Unbroken Thread: An Intimate Journal of the Daily Life in the Welsh Countryside of England's Best-loved Woman Novelist*. London, Rider, [1948]

Oliver Sandys ('Marguerite Caradoc Evans'), *The Miracle Stone of Wales*. London, Rider, 1957

ARCHIVAL HOLDINGS

The National Library of Wales (NLW) at Aberystwyth holds almost all of the archival material relating to Caradoc Evans. Following her husband's death, Marguerite Evans roughly divided his papers, donating half to the National Library (1946/47) and giving half to Professor Gwyn Jones, this on the understanding that his half would eventually join hers in the national repository. He fulfilled her wishes: his Caradoc Evans archive, enhanced by valuable additions he acquired independently, now form part of the voluminous Gwyn Jones Papers at NLW. Details of Caradoc Evans archive holdings are available via NLW's online catalogue.

ABBREVIATIONS

CB Countess Barcynska, pen name of Marguerite Evans
CB: *ILF I Loved a Fairy*
CE Caradoc Evans
CN Cambrian News
DD Duncan Davies, Evans's early London friend
EGATA Caradoc Evans, *The Earth Gives All and Takes All*
FNLU Caradoc Evans, *Fury Never Leaves Us*
GG George Green, educational psychologist and university lecturer at Aberystwyth
GJ Gwyn Jones, Rendel Professor of English, Aberystwyth
JH John Harris, biographer
MD Monica Dunbar, daughter of Malcolm and Helen (Nell) Dunbar and, like her parents, a long-time friend of Marguerite's.
ME Marguerite Evans, Evans's second wife, who went under various names in her professional and personal life
ND Helen (Nell) Dunbar; always Nell to Marguerite
NLW National Library of Wales, Aberystwyth
OS Oliver Sandys, pen name of Marguerite Evans
OS: *CE* Oliver Sandys, *Caradoc Evans*
OS: *F&F* Oliver Sandys, *Full and Frank*
OS: *MSW* Oliver Sandys, *The Miracle Stone of Wales*
OS: *UT* Oliver Sandys, *Unbroken Thread*
PB Paula Block, the Evanses' wartime general maid
TPCW T.P.'s & Cassell's Weekly
UWP University of Wales Press
WM Western Mail

NOTES

Chapter 1. "I Remember Things" : Family and Boyhood in Rhydlewis

1. *Ideas*, 7 April 1916, 24.
2. David Jenkins, 'Community and Kin: Caradoc Evans "At Home"', *Anglo-Welsh Review* 24.53 (1974), 43-57.
3. D. Jacob Davies, 'Family Feuds', *Planet* 1 (1970), 71-4.
4. Cutting from the *South Wales Daily News* [1921?]. NLW Minor Deposit 897B.
5. Annie Rees to W. Anthony Davies, 22 June 1948. NLW Papers of T. Rowland Hughes & W. Anthony Davies.
6. One is tempted to think it an instance of the "obscure magic that gives famous people appropriate names" which Paul Ferris saw at work with Dylan Thomas.
7. Annie Rees, reminiscences [1948]. NLW Papers of T. Rowland Hughes & W. Anthony Davies.
8. J. Seymour Rees, 'Caradoc Evans', *YrYmofynnydd* 52.12 (1952), 204.
9. CE, 'My Preachers', *Sunday Express*, 25 October 1925, 13.
10. Jenkins, 'Community and Kin', 51.
11. *Cardigan and Tivy-Side Advertiser*, 27 July 1934, 6.
12. Howell Evans to ME, 6 February 1945. NLW Gwyn Jones Papers.
13. Edward Wright, 'Caradoc Evans', *Bookman*, October 1917, 6-7.
14. Maud Ellen Davies (née James), a daughter of Twrgwyn farm, Rhydlewis, who knew Mary Evans and wrote these words in a short profile of CE (probably in the 1970s).
15. Annie Rees to W. Anthony Davies, 22 June 1948.
16. It so happened that Hawen's longest individual ministry was followed by its shortest. The Revd Thomas Alban Davies arrived at Rhydlewis from Ton Pentre in summer 1929 and lasted a matter of months. His move had been a dreadful mistake: he missed industrial Rhondda's buzz and could not adjust to Cardiganshire rural life (it didn't help that the family's much loved dog was shot for worrying sheep). Fortunately, the pulpit of Bethesda, the great Congregational temple at Ton Pentre, remained untenanted and by 1930 Alban Davies had been reinstated there.
17. Miss Evans (Derlwyn, Rhydlewis), interview with JH. She recalled how Josi would gesticulate in chapel, urging Twrgwyn members to hurry up service proceedings.
18. David Jenkins, interview with JH, 6 February 1987; Howell Evans, interview with JH, 13 February 1987.
19. According to Howell Evans (son of Caradoc's sister Sarah), it seems that a man called at Caradoc's Fleet Street office and learning that Caradoc was at lunch said that he was his brother and would call again. He never did. "One can only imagine he was William. If his mother's surmise about the earthquake was right, of course, Caradoc's caller was a fraud." (Howell Evans, letter to ME, 6 February 1945.)
20. Howell Evans to ME, 6 February 1945. NLW, Gwyn Jones Papers.
21. Annie Rees to W. Anthony Davies, 10 August 1948. NLW Papers of T. Rowland Hughes & W. Anthony Davies.
22. K.O. Morgan, 'Cardiganshire Politics; the Liberal Ascendancy 1885-1923', *Ceredigion* 5 (1967), 311-46; Anita Arter, interview with JH, 21 December 1995.
23. Annie Rees to W. Anthony Davies, 10 August 1948.
24. Stanley. J. Kunitz & Howard Haycraft, *Twentieth Century Authors: A Biographical Dictionary* (New York,

H.W. Wilson, 1942), 430-1.

25. NLW Cardiganshire Local Education Authority Records 76a and 76b. Reference to an entry is made through its date in the log book.

26. Maud Ellen Davies (née James), 'Saturdays in Cardiganshire', manuscript essay. Private collection.

27. As David A. Pretty notes, rural school boards were dominated by shrewd-minded farmers who often themselves employed these young offenders; by turning a blind eye to absenteeism they "guaranteed yet another generation of docile workers and cheap labour". (*The Rural Revolt That Failed: Farm Workers' Trade Unions in Wales, 1889–1950*, Cardiff, UWP, 1989.)

28. GG, 'Caradoc', in *EGATA*, xv.

29. *Ideas*, 14 July 1916, 23.

30. CE, 'Self-Portrait', *Wales* 3 (1944), 83; *FNLU*, 104.

31. *Ideas*, 19 November 1915, 28.

32. D. Jacob Davies, 'Family Feuds'.

33. *Ideas*, 11 August 1916, 23.

34. CE, interview with the London *Star*, reprinted in *Carmarthen Journal*, 16 April 1915. On retirement from teaching, Crowther settled in Cardiff before moving to Solva, Pembrokeshire. He died aged 80 in February 1928 and is buried at Hawen, Rhydlewis.

35. 'Self-Portrait', 83.

36. 'Caradoc', *EGATA*, xvi.

37. Nest Lloyd (Llandysul), letter to JH, 16 September 1992.

38. 'Caradoc Evans', *Yr Ymofynnydd*, 52.12 (1952), 204-8.

39. A commemorative plaque marks her birthplace, Moylon farm, Rhydlewis. Caradoc nowhere mentions Moelona (1877-1953; Elizabeth Mary Jones on marriage); presumably he placed her among those writing "nice, false" novels of Wales. She is best remembered for her children's novel *Teulu Bach Nantoer* ('The Little Family of Nantoer'). Published in 1913 (two years before *My People*), it was regularly reprinted, achieving sales estimated at over 30,000.

40. Annie Rees, reminiscences [1948].

41. *Ideas*, 28 July 1916, 23.

42. J.N. Crowther, letter to *TPCW*, 10 October 1925, 803.

43. *Ideas*, 28 July 1916, 23.

44. 'Caradoc Evans's Boyhood Days', *Wales* 27 (December 1947), 381.

45. 'Self-Portrait', 83.

46. John Crowther, 'The late Rev David Adams', *Cardigan and Tivy-Side Advertiser*, 14 July 1922, 6.

47. J.N. Crowther, *Cardigan and Tivy-Side Advertiser*, 14 July 1922, 6.

48. J.T. Jones, *WM*, 18 July 1924, 6.

49. David Adams, 'Creed and Character', *University College of Wales Magazine* 1 (November 1878), 27-31.

50. Translation by David Jenkins, *The Agricultural Community in South-West Wales at the Turn of the Twentieth Century* (Cardiff, UWP, 1971), 217.

51. Jenkins, *Agricultural Community*, 217.

52. *People*, 20 July 1924, 13.

53. J.T. Jones, *WM*, 18 July 1924, 6.

54. Idwal Lewis, 'John Newton Crowther (Glanceri, 1847-1928)', *Dictionary of Welsh Biography*. Available online.

55. CE, 'Things That Anger Me', *Daily Express*, 8 April 1930.

56. John Crowther, newspaper cutting. NLW Minor Deposit 897B.

57. He succeeded in bringing together for teaching purposes two distinct chapel choirs. David Jenkins remarks that delicate tasks of this kind were best achieved by an "institutionalized outsider", a person whose background and occupation identified him with no particular local faction. (*Agricultural Community*, 201.)

58. *Cardigan and Tivy-Side Advertiser*, 15 March 1889, 4.

59. 'Caradoc Evans', *Bookman*, 6-7.

60. See M. Euronwy James, *Annibynwyr Pisgah a Phenrhiwgaled, Ceredigion* (Llandysul, Gomer, 1971), 87-93.

61. 'Joshua Powell, MRCS, LSA', *British Medical Journal*, 27 October 1917, 569. Obituary.

62. Thus in a Cardiganshire minority: "Only the peer, the priest and the publican will rally to the Conservatives," thought the *Cambrian News* (31 December 1909), anticipating the 1910 general election; "the only question is the size of the Liberal majority." (In the event, the Tories polled almost a third of the vote.)

63. Howell Evans to ME, 13 April 1945. NLW Gwyn Jones Papers.

64. Miss Evans (Derlwyn, Rhydlewis), interview with JH.

65. Dr Powell died a wealthy man. The *Cardigan and Tivy-Side Advertiser* (11 January 1918) carried a notice of his house and effects. Line after line list the choicest possessions, the auctioneer finally resorting to "and other articles too numerous to mention". Powell's will valued personal effects at more than £6,000.

66. George Bullock, 'Caradoc Evans', radio talk, 23 March 1948. NLW BBC Wales Archives: Scripts.

67. *Ideas*, 1 September 1916, 23.

68. Barbara Prys-Williams, 'Fury Never Left Him: the Psychology of Caradoc Evans', *New Welsh Review* 31 (1995-96), 60-2. A psychoanalytical reading laying stress on the trauma of Caradoc's father's early death.

Chapter 2. Draper's Assistant, Apprentice Journalist

1. 'Impertinent Interviews', *London Mail*, 20 February 1926, 25; S.J. Kunitz & H. Haycraft, *Twentieth Century Authors* (1942), 430.

2. W.J. Rees, 'Inequalities: Caradoc Evans and D. J. Williams: A Problem in Literary Sociology', *Planet* 81 (1990), 69-80.

3. CE, 'The Living Welsh Language', *Sunday Times*, 29 January 1928, 14.

4. DD to ME, 24 February 1945. NLW Gwyn Jones Papers.

5. Howell Evans to ME, 6 February 1945.

6. Speaking of bogus apprenticeships, H.G. Wells recalled that in his day every draper's shop had from four to ten apprentices whose parents had paid between twenty and fifty pounds, believing that they were making little gentlemen of their sons. "The employer undertook to teach them the trade. I learned nothing." (*Manchester Guardian*, 6 April 1931.)

7. "Impertinent Interviews", 25.

8. *National Amalgamated Union of Shop Assistants, Warehousemen and Clerks Annual Congress, Cardiff, Easter 1908, Official Programme and Souvenir*. NLW XHD 6668. Contains a survey, 'Cardiff and the National Union', by A. Parr.

9. Sewell Stokes, *Personal Glimpses* (T. Werner Laurie, 1924), 139.

10. T. Michael Pope, 'Caradoc Evans', *Current Literature* 260 (August 1930), 306.

11. CE, 'Children and News', *Cassell's Weekly*, 19 May 1923, 327; *FNLU*, 106-8.

12. His letters to ME, 1945-46. NLW Gwyn Jones Papers.

13. DD to ME, February 1945.

14. T.P. O'Connor, 'Men, Women, and Memories', *Sunday Times*, 5 September 1926, 9.

15. DD to ME, February 1945. P.C. Hoffman, *They Also Serve: The Story of the Shop Worker* (Porcupine Press, 1949) provides a graphic account of 'living in'.

16. David Muspratt of the Working Men's College kindly supplied details of CE's time there.

17. 1900 to 1914 saw a major expansion in university and adult education; W.D. Caröe, the architect of the new building, also designed University College, Cardiff.

18. Howell Evans to ME, 13 April 1945.

19. DD to ME, February 1945.

20. Both extracts are quoted in Quentin Bell, *Virginia Woolf: A Biography*. Vol. 1 (Hogarth, 1972), 106, 203. The first is from a letter to Violet Dickinson and the second from a report prepared by Woolf in July 1905.

21. Quoted in Stanley Pierson, *Marxism and the Origin of British Socialism* (Cornell UP, 1973), 151-2.

22. Pierson, 55.

23. T.S. Eliot, 'In Memoriam: Marie Lloyd', *Criterion*, January 1923, 192-5.

24. CE, 'Self-Portrait', *Wales* 3 (1944), 85; *FNLU*, 104-6.

25. *The Autobiography of Arthur Machen* (Richards Press, 1951), 72.

26. DD to ME 3 March 1945.

27. DD to ME, 24 February 1945 and 12 November 1946.

28. DD to ME, 24 February 1945.

29. From Burke's 'Caradoc Evans: the Man and His Work', printed on the dust jacket of the American edition of CE's *Nothing to Pay* (New York, Norton, 1930).

30. One thinks of Dylan Thomas's 'The Orchards', according to Vernon Watkins "written in minute handwriting on the inside cover of a cardboard box. He [Thomas] told me that it helped him to see the whole story in one place as he wrote it, and pages were less good for this than box-covers." (Introduction, Dylan Thomas, *Letters to Vernon Watkins*, 1957.)

31. DD to ME, February 1945.

32. 'The Road with One Fingerpost', *TPCW*, 26 July 1924, 466; *FNLU*, 120 CE here writes of the acceptance of Thomas Burke's first story.

33. Working Men's College Entries: Fifty-second College Year, 1 August 1905 to 31 July 1906.

34. Letter in *Western Mail Jubilee Supplement*, 1 May 1919.

35. Howell Evans to ME, 6 February 1945.

36. *Cassell's Weekly*, 19 May 1923, 327.

37. *Autobiography of Arthur Machen* (1951), 67-9.

38. CE, 'A Bundle of Memories', in *The Book of Fleet Street*, ed. T. Michael Pope (Cassell, 1930), 92; *FNLU*, 111-6.

39. DD to ME, 24 February 1945.

40. D.L. Evans, *WM*, 24 April 1952, 6.

41. Edward Wright, 'Caradoc Evans', *Bookman*, October 1917, 7.

42. *With Northcliffe in Fleet Street: A Personal Record* (Hutchinson, 1932), 38-9.

43. Journalist, novelist, sailor and tramp.

44. J.A. Hammerton, *Child of Wonder: An Intimate Biography of Arthur Mee* (Hodder, 1946), 114.

45. T. Michael Pope, 'Caradoc Evans', 306.

46. Desmond Hawkins, *When I Was: A Memoir of the Years Between the Wars* (Macmillan, 1989).

47. J.A. Hammerton, *Books and Myself*, 207-8.

48. OS: *CE*, 77.

49. CE, 'A Bundle of Memories', 93.

50. DD to ME, 12 November 1946.

51. CE, 'Downtrodden Actors', *Sunday Express*, 20 September 1925, 7.

52. CE, 'My Preachers', *Sunday Express*, 25 October 1925, 13; *FNLU*, 108-11.

53. 'My Preachers', 13.

Chapter 3. Earliest Stories: Cockney and Welsh

1. DD to ME, dated February 1945.

2. CE, 'Self-Portrait', *Wales* 3 (1944), 85.

3. Reprinted in Trevor L. Williams, *Caradoc Evans* (1970), 31-7.

4. Ieuan Gwynedd Jones, 'Language and Community in Nineteenth-century Wales', in *A People and a Proletariat,* ed. David Smith (Pluto Press, 1980), 53.

5. Except that the usually reliable Duncan Davies speaks of Evans as keeping up his freelance writing. "One of the editors who took a good deal of his work was Frank Harris, and Caradoc had many amusing stories to tell of his connection with that extraordinary character." Despite extensive searching, no Evans pieces in journals associated with Harris have so far come to light.

Chapter 4. "A Wild Welsh Editor Chained Up" Evans at *Ideas*

1. Swaffer's memoir of Caradoc appears as an appendix to OS: *CE*, 147-9.

2. Margaret Lane, *Edgar Wallace: The Biography of a Phenomenon* (Heinemann, 1938), 197.

3. CE, 'A Bundle of Memories', 94.

4. *Edgar Wallace: A Short Autobiography* (Hodder & Stoughton, 1926).

5. 'Up to Easter', *Nineteenth Century* 21 (1887), 638.

6. See the prefaces ('The Trend in Fleet Street') to Mitchell's annual *Newspaper Press Directory*, 1916, 1917.

7. Evans's own salary at this time must have been around the £10 a week *Ideas* paid Edgar Wallace.

8. CE, interview with the *Evening News* (London), 12 November 1915.

9. 'A Bundle of Memories', 94.

10. Edith Nepean, 'Caradoc Placed My Feet on the Ladder', *WM*, 16 January 1945, 3.

11. GJ, *The First Forty Years: Some Notes on Anglo-Welsh Literature* (Cardiff, UWP, 1957), 9.

Chapter 5. *My People*: "Banned, Burned Book of War"

1. Howell Evans to ME, 6 February 1945.

2. Maud Ellen Davies (née James), a daughter of Twrgwyn farm, Rhydlewis.

3. Edith Nepean, 'Caradoc Placed My Feet on the Ladder', *WM*, 16 January 1945, 3.

4. The paper explained (26 September 1913) that the letter had come its way via a Hong Kong reader who had found it the *South China Morning Post* (a Hong Kong paper taking syndicated material from all corners of the world).

5. DD to ME, February 1945.

6. D.T. Davies, *WM*, 30 August 1924.

7. Austin Clarke, 'The Bitter Word', *Irish Times*, 29 March 1947. Duncan Davies thought it important that "for a long time, Caradoc had confined his reading to the great realistic writers, Ibsen, Zola,

Chekhov, Shaw, George Gissing, etc.: and he had deliberately made up his mind to keep his stories drab and sordid. He would have nothing to do with my suggestion that occasionally a simple and innocent peasant might be allowed to creep in and leaven the picture. No, he had finally made up his mind on that matter." (DD to ME, 12 November 1946.)

8. 'David Caradoc Evans' appears as the author of 'Two Welsh Studies', the umbrella title for 'The Man who Walked with God' (later re-titled 'A Father in Sion') and 'Be This Her Memorial'. For two further stories in the *English Review* (July 1915) 'Caradoc Evans' is preferred; henceforth 'David Caradoc' would be confined to Evans's letters to the press.

9. A prominent Swansea public figure and keen promoter of Welsh art, Williams later at the *South Wales Daily Post* made Dylan Thomas a cub reporter. In 1936 heart failure caused him to fall to his death while mountain climbing in Snowdonia.

10. Peter Lord, *Winifred Coombe Tennant: A Life through Art* (Aberystwyth, NLW, 2007), 56.

11. *Y Geninen* instances the pastoral fund, the chapel debt fund, the chapel bank fund and the denominational fund, in addition to the Sunday School fund and the standard Sunday evening collection.

12. More recently, commentators have stressed the importance of the treacherous 1847 'Blue Books' in shaping Welsh responses to Caradoc Evans. Widely quoted at the time, these blue-bound volumes of *Reports of the Commissioners of Inquiry into the State of Education in Wales* passed into folk memory largely on account of reports, by three non-Welsh-speaking Anglican commissioners, on the backwardness and immorality of the Welsh, a consequence (so they believed) of Welsh religion and the Welsh language. "The brouhaha over the Blue Books was paradoxical and contradictory," writes the historian Prys Morgan; "On the one hand it made the Welsh more nationalistic and Anglophobe... on the other it made the Welsh concerned to answer the criticisms of the Commissioners by becoming more like the English, by turning themselves into practical, hard-headed, business-like English-speaking Britons." From feelings of victimisation sprang healing self-praise and a remarkable appropriation of Welsh culture by a united Nonconformist front of preachers, politicians, publishers and press. Nonconformity came to stand for Welshness itself. Romantic myths evolved – Evans's "sorry illusions of Wales" – among them the notion of the spotless rural heartlands, the nation's spiritual home. If in 1915 the treacherous *My People* brought the Blue Books to mind, its opponents did not mention them. Their Anglophobia was freely displayed and their extraordinary concern for how the book would appear to the English, a people thought to be all too ready to believe the worst of Wales.

13. Martha S. Vogeler, *Austin Harrison and the English Review* (Columbia, University of Missouri Press, 2008), 171.

14. Stanley Unwin, *The Truth About Publishing: An Autobiographical Record* (Allen & Unwin, 1960), 133.

15. Russell Davies, 'Inside the "House of the Mad": the Social Context of Mental Illness, Suicide and the Pressures of Rural Life in South West Wales, c. 1860-1920', *Llafur: Journal of the Society for the Study of Welsh Labour History* 4.2 (1985), 20-35, explores the records of the Joint Counties Lunatic Asylum at Carmarthen (Evans's 'House of the Mad').

16. Russell Davies, '"In a Broken Dream": Some Aspects of Sexual Behaviour and the Dilemmas of the Unmarried Mother in South West Wales, 1887-1914', *Llafur: Journal of the Society for the Study of Welsh Labour History* 3.4 (1983), 24-33.

17. David Jenkins, *Agricultural Community*, 231.

18. CE, 'Chapel Prussianism', *New Witness*, 8 February 1917, 434. Review of Mary Webb, *The Golden Arrow* (1916).

19. Alun Richards, *Days of Absence* (Michael Joseph, 1986), 27.

20. D.M. Davies, *Hanes Eglwys Annibynol Hawen, Ceredigion* (Llandysul, Gomer, 1947), 22; S. Gwilly Davies, *Dyffryn Troedyraur* (Llandysul, Gomer, 1976), 40. David Jenkins, 'Community and Kin', 52, mentions that Nanni was "a woman who lived almost within a stone's throw of Caradog's home".

Chapter 6. *My People*: Public Reaction

1. As recounted by GG, *EGATA*, xxiv.
2. CE, *WM*, 27 November 1915, 4.
3. J.B. Priestley to ME, 7 March 1945. NLW Gwyn Jones Papers.
4. Thought to be Norman Douglas, the *English Review's* assistant editor who had helped bring Evans's work to prominence and had favourably reviewed *My People*. "Douglas liked people of character, people whose idiosyncrasies had not been worn away to polished surfaces," remarks his biographer Mark Holloway.
5. As quoted by CE, *WM*, 15 March 1916, 7.
6. CE, interview with the *Globe*, 21 January 1916.
7. CE, 'The Banned Book', *WM*, 22 January 1916, 6. This letter, setting out the Evans/Melrose position, also appeared in the *Globe*, the *Pall Mall Gazette*, the *Weekly Dispatch*, the *Liverpool Post* and the *Yorkshire Post*.
8. A fourth impression of the book (February 1916) shows a redesigned dust jacket. Extracts from favourable reviews fill its front cover. The back carries Melrose's original note, below which is appended: "N.B. The above was written before the Press had seen the book. The reviews which appear on the front of this cover show how completely the publisher's note has been justified."
9. CE, *WM*, 22 January 1916.
10. Of Australian descent, Lynch had fought against the British in the second Boer War and was afterwards tried for high treason, sentenced to death, and imprisoned for life after commutation. Following a year's intense petitioning, he was pardoned in 1907 and two years later became West Clare's MP.
11. British Library Add. 57016 Society of Authors letter book.
12. CE, 'Cardiff Police and "My People"', letter to *WM*, 15 March 1916, 7.
13. CE, *NewWitness*, 17 February 1916, 484.
14. *Labour Voice*, 6 November 1915, 5.
15. Joseph Keating, 'The Fascinating Welshman', *WM*, 27 December 1916, 4.
16. [Lewis Giles], *Carmarthen Journal*, 17 December 1915, 7.
17. Thomas Owen, letter to *WM*, 13 April 1953, 8.
18. David L Evans, letter to *WM*, 24 April 1952, 6.

Chapter 7. *Capel Sion*

1. CE, typescript of an address to the Tomorrow Club, November 1926. NLW Gwyn Jones Papers. An abbreviated version in *WM*, 5 November 1926, 8.
2. Printed as an appendix to *Capel Sion* (Bridgend, Seren, 2002), 103-7.
3. CE, 'Welshmen as Self-Advertisers', *WM*, 10 February 1925, 6; *FNLU*, 137-8. From an address to the Publicity Club of London.
4. DD to ME, 3 March 1945.
5. Andrew Melrose to Mrs Harold Eastwood, 21 February 1917. NLW MS 20018C.
6. CE, 'Mary Webb', *Colophon* 3 (1938), 123.

7. Hannen Swaffer, *Weekly Dispatch*, 14 December 1916.

8. David A. Pretty, *Rural Revolt That Failed*, 213.

9. Andrew Melrose to Mrs Harold Eastwood, 21 February 1917.

10. CE, 'The Welsh People', *Faculty of Arts Journal* [University of London] 4 (February 1925), 57.

11. CE, 'The Welsh Miner', *New Witness*, 7 December 1916, 4; *FNLU*, 154-6.

12. Quotations in this paragraph are taken from CE, 'Men and Women 2: W.H. Davies', *Welsh Review* 3.3 (1944); *FNLU*, 126-30.

13. CE, 'Tramp and Poet', *WM*, 15 January 1916, 7.

14. CE, *New Witness*, 17 February 1916, 184.

15. CE, *New Witness*, 8 February 1917, 434.

16. Grant Uden, "'Thomas Burke of London', *Antiquarian Book Monthly Review* 11 (1984), 482-5.

17. CE, 'The Road with One Fingerpost', 466.

18. CE, 'A Bundle of Memories', 94.

19. *WM*, 9 November 1916.

20. *The Private Diaries of Sydney Moseley*, 163.

21. 'Notorious Pest Deported', *The Times*, 14 June 1915, 3.

22. H. Simonis, *The Street of Ink: An Intimate History of Journalism* (Cassell, 1917), 92.

Chapter 8. "Bright and Lively and Humble": A *Mirror* Man

1. Austin Harrison, 'The old "English"', *English Review* 36 (1923), 512-3.

2. His support for Evans rebounded when in the "khaki election" of December 1918 he took on Lloyd George in the Prime Minister's safe haven, Caernarvon Boroughs. With no hope of victory, Harrison chose to stand as an Independent, largely as the advocate for a League of Nations. Local papers dismissed an intruder and "His publication of Caradoc Evans's hostile portraits of the Welsh was held against him." Family legend held that he narrowly avoided a ducking in the river. (Martha S. Vogeler, *Austin Harrison and the English Review*, Columbia, University of Missouri Press, 229.)

3. Anita Arter (nee Davies), interview with JH, 21 December 1995.

4. *Everyman*, 23 February 1917, 398.

5. Ada Chesterton, 'Tabletalk', *Everyman*, 26 October 1917, 58.

6. CE, letter to *WM*, 15 November 1917, 2, in answer to G.N.W. Thomas, 12 November, 4.

7. Howell Evans, in conversation with JH.

8. CB, *I Loved a Fairy* (Hurst & Blackett, 1933), 162. Written by ME soon after her marriage to CE, this epistolary novel, largely set in 1922, clearly shows his hand.

9. 'In Praise of Journalists', in Gerald Gould, *The Musical Glasses and Other Essays* (Methuen, 1929), 13-9.

10. Howell Evans, in conversation with JH.

11. Edward Wright, 'Caradoc Evans', 6-7.

12. Gerald Cumberland, *Written in Friendship: A Book of Reminiscences* (Grant Richards, 1923), 39-40.

13. Hannen Swaffer, 'Caradoc', in OS: *CE*, 148.

14. Augustus John, *Autobiography* (Cape, 1975), 403.

15. Howell Evans to ME, 16 February 1945.

16. Annie Rees to W. Anthony Davies, 30 August 1948. In Welsh.

Chapter 9. *My Neighbours*

1. They are appended in the Seren edition of *Capel Sion* (2002).

2. Glyn Roberts, *I Take This City* (Jarrolds, 1933), 263.

3. Quoted in Greg Hill, *Llewelyn Wyn Griffith* (Cardiff, UWP, 1984), 22-3.

4. *Starrett vs. Machen: A Record of Discovery and Correspondence*, ed. Michael Murphy (St Louis, Autolycus Press, 1977), 63-4.

5. Letter to Colin Summerford, 25 September 1945, in Arthur Machen, *Selected Letters: The Private Writings of the Master of the Macabre*, ed. Roger Dobson and others (Wellingborough, Aquarian Press, 1988).

6. C. Marshall Rose, *Mortlake in the 17th Century and the History of its Congregational Church, 1662-1950* (1995). Privately printed.

7. Ben's Birds' Rock peroration echoes Lloyd George at Queen's Hall (19 September 1915). Michael Macdonagh describes this electrifying performance before the London Welsh, Lloyd George in summery light grey suit striding to the platform, exuding confidence; behind him the flags of the Allies drape the great organ while a choir of Welsh women, robed in white, leads the fervent gathering through 'Land of My Fathers'. (*In London During the Great War: The Diary of a Journalist*, 1935, 28.)

8. P.C. Hoffman, *They Also Serve: The Story of the Shop Worker* (1949), includes a vivid account of the living-in system and its eventual demise.

9. 'Wisdom' and 'The Lantern Bearer' are printed as an appendix in CE, *My Neighbours* (Aberystwyth, Planet, 2005).

10. The letter recalls Llewelyn Williams, a prominent anti-Lloyd George Liberal, on the thirst for honours among Welsh MPs: "You get into the House to get on; you stay in to get honours; you get out to get honest."

11. "There was a custom of 'cadw'r mis' [to keep the month]. This meant that all farmers took their turn to supply food for the visiting minister every Sunday for a month. This was taken to the 'Ty Capel' – the chapel house – on the Saturday evening for the caretaker to prepare for the preacher's Sunday lunch and tea. It usually consisted of a chicken & vegetables, an apple pie or milk pudding, home made bread and butter, eggs and cakes, honey and jam. There was a time when an ounce of tobacco was taken too but that was before my time but I well remember Nain [grandmother] saying about it." (Maud Ellen Davies [née James], 'Saturday in Cardiganshire', a manuscript essay, privately owned.)

12. 'The Sahara of the Bozart', in H.L. Mencken, *Prejudices: Second Series* (Cape, 1921), 136-54.

13. H.L. Mencken, *The American Scene: A Reader* (New York, Knopf, 1977), 157.

Chapter 10. *Taffy*: Novel and Play

1. Edward Wright, 'Caradoc Evans', 6-7.

2. *WM*, 10 May 1922, 9.

3. The unfinished *Taffy* comprises thirty short chapters, most of which survive in draft (part manuscript, part typescript). Following Evans's death a portion of the text went to NLW and a portion to GJ, an assiduous collector of Anglo-Welsh literary papers. These portions are now at NLW (MS 20031B, MS 21624B) and quotations in this chapter are taken from them.

4. The youthful preacher's forename derives from Charles Haddon Spurgeon, the immensely popular nineteenth-century Baptist minister who frequently visited Wales and whose writings were translated into Welsh. Behind Ben Woodenleg lies Rhys Davies (Y Glun Bren, or Wooden Leg), a Congregationalist preacher of the locality who lost a leg at a religious gathering when, in an excess of fervour, a heavily built enthusiast accidentally trod on his foot.

5. CE, interview with *Daily Graphic*, 26 February 1923.

6. From a June 1917 article, reprinted in H. Dennis Bradley, *Not For Fools* (Grant Richards, 1920).

7. The fullest report of the performance is probably the *Daily Graphic's*, 27 February 1923; Berta Ruck, *A Trickle of Welsh Blood* (Hutchinson, 1967), provides a further eyewitness account.

8. Report dated 12 February 1923, British Library Lord Chamberlain's Plays: Correspondence, *Taffy* 1923/4723. The licensed copy of the play is also on file at British Library, Lord Chamberlain's Playscripts, Taffy, 1923.

9. *Daily Graphic*, 27 February 1923.

10. *Sunday Express*, 4 March 1923, 6.

11. Edwin Pugh, 'Mary Webb', *Bookman*, July 1928, 193-6.

12. Augustus John to CE, 27 February 1923, NLW MS 20034D.

13. Margot Asquith to CE, 27 February 1923, NLW MS 20034D.

14. *Saturday Review*, 3 March 1923, 185-6.

15. *English Review*, April 1923, 350.

16. *The Times*, 27 February 1923. Trewin, *Edith Evans*, 20, has a photograph of the actress as Marged.

17. John D. Lewis, 'Libel on Life in Wales', *WM*, 27 February 1923, 6.

18. 'Caradoc Evans's "People"', *WM*, 5 March 1923, 8.

19. *WM*, 3 March 1923, 7.

20. "Do I Insult the Welsh", *Sunday Express*, 4 March 1923; *FNLU*, 156-7.

21. 'Caradoc Evans's Monsters', *South Wales Daily News*, 6 March 1923, 5; 'Way Down West: "The Sweet Shire of Cardigan"', *WM*, 2 June 1923, 9.

22. William D. Jones, *Wales in America: Scranton and the Welsh, 1860-1920* (Cardiff, UWP, 1993) documents the near-hysterical American-Welsh reaction to CE.

Chapter 11. "The Best-Hated Man in Wales"

1. *Cassell's Weekly*, 21 March 1923.

2. CB: *ILF*, 66.

3. This and the succeeding two quotations are from a draft article on O'Connor. NLW Gwyn Jones Papers. A version appeared as 'Men and Women, 3: T.P. O'Connor', *Welsh Review* 4.1 (1945), 34-5.

4. 'Downtrodden actors', *Sunday Express*, 20 September 1925, 7.

5. Austin Clarke, *A Penny in the Clouds: More Memories of Ireland and England* (Routledge, 1968), 181. Poppin's, also known as the Compositors' Arms (it stood opposite the offices of the union of printers and compositors), is the subject of Clennell Wilkinson's contribution to T. Michael Pope's collection *The Book of Fleet Street* (1930), 271-9. Wilkinson lists the Fleet Street familiars who gathered there in the early 1920s, CE among them.

6. Reginald Pound, *Their Moods and Mine* (Chapman & Hall, 1937), 259.

7. Sewell Stokes, *Personal Glimpses*, 135-6, 137. Journalist, biographer, co-author of the first play about Oscar Wilde, Stokes worked briefly for CE on *T.P.'s Weekly*.

8. Con O'Leary, *TPCW*, 20 September 1924, 690.

9. Arthur Machen, letter to J. Leslie Miller, 22 February 1937. In Arthur Machen, *Selected Letters: The Writings of the Master of the Macabre* (1988).

10. CB: *ILF*, 83.

11. This and the succeeding quotation are from Machen letters to CE. NLW MS 14935C.

12. Arthur Machen to ME, June 1945.

13. H. Dennis Bradley, *Towards the Stars* (T. Werner Laurie, 1924), 169.

14. *Towards the Stars*, 210-1.

15. The case is reviewed in J. Gwyn Griffiths, *Atlantis and Egypt* (Cardiff, UWP, 1991), 266.

16. The incident is recounted in J. Seymour Rees, 'Caradoc Evans', *YrYmofynnydd* 52.12 (1952), 204-8.

17. CE, letter to *Review of Reviews*, June-July 1924, 542.

18. Specifically by Olive Ely Hart, who interviewed CE for her thesis *The Drama in Modern Wales* (Philadelphia, 1928).

19. 'The Welsh People', *Faculty of Arts Journal* [University of London] 4 (1925), 56.

20. J.H. Evans, *WM*, 12 June 1924.

21. The *Mail's* publicity given to Evans had its own unforeseen impact: on 1 July 1924 the Library Committee of Abergorki Workmen's Hall and Institute recommended purchase of *My People* and *Capel Sion*.

22. 'The Transactions of Our Village Eisteddfod', *Welsh Outlook*, January 1922, 7.

23. Quoted in Huw Ethall, *R.J. Berry* (John Penry, 1985), 34.

24. See *WM*, 25 and 26 July 1924.

25. David Powell, letter to *WM*, 26 July 1924.

26. The pub here alluded to is presumably the Ffostrasol Inn.

27. D.T. Davies, 'Caradoc Evans: a Defence and an Appreciation', *WM*, 30 August 1924, 5.

28. Berta Ruck, *A Trickle of Welsh Blood*, 162.

29. Extracts from CE's address appeared in the *WM* and the *Liverpool Daily Post*, 8 November 1924. The *WM*, 10 November, further describes student reaction.

30. In a broadcast, 'Caradoc Evans and the BBC', Radio Wales, March 1987.

31. *Magazine of the University College of North Wales* 33.1 (December 1924), 36-7.

32. Letter to the *Liverpool Daily Post*, 10 March 1987.

33. Moses Gruffydd, who within a year would be one of the six people at the meeting that founded Plaid Cymru (8 August 1925).

34. T. Ceiriog Williams to JH, 10 April 1987.

35. There are reports of the occasion in *WM*, 2 and 3 December 1924.

36. *Personal Glimpses*, 135.

37. The text is partly reported in *WM*, 10 February 1925.

38. The fullest printed version of this talk, taken from Evans's surviving typescript, appears in *FNLU*, 131-6.

39. The November 1925 issue of the *Writer* carried a cover sketch of Evans by 'Sava', the caricaturist and portrait sculptor Anasta Botzaris Sava (1894-1965; born in Belgrade, he settled in London in 1920, emigrating to Venezuela in 1941). The sketch was to accompany an article on Evans by one Ashley Belbin; listed in the contents of the November issue, it seems not to have been published.

40. Michael Holroyd, *Bernard Shaw. Vol. 3. 1918-1950: The Lure of Fantasy* (Chatto & Windus, 1991), 177.

41. CB: *ILF*, 104.

Chapter 12. *Taffy* at the Royalty: "An Early Closing Show"

1. CE, interview with *WM*, 2 September, 1925, 7.

2. *Review of Reviews*, November-December, 1924, 457.

3. Evidence of the acting version survives in a marked-up copy of the 1924 printed edition used in the Q Theatre production (NLW MS 21634B). Signed by Rosmer and the cast, the book was

offered as a gift 'To his friend the ideal Ester (Winifred Evans) from Caradoc'. CE's original typescript of the play has also survived (NLW G.V. Roberts Papers MS 18431C).

4. *WM*, 9 September, 1925, 7; 10 September 1925, 6.

5. CE, 'My Dear Old Welsh Bible', *Sunday Express*, 13 September 1925, 7.

6. *WM*, 9 September, 1925, 7.

7. CE, interview with *WM*, 22 September 1925, 6.

8. David Pretty, *The Rural Revolt That Failed*, 213-4.

9. An English translation (by Meic Stephens) appears as 'The late Lemuel Parry, Esq., JP, OBE', *New Welsh Review* 24 (1994), 39-42.

10. W.J. Gruffydd, 'Is Caradoc Evans Right?', *TPCW*, 17 October 1925, 815.

11. The Jewish reference is to Sir Alfred Mond, Liberal MP for Swansea (1910-23) and Carmarthen (1924-28). Later he joined the Conservatives.

12. From the typescript of his Bangor address. NLW MS 20033C.

13. CE, 'The Captive Welsh', *Sunday Express*, 16 August 1925, 5.

14. For reports see *WM*, 25 September 1925, 9; *Daily Mail*, 25 September 1925, 9; *Daily News*, 25 September 1925, 7.

15. *WM*, 25 September 1925, 9.

16. *Daily Mail*, 26 September 1925, 6.

17. CE, 'Downtrodden Actors', *Sunday Express*, 20 September 1925, 7.

18. 'Caradoc Again', *WM*, 15 January 1930, 9. Partial text of CE's talk to the Hounslow Science and Arts Club.

19. Gruffydd, *TPCW*, 17 October 1925, 815.

20. Stirred by this declaration, T.P. O'Connor announced a competition for the best letter on the subject of Evans and Wales; Ernest Rhys, Lord Howard de Walden, the Rt. Hon. J.H. Thomas and T.P. himself would award the ten-guinea prize. Entries poured in, from as far away as China.

21. J.N. Crowther, *TPCW*, 10 October 1925, 803.

22. A report of the talk appears in *WM*, 19 October 1925.

Chapter 13. Editing *T.P.'s Weekly*

1. Actually, *T.P.'s and Cassell's Weekly* from 27 October 1923 until 17 September 1927; the shorter title took effect from 24 September 1927.

2. CE, 'A Bundle of Memories', 98.

3. Clarke, *A Penny in the Clouds*, 185.

4. Thomas Burke, 'Old Bloke', in OS: *CE*, 155.

5. CB: *ILF*, 163.

6. Anthony West, *H.G. Wells: Aspects of a Life* (Hutchinson, 1984); Dilys Powell to JH, 1 May 1988.

7. *The Letters of D. H. Lawrence*, Vol. 6, 1927-28, ed. James T. Boulton and others (Cambridge UP, 1991), 182.

8. An obituary of Caradoc in the Norwich *Eastern Daily News* (13 January 1945) provides one picture of him in the *T.P.'s Weekly* driving seat. At a dinner party Caradoc had been seated next to a lady whose conversation entertained him. "Before they parted he observed, in the patronizing way which I am afraid was habitual with him: 'If you write as well as you talk you should make some money by your pen.'" The lady confirmed her name as Miss Smith. "Well Miss Smith," said Caradoc, "if you will write something and let me see it we may not be able to publish it as it is, but perhaps I can give you some advice." He then asked for Miss Smith's address. "The flattered lady handed

him her card, on which he read Sheila Kaye-Smith. He is said to have been embarrassed, but I find that hard to believe."

9 George Blake, *The Press and the Public* (Faber & Faber, 1930) and Sidney Dark, *Not Such a Bad Life* (Eyre & Spottiswoode, 1941) briefly discuss *John O'London's Weekly*.

10. The democratic ethos resonated with one latter-day editor, Michael Schmidt, who has explained that his *Poetry Nation* was abbreviated to *PN Review* in the spirit of *T.P.'s Weekly*, the intention being to evoke "a republic not a tyranny of letters".

11. *Cassell's Weekly*, 3 May 1923.

12. CB: *ILF*, 104.

13. John Rayner, *TPCW*, 29 September 1928.

14. In April 1926 he likewise found room for Austin Harrison's memories of Gissing, having earlier offered to approach Cassell's about publishing Harrison's *Pandora's Hope*, "a study of woman" accepted by Heinemann in 1925. (Martha Vogeler, *Austin Harrison*, 284.)

15. Dilys Powell to JH, 1 May 1988.

16. Glyn Roberts, *I Take This City*, 37.

17. CB: *ILF*, 162.

18. Frank Morley, 'An American Looks at Fleet Street", in Pope, *The Book of Fleet Street*, 159-60.

19. Clennell Wilkinson, 'The Compositors' Arms' in *The Book of Fleet Street*, 272.

20. Austin Clarke, *A Penny in the Clouds*, 186.

21. George Blake, 'Strangers within the Gate', in *The Book of Fleet Street*, 60.

22. *A Penny in the Clouds*, 185.

23. James Agate, *Brief Chronicles: A Survey of the Plays of Shakespeare and the Elizabethans in Actual Performance* (Cape, 1943), 22.

24. Reginald Pound, *Their Moods and Mine*, 92.

25. T. Michael Pope, 'Caradoc Evans', *Current Literature* 260 (August 1930), 314.

26. From 'Caradoc Evans: The Man and His Work', printed on the book jacket of the American edition of *Nothing to Pay* (New York, 1930).

27. 'Strangers Within the Gate' 61.

28. Quoted in Paul Davies, *Link* 53 (1986), 3-4.

29. CE, *New Witness*, 8 February 1917, 434.

30. CE published a memoir of Mary Webb in the *Colophon* 3.1 (1938), 63-6, and revised it for the *Welsh Review* 3.1 (1944). Unless otherwise indicated, quotations in this section are from these two sources.

31. CE, *TPCW*, 31 December 1927, 363. Obituary notice of Mary Webb.

32. Mary Webb to Andrew Dakers, 4 July [no year]. Stanford University Mary Webb Digital Archive, item LM001. At this point Dakers was working as a literary agent.

33. Gladys Mary Coles, *The Flower of Light: A Biography of Mary Webb* (Duckworth, 1978).

34. 'A Bundle of Memories', 96.

35. As in the second edition of the *Handbook* (1930).

36. Dewi Emrys to J. Seymour Rees, January 1926. NLW J. Seymour Rees Collection.

37. A partial text of the address appeared in *WM*, 5 November 1926, 8.

38. As in the copy of Tennyson's *In Memoriam* he gave to Desmond Flower, son of Sir Newman Flower. (Desmond was a bibliophile, and the copy given was of the 1914 Medici Society edition.)

39. 'Caradoc on – Himself', *WM*, 24 February 1927, 6.

40. CE, 'The Living Welsh Language', *Sunday Times*, 29 January 1928, 14.

Chapter 14. Enter Marguerite

1. This and all subsequent Hooley references to CE are from Hooley's letter to GJ, 7 January 1946. NLW Gwyn Jones Papers.

2. 'Rock Flowers' and 'The Realist' appear in *Eve, and Other Poems* (1930) and 'Traitor' in *Orchestra, and Other Poems* (1935).

3. *The Amis Anthology* (Hutchinson, 1988), 228.

4. She is accorded a full-page portrait in *Modern Society*, 16 August 1913, to mark her new Oliver Sandys serial 'The Woman in the Firelight' (she is "Mrs Arminger [sic] Barclay in private life" the caption runs). "Me !!!", Marguerite annotated the portrait in her copy, double-underlining the "Me".

5. Elaine Jackson, '*Sievier's Monthly* (1909): Pseudonyms and Readership in Early Twentieth-Century Popular Fiction', in *Book Trade Connections from the Seventeenth to the Twentieth Centuries*, ed. John Hinks and Catherine Armstrong (Oak Knoll Press/British Library, 2008), 245-62.

6. ME to Nell Dunbar, 28 November 1917. NLW Gwyn Jones Papers.

7. OS, *Full and Frank: The Private Life of a Woman Novelist* (Hurst & Blackett, 1941), 65.

8. OS: *F&F*, 64-5.

9. Monica Dunbar to GJ, 8 January 1981. NLW Gwyn Jones Papers.

10. ME to ND [1914].

11. ME to ND, 13 August 1914.

12. OS, *Unbroken Thread: An Intimate Journal of the Daily Life in the Welsh Countryside of England's Best-Loved Woman Novelist* (Rider, 1948), 54.

13. Sarah Clynch, in conversation with JH, June 1992.

14. ME to ND [1916].

15. MD to JH, June 1986.

16. ME to ND, 28 November 1917.

17. MD to JH, 6 January 1987.

18. ME to ND [1920].

19. ME to ND [April 1914].

20. She signs herself 'Marguerite Lovell' on headed notepaper that lists her books and films and at the top displays a small crest with a banner inscribed 'Venale Nec Auro' ("Not to be Bought with Gold"). This was the motto of Sir John Jervis (1802-56), judge and member of the family of the Earls of St Vincent, from whom Marguerite believed her father was descended. Sir John's *Dictionary of National Biography* entry states that the family name is often wrongly pronounced Jarvis.

21. CB: *ILF*, 137-8.

22. DD to ME, 12 November 1946.

23. CE to ME, 9 June 1930, reproduced in OS: *CE*, 143.

24. OS: *CE*, 68-9.

25. OS: *UT*, 106-7.

26. Michael Holroyd, *Lytton Strachey: The New Biography* (Pimlico, 2011).

27. Peter Lord, *Winifred Coombe Tennant*, 48, 58, 149.

Chapter 15. *Nothing to Pay*

1. Morley had urged that 'Anna Livia Plurabelle' be separately published as a shilling pamphlet ("Buy a book in brown paper / From Faber and Faber / To see Annie Liffey trip, tumble and caper", Joyce suggested as advertising copy). Posting the published pamphlet (Criterion Miscellany, no.

15) to Evans, Morley wrote "You were the first to give us a hand for proposing to do Joyce in the Miscellany and should rightly be the first to have an advance copy" (23 May 1930). Morley threw in a copy of Herbert Read's *Ambush* (Criterion Miscellany, no. 16) for good measure.

2. CE to Herbert M. Vaughan, 18 April 1930. NLW G.V. Roberts Papers MS 18428E.

3. Frank Morley to CE, 9 April 1930. The Faber Archive preserves CE's correspondence with Morley.

4. The W.W. Norton edition (New York, 1930) additionally corrects a few misprints and shows minor textual revision. (The 1989 Carcanet reprinting follows the Norton text.)

5. CE to Frank Morley, 16 July 1930.

6. Faber's publicity put a title to one story, 'The Road that Strangled the Mountain' (covering the journey to Holyhead, chapter 8).

7. Swaffer, 'Caradoc", in OS: *CE*, 149.

8. 'Another Outburst on My People', *WM*, 5 November 1926, 8. The partial text of a talk, "People – and Things", given to the Tomorrow Club. A fuller typescript version is held at NLW Gwyn Jones Papers.

9. Compare this, written almost forty years later: "Further down the houses begin, the rows of drab dwellings, wrenched from the slopes, with wet roofs, permanently wet. Their plots marked off with slate fences. Places of spittle and cold phlegm. Women swab the steps that are never dry. Late, lonely buses climb up to them, a brief gaudiness in a vast gloom. These people know the mountains but do not ascend them. They gnaw at them for small pay, and die early, silted up. The bare, hideous chapels ache for an hour with sad words and fierce singing; the futile memorials are planted in rows." (R.S. Thomas, *The Mountains*, New York 1968, 14.)

10. The argument advanced in the first paragraph was offered in a January 1930 talk at Hounslow where Evans spoke of a new kind of politico-religious oppression and the spiritual inheritance of those (like Amos) born into late nineteenth-century rural Wales. He claimed that, "Liberal-Nonconformity drove the squire from his land and set in his place the draper, grocer, lawyer, or preacher. It sought the people's help to do so by empty promises and lies. When the squire was driven away, what happened? Rents were raised, wages lowered, and field paths, which had been trodden by generations of our people were fenced in. The new squire is a Liberal and a Nonconformist and a man of business, and every foot of his land must show a dividend." (*Western Mail*, 15 January 1930, 9).

11. A text of the speech appears in the *Shop Assistant*, 18 April 1931, 7.

12. H.G. Wells, *Experiment in Autobiography*, vol. 1 (Faber & Faber, 1984), 147-8.

13. CE to FM, 18 November 1930.

14. CE to FM, 21 November 1930.

15. FM to CE, 25 November 1930.

16. A.D. Peters to FM, 21 November 1930. Faber Archive.

17. Allen Lane, *King Penguin: a biography* (Hutchinson, 1979).

Chapter 16. Leaving London

1. R.B. Marriott, 'Caradoc Evans', *Wales* 5.7 (Summer 1945), 61-4.

2. CE to Glyn Roberts, 5 October 1930. NLW L.J. Roberts Papers.

3. Marriott, 'Caradoc Evans', 61-4.

4. Evans's high regard for Machen was far from shared by the English-language writers of Wales (apart from Keidrych Rhys, who hailed one Welshman who lived by the pen, and Gwyn Jones, who did his best to promote a fellow author from Gwent). Machen thought literature "the sensuous

art of causing exquisite impressions by means of words"; he set his face against literary realism, against the contrivances of plot and character, against the notion of "subject matter" even. He made much of his Welshness, of personal myths surrounding Celtic literature and religion, but Welsh concerns of the Thirties totally failed to touch him. His contribution to *Authors Take Sides on the Spanish Civil War* (1937) suggests how far he stood apart: he was, and always had been, "entirely for General Franco".

5. George Blake, 'Strangers within the Gate', in Pope, *The Book of Fleet Street*, 61.

6. CE, 'Things that Anger Me', *Daily Express*, 8 April 1930.

7. Kenneth O. Morgan, *Rebirth of a Nation:Wales 1880-1980* (Clarendon/UWP, 1981), 235.

8. CB: *ILF*, 81-2.

9. CB: *ILF*, 54-5.

10. Arthur Machen, *The London Adventure or The Art of Wandering* (Martin Secker, 1924), 100.

11. Edward Shanks, 'A Fool i' the Forest', in *The Book of Fleet Street*, 210.

12. James Bone, *The London Perambulator* (Cape, 1925), 176.

13. Martin Armstrong, 'The Journalist at Play', in *The Book of Fleet Street*, 4.

14. OS: *CE*, 97.

15. OS: *F&F*, 119.

16. David Higham, *Literary Gent* (Cape, 1978), 234.

17. *Voices of Scotland*, December 1948, 2.

18. In January 1931 Dylan Thomas was still at school. He left in July 1931 (a little short of his seventeenth birthday) and was recruited by the *South Wales Daily Post*, Swansea's evening paper, where he remained until December 1932. Apparently he "doodled" for the paper before officially becoming a reporter.

19. *South Wales Evening Post*, 22 April 1932, 6.

20. *South Wales Evening Post*, 4 May 1932, 5.

21. *WM*, 5 May 1932, 10.

22. CB, *Sweetbriar Lane* (Hutchinson, 1938), 32.

23. OS: *CE*, 98.

Chapter 17. *Wasps*

1. The fullest account of the Gloucestershire period is ME's biography, *Caradoc Evans*, pp. 96-110. It is the source of this and most of the quotations that here follow.

2. CE to Evelyn Lewes, 3 April 1932. NLW Evelyn Lewes Bequest.

3. Glyn Roberts, *London Welsh News*, 9 December 1932.

4. Unidentified newspaper cutting (ms. dated 28 January 1933). NLW D.R. Davies Scrapbook 43.

5. OS: *F&F*, 121.

6. "Happily married people can live without kissing," so Caradoc recorded in his notes.

7. The 'Hélène' is something of a surprise: it was an embellishment of Armiger's. He argued that "Countess Barcynska must remain a veiled figure – a shadow. She lived 'somewhere in France.' Her Christian name was Hélène. Armiger typed all her letters and signed them Hélène Barcynska." (OS: *F&F*, 85.)

8. Clifford Evans to JH, 28 November 1980.

9. T.L. Williams spots another barb in the choice of this character's name: the initials E.B. were Edith's before marriage. She was the daughter of John Bellis, sometime Overseer of the Poor in Llandudno.

10. John Gawsworth, preface to his *The Life of Arthur Machen*, ed. Roger Dobson (Tartarus, 2005).

11. Evans had made a Rich & Cowan appearance three months earlier by way of 'The Coffin', reprinted in *Full Score*, a short-story collection edited by Fytton Armstrong.

12. This passage was a favourite of Marguerite's. In the Hurst & Blackett text Dame Edith, on hearing it read in Penetralia, sighs like "parched earth in summer heat". The Patriarch interprets her response: "for women chastity is a burden and... in every woman's mind there lodges a lover and the face of the lover is ever on her pillow."

13. Ronald Matthews, *English Messiahs: Studies of Six English Religious Pretenders, 1656-1927* (Methuen, 1936), 163-91 (on the Abode of Love).

14. Unidentified newspaper cutting (ms. dated 27 May 1933). NLW D.R. Davies Scrapbook 43.

15. Glyn Roberts, letter to the *Star*, undated newspaper cutting [June 1933]. NLW L.J .Roberts Papers.

16. 'London Letter', *Daily Dispatch*, undated newspaper cutting. NLW L.J. Roberts Papers.

Chapter 18. Return to Wales

1. H.V. Morton found the town distinctive in another way. "Aberystwyth is leading a double life. It is not the simple seaside town praised on the railway posters. Behind its hotels and boarding houses, its pretty hills, its inadequate pier and its half-moon of blue-grey shingle is something even more important than holidays: it the oldest University town in Wales.... It welcomes the outside world with a smile, but it has a deeper significance: it is one of the corner-stones of the Welsh nation." (*In Search of Wales*, 1932.)

2. OS: *F&F*, 111.

3. *WM*, 22 June 1933, 9.

4. 'Cymro', typescript obituary of ME. NLW D.R. Davies Scrapbook 31.

5. *CN*, 8 December 1933, 10; *WM*, 7 December 1933, 11.

6. Nick played opposite Connie Ashley-Jones (playing Chappie) in what was regarded as Marguerite's attempt to bring the two closer together. Neither could really act but the audience loved it, knowing the off-stage situation – that Connie (daughter of a local hairdresser) would have nothing to do with Nick.

7. OS: *CE*, 111.

8. *Welsh Gazette*, 17 May 1934, 8; *CN*, 18 May 1934, 5.

9. OS: *The Miracle Stone of Wales* (Rider, 1957), 14.

10. OS: *MSW*, 50-1.

11. Her autobiography underlines this: "In making a name I entertained a number of people. This is nothing very much. Anyone will pay to be entertained. I do, because my writings are cheerful and I hope not untinged with the beauty that means everything to me, comfort the sick and the infirm and even the blind. That is on the credit side." (OS: *F&F*, 174.)

12. OS: *F&F*, 174.

13. OS: *UT*, 111.

14. Sarnicol [Thomas Jacob Thomas], 'Caradoc Evans in a New Light', *WM*, 20 July 1933, 11.

15. OS: *UT*, 112.

16. GG, 'Caradoc', *EGATA*, ix-x. Quotations in this section are taken from this, GG's introductory essay, or from his obituary notice in OS: *CE*, 156-7.

17. GG, 'Caradoc', OS: *CE*, 156.

18. The gallery appears in *Aberystwyth* (1996), 113, a compilation of the Aberystwyth Postcard Club.

19. Jack Griffith, '"Soak Yourself in the Russians": Caradoc Evans Remembered', *Wales* 39 (April 1959), 67-70.

20. "I do not quarrel with those who pay tribute to Caradoc Evans's characteristics as a man. But those who knew him in private life must agree that he could be ruthless as well as generous; crude as well as gracious." (Pseudonymous correspondent, *Western Mail*, 6 May 1952.)

21. "Funerals are a vastly popular institution in Wales, and everyone in the district is expected to attend…. There is, I suppose, not a prouder man to be found than a Welsh Nonconformist with a corpse in his house." (Sabine Baring-Gould, *South Wales*, 1905, 250.)

22. Anne Rees, to W. Anthony Davies, August 1948.

23. Howell Evans, in conversation with JH.

24. OS: *CE*, 34.

25. OS: *CE*, 118.

26. OS: *F&F*, 124.

27. CE to William Evans, 12 July 1934. NLW Wil Ifan Papers.

28. NLW Gwyn Jones Papers.

29. OS: *CE*, 11.

30. Glyn Jones describes this visit and its background in his *The Dragon Has Two Tongues: Essays on Anglo-Welsh Writers and Writing*, ed. Tony Brown (Cardiff, UWP, 2001).

31. Gwen Watkins, *Portrait of a Friend* (Llandysul, Gomer, 1983), 34.

32. In the draft of an unpublished essay of the 1950s, Glyn Jones writes: "Sometimes I am tempted to think that Caradoc's truly appalling vision of life is not to be explained by the facile reasons often given for it. In his stories he is not paying back the insults and humiliations of his first thirty years. He is not taking a diabolical delight in pillorying individuals or the vices of community. Sometimes, I am almost persuaded, his best stories are less those things than a *cri-de-coeur*, an agonised cry of protest and indignation at the horror of life itself. Or they are attempts to objectify, to make something out of, the emotions of bitterness with which the spectacle of existence on this planet have filled him." (Quoted in Glyn Jones, *The Dragon Has Two Tongues*, 2001, 203.)

33. Jones, *The Dragon Has Two Tongues*, 61.

34. OS: *MSW*, 14-15; see also ME's 'Caradoc Picked Out Genius', *Empire News*, 6 March 1955, 4.

35. This last quotation comes from ME's third account of the meeting, part of her foreword to T. Howard-Lloyd, *Sun on Merlin's Pool: Poems* (Portsoken Press, 1964).

36. Glyn Jones, in conversations with Paul Ferris and with JH.

37. *The Collected Letters of Dylan Thomas*, ed. Paul Ferris (Dent, 1985), 117.

38. Wim Van Mierlo, 'James Joyce and Caradoc Evans', *Genetic Joyce Studies* [electronic journal] 7 (2007). http://www.antwerpjamesjoycecenter.com /GJS7/GJS7mierlo2.html.

39. Frank Morley, *Literary Britain: A Reader's Guide to Writers and Landmarks* (Hutchinson, 1980), 474-5.

40. Roberts slightly misquotes this passage. The omitted sentences run: "The working man has an intellect higher developed than the little farmer in England. This, in a measure, is due to his being bilingual. The acquisition of a second tongue undoubtedly gives a flexibility to his mind. No English labourer dreams of learning another language than his own, but the Welsh peasant must do this, and this fact gives his mind aptitude for fresh acquisitions and affords a spur to learning." (Baring-Gould, *A Book of North Wales*, 1903, 213.)

41. An epistolary novel gave him chance to discourse on the love letter (with his own to Marguerite in mind): "You say you keep my letters. Don't kid yourself that my letters are of any literary value.

The man who tries to write literary letters to the girl he adores is a *poseur*. A man in love expresses himself in temperatures and his style can go to hell."

42. Words like boodle, complane, drailed, drumblish, dwale, faddled, fleered, glavering, hankled, jill-flirt, jimmeries, lapling, menseless, mopsical, prossing, roytish, ruth, shogged, spact, twattled, wambling, whim-wham and yerking.

43. Andrew Dakers to CE, 12 April 1934. NLW Professor Gwyn Jones Papers.

Chapter 19. Rogues & Vagabonds

1. OS: *MSW*, 17.
2. *CN*, 17 May 1935, 5.
3. Taken from her *Stage* advertisement, 7 November 1935.
4. *CN*, 17 May 1935, 5.
5. OS: *CE*, 113.
6. *WM*, 20 June 1935, 13; *CN*, 21 June 1935, 5; *Welsh Gazette*, 27 June 1935, 5.
7. *WM*, 16 December 1936.
8. *CN*, 7 June 1935, 7.
9. Unidentified newspaper cutting, ms. dated 1 July 1935. NLW D.R. Davies Scrapbook 44.
10. Unidentified newspaper cutting, ms. dated 24 July 1935.
11. *CN*, 26 July 1935, 9.
12. Unidentified newspaper cutting, ms. dated 24 July 1935; *Welsh Gazette*, 25 July 1935, 5.
13. Evan Andrew, 'Countess Barcynska', in *Aberystwyth Voices*, ed. William Troughton (Stroud, Tempus, 2004), 92-3.
14. OS: *F&F*, 130.
15. *Welsh Gazette*, 1 August 1935, 5.
16. *WM*, 3 September 1935, 13.
17. Wife of the better known actor Cyril Luckham, Violet (nicknamed 'Twin') died in 2009. Among her possessions was a presentation copy of a book inscribed, "You have the grace, humour and the genius that goes with art. Greetings and llwyddiant [success], Caradoc Evans". Violet's copy of Marguerite's *The Show Must Go On* (1936) carried the inscription "For Violet Lamb (Twin) the nicest girl & the nicest actress any management could have wished to have as a member of its company, in love & recognition, from Oliver Sandys."
18. Violet Luckham, interview with JH, April 1995.
19. *Welsh Gazette*, 12 September 1935, 5.
20. *CN*, 16 August 1935, 8.
21. OS: *F&F*, 129-30.
22. OS: *MSW*, 57.
23. OS: *F&F*, 130.
24. Unidentified newspaper cutting, ms. dated 11 September 1935. NLW D.R. Davies Scrapbook 44; *Welsh Gazette*, 12 September 1935, 5.
25. George Rowell and Anthony Jackson, *The Repertory Movement: A History of Regional Theatre in Britain* (Cambridge UP, 1984), 176.
26. Rhys Davies, letter to R.B. Marriott, 22 October 1936. NLW MS 20897E; Rhys Davies, *My Wales* (Jarrolds, 1937), 161.
27. Unidentified newspaper cutting, ms. dated 11 September 1935.
28. Foremost among the doubters must have been Caradoc and one imagines that a mighty flare-up

lay behind his reassuring letter of 5 September 1935. "My little one," he writes to Marguerite, "I loved you from the first moment I saw you and since then it has grown and grown and grown and will outlast eternity…. I love your company and I shall never want to part from it, however wild will be the periods of storm" (OS: *CE*, 144). Marguerite mentions that whenever they had something intimate to say, they preferred to say it by letter.

29. Reproduced in Peter Lord, *Winifred Coombe Tennant*, 151, where the diary entry also appears.

30. A concert hall, latterly known as the Quarryette Pavilion, had occupied the site in the early 1920s, housing concert parties, dances and the occasional play. The Parc Craiglais housing development now stands on the site.

31. Unidentified newspaper cutting, ms. dated 24 October 1935. NLW D.R. Davies Scrapbook 44.

32. 'Theatres of Wales' (typescript). NLW Evelyn Lewes Bequest.

33. *WM*, 23 October 1935.

34. "The Rogues & Vagabonds played as sincerely to ten people as to one hundred," OS: *F&F*, 136.

35. *Welsh Gazette*, 19 December 1935, 4. A still from the Quarry production appears in OS: *F&F*, 113.

36. OS: *UT*, 49.

37. *WM*, 31 July 1936, 10.

38. Having joined in 1928, Howell remained at the *Cambrian News* until 1934. He remembered "witnessing the Board of Guardians at Bronglais [workhouse], with gold watch chains along their rounded beer bellies, gold rings on their fingers and all that, having a long discussion before granting a 6d increase on the 3/6d weekly allowance of a small, timid, half-starved woman" (*Cambrian News*, 31 October 1986, 5). In 1934 at Aberystwyth he was earning 30 shillings a week (he would join the *Western Mail* as a sub-editor on £4.50 a week).

39. OS: *F&F*, 136.

40. *CN*, 25 December 1936, 10.

41. OS: *CE*, 114.

42. OS: *CE*, 114.

43. OS: *MSW*, 18.

44. OS: *F&F*, 132.

45. OS: *MSW*, 16.

Chapter 20. Aberystwyth Gadfly

1. OS: *MSW*, 29.

2. *Daily Express*, 29 January 1937, 5.

3. OS: *MSW*, 30.

4. http://www.museumwales.ac.uk/en/rhagor/article/witch_bottles/

5. OS: *F&F*, 126.

6. In yet another retelling of the story, this one in person to David Conway and his parents, Marguerite stated that besides her own writer's block, Caradoc at the time had succumbed to "a protracted bout of depression". (David Conway, *Magic Without Mirrors*, 35.)

7. Juliette Wood, 'The Miracle Stone and Welsh Legend Formation', http://www.juliettewood.com/papers/miraclestone/pdf.

8. OS: *F&F*, 186.

9. OS: *CE*, 119. Other sources give the original title of *Mother's Marvel* as *Kitty Shore's Magic Cake*.

10. Griffiths's talk is reported in *WM*'s 'Our London Letter' column, 26 April 1953.

11. Lam is something of a critic, praising a film script where "every line is conducive to the plot" and

declaring that "In creative work... love and hate should be blended if the artist is to produce the mean that is like life" – advice that Evans had heard (and ignored) all his life.

12. Ernest Betts, *The Film Business: A History of British Cinema, 1896-1972* (Allen & Unwin, 1973). Chapter 7 covers Wardour Street and the structure of the industry.

13. L.J. Roberts, Glyn's father, read history at Oxford and became an H.M. inspector of schools in Wales. He was also a notable musician.

14. *Welsh Nationalist*, July 1950, 4.

15. Menai's three letters to *WM* here quoted appeared on 8, 17, 20 April 1935. (Two further letters were published on 25 and 29 April.)

16. CE, 'A Nation of Penny Whistlers', *Evening News* [Glasgow], 10 August 1935 [Saturday Supplement], 1.

17. Geraint Goodwin, 'Are Celtic Festivals Worthwhile?', *Evening News* [Glasgow], 24 August 1935 [Saturday Supplement], 1.

18. *WM*, 9 July 1936, 9.

19. 'Caradoc at Machynlleth', *WM*, 10 July 1936, 8.

20. Gilbert Norwood, 'A Welsh Gadfly', *WM*, 14 July 1936, 8.

21. Another notable classicist seems to have taken to Evans: Baptist-bred W.H.D. Rouse, co-founder of the Loeb Classical Library, possessed a copy of *My People* inscribed and signed by the author (on 14 January 1916).

22. The eight adjudicators were Cassie Davies (Barry), Mary Davies (Llanishen), W.J. Gruffydd (Cardiff), Thomas Jones (Aberystwyth), Thomas Parry (Bangor), Iorwerth Peate (Cardiff), Prosser Rhys (Aberystwyth) and R.J. Rowlands (Caernarfon). It is unlikely that Caradoc Evans played any part in W.J. Gruffydd's thinking, and Revd Fred Jones (Talybont), another adjudicator who resigned, had been a leading advocate for the selection of Caradoc.

23. *WM*, 20 February 1937, 13.

24. CE, interview with *WM*, 11 March 1937, 10.

25. *WM*, 5 March 1935, 5.

26. *WM*, 16 August 1935, 10.

27. *WM*, 31 March 1936, 10.

28. *WM*, 31 March 1936, 10.

29. The talk was finally broadcast on BBC Radio Wales in March 1987, fifty years after its original rejection. Intelligently read, in Evans's accent and manner (as remembered), it came across well. The *Western Mail* text was used, Caradoc's original manuscript not having survived.

30. Jack Jones, 'Welsh Writers and Critics', *WM*, 26 February 1937, 11.

Chapter 21. Ruislip and Broadstairs: Gathering Storms

1. 'A Mighty Man in Sion', in GJ, *Background to Dylan Thomas and Other Explorations* (Oxford UP, 1992), 85.

2. OS: *MSW*, 51-3, and ME's foreword to T. Howard-Lloyd, *Sun on Merlin's Pool*; see also her 'Caradoc Picked Out Genius', *WM*, 6 March 1955, and Nicholas Sandys, 'Dylan and the Stormy Petrel', *WM*, 7 January 1961.

3. A Hutchinson's chairman recalled: "There appeared to be no consultation other than with Mrs Webb; there was no planning other than that imposed by Mrs Webb; there was no authority other than that exerted by Mrs Webb... the glue holding the whole enterprise together." (Robert Lusty, *Bound to be Read*, 1975.)

4. OS: *CE*, 119.

5. OS: *F&F*, 137.

6. ME to Glyn Roberts, 7 October 1937. NLW J. Glyn Roberts Papers.

7. As a literary label 'Anglo-Welsh' seems first to have been used by Idris Bell in *Welsh Outlook*, August 1922. On 24 July 1931, the *Western Mail* employed it "for want of a better term" and the label became increasingly common in the 1930s as a convenient tag for the body of Welsh authors and their writings in English then coming into prominence. By the 1980s the term had fallen out of use, save in reference to a specific phenomenon, the Welsh literary flowering of the 1930s and early 1940s.

8. OS: *CE*, 56.

9. Letter to Keidrych Rhys, 25 July 1937. NLW MS22745D.

10. Glyn Jones, *The Dragon Has Two Tongues* (2001), 32.

11. *Dragon*, 62.

12. Rhys Davies to Keidrych Rhys, 8 December 1937. NLW MS22745D.

13. Keidrych Rhys, 'Modernism in Wales: Literature', radio talk, 13 July 1937. NLW BBC Wales Archives: Scripts.

14. 'A Might Man in Sion', *Explorations*, 85.

15. 'A Might Man in Sion', *Explorations*, 85.

16. Keidrych Rhys, 'Modernism in Wales: Literature'.

17. Idris Davies to Keidrych Rhys, 8 December 1937. NLW MS22745D.

18. GJ, 'Welsh Writing: 1938-1948', radio talk, 7 September 1948. NLW BBC Wales Archives: Scripts.

19. Goronwy Rees, a writer often thought to be 'anti-Welsh', could say (in a June 1938 talk on radio): "my people seem to me to possess more of those qualities I admire, of passion, intelligence, individualism, and a natural devotion to culture than almost any other I have known" (the Jews were his exception).

20. *Heddiw*, 3.1 (1937), 37.

21. A reference to the Methodist children's magazine, *Trysorfa y Plant*, popularly known as the *Trysorfa Fach* to distinguish it from *Y Drysorfa*, the Calvinistic Methodist monthly.

22. The case is reported in *WM*, 3 December 1937, 4; see also *Welsh Gazette*, 9 December 1937 and *CN*, 10 December 1937.

23. *CN*, 10 December 1937, 11.

24. *WM*, 9 February 1938, 12; *Liverpool Daily Post*, 9 February 1938, 9; *CN*, 11 February 1938, 6.

25. CE to F.B. Adams Jr, 17 June 1938. Stanford University Mary Webb Digital Archive, LT001.

26. OS: *CE*, 120.

27. OS: *F&F*, 132.

28. OS: *CE*, 120.

29. OS: *MSW*, 55.

30. OS: *CE*, 120-1.

31. *WM*, 9 March 1938, 6.

32. OS: *CE*, 121.

33. OS: *CE*, 105.

34. ME to ND, 19 September 1938.

35. ME to Evelyn Lewes [March 1939]. NLW Evelyn Lewes Bequest.

36. *A Kentish Lad: The Autobiography of Frank Muir* (Bantam Press, 1997), 37. Muir's memory plays him false regarding the year of his sightings of ME.

37. ME to Evelyn Lewes [March 1939].

38. OS, *Calm Waters* (Hurst & Blackett, 1940), 119.

39. OS: *F&F*, 144.

40. ME to Evelyn Lewes [March 1939].

41. ME to Evelyn Lewes [March 1939].

42. OS: *CE*, 10.

43. A portion of Bullock's memoir 'Caradoc Evans' appears in *Wales on the Wireless: A Broadcast Anthology*, ed. Patrick Hannan (Llandysul, Gomer, 1988), 31-3. His complete radio script, broadcast 23 March 1948, is held at NLW BBC Wales Archives: Scripts.

44. John Glyn Roberts died of tuberculosis, aged twenty-eight, at Welwyn Garden City in December 1938 and was buried at Hatfield Hyde Cemetery (Welwyn's Male Voice Choir laid a wreath). Latterly he was film critic of *Tribune* whose obituary praised him as "incapable of delivering a merely 'fashionable' or superficial judgment.... His ability to analyse social and political trends in the modern cinema gave a particular left wing quality to his criticisms and earned him special distinction in the film world." No one seemed to have been aware of Glyn Roberts's *The Most Powerful Man in the World: The Life of Sir Henri Deterding*, a hefty, hostile analysis of the oil industry and the activities of the long-time chairman of the Royal Dutch/Shell oil company. Victor Gollancz thought it "quite brilliant" but "too dangerous" to publish – he feared a libel action that could put him out of business. The book appeared in 1938 – under a New York imprint. "No ordinary person could produce a work of this quality and magnitude", wrote a *Journal of Politics* reviewer, noting the book's dedication to Ralph Fox, who had agreed to write a life of Deterding but fell in the Spanish Civil War.

45. Quoted in *Wales* 8/9 (August 1939), 243.

46. Harold Harris, 'Hutchinson and Company (Publishers) Limited', in *British Literary Publishing Houses, 1881-1965* (*Dictionary of Literary Biography*, vol. 112), ed. Jonathan Rose and Patricia J. Anderson (Gale, 1991), 162-72.

47. OS, *Calm Waters*, 135; see also OS: *F&F*, 148.

48. Exactly when it closed is uncertain: the *Stage* (31 August 1939) carries a complementary report of the Playhouse production of *Night Must Fall*.

49. ME to ND, 23 August 1939.

50. OS: *F&F*, 161.

Chapter 22. Brynawelon: "That Private Madhouse"

1. OS: *F&F*, chapter 21, describes the return to Wales and the months at Abermâd.

2. ME to ND, 23 August 1939.

3. The fullest version of CE's journal is to be found in his *Morgan Bible & Journal 1939-44*.

4. GG, 'Caradoc', *EGATA*, xxxiii.

5. *Morgan Bible & Journal*, 124, 125.

6. OS: *F&F*, 182.

7. *Morgan Bible & Journal*, 127.

8. The *Welsh Short Stories* exchange is preserved in NLW Gwyn Jones Papers.

9. 'A Mighty Man in Sion', in GJ, *Explorations*, 72. Succeeding quotations in this section are taken from this source.

10. GJ, 'The Welshman Who Became a Legend', *Listener*, 17 January 1946, 79, 87.

11. In his funeral tribute – Alice Jones died in January 1979, aged seventy-four – R. George Thomas spoke of her warm, hospitable friendliness and ready sense of fun; and of one moment at a pre-

sentation to her distinguished husband. "'Mrs Jones,' someone suggested, 'this must be the proudest moment of your life?' Came her unforgettable reply: 'Our life together has been full of proud moments – and the other kind.' This honesty of statement reflected her acute judgement of people and things which Gwyn had come to trust implicitly." In relations with Marguerite it helped that Alice was not in the least academic, and a true dog-woman. In 1945 she would tell Marguerite how she felt on the death of her corgi Tivy: "Whilst he was alive I was terribly tied – he couldn't be trusted far off the lead because he would fight. He nipped people. My life with him was turbulent like yours with Caradoc. Yet now he is gone and there is no row, all is quiet – and how I hate it! I ought to be relieved, but I'm not. I hate the calm – hate it." (OS: *UT*, 62.)

12. Quotations in this and succeeding paragraphs are taken from Paula Block's letters to GJ and to Trevor Williams, 9 February 1969 and 29 May 1969. NLW Gwyn Jones Papers.

13. Pauline Block made herself known in February 1969 after her brother, a *TLS* reader, sent her Gwyn Jones's article on Caradoc in the 9 January 1969 issue. Paula got in touch with Jones and eventually gave him Marguerite's letters to her on the understanding that they, together with Paula's brief Brynawelon diary, would be deposited in the National Library of Wales.

14. Still classed as 'friendly', Category B aliens posed 'a slight risk' and were denied possession of a camera and bicycle and barred from travelling more than five miles from their home. Of some 73,000 persons assessed, just 569 were deemed Nazi sympathizers posing 'a significant risk'; placed in Category A, they were immediately incarcerated.

15. Paula Block's diary of January 1942 is deposited at NLW Gwyn Jones Papers, together with a covering letter to GJ, dated 7 November 1978.

16. *Morgan Bible & Journal*, 153.

17. Paula would not have been surprised. Her diary entry for 2 January 1942 (augmented in translation) runs: "Visitors again. Caradoc very graceful and sociable to visitors. Marguerite rushed upstairs to powder and paint her face, framed by her straw coloured hair. Dr George Green the Professor of Psychology came often from Aberystwyth. But was there a Mrs Green? I never saw one." There *was* a Mrs Green – Sophia – but unlike the Evanses, the Greens enjoyed a measure of independence from each other in their social lives.

18. PB to GJ, 26 October 1978.

19. OS: *F&F,* 196.

20. The hymn, 'Pererin wyf mewn anial dir' by William Williams (Pantycelyn), is usually sung to the tune of 'Amazing Grace'. 'A pilgrim in a desert land' would be a more accurate translation.

21. Published as recently as August 1939 in *Wales*, 'Your Sin Will Find You Out' underwent revision for its appearance in book form. The changes, individually minor (altering of words, word order and the positioning of phrases), are numerous in total.

22. *WM*, 5 February 1943, 3.

23. 'Starting a Publishing House in War Time', *Bookseller*, 9 November 1939, 680-1.

24. Besides his career as a literary agent and afterwards in publishing, Andrew Dakers (1887-1966) authored a brief life of Robert Burns, popular studies of Oliver Cromwell and Mary Queen of Scots, and a novel published pseudonymously.

25. Andrew Dakers to GG, quoted in GG's "Caradoc", *EGATA*.

Chapter 23. Brynawelon: The Last Phase

1. Arthur Machen to John Gawsworth, 30 March 1931. Newport Central Library Arthur Machen

Collection. Subsequent letters quoted in this paragraph are also housed in Newport Library's Machen Collection.

2. GJ to Colin Summerford, February 1943.

3. Colin Summerford to GJ, 23 February 1943.

4. ME to Colin Summerford, 23 February 1943.

5. ME to PB, 5 November 1942. NLW Gwyn Jones Papers.

6. Trevor L. Williams plausibly sees in this choice of title a reference to the Bishop Morgan's Bible, the Welsh Bible of 1588 translated by William Morgan. (Williams, *The Life and Works of Caradoc Evans*. PhD Thesis. University of Wales [Cardiff], 1970.)

7. The quotations are from Robin Chapman's translation of Lewis's review. The vocabulary of the original was seemingly beyond Caradoc whose own request for a translation was met by T.E. Nicholas (Niclas y Glais), then living at Aberystwyth.

8. OS: *CE*, 38.

9. CE to Tom Beynon, 6 July 1940. NLW Calvinistic Methodist Archive.

10. CE to Tom Beynon, 8 November 1943. NLW Calvinistic Methodist Archive.

11. GG, 'Caradoc', *EGATA*, xxxi.

12. OS: *F&F*, 161-2.

13. 'How Green are Welsh Authors?', *WM*, 8 August 1942, 3.

14. T. Rowland Hughes to GJ [1942]. NLW Gwyn Jones Papers.

15. "I am afraid it is too true that as a people our Welsh folk are prone to fatalism," said James Griffiths, Labour MP for Llanelli, in parliamentary debate on the 1939 report of an Inquiry into the Anti-Tuberculosis Service in Wales; "No one who knows me would charge me with not appreciating the tremendous contribution of our religious teaching to Welsh life and Welsh culture, but I am bound to admit that some of our religious teaching is responsible for this fatalism, for regarding this disease as some terrible plague which we cannot overcome. We are not facing a predestined fate, we are facing a social problem, and if my words can reach the people of Wales I would say to them in the language of religion which they know best, that we must work out our own salvation."

16. In the New Cross area (one is told) most sheepdogs would have been fed, but dogs that killed sheep were indeed sometimes hanged.

17. ME, *WM*, 19 May 1944, 4; 1 June 1944, 3.

18. ME to PB, 26 May 1942.

19. Caradoc consistently refers to Taffy as though he were male while in *Full and Frank* Marguerite makes clear that Taffy was a bitch and would speak of her always as such.

20. OS: *UT*, 158.

21. GJ to Meic Stephens, 24 November 1968. NLW Gwyn Jones Papers.

22. Marguerite alludes to this "ridiculous rumour", positing that it might have been "mixed up with the actual fact that Ribbentrop, as a traveller in wines, had frequently put up in the town". Though for years a wine merchant, there is no record of Ribbentrop ever having visited Aberystwyth.

23. GG, 'Caradoc', in OS: *CE*, 157.

24. OS: *UT*, 95.

25. Berta Ruck, *A Trickle of Welsh Blood*, 162.

26. Frank Lewis, 'The Gentle Art of Making Friends: an Impression of Caradoc Evans', in OS: *CE*, 160-1.

27. Anita's mother was Mrs Maud Ellen Davies; born the youngest child of James and Ellen James, Twrgwyn, Rhydlewis, she became friendly with Caradoc's mother. In later years she took to

writing and (as has been mentioned) left an account of Caradoc and an interesting (unpublished?) piece on 'Saturday in Cardiganshire' as she recalled it and the shadow it cast over Sunday. (Anita, who married the Revd James Arter, died in 2006.)

28. Anita Arter, in conversation with JH, 21 December 1995.

29. ME to Herbert M. Vaughan, 10 June 1942.

30. Two versions of this story appear in the typescripts of talks given by Evans in the mid-1920s. NLW Gwyn Jones Papers.

31. So called because he carried an umbrella when wearing his Sunday clothes, John Evans was a semi-recluse living alone in a cottage where everything he possessed – furniture, ornaments, pictures – had a label attached. "They are the names of my heirs," he explained to Marguerite; "There will be no quarrelling after I am dead."

32. GJ's letter to Rhys, 16 November 1943, was published in *Wales* 3 (1944), 104.

33. CE, 'Self-Portrait', *Wales* 3 (1944), 83-5.

34. Keidrych Rhys to JH, 5 March 1981.

35. Davies in the 1930s, employed as a publishers' traveller, had more than once written from Cardiff to Caradoc at Queen's Square House and received no reply. He'd also spent two wartime holidays in Aberystwyth, hoping he might encounter Caradoc in the street or on the 'front'; but he never did. "At the time I felt sure that I must have done or said something which he resented, and therefore did not care to call on him," Davies told Marguerite, in February 1945. She then sent him a jug that had belonged to Caradoc ("I shall treasure [it] as a memento of my dear old friend") and some honey for Mrs Davies.

36. GJ, 'A Mighty Man in Sion', *Explorations*, 82

37. Quotations here are from letters in the NLW Gwyn Jones Papers: *Welsh Review* archive.

Chapter 24: "The Earth Gives All and Takes All"

1. ME to PB, 23 September 1943.

2. OS: *CE*, 15.

3. CE to Tom Beynon, 8 November 1943. NLW Calvinistic Methodist Archive.

4. OS: *MSW*, 22.

5. ME to Mrs Beynon, 3 January 1944. NLW Calvinistic Methodist Archive.

6. OS: *CE*, 20.

7. OS: *UT*, 66.

8. Quoted by GG, EGATA, xxxii.

9. ME to Alice Jones, [1946].

10. 'The Bitter Word', *Irish Times*, 29 March 1947.

11. His composite review also welcomed Philip Larkin's *A Girl in Winter*.

12. 'The People and the Latent Wish', *Wales* 27 (December 1947), 356-7.

13. ME to ND, 6 July 1944.

14. MD to JH, June 1986.

15. MD to JH, 11 January 1989.

16. MD to JH, 26 June 1986.

17. MD to JH, 23 February 1987.

18. CE to MD, 13 May 1942.

19. ME to ND, 5 January 1944.

20. MD to Noreen Bray, 5 December 1980.

21. Memory of this incident prompted Monica in December 1980 to write to Broadcasting House, Cardiff. She had heard a radio programme that she thought did less than justice to "the nice side" of Caradoc. She was also greatly distressed to learn of the "ruinous condition" of his grave. It would be an honour, she told the BBC (and the *Western Mail*) to be allowed to contribute to its upkeep. In fact, she ensured its upkeep for the next five years at a cost of £50, "a very small repayment for a large debt of kindness owed to these three dear friends".

22. GJ, 'Caradoc', *Welsh Review* 4.1 (March 1945), 25.

23. Glyn Jones, *The Dragon Has Two Tongues* (2001), 75.

24. *Dragon*, 137.

25. *Dragon*, 61.

26. GJ to PB, 7 October 1978.

27. GJ to PB, 7 October 1978.

28. ME to Alice Jones [1944].

29. OS: *CE*, 79.

30. Ronnie Hughes, in conversation with JH.

31. Both were drawn to white witchcraft and Hughes would develop an interest in the rituals and practice of exorcism.

32. Nicholas Sandys, 'Dylan and the Stormy Petrel', *WM*, 7 January 1961.

33. Nick indeed turned to writing and managed to place a couple of poems with the *Western Mail*. Later Caradoc sent Gwyn Jones some more of Nick's poems for possible inclusion in the *Welsh Review*. He had no great hopes of them, but "If you like even one well enough to print God bless you," he wrote to Jones (3 January 1944). All were rejected.

34. Professor Edmund Fryde, in conversation with JH.

35. Letter to Alice Jones [1946].

36. OS: *CE*, 15-6.

37. OS: *CE*, 88-9.

38. *Listener*, 17 January 1946, 79, 87.

39. GJ to PB, 7 October 1978.

40. GJ additionally served as Lieutenant in the 1st Cardiganshire Home Guard having undergone weapon training at Liverpool.

41. OS: *UT*, 44.

42. GJ to PB, 7 October 1978.

43. Beti Richards, in conversation with JH.

44. GJ, in conversation with JH.

45. David Conway, *Magic without Mirrors: The Making of a Magician* (2011), 14-5. Accessed online.

46. OS: *MSW*, 53-4.

47. OS: *CE*, 13; ME to GJ [1952].

48. OS: *UT*, 105.

49. OS: *CE*, 17. ME's biography has much on CE's hospitalisation and death.

50. OS: *CE*, 145.

51. The wounded were probably American servicemen after a coach crash on the Devil's Bridge road.

52. From his obituary, *British Medical Journal*, 25 June 1977, 1668.

53. In one of her spirit conversations with Caradoc (nine months after his death), she passes on what Dr Burrell had told her about penicillin's efficacy: "Syphilis — all clear in three weeks. Nothing experimental — a fact. As soon as this is generally known — as it is bound to be — what is going to

be the effect on morals." OS: *UT*, 43.)

54. OS: *UT*, 8.

55. This may be the place to mention the ugly rumour that Marguerite offered to pay local people to attend her husband's funeral. The story surfaces in T. Llew Jones's *Fi Mhobol i* (2002) where the author speaks of having heard from J.R. Evans, headmaster at Llanilar, that he [J.R. Evans] on the eve of Caradoc's funeral had been contacted by Countess Barcynska "asking him to hire some local people who would be willing to act as mourners at the funeral. She said she was willing to pay a pound each to any who might come." (See also Diarmuid Johnson, *Pen and Plough: 20th Century Poets and Bards of Ceredigion*, 2016, 74). This is highly improbable. *The Oxford Companion to the Literature of Wales* has John Roberts Evans teaching in London until 1947 when he took up a post at Penuwch; his Llanilar appointment dates from 1954. Marguerite Evans nowhere mentions him. She does, however, mention J.L. Evans, the man in whose his hands she placed Caradoc's funeral entirely ("arrange everything – please"); and it was almost certainly John Lewis Evans who recruited local bearers to carry the coffin to Horeb's cemetery top. It would have been wholly in keeping with her generosity had Marguerite offered them each a pound as a token of thanks.

56. Edith Nepean, 'Caradoc put my Feet on the Ladder', *WM*, 16 January 1945, 3.

57. OS: *CE*, 15.

58. Aberystwyth Ceredigion Archives, Papers of Miss Florrie Hamer. ADX/415.

59. OS: *CE*, 50.

60. *WM*, 17 January 1945, 3.

Postscript

1. GJ, 'Nick & the Sublime Posture'. NLW Gwyn Jones Papers.

2. ME to Alice Jones [1946]. The further letters from ME quoted in this postscript are likewise held in the Gwyn Jones Papers at NLW.

3. John Edmunds, *Master of None: Memoirs of a Dithering Man* (2008), 53. Privately published.

4. Marguerite's biography of her husband and her Penrhyncoch journal freely reproduce their chats together after his death. She writes as if under his direction and there is little doubt that this was her belief; she had long been drawn to supernaturalism, kept a shelf of books on spiritualism, and seemingly possessed some occult gifts herself. Her biography's dedication "To the wayward spirit of my husband Caradoc" imagines him "in the fields of God's universe now free for your roaming", while its epigraph quotes Lucretius, *De Rerum Natura*, Book I: "Thus it was that the vital force of his mind achieved a way so that he went long beyond the burning walls of this world and with mind and spirit journeyed throughout the immense whole." Most readers will prefer to consider Marguerite's conversations with Caradoc not as literal truth but the result of her having completely absorbed and internalized her husband's thoughts and opinions and his striking turns of phrase. He had possessed her. (One thinks of Cathy and Heathcliff: "Nelly, I am Heathcliff! He's always, always in my mind: not as a pleasure, any more than I am always a pleasure to myself, but as my own being.")

5. ME to Alice Jones [1952].

6. Keidrych Rhys, postcard to JH, 12 March 1981.

7. ME to Gwyn Jones [1951].

8. At Christmas 1956 Monica Dunbar received from Marguerite a copy of *Letters from Abelard to Heloise* (Dublin 1769) inscribed: "I can think of no more precious thing to give you for this Holy

Day than the first little gift Caradoc gave to me. In my lifetime I am giving away such little treasures lest after my passing they may find their way to a second hand stall. The pencil scrawl at the back are some notes he must have made." The book is now in the National Library of Wales. Marguerite donated Evan Walters's charcoal sketch of Caradoc to Aberystwyth town library (where it can no longer be found).

9. In letters to JH, Margaret Austin has generously shared her knowledge of the Shropshire migration, the result of research undertaken through interviews with those who knew ME and Nick at Church Stretton (pre-eminently Eileen Bound, Helen Bower and Peggy Howells).

10. ME to MD, 3 June 1957.

11. ME to Alice Jones, 30 June 1953.

12. Among David Conway's delightful vignettes is one of Marguerite in Hewitt's company soon after they had met: "Rarely did she call on us without bringing new tidings from the Afterlife, mainly imparted to her by her late husband. It was a great surprise therefore when one day she turned up on the arm of an elderly gentleman, introduced as Captain Hewitt, with her habitual seriousness replaced by girlish smiles and tinkling laughter. The change was disconcerting, but not entirely unwelcome. My father put it down, no doubt correctly, to the advent of the Captain." (*Magic Without Mirrors*, 39.)

13. Keidrych Rhys to JH [February 1981].

14. From a note by Marguerite inside Margaret Austin's copy of *The Miracle Stone of Wales*.

15. ME to ND, 13 August 1956.

16. ME to MD, 3 June 1957.

17. ME to MD, 10 September 1960. Postcard.

18. ME to GJ, 29 December 1963.

19. From time to time Marguerite had looked to Richard Burton as someone who might help keep Caradoc's name before the public. A year before she died she sent him a copy of *The Miracle Stone of Wales*. Burton's letter of thanks (2 April 1963) has the postscript: "One of these days we will put C.E. on the screen or stage – as himself if that is possible."

20. ME to MD, 27 May 1963.

21. Sarah Clynch, in conversation with JH, June 1992.

22. Patricia Crowther, *One Witch's World* (Robert Hale, 1988), 116-7. By 1972 Nick was describing himself as an occultist and quoting the "as above, so below" maxim from *The Emerald Tablet of Hermes Trismegistus* (in the Hermetical tradition expressive of the fundamental unity of macrocosm and microcosm). He was led to this source by Aleister Crowley, whom he personally knew and respected; "a very strange man indeed", he told Monica Dunbar, but one whose occult research was outstanding ("as was his physical courage").

23. 'Forty Years Later He Turns Up To Be – a Witch!', *CN*, 29 February 1980.

INDEX

References to endnotes consist of the page number followed by the letter 'n' followed by the number of the note. When the author or subject mentioned in the endnote is not directly identified in the main text, the text page is added in brackets, e.g. 362n20 (131) refers to endnote 20 on page 362, and the note number is to be found in the main text on p. 131.